Haitian Creole

Haitian Creole

Structure, Variation, Status, Origin

Albert Valdman

SHEFFIELD UK   BRISTOL CT

Published by Equinox Publishing Ltd.

UK: Office 415, The Workstation, 15 Paternoster Row, Sheffield, S1 2BX
USA: ISD, 70 Enterprise Drive, Bristol, CT 06010

www.equinoxpub.com

First published 2015

© Albert Valdman 2015

All rights reserved. No part of this publication may be reproduced or transmitted in any form or by any means, electronic or mechanical, including photocopying, recording or any information storage or retrieval system, without prior permission in writing from the publishers.

ISBN   978-1-84553-387-8 (hardback)
        978-1-84553-388-5 (paperback)

British Library Cataloguing-in-Publication Data

A catalogue record for this book is available from the British Library.

Library of Congress Cataloging-in-Publication Data
  Haitian Creole : structure, variation, status, origin / Albert Valdman.
     pages cm
  Includes bibliographical references and index.
  ISBN 978-1-84553-387-8 (hb) — ISBN 978-1-84553-388-5 (pb)
  1. Creole dialects, French — Haiti. 2. Creole dialects, French — Haiti — History.
  3. Creole dialects, French — Social aspects — Haiti. 4. Haitians — Languages.
  5. Native language and education — Haiti. I.Title.
  PM7854.H3V33 2014
  447'.97294 — dc23
                        2013046626

Typeset by CA Typesetting Ltd, Sheffield, www.sheffieldtypesetting.com
Printed and bound in Great Britain by Bell & Bain Ltd, Glasgow, www.bell-bain.com

Contents

In Memoriam	viii
Preface	x
Acknowledgments	xvi

1	**Introduction**	**1**
	1.1 What Is a Creole?	1
	1.2 Haiti and Haitian Creole	5
	1.3 The Description of Haitian Creole	15
	1.4 Other French-based Creoles	19
2	**The Phonological System**	**59**
	2.1 The Phonemic Principle	59
	2.2 The Consonant System of HC	61
	2.3 Semivowels (Glides)	66
	2.4 The Vowel System of HC	67
	2.5 Front Rounded Vowels	72
3	**Variation in the Forms of Words**	**79**
	3.1 Introduction: Morphophonology: Alternations in Form	79
	3.2 General Morphophonemic Rules	80
	3.3 General Morphophonemic Processes in HC	81
	3.4 Variation in Form of the Post-posed Determiner la	87
	3.5 Variation in the Possessive Construction in Northern HC	90
	3.6 A Sample of Running Text	91
4	**Toward a Systematic Autonomous Spelling**	**95**
	4.1 Introduction	95
	4.2 Phonological Constraints on Orthographies	97
	4.3 The Evolution of Etymologically Based Representations in HC	99
	4.4 Systematic Autonomous Orthographies for HC	116
	4.5 Normalization	124
	4.6 Demarcation of Word Boundaries	132
5	**The Structure of the Haitian Creole Lexicon**	**139**
	5.1 The Problem of the Definition of the Word	139

	5.2 Morphemes and Lexemes	140
	5.3 Creative Processes in the HC Lexicon	143
	5.4 Gender in Haitian Creole	161
	5.5 Borrowing	163
6	The Origin of the Haitian Creole Lexicon	166
	6.1 On the Perils of Etymological Research	166
	6.2 Le Vocabulaire des Isles	169
	6.3 Colonial French	170
	6.4 Vocabulary of French Origin	171
	6.5 The Contribution of Other Languages	182
7	Basic Sentence Structure	189
	7.1 Introduction	189
	7.2 Multifunctionality of Words in HC	190
	7.3 Predicate Types in HC	192
	7.4 Phrase-final Emphatic Markers	206
8	The Verbal System	209
	8.1 Semantic Structures and Structural Mechanisms	209
	8.2 The HC TMA System	215
	8.3 Auxiliary Verbs	227
	8.4 Modal Introducers	237
	8.5 The Case of pou	239
	8.6 Serial Verbs	241
9	The Structure of Noun Phrases	253
	9.1 The General Structure of Noun Phrases (NPs)	253
	9.2 The Determiner System	257
	9.3 Pronouns	268
	9.4 Possession	274
	9.5 Summary of Post-posed Determiners	280
	9.6 Pre-posed NP Elements	280
	9.7 Adjectives	281
	9.8 Sex Reference	285
10	Complex Sentences: Coordination, Subordination, and Clefting	288
	10.1 Coordination	288
	10.2 Embedding	289
	10.3 Reduplication and Clefting: Topicalization and Focalization	300

11	Variation in Haitian Creole	315
	11.1 Types of Variation	315
	11.2 Geographical Variation	316
	11.3 Sociolinguistic Variation	331
	11.4 The Sociolinguistic Continuum	351
12	Language Planning and Language Choice in Education	357
	12.1 Introduction	357
	12.2 Language Planning in Haiti	358
	12.3 The Linguistic Ecology of Haiti	362
	12.4 Attitudes Toward French and HC	367
	12.5 Language and Education in Haiti	371
13	The Genesis and Development of Haitian Creole	395
	13.1 Theories about Creole Genesis	395
	13.2 The Genesis of French-based Creoles	404
	13.3 The Role of Substrate Transfers in the Genesis and Development of Haitian Creole	424
	References	444
	Subject Index	466
	Author Index	474

In Memoriam

I dedicate this book to the memory of four individuals who have played a crucial role in the promotion of Haitian Creole and in the development of a standard variety of the language suitable for all types of written texts. In various ways, all of them extended generous assistance and counsel to me in the early stages of my study of Haitian Creole and inquiry into its role in basic education.

Charles-Fernand Pressoir, a journalist, authored the spelling system for Haitian Creole that served as the canon for three decades before being replaced by a slightly modified one, promulgated by the government of Jean-Claude Duvalier in 1979. When Haitian intellectuals favorably disposed to transforming Haitian Creole into a written medium rose in their opposition to the first systematic autonomous orthography for the language proposed by the Northern Irish Methodist pastor Ormonde McConnell, the well-read Pressoir discovered that in 1872 Auguste de Saint-Quentin, a judge in French Guiana, had proposed a spelling which met that high standard, while at the same time conserving many of the systematic aspects of French spelling. He astutely surmised that this orthographic system could gain the support of his compatriots and serve as a basic tool in transitional literacy programs leading to reading competence in both of Haiti's languages. It was this self-taught scholar who took me under his wing during my first stay in Port-au-Prince in 1966. He arranged meetings with all his colleagues and friends involved in the study and the valorization of the country's only shared language, notably, Pradel Pompilus and the Dejean brothers, Paul and Yves, who during their time as missionary priests assumed a pioneering role in the Catholic Church in translating religious material into Haitian Creole. Yves Dejean went on to complete a doctorate at Indiana University. His dissertation, 'Comment écrire le créole d'Haïti' (subsequently published), had a wide impact and contains a very detailed and noteworthy phonological description of the language. He is undoubtedly the most fervent and knowledgeable defender of the use of his native language in education today.

Pradel Pompilus ranks as the most versatile and productive of the native Haitian linguists. We owe to him the first description of the Haitian variety of French, produced in 1961, long before the Agence Universitaire de la Francophonie launched its program of descriptions of the lexical particularities of French varieties outside of France. As a supplement to this groundbreaking work, he compiled the first Haitian Creole–French bilingual dictionary. But undoubtedly his major contributions are his pedagogically oriented contrastive descriptions of the phonological and grammatical systems of French and Haitian Creole; works that make possible the teaching of French from the perspective of the convergent approach fostered by Robert Chaudenson. This innovative pedagogy aims to facilitate the acquisition of competence in French by focusing, as a starting point, on linguistic similarities between the two languages. As a professor in various units of the State University of Haiti and as a principal and teacher at the secondary level, he trained several generations of students. For him, his native language was more than a medium of communication. It was the means by which the bilingual élite might join in the project for national development. As he eloquently puts it himself in *Le problème linguistique haïtien,* in which he traces his progression from a defender and illustrator of French to a champion and analyst of Haitian Creole:

> [Le créole] représente à mes yeux ... un moyen d'opérer la réconciliation avec nous-mêmes, susciter le respect de nous-mêmes, gage du respect des autres ...

> [Creole] represents for me ... a means to conciliate our inner contradictions, to foster self-respect, and it is proof of our respect for others ...

Personally, I am indebted to him for the many kindnesses he showed me, for sharing many original insights on the structure of Haitian Creole, and for his realistic view of the relationship between the two languages on the road to economic development.

Carrié Paultre, an agronomist by training, exercised his profession for fifteen years, providing technical assistance to farmers in the Central Plateau region. In 1964, he was invited by the Comité protestant d'alphabétisation et de litérature to serve as editor and chief writer of a new monthly magazine, *Boucan* 'bonfire'. The first periodical in Creole to appear regularly, *Boucan* ceased publication after the death of its founding editor. Carrié Paultre's role in the development of his native language as a written medium rests in large part on his talent as a translator and author of novels describing the life of country folk cast in the country's historical context. Bryant Freeman, the noted specialist of Haitian studies, in characterizing Paultre's most famous and influential novel, *Tonton Libin* 'Uncle Liben', states: 'That novel can well be seen as the entire saga of Haitian history in this century, as told through the life of one peasant. *Tonton Libin* is a sort of Haitian everyman of his times who symbolizes the trials and tribulations of a people and of a nation.'

Joris Ceuppen was a Belgian missionary priest in the Congregation of the Immaculate Heart of Mary (CICM-Scheut). Founded in Scheut, a Flemish-speaking suburb of Brussels, the order has been very active in Haiti. Realizing in 1967, as the Methodist pastor Ormonde McConnell did before him, that the production of reading material suitable for new literates constitutes a fundamental part of literacy programs, Father Joris launched the second major periodical in Haitian Creole, the 16-page monthly *Bon Nouvèl*. With an initial run of 10,000 copies, and now in its thirty-fifth year, the magazine stands as the only existing periodical containing material exclusively dedicated to Haitian Creole.

Preface

Although interest in creole languages emerged toward the end of the nineteenth century with research by European scholars – Schuchardt, Coelho, Hesseling, Adam – the field of creole studies (creolistics) remained a relatively marginal one in the language sciences and it remained closely associated with historical linguistics. It was not until the 1970s that it became autonomous and began to be directly influenced by research in syntax, semantics, language change, first- and second-language acquisition, sociolinguistics, and educational linguistics. In return, it has contributed to theoretical issues in these fields of the language sciences.

The title of this book recalls one in French I wrote more than thirty years ago: *Le Créole: Structure, status et origine* (1978). That work, which treated all French-based creoles, was based on the erroneous notion that these languages differed little among each other and could be viewed as closely related dialects. Considerable research since that time has shown that, on the contrary, individual French-based creoles are fully autonomous languages. Although they do share some linguistic features and have arisen under comparable sociohistorical circumstances, today they differ significantly at all levels of linguistic structure as well as in the role they assume in their particular community. Thus, this book is limited to Haitian Creole, the language of ten million or more speakers living in the Republic of Haiti and in various diaspora communities, particularly in the Dominican Republic, the United States, and the Bahamas, who refer to their language as *kreyòl*.

Haitian Creole is undoubtedly the best-described creole language. It has benefited from numerous studies, although there exist in fact few general descriptions. The first book-length works, both by Haitian scholars (Jules Faine and Suzanne Sylvain) and written in French, appeared in 1936. It was not until nearly two decades later that another global description of the language, this time in English, was published by Robert Hall Jr. (1953). Although Sylvain, and particularly Faine, in addition to providing solid descriptions of the grammatical structure of the language, proposed diametrically opposed theories regarding the genesis of the language, neither they nor Hall dealt in any detail with geographically and socially determined variations of the language nor with language-planning issues, for example, its legal status with regard to French or its role in the country's educational system.

In the last thirty years our knowledge about the linguistic structure of Haitian Creole has expanded exponentially as a result of extensive research, much of which has been conducted by native speakers of the language. It has been enhanced by the most extensive investigation of geographical variation conducted for any creole language (Fattier 1998). Most importantly, in 1987 a new constitution promulgated Haitian Creole as the joint official language of the country with French and recognized it as the true national language. In addition, the domains of use of the language have been extended, including its use as instructional medium in basic education.

My own knowledge about the language and the role it plays in Haitian society and the diaspora communities in the United States has benefited from work conducted with colleagues and graduate students – some native speakers of Haitian Creole – in the preparation of bilingual dictionaries and pedagogical materials for the acquisition of the language by English speakers. Another important source of insights was my participation, in 1979, in a seminar held in Port-au-Prince at the time when an educational reform, the Réforme Bernard, was being launched to officially introduce the language into primary school classes, as well as my collaboration with a team of Haitian linguists and educators in the elaboration of a bilingual Haitian-Creole/French dictionary destined for school use in Haiti. In view of this personal experience, this book, while it provides a description of the linguistic structure of the language informed by current research, also deals with broad language-planning issues including the use of the language in education. In addition, and because a discussion of these issues cannot be separated from the linguistic relationship of Haitian Creole with French, the book ends with a review of the various hypotheses that have been put forward by creolists to account for its origin and development.

Organization of the Book

After the introductory chapter (Chapter 1), the remainder of the book is divided into five parts.

Chapter 1 opens with a general discussion of the difference between pidgin and creole languages. It then situates Haiti in the Caribbean and provides a short sketch of the history of the Republic of Haiti, with an emphasis on the French colonial period and a key event: the nineteen-year US Occupation. There follows a brief mention of the respective roles of French and Haitian Creole in Haiti and a list of the numerous linguistic studies bearing on the language, focusing on lexicographic resources. The final section of this lengthy chapter reviews the various French-based creoles in the Atlantic zone (Louisiana, the Caribbean, and French Guiana) and in the Indian

Ocean (Réunion, Mauritius, Rodrigues, and the Seychelles), with a brief mention of Tayo, a potential creole language spoken in New Caledonia.

The first part (Chapters 2 to 4) deals with the phonological structure of HC, the variation in the phonological forms of words, and the development of a suitable phonologically based orthographic system.

Chapter 2 opens with a discussion of the notion of phonemic distinction. The consonant and vowel systems of HC are presented in comparison with the corresponding systems of French and English. The description of each of the two phonological subsystems of the language is tripartite: inventory of phonemes, articulatory details, and distributional features. For the vowels, special sections are devoted to the treatment of the nasal vowels and the front rounded vowels.

Chapter 3 deals with **morphophonology**, variation in the forms of words found in the speech of all speakers of Haitian Creole. These include short and long forms of personal pronouns, vowel reduction in verb forms, vowel blending, the variants of the definite determiner, and the complex set of phonological processes that affect post-nominal possessive determiners in Capois (northern Haiti), the local dialect.

Chapter 4 opens with a general consideration of the nature and function of orthographic systems. It continues with a discussion of the principles of phonologically based orthographies. Within the context of the presentation of early notations for Haitian Creole (HC) based on the traditional French spelling, a sample is offered of written texts from the colonial and immediate post-colonial periods which used that spelling. Next, the chapter reviews the three autonomous phonologically based orthographies devised for HC after 1940. It ends with the introduction of the concept of normalization in handling the morphophonological variation presented in Chapter 3.

The next part (Chapters 5 and 6) covers the structure, origin, and development of the lexicon of the language.

Chapter 5 starts with a general description of morphological structure. There follow sections on lexicogenetic processes in HC: derivation (a listing and illustration of about twenty productive suffixes and prefixes), compounding, onomatopoeia, and borrowing.

Chapter 6 opens with a section that stresses the fact that the input to the creation of HC by the African slave population was Colonial French, a variety of the language highly distinct from Standard French. The next section presents the phonological processes that link forms of HC and French cognates; these are in fact the processes that account for differences between Colonial and Standard French. The next sections discuss the survival, in HC, of regional or vernacular French forms and semantic processes that have led to differences in meaning between HC forms and French cognates. The last section deals with the lexicon that originates in languages other than French.

The third part (Chapters 7 to 10) deals with the grammatical (**morphosyntactic**) structure of HC.

Chapter 7 opens with one of the central features of the language, the fact that many words serve multiple grammatical categories (**multifunctionality**). It then presents the structure of simple sentences: sentences formed with introducers, copula-type sentences, sentences with predicates containing transitive and intransitive verbs, and those with double objects. A section is devoted to middle verbs, which enter into constructions equivalent to French and English passive sentences. The final section deals with a notable structural feature of HC: the sentence-final emphatic markers *wi* and *non*.

Chapter 8 begins with a discussion of the semantic information – tense, aspect, mood – carried by verbs. It continues with a presentation of the structural features that carry this information: verb markers and auxiliaries (verbs that, unlike verb markers, have more lexical than grammatical meaning and are related to autonomous verbs). Special consideration is given to the form *pou* that functions as a preposition, a verbal marker, and nominal and verbal complementizer. The final section presents serial verbs, a grammatical feature that is a salient feature of the HC verb system.

Chapter 9 describes the structure of noun phrases. The first section presents their various constituents. The second section examines the semantic information conveyed by the various determiners and their functional role. It contains a detailed discussion of the semantics of the post-posed definite determiner and its extensive phonological variation. Another focus of this section is the syntactic expression of possession. The third section deals with personal and interrogative pronouns and the fourth with adjectives, their position in the noun phrase, and the expression of comparison. The chapter ends with the issue of sex reference in HC.

Chapter 10 covers the structure of complex sentences. The first section describes conjoining clauses with the use of coordinating conjunctions. The second section deals with the various means of embedding clauses into the main clause: the complementation of the verb of the main clause with another verb, the use of conjunctions expressing cause, condition, manner, etc., and the modification of noun phrases of the main clause with relative clauses. It contains a detailed discussion of the expression of temporal relations between the verbs of main and dependent clauses. The third section describes the very complex processes involved in clefting and reduplication to effect emphasis on particular sentence elements.

The fourth section (Chapters 11 and 12) deals with variation in HC and issues in language planning: the relationship between HC and French and the use of HC in basic education.

xiv   *Preface*

Chapter 11 describes geographical and sociolinguistic variation. The chapter opens with a discussion of how geographical variation is studied. It then describes two major geographical variation studies conducted in Haïti. Special attention is given to the more thorough study, *L'Atlas linguistique d'Haïti*, that bears on 2,000 variable words and constructions. Various illustrative maps of particular variants are provided. The second part reviews the small body of research on sociolinguistic variation. Two particular studies are described: the first, a pilot study of a phonological change in progress, the extension of nasalization in the post-posed definite determiner; the second, an extensive study of the influence of the standard (Port-au-Prince) variety of HC on the most divergent geographical variety, that of northern Haiti: Capois. In addition, Chapter 11 compares the variety of standard HC spoken by monolingual speakers to *kreyòl swa*, the one heavily influenced by French that is spoken by bilingual members of higher social classes.

Chapter 12 discusses language planning in Haiti and the relationship between French and HC in education. Two aspects of language planning are covered in the first section: **status planning**, in particular whether and how HC is mentioned in the various Haitian constitutions; **corpus planning**, the level to which HC is present in administration, education, and the media. The sections that follow describe to what extent monolingual speakers have access to French and the attitude of speakers, both monolingual and bilingual, toward the country's two languages. The final section reviews the various governmental programs that aim to introduce HC into literacy training and basic education. In particular, it examines the implementation of the Réforme Bernard that, in 1979, marked the official introduction of HC as an educational vehicle in the early grades of primary school.

The final part contains a single chapter, whose content differs markedly from the two chapters of Part IV. It deals neither with sociolinguistic research on HC nor with language planning or educational issues. Instead, it reviews the various theories put forward to explain the genesis of Haitian Creole.

Chapter 13 opens with a presentation of the various hypotheses put forward to account for the genesis of creole languages. It begins with those that view it somewhat as an exceptional process – the Creole Prototype, the Bioprogram, and the Relexification theories . It follows with the Superstratist approach, which views HC as the unguided acquisition of Colonial French in the special social context of seventeenth- and eighteenth-century plantation colonies. The next section attempts to account for the relationship among the French-based creoles of the Atlantic zone, with the support of historical evidence and early texts, as well as consideration of vernacular varieties of French, particularly those of the Americas. The final section returns to the issue of transfer from African substrate languages espoused by the Relexification hypothesis, some involving congruence between structures of the substrate and Colonial French, others pointing to an apparent total transfer.

Acknowledgments

Men anpil, chay pa lou 'many hands make light work' is an oft-cited Haitian proverb. I am indebted to many people who provided invaluable guidance and assistance in various ways as this book went through several drafts. Three graduate students in the French Linguistics Program at Indiana University – Kelly L. Farmer, Jason F. Siegel, and Michael A. Kunz – searched for references and specific data and made useful comments and suggestions at various stages of the preparation of the book, often providing original insights and new information. I have profited from the rigorous stylistic editing and suggestions about summarizing the history of Haiti provided by Thomas E. Davies, another doctoral student at Indiana University. David Tezil, instructor of the Haitian Creole courses at Indiana University, and Rogéda Dorce Dorcil, Dean of the Faculté de Linguistique Appliquée of the State University of Haiti, contributed native-speaker input on central features of the grammar of the language. The assistance of Jeannette Silva and Alice Jobard, secretaries of the Creole Institute, is also gratefully acknowledged.

Michael A. Kunz deserves particular credit and thanks for checking drafts several times, preparing the bibliography, as well as both the subject and author indices, and reviewing the entire manuscript. His assistance has been invaluable.

The innovative data bearing on sociolinguistic variation in Haitian Creole would not have been collected so efficiently without the support of the Faculté d'Education Regina Assumpta (FéRA) in Cape Haitian. I owe a deep debt of gratitude to the Dean of FéRA, Sister Zita Reuben-Charles, who made available the resources of the institution, facilitated contacts in the village of Thibeau, and recruited the FéRA students who took on various roles in the project: Nicolas Saint-Martin, Roseline Jean-Baptiste, Wilma Laurent, and Rony Saint-Martin all conducted first-level dyadic interviews; Solfils Telfort provided the primary transcriptions from the 126 recordings; and Odilson Sériphin supervised the safe transfer of material by Internet. Thanks are also due to Fernand Léger, currently at the University of Toronto, and Thomas E. Davies, then chief translator for the Lee County School District in Florida, both of whom were responsible for the second-level individual interviews. Thomas Davies also assisted in the logistics of the crucial initial period of data collection. A central role in the analysis and statistical treatment of the sociolinguistic Cape Haitian data was undertaken by Anne-José Villeneuve, currently at the University of Toronto, and Jason Siegel, who is assuming the direction of Caribbean lexicographic research at the University of the West-Indies, Cave Hill, Barbados. Anupam Das, Wendy Hill, and Scott Ledbetter assisted in the handling of the data from the study, funded by the US National Science Foundation, grant No. 0639482.

I have benefited immensely from the comments and suggestions proffered by fellow creolists: Robert Chaudenson, who in addition to putting forward the two-stage model for the development of French-based creoles in 1974, which has guided my discussion of the origins of Haitian Creole, provided broad-ranging comments on the genesis of the language; Salikoko Mufwene also offered valuable comments on the genesis of creoles, in addition to groundbreaking ideas on the relationship between second-language acquisition and creolization; and Dominique Fattier, whose monumental *Atlas linguistique d'Haïti* served as the basis for my coverage of dialectal variation, added useful comments related to that topic. The information for the chapter on spelling benefited from Marie-Christine Hazaël-Massieux's compendium of older texts and her comments on current scriptural practice. Benjamin Hebblethwaite provided feedback on his use of draft chapters for a course on the structure of Haitian Creole at the University of Florida-Gainesville. Thomas Klingler, the leading specialist on Louisiana Creole, also made valuable suggestions, especially on the link between that creole and the one that is the subject of this book. Although the advice and information provided by all these colleagues have helped to improve the book, all shortcomings remain my full responsibility.

Acknowledgment is made to the following for permission to reproduce material: University of Michigan Press, for the map in Figure 11.1; Editions Klincksieck for the map in Figure 11.3. Dominique Fattier gracefully allowed us to adapt material from her Doctorat d'Etat dissertation for the maps in Figures 11.4 to 11.11.

The copy-editing in the final stage of preparation of the book, for production by Equinox Publishers, was handled flawlessly by Sandra Margolies. Her judicious comments led to eliminating ambiguities while providing more precise formulations, as well as executing the final check on bibliographical coverage.

The deepest debt of gratitude, and one that I will never be able to fully repay, is owed to my wife, Hilde, who has given me unfailing support for more than a half century. Although she possesses greater pedagogical skill than I, she sacrificed her career in German literature to further my own. Importantly for this book, it was she who, when we first met and had just returned from filming a documentary in the Caribbean, full of enthusiasm for Haiti and Haitian culture, inspired me to begin the creole page of my career.

1 Introduction

1.1 What Is a Creole?

1.1.1 The origin of the term creole

The use of the term **creole** to refer to the vernacular language of Haiti is not fully satisfactory. It is at the same time a generic term, referring to a group of languages, and the label for a specific tongue. Today, there is a tendency among linguists and some speakers to identify such languages simply by the places where they are spoken: Mauritian or Haitian instead of Mauritian Creole or Haitian Creole. However, in the case of Haitian Creole, the overwhelming majority of native speakers call the language simply *kreyòl*. Therefore, in this book, the compound Haitian Creole (*kreyòl ayisyen*, abbreviated HC) will be adopted because of its wider use than the label Haitian.

The word 'creole' is derived from the Portuguese *criar* (from the Latin *creare*) 'to nurture, to raise, to bring up'. With the adjunction of a diminutive suffix, it became *crioulo* and referred to an African slave born in Brazil (Holm 1988: 9). The term was borrowed into Spanish in the second half of the sixteenth century under the form *criollo* to refer to natives of European parentage in the Spanish colonies of South America. For example, in his *Historia natural y moral de las Indias* (2002; first published in 1586) the Spanish priest J. de Acosta defines *criollos* as '*como alla llaman a los nacidos de españoles en Indias*' (as over there they call those born to Spaniards in the Indies). Acosta also uses the term to refer to fruit, presumably of European origin, grown in the Americas.

The term was then used by French writers with more or less the same senses: (1) any person of European parentage born in the colonies, both in the West Indies and in the Indian Ocean; (2) any person, including one of African origin, born in the colonies; (3) any living creature, plant or animal, specific to the colonies, as opposed to one imported from Europe. Interestingly, HC has preserved the etymological sense 'nurtured, raised'. The French version of the term, *créole*, first appeared in the form *criole*, adapted from the Spanish *criolo* and with the original meaning, as attested in one

2   Introduction

of the earliest dictionaries of the French language (Furetière 1690): '*criole. c'est le nom que les Espagnols donnent à leurs enfants qui sont nez aux Indes*' (criole, it's the name that the Spaniards give to their children born in the Indies [i.e. West Indies]). In his French–HC dictionary, the Haitian scholar Jules Faine (1974: 148) offers two examples illustrating this sense: *Moin cé créole Cam-Perrin* 'I am a native of Camp-Perrin', *tit poulain ça ha cé créole moin* 'that little colt is one I raised', and another exemplifying the related sense 'contemporary, raised during the same time': *Moin cé Créole Tirésias, papa'm té créyiole Salonmon, grand papa m meinme té créole Lempèrè* 'I am a contemporary of [president] Tirésias. My father was a contemporary of [president] Salomon, and my grandfather was a contemporary of emperor [Soulouque]'.[1]

The first attested use of the term 'creole' to refer to language is noted in 1688 in the diary of the French navigator Le Courbe.[2] He used the expression *langue créole* for a pidginized variety of Portuguese used by Senegalese traders that he likened to Lingua Franca, a contact language based on the Romance language, which was widely used at that time in the Mediterranean area. In 1785, the Swiss traveler J. Girod-Chantrans applied the term to the vernacular of French Saint-Domingue which, for him, was the most widely used speech variety in the colony. He declared that *créole* was not only the language of slaves of African origin but even that of the Whites residing in the colony, who according to him spoke it more readily than French, either by habit or because they found it more pleasing.

1.1.2 Pidgins and creoles

Are creoles exceptional languages?
Creoles are fully constituted languages. Their vocabulary and grammar are sufficiently developed and complex to meet all the communicative and cognitive needs of their speakers and the formation of linguistic communities. In this regard, they are not exceptional languages (DeGraff 2003). Some creolists (linguists specializing in the study of creole languages) consider creoles to form a class of languages defined by a small set of specific structural features, among which the major one is lack of inflection (McWhorter 1998). However, the consensus among creolists is that creoles, particularly those derived from French, do not differ substantially from other natural languages. It is only the socio-historical circumstances of their development and their sociolinguistic relationship with the other language(s) with which they co-exist that have set them apart. A linguistic analysis of HC would hardly identify any special 'creole' features. It is recognized as a

creole language because there is sufficient historical evidence that it did not develop gradually from some other speech form in the way, for instance, French developed from Latin, but developed relatively rapidly, within thirty to fifty years, in the special socio-historical context of a colonial plantation society.

Laymen definitions of creole languages tend to stress their hybrid nature. An extreme example of such erroneous views is illustrated by the following description of HC from a brochure published in the 1960s by the Ministry of Tourism of Haiti:

> Resulting from a unique blend of cultural traditions, Creole has developed as the unofficial second language. The only tongue which grew up spontaneously in the Western Hemisphere, Creole is derived from the simple syntax of English privateers; Norman French of the 16th and 17th century buccaneers [;] and native Indian language from which it borrows the names of flora and fauna. The Spanish contributed some grammatical features and names while the Africans gave the language its accent, modulation, tone, and the suppression of 'r' and 's'.

As will be shown in subsequent chapters, the Ministry of Tourism's definition of HC, concocted to make the language appear exotic to tourists, is grossly inaccurate, from the point of view of both the present-day structure of the language and the process of its historical development. For example, concerning the claimed African origin of the suppression of 'r', which in any case occurs only in syllable-final position, this originates not in African languages but in the vernacular French varieties that were the target for acquisition by the African slaves.

Another widely held view about Caribbean creoles is that they are composed of a European-based vocabulary cast in the syntax of western African languages. Indeed, a highly respected creolist, Claire Lefebvre (1998), has attempted to demonstrate that HC is the result of clothing the syntax of a specific African language, Fongbe, with French vocabulary. This proposal encounters many difficulties, a detailed discussion of which will be presented in Chapter 13, which deals with the genesis and development of HC. Suffice it to say that HC is not a linguistic cocktail but, like other natural languages such as English or French, an organic whole whose phonology, grammar, and vocabulary represent a coherent restructuring of linguistic material from multiple sources. Its linguistic structure is sufficiently developed to enable it to meet all the communicative and cognitive needs of its speakers.[3] The great Martinican writer, Aimé Césaire, provided the most insightful characterization of his native Martinique Creole when he declared: '*Le créole est une langue dont le corps est français mais l'âme africaine*' (Creole is a language whose body is French but whose soul is African). It would be simplistic to equate the body of a language with its vocabulary and its soul with its grammar.

Expanded pidgins and creoles

Creoles differ markedly from **pidgins**. These are indeed types of languages characterized by a limited vocabulary and reduced grammatical apparatus whose functions are limited. They serve primarily the instrumental, regulatory, and representational functions, generally for groups with no language in common. Pidgins may also develop when a socially subordinate group uses the language of a superior group for limited functions, as is the case of Tây Bôy, a pidgin based on French, formerly used by some members of the indigenous population of colonial Indochina (Phillips 1975). It was also used by French speakers in their relations with speakers of Indochinese languages with slave status.

There exist expanded pidgins, such as Tok Pisin, an English-based pidgin spoken in Papua New Guinea. Originally used in interactions between White plantation owners, overseers and laborers who spoke a variety of indigenous languages, the pidgin was expanded structurally when it became a means of communication between indigenous groups and within individual indigenous language groups in an urban setting (Sankoff 1977; Mühlhäusler 1986).

As will be pointed out in Sections 13.1.1 and 13.1.2, many creolists view creoles as expanded pidgins that become the primary language of a linguistic community and eventually expand their functions with an accompanying structural complexification. This transformation is labeled the 'creole cycle' (R. A. Hall 1966). According to this view, creoles are nativized pidgins. They are modified as they are acquired as a first language by children and transmitted to new generations by regular first-language acquisition processes. As the domains of use of an expanded pidgin increase, its vocabulary is enriched and its grammar complexified. Internal differences develop that enable differentiation among subgroups of the community. For example, in Zaire (currently the Republic of Congo) for the expression of past tense younger speakers of Kituba, the variety of Kikongo used by speakers of other languages, replace an analytic structure (word order) by a synthetic one (inflection): *munu imene kwenda* 'I went' > *mumekwenda*. The creole cycle ends by decreolization in situations where, bearing socially subordinate status, a creole is used together with the language from which the original pidgin was derived.

This is the case of HC in Haiti where, although it is legally recognized as a co-official language, it remains devalorized with respect to French.

However, the development of HC does not illustrate the creole cycle. As will be argued in Section 13.2, there is no persuasive evidence that HC and other French-based creoles started out as expanded pidgins. The missionary priests sent to the French Caribbean seventeenth-century colonies distinguished between a pidgin, which they labeled *baragouin*, employed by the Carib Indians in their dealings with Europeans, and approximative varieties of French spoken by newly imported African slaves, labeled *le langage des Nègres* (Chaudenson 1979: 12–16). Like its congeners in the Caribbean, French Guiana, and Louisiana, HC developed from the attempt of slaves to speak the vernacular variety of French spoken by the White colonists.

1.2 Haiti and Haitian Creole

1.2.1 Geography and demographics

Occupying the western third of Hispaniola, an island that it shares with the Dominican Republic, the Republic of Haiti has an estimated population of more than ten million in an area of 10,714 square miles, about the same size as the US state of Maryland. The name Haiti (*Ayiti* in Haitian Creole), coined in 1804, when the country gained independence from France, is derived from its name in the language of the indigenous Taino Indians. It means 'land of high mountains' and replaced Saint-Domingue, the name France had given to its colony. The largest city of Haiti by far, the capital Port-au-Prince, had a population exceeding two million when a devastating earthquake struck in January 2010. The next three largest cities: Cape Haitian, the former colonial capital; Gonaïves, where the country's independence was proclaimed in 1804; and Léogâne, located a few miles west of Port-au-Prince, have about 200,000 inhabitants each. Other notable cities are Jacmel, Les Cayes, and Jérémie, but these contain fewer than 50,000 inhabitants.

More than three million Haitians, or persons of Haitian origin, live outside of Haiti. Two million of this influential diaspora are located in the Dominican Republic, and another 900,000 live in the United States. There are an estimated 200,000 Haitians in Canada (mostly in Quebec Province), 80,000 in the Bahamas, and the same number in France and its overseas departments, French Guiana, Guadeloupe, Martinique, and Réunion. Considering that the total population of Haiti is estimated at only ten million, members of the diaspora communities who maintain close ties with their homeland wield considerable sway.

6   Introduction

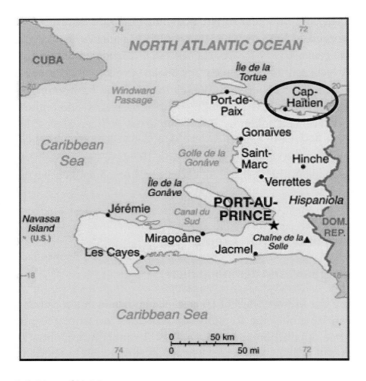

Figure 1.1. Map of Haiti

1.2.2 A short sketch of Haitian history[4]

On his initial voyage to the New World, looking for gold, Christopher Columbus first sighted and visited the island of San Salvador. The indigenous peoples directed Columbus to the much larger island of Hispaniola (Little Spain), which he himself named. Columbus sailed into the harbor, near what is now Môle Saint Nicolas at the extreme north-western tip of Hispaniola, on December 6, 1492. It was near there that he established the first European settlement in the New World, the Fort of the Nativity, constructed from the wreckage of one of his three ships, the *Santa Maria* (Heinl and Heinl 2005).

Within three decades of the initial European contact, the indigenous Taino population was decimated by contact with diseases to which it was not immune, especially smallpox, and general maltreatment. Starvation was another major contributing factor, because imported cattle devastated the native agricultural base (d'Ans 1968). For the Spaniards, Hispaniola served mainly as a staging base for their conquests in Mexico and South America.

Consequently, no major plantation economy emerged during their century-long control of the entire island.

Around 1625, English, French, and Dutch buccaneers established themselves on the island of Tortuga, north of Haiti. These pirates preyed on Spanish enclaves in the Caribbean and naval traffic across the Windward Passage between Cuba and Hispaniola. In 1665, after a troubled period of numerous Spanish attacks followed each time by the return of the pirates, the island came under full French control under the governorship of Bertrand d'Ogeron. Under d'Ogeron's guidance, the buccaneers and other colonists became *habitants* (owners of small homesteads) on the western part of Hispaniola and cultivated tobacco and indigo with the help of French indentured servants and a small number of slaves. When France was formally granted that part of the island by Spain in 1697, by the Treaty of Ryswick, White colonists numbered 4,441, with 3,358 imported African slaves. In the seventeenth century, in Saint-Domingue, the homestead phase of colonization in which slaves had relatively close contact with French speakers was replaced by the plantation phase.[5] The cultivation of crops such as tobacco and indigo, which did not require massive manpower, yielded to the production of coffee and especially sugar, an agro-industrial endeavor highly dependent on slave labor on a large scale. By 1739, there were ten times more African slaves than Whites (109,780 versus 11,699 respectively). During the last decades of French possession, 5,000 slaves were imported each year into Saint-Domingue, and 29,000 alone in 1791 (Cornevin 1982: 31). When the Haitian Revolution broke out in 1791, the slaves constituted 90% of the population in what had become the wealthiest European colony, termed the Pearl of the Antilles: 465,429 versus 30,826 Whites and 27,548 free Blacks or Mulattoes. That year half of the slaves were not native-born Creoles but newly imported *Bozals*.[6]

Despite the wealth it produced, the Saint-Domingue colony was rife with strife caused by the social diversity of a population with conflicting interests: administrators named by the French kings, who were transient but wielded most of the power; a small group of wealthy plantation owners who chafed under the mercantile economic system that excluded trading with other nations in order to serve the interests of the French state and French merchants; *Blancs manants*, poor Whites, who looked askance at the wealthier social group just above them; the Mulattoes and freed Blacks who owned 25% of plantations and possessed slaves; and the exploited slave masses. The French Revolution in 1789 brought all these latent conflicts to the fore. The Mulattoes, invoking the Declaration of the Rights of Man that had been proclaimed in Paris in 1789 and supported by a group of French legislators who called themselves *La Société des amis des Noirs* (The Society of the Friends of Blacks), demanded the political and social rights denied to them and equality with the Whites. In 1791, after a clandestine meeting in Bois Caïman (northern Saint-Domingue) called by a Vodou priest, Boukman, 50,000 slaves revolted. They devastated hundreds of sugar and coffee plantations and massacred about 1,000 Whites. This marked the beginning of the Haitian Revolution that lasted more than ten years and led to the creation in 1804 of the first Black republic in the world and the second independent state in the Americas.

In 1793, the French revolutionary government sent two commissioners, Santhonax and Polverel, with troops to restore order in Saint-Domingue. The commissioners declared that all enslaved Africans and Mulattoes were free and were to enjoy all the rights of French citizens but that they had to return to work on the plantations. A year later, the Convention, the first elected governing institution of the French Revolution, abolished slavery in all French colonies. England and Spain, who had declared war on France, now invaded Saint-Domingue. A freed slave and owner of a small plantation, Toussaint L'Ouverture, who had joined the rebellion, was granted a command by the Spaniards to fight the French. However, in 1794 he switched sides and eventually defeated the Spanish and English forces. In 1801, Toussaint had a constitution drafted that named him governor-general for life of the newly liberated Saint-Domingue.

In the meantime, in France, Napoleon Bonaparte, a very successful general, staged a coup in 1799 and assumed full power as First Consul. In 1801, Bonaparte, who envisaged re-establishing slavery, sent an expeditionary force of 86 ships and 22,000 soldiers, commanded by his brother-in-law Emmanuel Leclerc, to regain control of Saint-Domingue. In 1802, Leclerc concluded an uneasy peace with the former slaves, and Toussaint retired to his plantation. However, he was treacherously arrested and exiled to a prison in the Jura mountains in eastern France, where he died in 1803 of pneumonia and exposure.

Subsequently, the French expeditionary corps was decimated by an epidemic of yellow fever to which Leclerc himself succumbed. The insurrection was rekindled, and Toussaint's generals, Jean-Jacques Dessalines and Henri Christophe, continued a guerrilla war that led to the ultimate defeat of the French. Altogether nearly 50,000 French soldiers perished in the misguided effort to re-establish the plantocratic system dependent on slave labor. It is reported that during his forced exile on the African island of St Helena, Napoleon declared: *'C'était une grande faute que d'avoir voulu soumettre la colonie par la force, je devais me contenter de la gouverner par l'intermédiaire de Toussaint'* (It was a grave mistake to have attempted to gain control of the colony by force, I should have been satisfied to rule it through the intermediary of Toussaint).

The independence of Haiti was proclaimed by Dessalines in Gonaïves on January 1, 1804. The new leader assumed Toussaint's title of governor-general for life, then later that year that of emperor under the name of Jacques 1er. In 1806, he was betrayed, ambushed, and brutally killed as he attempted to put down a revolt in the south led by Alexandre Pétion, a Mulatto who had played a major role in the war of independence. Following Dessalines' demise, Haiti was divided into two parts: the northern kingdom under Christophe, who named himself king; and a republic in the south and west under the leadership of Pétion. After his death Pétion was succeeded by the commander of the presidential guard, Jean-Pierre Boyer, who united the country in 1820 after Christophe's suicide.

Boyer ruled for twenty-five years, the longest tenure of office in the country's history. In 1830, facing the presence of French warships off Haitian shores and the possibility of another French invasion, Boyer agreed to pay an indemnity of 150 million gold francs, ten times the country's annual revenue at that time, to compensate French colonists for the loss of their slaves and plantations. In exchange, France recognized Haiti as an independent nation. Reduced to 90 million gold francs (currently equivalent to about 20 billion dollars), the debt, a severe handicap for Haiti's economy, was not paid off until 1947. In 1822, Boyer decided to invade the less-populated eastern part of Hispaniola (currently the Dominican Republic), which had gained independence from Spain and where a major agro-industrial economy with attendant slavery never fully developed. The brutal nature of the twenty-year occupation resulted in constant friction between the two countries that still continues today.

Boyer was overthrown in 1843 and political instability ensued for a couple of decades. In 1867, a new constitution was drafted that assured a relatively smooth transition from one elected president to another and the country enjoyed economic development for a while, especially the production of coffee and some sugar. However, in 1911 a revolution broke out and Haiti slipped once again into turmoil. Between that year and 1915, six presidents were either killed in office or forced into exile. During this period, the United States State Department, in order to limit the influence of a sizeable German business community, backed the National City Bank of New York when it assumed control of the National Bank of Haiti. In 1915, during the Woodrow Wilson presidency, to guarantee loans issued by the US bank, as well as to prevent a possible German military presence, since World War I was raging, the United States sent in a military force of Marines under the pretext of restoring order after the mob lynching of President Vilbrun Guillaume Sam, who himself had massacred 167 political prisoners just days before. In fact, the US occupation, justified by the Monroe Doctrine, constituted another facet of the US imperialism of the late nineteenth and early twentieth centuries that included military interventions in Cuba, the Dominican Republic, and Nicaragua.

The US occupation lasted until 1934 and had mixed results. On the one hand, it led to an impressive infrastructure upgrade that included the construction of a remarkable number of new roads, bridges, irrigation canals, and port facilities, and the establishment of a public health service, as well as a national police force, the Gendarmerie d'Haïti, whose name was later changed to the Garde d'Haïti. On the other hand, the newly established police force was commanded by White American and Mulatto officers, and the labor force needed for all this construction was assembled through the system of *corvées*, forced labor, all of which smacked of a return to slavery under a White power structure.

The United States assumed full *de facto* political and administrative control, taking over stewardship of the financial institutions of the country, the collection of custom fees (a major source of income), and public health. In 1917, the US State Department drafted a new constitution, for which Franklin Delano Roosevelt, then Assistant Secretary of the Navy, claimed authorship. That constitution, for the first time, allowed foreigners to own land and, as a sop to the bilingual élite, declared French the official language of the country. When the legislature refused to ratify the constitution, adopted in a dubious plebiscite, in which only 5% of the population voted, it was dissolved. The USA appointed a new president, Philippe Dartiguenave, who served as a figurehead, until in 1922 he was succeeded by the duly elected Léon Borno. Borno wielded absolute political power for two six-year terms together with an US-appointed High Commissioner, the marine General John H. Russell, Jr. However, it was during the Russell–Borno rule that most of the impressive infrastructure development took place.[7]

In the area of education, the Americans found a dual system: a network of poorly run government schools for the general population and an efficient Catholic school system staffed by French clerics that primarily served the Mulatto élite. Focusing on the improvement of agriculture, they established a system of vocational schools, the Agricultural Extension and Teaching Service, called the *Service Technique*, It was administered by a White American director and staffed by American 'experts' of dubious educational competence, ignorant of Haitian culture and lacking proficiency in either French or HC. The US effort that favored vocational training in Haiti for the Black rural masses led to a clash of cultures because of the attachment of the influential élite to traditional, French-influenced educational goals (Heinl and Heinl 2005; Pamphile 2008).

Invoking the separation of church and state, the American administrators, who controlled the purse strings, disregarded the Catholic school system that assumed the major role in Haitian education. At the same time, they reduced the funding allotted to the public school system, which received far less support than the US-run *Service Technique*. To implement that institution's program for the improvement of Haitian farmers' agricultural practices the *Service Technique* provided relatively generous scholarships (*bourses*) to educated young Haitians. In 1929, in a deteriorating economic context, funding for the *Service Technique* was reduced. As was the case for many of his predecessors, Borno refused to step down upon the termination of his term in office. Confronted with a cut in his budget, Dr. Freeman, the head of the *Service Technique*, reduced the amount of the scholarship and required students to perform rural labor. The students, mostly from the élite, who were trained as instructors for the *Service Technique* at the Central School of Agriculture in Damien (north of Port-au-Prince), went on a strike that degenerated into general disorder.

Following this disorder and a growing resentment of the occupiers' economic and political policies, the US President Herbert Hoover appointed a Commission for the Study and Review of Conditions in Haiti to review the entire occupation. In its report to the president, the Commission recommended that the United States should liquidate the occupation of Haiti as expeditiously as possible, meanwhile rapidly 'Haitianizing' administrative services and the Garde and reducing US interference in Haiti's internal affairs (Heinl and Heinl 2005). In 1930, following the election to the presidency of Sténio Vincent, a long-time critic of the occupation, the USA began to withdraw its troops. The withdrawal was completed in 1934 during the presidency of Franklin D. Roosevelt as part of the new American 'Good Neighbor Policy'.

From their initial landing in Haiti in 1915, the Marines were opposed by peasant guerrillas termed *Cacos*.[8] These insurgents were led by a former officer in the Haitian army, Charlemagne Péralte, and operated mainly in the central plateau and the north. Using tactics reminiscent of those used by the slave-insurgents against French troops during the Haitian Revolution, the *Cacos* offered a stubborn resistance to the Marines. In 1919, Péralte was treacherously killed but the insurgency continued under the leadership of a former teacher, Benoît Batraville, who was killed in battle. By 1921, the Marines and the Garde d'Haïti had defeated the insurgents, more than 2,000 of whom were killed. Considered a martyr in the cause of Haitian nationalism, Péralte was honored by a national funeral in 1935 after his body was unearthed.

Summarizing the US occupation, Weinstein and Segal concluded that '… American reforms have few lasting direct effects of any kind, good or bad … linguistic differences and race prejudice limited communication … American techniques of rule contradicted expressed U.S. desires for stability, respect of law, and institutionalization' (1984: 28). Another dubious legacy of the US pacification of Haiti was the increased centralization of power in the 'Republic' of Port-au-Prince.

The US occupation, and in particular the outright racism displayed by the occupying troops and administrators, triggered on the part of leading Haitian intellectuals a nationalist reaction including the valorization of the African heritage and a re-assessment of the role of Vodou and HC in the country's culture. This reaction coincided with the Négritude movement in France.[9] The leader of this valorization was the anthropologist Jean Price-Mars, whose major work, *Ainsi parla l'oncle* (1928), constitutes the first extensive study of Haitian rural folk culture. Price-Mars's work inspired the founding of a quarterly journal *Les Griots*, one of whose editors was the future president François Duvalier.

The period following the US occupation was marked by struggles between the Mulatto élite, a rising Black middle class, and the leaders of the Garde d'Haïti, as well as the typical tendency of elected presidents, most of them generals, to seek autocratic power, extend their terms of office, and become president for life. The resulting instability gave an opening for the election in 1957 of François Duvalier, a rural doctor and former Minister of Health and Labor, known as 'Papa Doc'. He reduced the influence of the Mulatto élite, replaced the military with a thuggish militia loyal only to him, the *Volontaires de la Sécurité Nationale*, known as the *Tonton Macoutes* and, predictably, named himself president for life in 1961. Papa Doc's rule was corrupt, brutal, and repressive. It isolated Haiti on the international level and led to the massive emigration of the educated and skilled members of the élite and middle classes.

After the death of Papa Doc in 1971, power passed to his son, Jean-Claude (Baby Doc). His rule was less repressive than his father's, but much more corrupt, fully meriting the label of kleptocracy. However, international support flowed to the country and an attempt at educational reform (Réforme Bernard, see Section 12.5.2) was launched, one of whose central components involved the initial use of HC as instructional medium.

Pope John Paul II's visit to Haiti in 1983 was a catalytic event and eventually led to a rebellion, a *dechoukaj* 'uprooting', the exile of Baby Doc, and the seizure of power by the army.[10] The army maintained unsteady control of the government until 1990, when a Salesian priest, Jean-Bertrand Aristide, won the presidential election by a wide margin. The leftist populism of Aristide and his political movement, *Fanmi lavalas* ('the deluge family', evoking the projected sweeping reforms), alarmed several sectors of the Haitian population and some foreign governments. After a short year in office, he was deposed and the army regained control. In 1994, with US military intervention, Aristide was reinstated to complete his presidential term. In 1996, in a rare peaceful transition, a political ally, René Préval, succeeded him.

Upon the end of Préval's term, Aristide was re-elected but the opposition boycotted the election. In 2004, a revolt broke out in Gonaïves, spread to Cape Haitian, and the rebels threatened to march on Port-au-Prince. Aristide was forced to resign and leave Haiti under a cloud, including accusations of intervention by the French and US governments. At that stage, to ensure order, the United Nations sent a multinational armed force, the MINUSTAH (United Nations Stabilization Mission in Haiti) that is still operational.

In 2006 Préval was elected and completed his term of office in 2011, but not before a devastating earthquake struck the capital area, causing an estimated 300,000 deaths and leaving more than a million homeless. In the second round of a controversial election, Michel Martelly, a former singer with stated ties to the Duvalier regime, was declared the winner by an electoral commission.

As will be pointed out in Chapter 12, there is at present in Haiti a lively debate about the role that HC should play in the educational system and in the administrative sphere. The republic's latest constitution in 1987 declared HC and French equal official languages. However, in 2013 President Martelly refused to give legal status to a decision of the legislature for the creation of an organization charged with language planning and the standardization of Haitian Creole, the Académie Créole, as stipulated in the 1987 constitution, because the proposal was drafted in HC, without a French version.

1.2.3 Haitian Creole and French in Haiti

Haitian Creole (HC) comprises one of the five principal groups of French-based creole languages. The others are those in (1) Louisiana; (2) the Lesser Antilles – Dominica, Guadeloupe, Martinique, Saint Lucia, etc.; (3) French Guiana; and (4) the Mascarene archipelago (Réunion, Mauritius, and Rodrigues) and the Seychelles in the Indian Ocean. Since there are significant differences in vocabulary, as well as levels of grammar and pronunciation, these languages are not always mutually intelligible, especially from one zone to another. For example, there is little mutual intelligibility between the French-based creoles of the Indian Ocean and those of the New World. However, mutual comprehension is more easily attained between neighboring creoles, as for example between HC and Louisiana Creole, or those of French Guiana and the Lesser Antilles.

HC is the principal language of communication in the Republic of Haiti. All Haitians speak it, and it is the sole means of communication for the vast majority of the population. In the constitution of 1987, both French and Creole were promulgated official languages of the Republic of Haiti but a certain dominant/subordinate relationship exists between them. A mastery of

French is still highly valued by all segments of the population. Although the use of Creole continues to expand into all domains – the media, education, administration, literature – French is still often preferred for literary expression and in the educational and administrative sectors. On the other hand, HC is considered by all Haitians as the true national language of their country.[11]

The two languages differ little at the level of pronunciation. They also share a great deal of lexical items, many of which are false cognates, that is, words with the same form but different meanings. For example, the French adjective *fréquent*, like its English cognate, means 'frequent' but its HC cognate *frekan* means 'insolent, rude, and impertinent' and usually refers to people. However, the two languages differ substantially at the grammatical level, rendering them mutually unintelligible. Like its above listed congeners, HC arose in the social context of a slave-holding plantation society in which French was the language of most of the original European settlers, indentured servants, artisans, military personnel, and administrators.

The variety of French that evolved into the varieties of the language currently used in Haiti and North America (Quebec, the Maritime Provinces of Canada, and Louisiana) is usually referred to as Colonial French. In their attempt to acquire Colonial French without ready access to a proper model, the slaves modified its structure considerably. In the social context of the plantation colonies, the French available to them was highly variable, reflecting the everyday speech of uneducated people from different parts of France rather than the more standardized language of the educated élite. Imported slaves spoke a variety of African languages, which operated as filters through which Colonial French was interpreted. However, it is simplistic to characterize the language that developed from the attempt by the slaves to acquire Colonial French as a mixed language consisting of French vocabulary embedded in African grammar, as some have suggested. Instead, it is a language in its own right whose pronunciation, grammar, and vocabulary, though grounded in French, do show the influence of African languages.[12]

For the small minority of the population that is bilingual, the use of the two languages is largely determined by the interaction of two sociolinguistic variables: that of public versus private context, and that of formal versus informal situations. That complementary use of two languages, depending on social context of use, is referred to as **diglossia** (C. A. Ferguson 1959; Fishman 1971) and the relationship between the two languages as diglossic. In Haiti, because French is more highly valued in that diglossic relationship, it is termed the high language, and HC, the low language.

As is the case for all languages, HC shows geographical and sociolinguistic variation, manifesting itself primarily at the levels of pronunciation and vocabulary. The speech of the Cape Haitian region in northern Haiti differs most strikingly from that of the rest of the country, although there are also some salient differences in the speech of the western part of the southern peninsula. Differences also exist between urban and rural inhabitants of each region, but the sharpest differences are between the speech of the bilingual minority and that of the monolingual majority.

1.3   The Description of Haitian Creole

Haitian Creole (HC) is arguably the best and most described creole language. Many of the descriptions of the language and of the linguistic situation of Haiti are authored by native speakers of the language such as Faine, Sylvain, Pompilus, Racine, Etienne, Dejean, Vernet, Piou, Joseph, Zéphir, DeGraff, Vilsaint, and Lainy.[13]

1.3.1   Linguistic descriptions

HC benefits from several comprehensive descriptions of the language: Faine (1936), Suzanne Sylvain (1936), R. A. Hall (1953), d'Ans (1968), DeGraff (2007). Although it attempts to describe all French-based creoles, Valdman (1978) provides an extensive treatment of the structure of HC. Detailed descriptions of the phonological structure of the languages are contained in Tinelli (1970), Dejean (1980), and Cadely (1994). Lefebvre *et al*. (1982) focus on the syntactic structure of HC. Pedagogically oriented descriptions of HC, addressed primarily to a Haitian audience, have been authored by Pompilus (1973, 1976) and Damoiseau (2005a). Zéphir (1990) examines the variety of HC, *kreyòl swa*, spoken by the bilingual élite. These works are complemented and updated by numerous articles applying the latest theoretical constructs to the description of the syntactic, phonological, and lexical structure of the language. These are cited in the chapters of this book that deal with particular aspects of HC and the linguistic situation of Haiti. There also exist two descriptions of regional varieties of HC: G. Etienne (1974) for Northern HC and Racine (1970) for Southern HC. Fattier's (1998) monumental study provides an in-depth survey of the linguistic variation across the country on the basis of more than 2,000 words or grammatical features. Descriptive data about HC also appear in major publications dealing with general issues in creole linguistics, particularly Claire Lefebvre (1998), Chaudenson (1992, 2003), and DeGraff (2003).

1.3.2   Lexicography

There exist more than a dozen bilingual dictionaries that generally meet basic lexicographic standards. Except for Pompilus (1958), Faine (1974),

Bentolila *et al.*(1976), and Peleman (1976), most target English-speaking users.

Pradel Pompilus's 'Lexique créole-français' (1958), a complementary doctoral thesis presented at the University of Paris, stands as the first effort to provide an inventory of the lexical resources of HC. Although not published until 1974, Jules Faine's French–HC dictionary, as was the case with this pioneering Haitian linguist's two other works, *Philologie créole* (1936) and *Le Créole dans l'univers* (1939), was produced during the later years of his life prior to his death in 1958. In addition to being the only available major French–HC bilingual dictionary, Faine's last work provides interesting insights on the etymology of HC words and useful linguistic information about the language. The Bentolila *et al.* (1976) dictionary, modestly titled *Ti Diksyonnè* ('little dictionary'), is based on a corpus collected in the Saint-Marc area, north of Port-au-Prince. Like the Peleman work, it contains contextual examples that contribute to narrowing down the sense of individual words and expressions.

The noteworthy bilingual dictionaries destined for English users fall into two groups: those providing English glosses (lexical equivalents) for HC entries, which include Valdman *et al.* (1981), Targète and Urciolo (1993), Freeman and Laguerre (2006), Valdman *et al.* (2007), and Freeman (2010); and those providing information in the reverse order (English >HC), which include Vilsaint (1991), Vilsaint and Heurtelou (1994), Valdman *et al.* (1996), and Freeman (2011). These various bilingual dictionaries differ widely in their structure and the size of their **nomenclature**: the number of words and expressions that they treat. Valdman *et al.* (1981, 2007), Targète and Urciolo (1993), and Valdman *et al.* (1996) have the advantage of providing extensive illustrative examples, many of them of sentence length. For polysemic words and expressions, these examples provide information that helps to differentiate senses, and they also sometimes provide key grammatical information.

Another major difference between the dictionaries involves the treatment of homonyms (words with the same pronunciation but different meanings) and polysemes (words with multiple meanings). These differences of treatment are illustrated by comparing the two HC >English dictionaries with the larger nomenclatures: Freeman and Laguerre (1996, 1998, 2002, 2004, 2006), Freeman (2010), and Valdman *et al.* (2007). For example, the latter's nomenclature consists of 30,000 headwords, 26,000 subentries (expressions) and about 75,000 individual senses. The first of these two dictionaries regroups homonyms in the same article. The unfavorable result is that the subentries for the various homonyms do not appear with the appropriate headword:

1.3 The Description of Haitian Creole 17

ba *n.* stocking(s), hose; wooden pack-saddle; bar, stick, piece (metal, soap, etc.); bar (restaurant, café); snack bar; bar (river); line (drawn with pencil or pen); helm, tiller; peck, small kiss; stripe(s), epaulette; *adj.* low, short; very sick, weak; depressed, discouraged; *adv.* down; low; *prep.* to; for; see **bay~ chosèt** thick socks
~ **kilòt** pantyhose
~ **site** security bar
~ **vitès** gearshift lever
bay kout ~ to play a dirty trick (on s.o.); to deceive
demi ~ knee-high stocking(s)
fè ~ pou to kiss
mete ~ to give birth (animal), calve, have a litter
mete li nan ~ to put in a straitjacket
pa ~ from the rectum
pwen ~ that's final
vant ~ lying flat; to be flat on one's back, be in bad shape

In contrast, Valdman *et al.* (2007) list the homonyms under separate entries, clearly distinguish the sense of polysemic entries, and in addition provide illustrative examples where useful. This type of organization makes for a much richer and useful treatment of homonyms.[14]

ba¹ *adj.* **1** low *Branch yo twò ba.* The branches are too low. *Li kite travay la paske salè l te twò ba.* She quit her job because her salary was too low. **2** low, discouraged, depressed *Moral msye ba.* He is discouraged. **3** weak [unwell] *M santi m ba jodi a.* I feel weak today. **4** starved, ravenous *Msye te ba papa!* He was starved, man! •**bay kout ba** see **koutba** •**chapo** see **chapo** •**mache do ba** see **mache** •**pran kout ba** see **koutba** •**vant ba** see **vant** •**yanvalou do ba** see **yanvalou**

ba² *n.* F bas stockings •**ba chosèt (ba koton.** stocking (sport); thick stockings •**ba kilòt** pantyhose •**demi ba.** knee-high stocking(s)

ba³ *n.* pack saddle (wooden). cf *lekipay*

ba⁴ *n.* line [drawn with a pencil or pen] •**pwen ba** period [punctuation]

ba⁵ *n.*1 bar [metal, wood] **2** helm, tiller •**ba direksyon** steering shaft •**ba fè** steel bar **cf** feray •**ba fiks{paralèl}** parallel bars •**ba savon** soap bar •**ba van** wind barrier forming a rudimentary kitchen •**ba vitès** gearshift lever **cf** levye

ba⁶ *n.* stripe

ba⁷ *n.* snack bar, small restaurant **cf** restoran

ba⁸ *n.* peck, little kiss on the cheek **cf** bo •**fè ba pou yon moun** to kiss, give s.o. a kiss *Fè ba pou mwen.* Give me a kiss.

ba⁹ •**mete ba¹** to give birth [animal] *Manman bèf la met ba yè.* The cow gave birth yesterday. **cf** mete atè •**mete ba** to whelp, give birth [animal] *Manman bèf la mèt ba yè, li fè de ti vach.* The cow gave birth last night, she had two calves **cf** akouche, met atè, miba •**mete yon moun ba** to humiliate *Pouki ou mete pitit la ba konsa?* Why do you humiliate the child like that? •**mete ba lezam** to lay down arms, to stop fighting *Nou mande militè yo pou yo mete ba lezam*. We asked the soldiers to lay down their arms. •**pa ba** from the rectum *Yo ba l lavman an pa ba*. They gave her the enema from the rectum. •**pale ba** see **pale**

There exist two attempts to produce monolingual dictionaries for HC, both by Haitian professionals: Vilsaint and Heurtelou (1994) and Trouillot (n.d.). The latter is a sketchy attempt, marred by serious shortcomings, for example, in defining *bal* 'bullet' it provides: *Pwojektil ki ka touye yon moun ki resevwa l* 'a projectile that kills people who receive it'. First, *pwojektil* is not defined in the dictionary, and second, the definition does not differentiate between a bullet and an arrow. The latter is also a projectile capable of killing people. For another example, the definition of the homonym 'dance' is also extremely vague and problematic: *Prestasyon yon gwoup mizikal ap fè, men se sitou aswè* 'a service rendered by a musical group, but it's especially in the evening'. Worse still, the definition of *prestasyon* refers to a type of tax, not an entertainment event: **Prestasyon sosyal**: *Pòsyon lajan leta retire sou moun k ap travay* 'A portion of money the State deducts from people who work'.

The Vilsaint and Hourtelou dictionary generally avoids these problems. For example, the definitions of the two *bal* entries are passable and illustrative examples are sometimes provided, although the definition for 'dance, ball' is curious and tedious:

bal: n. 1. Dans, fèt ki gen danse ladan l. 'dance, party, that has dancing in it' Se lè yon gwoup moun reyini nan yon fèt epi yo danse epi yo deplase kò yo ak elegans pandan yo ap suiv kadans yon mizik. 'It's when a group of people get together for a party and they dance and move their body with elegance as they follow the rhythm of the music.' Mwen pa renmen bal sa a, pa menm gen bon mizik. 'I don't like this ball, there's not even any good music.' 2. Moso plon ki soti nan yon zam. Plon pou chaje fizi osnon revòlvè. 'A piece of lead that comes out of a firearm. Lead to load a rifle or a revolver'.

Both dictionaries run into the fundamental problem of monolingual lexicography: the development of a suitable metalanguage for the framing of definitions.

Another major problem is the importance of closing definitions so that any defining term is provided within the body of the dictionary. For example, in defining *lota* 'skin rash' the user is engaged in a wild-goose chase, because the last defining term is absent from the Vilsaint dictionary:

Iota	tach nan figi 'a scar, mark on face'
tach	mak 'mark, scar, spot, bruise'
mak	**sikatris** ki sou po yon moun aprezavwa moun nan te gen yon blesi ki geri 'that is on the skin of a person after that person had a wound that healed'
sikatris	(absent from the dictionary)

Actually, *sikatris* means 'scar'. Thus, in the final analysis the user would be hard put to differentiate any of these near-synonyms from each other.

1.4 Other French-based Creoles

French-based creoles, other than Haitian Creole, fall into four groups on the basis of their structure, their relationship with Standard French, and various sociolinguistic factors: (1) Louisiana Creole; (2) Lesser Antilles creoles, where one needs to distinguish those that have political ties with France from those that have been closely associated with the British Commonwealth; (3) Guianese Creole; (4) creoles spoken in Indian Ocean islands or archipelagoes. The latter section includes a discussion of Tayo, a contact speech variety located in New Caledonia whose status as a creole and relationship with Réunion Creole are not clear.

1.4.1 Louisiana

Compared to Louisiana French (LF), spoken widely in the south-eastern portion of the state (the Francophone Triangle), Louisiana Creole (LC) exists only in three relatively isolated localities: on the banks of the lower Mississippi, in the former Acadian and German Coasts (St. James, St. John, and Ascension parishes between New Orleans and Baton Rouge); in New Roads (Pointe Coupee parish, north of Baton Rouge), see Klingler (1992, 2003); further to the west, in the Bayou Teche area (St. Martin and St. Landry parishes), see Morgan (1959), Marshall (1982), Neumann (1985) and Valdman and Klingler (1997). There are pockets of speakers of LC in other areas of the Francophone Triangle and some in Texas and California, see Klingler (2003: xxvii). According to the 1990 census, there were 6,310 speakers of LC, as opposed to 261,678 speakers of LF. But Klingler considers this number to be too low because, in view of its undervalued status, speakers probably under-report their use of it. In Neumann's description of the creole spoken in Breaux Bridge, in the Bayou Teche area (1985), she provides an estimate of 60,000 to 80,000 speakers. The 2010 census shows that the number of LF speakers has dropped sharply to 138,672 but that

Table 1.1. Parental Choice of Speech Variety to Be Spoken by Their Children

Speech variety (or varieties)	Percentage
IF	38
IF+LF	29
LF	10
LC	2
IF+LF+LC	9

the number of Creole speakers has risen slightly to 6,927 compared to the 2009 figures. This may be due to the fact that the census does not differentiate varieties of French-based Creoles (FBCs) spoken in Louisiana. Some of the people who declared that they spoke Creole at home may have been speakers of Haitian Creole (HC). Indeed, the number of speakers of HC in the USA rose more than a third between the 2000 and 2010 censuses (Valdman 2010).

A study of parental attitudes toward International French,[15] LF, and LC in francophone Louisiana underscores the devalorized status of LC. In a survey in parishes where LF and LC are best preserved, Tornquist (2000) found that International French (IF) is by far the variety that parents would prefer their children to speak (Table 1.1). Both LF and LC are truly endangered languages since they are no longer being transmitted intergenerationally. The terms used for LC reflect its depreciated status because of its association with slavery: *nèg* 'negro', *français nèg* 'negro French', *nigger French*, *couri-vini*,[16] *gumbo*.

Formerly spoken much more widely in Louisiana, in New Orleans, as far as Natchitoches in the north and Mobile, Alabama, in the east (Marshall 1990), and close to the Texas border in the west, LC is used by Blacks, Whites, and a group referred to as Creoles of color. Many of the members of these groups are multilingual, using Standard French (SF), LF, LC, and English. The linguistic situation of Louisiana is even more complicated than this multilingualism suggests. What is referred to as LF subsumes different regional and social varieties: Cajun (Cadien) and Plantation French among others, as is reflected by the title of the most authoritative dictionary for the language: *Dictionary of Louisiana French: As Spoken in Cajun, Creole, and American Indian Communities* (Valdman et al. 2010).

The first European presence in Louisiana dates back to 1519 and 1530, when the Spaniards Alvarez de Piñada and De Soto explored the lower Mississippi valley. In 1682, Robert Cavelier, Sieur de La Salle, traveling down the Mississippi from the Great Lakes region, planted the French flag at the mouth of the mighty river. He claimed for France all regions drained by the Mississippi and named that vast territory Louisiane, in honor of his sovereign Louis XIV. When, two years later, starting from France, he sailed to the Gulf of Mexico trying to relocate the mouth of the Mississippi from the west, his expedition lost its way and landed far away in Texas. After many hardships endured by members of the failed expedition, La Salle was assassinated in March 1687 following a mutiny. In 1698, Pierre Le Moyne d'Iberville and his younger brother, Jean-Baptiste Le Moyne de Bienville, both born in Canada, established small French settlements in Biloxi, then others in Mobile, Natchitoches, Nachez, and finally in New Orleans in 1718.

The Louisiana colony had an inauspicious start. The early settlers, many of them vagabonds, criminals, and prostitutes were not well-suited for the cultivation of cash crops, except some from Germany and Switzerland who settled on the west bank of the Mississippi on the German Coast. By 1719 the importation of slaves from African began. From that date until 1731, 5,310 were imported: 3,719 from Senegambia, 1,297 from the Bight of Benin, and 294 from Angola (G. M. Hall 2000; Klingler 2003: 6). Between 1726 and 1732 the proportion of slaves to free persons had tripled: 1,468 versus 1,147 in 1721 to 3,395 versus 1,095 in 1732 (Klingler 2003: 12). Slaves were unevenly distributed in the colony. For example, in 1732, in Pointe Coupee there were only 75 slaves versus 56 free persons whereas closer to New Orleans, in Chapitoulas on the right (west) bank of the Mississippi, there were 1,227 slaves versus 237 free persons. Many homestead owners (*habitants*) had three or four slaves but some, particularly the élite, had 100 or more. Klingler (2003: 11) reports that one of the high officials, a certain Dubreuil, had accumulated 500 slaves. Thus, there co-existed early in the development of the colony what Chaudenson (1992) defines as the homestead phase (s*ociété d'habitation*), in which slaves had close contact with speakers of Colonial French (CF), and the agro-industrial phase (*société de plantation*), in which their linguistic input was provided by other slaves who had acquired an approximative version of CF or an early form of the local creole. Also, in New Orleans slaves worked on public construction projects or were servants; outside of the city, they had greater freedom for contacts with Whites and Amerindians beyond the homestead or the plantation (Klingler 2003: 13).

Having lost the Seven Year (French and Indian) War and been forced to surrender to England the territories of New France (chiefly present-day Quebec province) and the east bank of the Mississippi, except New Orleans, in 1762 (prior to the Treaty of Paris in 1763 that formalized the cession) Louis XV secretly gave Louisiana to Spain so that it would escape British control. Earlier, in 1713, by the Treaty of Utrecht, France had been forced to surrender its colony of Acadia (later renamed Nova Scotia) to England. Acadians refused to pledge allegiance to the British crown and, in an event termed *Le Grand Dérangement* 'The Great Upheaval', many were evicted and deported to England, France, Saint-Domingue, and the US colonies. From 1765, Acadian refugees were allowed to settle in Louisiana by its new Spaniard masters. They formed communities in the Acadian Coast, in the Bayou Teche region and later along the Bayou Lafourche in the Terrebonne and Lafourche parishes (Rottet 2001: 52–3). In the Bayou Teche region the Cajuns (Cadiens), as they were called, interacted with speakers of LC and influenced the development of that variety of the language.

The Spanish period that lasted until 1800, when Louisiana was retroceded to France, was marked by considerable development. The population grew from 11,000 (half slave and half free) in 1763 to about 50,000 (Neumann 1985; Rottet 2001: 51). Beginning with the Haitian Revolution until 1810, refugees from Saint-Domingue sought refuge in Louisiana, bringing along with them their slaves: 2,731 Whites, 3,102 free people of color, and 2,226 slaves. Most settled in New Orleans but many of the Whites established plantations on the banks of the Mississippi.

The main existing descriptions of CF (Neumann 1985 and Klingler 1992, 2003) distinguish two main varieties of LC, Bayou Teche Creole and Mississippi Valley Creole. Speedy (1994, 1995) claims a separate origin for the two varieties, suggesting that Bayou Teche Creole has its origin in the HC brought in by Saint-Domingue refugees who settled in that region. On the basis of both demographic and linguistic evidence, Klingler (2003: 71–92) refutes that claim and concludes that the differences between the two varieties are not profound and that they stem from the transportation of the language from the banks of the Mississippi westward.

Although LC does share linguistic features with HC, for example, the durative *ap(e)* and future *(v)a* verb markers versus *ka* and *ke*, respectively, for the Antillean French-based Creoles (FBCs), it differs widely from it in many respects.[17] As in the Indian Ocean FBCs and in Guianese Creole (GuiC), possession is marked by pre-posed determiners, as versus post-posed pronouns: *mo popa* 'my father' vs. *papa mwen/papa a mwen* in HC and the Antillean[18] FBCs. In the determiner system, LC shows significant decreolization, more so in Bayou Teche than in Pointe Coupee. For example, gender differentiation is variably marked by pre-posed differentiated determiners: *Li monde pou ki l kouto* [*l'couteau*] 'she asked whose knife it is' (Valdman and Klingler 1997: 117); *la fiy* [*la fille*] *vini reste avek mwa isi* 'the girl came to stay with me here' (Neumann 1985: 10).[19] In all varieties of LC, there is alternation between pre- and post-posed definite determiners and the marking of plural: *chyen-la trape lode lapen-la* 'the dog caught the scent of the rabbit', *le machin ...* [*les machines*] 'the machines' vs. *depèch-ye* 'the peaches' (Klingler 2003: 172–5). It is noteworthy that in Pointe

Coupee, but not in other areas, when it is post-posed, the definite determiner shows nearly the same morphophonological variation determined by the final phoneme of the preceding noun as in HC:[20] *piti-a* 'the child', *chyen-la* 'the dog', *letòf-lœ* 'the cloth', *la krèm-nan* 'the cream' (Klingler 2003: 173).

Klingler (2003: 25–46) offers sample extracts of court proceedings, registered in 1748, of a slave accused of killing a soldier. These clearly reflect approximative French:

(1)

Ou toy courir Charlot pendant que nous diner?	'Where did you go, Charlot, while we were eating?'
Moy Gagner Gillet.	'I have a vest.'
Cela n'est pas bon, si toy mourir, mourir seul et nia pas faire mourir monde qui ny'a rien faire avec toi.	'That is not good, if you die, die alone and don't make people die that have nothing to do with you.'

Neumann-Holzschuh (1987, 2011) offers a wide variety of nineteenth- and early-twentieth-century texts written in LC. An interesting example of early LC and of the diglossic nature of the relationship between that language and its lexifier is found in A. Mercier's novel, *L'Habitation Saint-Ybars* (1881). The first scene, situated in New Orleans, contains LC samples that demonstrate the alternation between the two languages on the part of bilingual speakers. It involves a newly arrived Frenchman who passes a shop where slaves are on sale and asks what is going on. A passer-by responds first in LC but, seeing that she wasn't understood, switches to French (Valdman 1979, 1992):

(2)

–Madame, je vous prie, qu'est-ce que cela?	'M'am, please, what's this?'
–Vou pa oua don, Michié ... ce nèg pou vende.	'Don't you see, then, it's negroes for sale.'
–Ce sont des nègres à vendre, Monsieur.	'They're negroes for sale, sir.'

The other sample, between a child of the plantation owner and his Black nanny, shows that White children entrusted to the care of Black house servants grew up speaking LC. Here the little boy, Démon, scolds a bird that he has just captured and is putting into a cage. He is reprimanded by the slave nanny, Mamrie:

(3)

    –Resté don tranquil, bête !   'Stay quiet, beast!'
    –To bon toi, **lui dit Mamrie,**   'You're funny,' Mamrie said to him,
    to ote li so liberté et to oulé [*vouloir*] 'you took away its freedom and you
    li contan. Mo sré voudré oua ça to sré want it to be pleased. I would like to see
    di, si yé [*eux*] té toi andan ain cage what you would say if they put you in a
    comme ça !   cage like that!'

At this stage, according to the written samples cited here, which might not reflect the full scale of variation of the language, LC did not differ substantially from the current varieties. For example, in the above extract the second person singular informal pronoun shows functional differentiation, *to* for subject and *toi* for object. The irrealis (conditional) marker *sré*, derived from the French conditional *serais, serait, seraient*, occurs rarely at present; it has been replaced by *se* (Neumann 1985: 220; Klingler 2003: 261).

However, there are three signal differences that reflect the more basilectal[21] nature of early LC. First, only the post-posed determiner appears: *si to gadé nan pi là enco* 'if you keep looking in the well' (Neumann-Holzschuh 1987: 29). Second, verbs have only a single form whereas in present-day LC there are two classes of verbs: those with a single stem and those with both a short and a long stem (Neumann 1985; Valdman and Klingler 1997; Klingler 2003). For two-stem verbs, which are generally non-stative (action) verbs, the long form carries the completive meaning. It is used with the various pre-posed verb markers: *mo lave mo figi* 'I wash my face', *m ape lave mo figi* 'I'm washing my face'. The short expresses the habitual or universal present and imperative: *vu lav li* 'you wash it (in general)', *lav li* 'wash it'. For single-stem stative verbs, the stem carries the habitual or universal present meaning: *to konen* 'you know'. For non-stative single-stem verbs, the meaning of the stem is variable but generally expresses completed actions: *nou kouri mene le flœr o simityèr* 'we took the flower to the cemetery' (Valdman and Klingler 1997: 124). Third, in older texts the negative adverb *pa* precedes the verb: *cofair to pa jité vilen Compair Lapin dans zéronce là* 'Why don't you throw nasty Brer Rabbit in the briar patch', *pa jité mouen dans zéronce* 'Don't throw me in the briars' (Neumann-Holzschuh 1987: 33). In current LC, *pa* precedes the long form and follows the short form of two-stem verbs: *ye pa mete fime* 'they didn't put fertilizer' versus *mo truv pa sa isi* 'I don't find that here'. For single-stem verbs, *pa* usually follows when they are used in the habitual or universal sense, *mo jwe pa li asté l* 'I don't play it now' but precedes it when they carry other meanings: *mo pa fe en zariko* 'I didn't raise a (single) bean' (Klingler 2003: 321).

The detailed descriptions provided by Neumann (1985) and Klingler (2003) contain extensive corpora of recorded material. *The Dictionary of Louisiana Creole* (Valdman *et al.* 1998) provides extensive contextual examples with an indication of the region where they were collected or the bibliographical source in which they were cited.

1.4.2 Lesser Antilles

Although in his three voyages to the West Indies Columbus 'discovered' and named most of the small islands that compose the Lesser Antilles archipelago that stretches east of Puerto Rico to the north-eastern shore of Venezuela, the Spaniards made few attempts to establish plantations for export cash crops like tobacco, indigo, coffee, or sugar. As their initial contacts in Hispaniola show, they were primarily interested in the extraction of gold and silver and establishing a base for further exploration on the American mainland. In addition, in contrast to the relatively peaceful Tainos who had settled in the Greater Antilles (Cuba, Puerto Rico, Jamaica, and Hispaniola) and created sedentary societies based on agriculture, the smaller Caribbean islands were inhabited by the fierce and warlike Caribs, who were hostile to the European invaders and did not engage in large-scale agriculture.

Throughout the sixteenth century, Dutch, English, and French pirates, many of them holders of official commissions from their respective countries' rulers as privateers (French *flibustiers* 'freebooters'), preyed on Spanish ports and ships transporting precious metals from Mexico and Peru to Spain. They also engaged in contraband to break the mercantilist trade laws that forbade trade between Spanish colonies and other European powers. Beginning in the seventeenth century, England, France, and the Netherlands began to establish permanent settlements on Caribbean islands, engaging in a constant struggle among themselves that reflected dynastic and religious conflicts in Europe. Most of the Lesser Antilles islands changed hands numerous times, resulting in the destruction of infrastructure and the displacement of colonists along with their slaves. An important aspect of interisland forced migrations is that plantation owners transported slaves and some equipment with them (Chaudenson 2003: 106–14).

In addition to Tortuga Island, north of Hispaniola, which served as a base for the multinational cohort of privateers, the first French implantation in the Caribbean was in St. Kitts (Saint-Christophe). The privateer Pierre Belain d'Estambuc established a settlement there in 1626. With Cardinal Richelieu as the primary shareholder, the Compagnie de St. Christophe was formed, later reorganized as the Compagnie des Iles d'Amérique. St. Kitts was shared with the English, who had established an earlier settlement and

26 Introduction

eventually gained full possession of the island in 1783. It was from St. Kitts that in 1635 d'Estambuc led a French expedition of about 150 men to Martinique. The same year 500 colonists from France, under the leadership of Charles Liénard and Jean du Plessis, obtained a commission to establish a settlement in Guadeloupe (Holm 1989: 364). By 1671, the French colony in St. Kitts was in the incipient stage of a plantation economy, *société de plantation* (Chaudenson 1979, 1992). The two censuses taken that year indicated a slight majority of slaves: 4,450 out of a total population of 8,089 in one and 4,281 out of 7,616 for the other (Calvet and Chaudenson 1998: 50). However, these authors emit doubts about the existence at that time in St. Kitts of an FBC that would have been exported to Guadeloupe and Martinique.

The numerous contacts among these first three major French plantation colonies account for the affinity and mutual intelligibility between Guadeloupean Creole (GC) and Martinican Creole (MartC). For example, both mark the durative (progressive) with the verb marker *ka* (MartC *man ka manjé*, GC *an ka manjé* 'I'm eating') versus HC *ap(e)* (*m ap manje*); the plural of nouns is expressed by pre-posed *sé* (*sé biten la* 'the things') versus HC post-posed *yo* (*bagay (la) yo*). It is this Lesser Antillean FBC, spread southward from Guadeloupe and Martinique, that is found in the later-established French settlements in Dominica, St. Lucia, and Grenada and that was exported to Trinidad. For an overall description covering all FBCs of this region, see Bernabé (1987), and for a survey of variants among Antillean FBCs, see Le Dû and Brun-Trigaud (2011)'s geographical atlas.

The overseas French departments and associated territories
Guadeloupe

Guadeloupe, whose Arawask name was Karukera 'land of the beautiful waters', consists, in fact, of two juxtaposed islands: the mountainous Basse Terre, featuring an active volcano, the Grande Soufrière, the highest mountain peak in the Lesser Antilles, to the west, and the flat Grande Terre to the east, separated by a narrow sea channel. The administrative unit of Guadeloupe also includes three smaller dependent islands, Désirade to the east, Marie-Galante to the south-east of Grande Terre, and the twin islands of Les Saintes (Terre de Haut and Terre de Bas) south of Basse-Terre. The total population of Guadeloupe is 503,000 (2011) in an area of 630 square miles. As is the case for the other three overseas French dependencies where a creole is widely spoken (Martinique, French Guiana, and Réunion), Guadeloupe was granted the status of a full-fledged department (département d'outre-mer, DOM) in 1946.

Guadeloupe's development as a plantation colony was hampered in the early period by strife with the Caribs and incursions by Dutch and English raiders. This was in a time of great conflict during the French Revolution when the White planters rebelled against the revolutionary regime and allied themselves with a British invading force. Dispatched from France to Guadeloupe as governor, Victor Hughes defeated the British. He brought along a guillotine and executed many of their French allies while emancipating the slaves. These events account in part for the relatively low percentage of the population of White origin (Chaudenson 1992: 29).

In the 1960s, Gérard Lauriette, a schoolteacher with unorthodox pedagogical views, initiated a transitional approach in which GC was used as the oral classroom language and French as the written one. For this initiative, opposed by many parents and the authorities, and other provocative ideas, he was fired on the grounds of *aliénation mentale* (mental illness). Eventually, he served as mayor of his town, Capesterre Belle Eau in Basse Terre. The issue of the introduction of GC and its role in Guadeloupean society continues to be debated. Its promotion is advocated by militants of the independentist movement. A sociolinguistic survey by Durizot Jno-Baptiste (1996) indicates that a majority of the population consider both French and GC as their native languages but it is the latter that expresses their cultural identity. Nonetheless, as Chaudenson concludes (1992: 29), the language situation of Guadeloupe is one of diglossia: French is used nearly exclusively in the official sphere and GC as vernacular.

GC is endowed with a variety of linguistic tools: a descriptive grammar (Germain 1976) and two GC–French dictionaries containing a French–GC index (Ludwig *et al.* 1990; Tourneux and Barbotin 1990);[22] the data for the latter were collected on the island of Marie-Galante, but the lead author affirms that the language described does not differ from that of the main island. An extensive and detailed lexicological analysis appears in Cervinka-Taulier (1992). There exists a set of learning materials for the language addressed to travelers distributed by the French publisher Assimil (Poullet and Telchid 1990). The most thorough structural description of GC appears in Bernabé's 1983 joint treatment of GC and MartC.

Martinique
Somewhat smaller and less populated than Guadeloupe (412,000 inhabitants on 430 square miles in 2012), Martinique is located between Dominica and St. Lucia in the Windward chain of the Lesser Antilles. In its early period, in the middle of the seventeenth century, the workforce of the colony consisted mainly of indentured servants. Their masters, the *habitants*, cultivated staples such as manioc, tobacco, achiote or annatto (a coloring agent; *roucou* in French), and indigo that did not require the intensive cultivation that sugarcane does. It was not until the end of the century that

imported African slaves began to outnumber Europeans: in 1699, the population was 13,799 Blacks and Mulattoes versus 6,252 Whites (Kremnitz 1983: 15). By then an agro-industrial economy (*société de plantation*) had been firmly established, and by the end of the eighteenth century the Whites constituted less than 10% of the total population. An important step in the development of the colony was the arrival in 1654 of 250 Dutch Jews, who brought their technical experience of the production of sugar in Brazil – Jews were later expelled from all French colonies by order of Louis XIV's minister Colbert.

Like its sister Caribbean DOM, Martinique came under British control several times. During the French Revolution, when the Legislative Assembly first gave equal rights to freed slaves and Mulattoes, and then abolished slavery in 1794, the planters in Martinique appealed for assistance from England. The British occupied the island off and on until after the fall of Napoleon in 1814. Initially, the freed slaves were returned to their owners. However, when England abolished slavery in its empire in 1833 an attempt was made to extend the proscription to Martinique. It was not until 1848 that, with the efforts of Victor Schoelcher, France officially abolished slavery in all its colonies.[23] Schoelcher later became a deputy in the French parliament, representing both Guadeloupe and Martinique.

Martinique's active volcano, Mont Pelée, erupted in 1792, 1851, and 1902. That last eruption caused the death of all of the 30,000 inhabitants of the former capital of Saint-Pierre except a shoemaker and a prisoner in the town jail. The capital was then moved south from the Caribbean coast to Fort-de-France. The eruption led many inhabitants to move to French Guiana (Chaudenson 1992: 31).

Several names in French literature are associated with Martinique: Aimé Césaire, who founded the Négritude movement of the 1930s with the Senegalese Léopold Sédar Senghor (later president of Senegal and champion of Francophonie), and the Guianese poet Léon-Gontran Damas. The Négritude movement, founded by Black writers and intellectuals, was formed in reaction to European colonialism and valorized the shared African cultural heritage of its founders. Césaire, author of *Cahier d'un retour au pays natal* (1939), later became mayor of Fort-de-France and a representative to the French National Assembly.

A younger group of Martinican and intellectual writers – Jean Bernabé, Patrick Chamoiseau, and Raphaël Confiant – distanced themselves from Négritude. In their manifesto, *Éloge de la créolité* (1993) they advocated a recognition of the diversity of Antillean culture distinct from the simple preservation of African cultural influences, just as creole languages represent the harmonization of disparate components into a single cohesive whole. In their literary works in French, Chamoiseau (whose novel *Texaco*, 1992, was awarded the coveted Prix Goncourt[24]) and Confiant introduced syntactic features and lexical items modeled on Martinican Creole (MartC), *créolismes*. The latter's early literary works were in MartC, first a set of short series, *Jik dèyè do Bondyé* (Just in the Back of God) in 1979 and subsequently several novels. Faced with a lack of readership for these works, in Confiant's words he switched from a bicycle to a car, that is, he abandoned MartC and began writing in French. His first novel in French, *Le Nègre et l'amiral* (1988) was a notable success. Confiant is also the author of the most comprehensive MartC–French bilingual dictionary (2007). Bernabé, a linguist affiliated with the Université des Antilles et de la Guyane campus in Schoelcher, Martinique, has written the basic linguistic descriptions of MartC (1983, 1987, 2001, 2003). In 1976, he founded the GEREC (Groupe d'Études et de Recherches en Espace Créolophone et Francophone), which devised a phonologically based spelling, based on the Faublas-Pressoir orthography.[25] It is used widely for all Antillean creoles and for Guianese Creole. With Confiant, he also promoted the extension of a diploma for the teaching of regional languages at the secondary school level (CAPES) to the FBCs spoken in the DOMs. However, a major problem with this extension of the CAPES is that it treats all these languages as a single language. Although there is a fair degree of mutual intelligibility among Guadeloupean, Martinican, and Guianese Creoles, there is little if any between this group of creoles and Réunion Creole.

Two German scholars, Kremnitz (1983) and March (1996), have conducted thorough sociolinguistic studies on the attitude of speakers toward French and MartC and their perception of the role they should play in their society, the former studying teachers and the latter, mothers and schoolchildren. March demonstrates that in the matrifocal Martinican society, as is the case in Guadeloupe, both the creole and French are considered native languages: the former as the expression of local cultural identity and the latter as the means to socio-economic advancement. However, the use of MartC is declining among younger speakers.

The first lexicographic study of MartC (Jourdain 1956) organizes the lexicon of the language in terms of semantic fields, for example, flora, fauna, entertainment, sports, sciences, travel. Confiant's work (2007) constitutes the most up-to-date and thorough bilingual dictionary (MartC→French) for the language.

Saint-Martin (Sint-Maarten)
Located east of Puerto Rico, this island was a former dependency of Guadeloupe. Since 2003 it has been a semi-autonomous Collectivité d'Outremer (COM), enjoying local rule and a looser association with France. In 1648, it was divided between the French and the Dutch. France administers the

northern part, 34 square miles in which 36,824 (2009 figure) inhabitants reside. With its hilly terrain, Saint-Martin did not lend itself to the development of an agro-industrial economy based on sugar production; its major attractions in the late seventeenth and eighteenth centuries were its salt flats and its strategic location at the northern end of the Lesser Antilles island chain. This explains why it changed hands among the Dutch, English, and French about a dozen times until the Franco-Dutch division was reinstituted in 1816. At present, especially on the Dutch side, the island is an attractive vacation spot, particularly for US tourists.

Although French is the official language of the part of the island administered by France, the vernacular language is not an FBC but a vernacular variety of English, 'English of the islands', which exists on a continuum with Standard English and is heavily influenced by US usage. FBCs are present but these are spoken by migrants from the French Antilles and Haiti (Martinez 1994).

Saint-Barthélemy (St. Barts)
Located a short distance to the south-east of Saint-Martin, the islet of Saint-Barthélemy (abbreviated as St. Barts in English and St. Barth in French) has a population of 8,902 (2009) within 8.5 square miles. Previously administered as a dependency of Guadeloupe, it is, like French Saint-Martin, a Collectivité d'Outremer (COM).

Currently a fashionable winter vacation destination, St. Barts is particularly noteworthy linguistically and anthropologically. First, some of its White inhabitants, descended from the original French settlers, speak a creole influenced by GC and MartC, St. Barts Creole (SBC); others use a French dialect that reflects Colonial French, St. Barts Patois (SBP). Second, there exists a high level of endogamy within each of these two groups, corresponding to a geographical separation: SBC speakers, engaged primarily in agriculture, are located in the eastern, relatively flat part of the islet, Au Vent (windward). The SBP speakers, primarily fishermen, live in the western hilly part, Sous le Vent (leeward). In the late nineteenth century, following a period of economic hardship, many St. Barts inhabitants from the two communities emigrated to St. Thomas, in the US Virgin Islands. Interestingly, these immigrants formed two separate communities, reflecting the division in the homeland: Carenage, a fishing community speaking SBP in the harbor of Charlote-Amalie, and Northside, a truck-farming community speaking SBC on the north side of the island (Morrill and Dyke 1965; G. Lefebvre 1976; Highfield 1979; Maher 1990, 1997; Calvet and Chaudenson 1998).

Most of the first French settlers sent from St. Kitts in 1648 were massacred by the local Caribs in 1656 (Du Tertre 1667, Vol. 1: 416; Calvet and Chaudenson 1998: 22). The French returned again from St. Kitts in 1659, and by 1671 the population numbered 300, of whom, according to the census, 59 were White servants and 46 Black slaves. Because of the constant state of warfare between the western European powers in the seventeenth and eighteenth centuries, there were constant movements of population from one island to the next, particularly in those like St. Barts characterized by a low level of development. In 1784, when the islet was ceded to Sweden in exchange for trading rights in Gothenburg, the population had reached only 739, of whom two-thirds were White (Calvet and Chaudenson 1998: 39). There was a spike in the demographic curve in 1812, to 5,482 inhabitants, followed by a sharp drop to 2,600 in 1885, explainable in part by the departure of Black slaves after emancipation in 1848 and by economic hardship (Maher 1996, 1997). These demographic facts explain why in the course of the eighteenth and nineteenth centuries there never developed in St. Barts a robust agro-industrial economy (*société de plantation*) that could spawn an endogenous variety of FBC.

The period of Swedish administration had little impact on the linguistic development of St. Barts, except for the introduction of English and a creolized variety of that language in the island's main town, Gustavia, an active free port. However, the town had little influence on the speech of neighboring communities. The following linguistic scenario is proposed for this part of the island by Calvet and Chaudenson (1998: 151). Colonial French was introduced by the original settlers, many of whom migrated from other Caribbean islands, especially St. Kitts, Saint-Vincent, and Guadeloupe. It was the speech of both the Au Vent and Sous le Vent sections. In the middle of the eighteenth century, there were attempts to develop cash crops such as indigo and cotton in the Au Vent section, which was more suitable for agriculture. Creole-speaking slaves were imported from Martinique and Guadeloupe to labor on small-scale plantations, leading to close contact between the Colonial French-speaking Whites and the slaves. As was the case in some areas of francophone Louisiana (Klingler 2003), the Whites eventually acquired what became SBC, which does not differ greatly from GC and MartC. When the Blacks left St. Barts, the Au Vent Saint-Barthians retained SBC as their primary speech variety.

When St. Barts was restored to France in 1874, it held only about 2,500 inhabitants: a number that remained constant for a full century. In the last three decades, the tourist boom has caused the population to quadruple, with the arrival of outsiders from the region and from metropolitan France who have swamped the descendants of the original settlers. At present, with the influx of people from France and generalized schooling, the speakers of both SBC and SBP are exposed to the strong influence of Standard French.

St. Thomas

Conquered by Denmark in 1666, this most populous of the Virgin Islands became a territory of the United States when its government purchased the entire archipelago from the Danes in 1916. The majority of the population consists of English-speaking descendants of African slaves imported to work on sugar plantations. Around 1870, when St. Barts experienced a severe economic downturn, men from both the St. Bart's French-dialect-speaking and Creole-speaking communities, followed eventually by their families, migrated to St. Thomas and, as indicated in the description of St. Barts above, formed two separate communities corresponding to those in their homeland. Morrill and Dyke (1965) estimated the Carenage community at about 1,000 and the Northside one at 500. However, invoking migration of younger members of the Carenage community to the US mainland, Highfield (1979) lowered the estimate of its population by half.

No study exists of the speech of the Northside community, so it cannot be determined to what extent it differs from that of the creole of St. Barts Au Vent. Highfield's (1979) description of Carenage French shows that it does not differ substantially from the speech of St. Barts Sous le Vent. His study provides the most detailed insight into the morphosyntax of St. Bart's French, given its similarity to Carenage French, as well as the most extensive published corpus of recorded material. There was little contact between the Carenage and Northside communities because of their occupational differences, poor communications between distant localities in the earlier period of settlement, and linguistic differences. In the few interactions he witnessed, Highfield (1979: 19) reports that local English serves as the basic common speech medium but speakers often switch to their own vernacular, Carenage French and Northside Creole, respectively, which their interlocutor(s) appear to understand.

The British-influenced West Indies

Dominica

Located south-south-east of Guadeloupe, Dominica's 750 square miles hold a population of 71,293 according to the 2011 census. The island was discovered by Columbus on Sunday, November 3, 1493, hence its name from the Latin for Sunday. It was first claimed by France in 1635, but a French settlement was not established there until 1715. As was the case with St. Lucia, ownership of the island was constantly disputed with Great Britain for nearly a century; it was finally ceded to that country in 1783. Part of the short-lived West Indies Federation, Dominica was granted independence from the United Kingdom in 1978.

Because of the relatively low level of French and British settlement, many of the indigenous Carib population remained in Dominica. A Carib reservation was established in the eastern part of the island; today, about 3,000 members of the Garifuna tribe of Arawak and Carib origin remain. The French missionary priest Raymond Breton, who lived among the Caribs for ten years, authored the first dictionaries for the language (1665,1666). He also wrote a catechism in Carib (1664) and a grammar (1664). According to Douglas Taylor (1977), a British linguist who lived for forty years on the island, the language described by Breton was Arawak, although it does contain many Carib elements.

Taylor provided most of the descriptions of current Dominican Creole (1951, 1962). There exists a dictionary of the language containing only about 6,000 words without contextual examples (Fontaine and Roberts 1991). These authors point out that the language shows wide regional variation, with influence from GC in the north and MartC in the south. In the dictionary, they list *mwen* as the first-person pronoun but in a small set of simple sentences contained in a brief introduction they use the variant *mon* alternating with *mwen* as subject (*mon fen* 'I'm hungry', *mwen ni ven nanné* 'I'm twenty years old') and *mwen* as possessive (*non mwen sé Paul* 'my name is Paul').

St. Lucia
This volcanic island located about 25 miles south of Martinique has a surface of 620 square miles and a population of 174,000 (2010 census), one-third of which lives in the capital, Castries. Although it had been visited by various Europeans from about 1550, a French settlement was not established there until 1643 under the leadership of Jacques du Parquet, governor of Martinique. Unlike the British, who had attempted several previous small-scale settlements, the French had relatively harmonious relations with the fierce Carib Amerindians (Chaudenson 2003: 30). In 1765, the first sugar plantation was established in Vieux Fort, on the southern tip of the island. By 1772, the total population had reached 15,476, of whom only 13% were Whites (Le Page and Tabouret-Keller 1985: 57). As was the case for the islands in the Lesser Antilles, control of St. Lucia, where a plantation economy developed with the importation of African slave labor, was contested between England and France for more than a century. The British finally gained ownership of the island in 1804. Having joined the West Indies Federation (1958–62), it gained full independence in 1979.

Because of the predominant presence of French plantation owners, many of them migrants from Martinique, French held a dominant position until the proclamation of English as the official language in 1840. Most place names in St. Lucia evoke the former French presence: town names – Castries, Vieux Fort, Gros Islet, Choiseul; bays – Anse l'Ivrogne ('drunkard's bay'), Anse La Voutte; the famous active volcano, Souffrière. However, Saint Lucian Creole, locally termed Patois or Kwéyòl, was spoken by nearly the entire population. In 1911, only about 3% of the population spoke English (Carrington 1984: 4). Today, many Saint Lucians are bilingual in English and Kwéyòl (Cadette-Blasse 2008: 203–16). Long unvalued, as the label Patois reflects, the language now benefits from promotion at the highest level of government.[26] The Governor-General of the country,[27] Dame C. Pearlette Louisy, founded the association that promotes the use and development of the language: Mouvman Kwéyòl Sent Lisi. St. Lucian Creole is one of the best-described FBCs in the British-influenced Caribbean, benefiting from a descriptive phonology and morphosyntax (Carrington 1984) and two dictionaries (Mondésir and Carrington 1992; Frank 2001). Nonetheless, pressure from English, the language dominating the media and the educational medium, as well as the creolized English vernacular speech ('English of the islands'), is causing St. Lucian Creole to recede.

Grenada and Carriacou
Stretching southward from St. Lucia are the Windward Islands, Saint-Vincent, the Grenadines, Carriacou, and Grenada. Of these, only in the latter two does an FBC remain, albeit severely endangered. With a population of only 8,000 on 13 square miles Carriacou is a dependency of the larger Grenada, which has 344 square miles and a 2010 population of 104,000. In 1649, after an unsuccessful first French attempt at settlement in 1638, Jacques Du Parquet led an expedition from Martinique to Grenada, which was occupied by the Caribs, as was the case for most islands of the Leeward and Windward archipelagoes. The French held the island for about a century and introduced the cultivation of indigo and sugarcane and the accompanying importation of African slaves. The two islands were surrendered to Britain in 1783 by the Treaty of Versailles. Grenada became a British crown colony in 1877 and gained its independence in 1974. A notable political event was the intervention in 1983 by US forces, with support from some English-influenced Caribbean nations, following a military coup which overthrew the existing leftist government.

Robert Le Page (Le Page and Tabouret-Keller 1985: 52) states that Grenadian Creole, termed Patois locally, was in vigorous use among older speakers when he did fieldwork on the island in 1950. However, Holm (1989: 376) reports that it is spoken by only a few older speakers in Carriacou and the northern part of Grenada. The only descriptions of the language are Peter Roberts's 1971 University of the West Indies MA thesis on the verb system and Kephart's (1991) presentation of texts.

Trinidad and Tobago
The largest island in the eastern Caribbean, located less than a dozen miles from the South American mainland, Trinidad and its smaller dependency of

Tobago have a 2013 population of 1,225,225 in an area of roughly 1,841 square miles. Trinidad was discovered by Columbus in 1498 during his third American voyage. It remained a scarcely populated and poorly developed colony until the 1770s, when the Spanish encouraged immigration by Catholics from countries allied with Spain by means of a *cédula de población* (population bill) that granted land and exemption from taxation (Buscher 1969: viii–ix; Holm 1989: 377). In 1783, four years before the seizure of Trinidad by England in 1787, a French planter from Grenada, Philippe Rose Roume de Saint-Laurent, impressed with the promising economic opportunities offered by the island, persuaded the Spanish rulers to propose a more generous *cédula*. He encouraged French settlers from the region to take advantage of the new provisions and establish plantations.[28] French planters and their slaves came from the Leeward and Windward islands, especially after the French Revolution brought unrest in Guadeloupe and Martinique. From about 1,000 inhabitants in 1773 the population had grown to 18,627 according to the census taken by the British in 1798 (Buscher 1969).[29]

Tobago, the smaller of the two islands of the current Republic of Trinidad and Tobago, was a territory hotly disputed by the Dutch, English, French, Spanish, and Swedish; it changed hands thirty-three times prior to its official cession to England in 1814. The French occupied Tobago for about thirty years after their capture of it in 1781.

French and, for the laboring majority of inhabitants, an FBC similar to that of the Caribbean islands remained the dominant languages of Trinidad and Tobago until the influx of people from the British eastern Caribbean and massive arrivals of Chinese, Portuguese, and especially Indian indentured servants after passage of the Slavery Abolition Act of 1833 in England (Borde 1876). English was declared the official language in 1821.

With the spread of education and the impact of the mass media, Trinidadian Creole (also termed Patois) has continuously lost ground to English. It is still spoken by older people in small isolated regions of the island, for example, in Paramin, a village in the northern range above the Maraval Valley. I collected some Patois material in that area in 1966.[30] Trinidadian Creole has the distinction of being the first FBC to benefit from a systematic description, John Jacob Thomas's, *The Theory and Practice of Creole Grammar* (1869). Born in humble circumstances, the Afro-Trinidadian Thomas's 'most impressionable years were spent among those who themselves had known the indignities of servitude and the excited hopes of emancipation, and some of these in their memories could reach back to Africa' (Vidale 2005). He attended a teacher training college and became a schoolmaster in rural areas. Thomas was one of the first Black Trinidadians to sit the competitive examination for administrative posts. In 1867, he was successful and obtained a minor administrative post in Port of Spain. Later, the governor of the colony appointed him Secretary to the Board of Education and then Secretary to the Council of Queen's Royal College. He was invited to England by the Philological Society and, at one of its meetings, he delivered a lecture on 'Some peculiarities of the Creole language'. He was then elected member of that august society (Vidale 2005). In 1888, in poor health, he returned to England for treatment and died of tuberculosis the next year at age forty-nine. Before his death, he wrote his most famous book, *Froudacity: West Indian Fables by James Anthony Froude* (1889), in which he showed the inaccuracies in that famous historian's account of British colonization of the West Indies and highlighted its deep racism. For example, Froude deemed Black West Indians incapable of self-government (Froude 1888).

As Goodman assessed, 'Thomas' treatment of the grammar per se is generally clear and thorough' (1964: 119), although he often confuses descriptive and historical analyses. Unlike Saint-Quentin (1872), whose description of Cayenne Creole would soon follow, Thomas adopted an etymological rather than an autonomous phonologically based spelling. But he did provide guidance in its interpretation. For example, he points out his use of CH for a sound not heard in French, the palatal voiceless fricative /tʃ/ which replaces French /k/ before front vowels: *cuite* > *CHuite* 'cooked', although he mischaracterizes that phoneme as a 'guttural' (Goodman 1964: 3).

Thomas also notes differences between Trinidadian Creole (TC) and that of other FBCs, for example, the use of the preposition *à* with post-posed pronouns in possessive constructions in GC: *bitin à-ou* 'your baggage' versus TC *bitation nous* 'our estate'. This suggests that in its development TC was more subject to the influence of the other Lesser Antilles FBCs than Guianese Creole (Thomas 1869: 38). In some sense, Thomas's description of TC constitutes a sort of contrastive analysis of TC versus French and English. For example, he points out that unlike French, where a determiner must be used with nouns in all instances, TC like English uses the plural definite determiner only to mark definiteness. To account for the contrast between '*moèn voèr* zanneaux *et-pis* bouacelets *nans yon magazin* 'I saw *ear-rings* and *bracelets* in a store' versus *ces anneaux* la *te bien nans goût moèn; main moèn pa té content ces bouacelet*s la, 'the ear-rings were much to my taste; but I did not like the bracelets', he states: 'We use the definite *ces-la (the)* in these instances, because *zanneaux* and *bouacelets* have, by the second mention of them, become determinate and specific' (1869: 24).

French creoles in Venezuela
Güiria Creole (Patois)
There exists, in the town of Güiria, located in the Paria peninsula in the north-western Venezuelan state of Sucre, a creole related historically and linguistically to Trinidadian Creole (Hancock 1985; Neumann-Holzschuh

2007). Spoken by a population of only about 1,000, and in the absence of intergenerational transmission, Güiria Creole, termed Patois locally, is seriously endangered.

When Trinidad was annexed by Great Britain in 1797, French plantation owners, with their slaves, fled the island and established plantations in the Paria peninsula that points to the western coast of Trinidad. Others from the Lesser Antilles then joined these colonists. Throughout the nineteenth century, an agro-industry based on the production of coffee and cocoa flourished in Güiria, and an FBC served as the most important vernacular on the plantations (Neumann-Holzschuh 2007: 102–3).

As described in Neumann-Holzschuh's sketch of Güiria Creole (2007: 105–13), its structure differs little from that of Trinidadian Creole and Lesser Antilles FBCs in general. The definite determiner is post-posed *la/a* and the plural marker pre-posed *se* [se]: *kai-la* 'the house', *se Mayi-a* 'the Magus'. The possessive construction consists of the post-posed pronoun, with alternation between the use of the preceding proposition *a* or the sole pronoun: *kai a tant mue* [house + PREP + aunt + PRO 1SG] 'my aunt's house' versus *kai mamá mue* 'my mother's house'.[31]

The verb marker system also accords very much with that of the Lesser Antilles and Trinidadian creoles: *ka* expresses the durative, the iterative, and the habitual aspects but also the future, *ke* marks the future, and *te* anteriority. At the phonological level, initial and intervocalic /r/ is replaced by /g/: *guesté* 'to stay' (French *rester*), *bouguik* 'donkey' (French *bourrique*). The only influence of Spanish appears to manifest itself in alternations between /b/ and /v/ because in that language there is no real contrast between these two consonants. There is a single phoneme /b/ with two phonetic realizations (allophones): the labial stop [b] in initial position (*boca* 'mouth') and the labial fricative [β] within a word (*cabo* 'rope, cable'). Thus, one finds in Güiria Creole: *lavé* 'abbot' (French *l'abbé*), *dubá* 'in front of' (French *devant*).

1.4.3 French Guiana and South American French-based creoles

French Guiana

French Guiana, like Guadeloupe and Martinique, an integral part of France as a DOM, is located on the north-eastern coast of South America between Surinam and Brazil. Its 35,135 square miles hold an estimated (in 2005) population of 191,000, of which 113,000 reside in the capital city of Cayenne. There are more than a dozen regional languages spoken in addition to Guianese Creole (GuiC; *Guianais* in French) belonging to three different groups: (1) three sets of Amerindian languages: Arawak and Palikúr

(Arawak), Kali'na (formerly Galibi) and Wayana (Carib), Teko (formerly Emerillon) and Wayampi (Tupi); (2) English-based Maroon[32] creoles: Aluku, Ndjuka, Paramaka, Saramaccan; (3) Asian: Hmong (Renault-Lescure and Goury 2009). Saint Jacques Fauquenoy (1972) reports the existence of five diatopic (geographic) varieties of GuiC: Cayenne (the oldest variety and the one in closest contact with French), Oyapock-Approuague, Mana-St. Laurent, Sinnamary, and Roura. About half of the population consists of native speakers of these languages. In addition to the languages enumerated above, French and GuiC are in contact with those spoken by recent immigrants from Surinam (Sranan), Brazil (Portuguese), Saint Lucia (Saint Lucian Creole), and Haiti (Haitian Creole) who constitute approximately 60% of the population.

The French first attempted to establish a plantation colony in French Guiana (which was referred to as Cayenne from the name of the first settlement) in 1604. This and subsequent efforts throughout the seventeenth century were plagued by internal dissension among the leaders of the settlers, constant warfare between France and the Netherlands during that century, raids by marauding Dutch and English pirates, and the health hazards of a tropical climate, notably malaria. Dutch colonists and Sephardic Jews expelled by the Portuguese from Dutch settlements in Recife, Brazil, established a fairly successful foothold in 1654. They were forced to leave when the French recaptured Cayenne in 1664. Despite incursions by the Dutch and British, Cayenne prospered modestly, in comparison with the richer Antillean colonies, by the cultivation of indigo, achiote, cloves, coffee, and sugar. According to the first census in 1665 there were only 260 Blacks (presumably slaves) and 610 Whites (Chaudenson 2003: 112), which suggests that it took some time before the colony reached the *société de plantation* stage. From 1763 the population of Whites, slaves, and free people of color grew considerably (Marchand-Thébault 1986: 58):

	1704	**1763**	**1788**
Whites	264	575	1,346
Free colored		64	483
Amerindians		83	1,279
Slaves	1,137	6,996	10,430

Throughout the nineteenth century and the twentieth century up to 1965, the size of the population remained relatively stable, with about 33,000 inhabitants in 1961. Abolished in 1792 during the French Revolution but reinstated by Napoleon in 1802, slavery was permanently abolished in 1848, as it was in the French Antilles. However, beginning in 1855 the production of cash crops became a marginal economic activity in French

1.4 Other French-based Creoles

Guiana as France installed major penitentiaries there, including the infamous Ile du Diable (Devil's Island). The same period saw the beginning of the gold rush (*arpaillage*[33]), with its negative consequences for the ecology and the Amerindian communities. The creation of the French space center in Kourou in 1965 triggered a demographic boom resulting from massive immigration.

A detailed inventory of the slaves held in the Noël sugar plantation in Rémire, a few miles from Cayenne, made in 1690 by a certain Groupy des Marets, provides invaluable information about the size of Cayenne plantations and the provenance of the slave population of the period (Karam 1986: 68; Jennings 1995). Caution must be exercised in inferring ethnic affiliation and language spoken from the provenance label, for example, Bambaras and Sénégals (Senegambia), Foins (Fons), Aradas, Petits-Popos (Slave Coast), or Congos (Angola). Slaves from the Slave Coast were more likely speakers of Kwa languages (Yoruba, Fon, Gun, etc.) but as pointed out by Manessy (1995) and especially Chaudenson (1992, 1996, 2003), the ethnic origin of slaves cannot always be inferred from the port of embarkation since many were captured far inland before being brought to the coastal areas for sale to European traders. Of the 117 slaves (including eight deceased) listed in the Rémire inventory, 29 were locally born (Creoles) of whom 22 were children younger than fourteen, half boys, half girls. Of the African slaves, 40 were from the Slave Coast, 11 from Angola and 19 from Senegambia. Four slaves were Amerindians and six of unknown origin.

In addition to the name, provenance, age, and sex of the slaves, the Groupy de Marets inventory lists, for some, the ship on which they arrived or the merchant from whom they were bought, as well as physical characteristics, among other details. For example, the slave Jean le Juif (Karam 1986: 66) is described as follows:

> *Jean, dit le Juif, appelé par les Noirs Fancholadé, âgé de cinquante-quatre ans, est de Oloco, Royaume de Fon, il est venu dans Vernal* [name of the Dutch slave ship captain] *qui l'a vendu au nommé Gras, un Juif qui luy a fait servir ses enfants et un de ses fils appelé Jacob quy l'a enfin vendu à la Compagnie après la prise de l'île par les Anglais ansuitte de quoy M. de Chevalier de Lezy l'a vendu à MM. de la Touche et de Boulac. Ce noir est sucrier, cieur de long et bonne hache.*

> Jean, alias the Jew, called Fancholadé by the Blacks, fifty-four years old, is from Oloca in the Fon Kingdom, he came in the Vernal [name of the Dutch slave ship captain] who sold him to one Gras, a Jew who had him serve his children and one of his sons called Jacob eventually sold him to the Company after the capture

of the island by the English after which M. Chevalier de Lezy sold him to MM. de la Touche and de Boulac. This Black is a sugar-mill worker, pit sawyer and lumber man.

The background of this slave provides some insight into the linguistic situation of the early period of the Cayenne colony since his arrival there in about 1660. Transported by a Dutch slave trader, then bought by a Jew who came from Brazil, he was, on his arrival in the New World, first exposed to Portuguese or an approximative or creolized variant of the language. It is not clear what language he spoke with twelve of the slaves originating in Foins (Fon) or those from other regions of Africa. In view of the disproportion of the slave versus White population, as indicated by the 1704 census above, it is doubtful that the slaves had close contact with speakers of Colonial French. Given the linguistic diversity of the slaves on this plantation, even taking into account the multilingualism that existed and still exists in West Africa, it would appear that an approximative variety of Colonial French was the medium of communication. A 1744 citation of a letter written by an Amerindian (Saint-Quentin 1872: 195) suggests that a local FBC had developed by that time in Cayenne: *anglai pran Yapoc, yé mené mon père alé toute blang foulkan mawon danboi* 'the English took Ayapock, they carried away the priest, all the Whites ran away in the woods'.[34]

GuiC and TC (Thomas 1869) both benefit from early linguistic descriptions. The description of GuiC is all the more noteworthy because its author, Auguste de Saint-Quentin (1872), devised a systematic phonological-based spelling, adopted in Haiti in the 1940s (see Section 4.4.2). Recognizing GuiC's status as an autonomous language, he rejected the etymological spelling used generally for all FBCs until the middle of the twentieth century, arguing that it gave the language: *l'apparence d'un français corrompu et mal parlé* 'the appearance of a corrupt and badly spoken French'. More recent descriptions of the language are given by Saint Jacques Fauquenoy (1972), Peyraud (1983), Damoiseau (2005b, 2007), and Honorien (2009). A very rudimentary bilingual dictionary of the language is available (Barthélémi 2007). In 1882, there appeared a novel, *Atipa*, in GuiC using an etymological spelling, that describes the political and social scene of French Guiana in the second half of the nineteenth century. Written under the pseudonym, Alfred Parépou,[35] it was attributed to Saint-Quentin's uncle Alfred because of the shared first name, but the author is more likely to have been a French navy official, a native of Cayenne, Pierre Félix Athénodor Météranu (Méteyrand).

GuiC shares with GC and MartC the durative markers *ka* and *ké*, respectively: *li ka dromi* 'he/she is sleeping'. The current irrealis (future) marker is borrowed from these two FBCs: *to ké manj* 'you'll eat'. The latter verb marker shows variants *kay*, presumably influenced by Saint Lucian Creole, and *wa* (similar to HC *va*), an older form noted by Saint-Quentin (Saint Jacques Fauquenoy 1972: 83). Like LC, it differs from all Antillean varieties and HC by having pre-posed possessive determiners rather than post-posed pronouns: *mo, to, so, nou, zòt, yé* **zanmi** 'my, your, his/her friend' versus HC **zanmi** *mwen, ou, li, nou, yo*. The definite determiners are *-a* in the singular, *fanm a* 'the woman', and *-ya* in the plural, *oranj-ya* 'the oranges'. The latter appears to be an evolved form of the combination *yé la* (which occurs in LC and is the reverse of the older HC combination *la yo*). In these three FBCs, the plural marker coincides with the third-person plural pronoun.

Karipúna

Varieties of FBCs closely related to, if not varieties of, GuiC are spoken by Amerindians in the north-eastern Brazilian state of Amapá, specifically, in the region of Uaçá, which is located to the east of French Guiana (J. S. Tobler 1983; Anonby 2007; Ferreira and Alleyne 2007). The two latter authors distinguish two varieties of Karipúna Creole: Karipúna Creole proper (KC) and Galibi Marwono Creole (GMC). Tobler estimates the number of speakers of KC at about 500 to 600 but both Anonby and Ferreira and Alleyne list a much higher number: 1,726 for KC and 1,987 for GMC. As Ferreira and Alleyne point out (2007: 351), these creoles constitute the rather unusual case of a creole language first adopted as a second language which then became the native language of a linguistic community.

As described in Tobler's detailed grammatical analysis of KC, the signal differences between it and GuiC seem to be in the determiner system. There is a zero indefinite determiner corresponding to GuiC *un*: *li èg sanble sithon* 'it's as sour as a lemon' vs. *un bon lasoup* 'a good soup'.[36] Corresponding to the GuiC post-posed determiner Karipúna shows either zero or what Tobler labels the Ind (indicator) *la*: *li te asi* **la** *sou ban* 'she sat there on the bench', *vini gade tchizozo* **la** atò 'come and look at the bird now' vs. *a fanm a* 'it's the woman', *wòm ki vini-a* 'the man who came'. However, Ferreira and Alleyne indicate it to be post-posed *la*: *tab* **la** *so jam* 'the leg of the table'. Tobler shows variable marking of plural in nouns: *ou ké fèt bèt manje, non?* 'Didn't you give food to the animals?' vs. *sa fanm ya* 'these women'. These structural features of the noun phrase give credence to Corne's comment that KC reflects a nineteenth-century GuiC (1995: 234). Indeed, in one of the folktales reproduced in Saint-Quentin (1872: 45) there is no overt definite determiner or plural markers: *pendan chien katorné- viré landan chamb, limé difè, lavé gniam mété la chouguiè ké dilo* 'while DOG was going back and forth in the room, lighting the fire, washing the yams, putting them in the pot'.

There exists a creole in the capital, Macapá, in the southern part of the state, labeled Amapá French Creole or, locally, Lanc-Patua (Patois Language), which Andrade (1984) describes in great detail. She reports that it is spoken by migrants from French Guiana and the Lesser Antilles, especially St. Lucia. The original migrants, established in Brazil from the 1940s onward, were attracted to the region by the gold mines. They all have competence in Portuguese, and their children are schooled in the language. Grimes (1996) indicates that Amapá French Creole has 25,000 speakers but Ferreira and Alleyne report that they did not find any during their research that took place in the late 1990s.

Lanc-Patua appears heavily influenced by Saint Lucian Creole. For example, it shows *kay* instead of *ké* as future verb marker. Also, in contrast to Karapúna, the definite determiner is *–a/-an* (vs. *–la* for the Uaçá creoles) and the indefinite determiner is *yon* (vs. *un*): *yon nom* 'a man', *bo mwen chapo a* 'give me the hat', *timoun an* 'the child'. The possessive determiner is post-posed, *chapo li* 'his hat' in contrast to the Uaçá creole pre-posed equivalent *so chapo* 'his hat'.

1.4.4 Indian Ocean French-based creoles

The Indian Ocean FBCs are less basilectal compared to their Caribbean counterparts. That is, they differ less markedly from Colonial French. At the morphosyntactic level they all show four major linguistic features: (1) as in Louisiana and Guianese Creoles possession is expressed with pre-posed possessive determiners rather than post-posed genitive constructions, e.g., RC[37] *mo frer* 'my brother' (French *mon frère*) vs. HC *frè mwen*, Northern HC *frèr an mwen*; (2) the plural marker is derived from the French lexeme *bande* 'group, lot of', RC *bann lisyen la* 'the dogs' (French *une bande de chiens* 'a group of dogs') instead of from a function word, the pre-posed plural demonstrative determiner *ces* in the Antilles, *se chen la*, or the third-person plural pronoun *eux*, HC *chen yo*, LC *chen ye*, GuiC *chen yan*; (3) the insertion of the particle *i* in predicates, MartC *bonom i dir avek li* 'the old man told him' (Papen 1978: 308), although this insertion is subject to various constraints differing among the individual creoles; (4) as in Louisiana, the alternation of two stems for most verbs, subject to various constraints, such as the morphosyntactic environment: short form before a noun phrase object, RC *mwen la sant en romans* 'I sang a song', long form before an adverbial complement, MC *Zot komans rode partou* 'they begin looking everywhere' (Papen 1978: 416–17). Unlike the Atlantic FBCs, for non-stative (action) verbs, a bare stem does not signal past tense but present: *mo travay lakaz* 'I work at home'. Past tense is signaled by the verb marker *ti*: *mo ti trouv Mari ier* 'I saw Mary yesterday' (Papen 1978: 334, cited by Klingler 2003: 269).

At the phonological level, Indian Ocean FBCs show two salient differences with respect to Atlantic Ocean FBCs. First, the retention of /r/ in final and post-vocalic position, which draws them closer to CF. In that position /r/ is realized as lengthening of preceding low vowels (*kar* [ka:] 'quarter') or as a central glide, represented by the superscript [ə] (*defer* [defeə] 'to undo') (Papen 1978: 100–5). Second, the replacement of the palatal fricatives by their dental equivalents, unlike that of the CF input: /s/ for /ʃ/: Indian Ocean Creoles *simen* vs. Atlantic Ocean Creoles *chimen* 'way, road' and /z/ for /ʒ/: Indian Ocean Creoles *zour* vs. Atlantic Ocean Creoles *jou* 'day'. These features are attributable, at least in part, to the Malagasy substrate in which palatal fricatives are absent, although Chaudenson (1981: 156) points out that alternations between palatal and dental fricatives occur in regional varieties of French and local dialects: *chaze-femme* for *sage-femme* 'midwife' *sanger* for *changer* 'to change', *chesser* for *sécher* 'to dry'.

Another major difference between the Indian Ocean Creoles and their Atlantic Ocean counterparts resides in their settlement history. In the Atlantic French colonies, the slave population originated primarily in West Africa. There, the importation of indentured servants from India and China, after the abolition of slavery, did not involve a major demographic shift. In the Indian Ocean territories, on the contrary, indentured servants were numerous; in Mauritius, they constituted the majority of the population.

According to Robert Chaudenson (1974, 1979, 1981, 2003), a creole developed during the late seventeenth century first in Réunion Island (called Isle de Bourbon at that time) from approximative varieties of CF spoken by slaves from Madagascar, India, and West Africa. In its early stage, when it was becoming distinct from CF, this speech variety, which Chaudenson labels Bourbonnais, was introduced in Mauritius (named Isle de France at that time). The creole that developed on that island, in part from that original input, influenced the formation of RodC and, with some contacts from Réunion and the Seychelles. In Mauritius, during the eighteenth century, the development of an agro-industrial economy (*société de plantation*), based on the production of sugar, led to the massive arrival of indentured servants speaking languages different from slaves imported into the Mascarene islands. In that island, unlike in Réunion, in the initial period of settlement slaves were imported mainly from West and East Africa. In the case of the Seychelles, where an intensive agro-industrial economy did not develop, the working force consisted mainly of African slaves freed from ships involved in the illegal post-emancipation slave trade. There was little immigration to Rodrigues after the initial eighteenth-century settlement from Mauritius (Chaudenson 1981: 243–7).

Baker and Corne (1982) distinguish between RC and the other three Indian Ocean creoles, which they label Isle de France creoles. They claim that the first of these to emerge, MC, arose with little to no direct input from the earlier Bourbonnais speech. As pointed out above, Chaudenson holds an opposite view that stresses the importance of an initial input from Réunion (Bourbon). A. Bollée's etymological dictionary covering all Indian Ocean FBCs (1993, 2000) shows a large proportion of shared lexical items, especially between RC and MC. However, RC differs significantly from the Isle de France creoles. Among the differences listed by Papen (1978: 598–9), the most important are: (1) an overt copula that shows tense variation; (2) a verb system where tense rather than aspect distinctions predominate and where inflections appear, for example, -*ra* for the negative future; (3) the distinction between subject and object pronouns; (4) fewer agglutinations.

Réunion
Located about 450 miles east of Madagascar, the island of Réunion holds a population of 833,000 (as of 2010) in an area of 970 square miles. Since 1946, it has been an overseas department, *département d'outre-mer* (DOM), like Guadeloupe, Martinique, French Guiana, and Mayotte.[38]

There are records of Arab traders having sighted and visited uninhabited Réunion and the neighboring islands of Mauritius and Rodrigues in the eleventh century, but the first European contact occurred in the early years of the sixteenth century when Portuguese navigators, on their way to India, discovered these islands. One of them, Pedro Mascarenhas, gave the archipelago his name (in English Mascarenes and French Mascareignes) and Réunion island the name Santa Apolonia. Later on Dutch and English ships stopped at the island. The first French contact occurred in 1638 and four years later Jacques de Pronis, governor of the French trading post of Fort Dauphin in southern Madagascar, officially claimed the island and named it Mascarin. In 1649, de Pronis' successor as governor of Fort Dauphin, Etienne de Flacourt, changed the name to Bourbon Island, in honor of the newly crowned Louis XIV.

It was not until 1665 that a fully fledged settlement effort was undertaken under the aegis of the French East India Company (Compagnie des Indes Orientales) for the cultivation of spices and coffee. This initiative was feeble, as the 1686 census attests. There existed a total population of 269: 82 Whites, 70 Malagasies, 24 Indo-Portuguese, and 93 Creoles, i.e., persons born on the island (Papen 1978: 9; Chaudenson 1981: 148). By 1704, the population had only increased to 734: 423 Whites and 311 slaves, of whom 102 were Creoles and 208 were imported – 110 Malagasies, 45 Indians, 42 East Africans, 10 West Africans, and 1 North African. Only in the eighteenth century did Bourbon Island attain the agro-industrial phase (*société de plantation*), where the slave population greatly outnumbered that of Europeans, as shown by the demographic statistics in Table 1.2.

Table 1.2. Population Statistics in Réunion in the Eighteenth and Early Nineteenth Centuries

	Total population	Whites	Slaves	Freemen
1717	2000	910	1100	
1735	8289	1716	6210	363
1789	69,200	10,000	50,000	1,200
1818	89,896	16,400	70,000	3,496

Between 1725 and 1735 one-third of the slaves originated in Madagascar, India, and West Africa.

The initial homestead phase (*société d'habitation*) lasted about fifty years, from 1665 to 1715 (Chaudenson 2003). According to this author, during this period Whites were more numerous than slaves. The latter were closely integrated into the homesteads, working side by side with their masters. Also, they were relatively young upon their arrival on the island. Most were Malagasy or Indo-Portuguese, in particular the women, the majority of whom married Whites. In this social context, CF was relatively accessible to the slave population, rendering unlikely the emergence of a creole. As was the case in the Atlantic Ocean Creoles, during that phase of colonization, the slaves spoke a highly variable approximative version of CF. With intensive cultivation of coffee and then the production of sugar, the more numerous slaves' linguistic target shifted from CF to the imperfect reproduction of it and then to the creole that had developed. As was the case in Louisiana (see Section 1.4.1 above), most of the early attestations of Réunion Creole are excerpts from court proceedings where the scribe's notations (in bold face below) precede the slave's statement (Chaudenson 1981: 3–5):

1734   *Toutes les nuits le dit Jouant était à grater à la porte*
'Every night the said Jouant was scratching at the door.'

1799   **Pierre lui a dit** '*si toi y veut, moi y va te donner quelque chose pour sortir des mains de ton maître.*' **Que lui répondant a encore répliqué** '*moi y en pas besoin parce que mon maître ne fait pas misère à moi.*'

Pierre said to him, 'If you wish I'll give something to free yourself from your master's control.' **To which he responded again,** 'I don't need to because my master is not mean to me.'

Following the French Revolution, in 1794, the name of the island was changed to Isle de la Réunion to commemorate the joining of revolutionaries from Marseille with the Paris National Guard. But, with Napoleon Bonaparte's accession to the throne of France in 1804, the island was renamed Ile Bonaparte in 1806. After the restoration of the Bourbon royal dynasty following Napoleon's final defeat, the name Bourbon was restored. The 1848 Revolution brought the final name change, back to the republican Ile de la Réunion. Even before the abolition of slavery in 1848, with the development of intensive sugar production, plantation owners began to turn to Indian and Chinese indentured servants. A major social change in Réunion was the impoverishment of a large number of Whites due to the division of landholdings among heirs and the shift to sugar production, which required extensive capital (Papen 1978: 13). The poor Whites left the lowlands for the highlands of the interior of the island, hence their name *Blancs des Hauts* 'highland Whites'.[39] After the abolition of slavery, about 30,000 Black slaves left the lowland plantations for the highlands (Baker and Corne 1982: 108).

Volcy-Focard (1884) distinguished three varieties of RC: *créole des Hauts*, spoken by the highland Whites; *vrai créole* or *créole des Indigènes*, spoken by the Black population that remained in the lowlands; *créole des Cafres et Malabars*, spoken as an acquired language by later arriving Indian indentured servants. Chaudenson (2003) reduces it to two varieties, what he terms the basilectal creole (or *créole des Bas*), closer to the creole of the colonial period and spoken by the lowland population, and the acrolectal or frenchified creole spoken by the highland Whites (*créole des Hauts* or *français créolisé*), closer to French, as the second term indicates. Today, as a result of social and economic changes that began in the 1960s, there exists a continuum of variation between the *créole des Bas* and the *créole des Hauts*, as well as extended contact of all groups with Standard French through the media and schools (Chaudenson 1979). However, as Chaudenson (2003) asserts contra Holm (1989: 395), RC does not qualify as a 'semi-creole' but as a full-fledged one that, because of the socio-historical context of its genesis – the higher proportion of Whites in an extended period of homestead economic development (*société d'habitation*) – has remained closer to its CF origin.

The two varieties of RC share the same lexicon and differ primarily at the phonological and morphosyntactic levels. *Créole des Hauts* speakers contrast dental and palatal fricatives (/s/ vs. /ʃ/, /z/ vs. /ʒ/) and have the front rounded vowels /y ø œ/. For the equivalent of the French imperfect, they use an inflected form preceded by the short form of the pronoun and the reprise *i* (*m i dansé* 'I was dancing') whereas *créole des Bas* speakers use the periphrastic construction formed with the verb stem, *être*, the full variant of the pronoun and *ki* (*mouin létait ki dans*). As Chaudenson (2010: 62) points out, interestingly, the latter construction coincides with that found in the St.-Bart French dialect. Also, it is identical with that attested in the early stage of the language. One salient feature that makes *Créole des Hauts* especially closer to French than its other congeners is the presence of a wide variety of inflected forms (Table 1.3).

Table 1.3. Inflected Verb Forms in *Créole des Hauts* (Réunion)

	eat	serve	say
Present	*manz*	*serv*	*di*
Past	*manze*	*serve*	*dize*
Negative future	*manzra*	*servira*	*dira*
Past participle	*manze*	*servi*	*di*
Infinitive	*manze*	*servir*	*dire*

RC ranks with HC as one of the best-described FBCs. Chaudenson's 1974 *Le lexique du parler créole de la Réunion* has the distinction of being the only lexicographic description of any FBC. It is complemented by a linguistic atlas (Carayol *et al.* 1984, 1989, 1995). Detailed descriptions of the verbal system – the part of the language that sets it apart from all other FBCs – are provided by Chaudenson (1974), Papen (1978), Corne (1982) and Watbled (2003).

Mauritius
Located north-east of Réunion, Mauritius encompasses an area of 788 square miles and holds an ethnically diverse population of 1,291,456 (in 2012), nearly two-thirds of which is of Indian ancestry (Buddhists and Muslims). The remainder has origins in Africa, China, Madagascar, and Europe. English is the *de facto* official language of the island, but multilingualism is widespread, with more than a dozen different languages spoken: Arabic, Bhojpuri, Hakka Chinese, Hindi, Marathi, Mandarin, Cantonese, Sanskrit, Tamil, Telugu, and Urdu. French, the former dominant language, is widely spoken but MC is the most widely shared mother tongue (for 60–65% of the population) and serves as the country's lingua franca. French and English rank second and third, respectively, among the languages spoken (Baggioni and de Robillard 1990: 47).

As was the case with Réunion, there is evidence of the sighting of Mauritius by Arab sailors (Papen 1978: 7). The first Europeans to discover, in 1507, what was then an uninhabited island were the Portuguese. But it was not until more than a century later that the Dutch established the first settlement (an initial attempt was made in 1638 and a more permanent, though short-lived, one in 1664) and named the island Mauritius in honor of the then-ruler of the Netherlands, Stadhouter Maurits (Maurice) of Nassau. The French took over in 1715 and renamed it Isle de France. During the Napoleonic wars England conquered Isle de France, which was ceded to them by the Treaty of Paris (1814). Its original name, Mauritius, was then restored. The establishment of an agro-industrial economy based on sugar production developed rather rapidly, as did consequently the slave population: in 1737 there were 132 White owners of 1,033 slaves (Baker and Corne 1982: 17). In 1819, after England had assumed control of Mauritius, the population had grown to 77,768: 65,367 slaves, 5,912 freed persons of color, and 6,489 Europeans. In 1835, following the abolition of slavery, the British imported indentured servants from various parts of India, nearly 500,000 in the course of the nineteenth century, with massive arrivals in 1843 (34,625) and 1859 (44,397) (Chaudenson 1981: 244). Mauritius became an independent nation within the British Commonwealth in 1968 and a republic was proclaimed in 1992.

In 1721, when the French East India Company decided to establish a colony on Isle de France, it recruited 36 Whites and slaves from Bourbon Island to:

> *Instruire les nouveaux colons dans la culture des cafés et des autres productions et prendre les saisons convenables pour planter et semer vu que la situation des deux isles est presque la même.* (To instruct the new settlers in the cultivation of coffee and other products and choose the appropriate seasons to plant and sow since the situation of the two islands is almost the same.) (Chaudenson 1992: 57–61)

These recruits stayed for more than a year. On this basis, Chaudenson argues that Bourbonnais (the approximative French speech used in Bourbon) served as the basis for the development of MC. Baker and Corne (1982) claim an independent genesis. They stress the predominance of the more highly valued slaves from West Africa and suggest the possible influence of a French-based pidgin in West African ports of embarkation on the development of a local pidgin that would serve as the basis for MC. What is undisputed is that the agro-industrial phase emerged rapidly in Mauritius. As the demographic figures above attest, the slave population constituted nearly 90% of the population less than twenty years after the initial settlement. In that social context, unlike in Réunion, the slaves had fewer opportunities to acquire CF.

Although they are not extensive, the first attestations of MC are not linguistically distant from the present-day language (Chaudenson 1981: 77–8). The first sample is contained in an English text (*Letters from Mauritius in the Eighteenth Century*) written in 1749 by Baron Grant in which he quotes some Malagasy slaves who identify the location of Madagascar:

> ... in their corrupted French: *ça blanc là li beaucoup malin, li couri beaucoup dans la mer là-haut; mais Madagascar li là* 'that white man he's very smart; he travelled a lot in the sea over there; but Madagascar is there ...'

A later sample is provided by the writer Bernardin de Saint-Pierre in *Voyage à l'Ile de France* (1773), who cites the *mauvais patois* 'bad dialect' of the owner of a canoe (*pirogue*):

> *ça n'a pas bon, Monsié ... Si nous n'a pas gagné malheur, ça bon*
>
> 'that's not good, Sir ... If we don't have a mishap, that's good.'

Baker (1972, 1982) identifies four varieties of MC: (1) Ordinary Creole, spoken by primarily monolingual speakers; (2) Refined Creole, spoken by speakers of ordinary Creole who attempt to imitate the third variety; (3) French-Influenced Creole; (4) Bhojpuri-Influenced Creole, which shows phonetic features and lexical items of that language. French-Influenced Creole refers to that of speakers of French as a first language and is marked by the contrast between dental and palatal fricatives and the presence of front rounded vowels.

The lexicon of MC is inventoried in several dictionaries, in particular those of Baker and Hookoomsing (1987) and Carpooran (2009). The latter stands as the best of the few monolingual dictionaries produced for any FBC: it provides English and French glosses for entries together with definitions in MC and illustrative examples. There are several complete linguistic analyses, notably those of Baker (1972) and Corne (1977), as well as numerous articles dealing with specific morphosyntactic and lexical features, e.g., Syea (1992, 1994, 1997). Stein (1982) provides an in-depth study of language contact in the multilingual Mauritian context. Baggioni and de Robillard (1990) offer an overview of the role and status of French, the socially dominant language in Mauritius. Because it contains an analysis of the diachronic development of the Indian Ocean Creoles, Chaudenson (1981) constitutes an important source for early texts in MC, supplemented by studies of specific aspects of that development for MC in Baker and Fon Sing (2007). Carpooran (2002) has produced a set of materials for learning MC destined for travelers, similar to those for Guadeloupean and Martinican creoles. The issue of the relationship between Réunion and Mauritian Creoles is discussed in Baker and Corne (1982) – 'independent genesis' – and Chaudenson (2010) – strong influence of Bourbonnais.

Rodrigues Island

Named after the Portuguese navigator Diogo Rodrigues who, with other compatriots, sighted it in the early sixteenth century, this island is located about 400 miles east of Mauritius. Its 40 square miles hold a population of 37,922 (in 2011). Formerly part of the Republic of Mauritius, it was granted autonomy in 2002.

In 1691, a French Huguenot, François Leguat, who had sought refuge in the Netherlands after the Revocation of the Edict of Nantes that granted Protestants freedom of worship, led a small group of eight settlers to engage in farming. This endeavor proved unsuccessful and these pioneers abandoned Rodrigues. It was not until 1735 that French colonists from Mauritius established small-scale plantations with imported slaves of mostly Malagasy and African origins. In 1809, like Mauritius and the Seychelles, Rodrigues came under English rule. The low level of development was reflected by low demographic growth: the population reached only 125 in 1831 and 495 in 1851 – 350 Malagasy or African slaves, 100 identified as Mauritians, and 45 Europeans (Jauze and Yeung Ching Yung 1998). However, by the end of the nineteenth century Rodrigues was inhabited by 3,000 people. The only major descriptive work that focuses on RodC is a linguistic atlas (Chaudenson *et al*. 1992).

The Seychelles

As is the case with the Mascarene Islands, the Seychelles were inhabited when Arab traders first sighted them. The first European contact dates back to 1502, when the famous Portuguese navigator Admiral Vasco de Gama named the archipelago after himself, the Amirantes (Admiral Islands). The Seychelles archipelago consists of about 100 islands, some granitic and others coral, the largest of which, Mahé (55 square miles), holds about 80 to 90% of the 90,024 inhabitants (in 2012) of the archipelago. One-third of Mahé's population lives in the capital, Victoria. Ceded by France to England together with Mauritius and Rodrigues in 1814, the Seychelles, previously administered by England from Mauritius, became an independent member of the British Commonwealth in 1976.

In 1744, the governor of Isle de France sent Lazare Picault to explore the archipelago. Picault identified Mahé as the most propitious site for a settlement. France officially claimed the archipelago in 1756 and named

Table 1.4. Early Population Statistics for the Seychelles

	Europeans	Slaves	Freed slaves
1788	20	221	9
1791	74	487	29
1810	317	3,015	125
1825	582	6,058	323

it Séchelles in honor of Louis XV's minister of finance, Jean Moreau de Séchelles. When the British took control of the island, they practiced what Lionnet (1972, cited by Bollée 1977: 3) characterized as 'passive imperialism' because of the low level of economic development. The name of the territory was slightly anglicized to Seychelles. Prior to emancipation in 1835, the demographic composition of the Seychelles conformed to the typical *société de plantation* pattern, with a predominant slave population (Bollée 1977: 3; and see Table 1.4).

The majority of the early settlers were European Creoles, that is, native-born in Réunion and Mauritius; they arrived with slaves, many of whom by that time were also Creoles. Between 1701 and 1810, most of the new-comers to the Seychelles originated in Réunion. Later on, imported slaves, termed Mozambiques, originated in East Africa. After the abolition of slavery, the English intercepted slave-trading ships and brought an estimated 2,400 freed slaves to the Seychelles, thus raising the level of the population of African origin (Bollée 1977: 5).

Saint-Jorre and Lionnet (1999) provide an inventory of the lexicon of Seychellois Creole (SC). Its linguistic structure is described in Corne (1977) and, in a broader treatment, in Bollée (1977), which includes an extensive collection of texts. Michaelis (1993) provides a detailed discussion of the tense and aspect system of the language. A discussion of the role of SC in the educational system appears in Chaudenson and Vernet (1983).

The 1979 constitution declared English, French, and SC to be the official languages. English holds a dominant place in administration (Chaudenson and Vernet 1983: 92), as well as in the media. According to a 1973 survey mentioned by these authors, the use of the languages on the radio was:

> English 65%, French 10%, SC 15%, with an increasing use of the latter. SC is the initial classroom language and English assumes that role after students learn to read and write.

Chagos Archipelago

The Chagos Archipelago consists of seven coral atolls consisting of more than 60 islands located south of the Maldives Archipelago and 1,200 miles north-east of Mauritius. Sighted by Arab sailors (Papen 1978: 7) and discovered by Portuguese seafarers in the early 1500s, who named it the Bassas de Chagas, from the Portuguese *chagas* ('wounds') referring to the Holy Wounds at the crucifixion of Jesus, and its main island, Diego Garcia, for a famed Spanish navigator. The archipelago was first claimed by France toward the end of the eighteenth century but ceded to England by the Treaty of Paris (1814) at the end of the Napoleonic Wars. Diego Garcia served primarily as a coaling base for ships crossing the Indian Ocean from the Suez Canal to Australia and for the cultivation of coconuts.

In 1778, a certain Dupuit de la Faye was granted Diego Garcia by the governor of Mauritius. There were sporadic visits to the island for gathering coconuts, fish, and turtles. The island then served as a reserve for lepers, presumably because it was thought that turtle meat cured leprosy. In 1793, the French established a permanent settlement with imported slaves; they cultivated coconut trees and exported sea cucumbers (appreciated in East Asia as a delicacy). The inhabitants of the Chagos Archipelago, called Ilois (Zilwa), from the French for 'islanders', or Chagossians, originate from Madagascar, Africa, and India and were shipped or migrated from Mauritius, the Seychelles, or Rodrigues island. Robert Papen, the only linguist to have provided information on the creole that developed in the archipelago (Chagossian Creole), indicates that it resembles closely the conservative variety of Rodrigues Creole at the phonological and syntactic levels (1978: 82).

The Chagos Archipelago remained administered from Mauritius until 1965. In that year, in the context of the creation of a joint UK–USA mutual defense strategy, the Chagos were purchased from newly independent Mauritius to become ultimately an uninhabited area, the British Indian Ocean Territory, to serve as a marine reserve and military base. Between 1967 and 1973 the entire population, numbering about 1,800 (Holm 1989: 403), was forcibly removed from the entire archipelago because it was felt that their presence posed a potential danger for the major US strategic base created on Diego Garcia. The evicted Chagossians were resettled in Mauritius and the Seychelles.

Tayo

This contact vernacular arose in the village of Saint-Louis located close to Nouméa, the capital of New Caledonia. Classified as a *collectivité d'outre-mer* (COM), like Saint-Martin, New Caledonia is located about 900 miles east of Australia and approximately 1,200 miles north of New Zealand. It was claimed by France in 1857 although, as its name suggests, its first European visitors were British and there were also many contacts with Australia. Its population is nearly equally divided between Austromelanesians (Kanaks) and Europeans, according to the 2009 census – 99,098 and 71,721 respectively. French is the official language but a large number of Austronesian languages, not all mutually intelligible, are spoken by the indigenous Kanak population.

Tayo, also referred to as Patois de Saint-Louis or simply Patois, developed from a pidginized version of the local variety of French used as a lingua franca by speakers of several Kanak languages. In 1860, Marist missionaries in Saint-Louis established a settlement for new converts that included a school, a church, and a training center for new catechists. The members of this community also worked in a sawmill, in rice paddies, and in sugarcane fields. The speech variety that developed from the contact between New Caledonian French and mainly three different Kanak languages (Drubéa, Xârâcùù, and Cèmuhî) attained a somewhat stabilized form by 1920. According to Ehrhart (1993), it is estimated that there are about 1,000 speakers of Tayo and intergenerational transmission appears to be limited.

Despite its small number of speakers, Tayo provides interesting insights into the genesis of FBCs. Unlike all other FBCs, its substrate languages are clearly identified, and one can determine to what extent specific features of these languages are reflected in the structure of the speech form that emerged in this contact situation. Among the features Corne (1989, 1995, 1999) identifies as transfers from the Kanak languages present in the Tayo-speaking community, two salient ones are dual personal pronouns and subject indexes. Dual personal pronouns, contrasting with singular and plural pronouns, are derived by prefixing the French numeral *deux* 'two' (see Table 1.5). Dual personal pronouns are a general feature of all Melanesian languages. They occur, for example, in Tok Pisin, the expanded pidgin language used in New Guinea.

Table 1.5. Tayo Personal Subject Pronouns

Person	Singular	Dual	Plural
1st	*ma/mwa*	*nude*	*nu*
2nd	*ta*	*(b)ude*	*(v)uso(t)*
3rd	*la*	*lede/de-la*	*sa/sola/lesot*

Subject indexing occurs with noun phrase subjects: *le kreve tu sel lãp-la.* 'The lamp went out by itself'. The Standard French (SF) translation would be *La lampe s'est éteinte toute seule.* However, the equivalent in vernacular French, the likely source of the Tayo utterance, is *Elle s'est crevée toute seule la lampe-là.* This sentence involves the focalization and fronting of the predicate with the use of the corresponding third-person pronoun and the stranding of the subject noun phrase in the original sentence, a very productive emphatic structure in vernacular French, e.g., *Mon frère est parti* 'My brother left' > ***Il est parti*** *mon frère* 'The fact is that my brother left'. The Tayo subject index *le* coincides with the combination of the third-person singular pronoun and copula of vernacular French. Thus, this constitutes a convergence between vernacular French and the substrate Kanak structure, as Jeff Siegel (2008) indicates:[40]

> ... transfer can only occur if there is a feature in the L2 [target second language] superficially similar enough to a feature of the L1 [acquirer's first language] that it can be misinterpreted or reanalyzed to correspond to L1 rules.

However, Chaudenson (1994; 2003: 85–8) makes a strong case for the influence of Réunion Creole on the development of Tayo that he did not label specifically as a creole. He pointed out the establishment, in the region of Saint-Louis, of villages in which resided Indian workers (Malabars) who specialized in the production of sugar imported from Réunion. He, together with Speedy (2007), adduces various structural similarities between Réunion Creole and Tayo. For example, with regard to the subject indexing mentioned above, Speedy (2007: 221) cites the use of the overt RC copula *le* attributed to a Black Réunion Creole from Mozambique brought to New Caledonia to work in a sugar plantation, who escaped and lived in a Kanak village: *Blanc l'est malins* [White COPULA cunning] 'The Whites are cunning'.[41] The Tayo subject index (SI) *le* converges with the RC copula: *lia le fu* [3SG SI crazy] 'He is crazy' (Corne 1995: 174), cited by Speedy (2007: 221). The presence of RC in the Saint-Louis area renders complex the context in which Tayo was formed. In addition to New Caledonia French, RC might have constituted a learning target or at least a major influence in the contact situation in Saint-Louis. This questions Corne's conclusion that: 'Tayo today is a language whose phonological and lexical material comes essentially from French but whose syntax is largely Kanak' (1999: 42).

Notes

1. In the present officialized spelling, these three sentences would be represented as: *Mwen se kreyòl Kan-Peren, ti poulen-sa-a se kreyòl-mwen,* and *Mwen se kreyòl tiresyas, papa m te kreyòl Salonmon, granpapamwen te kreyòl Lanpèrè.* Note the inconsistency in the representation of *kréyòl.*
2. *Premier voyage du Sieur De La Courbe Fait à La Coste d'Afrique 1695* (First voyage of Mr. De La Courbe made on the African coast 1695), published in 1913.
3. M. A. K. Halliday (1973) identifies nine functions assumed by languages: (1) instrumental: manipulation and control of the environment; (2) regulatory: control over other individuals; (3) interactional: enabling the identification and cohesion of a group; (4) personal: enabling speakers to define themselves; (5) heuristic: using language as a means of discovery and learning; (6) imaginative: enabling speakers to create their own environment; (7) representational or informational: using language for the communication of messages about the real world; (8) ludic: playful use of language, for example, puns, recoded varieties of a language (Pig Latin, etc.); (9) ritual: use of language to define social groups by setting norms.
4. Various detailed treatments of Haitian history and politics are offered in James (1938), Heinl and Heinl (2005), Nicholls (1979), Weinstein and Segal (1984), and James Ferguson (1987).
5. For a discussion of the transition between the homestead phase to the plantation phase and the inception of an agro-industrial economy, see Section 13.1.5.
6. This term, originating in the Spanish word *bozal* 'muzzle to prevent animals from biting; horse bridle or halter', was used from the sixteenth century to refer to slaves newly imported to the colonies from Africa. It also labels approximative forms of Spanish found in Central and South America (see Lipsky 1986).

    This massive demographic input reflects the high level of mortality of slaves in what was no doubt the most brutal slavery system in the Americas.
7. Borno was the first Haitian president to authorize the use of HC in education.
8. Originally, the Cacos were peasant mercenary bands that, beginning during the troubled years of the second half of the nineteenth century, were recruited by northern claimants of presidential power.
9. Négritude was a literary and ideological movement launched in Paris in the 1930s that denounced European colonization and stressed African and Africa-related cultural values. Its founders were the Senegalese Léopold Senghor – who became a long-serving president of his country, the Martinican writer and politician Aimée Césaire, and the French Guianan poet and politician Léon-Gontran Damas, who were all living in the French capital during that time. An influential forebear was the Haitian anthropologist Anténor Firmin, who had studied in Paris and authored a refutation of Arthur de Gobineau's manifesto on the superiority of the White race, *Essai sur l'inégalité des races*

56 *Introduction*

       humaines (1885), with his own *De l'égalité des races humaines* (1885). As minister, Firmin opposed the US proposal to establish a naval base in the Môle Saint-Nicolas and wrote a book in 1905 in which he predicted an eventual US occupation of his country: *M. Roosevelt, président des États-Unis et la République d'Haïti*.

10. In a homely the Pope declared: '…Christians cannot be unaware of the injustice, the excessive inequality, the degradation of the quality of life, the misery, the hunger, the fear suffered by the majority of the people' (J. Ferguson 1987: 75).

11. Chapter 12 presents a detailed discussion of the relationship between French and HC in Haitian society and the use of the two languages in basic education.

12. Sections 4.3.1 to 4.3.3 offer samples of the precursor of HC, Saint-Domingue Creole, as it was developing and represented in texts of the colonial period.

13. These authors are listed chronologically, and references to their works are provided in the bibliography.

14. Note that there is little difference in the lexical coverage provided by these two dictionaries. Whereas Freeman (2011) does not list the subentry *mete ba* 'to humiliate', it does provide the subentry *mete li nan ba* 'to put s.o. in a straitjacket', which is missing from Valdman *et al.* (2007). The latter dictionary provides cross-listing to synonyms keyed by the symbol **cf.**; for *ba³* 'pack saddle', the user is referred to *ekipay*. Also, to avoid repetitious listings, subentries are listed under the headword to which the user is directed by **see**. For example, under **ba¹**, the subentry **vant ba** refers the reader to the head noun, *vant* (see **vant**): **vant ba** afflicted, distressed *Nouvèl lanmò Bòb la kite m vant ba*. 'The news of Bob's death distressed me.'

15. In Louisiana, the standard variety of the language, as versus the local forms, is referred to as International French.

16. The term *couri-vini* reflects the use of serial verbs in LC; see Section 8.6 for a discussion of this feature in Haitian Creole. Gumbo is a typical southern Louisiana dish. Two etymologies have been proposed for the word, both of which refer to essential ingredients of the dish: okra (Bantu *ki ngombo* or *quingombo*) or filé, a spice made from ground sassafras leaves (Choktaw *kombo*).

17. Following Klingler (2003), LC forms are represented with the official spelling for HC. Note that in this system [e] is represented by *e* rather than by *é*, as is the case in the spelling used for most FBCs.

18. Klingler notes a single occurrence of the N +*a* + Pronoun construction: *Mo te gen bon lenj a mon* 'I had my good clothes (dress)' (2003: 289).

19. Neumann's examples, cited with a modified IPA (International Phonetic Alphabet), are retranscribed here with the IPN spelling officialized in Haiti. Those from Neumann-Holzschuh (1987) are represented in the original etymological spelling.

20. For a description of the HC system, see Section 3.4.

21. The term basilectal refers to varieties of FBCs that are most deviant from French.

22. It appears that Tourneux misappropriated a previous work by Barbotin strictly limited to the lexicon of Marie-Galante. That work appears in Barbotin (1994).
23. Born in Paris into a middle-class family, Schoelcher started his career as sales representative for his father's business. In 1828, during a business trip to Mexico, the USA, and Cuba, he confronted the reality of slavery. Upon his return to France, he became a journalist and music critic. Although he supported slavery at first, he later became a leader among French abolitionists. Named Minister of the Colonies and the Navy in 1848, he was instrumental in the formal abolition of slavery in the French Atlantic colonies of the time: Guadeloupe, French Guiana, and Martinique.
24. This award, instituted in 1903 by the Académie Goncourt, is awarded to the author of the best and most imaginative prose work of the year. Among its recipients have been Marcel Proust and André Malraux.
25. Notably, it uses the symbol *é* for /e/ instead of *e*.
26. The author who first mentioned St. Lucian Creole, an English resident of the island, cast aspersions on the language that have long endured (Breen 1844, cited by Carrington 1984: 3): '... as a patois, it is even more unintelligible than that spoken by the Negroes of the English colonies. It is in short, the French language, stripped of its manly and dignified ornaments and travestied for the accommodation of children and toothless women. I regret to add that it has now almost entirely superseded the use of the beautiful French language even in the highest circles of colonial society.'
27. In countries belonging to the British Commonwealth the Governor-General is the direct representative of the Queen of the United Kingdom. It is, like the Queen's, an honorific title.
28. Roume eventually returned to France and in 1791 was appointed by the revolutionary government as one of three commissioners to Saint-Domingue during the colony's slave revolution. Later, at the request of Toussaint L'Ouverture, he returned as the sole French agent but, following rifts between them, he returned definitively to France in 1799.
29. Citing Wood (1968), Holm (1989: 377) states that when the English captured Trinidad in 1787 the population numbered 28,000, of whom 20,000 were slaves.
30. This brief visit led to an amusing episode. When I taught at the Mona, Jamaica, campus of the University of the West Indies in 1965–66, I was told by students and colleagues from Trinidad that the Patois was extinct. But in 1966, I stopped off in Port of Spain and, in the hotel where I stayed, I discovered that many of the employees spoke creole. But they all declared that it was not the true creole, which was spoken only in Maraval. In Maraval, too, people told me that they didn't speak the real creole, which was to be found up in the hills above Morne Coco Road. Arriving there, I was told that the rare creole was spoken only by a single person, an elderly widower, Mounounque Mendez ('uncle Mendez'). I walked half a mile uphill to his house lugging my heavy Uher tape recorder. I recorded Mounounque

58   Introduction

Mendez for about an hour but his creole didn't seem different from what I had heard in Port of Spain or Maraval. I pointed this out to him, and he responded: 'You want to hear the "real" creole?', whereupon he had his son bring him some yellowed sheets. Then he began to sing some hymns that were unintelligible to me. Puzzled, I glanced at the sheets of paper. He had been singing French hymns! The 'real' creole turned out to be approximative French: Mounounque Mendez was the surviving member of a choir formed by a French priest who had taught its members these French hymns.

31. The acute accent indicates word stress falling on the final syllable rather than on the penultimate (next to last) one.
32. Maroons (from the Spanish word *cimarrón* 'fugitive, runaway', literally, 'living on mountaintops', from Spanish *cima* 'top, summit') is the term that refers to slaves escaped from European plantation colonies in the Caribbean and South America. In some colonies, notably Jamaica and Surinam, Maroon slaves formed permanent settlements in remote areas. Today, the term Maroon refers to the descendants of these escaped slaves. Maroons who escaped from plantations in Surinam developed creole languages different from that of Surinam, Sranan.
33. *Arpaillage* refers to the non-industrial search for gold in rivers practiced by individuals, *orpailleurs*. It is a very intensive activity in French Guiana but one that, because of the use of mercury to fix gold particles, pollutes the environment.
34. Presumably Auguste de Saint-Quentin retranscribed the text using the phonological orthography he devised.
35. *Parépou* is the peach-palm tree, of which the fruits are salted and boiled as a staple of the Guianese diet.
36. For convenience, the Karapúna data and the citation from Saint-Quentin (1872) have been retranscribed using the GEREC spelling.
37. The following abbreviations will be used to refer to the various Indian Ocean FBCs: Réunion Creole (RC), Mauritian Creole (MC), Seychellois Creole (SC), Rodrigues Creole (RodC).
38. Mayotte became an overseas department of France only in 2011.
39. These are also termed Petits Blancs, as a reflection of their low social status compared to the wealthier White plantation owners.
40. The notion of convergence was originally proposed by Andersen (1983) as 'transfer to somewhere,' to account for transfer in second-language acquisition.
41. RC material produced by this escaped indentured worker (Maroon), Socrates, is provided by Georges Baudoux in a book first published in 1979 but depicting events that occurred in the 1890s. Extensive excerpts are reproduced and analyzed in Speedy (2007).

2 The Phonological System

In this chapter, I will describe the sound system of HC from a triple perspective. First, I will identify the minimally contrastive units of the system in preparation for the discussion of the issue of spelling (see Chapter 4). Second, I will consider differences between the sound system of HC and that of English in order to identify potential acquisition problems of English speakers learning HC and, conversely, those of HC speakers attempting to speak English. Third, I will make some comparisons between HC and French because, given the diglossic relationship between these two languages for part of the Haitian population, their phonological systems mutually influence each other. A discussion of moot points about the phonology of HC, namely, the status of the nasal consonants [ɲ] and [ŋ], the nasal vowels [ĩ] and [ũ] and the front rounded vowels will follow.

2.1 The Phonemic Principle

2.1.1 What is a 'phonetic' writing system?

There are two perspectives in the description of the sound system of a language: (1) its general phonetic characteristics, its **accent**; (2) its set of contrastive sounds, its **phonemic inventory**. When foreigners attempt to speak our language, we are aware of an accent so specific that it identifies particular linguistic groups. For example, the accent in English of a native speaker of Spanish differs markedly from that of a German speaker. Accents are composites resulting from the superimposition of the intonation, stress, and rhythm of one language on another, as well as from the transfer of particular phonetic habits, for example, the way of pronouncing *r* sounds. Speakers of Spanish might conserve a trilled *r* (pronounced with the tip of the tongue touching the back of the upper front teeth) whereas most speakers from France might retain a velar *r* (produced by contact of the back of the tongue against the soft palate). A foreign accent does not generally interfere with the communication of a message unless the foreign speaker also has failed to acquire the small stock of distinctive sounds of the target language. For example, in English, the vowel sound of *beet* must be differentiated from that of *bit*. To confuse these two sounds would not only lead to accented speech, but it would make it difficult for native speakers to clearly identify messages; *bit* and *beet* cannot be freely substituted in the utterance *Pass me the bit, will you, so that I can drill the hole*. In addition to acquiring a good accent in a foreign language, it is necessary to learn to distinguish among the distinctive sounds or **phonemes** of the target language.

The identification of the phonemes of a language is central in the devising of writing systems. Although it cannot be established as a universal principle, generally, a writing system is preferable wherein each phoneme is always represented by the same symbol and wherein, conversely, the same symbol always denotes the same phoneme. This convention provides for a **bi-unique representation**, and writing systems based on this convention are described as phonologically based. In popular parlance, phonologically based representations are called phonetic, and the language is also termed **phonetic**. Of course, this property does not pertain to the language itself but more specifically to the relationship between the sound system and the spelling.

2.1.2 Distinctive and non-distinctive features

The key to the discovery of the phonemic stock of a language is in **minimal pair** contrasts. For two sounds to be distinctive, they must produce differences in meaning when they are substituted for one another in the same phonological environment, that is, in the presence of the same phonemes, in the same position in the word, etc. Consider the *th* sound of *thin*: [θ]. That it contrasts with *f, t, s*, its closest articulatory neighbors, can be demonstrated by the minimal pairs: *thin/fin, thin/tin, thin/sin*. To show that there are two phonemes in English represented by the same spelling *th*, /θ/, as in *thin*, and /ð/, as in *then*, is a bit more difficult because of the relatively low frequency of these two phonemes in speech. But consider the two pairs of words, *thin* and *then*, and *author* and *other*. If you pronounce these pairs, you will note that in the second example *th* represents a **voiced** sound. If you touch your Adam's Apple as you begin to pronounce each word, you will notice that there is vibration for *then* and *other*, but none for *thin* and *author*. While these are not minimal pairs (the vowels of *thin* and *then* differ, as do, for some speakers, the first vowels of *author* and *other*), they do enable us to show that voiceless *th* [θ] and voiced *th* [ð] are distinct phonemes in English. For that reason, in a phonemic transcription, they would be represented by different symbols: /θ/ and /ð/, respectively. The use of slashes here signifies that these two sounds contrast; until it is demonstrated that two sounds contrast, the symbols that represent them are noted between square brackets [ ], denoting that the contrast is phonetic and not phonemic.

Not all phonetic differences are distinctive. Careful listening, unaided by instruments, will reveal that there are at least three phonetically distinct varieties of *t* in English. Compare the pronunciation of *t* in *tin* and *stint*. If you place the palm of your hand in front of your mouth, you will notice that *tin* is produced with a strong puff of air: **aspiration**. That aspiration is lacking in the *t* of *stint*. When it occurs in a final position, as in *kit*, *t* is usually produced without aspiration. In fact, the articulation is not released. The tip of the tongue approaches the alveolar ridge located behind the upper front teeth but does not make and then break contact with it. The articulation is released when we enunciate clearly, but this is only in the careful pronunciation required in formal situations or when we make an effort to be especially precise. Thus, there are not three *t* phonemes in English, because these three different sounds do not contrast, that is, substituting them for one another does not lead to different words. Indeed, the aspirated and the unaspirated *t* never occur in the same environment: the unaspirated variant occurs only after *s* and before an unstressed vowel, the aspirated one before a stressed vowel. In final position, unreleased *t* and released (aspirated) *t* are in **free variation**: they may be freely substituted for each other without causing changes in meaning. Speakers of some varieties of English also have a flap *t* in the middle of words before unstressed vowels: *butter*, *painter*, *automobile*, etc. The tip of the tongue moves toward the upper gum ridge but does not make firm contact. Despite the fact that they do not have a flap variant, *p* and *k* pattern like *t*:

Aspirated	**Unaspirated**	**Unreleased**
Before stressed vowel	*After s*	*Final*
tin	stint	pit
pin	spin	tip
kin	skin	tick

Languages differ with regard to the functional value they assign to the same sound; in one language, it may be distinctive, in another, conditioned by the environment and, thus, without contrastive function. As I will show in Section 2.4.3, this is the case, for instance, for the nasalization of vowels.

2.2 The Consonant System of HC[1]

HC and English have very similar consonant systems. As is the general practice, I will classify consonants on the basis of their **manner** and **place** of articulation. Place of articulation refers to the place in the mouth cavity where there is closure (in the case of stops) or constriction (in the case of other consonants). Manner of articulation describes how the consonant is produced: **stops** (or occlusives) involve the brief closure of the mouth cavity at a particular point; **fricatives** are marked by constriction that produces noise; **resonants** are produced with slight constriction not generating noise. Voiced and voiceless describe the presence or absence, respectively, of vibration of the vocal chords. **Liquids** are *l*-type sounds and **nasals** are produced by lowering the back part of the soft palate (velum) so that the passageway between the nasal cavity and the back of the mouth is open. Although they are produced with closure at some point in the mouth cavity, they are not occlusives since the passageway between the oral and nasal cavity provides an opening. Sounds consisting of a stop followed by a fricative, as at the beginning of English *chin* and *jean*, are termed **affricates**.

Labels used to specify place of articulation refer to the conjunction of a stationary point and a moving articulator; for example, a dental involves the movement of the tip or the blade of the tongue against the upper front teeth or the gum ridge. **Labials** are produced with closure or constriction involving the lips, **dentals** involving the teeth, **palatals** involving the hard palate, and **velars** involving the soft palate. **Glottal** sounds are produced with constriction in the upper throat. The left-to-right order in the tables below reflects movement from the front to the back along the roof of the mouth.

The consonants of HC are listed in Table 2.1 (for the sake of convenience, I list individual phonemes in the standard Haitian spelling; where these differ from standard phonetic notation, I provide the latter between slashes). Except for the velar nasal (see the discussion below), there is general agreement among the various phonological analyses of the consonantal system of HC (Tinelli 1970; d'Ans 1968; Pompilus 1973; G. Etienne 1974; Férère 1974; Valdman 1978, 1980).

Table 2.1. Consonant System of HC

	Labials	**Dentals**	**Palatals**	**Velars**	**Glottal**
Stops					
voiceless	p	t		k	
voiced	b	d		g	
Affricates					
voiceless			tch /tʃ/		
voiced			dj /dʒ/		
Fricatives					
voiceless	f	s	ch /ʃ/		(h)
voiced	v	z	j /ʒ/		
Resonants					
nasals	m	n		ng /ŋ/	
liquids		l		r /ʁ/	
semivowels	w		y /j/, u /ɥ/		

The following evidence from minimal pairs may be adduced to support this inventory of consonant phonemes. Since there are few problems of analysis, the demonstration is meant to be illustrative rather than exhaustive:

Contrast	Distinctive features	Minimal pairs	
f/v	voiceless/voiced	*fini* 'to finish'	*vini* 'to come'
f/s	labial/dental	*fann* 'to split'	*sann* 'ash'
f/p	fricative/stop	*fè* 'to do'	*pè* 'priest'
f/b	fricative voiceless/labial voiced	*fèt* 'feast'	*bèt* 'animal'
f/w	fricative/semivowel	*fo* 'false'	*wo* 'tall'

2.2.1 Particular remarks

1. **Affrication in *t* and *d*.** HC voiceless stops, unlike those of English (see Section 2.1.1), are always unaspirated and fully released in all positions. However, *t* and *d* are produced with palatal contact before the vowel *i*. This palatal contact is perceived as a short *y* or *s* sound following the consonant: *pitit* 'child' is heard as /pit^{j}it/ or /pit^{s}it/, *dis* 'ten' is heard as [d^{j}is] or [d^{s}is]. That this affrication reflects the origin of HC in vernacular rather than Standard French finds support in the presence of affrication of *t* and *d* before high front vowels in the French varieties spoken in Quebec and some parts of Louisiana.

2. **Velar nasal.** Many linguists, both native speakers and foreigners, have posited for HC a velar nasal consonant phoneme /ŋ/, for example, Tinelli (1970), Pompilus (1973), and G. Etienne (1974). Indeed, this sound does exist in a few words, for example, *pinga* [pĩŋga] 'watch out'. However, because it is preceded by the nasalized vowel [ĩ], it is best to interpret that sound in terms of the sequence /ng/, as does Dejean (1980: 117), not a unitary phoneme /ŋ/, and transcribe *pinga* as /pinga/. The nasalized [ĩ] is then analyzed as an allophonic variant of /i/ resulting from the regressive (backward, i.e. a phoneme influences the pronunciation of the preceding one) assimilation of the nasality of the following /n/. In turn, the sound [ŋ] is analyzed as an allophonic variant of /n/ resulting from the regressive assimilation to the following velar /g/.

3. **Nasalized *j*.** When it occurs in the middle of words between nasal vowels or at the ends of words after a nasal vowel, *j* is nasalized in HC: *benyen* 'to bathe'; *zonyon* 'onion'; *peny* [pẽj̃] 'comb'; *liny* [lĩj̃] 'line' (Dejean 1980).

64   *The Phonological System*

4. **Weakened medial consonants**. In the middle of words, the voiced stops *b, d, g* may be produced with reduced force of articulation; in which case, they are nearly inaudible, for example, *bagay / baay/* 'thing'. The voiceless stops *p, t, k* may also be voiced in the same environments: *kapab* /kabab/ 'able' (this word is usually pronounced as *kap, kab*, or *ka* when it serves as a modal verb: *yo ka pati* 'they may leave').

5. **r**. This HC phoneme has severely limited distribution (see Section 2.2.2 below). When it is pronounced, at the beginning and in the middle of words, HC /r/ differs phonetically from both French and English corresponding phonemes. For that reason, I note it with the symbol /ɤ/. It is a weak resonant produced with slight constriction involving the back of the tongue and the front part of the soft palate, that is, it is a front velar. In French, the phonetic nature of /ʁ/ varies greatly depending on sociolinguistic and geographical factors and position in the word. In the prestige variety of Standard French, it is a back velar weakly articulated in final position. Some lower-class Parisian speakers may produce the /ʁ/ as far back as the pharynx. In fact, there are several structural features of HC /r/ that might lead one to categorize it as a semivowel, as does Cadely (1988). The substitution of the HC /ɤ/ for the French /ʁ/ results only in an accent. Indeed, it is one of the most salient marks of Haitian French.

2.2.2   Distribution of phonemes

1. Consonant clusters. Compared to English and French, HC has few consonant clusters such as those that occur in English *necks* /ks/, *lapsed* /pst/, *calms* /lmz/ or French *porte* /ʁt/, *table* /bl/. On the other hand, HC has some initial consonant clusters that occur neither in English nor in French. These involve the resonants *m, n,* and *l* found in the short form of the pronouns for the first person singular, the first person plural inclusive (that is to say, *we, you*, or *we and you*), and the third person singular, respectively: *epi m̩ te sòti* 'then I had left', *se pou n̩ rele l* 'we/you have to call her', *lè sa a l te pati* 'at that time he had left'. Of these three consonants, *m* is the only one that occurs most frequently before another consonant in utterance-initial position, for example, *m̩ benyen, m̩ bwose dan m* 'I wash myself, I brush my teeth' (Valdman 2008) and word-initially, *m̩sye/ m̩che* 'the guy, he'. When the consonants *m, l,* and *n* occur in initial position before another consonant, specifically in the 1st and 3rd person singular pronouns and in the 1st/2nd person plural pronoun, respectively, they actually do not form initial consonant clusters. Instead, they have full syllabic value, indicated here for convenience by the subscript dot. Thus, for example, *m̥sye* has the CVCV structure, with the initial *m* counting as a full syllable (Valdman 1978: 71–2). Of these three syllabic consonants, *m* occurs most frequently.

In Table 2.1, I have included, under the label 'affricates', the phonemic sequences *tch* /tʃ/ and *dj* /dʒ/. Phonological analyses of HC differ with regard to their phonological status: do they constitute unitary phonemes, like the other consonants, in which case they should be transcribed as tʃ and dʒ, respectively (Pompilus 1973), as done for English (see Table 2.1), or do they function as biphonemic sequences as the transcription suggests (R. A. Hall 1953; Tinelli 1970; d'Ans 1968; Valdman 1978; Dejean 1980)? In the most detailed discussion about this issue, Dejean (1980: 103) constructs a strong argument for the biphonemic solution. First, unlike all consonants, these sequences occur infrequently in final position, generally in English loanwords: *match* 'match', *gedj* 'gauge'. Second, both sequences alternate freely with the sequences *dy* and *ty*: *djòl /dyòl* 'mouth of an animal', *tchoule/tyoule* 'to move back'.

2. The liquid r. In contrast to its corresponding French phoneme /ʁ/, HC *r* does not occur in final position or after a vowel within a word.[2] For example, note the following correspondences between French and HC:

French			**HC**
la porte	'the door'	/pɔʁt/	*pòt*
la carte	'the card'	/kaʁt/	*kat*
le frère	'the brother'	/fʁɛʁ/	*frè*
la cour	'the yard'	/kuʁ/	*lakou*
venir	'to come'	/vəniʁ/	*vini*
sortir	'to go out'	/sɔʁtiʁ/	*soti*
parler	'to speak'	/paʁle/	*pale*

The loss of final and post-vocalic *r* probably does not fully reflect an autonomous development of HC. A weakened /ʁ/ and loss of that phoneme in these positions is a well-attested phenomenon in French dialects and, in fact, during the sixteenth and seventeenth centuries it even affected the Paris dialect. That French phoneme, often realized as length of the preceding vowel, is found in some varieties of Louisiana French and in Northern Haitian Creole (NHC). See Chapter 11 for a detailed discussion of the differences between this dialect and the Port-au-Prince variety on which the standard spelling is based.

In addition, *r* does not generally occur before rounded vowels *(ou, o, ò, on)* and, as a consequence, it does not contrast with the semivowel *w* in these environments. Note the distribution of *r* and *w* in HC presented below:

Before front unrounded vowels		Before central unrounded vowels		Before rounded back vowels	
ri	'street'	*rat*	'rat'	*gwo*	'large'
wi	'yes'	*wat*	'watt'	*wouj*	'red'
rete	'to remain'	*ranp*	'slop'	*wòch*	'stone'
wete	'to take away'	*wanp*	'whack'	*won*	'round'

Especially in northern Haiti, speakers do optionally replace *r* by *w* before unrounded vowels and after labial and labio-dental consonants (see Chapter 11 and Dejean 1980: 97). For example, whereas speakers from the Port-au-Prince region generally say *pran* 'to take', *bra* 'arm', *vrè* 'true', and *frè* 'brother', their northern compatriots may pronounce these words as *pwan, bwa, vwè,* and *fwè* respectively. In southern Haiti, for some words, many speakers replace the velar resonant *r* with the glottal aspirate /h/ that is identical phonetically to the corresponding English sound in *him*, for example. So instead of *rad* 'clothing', *rèl* 'cry, shout', or *raje* 'bushes', these speakers say *had, hèl* and *haje* respectively. Before rounded vowels, for words that correspond to French words with /ʁ/, these speakers will have *h* instead of *w*, for example, *hou* 'hoe' instead of *wou*. Note that these speakers have *r* and *w* in other words. They contrast *r* and *h* in, for example, *hèl* 'cry' vs. *rèl do* 'backbone', and *h* and *w*, for example, in *hou* 'hoe' vs. *wou* 'you' (*se wou* 'it's you').

2.3 Semivowels (Glides)

There are three semivowels (also termed glides) in HC. The most frequent, *w* and *y* /j/, are pronounced like their English near-equivalents. These two semivowels occur in all word positions: *yo* 'they', *wè* 'to see', *dèyè* 'behind', *dèyò/dèwò* 'outside' and *kay* 'house', *kaw* 'blackbird'. They also occur before vowels: *pye* 'foot', *lwen* 'far'. In this position, they form a single syllable with the following vowel. If the occurrence of *w* word-finally is rare, it is very frequent syllable-finally because the 2SG pronoun, *ou*, is generally realized as /w/ after a vowel: *m ap di w* 'I'm telling you', *avò w* 'with you'.

We have seen above that *r* and *w* do not generally contrast before rounded vowels and, sometimes in NHC, after labial and labio-dental consonants, as in *pwan* 'to take' instead of HC *pran*. In the most widely spoken variety of HC, i.e., the one reflected by the standard spelling and by the speech of monolingual speakers of the Port-au-Prince region, the word for 'arm' is generally *bra* and that for 'wood' is *bwa*, but some speakers, especially those from northern Haiti, freely substitute *w* for *r* in *bra* 'arm'. In addition, they will say *bra* as well as *bwa* for 'wood'. Since the use of *r* characterizes the standard variety of HC, that pronunciation is viewed as the more correct one in words such as *bra*. Those speakers who replace *w* with *r* tend to overreact by substituting *r* for *w* even in words that have the semivowel in the standard pronunciation.

The absence of *r* in the environment of labials and rounded vowels suggests a structural relationship between it and the semivowel *w*. The latter is the semivowel corresponding to the back rounded vowels *ou* and *o*, just as *y* is the semivowel that corresponds to front unrounded *i* and *e*. Interestingly, as pointed out above, *w* rarely occurs in word-final position and in the standard dialect *r* is absent in that position too. Furthermore, as will be shown in Chapter 3, although it occurs finally in NHC, it is followed by the post-vocalic **allomorph** (morphological variant) of the definite determiner, namely *a,* not the post-consonantal one *la*. This supports the claim that it functions as a semivowel rather than a liquid resonant consonant (Cadely 1988). Of course, a major difference between *w* and *r* is that there is no corresponding relationship between the latter and any vowel.

In sequences of two successive vowels, depending on the nature of the vowels in contact, a transitional glide is inserted between them. This glide is shorter and less perceptible than those that occur in other positions. After high front vowels (*i, e, en*), the transitional glide is front [j]: *diri a* [diriʲa] 'the rice', *pye a* [pyeʲa] 'the foot', *chen an* [ʃẽʲã] 'the dog'. After the rounded vowel (*ou, o, on*), the back transitional glide [w] is inserted: *wou a* [wuʷa] 'the wheel', *dlo a* [dloʷa] 'the water', *pon an* [põʷã] 'the bridge'.

The third HC semivowel /ɥ/, noted *u*, occurs in sequences with *i: uit* 'eight'. However, in most cases, it alternates with /w/: *lannuit/lanwit* 'night', *kuit/kwit* 'cooked'. In the frenchified variety of HC, termed *kreyòl swa*, *u* is more likely to occur.

2.4 The Vowel System of HC

As does French, unlike English, HC distinguishes nasal from non-nasal vowels. Because of the complexity of this HC vocalic subsystem, there is no general agreement among linguists concerning their analysis. Here, the focus will be on the contrast between them and corresponding oral (non-nasal) vowels. There also exist divergent opinions about the status of the front rounded vowels /y, ø, œ/. Some linguists claim that these are an integral part of the sound system of HC; others see them as marginal elements borrowed from French. This issue will be taken up in Section 2.5. In this section, I deal primarily with the other oral vowels.

2.4.1 Oral vowels

There is general agreement about the existence of seven oral vowel phonemes in HC. Vowels are usually described in terms of: (1) the relative position of the tongue from front to back in the mouth cavity (front/back); (2) the position of the tongue relative to the roof of the mouth (high/mid/low); and (3) the lip setting (rounded/unrounded) (see Table 2.2). The vowels are represented in Standard Haitian spelling, with phonetic symbols provided where that spelling and the phonetic notation differ. Sample minimal pairs are given as illustrations in Table 2.3.

Table 2.2. Oral Vowel System of HC

	Front	Back
High	i	ou /u/
High-mid	e	o
Low-mid	è /ɛ/	ò /ɔ/
Low	a	
	Unrounded	Rounded

Table 2.3. Minimal Pairs Illustrating the HC Oral Vowels

li di	'he says'	*li dou*	'it's sweet'
pe bouch ou	'be quiet'	*se yon pè*	'it's a priest'
se yon abi	'it's a man's suit'	*se yon abe*	'it's a cleric'
se yon mè	'it's a nun'	*se yon ma*	'it's a mast'
li fo	'it's false'	*li fò*	'he's strong'

2.4.2 Nasal vowels

Nasal vowels, like nasal consonants, are produced with the velum lowered and, consequently, an open passageway between the back of the mouth and the nasal cavity. The salient feature of nasal vowels is not so much that the air passes through the nose but that a small cavity is formed in the area of the velum. The formation of that cavity produces a specific acoustic effect: **nasal-**

ization. The nasal vowels constitute the most complex aspect of the sound system of HC. As is the case in French, nasal and oral vowels contrast. But, in addition, vowels tend to be nasalized automatically in the environment of nasal consonants. This type of spreading of a pronunciation feature, forward or backward, from one phoneme to an adjacent one is termed **assimilation**, and it is quite common in languages of the world. Another complicating factor stems from the use of a nasal twang in various roles linked to Haitian folklore and in the representation of certain Vodou spirits. In folktales, the first of the two protagonists of traditional Bouki (Brer Bear or the hyena) and Malis (Brer Rabbit) stories is represented as speaking with a nasal tone. Overall nasality is also associated with the speech of *gede*, spirits in contact with the dead and associated with funeral rites, and *zombis*, the walking dead.

2.4.3 The primary nasal vowels

HC has three primary nasal vowels. These occur with high frequency, and their phonemic status is clear; they contrast with corresponding oral vowels in both free and checked syllables (see Table 2.4). Checked syllables end in a consonant and free syllables in a vowel (Valdman and Iskrova 2003).

Table 2.4. Distribution of the Primary Nasal Vowels in HC

Free syllables		
pe /pe/ 'be quiet'	*pè* /pɛ/ 'priest'	*pen* /pẽ/ 'bread'
po /po/ 'skin'	*pò* /pɔ/ 'harbor'	*pon* /põ/ 'bridge'
sa /sa/ 'that'		*san* /sã/ 'blood'
Checked syllables		
sèt /sɛt/ 'seven'	*sent* /sẽt/ 'saint'	
dòk /dɔk/ 'dock'	*donk* /dõk/ 'therefore'	
pat /pat/ 'paw'	*pant* /pãt/ 'slope'	

This system differs from that of French by the fact that some speakers of the latter language have a fourth nasal vowel, *un* /œ̃/ in such words as *lundi* 'Monday', *parfum*, 'perfume' or *brun* 'brown'; the latter word contrasts with (*le*) *brin* 'bit' (of grass). Also, the exact articulation of corresponding vowels differs: HC *en* is higher than French /ɛ̃/, *an* is more central than French /ã/, and *on* is lower and less tense than French /õ/; as a cautionary note, it should be pointed out that the pronunciation of nasal vowels varies greatly within France and between France and other French-speaking regions and countries, especially North American varieties found in Canada, New England, and Louisiana.

2.4.4 Distribution of nasal vowels

However, the major difference between the nasal vowel systems of HC and French resides in their respective distribution. In French, nasal vowels are by and large excluded from the environment of nasal consonants. There are many grammatical distinctions and pairs of words involving the contrast between a nasal vowel in final free syllables and the corresponding non-nasal vowel before a nasal consonant:

il est bon /bõ/	'he's good'	*elle est bonne* /bɔn/	'she's good'
Jean /ʒɑ̃/	'John'	*Jeanne* /ʒan/	'Jean'
il vient /vjɛ̃/	'he is coming'	*ils viennent* /vjɛn/	'they are coming'
un /œ̃/	indef. article, masc.	*une* /yn/	indef. article, fem.

In HC, as is the case in English, vowels tend to be nasalized, that is, produced with the velum lowered, before nasal consonants. However, corresponding oral and nasal vowels may contrast in this environment. In other words, nasalization is not automatic, and one must know whether a word may be pronounced with an oral vowel, a nasal vowel, or with either type of vowel followed by a nasal consonant. These facts are summarized in Table 2.5.

In word-initial or word-medial position, generally, vowels are nasalized in the environment of nasal consonants, but the fact that nasalization is not automatic is demonstrated by numerous words where the vowel remains oral, including some minimal pairs. Some cases of obligatory nasalization in the speech of monolingual speakers are *kanson* 'trousers', *panyen* 'basket', *zonyon* 'onion', *benyen* 'to bathe'; cases of obligatory non-

Table 2.5. Oral Versus Nasal Vowel Contrasts in HC

Free syllable			Syllable checked by a nasal consonant	
Oral vowel	**Nasal vowel**		**Nasal vowel**	**Oral vowel**
pe 'be quiet'	*pè* 'priest'	*pen* 'bread'	*lapenn* 'grief'	*pèn* 'our priest'
po 'pot'	*pò* 'harbor'	*pon* 'bridge'	*ponn* 'to lay eggs'	
mo 'word'	*mò* 'dead person'	*mon chè* 'Man!'	*lemonn* 'world'	*mòn* 'hill'
ko 'already'	*kò* 'body'	*konsa* 'thus'	*konn* 'to know'	*kòn* 'horn'
pa 'step'		*pan* 'peacock'	*pann* 'to hang'	*pàn* 'breakdown'

nasalization include *emab* 'nice', *somèy* 'sleep', *nèg* 'guy', *limonad* 'lemonade'. The following minimal pairs illustrate the phonemic contrast between oral and corresponding nasal vowels: *lanmè* 'sea' vs. *lamè* 'older woman', *chay* 'load' vs. *chany* 'shoeshine boy', *peye* 'to pay' vs. *penyen* 'to comb'. As may be expected, except for the words listed previously, there is considerable variation in the pronunciation of words containing vowels in the environment of nasal consonants: *famiy/fanmiy* 'family', *demon/denmon* 'devil'. In other cases, related words show different vowels, for example, *zanmi* 'friend' but *amitye* 'climbing plant', *amou* 'love' but *fè lanmou* 'to make love'.

It should be emphasized that although some words may be pronounced with either a nasal or an oral vowel, foreign learners cannot blithely alternate between oral and nasal vowels. They must know whether a word always has a nasal vowel (*lanm* 'wave'), never has a nasal vowel (*lam* 'breadfruit'), or may be pronounced with either (*famiy/fanmiy*). Lack of knowledge of the underlying form of a word can result in serious mispronunciations, for example, when *anmè* 'bitter' is produced as *amè or *anmen (the asterisk denotes ungrammatical forms). The issue of obligatory versus optional nasalization will be taken up again in Chapter 3.

2.4.5 The marginal nasal vowels: *in* and *oun*

There are two relatively infrequent nasal vowels whose status is the object of controversy among linguists, the high vowels [ĩ] and [ũ]. The problems of analysis these pose stem from their relatively low frequency of occurrence, but also from difficulties in perception.[3] It is more difficult to perceive nasalization with high vowels than mid and low vowels. Another confounding factor is that the postulation of these two vowels leads to complications in the elaboration of a suitable phonologically based spelling system for HC. We will return to this problem in the chapter devoted to spelling, Chapter 4.

The vowel /i/ occurs in nasalized form [ĩ] in such words as *kachimbo* 'earthenware pipe', *pinga* 'take care not to', *mi* 'ripe', *pitimi* 'little millet', or *liy* 'line'. Note that in these words, the vowel occurs in the environment of a nasal consonant; these are cases of regressive nasal assimilation, that is, the influence of a following phoneme. With regard to *pinga* and *kachimbo*, some speakers produce these words with oral *i* + nasal consonant, others with the nasal vowel [ĩ]. An important consideration in resolving this issue is the existence of near-minimal pairs such as *liy* [lĩy] 'line' and *fiy* [fiy] 'girl, woman'. However, this limited contrast cannot be accounted for by positing a nasal semivowel *y* (/j̃/) and claiming that /i/ becomes nasalized in the vicinity of that nasal consonant. Note, however, that *i* is not automatically nasalized before the other nasal consonants, for example, in *machin* 'machine'.

Evidence in favor of a phoneme *oun* /ũ/ is somewhat more persuasive, although minimal pairs are also lacking. Nasal *oun* occurs in free syllables in words related to the Vodou religion: *oungan* [ũgã] 'Vodou priest', *ounfò* [ũfɔ] 'Vodou altar', *ounsi* [ũsi] 'female Vodou assistant or initiate'. In these words, it also varies freely with non-nasal *ou*. An important word that is always pronounced with [ũ] is the pronoun *nou* (this is the official spelling that does not note nasal [ũ]); other words that are often pronounced with this vowel are *kouman* 'how' and *youn* 'one'.

2.5 Front Rounded Vowels

Bilingual speakers of HC make three additional vowel distinctions. These are the front vowels produced with lip rounding, which constitute one of the marked characteristics of French and are, in fact, one of the most difficult aspects of the phonological system of that language for foreigners to master. These vowels – [y], [ø], and [œ] – are for the sake of convenience represented here as *u*, *eu*, and *eù* respectively. However, it should be stressed that the representation of these vowels has not been provided for by the standard spelling (see Chapter 4).

These three vowels are produced by starting from the articulatory positions of *i*, *e*, and *è* respectively and rounding the lips. They occur in such words as *ji/ju*, 'juice', *zeu/ze* 'egg', *seù/sè* 'sister'. Bilingual speakers are able to differentiate the two sets of front vowels, and they contrast such minimal pairs as *di* 'to say' vs. *du* 'hard', *ble* 'wheat' vs. *bleu* 'blue', and *pè* 'priest' vs. *pèu* 'fear'. Most monolingual speakers of HC cannot usually differentiate these minimal pairs, and they pronounce both words with the front unrounded vowel.

The controversy that surrounds the status of these three vowels in HC no doubt stems from the relationship between French and HC in Haiti and the fact that proficiency in French and in the variety of HC spoken by bilingual speakers serves as a marker of social class; for a more detailed discussion of these issues see Chapter 12. As we shall see in Chapter 4, the controversy is also linked with the elaboration of an orthography and the choice of a written norm. Those persons who opt for a norm determined by the speech of monolingual rural and lower-class urban speakers tend to deny their existence in the speech of monolingual speakers. However, empirical observations and statements of some Haitian analysts do reveal their consistent presence among monolingual speakers of HC, at least in northern Haiti.

2.5 Front Rounded Vowels

The Haitian folklorist Michelson Hyppolite (1951–6), who transcribed folktales in northern Haiti, generally notes front rounded vowels in HC words whose corresponding French words have these vowels, for example, *pèdu* (French *perdu*) 'lost', *li fè kum* (French *écume*) 'it foams', *msyeu* (French *monsieur*) 'man', *fiyeùl* (French *filleul*) 'godson'. He did indicate some variants with front unrounded vowels, for example, *li kimen* (French *elle écumait*) 'it foamed'. In the most authoritative study of geographical variation in HC, conducted in the early 1980s, the *Atlas Linguistique d'Haïti* (Linguistic Atlas of Haiti), the author, Dominique Fattier (1998), noted the occurrence of front rounded vowels alternating with corresponding unrounded vowels: 197, *oteùr* 'height', 209 *kwochu* 'crooked', 210 *cheuveu* 'hair', 220, 221, 222, 225, 227, 230 *zyeu*, 'eye', 90 *lalun* 'moon', 420 *postum, potsum* 'pus' (the numbers refer to the listing of the particular variable in the study).[4] Of particular significance is the form *zyeu* 'eye', which occurs as *je* even in the speech of bilingual speakers in the capital city.[5]

In stays in Haiti from 1966 to 1985, I have myself noted the occurrence of the three front rounded vowels in random observations made in the Cape Haitian region. These observations have been supported by recent empirical data collected by local interviewers (Valdman 2004, 2008). In 2001, Jacques Pierre, a native of Cape Haitian, recorded interviews with a dozen adult illiterate monolingual rural speakers in L'Anglaise, a village near the town of Limbé. The recordings, totaling about ten hours, transcribed by the interviewer and checked by me, show instances of front rounded vowels, for example, *duri* 'rice', *sèur* 'sister'. Often these vowels alternated with their front unrounded corresponding vowel: *bleu/ble* 'blue', *sèul/sèl* 'alone'. A contextual example, in which the interviewer elicited words for colors, is particularly revealing: *Bleu, bleu. Gen ki ble et blan. Li gen bleu senp* 'Blue, blue. There are some that are blue and white. There are some that are all blue'. However, there are cases where, although the French etymon contains front rounded vowels, forms showing the corresponding unrounded vowels were more numerous, for example, *lalin* 'moon', *jije* 'to judge', *dife* 'fire', *lye* 'place', *bèf* 'cow, ox', *fèy* 'leaf'. To be sure, there were also cases of **hypercorrection** (the production of the prestige form in the wrong word). For example, a fifty-year-old woman produced *beu* instead of the correct *be* 'the letter b' in the utterance: *M pap fè beu, m pap fè se* 'I don't do B, I don't do C', that is, 'I don't do anything'. The following conversational exchange is particularly interesting, for she hypercorrects the correct form provided by the interviewer and inserts a post-vocalic *r*:

Interviewer: Eske ou fèt nan batis, ou byen ou te katolik anvan ou vin *konvèti* (French: *converti*) nan batis?
'Were you born a Baptist, or were you a Catholic before you converted to a Baptist?'

Speaker: M te katolik anvan, apre sa m vin *konvèrtu* kounyè a.
'I was Catholic before, after that, I've become converted now.'

In 2007 and 2008, a more extensive corpus was collected from 135 speakers: 30 rural monolingual adults, 30 urban monolingual adults, 30 rural teenagers enrolled in the sixth year of the basic education cycle, 15 urban teenagers also enrolled in the sixth year of the basic cycle, and 30 teenagers enrolled in the ninth year of the basic cycle (Valdman 2008).[6] The teenagers were partially bilingual, the older urban ones showing a higher level of competence in French than their rural peers and younger urban peers. All the adolescents had passed a national test designed to evaluate their mastery of standard spelling, in both reading and writing. Local secondary and primary schoolteachers conducted the primary interviews of this later study. They were transcribed independently twice by local bilingual teachers who had attained a Bachelor of Education degree from the Faculté d'Education Regina Assumpta in Cape Haitian (FERA).[7] The second interview was transcribed in collaboration with a trained non-native linguist fluent in HC. All the adult rural speakers in the 2007 study produced relatively few front rounded vowels. For example, in a two-hour sample from two male and two female speakers, the following eleven instances occurred: *bleu* 'blue' (4), *zyeu* 'eye', *sèul* 'alone' (2), *dur* 'hard' (2), *Duvalye* 'Duvalier', *sujè* 'subject'. In half of the occurrences of *bleu* and *dur* and in *Duvalye*, the rounding is partial and the vowel quality is intermediate between [i] and [y]. There were no cases of hypercorrection but one of free variation: *dir/dur*. In addition, there were a considerable number of words whose French etymon contains a front rounded vowel that were pronounced with the corresponding unrounded vowel: for example, *doktèr/dòktè* (*docteur*), *Bondje* (*Bon Dieu*) 'God', *pèrdi/pèdi* (*perdu*) 'lost'.

In contrast, the urban adolescents produced more than 100 cases of front rounded vowels and a small number of hypercorrections: *musyeu (*monsieur* [møsyø]) 'sir, guy, he', whose standard form is *mesye/msye*, *sutiye (*situé*) *sitiye* 'located', **etuduye/*etiduye* (*étudier*) *etidye* 'to study'. They also inserted occasional French code switches, for example, *o zyeu de yon moun* (*aux yeux d'une personne*), instead of more general HC *nan je yon moun* 'from the point of view of someone, literally, from the eyes of a person' and they showed extensive use of the preposition *de*, a feature associated with, but not limited to, *kreyòl swa* (bilingual HC).[8] This form was produced with both the rounded and the unrounded vowels: *nonm de tan* 'a number of times' vs. *on mank deu respè* 'a lack of respect'. In observations made in 1966, Dejean (1980: 124–6) documents the influence of rudimentary schooling (two or three years of primary school) on the production of hypercorrected front rounded vowels. He contrasts the reading of the sentence *ti fi a te li liv la* 'the girl read the book' by two adult women, the first of whom, illiterate, was being taught to read creole and the second of whom had been taught to read French forty years earlier. The first pronounced the front vowels correctly, the second erroneously changed them all to the corresponding rounded vowels: **tu fi a teu lu luv la*.

The vowels *i*, *eu*, and *eù* constitute a salient feature of bilingual HC and, consequently, they have high prestige. In a sense, to be able to produce them is viewed as reflecting competence in French. Consequently, monolingual speakers might strive to produce them in situations that demand the most frenchified form of HC they can muster. As may be expected, this is an area of the sound system of HC where hypercorrection is likely to occur. Bilingual speakers are not only able to consistently differentiate *i* and *u*, *e* and *eu*, and *è* and *èu*, but they also know which words potentially have a dual pronunciation. That is, they know that the word for 'juice', which they generally pronounce *ju*, is pronounced *ji* by most monolingual HC speakers, and they might alternate between the two pronunciations. On the other hand, they know that the word for 'to say' may only be pronounced *di*. Monolingual speakers and, in particular, those who have had some exposure to French instruction, do not always know to which of the two classes (dual pronunciation or single pronunciation) individual words belong. Since they know that the pronunciation with a rounded vowel is more prestigious, they will extend that pronunciation to all words containing *i*, *e*, and *è* and thus produce hypercorrections.

With the paucity of detailed empirical studies of language variation in Haiti, it is difficult to state how widespread the distribution of front rounded vowels has become. However, because it is widely attested among some monolingual speakers, especially in northern Haiti, it is arbitrary to exclude them from the vowel system of monolingual HC on the grounds that they reflect the influence of French.

As education, still conducted primarily with French as the classroom vehicle, becomes more available to urban and rural monolingual HC-speaking children, and with the greater exposure of the population to radio and television broadcasts, the frequency of occurrence of these vowels is likely to increase. On the other hand, as will be pointed out in Chapter 12, the domains of use of HC are broadening, resulting in an increased exposure to the standard spelling that does not provide representation of the front rounded vowels (see Chapter 4). Finally, for regions of Haiti where these vowels appear to be a feature of the monolingual speech of illiterates or semi-illiterates (individuals with limited schooling), with their spread from above, i.e., from contact with French and bilingual HC, it becomes more difficult to determine whether they reflect an older stage of HC, Saint-Domingue Creole which was overall closer to French, or are the result of more recent trends.

Summary

The phonological system of HC does not differ widely from that of French. At the consonantal level the main differences are the occurrence of the palatal sequences /tʃ/ and /dʒ/ but these alternate with the sequences /tj/ and /dj/, respectively: *tchoule/tyoule* 'to move', *djòl /dyòl* 'mouth of an animal'. Also, /t/ and /d/ are produced with affrication: *pitit* 'child' [pitʲit] or [pitˢit], *dis* 'ten' [dʲis] or [dˢis]. Another phonological particularity is the nasalized glide [j̃]. As it occurs after nasal vowels, it is best analyzed as progressive nasal assimilation: *peny* /pẽj/ 'comb'.

The signal feature of HC at the consonantal level is the phonetic nature and the distribution of *r*. Phonetically, it is a very weak resonant produced further forward than the corresponding French phoneme. Except for the dialectal variety of the Cape Haitian region, Capois, it does not occur in post-vocalic position. It is replaced by /w/ before rounded vowels: *wouj* 'red', *wòb* 'dress'. Capois speakers tend to extend that replacement after labial consonants: *pwan* 'to take', *bwa* 'wood', *fwè* 'brother'. In southern Haiti, in some words, *r* is replaced by the glottal aspirate /h/: *rad* [had] 'clothes'.

Because of the favored CVCV nature of HC, after high vowels transitional glides are inserted to eliminate two successive vowels: [j] after the front vowels *i, e, en*: *diri a* [diriʲa] 'the rice', *pye a* [pyeʲa] 'the foot', *chen an* [ʃẽʲã] 'the dog' and [w] after the rounded vowel *ou, o, on*: *wou a* [wuʷa] 'the wheel', *dlo a* [dloʷa] 'the water', *pon an* [põʷã] 'the bridge'.

Monolingual speakers do not produce the front rounded vowels found in the speech of bilinguals (*kreyòl swa*) and some Capois speakers in such words as *diri* /dyri/ 'rice', *ze* /zø/ and *se* /sœ/. Because of the prestige attached to bilingual speech, monolingual speakers occasionally hypercorrect: *konvèti* /kõvɛty/ 'converted', *ble* /blø/ 'wheat'. Otherwise, the oral vowel system of HC with its seven phonemes does not differ from that of Standard French, except that, because of the absence of post-vocalic *r*, there is a phonemic distinction between high and low mid vowels in open syllables, that is, those syllables ending with the vowel. Compare French *père* /pɛr/ 'father' and *fort* /fɔr/ 'strong' to HC *pè* 'priest' and *fò* 'strong'. Consequently, in HC, these two words contrast with *pe* (*bouch ou*) 'be quiet' and *fo* 'false', respectively.

Like French, HC has nasal vowels that contrast with corresponding oral vowels, for example, *pa* 'step' vs. *pan* 'peacock'. But whereas in French nasal vowels do not generally occur before nasal consonants, in HC they do contrast with oral vowels in this position: *pàn* 'breakdown' vs. *pann* 'to hang'. The phonetic high nasal vowels [ĩ] and [ũ] in such words as *pinga* 'take care not to', *mi* 'ripe', *liy* 'line', and *oungan* 'Vodou priest' are best analyzed as conditioned by a following nasal consonant, a case of regressive assimilation.

Notes

1. As will be shown in Chapter 4, the spelling system currently in use in Haiti is phonologically based. For that reason, I will use the letters of that system to represent the phonemes of HC. The table below provides the correspondences between these letters and the symbols of the International Phonetic Association (IPA) represented below:

    Consonants: p /p/, t /t/, k /k/, b /b/, d /d/, g /g/, ch /ʃ/, j /ʒ/, tch /tʃ/, dj /dʒ/, s /s/, z /z/, m /m/, n /n/, ng /ŋ/, l /l/, r /ɣ/
    Semivowels: y /j/, u /ɥ/, w /w/
    Oral vowels: i /i/, e /e/, è /ɛ/, a /a/, ou /u/, o /o/, ò /ɔ/
    Nasal vowels: en /ẽ/, an /ã/, on /õ/

    I will refer to the spelling system currently used in Haiti and in the Haitian diaspora as the **standard spelling**, proclaimed as official in 1979 during the rule of Jean-Claude Duvalier.

2. In the speech of northern Haiti, especially the area of Cape Haitian, Northern Haitian Creole, henceforth NHC, it appears that some speakers do have *r* before rounded vowels. However, the difference between *w* and *r* is often difficult to hear and not readily amenable to acoustic analysis. Interestingly, the same speakers, who appear to have *r* in this position, replace it with *w* after a labial consonant.

3. The phonemic status of these two nasal vowels is proposed by both native and foreign linguists (Pompilus 1973; Férère 1974; R. A. Hall 1953; Orjala 1970) but is rejected categorically by the native linguist Yves Dejean (1980: 120), who invokes naïve native-speaker perception. He argues that, whereas the average native HC speaker can easily perceive the difference between pairs involving the primary nasal vowels and their oral counterparts, for example, between invented minimal pairs like *[vila] vs. *[vilã], they would be unable to hear the differences between *[vili] vs. [vilĩ] or between *[vilu] vs. *[vilũ]. This is not a totally persuasive argument because we must assume that trained linguists' perception trumps that of ordinary speakers, particularly when the linguists happen to be native speakers. Dejean grants, however, that these two nasal vowels might have in some cases allophonic status. That is, the

78   The Phonological System

nasalization is the result of regressive assimilation triggered by the following nasal consonant. Also, there might be free variation between the oral and nasal counterparts. As I have pointed out above, the oral vs. nasal distinction is less salient for high vowels like *i* and *ou*. Also, Dejean's views may be influenced by the underlying objective of his analysis and the title of his book: *Comment écrire le créole d'Haïti* (How to write the Creole of Haiti). The spelling system he supports in the book does not provide symbols for these two infrequently occurring vowels – a reasonable position – nor does the standard spelling.

4. These numbers refer to maps in Fattier's study (1998), which is discussed in Chapter 11.

5. Yves Dejean (1980: 121), who absolutely denies the phonemic status of front rounded vowels in HC, characterizes Hyppolite's observations as 'vague and incomplete'. This judgment must be tempered by the fact that he grants that Hyppolite's perception of post-vocalic *r*, a very weakly articulated sound, is accurate. Dejean also misinterprets Pressoir (1947: 66), another Haitian author, whom he cites as denying the existence of front rounded vowels in the speech of monolingual speakers. In fact, to the contrary, Pressoir criticizes the creator of the first phonologically based spelling for HC, McConnell (McConnell and Swann 1945a and b), for failing to provide a representation for these vowels:

> [McConnell] ne connaissant pas assez notre idiome pour en saisir les nuances, ne s'appliqua à rendre que les voyelles du « gros créole » sans tenir compte des doublets en usage non seulement dans le parler des Haïtiens cultivés mais encore dans la langue d'un nombre considérable de prolétaires mêlés à la masse de ceux qui parlent le « gros créole ». Ainsi, *i* élimina *u* (diri, jamais *duri*), *è* élimina *eu'* (kwafè, jamais *kwafeu*'), *é* élimina *e* (ké et jamais *ke*) (Pressoir 1947: 66).

> With an insufficient knowledge of our language to be able to perceive all its variations, he [McConnell] strove only to render the vowels of the 'highly marked rural creole', without taking into account the alternate forms used not only by cultivated Haitians but also by a considerable number of working-class people who mingle with the masses who speak the highly marked rural creole. Thus, *i* eliminated *u* (diri, never *duri*), *è* eliminated *eu'* (kwafè, never *kwafeu'*), *é* eliminated *e* (ké and never *ke*).

It is quite clear from this citation that Pressoir recognized the presence of these vowels in the speech of some monolingual speakers.

6. For other aspects of this study, see Chapter 11.

7. In fact, the degree is conferred officially by Sherbrooke University in Quebec province, with which FERA has a collaborative relationship.

8. In the Cape Haitian area, the word for 'eye' is often pronounced *zyeu* when it occurs in isolation but as *je* in the possessive construction *janm* 'my eye' (see Chapter 11).

3 Variation in the Forms of Words

3.1 Introduction: Morphophonology: Alternations in Form

All languages show obligatory alternations in the forms of words that occur in the speech of an individual speaker. Although these variations are usually tied to certain types of speech styles, they are generally independent of social factors, such as social class or geographical location. Very often speakers are not aware of these alternations, some of which affect most of the words in a language and are based on fundamental phonological processes of the particular language. Awareness and understanding of variation in forms is central to the evaluation or elaboration of spelling systems.

We have seen in Chapter 2 that HC shows some free variation in the pronunciation of individual words. Speakers may say *famiy* /famij/ or *fanmiy* /fãmij/ 'family'; *chwal* /ʃwal/ or *cheval* /ʃeval/ 'horse'; *kounyea* /kunjea/, *konyea* /kũnjea/, *koulyea* /kuljea/, *kouliyeya* /kulijeja/ 'now'. Analogous alternations in English are the pronunciations /iðər/ or /ayðər/ for 'either'. These alternations affect individual words; they are not reducible to rules that apply to large sets of words that may be formulated in terms of phonological or grammatical factors. The latter are precisely the types of alternations that are the central concern of learners of a foreign language or those involved in the evaluation or elaboration of spelling systems.

The level of language involving systematic alternations in the form of words is called **morphophonology**, from **morphology**, the study of the structure of words, and **phonology**, the study of sound systems. At the core of morphophonology is the fact that there is not always a straightforward relationship between a word or grammatical form (**morpheme**) and its phonological representation. Some words do have an invariable spoken form, for example, 'boy, girl, and cat' in English. But often a word has several alternant forms determined by fairly general rules and, inversely, the same phonological material may represent more than one word or grammatical form. In this chapter, in order to illustrate some general morphophonological processes of Haitian (HC), I first provide examples of some general rules in English and French. I follow with a description of general rules in Standard Haitian Creole (SHC) and end the chapter with the presentation of alternations involving individual SHC forms.

80 Variation in the Forms of Words

3.2 General Morphophonemic Rules

3.2.1 Stress alternations in English

The most extensive systematic alternation in English involves changes in vowel quality related to the placement of stress on words. Compare the following matched pairs:

Full vowel with main stress		Reduced vowel with reduced stress	
I can.	/kæn/	I can do it.	/kən/
And you?	/ju/	Did you do it?	/jə/

In the utterances on the left, the words 'can' and 'you', which occur with main stress, contain a full vowel, namely /æ/ and /u/, respectively. In the utterances on the right, the same words are produced with reduced stress, and the vowel shifts to the reduced, neutral vowel /ə/. Interestingly, when attempting to note these alternations, non-academic or literary writers will use the letter *a* to indicate vowel weakening, for example, *didja* (did you). Note that this morphophonemic rule is quite general in English, affecting all types of forms. Although reduction of word stress typifies so-called fast speech (in fact, normal conversational style), it is present in all styles except highly artificial word-by-word pronunciation.

3.2.2 Liaison in French

The most general morphophonemic phenomenon in French is **liaison** 'linking'. Certain words of this language have the potential for dual pronunciation, with one spoken form ending in a final consonant and another produced without the consonant. The variation involves the potential pronunciation of certain final consonants depending on whether the following word begins with a vowel or a consonant and on grammatical and stylistic factors. Liaison involves the pronunciation of these consonants. In Table 3.1, the consonants subject to liaison are indicated in boldface type.

Table 3.1. Contrasts between Pre-vowel and Pre-consonant Variants

Consonant pronounced (liaison)		Consonant not pronounced	
French	Gloss	French	Gloss
nou**s** avons /z/ /nuzavɔ̃/	we have	nous savons /nusavɔ̃/	we know
o**n** a /n/ /ɔ̃na/	one has	on va /ɔ̃va/	one goes
le**s** hommes /z/ /lezɔm/	the men	les femmes /lefam/	the women
un peti**t** oiseau /t/ /œ̃ptitwazo/	a small bird	un petit chien /œ̃ptiʃjẽ/	a small dog

When the forms *nous, on, les,* and *petit* occur before a word beginning with a vowel sound, their final consonant must be pronounced. When they occur before a word beginning with a consonant or at the end of a phrase, the consonant does not appear. Liaison potentially affects a few dozen words of the language, including many of the important function words such as pronouns, articles, and common adjectives, as well as grammatical endings. For example, the 1st and 2nd person plural verb endings, *-ons* and *-ez*, respectively, may be pronounced with the consonant /z/ before a vowel, but that consonant never appears before a consonant or at the end of a phrase. Compare: *vous pouvez* /vupuve/ 'you may' and *vous pouvez partir* /vupuvepaʁtiʁ/ 'you may leave', in which /z/ cannot appear, to *vous pouvez entrer* /vupuvezɑ̃tʁe/ 'you may come in', where it may be pronounced. However, in this particular grammatical context the liaison is optional.

3.3 General Morphophonemic Processes in HC

One of the basic features of the phonological system of HC is that two successive vowels generally do not occur, either within individual words or across word boundaries. There are various morphophonological processes that conspire, as it were, to eliminate such combinations.[1] The most widely distributed one is elision, the deletion of a word-final vowel before a vowel-initial word. Unlike French elision, which applies primarily to the unstable E (mute e) and occurs only before a following vowel, for example, *je vais* 'I go' vs. *j'ai* 'I have', *il me voit* 'he sees me' vs. *il m'aime* 'he loves me', HC elision involves a variety of vowels. Other morphophonemic processes are truncation, nasal assimilation, and vocalic assimilation or blending.

3.3.1 Vowel loss in personal pronouns

In HC, the five personal pronouns occur in a single form (morpheme) no matter what function they serve in a sentence; in English and French, pronouns have different subject, object, and possessive forms; for example, in English: *I see, she sees me, that's my book, it's mine*; in French *je vois* 'I see', *elle me voit* 'she sees me', *c'est moi* 'it's me', *c'est mon livre* 'it's my book', *c'est le mien* 'it's mine'. The basic forms of the five HC personal pronouns are:

	Singular	**Plural**
1st person	*mwen* /mwɛ̃/	*nou* /nu/
2nd person	*ou* /u/	*nou* /nu/
3rd person	*li* /li/	*yo* /jo/

Note that there is no distinction between 1st and 2nd person plural pronouns: *nou* means 'we', 'you all', and 'we and you all'. HC pronouns are subject to loss of a vowel in certain situations. There are two types of vowel loss: (1) truncation and (2) elision. The latter involves vowel loss before a following vowel. Unlike French elision, which applies primarily to the unstable E (mute e) and occurs only before a following vowel, HC elision involves a variety of vowels and occurs in several environments. Truncation affects vowels occurring in phrase-final position. However, the same word may be affected by truncation and elision, depending on the environment in which it finds itself. For example, the vowel of *nou* /nu/ undergoes truncation in *Sa se manje n* /sasemãʒen/ 'That's our food' but elision in *Papa n ale Okap* /papanaleokap/ 'Our father went to Cape Haitian'.

Truncation in post-position

HC personal pronouns occur in pre-position or in post-position. They are pre-posed when they serve as subjects of verbs. In post-position, they assume three functions: (1) the equivalent of possessive adjectives after nouns;[2] (2) the object of verbs; (3) the object of prepositions. In post-position, after words ending with a consonant, personal pronouns occur in their full form.

Possessive adjective	Object of verb	Object of preposition
matant mwen	Yo bat mwen.	ak mwen
'my aunt'	'They beat me.'	'with me'
chanm ou	Li konn ou.	avèk ou
'your room'	'He knows you.'	'with you'
bèf li	Yo jwenn li.	kont li
'his cow'	'They found her.'	'against her'
chat nou	Li tann nou.	ak nou
'our cat'	'She waited for us.'	'with us'
milèt yo	M a reponn yo.	avèk yo
'their mule'	'I'll answer them.'	'with them'

In most cases, after a vowel, full and elided forms freely alternate:

frè m/mwen	'my brother'	Yo wè m/mwen.	'They saw me.'
papa n/nou	'our father'	Li rele n/nou.	'She called us.'
chen l/li	'his dog'	Yo touye l/li.	'They killed her.'

However, in post-position, *yo* remains invariable and always appears in its full form:

| tonton yo | 'their uncle' | M a pran yo. | 'I will take them.' |

3.3 General Morphophonemic Processes

Since it consists of a single vowel, the 2nd person singular pronoun *ou* cannot be elided. Instead, it alternates with the corresponding semivowel *w*, as well as an emphatic form pronounced with a preceding *w*: /wu/:

kaye w/wou   'your notebook'   *Yo rayi w/wou.*   'They hate you.'

After certain forms, such as the negative form *pa*, the introducer *se* 'it is', and the prepositions *sou* 'on' and *pou* 'for', only the full form may be used. The asterisk indicates that the combination of forms is ungrammatical.

Se li.   'It's her.'   **Se l.*

Li fè l pou mwen.   'She did it for me.'   **pou m*

Nèg la vire sou nou.   'That guy turned in our direction.'   **sou n*

Elision in pre-position

The analysis of elision of pronouns in pre-position is complicated by the effect of rhythmic and phonetic factors not yet fully elucidated. Generally, however, in pre-position, pronouns fall into three groups: (1) those containing an initial consonant: *mwen*, *nou*, *li*; (2) *yo*, which begins with a semi-vowel; (3) *ou*, which consists only of a vowel. For the first group, either the full or elided form may occur. The full form is more likely to occur at the beginning of a phrase before a consonant, and the short form must be used obligatorily before the verb markers *ap* 'progressive' and *a* 'definite future' (see Table 3.2).

Table 3.2. Elision of Vowels in Pre-position

Phrase-initial	Elsewhere before a consonant	Elsewhere before a vowel	Before *ap, a*
Mwen(/m) pati. 'I left'	*Epi mwen/m pati.* 'And then I left.'	*Mwen/m ale.* 'I'm going.'	*M ap tann.* 'I'm waiting.'
Nou(/n) wè. 'We saw.'	*Epi nou/n wè.* 'And then we saw.'	*Nou/n ale.* 'We're going.'	*N a reponn.* 'We will answer.'
Li rele. 'S/he yelled.'	*Epi li/l rele.* 'And then s/he yelled.'	*Li/l ale.* 'S/he's going.'	*L ap tann.* 'S/he's waiting.'
Ou pati. 'You left.'	*Epi ou/w pati.* 'And then you left.'	*Ou/w ale.* 'You're going.'	*W a rele.* 'You will yell.'
Yo manje l. 'They ate it.'	*Epi yo manje l.* 'And then they ate it.'	*Yo/y ale.* 'They're going.'	*Y ap reponn.* 'They will answer.'

84   *Variation in the Forms of Words*

A following vowel serves as a strong factor in triggering elision, whereas a following consonant favors retention of the final vowel. As pointed out in Chapter 2 (Section 2.2.2), in phrase-initial position, generally only /m/ combines with a following consonant, e.g., *M rele* 'I called'; *l* and *n* are excluded. *Ou* patterns like the first group of pronouns, except that its full form is *ou* and the form corresponding to the elided forms *m*, *n* and *l* is the semivowel *w*. The 3rd person plural pronoun *yo* occurs in its full form before a consonant, in either its full or elided form before a vowel, and in its elided form (consisting of the semivowel *y*) before *a* and *ap*.

As pointed out in Section 2.2.2, when they occur in initial position before a consonant the elided forms *m*, *l*, and *n* receive full syllabic weight. In other words, they constitute full syllables. This is indicated by the subscript dot (Valdman 1978: 72–3):

ṃ rele	'I call'
ḷ krwè sa	'he believes that'
ṇ pa ka pab	'we're not able …'

3.3.2 Vowel truncation in verbs

A small number of verbs lose their final vowel in utterance-medial position; the vowel must be retained, however, in utterance-final position. Because the vowel loss occurs before consonants and vowels, it is best viewed as a case of truncation rather than elision. Compare:

Sa ou **gade**?	'What are you looking at?'
M **gad** ou.	'I look at you.'
Kote li **rete**?	'Where does he live (stay)?'
Li **ret** anndan.	'She stayed inside.'
Yo pa vle **ale**.	'They didn't want to go.'
Y **al** lakay yo.	'They went home.'

Other verbs subject to truncation are *fini* 'to finish', *mete* 'to put', *pote* 'to carry', *sòti* 'to go out', *vini* 'to come', and *wete* 'to take off'. *Genyen* 'to have' is reduced to the first syllable: *gen*. The latter form is the one most commonly used. Several of these verbs have corresponding short forms that function as modal verbs, in which case truncation is obligatory. In a sense, a claim could be made that as modals, they represent different verbs:

fini	to just do so	Li **fin** ranje machin nan.	'He's just repaired the car.'
konnen	used to	Yo **konn** danse anpil.	'They used to dance a lot.'
mete	may	Ou **met** rete isit.	'You may stay here.'
sòti	to just have done	Nou **sòt** manje.	'We've just eaten.'

vini	to become	*Li **vin** gwo.*	'He became fat.'

Kapab 'to be able to', another modal verb that has no corresponding full verb, is also subject to truncation. Like *genyen* it does not undergo normal vowel reduction; there are two reduced variants, *kab* and *ka*. In addition, the full form may also be used: *Li pa kab (kapab, ka) travay* 'She isn't able to work.'

3.3.3 Elision in function words

The negative adverb *pa*. The negative adverb *pa* undergoes elision before the progressive marker *ap*, yielding the combination *pap*: *Li pap aprann anyen* 'He isn't learning anything'. That form shows no elision before other vowel-initial words: *Li pa aprann anyen* 'He doesn't/didn't learn anything.'

Verb markers. The past (anterior) marker *te* obligatorily loses its vowel before the progressive and definite future markers *ap* and *a*, respectively, as well as after the negative adverb *pa*: *Yo t ap (te + ap) bay kòb* 'They were giving money', *Nou ta (te+a) fè l* 'We would want to do it'. After *pa*, elision is optional: *Li pa t la / Li pa te la* 'She wasn't there', *Yo pa t gen bèf / Yo pa te gen bèf* 'They didn't have cows.'

The complementizer *ki*. The complementizer *ki* used to construct complex sentences elides optionally when it is followed by a vowel and undergoes truncation when it is preceded by a vowel: *sa ki ale lavil / sa k ale lavil* 'the one that went to town', *Kilès ki ap rele? / Kilès k ap rele?* 'Who's calling?', *sa ki te pati a / sa k te pati a* 'the one who left'. Note that this form does not generally elide in other environments: *Kilès ki rele?* 'Who called?'

The indefinite determiner *yon*. The indefinite determiner occurs in a variety of forms. It may appear with an initial *y* or without it, and the nasal vowel varies between /ɔ̃/ and /ũ/. In everyday speech, the usual form contains only the vowel. Before that reduced form, vowel-final verbs usually elide:

Se yon bagay. /sejɔ̃bagaj/	*S on bagay.* /sɔ̃bagaj/	'It's a thing.'
M gen yon kabrit. /mgɛ̃jɔ̃kabrit/	*M g on kabrit.* /mgɔ̃karit/	'I have a goat.'
M wè yon ti kay. /mwɛjɔ̃tikaj/	*M w on ti kay.* /mwɔ̃tikaj/	'I see a little house.'

The introducer se. The vowel of the introducer *se* usually elides before the indefinite article *yon*:

Se yon moun > *S on moun* /sõ mun/   'It's a person'

3.3.4 Elision in sequences of identical vowels

A combination of successive identical vowels across word boundaries may be replaced by a long vowel (the symbol ':' represents the lengthened vowel):

Papa ale.	*Papa: le.*	'Father went away.'
kaye elèv yo	*kaye: lèv yo*	'the pupils' notebooks'
Mari isit.	*Mari: sit.*	'Mary's here.'
Li nan gou ouvriye a.	*Li nan gou: vriye a.*	'It's to the worker's taste.'

3.3.5 Vowel blending

When they occur before the personal pronoun *ou*, in its short form *w*, the front vowels *i, e, è,* and the central vowel *a* take on the lip-rounding feature of the following semivowel. In other words, they are replaced by corresponding back rounded vowels: *ou, o, ò*, respectively; *ò* corresponds to both *ò* and *a*:

M ap di ou.	*M ap douw.*	'I'll tell you.'
Ou boule je ou?	*Ou boule jow?*	'Did you burn your eye?'
Li vle al avè ou.	*Li vle al avòw.*	'She wants to go with you.'
Lè ou vini.	*Lòw vini.*	'When you come …'
Sa ou vle?	*Sòw vle?*	'What do you want?'

Within phrases, when the high and high-mid vowels *i, ou, e,* and *o* occur before another vowel, they may optionally be replaced by the corresponding semivowels:

Toto ale.	*Totwale.*	'Toto went away.'
Pou a grate l.	*Pwa grate l.*	'The louse makes her itch.'
Bouki ale.	*Boukyale.*	'Bouki went away.'
Pope a bèl.	*Popya bèl.*	'The doll is beautiful.'

3.3.6 Nasal assimilation

In Chapter 1, I pointed out that vowels are often nasalized before a nasal consonant (regressive assimilation) but that, because there are contrasts such as *cham* 'Vodou charm' vs. *chanm* 'room', nasal assimilation does not operate automatically in HC. However, there are cases of nasal assimilation across word boundaries. The most salient cases affect the forms of the definite determiner (see Section 3.4) and of the possessive adjectives in NHC (Capois) (see Section 3.5). Two other forms are also subject to nasal assimilation: the verb and preposition *ba* 'to give to' and the 3rd person singular pronoun *li*.

In these forms, nasal assimilation is limited to very specific cases. For *ba* it occurs before the pronouns *mwen/m* and *nou/n*. Compare *Ban m mango sa a* 'Give me this mango', *Pote liv la ban mwen* 'Bring that book to me', *Li ban nou wou a* 'He gave us the hoe', and *M ap pote chwal la ban nou* 'I'll bring that horse to you' to *Li ba li lèt la* 'He gave them the letter' and *Li pote dlo a ba manman li* 'He brought the water to his mother'. The *l* of *li* is optionally nasalized to *n* after words ending in a nasal consonant. Compare: *pitit li* 'his child' to *madanm li/ni* 'his wife' and *machin li/ni* 'his car'.

3.4 Variation in Form of the Post-posed Determiner *la*

The phonological representation of particular language forms may be determined by the operation of several morphophonological processes. A noteworthy example is the pronunciation of the English endings for the plural of nouns and for the 3rd person singular of the present tense. Both of these are represented by *-s* and *-es* in conventional spellings, the choice of which is determined by the application of two rules.

Plural		**3rd person singular**	
boys	/z/	she reads	/z/
cats	/s/	she kicks	/s/
horses	/əz/	she passes	/əz/

Both of these endings are represented by three different phonological forms, each of which is predictable from the nature of the last sound of the word to which it is affixed. The rules that determine the spoken form of these endings are parallel. For both endings, the basic form is the voiced fricative /z/. That consonant is devoiced, that is, replaced by its voiceless counterpart, /s/, after a voiceless consonant for example: /p/ *he helps*, *the tips*; /t/ *she sits*, *the cats*; /k/ *it picks*, *the sacks*. After sounds that are phonetically similar to /z/ and /s/, namely, /s, z, ʃ, tʃ, ʒ, dʒ/, the neutral vowel /ə/ is inserted to break up what are nonpermissible consonant clusters: *he passes*, *the buses*; *it buzzes*, *the roses*; *she catches*, *the beaches*; *he judges*, *the edges*; *he cashes*, *the dishes*.

88   Variation in the Forms of Words

The most variable function word in HC is the post-posed definite determiner, whose meaning and function are intermediate between those of the English definite and demonstrative determiners. It occurs in five different forms: *la, lan, nan, a, an*. Consider the following examples:

pitit la	'the child'	*fi a*	'the girl'
liv la	'the book'	*wou a*	'the wheel; the hoe'
kay la	'the house'	*dlo a*	'the water'
kaw la	'the blackbird'	*mache a*	'the market'

The definite determiner (listed henceforth in its basic form *LA*) has the form *la* after a consonant and *a* after a vowel. The case of the deletion of *l* is puzzling because it results in the creation of a two-vowel sequence. As was mentioned in Section 3.3 and will be discussed in Section 3.5, there are various morphophonological processes that eliminate these sequences. However, in the case of *fi a* and *wou a*, an intervocalic glide is inserted after high vowels (*i, e, ou, o, on*) that eliminates the two-vowel sequence but is not indicated in the official spelling (see Section 2.3): /fi^{y}a/ 'the girl', /wou^{w}a/ 'the hoe'. Now examine the following forms:

lang nan	'the language'	*chen an*	'the dog'
lalin nan	'the moon'	*pon an*	'the bridge'
madanm nan	'the woman'	*van an*	'the wind'

A preceding nasal vowel triggers **progressive** (forward) nasal assimilation. *LA* becomes *an* after a nasal vowel and *nan* after a nasal consonant. After a consonant, nasal assimilation may only affect the vowel, and the /l/ remains unchanged: *lang lan, lalin lan, madanm lan*. The forms *lan* and *nan* vary freely in this environment.

There are cases of nasal assimilation that are not readily accounted for in terms of the last sound of the preceding word. First, compare:

| *pòt la* | 'the door' | *mont lan* | 'the watch' |
| *bak la* | 'the tray' | *bank lan* | 'the bank' |

Here, it is the preceding vowel that triggers nasal assimilation, and the latter 'jumps over' the final non-nasal consonant. Now compare:

| *kou a* | 'the blow' | *jenou an* | 'the knee' |
| *tapi a* | 'the rug' | *pitimi an* | 'the millet' |

In this case, nasal assimilation is triggered by two factors: (1) the high final vowels *i* and *ou*; and (2) the nasal consonant preceding the vowel. In the speech of bilingual speakers, the front rounded vowel *u* preceded by a nasal consonant also triggers nasal assimilation: *mango mi an* 'the ripe mango' (as opposed to monolingual speech *mango mi a*).

There are some indications that the explanation in terms of nasal assimilation 'jumping' over non-nasal segments may not be the best one. After observing instances of nasalization of *LA* where no nasal segment is present in the preceding word, for example, *chat lan* 'the cat', *dlo an* 'the water', I conducted a study in Haiti that revealed that pervasive nasalization characterized the speech of younger bilingual speakers belonging to the middle class (Valdman 1991). Two groups of speakers from this social group were interviewed: senior speakers, whose ages ranged from 40 to 60, and young adult speakers, whose ages ranged from 18 to 25. The data in Table 3.3 show that the latter group displays significant nasalization of *LA* in non-nasal contexts; the group average was 42.9%, with nasalization more frequent after a consonant than after a vowel. On the other hand, for senior speakers the group average of unexpected nasalization was only 3.6%, again with higher levels after a consonant. These data suggest that younger bilingual upper-

Table 3.3. Nasalization in the Determiner among Middle-class Port-au-Prince Speakers

Speaker			Vowel frequency	%	Consonant frequency	%	Total frequency	%
Juniors								
13	M	2+	13/21	61.9	49/52	94.2	62/73	84.9
14	F	2+	13/20	6.4	42/47	89.7	55/67	82.1
16	F	2+	23/31	74.2	28/42	66.17	5/73	69.9
18	M	1	21/43	48.8	39/47	83	60/90	66.7
3	F	2	18/60	30	39/60	65	57/120	47.5
1	M	1	27/105	25.7	69/103	67	96/208	46.1
4	F	1	8/57	14	6/57	10.5	14/114	12.3
2	M	2	2/105	2	13/105	12.4	15/120	7.1
			125/442	28.3	285/513	55.5	410/955	42.9
Seniors								
17	F	1	5/18	27.8	4/25	16.3	9/4	20.9
12	F	2	1/11	9.1	3/29	10.3	4/40	10
15	M	1	1/21	4.8	3/35	8.6	4/56	7.1
8	M	1	0/44	0	3/44	6.8	3/88	3.4
7	F	2	1/78	1.3	4/79	5.1	5/158	3.2
5	F	2	1/91	1.1	1/91	1.1	2/182	1.1
6	M	2	0/91	0	1/91	1.1	1/182	.5
11	M	2	0/2	0	0/25	0	0/27	0
			9/357	2.5	19/419	4.5	28/776	3.6

The first three columns (under the heading 'Speaker') provide information about the speaker identification (1 to 18), the sex (male or female), and the estimated social-class level: 1 for lower-middle class, 2 for middle class, and 2+ for upper-middle class.

middle-class speakers were leading a linguistic change that took the form of generalization of the nasal variants *an*, *lan*, and *nan*. The result of this change is to simplify the structure of the language by reducing the number of variant forms of *LA*. It appears that the change is currently spreading, for it has been the subject of some negative comments, wherein, for example, some Haitian educators denounced it as a corruption of the language.

3.5 Variation in the Possessive Construction in Northern Haitian Creole

In the HC variety spoken in the Cape Haitian region, NHC (Capois), the possessive adjective is expressed with the use of a connecting element *a* instead of the simple conjoining of the personal pronoun to the main noun. When the noun ends with a vowel, a wide range of two-vowel sequences result. Many morphophonemic changes reduce and/or change these vowel sequences in everyday speech. As a result, the phonological realization of the possessive adjective construction differs markedly from that of the standard (Port-au-Prince) variety of the language, Standard Haitian Creole (SHC). Table 3.4 provides a comparison of sample SHC and NHC possessive constructions consisting of nouns modified by the singular pronouns. For SHC, reduced and unreduced variants are shown, but for NHC, only reduced variants.

Table 3.4. Possessive Constructions in NHC/SHC

Final segment	Gloss	1SG SHC	1SG NHC	3SG SHC	3SG NHC	2SG SHC	2SG NHC
Consonant	feast	*fèt mwen*	*fetanm*	*fèt li*	*fètay*	*fèt ou*	*fètòw*
	leg	*janm mwen*	*janmanm*	*janm li*	*janbay/janbèy*	*janm ou*	*janbòw*
Vowel							
-i	husband	*mari m/mwen*	*maranm*	*mari l/li*	*maray*	*mariw/ou*	*maròw*
-e	eye	*je m/mwen*	*janm*	*je l/li*	*jay*	*je w/ou*	*jòw*
-a	father	*papa m/mwen*	*papanm*	*papa l/li*	*papay*	*papa w/ou*	*papòw*
-an	mother	*manman m/mwen*	*manmanm*	*maman l/li*	*manmany*	*manman w/ou*	*manmòw*
-en	hand	*men m/mwen*	*manm*	*men l/li*	*many*	*men w/ou*	*mòw*
-on	name	*non m/mwen*	*nwanm*	*non l/li*	*nwany*	*non w/ou*	*nwòw*
-o	back	*do m/mwen*	*dwanm*	*do l/li*	*dwany*	*do m/mwen*	*dòw*
-ou	neck	*kou m/mwen*	*kwanm*	*kou l/li*	*kwany*	*kou w/ou*	*kwòw*
-è	sister	*sè m/mwen*	*sèranm*	*sè l/li*	*sèray*	*sè w/ou*	*sèròw*
-ò	body	*kò m/mwen*	*kòranm*	*kò l/li*	*kòray*	*kò w/ou*	*koròw*

Table 3.5. Morphophonological Rules in the Production of NHC Possessive Constructions

	Basic form			
	je a mwen	*mari a mwen*	*do a mwen*	*sè a mwen*
1. Vowel reduction	*je a m*	*mari a m*	*do a m*	*sè a m*
2. Nasal assimilation	*je an m*	*mari an m*	*do an m*	*sè an m*
3. Vowel elision	*j an m*	*mar an m*	———	———
4. Semivowel replacement	———	———	*dw an m*	———
5. R-insertion	———	———	———	*sèr an m*
Phonological realization	*janmanm*	*maranm*	*dwanm*	*sèranm*
6. SHC	*je m*	*mari m*	*do m*	*sè m*

Table 3.5 demonstrates how possessive constructions of the noun and the 1SG pronoun *mwen* can be accounted for by the application of several rules to the unreduced variant used in careful speech, namely: Noun + *a* + Pronoun 1SG pronoun. These rules are: (1) vowel reduction that changes *mwen* to *m*, *ou* to *w*, and *i* to *y;* (2) regressive nasal assimilation triggered by the following *m*; (3) vowel elision in the case of the front vowels *i, e, en*, and the low central vowel *a*; (4) semivowel replacement for the rounded vowels *ou, o*, and *on;* (5) *r* insertion in the case of the low vowels *è* and *ò*. In Table 3.5 I illustrate the sequential application of these rules in the production of various combinations of nouns and the 1st singular pronoun *mwen*.

Chapter 11 will provide a discussion of the sociolinguistic aspects of the NHC variants, specifically, the effect of such social factors as location (urban vs. rural), age, and sex on their retention under the pressure of SHC, on which the written form of HC is based.

3.6 A Sample of Running Text

Below are samples of the various morphophonological phenomena discussed in this chapter, particularly vowel reduction and blending. The excerpts are from speech recorded during interviews with speakers of NHC in 2007 and 2008. The full forms are given within brackets. Note in particular the NHC variant forms for the 3rd person singular, *i* (reduced form *y*) versus Central HC *li/l*, and the verb 'to go' – *ay* (with vowel raising before *y, èy*) versus Central HC *ale/al*.

92 *Variation in the Forms of Words*

Donk nan peryòd pa gen lekòl konsa, ki aktivito [aktivite] w [ou], sò [sa] w [ou] fè pandan jounen? Di m [mwen] tout bagay ou fè, depi lò [lè] w [ou] leuve nan kabann ou, juskaskeu w [ou] al [ale] dòmi nan aswè a. M [mwen] ap kito [kite] w [ou] pale.

So, at the time when there isn't any school, what's your activity, what do you do during the day? Tell me everything you do, from the time you get out of bed, until you go to sleep in the evening. I will let you speak.

Lè y [i] parèt i pa w [wè] anyen ... Men gen [genyen] lè msye te blese. San an tonbe n [nan] on [yon] bèèy [bagay], men g [genyen] on [yon] ti gout san ki tonbe n [nan] on [yon] boutèy kola, i pr [pran] on [yon] mouchwa i siye y [i].

When he appeared, he didn't see anything ... But there was a time when he was wounded. The blood fell on a thing, but there was a drop of blood that fell on a soft-drink bottle, he took a handkerchief, he wiped it.

Nou t [te] èy [ay] pwet [pwete] on [yon] boul pou nou te jwe. Apre nou t [te] èy [ay] remèt boul la, nou pa t [te] ap f [fè] anyen ankò ... Apre lè y [i] inè n [nou] èy [ay] benyen, mw [mwen] ake y [i], m [mwen] vin [vini] avè y [i] la

We went to borrow a ball to play with. After that we went to return the ball, we didn't do anything then ... Afterwards, when it was one o'clock, we went swimming, me and him, I went there with him.

Si n [nou] rive n [nan] on [yon] moman nou vin [vini] bloke pou n [nou] ale nan doktè, s [se] on [yon] kabrit pou nou vann. Sou [si] w [ou] g [gen] on [yon] bèt, se bèt la ki kanaw [kanè a ou] ... W [ou] apr [apral] acht [achte] on [yon] gode diròw [diri a ou] pou trant kòb ... M [mwen] konn ay nan jad [jaden] a papanm [papa a mwen] nan.

If there came a time when we became stuck [short of cash] to go to the doctor, it's a goat we would sell. If you have an animal, it's the animal that is your bank account ... You would buy your measure of rice for thirty cents ... I used to go to the fields of my father.

Summary

In HC, several general phonological processes lead to a variety of alternations in the form of words (morphophonology). Overall, these differ significantly from the two main morpho-phological features of French: elision and liaison. In this language, elision generally affects the so-called mute e (schwa): *le chat* 'the cat' vs. *l'oiseau* 'the bird', as well as the feminine singular definite determiner *LA*: *la table* 'the table' vs. *l'assiette* 'the dish'. In French, liaison entails the presence in a word of a latent consonant, that is, one that is pronounced or not depending on a variety of phonological and grammatical factors. Liaison consonants are obligatorily pronounced before words beginning with a vowel but deleted before those beginning with a consonant. Typically, liaison, the pronunciation of the consonant, occurs obligatorily between words involved in syntactic dependency, for example, a pronoun and a verb: *nous avons* /nuzavõ/ 'we have' vs. *nous savons* /nu savõ/ 'we know', or between a determiner and a noun: *les enfants* /lezãfã/ 'the children' vs. *les femmes* /lefam/ 'the women'.

Elision in HC differs significantly from that in French. In the case of the latter language, it affects primarily what is termed the mute e (schwa): a morphophonological phenomenon (represented as E in Valdman 1976) that is deleted before a vowel, as shown above, as well as word internally (see Table 3.1 above), and which is subject to a variety of phonological and stylistic factors (*je ne te le redemande pas* /ʒEntElrEdmãdpa/ 'I don't ask you for it again'). In HC, it optionally affects a variety of vowels, those of the personal pronouns when they occur initially before a vowel (*m ale*) but, except for *ou* and *yo* , also before a consonant in initial and medial position : *m rele, epi n pati* 'I called and then we left'. In medial position and before a consonant, *m, l,* and *n* have syllabic value; for *m̩,* that syllabic extends to word-initial position More restricted instances of elision occur with the negative *pa,* the verb markers *ape/ap/pe* and *te/t,* and the complementizer *ki.*

Another morphophonological feature is truncation, the optional deletion of vowels in a variety of positions in utterances and word classes. In the case of pronouns, truncation takes place after a vowel in final position: *papa m* 'my father', *m rele l* 'I called her'. In the case of verbs, it affects those that take on a modal function, in which case their meaning differs from that of their use as full verbs: *li fini* 'he finished' vs. *li fin ranje* 'he finished storing (things)'.

In HC, the favored structure of words in terms of syllables is CV(CV). When the high and high-mid vowels *i, ou, e,* and *o* occur before another vowel, they optionally undergo blending, that is, they may be replaced by the corresponding semivowels: *Toto ale > totwal, Bouki ale > Boukyale.* Related to this is insertion of a transitional glide in *pye(ʲ)a* and *wou(ʷ) a* that is not represented by the spelling. Northern Haitian Creole shows a variety of morphophonological processes that result in the elimination of consecutive vowel sequences that occur in the possessive construction, in which the preposition *a* is intercalated between the noun and the personal pronoun.

Finally, the most variable function word in HC is the post-posed definite determiner, whose form depends on the last or next-to-last segment of the preceding word. Interestingly, it appears that progressive nasal assimilation is gaining ground, as reflected by a linguistic change led by younger bilingual speakers. What is noteworthy and puzzling is why the *l* of *LA* is deleted after a vowel. This creates VV sequences (*flè a, wa a, pò a*), which, as we have seen, are in many cases eliminated by elision. As discussed in Section 3.5. above, in the case of NHC, these are eliminated by a variety of morphophonological processes. In the case of the standard variety of HC, two-vowel sequences (VV), where the second vowel is one of the high front vowels /i/ or /e/, are eliminated by a transitional glide /j/ (*fi(ʲ)a* 'the daughter', *kle(ʲ)a* 'the key'), and where it is the high back vowel /u/ or /u/ by a transitional glide /w/ (*wou(ʷ)a* 'the wheel', *dlo(ʷ)a* 'the water'). VV sequences remain in the case of other vowels (*papa a* 'the father', *dan an* 'the tooth').

Notes

1. See Section 3.4.1 for the case of two successive vowels created by the deletion of the *l* of the definite article, *la*.
2. Strictly speaking, these are not possessive adjectives but the use of personal pronouns in possessive constructions.

4 Toward a Systematic Autonomous Spelling

4.1 Introduction

4.1.1 General considerations

Any language can be reduced to writing in a systematic manner. The precise spelling system devised and the alphabet adopted depend on a multitude of factors. In addition to the nature of the sound system and the types of alternations in the form of words (see Chapter 3), a variety of social, political, and practical factors must be taken into consideration. For example, what alphabets are employed for the other languages in use in the community or that exert a cultural influence on it? For example, in Tajikistan, when it was part of the former Soviet Union, Tajik was written in the Cyrillic script used for Russian. However, in Iran, for religious, social, and political reasons, the language is represented with the Arabic alphabet that is used for Persian and the other languages of the country. As we shall see in the case of the elaboration of a systematic orthography for HC, even such practical considerations as the character of typefaces available to printers are not alien to the selection of an appropriate spelling system. However, the fundamental issues in the devising of orthographic systems are: (1) who are the intended beneficiaries of a written representation of the language and (2) what purposes is it intended to serve, for example, improving basic education, providing certain social groups with access to the written word, etc. (Faraclas et al. 2010). It is important to realize that orthographies are not transcriptions whose primary purpose is to faithfully note the pronunciation of words but more global systems that, in the act of reading, enable native speakers of a language to recover the meaning of words in context (Valdman 1989; M.-C. Hazaël-Massieux 1993). Of course, orthographies also enable native speakers to draft written texts but, as will be pointed out below, especially in Section 4.5, a non-purist approach within writing systems with some degree of abstraction (i.e., that are not viewed as transcriptions) allows speakers a certain degree of variance that might reflect geographical (**diatopic**) sociolinguistic (**diastratic**) variations, or stylistic/register (**diaphasic**) distinctions.

4.1.2 Orthographical standardization

Western societies place a premium on a high degree of uniformity in spelling. Spelling systems are highly codified, and total adherence to orthographic conventions is usually required. In the case of English, even such minor departures from convention as *nite* for *night* and *thru* for *through* are frowned upon. In our educational systems, much time and effort is invested in learning to spell, and spelling errors are viewed as reflecting lack of academic achievement, if not a low level of intelligence or low social status. There is no inherent virtue in highly standardized spellings and, in fact, concern for strict adherence to orthographic conventions is a relatively recent phenomenon that appeared with the extension of education to larger segments of populations. In earlier periods, when education and literacy were restricted to the élite, there existed great tolerance for orthographic idiosyncrasies. Such renowned writers as Pope in England and Voltaire in France had execrable spelling habits by today's standards. In France, for example, in the seventeenth century, upon being admitted into the august Académie française, one of Louis XIV's most distinguished generals, the Maréchal de Saxe, wrote, *'Il veule me fere de la Cadémie; cela miret come une bage à in chas'*, instead of *'Ils veulent me faire de l'Académie; cela m'irait comme une bague à un chat'* (They want to make me a member of the Academy; that would be as fitting for me as a ring for a cat). Every French schoolteacher today would be scandalized by this case of orthographic 'lack of restraint.'

4.1.3 Objectives of orthographic systems

Since there are numerous possible adequate systematic representations for a given language, an orthographic system can be evaluated only in terms of stated objectives. For what reasons is a writing system devised? What functions would it serve? For whom is it intended? In Haiti, at first, a systematic spelling system was mainly designed to provide monolingual speakers of HC with access to information and to a means of communicating in writing. It was also viewed by most of the people involved in the elaboration of a suitable orthography, not as a fully autonomous system, but as one that would facilitate the transition to literacy in French. In general, a satisfactory writing system is one that can be mastered easily by illiterate adults and by children who are being taught to read and write; it should avoid abstract conventions and adhere as much as possible to the bi-uniqueness principle (see Section 4.2.1 below). Were most Haitians bilingual in French and HC, a good case could be made for an orthography that made maximum use of French conventions. Thus, the spelling issue cannot be divorced from broader educational questions and from socio-political factors. In Haiti, given the fact that, although both HC and French are recognized by the country's latest constitution as equal official languages, French still retains higher prestige and is the conduit for economic, political, and social advancement. In addition, there is much more reading material available in French than in HC. Consequently, in devising a suitable orthography for HC a case could be made for taking into consideration, whenever possible and justifiable, those spelling conventions of French orthography that are systematic. This explains why certain proponents of orthographic systems introduced conventions of French spelling. On the other hand, it is important to take into consideration the fundamental objectives of a spelling system and the communicative needs of the intended beneficiaries. In the case of HC, these are not members of the bilingual middle and upper classes but illiterate monolingual speakers of HC.

In Section 4.2, I first examine principles for the elaboration of spelling systems that derive from phonological structure, namely, the notion of bi-uniqueness. In Section 4.3, I review the history of the development of a spelling system for HC. In particular, I examine attempts during the colonial and early post-colonial periods to represent Saint-Domingue Creole (SDC) with an etymological spelling closely based on that of French. In Section 4.4, I discuss the various systematic autonomous phonologically based orthographic systems proposed for HC since the 1940s. I end the chapter, in Section 4.6, by pointing out the complexities introduced by morphophonological variation and the difficulty of identifying words within the speech chain.[1]

4.2 Phonological Constraints on Orthographies

4.2.1 The bi-uniqueness principle

Social, political, and practical considerations aside, the best spelling for a language is one that provides a straightforward representation of the phonemes of the language. Ideally, a spelling system should be based on bi-uniqueness: each phoneme should always be represented by the same symbol and, conversely, each symbol should always represent the same phoneme. A representation that provides such one-to-one matching is termed bi-unique, although the usual lay term is a 'phonetic spelling'. The spelling systems for Spanish and Italian come close to providing this bi-unique matching, but both the English and French systems are lacking in this respect. In the latter language, for example, the nasal vowel /ẽ/ is represented by a half-dozen different letter combinations: *vin* 'wine', *vain* 'vain', *plein* 'full', *agenda* 'appointment book', *impot* 'tax', *faim* 'hunger': in addition, the letter sequence *en* stands for two different nasal vowels: /ɛ̃/ in *pensum* 'additional work given as a punishment' and /ã/ in *vent* 'wind'. In English, the vowel /i/ is spelled *ea* in *seat*, *ee* in *seed*, *ie* in *siege*, *ei* in *receive*, and *i* in *machine*. These inconsistencies in the notation of phonemes led the Anglo-Irish writer George Bernard Shaw to quip that the best way to write *fish* would be *ghoti*: *gh* for /f/, as in *rough*; *o* for /i/, as in *women*; *ti* for /ʃ/, as in *nation*.

There are cases where departure from strict bi-uniqueness is well advised. In languages that have extensive alternation in form determined by very general rules, as in the case of French liaison, for instance, it may be preferable to provide a single written representation for variant forms. The generality of the rules accounting for the variant forms enables speakers to recover spoken forms effortlessly if the relationship between written and spoken forms is not too abstract. Consider, for example, in French, the representation of the 1st person plural pronoun forms /nu/ and /nuz/ by a single invariable spelling *nous*. In this language, in plural personal pronouns, the **latent consonant** (a consonant that is potentially pronounced under certain circumstances), represented by *s,* is always pronounced as /z/ before words beginning with a vowel (*nous allons* /nuzalɔ̃/ 'we go') but corresponds to zero before a consonant (*nous partons* /nupaʁtɔ̃/ 'we leave') or at the end of a phrase (*avec nous* /avɛknu/ 'with us'). The pronunciation or non-pronunciation of the /z/ is automatic for native speakers and *s* is a fairly consistent notation for that liaison consonant.

4.2.2 Simple and complex symbols

The ideal bi-unique system is one in which phonemes are represented by unitary symbols. Given the constraints of a particular alphabet and various non-linguistic considerations, adherence to this principle is not always possible. For example, the Roman alphabet provides only five vowel symbols, *a, e, i, o,* and *u*. To adequately represent systems containing more than five vowel contrasts, other conventions must be adopted. One alternative is to use combinations of vowel letters, usually two, **digraphs**. Thus, French distinguishes between /y/, as in *du* and /u/ as in *doux* by the use of the combination *ou* for /u/ versus the use of *u* for /y/. Another solution is to use **diacritics**, as is done in French: accents (*é, è, ê*), the umlaut or dieresis (*ü*), and the cedilla (*ç*). In general, unitary symbols are preferable because they facilitate the task of the reader and the writer, and they reduce ambiguity in the relationship between sound and spelling.

4.3 The Evolution of Etymologically Based Representations for HC

It is only after a language has achieved a certain level of development, for example, when it begins to serve a variety of functions in a community – use in trade, education, administration, etc. – that a relatively uniform standard form of it emerges and that its users feel the need to write it down. For example, French had emerged as a language clearly distinct from Latin for several centuries before it appeared in written texts. Even after French had displaced Latin as the dominant language in the administrative, literary, scientific, and technical domains, its written representation was not fully fixed. For varieties of French not used for elevated purposes, especially regional rural dialects and the speech of the urban lower classes, there were no compelling reasons to write them down. Authors represented them in plays and novels mainly for comic purposes or, more rarely, in nonfiction, to document them for the interest of learned individuals. For these limited purposes, they simply adapted the spelling conventions used for the standard form of the language, the one they held to represent the language in a relatively uniform way.

As languages closely associated with slavery or viewed as a devalued variety of French used in the overseas colonies, it was likely that French-based creoles would be treated like the non-prestigious varieties of metropolitan French. Indeed, as one would expect, in the early written representations of the language found in missionaries' and travelers' accounts of life in the West Indian French colonies (Guadeloupe, Martinique, Saint-Domingue), although the authors attempted to portray these languages with accuracy, they did not try to devise autonomous phonologically based spellings. In other words, they made use of an etymological spelling that reflected French conventions. The objective of the writers was generally to inform readers about the evolving creoles in the plantation colonies, not to teach their speakers to read texts representing these languages or to compose written texts.

4.3.1 First texts from the early colonial period

The first texts from the early French colonial period reflect the fact that the French-based creoles had not yet emerged as relatively uniform stabilized varieties.[2] These texts, produced mostly by French missionaries assigned to the Guadeloupe and Martinique colonies in the second half of the seventeenth century, depict either a trade pidgin that was first used in contact with the Carib Indians or a pidginized French, perhaps based on **foreigner talk**, a simplified version of their language that native speakers may use in addressing certain categories of foreigners. In addition, as was noted in Section 4.1.2, in the seventeenth and eighteenth centuries, French orthography was not fully standardized and there was limited pressure for orthographic accuracy. Typical of such texts is a model that missionary priest André Chevillard (1659) provides for evangelizing Caribs (Text 1).

Text 1

| Toy sçavoir qu'il y a UN DIEU: luy grand Capitou: luy sçavoir tout faire sans autre pour l'ayder: luy donner à tous patates: luy mouche manigat pour tout faire, non point autre comme luy. | You know that there is a God: him big Chief: him know do everything without other to help him: him give to all sweet potatoes: him very powerful to do all, none like him.[3] |

This text reflects a general French foreigner talk, characterized by the use of an invariable form for verbs, usually the infinitive, the reduced use of function words, like articles, and a single form for personal pronouns (Valdman 1980). The same conventions are used in a report about the sighting in 1671 of an unusual animal, most likely a manatee, found in official archives in Martinique (Carden *et al.* 1991). The only significant feature is the use of the past participle alternating with the infinitive in representing verbs (see Text 2).

Text 2

| … moi mirer un homme en mer du Diamant. moi voir li trois fois. li tini assés bon visage et zyeux comme monde. li tini grande barbe grise, li sorti hors de l'eau, regardé nous tous. moi prendre ligne pour prendre li, moi teni petit peur. | … me look at a man in the Diamant sea. me see him three times. him had good enough face and eyes like people. him had big gray beard. him got out of the water. looked at all of us. me take line to take him, me had little fear. |

4.3.2 The first reliable documentation of Saint-Domingue Creole

The first extensive text representing a French-based Caribbean creole is an intriguing manuscript discovered serendipitously in 1986. It contains an adaptation of the Passion of Jesus Christ, *La Passion de Notre Seigneur selon Saint-Jean en Langage Nègre*.[4] The late Guy Hazaël-Massieux (1994), who had first access to the manuscript and devoted several years to elucidating its origin, placed it around 1750–60, but his wife, Marie-Christine Hazaël-Massieux (2008), after extensive research, pinpointed the date to between 1720 and 1740. She provides convincing evidence to suggest that the original author and scribe was a Jesuit priest, Pierre Boutin, who had the reputation in the French colony of Saint-Domingue of being 'le curé des Nègres' ('the priest of the Negroes'). From the time of his arrival in the capital of Saint-Domingue, Cap-Français (today Cape Haitian), in 1705 until his death in 1742, Boutin no doubt had ample opportunity to learn the language of the slaves to whose spiritual needs he ministered. He also regularly celebrated a mass in their language. The text was designed to be read to Saint-Domingue Creole (SDC)-speaking slaves by other members of the Jesuit order, either in Saint-Domingue only, or more widely in the French Caribbean plantation colonies where Jesuits served. The short excerpt of the *Passion* in Text 3 demonstrates that by this period SDC had emerged as a stabilized language quite distinct from the pidginized versions of French of the preceding century. The scribe attempts to represent modifications of the pronunciation of French words and accurately notes major grammatical features of the language whose reflexes characterize present-day HC and Caribbean French-based creoles in general. I use boldface to identify the notable departures from French spelling used by the scribe to represent actual pronunciation, and I underscore grammatical features that show structural development;[5] in addition to the English translation, I provide an equivalent in informal French.

Text 3

dans tems la, comme jour paque **té** proche, tous pères **jouifs** la ïo tous faire complot pour **quiember jesi**; mais ïo té bin **barassés**. ïo té dire, 'comment nous va faire? si nous faire **touyé li** dans tems grand fête comme ça, tout **moune** va lévé la sous nous pour prendre **pati pou** li'... Pendant ïo té qu'a **palé** comme ça, **ïon** camarade dans mitan ïo tous la té dis faire **macé** avec pères **jouifs** pour **quiember jesi** ... **jesi vini rivé** avèc **zapotes** li ... drèt li **rivé**, li **mandé** si ïo pas encore **metté** couvert ? ... pendant ïo té qu'a mangé, **jesi** prend pain, cassé li, séparé ba ïo tous; di ïo ... 'prend **li**, mangé, **cila** sé corps moé, vous **tende** ?' ... li té **metté di** vin ... li dire ïo; 'boire ça, c'est sang a moé'...

Dans ce temps-là, comme le jour de Pâques était proche, tous les prêtres juifs, eux tous ont fait un complot pour capturer Jésus; mais ils étaient bien embarrassés. Ils ont dit, comment nous allons faire? Si nous le faisons tuer pendant le temps de la grande fête comme ça, tout le monde va se soulever contre nous pour prendre parti pour lui ... Pendant qu'ils parlaient comme ça, un camarade parmi eux tous a fait un marché avec les prêtres juifs pour capturer Jésus ... Jésus venait d'arriver avec ses apôtres ... Dés qu'il est arrivé, il a demandé s'ils n'avaient pas mis le couvert ... Pendant qu'ils mangeaient, Jésus a pris du pain, il l'a cassé, l'a divisé pour eux tous; il leur a dit ... 'Prenez-le, mangez, cela c'est mon corps, vous entendez?' ... Il a mis du vin ... il leur a dit; 'Buvez ça, c'est mon sang'...

During that time, because the day of Easter was near, all the Jewish priests, all of them plotted to seize Jesus; but they were very troubled. They said: 'How are we going to do it?... If we have him killed during the period of the high holiday like this, everybody will rise up against us to take his side.'... While they were speaking like that, one of the comrades among them made a deal with the Jewish priests to seize Jesus ... Jesus arrived with his apostles ... As soon as he arrived, he asked whether they had set the table ... While they were eating Jesus took some bread, he broke it, divided it for all of them. He said to them ... 'Take it, eat, that's my body, you understand?'... He put some wine ... he said to them, 'Drink that, that's my blood.'

This sample shows that the verb system had evolved into the use of tense-mood-aspect markers preceding a relatively invariable verb stem, usually the infinitive or the past participle, as was the case in the pidginized French illustrated in Text 2. For active (versus stative) verbs, the bare stem denotes past actions or is unmarked for tense; *qu'a* marks the progressive aspect, *va* marks futurity, and *té* is used to mark past tense in copulative predicates and in combination with the aspect marker. *LA* functions like its French etymon, the locative adverb *là*, but it has also evolved into a postposed definite determiner, occurring in this excerpt in combination with the plural marker *ïo*. The latter form also serves as the 3rd person plural personal pronoun. Post-posed invariable personal pronouns also function as possessives; note in particular the alternation between straight affixation, *corps moé*, 'my body', reflecting current HC, and the use of the preposition *a*, reflecting current NHC, *sang a moé*. Especially notable is the serial verb construction, *vini rivé*, which indicates the immediacy of the action. The verb *bailler* 'to give', reduced to *ba*, has been grammaticalized into a prepositional use equivalent to 'for'.

As will become apparent after my presentation of other SDC texts from the colonial period, the *Passion* is remarkable for the information it provides about pronunciation. Of course, the spelling conventions followed by the scribe are not totally systematic – recall that in the eighteenth century French spelling was not fully standardized. For example, there are variant spellings for the same words: *maite/maitre* (*maître*) 'master', *giable/quiable* (*diable*) 'devil'. Final consonant clusters, usually reduced in everyday spoken French, are represented in full or reduced form, e.g., *vente* (*ventre*) 'belly', *zapotes* (*apôtres*) 'apostles' versus *chambre* 'room', *répondre* 'to answer', and *ensemble* 'together'. The following examples are notable deviations from French spelling that reflect pronunciations differing from those of Standard French. Note, however, that they do not necessarily indicate changes from the speech on which the creators of SDC targeted: some reflect the vernacular and regional French of the period, e.g., *moun* /mun/ < /mõn/ *monde* 'person', by the change of the final /d/ to /n/ when it follows a nasal vowel, a case of nasal assimilation.

1. Replacement of front-rounded vowels: *jezi, di vin, vini*. In some cases, the front-rounded vowel /y/ is replaced by the back vowel /u/ (*tuer* > *touyé*) and the semi-vocalic equivalent of /y/ (/ɥ/) by /w/: *juif* > *jouif*. The same type of replacement accounts for the 3rd person plural pronoun form *ïo*, presumably derived from the stressed form *eux* /ø/, pronounced as /jø/ in some northern French dialects.
2. Loss of final and post-vocalic *r: mace* (<*marché*), *pati* (<*partie*). The fact that most post-vocalic *r*'s are retained, and the alternation in the spelling of *pour* (*pour/pou*) 'for' suggests that the loss of *r* was not categorical. This happens to still be the case for present-day NHC.[6]
3. Palatalization of dental stops: etymological /t/ and /d/ are palatalized in the context of a high or high-mid front vowel and /j/: *quiember*, presumably from *tiens bien* 'hold well', present-day HC *kenbe* 'to hold'.
4. Agglutination of French determiners, either fully or partially: *zapotes* (<*les apôtres*), *di vin* (<*du vin*). Although the scribe writes it as two words, it is in fact a simplex, reflected by current HC *diven*.
5. Aphaeresis: in words with initial vowels, the vowel is deleted so that apparently a more natural syllable structure CV(X) results: *barassés* (<*embarrassés*), *rivé* (<*arrivé*), *tende* (<*entendre*).
6. Absence of vowel lowering: the use of *moé* /mwe/ instead of *moi* /mwa/ indicates that in the target variety of French, the lowering of the syllable nucleus from /we/ to /wa/ was not yet complete.[7]

4.3.3 Later colonial Saint-Domingue Creole texts

At the turn of the nineteenth century, there appeared numerous texts that attempted to represent SDC, either as it was actually spoken or as it was perceived by the European scribes who chose to write it down. To what extent these texts reflect the speech of field slaves with little or no competence in French is conjectural. Because the SDC of these texts was filtered through the perception of educated French speakers, some authors refer to it as *créole de salon* 'upscale creole' (Alleyne 1971) or *créole des blancs* 'white people's creole' (M.-C. Hazaël-Massieux 2008). These texts fall into four categories: (1) poems and songs, (2) *vaudevilles*, a type of musical play, (3) lessons in the form of dialogues destined for newly arrived plantation owners, and (4) proclamations drafted by French officials and intended to be read to the populace.[8]

As a form of entertainment, Saint-Domingue society was fond of lovers' complaints in the form of poems and songs attributed to members of the slave population but, of course, composed by well-educated members of the colonial society. One such song, *Lisette quitté la plaine* 'Lisette left the countryside', is particularly interesting because it has survived in three different versions: Moreau de Saint-Méry (1797), Ducœurjoly (1802), and *Idylles et chansons, ou, Essais de poësie créole par un habitant d'Hayti* (1811). In Text 4, I reproduce the first two and the fourth stanzas of the 1797 and 1811 versions. Noteworthy features appear in boldface.

Text 4

Moreau de Saint-Méry (1797) *Idylles et chansons* (1811)

Lisette quitté la plaine,
Mon perdi **Bonher** à **moué**
Gié à moin semblé fontaine,
Dipi mon pa miré **toué**.
La jour quand **mon** coupé canne
Mon songé **zamour** à moué;
La nuit quand **mon** dans cabane,
Dans **dromi mon quimbé toué**.

Lisette **toi** quitté la plaine,
Mo perdi **Bonheur** à **moi**,
Gié à moi tourné fontaine,
Dipi mo pa miré **toi**.
La jour quan **ma** coupé cane
Mo songé **zamour** à moi,
La nuit quan **mo** dan cabane,
Dans **Dromi ma** songé **toi**.

Si **to** allé à la ville,
Ta trouvé **geine** Candio
Qui gagné pour tromper filles.
Bouche doux passé sirop.
To va crer **yo** bin sincère
Pendan **quior** yo coquin tro;
C'est serpent qui contrefaire,
Crié rat, pour tromper yo.

Laut' jour **m**'alé à la ville,
Mo conté **Jeune** Candios.
Yo gagné pour trompé filles.
Bouche dous passé sirop.
Yo va semblé **to** sincère
Pendan yo coquin trop,
Cé couleuve qui contrefaire,
Cri à rat pour trapé yos.

... Mon maigre tant com' **gnon** souche
Jambe à **moin** tant comme Roseau;
Mangé **na** pas doux dans bouche,
Tafia même c'est comme **dyo**
Quand **mon** songé, **toué Lisette**
Dyo toujours dans **jié** moin.
Magner moin vini trop bête
A force chagrin magné **moin**,

... Mo maigre tan comme **yon** boi
Jambe à **moi** tan comme Roseau,
Mangé pas dous dans bouche **à moi**,
Tafia même **cé** comme **dio**,
Quand **moi** songé **toi** Lizette
Dio toujours dan **gié moi**,
Magnière à moi vini trop Bette
A force chagrin magnié **moi**.

Lisette has left the countryside
I've lost my happiness;
My eyes are like a fountain,   *... have turned into a fountain.*
Since I have not looked at you.
In the daytime, when I cut cane,
I think of my love;
At night, when I am in my bed,
In my sleep I hold you tight.   *... I think of you.*

If you go to town,   *The other day I went to town,*
You will find a young whippersnapper   *I met young whippersnappers*
Who has to fool women   *Who have ...*
A mouth sweeter than syrup.
You will think them very sincere   *They will seem ...*
Although their heart is very roguish;
It's a snake that imitates
Crying out like rats to fool them.   *The cry of rats...*

... I'm skinny as a tree stump   *... like a tree*
My legs are like reeds
Food is not sweet in my mouth
Even rum is like water
When I think of you Lisette
Water is always in my eyes.
My mind becomes very dull
So much does grief overcome me.

As pointed out in Section 4.1.2, some of the divergences in spelling between these two versions reflect the less-rigorous orthographic conventions of the period. Although both scribes remain close to corresponding French forms, they attempt to note SDC's divergences by modifying the French spelling, although not as extensively as in the *Passion* text. The 1811 version adheres more closely to French spelling than Moreau de Saint-Méry's: *moi* instead of *moué* or *moin*, *Jeune* instead of *geine*, *dio* instead of *dyo*, *magnière* instead of *magner*, *bonheur* instead of *bonher*. Moreau de Saint-Méry, a native of Martinique and a long time resident of Saint-Domingue, seems more attuned to SDC forms and is more successful in rendering their pronunciation accurately. For instance, he notes the nasalization of the subject form of the 1st person singular pronoun, *mon* instead of *mo*, as well as the one case of *moin* alternating with *moué* instead of *moi*. He shows the replacement of front rounded vowels by their unrounded counterparts, e.g., *bonher* instead of *bonheur*. As was the case in the *Passion* text, these scribes indicate agglutinations (*zamour* for *amour*), palatalizations (*quior* for *cœur*), and aphaeresis (*trapé* for *attrapé* and *conté* for *rencontré*). Both fuse the subject pronoun and the future marker *a*: *ta* (<*to a*), *m'a* (<*mo a*).

Similar modifications of conventional French spelling also characterize the other types of texts from the colonial period. Of particular interest is *Jeannot et Thérè*se, a sort of musical comedy, termed in this period *opéra en vaudevilles*, that M.-C. Hazaël-Massieux (2008) dates to 1753. Subtitled *Parodie du Devin du Village* 'Parody of the *Village Magician*' [an opera written by Jean-Jacques Rousseau the preceding year], this piece, written by a certain Clément, was in fact an adaptation of a parody in a French dialect (patois) of the Rousseau opera, *Bastien et Bastienne*, performed in Paris. First presented in the capital of Saint-Domingue, Cap-Français (today Cape Haitian), this musical comedy, whose actors were Europeans, garnered wide success before White audiences. With regard to spelling conventions, it differs little from the various versions of *Lisette*, although it does contain grammatical features that occur in present-day HC (see Text 5).[9]

Text 5

Papa Simon	Papa Simon
si moi crié moi ben raison	if I cry, I have good reason
vous qui conné dans zaffaire	you who know things
passé negre passé blanc	better than Blacks, better than Whites
dis moi ça bon pour faire	tell me what's good to do
qior à moi dans grand tourment	my heart is very troubled
gagné pitié moi t'en prie	have pity on me please
ba moi gnon piti ouanga	give me a little charm
pour moi conné la tromperie	for me to know the unfaithfulness
de Jeannot quienne à moi la	of that Jeannot of mine

Another type of text was produced during the Revolutionary period, between 1794 and 1802, when the French were trying to put down insurrections on the part of various segments of the population of Saint-Domingue, as well as the slave revolt which was to lead to the defeat of the French and the establishment of the new independent state of Haiti. These were proclamations, signed by French officials, but no doubt produced by local Whites, that were posted in public places and were meant to be read aloud to the populace. The use of SDC rather than French in these proclamations suggests that the former was the colony's most widely shared speech form. As such, it was utilized by those who wished to mobilize the population for common endeavors. These proclamations reflect the attempt, granted not a very successful one, to adapt SDC to administrative use. The first excerpt is from a proclamation issued in Cap-Français, on June 3, 1796, by Léger-Félicité Santhonax, who had been delegated by France's ruling body of the period, the Directorate. Its objective was to rally the slaves, to whom freedom had previously been granted, to support the central government, now being attacked by the royalists aided by an English expeditionary force.

Text 6

An nom de la République Française Proclamation à tous les Citoyens de la Colonie

In the name of the French Republic Proclamation to all the citizens of the Colony

Yo sorti verti nous que gagné monde méchand, zamis des anglais, monde qui pas voulé voir vous autes libre, qui cherché trompé vous, et faire craire que la République pas gagné encore l'intention de soutenir liberté vous-autes: nous conné que ces monde malouc la, yo après parlé mal la sous compte commissaire, et que yo dis vous mensonge en pille la sus compte nous, nous conné que yo dis vous-autes que la République voyés nous ici pour mettés vous encore dans l'esclavage.

They have just warned us that there are evil people, friends of the English, people who do not want to see you free, who seek to deceive you, and make (you) believe that the Republic does not have the intention to support your freedom: we know that these evil people, they are speaking ill about the commissioner, and that they tell you many lies about us, we know that they tell you that the Republic has sent us here to enslave you once again.

The second excerpt is from a proclamation signed by Napoleon Bonaparte and posted in Cap-Français after the French expeditionary forces landed in the fall of 1802 under the command of Bonaparte's brother-in-law, General Leclerc. With his typical cynicism, Bonaparte, who decided to restore the colonial plantations to the ownership of the dispossessed French owners, promises liberty and equality to the rebelling former slaves.

Text 7

Qui ça vous tout yé, qui couleur vous yé, qui coté papa zote vini, nous pas gardé ça; nou savé tan seleman que zote tout libre, que zote tout égal, douvant bon Dieu et dans zyé la Répiblique ...

Whoever all of you are, whatever your color is, wherever your father came from, we are not concerned with that; we only know that all of you are free, that you are all equal, before God and in the eyes of the Republic ...

Like the versions of *Lisette quitté la plaine,* these proclamations show drift from French cognates. The scribes' usage fluctuates and displays inconsistencies, although the second sample, less frenchified than the first, is more felicitous in its attempt to reflect the speech of the primary speakers of SDC: the slave population. In these texts, the simplification of French final consonant clusters is not always indicated; compare *autes* and *libres*. Sometimes the front rounded vowels /y/, /ø/, and /œ/ are reflected in the spelling, sometimes not: compare *République* and *zyé* to *couleur* and *Dieu*. In both texts, the agglutination of the preceding liaison consonant to the following noun is clearly marked: *zamis* (*les amis*), *zote* (*vous autres*). SDC forms that do not have obvious French cognates are represented 'phonetically' by the use of simple French spelling conventions: *yo* /jo/ '3rd person plural', *ye* 'to be' (derived in fact from French *est*). They also contain forms where straightforward representation of sound values is attempted: *craire* and *crère* for *croire* 'to believe', *ba*, the short form for *baille* 'to give', *conné* for *connaître* 'to know', *douvant* for *devant* 'in front of'.

These minor divergences notwithstanding, the representations of the predecessor of HC in colonial texts are etymologically based; they always attempt to mirror corresponding French forms. Even such scribes as Moreau de Saint-Méry – who was prepared to grant the local creole a certain dignity – viewed the folk speech as an adulterated form of French, at best a highly variable dialect, but not a language in its own right. As a variant of French, it was expected to reflect the original model.

The work that best reflects late Saint-Domingue Creole is the remarkable *Manuel des habitants de Saint-Domingue* by S. J. Ducœurjoly published in Paris in 1802, although it was no doubt begun much earlier. In addition to a description of the history and current situation of the colony, it was intended, as the term *manuel* suggests, to be a sort of handbook for prospective farmers (*habitants*). As such, it contains a series of dialogs dealing with typical communicative situations, as well as the first bilingual dictionary for a French-based creole. The first three dialogs between the captain of an incoming ship from France and, respectively, a dock-worker hired to unload the ship, a carpenter, and a plantation owner represent artificial situations. It is unlikely that the captain would have had a knowledge of the Saint-Domingue vernacular. No doubt, as the author indicates in the description of this handbook, it is to '*donner une idée de langage*' ('to show what this language is like'). The other two dialogs, between plantation owners and, first, a Black sugar plantation foreman (*commandeur*) and, second, a slave on a coffee plantation, especially aim to enable European plantation owners to communicate with the slave speakers of the language, '*se faire entendre des Nègres*' ('to be understood by the Negroes').

Text 8 is an excerpt of a conversation between a sugar plantation owner and his foreman. In this excerpt the French original precedes the SDC

4.3 Etymologically Based Representations

equivalent provided by Ducœurjoly; P. is the plantation owner and Th. (*Thélémaque*), the foreman.

Text 8

P. La terre est-elle bien mouillée, bien bien humide, peut-on planter des cannes, et des vivres?	**P.** Terre-là ben mouillée, yo savé planté canne acque vivres?
Th. Oui, Monsieur.	**Th.** Oui, Mouché.
P. Ah bien! Tu iras demain avec le grand atelier, fouiller la pièce No. 8, le petit atelier ira chercher du plant.	**P.** Ah ben! To va alé demain acque grand atelier, fouiller la pièce No. 8, le pitit atelier ira chercher plant.
Th. Que ferons-nous avec les nourrices, et les vieux?	**Th.** Ça nous va faire acque nourrices, et vieux monde?
P. Les vieux çarcleront les haies, et les nourrices jetteront ou sèmeront le plant.	**P.** Vieux-là-yo va sarclé hayies-là-yo, et nourrices-là-yo va semé plant.
Th. Monsieur, la pièce No. 5 est bientôt bonne à couper, nous pourrons la rouler aussitôt que nous aurons fini de planter le No. 8.	**Th.** Mouché, pièce No. 5 bentôt bon pour coupé, nous savé roulé-ly sitôt nous caba plante No. 8.
P. Tu as raison, je l'aurais commencé aujourd'hui, mais les mulets sont fatigués des charrois que nous avons fait à l'embarcadaire de la dernière étuvée, et je veux profiter de l'humidité de la terre planter les cannes et les patates.	**P.** To gagné raison, mo séré té coumencé ly jordy, mais milets-là-yo fatigués charrois-là-yo nous sorti faire l'embarcadaire pour dernière n'étivée, et pi mo vlé profiter pendant terre la mouillé pour planté cannes acque patates.

P. The soil is quite moist, can one plant sugar cane and starchy vegetables?

Th. Yes, Sir.

P. O.K.! You'll go tomorrow with the large work crew to till lot No. 8, the small work crew will go get plants.

Th. What will we do with the nursing mothers and the elderly?

P. The elderly will hoe the undergrowth and the nursing mothers will plant the seedlings.

Th. Sir, lot No. 5 is nearly ready for cutting, we can harvest it as soon as we have finished planting No. 8.

P. You're right, I would have begun today but the mules are tired from the hauling we did to load the last sugar juice, and I want to take advantage while the soil is wet to plant sugar cane and starchy vegetables.

The dictionary section of Ducœurjoly's handbook is more encyclopedic than properly linguistic. Although it does provide SDC equivalents for French entries, the emphasis is on defining the SDC term via the French entry. It is particularly useful for information about the fauna, flora, and social customs of Saint-Domingue. For example, *calinda,* adopted in French as a masculine noun, is defined in French as follows:

> *bal que donnent les Nègres sur les habitations, où l'on danse au son du bambala et du banza*
>
> 'ball that the Negroes organize on the plantations, where one dances to the sound of the bamboula [a type of drum] and the banza [a rudimentary banjo made with a calabash or gourd]'

On the other hand, for verbs, adjectives, and function words, Ducœurjoly offers short contextual examples that provide useful grammatical information:

Text 9

DEMANDER, v.a. [transitive verb] prier quelqu'un d'accorder quelque chose, – je vous demande votre amitié, – il lui a demandé la vie, ... – il demande ly communication des pièces, – il ne demande pas mieux, – monsieur un tel est venu vous demander.

Mandé – mo mandé l'amitié à vous, – ly mandé ly la vie, —mo mande vou en grace– ly mandé communication à – pas mandé mior – monsieur nion tel vini mandé vous.

TO ASK, v.a. to request someone to grant something, – I ask for your friendship, – he asked him for his life, ... – he asks for the handing over of the documents, – he doesn't ask for anything better, – Mr so-and-so came to ask for you.

It is noteworthy that the plural of French *pièces* is rendered in the SDC equivalent by the singular *pièce* followed by the post-posed plural marker *yo*, which at this stage of SDC was obligatorily preceded by the deictic determiner *là*. Although the author adheres closely to conventional French spelling, in contrast for example to the earlier *Passion*, the *Manuel* does display a significant evolution away from what may be characterized as approximate French. Note, for example, the use of *caba* and *sorti* as auxiliary verbs to express completed action and the verb marker combination *seré té* to express the conditional perfect.[10]

In colonial texts, a distinction must be made between texts written by local scribes, either native-born 'Creoles' or settlers with long and direct exposure to SDC, and those written by travelers with merely occasional contact with the local speech, as well as Europeans who had only secondhand acquaintance with SDC. The best-known early example of this latter tradition is a passage in a Swiss-French visitor's account of his travels in the French colonies of the New World, J. Girod-Chantrans' *Voyage d'un Suisse dans différentes colonies d'Amérique* (1785). The short sample (Text 10), designed to illustrate what the author perceived as a reduced form of French, which he observed to be widely used by all segments of Saint-Domingue's population, purports to represent a letter written by a Mulatto woman to explain to her lover how she was forced to be unfaithful to him against her will. This stereotypic French foreigner talk clearly does not represent late-eighteenth-century SDC.

Text 10

Moi étois à la case à moi; moi étois après préparer cassave à moi; Zéphir venir trouver moi, li dit que li aimer moi, & qu'il vouloit que moi aimer li tout. Moi répondre li que moi déja aimer mon autre & que moi pas capable d'aimer deux ...	I was in my hut; I was preparing my cassava; Zéphyr came to join me, he said he loved me and that he wanted me to love him too. I answered that I loved my other one and that I was not able to love two [men] ...

It is clear that Girod-Chantrans' sample was intended to acquaint educated readers of French with what he considered to be a quaint folk speech, a debased version of Standard French undeserving of serious study or of a systematic autonomous representation. Interestingly, that author noted that the creole was widely used by Europeans. L. E. M. Moreau de Saint-Méry, a self-described 'Creole' born in Martinique and actively involved in the cultural and political life of pre-revolutionary Saint-Domingue, remarked that Girod-Chantrans had failed to capture the local vernacular in all of its authenticity (1797/1958). He stated that the folk language of the French West Indies was not a *jargon maussade* 'a sorry pidgin', as Girod-Chantrans imagined, but a graceful dialect containing many subtleties that even some locally born Europeans could not fully master.

4.3.4 Post-colonial texts

One might expect that, when the new state of Haiti gained its independence in 1804, the only language shared by all members of the community would be given some sort of official recognition. After all, although the Mulattoes and some of the Black military leaders were bilingual, the majority of the slaves were monolingual speakers of SDC or, since a large proportion of slaves were *Bozals* newly arrived from Africa, approximative versions of it. However, the new leaders simply continued the colonial linguistic policy and used French exclusively in all spheres of public life and for all administrative purposes. Indeed, they were stauncher defenders of the linguistic *status quo* than some of the French, for they wanted to show to the world that liberated Blacks were fully capable of handling the most prestigious language of the period with grace and effectiveness. Few texts of the post-independence period contain extensive samples of the vernacular language. Typically, the latter take the form of occasional material inserted in French works to provide local color or, in the case of plays, to provide comic relief, and sometimes merely to inject socio-linguistic authenticity. The earliest example of this type of text is found in two works glorifying King Christophe, written by the official court poet, Juste Chanlatte, who held the title of Comte de Rosiers: a play with musical interludes (a *vaudeville*), *L'Entrée du Roi en sa capitale en janvier 1818* 'The entry of the King into his capital in January 1818', and a three-act opera performed in 1820, *La Partie de chasse du Roy* 'The King's hunting party'. In the play, the author adopts a device, used by Molière and other French playwrights in the seventeenth and eighteenth centuries, which consists in having domestics or other lower-class secondary characters speak in vernacular varieties, except that in this play, one of the two main characters, Valentin, a tinsmith, is presented as elevating his style of speech for a song dedicated to the king by the use of pseudo-dialectal French. The extract in Text 11 is from a speech in SDC by Marguerite, a maid, the paramour of Valentin.

Text 11

Dire moé donc, Valentin. Io dire nous bon papa à nous va rivé; cé pas pitit contents n'a contents ça, n'a voir bon maman à nous, bon Roi à nous, bel pitit Prince Royal à nous acqué toutes belles Princesses Royales à nous io. Mo ta voudré io dija passé, tant cœur à moé té va content; m'après langui, séché doubout à force moé ta voudré voir io paraîte.	Tell me, Valentin. They say that our good father is going to come; it's not a little joy we'll experience; we'll see our good mother, our good King, our handsome little Crown Prince and all our royal Princesses. I wish they had already passed by, so much will my heart be glad; I'm languishing, I'm dying of impatience [literally, drying up as I stand], so much do I want them to see them appear.

Although, with regard to the orthography, Chanlatte adheres closely to French, more closely in fact than did colonial texts, his representation of SDC departs from it from a structural perspective. The extract in Text 11 shows the expression of tense, mood, and aspect with pre-posed verb markers, *va/a* for the future and *té va/ta* for the conditional; as is the case in present-day HC, the latter mood is expressed by the combination of the anterior marker *té* and the future marker *va*, except that in Text 11, unlike present-day HC, the two markers do not always appear in the fused form *ta* but as two words: *té va*. Another structural feature, typical of present-day HC, is the focalizing construction involving the fronting of the reduplicated predicate: *cé pas pitit content n'a contents*. In addition, Chanlatte's texts contain several of the variants characteristic of NHC: the consistent use of the preposition *à* for the possessive construction, *cœur à moé* 'my heart' (present-day NHC *kèr a mwen* or, in normal speech, *kèranm* vs. HC *kè m/wen*) and *acqué* 'with' (present-day NHC *ake* vs. HC *ak, avè/k*). Chanlatte's plays provide strong evidence that by the beginning of the nineteenth century, HC had attained a stabilized form.[11]

4.3.5 Toward a more systematic etymologically based spelling

In the late nineteenth century and during the first half of the twentieth century Haitian writers used various etymological spellings in the representation of HC in their works, for example, Owald Durant in the famous poem *Choucoune* and Justin Lhérisson in novels written in French but with dialogs in HC.[12] Eminently representative of these attempts is the work of Georges Sylvain, a French-educated member of the Haitian cultivated bilingual élite, in a bilingual collection of fables adapted from La Fontaine, *Cric? Crac!* (1901). Sylvain's stated principle was, to quote the author, to 'preserve, as much as possible, in words derived from French, their French physiognomy, but without ever sacrificing phonetic form to etymology.' Interestingly, in the title page of the book, in order to stress the authenticity of the language, Sylvain ascribes the authorship of the fables to a fictitious monolingual rural speaker: *Fables de La Fontaine racontées par un montagnard haïtien et transcrites en vers créoles* 'La Fontaine fables narrated by a Haitian highlander and transcribed in Creole verse'. The sample in Text 12 is from the beginning of Sylvain's adaptation of the fable of the Wolf and the Lamb; Sylvain's French rendition, also in verse, is provided.

Text 12

Douvan poul' ravett pas janmain　　« Devant une poule, ravet jamais
G'ain raison. Grann moin té connin　　N'eut raison ». Ma grand'mère avait
Dit ça souvent: eh! ben, gadé　　coutume
Si mots longtemps pas vérité!　　De dire souvent cela: eh! Bien, voyez
　　Si les propos d'autrefois ne sont pas vérité!

Gnou mouton tout piti, gnou jou　　Un tout petit mouton, un jour,
T'apé bouè d'leau nan la-riviè.　　Buvait de l'eau dans la rivière.
Nan mainm moment, gnou gros loup　　Au même moment, un énorme loup
Soti nan bois tou, pou li bouè　　Sortit du bois, pour boire aussi.

– Zott pas janmain ouè bett ça-là?　　– Vous n'avez jamais vu cette bête-là, vous autres?

Before the chicken the cockroach
Never was right. My grandmother
Used to say that often. Well, see
If the old adages are not the truth!
A very young sheep, one day,
Was drinking water from a river.
At the same moment, a huge
wolf came out of the woods, in order also to have a drink.
—Have you (pl.) never seen this animal?

Sylvain introduces three signal innovations that result in a more reliable indication of pronunciation:

1. Final pronounced consonants are represented by doubling, in the case of words with an etymologically silent consonant: *ravett*, or by an apostrophe where the French cognate contains a final *e*: *poul'*. All other final consonants are silent: *souvent*, *loup*, except for c, q, r, l, and f, which are generally pronounced in French.
2. Non-etymological nasal vowels are indicated: *jamain* vs. *jamais*, *connin* vs. *connaître*, *mainm* vs. *même*.
3. Etymological determiners that have become fused with nouns are agglutinated: *lariviè*, 'river', *d'leau* 'water'; note that in HC definiteness is expressed by a post-posed form: compare 'the water' *dlo a* vs. 'some water' *dlo*.

The use of etymological spellings found in the early texts reproduced in Section 4.3.2 was independent of any educational, political, or social considerations. Those who produced these texts, like Sylvain, certainly did not intend to use the spelling they devised to impart literacy skills to monolingual

4.3 Etymologically Based Representations

Table 4.1. Samples of Berry's Etymological Spelling

Pronunciation	Berry notation	French cognate	English
mwẽs	moince	moins	less
suje	suyè	essuyer	to wipe
amizmã	amusement	amusement	amusement
nasjõ	nacion	nation	nation
pu	pour	pour	for
pati	parti	partir	to leave
nɥit	nuite	nuit	night
bèf	bœuf	bœuf	cow (ox, beef)
movè	movai	mauvais	bad
rele	rhélé	héler	to call
fãmi	fanmille	famille	family
kõnẽ	connen	connaitre	to know

speakers of HC; for a later example of such texts, see Morisseau-Leroy (1953). Such, however, was the objective of the Haitian educator Frédéric Doret (1924), an author, like Sylvain, of an adaptation of the fables of La Fontaine, but in a pedagogically oriented text: *Pour amuser nos tout petits: initiation aux fables de la Fontaine, avec une introduction sur le créole.* Doret's intention is stated clearly: '... *amener nos enfants vers le français en passant par le créole qui en dérive* (... to lead our children toward French by going through the creole that is derived from it)'. A more explicit etymologizing spelling was proposed within the same transitional tradition by Paul Berry (1964), an American Quaker missionary.[13] Berry retained several of Sylvain's conventions but, in general, adhered more closely to the French cognates (see Table 4.1).

Berry justifies his adoption of an etymological spelling and his rejection of an autonomous phonologically based orthography on the basis of three arguments:

1. In order not to alienate the support of the bilingual élite, any spelling system for HC should be relatively accessible to a reader of French.
2. Any monolingual HC speaker who has been taught to read his own language should be able to transfer his newly acquired literacy skills to French; in other words, the spelling system should form a 'bridge' to French. At the very least, the neo-literate should be able to read signs and posters in French.

3. However, since any spelling system for HC is designed primarily for illiterate monolinguals, it should be made easy for them to learn it.

An etymological writing system, simpler than Berry's, has been proposed for the creoles of the French Antilles by M.-C. Hazaël-Massieux (1993).[14] Because most speakers of Guadeloupean and Martinican Creoles have bilingual proficiency in French and schooling in French is free and compulsory (unlike in Haiti), that system is eminently reasonable. It has the overwhelming support of individuals in favor of some use of the local creole in schools, except for those intellectual activists who support the concept of **maximal differentiation**,[15] both in the devising of a writing system and in a written standard (Bernabé 1976). But within the Haitian educational and social context, where an estimated 90% of the population are monolingual in HC, if the primary objective of the creation of a writing system and the development of a standard written norm for the language is to render that group literate, the problem with a transitional system such as Berry's is that it places the burden of learning on the segment of the Haitian population that is the most educationally disadvantaged. That burden should more properly be placed on the shoulders of the bilingual élite. Since they are already literate, it should not be difficult for them to transfer their skill and learn to use a systematic phonologically based orthography.

From a linguistic perspective, the main flaw of any etymological spelling that attempts to include phonologically based conventions is that it is arbitrary. How can one reconciliate contradictory etymological and phonological criteria? For example, in representing /se/ so that it mirrors its French cognate *c'est*, why stop with the use of *c* for /s/ and the use of *é* for /e/? In the final analysis, only two alternatives lead to consistent and non-arbitrary spelling conventions: total reference to etymology or a bi-unique phonologically based notation. Thus, one writes /se/ either as *c'est* or as a sequence of two segments each of which receives an invariant representation, for example, *sé*.

4.4 Systematic Autonomous Orthographies for HC

The development of systematic and autonomous (i.e., non-etymological) writing systems for HC must be framed in a socio-political context. Whereas the putative beneficiaries of devising a suitable writing system for HC are the monolingual speakers, it would be unwise not to take into account the attitudes of that segment of the Haitian population that holds political power and social prestige, namely, the bilingual élite for whom proficiency in

French confers advantages that any social group is loath to give up (Schieffelin and Doucet 1994). Also, as pointed out earlier, the objectives of reducing a language to writing must be clearly stated.

4.4.1 The McConnell-Laubach orthography

The first systematic phonologically based spelling that started from the premise that HC was an autonomous language appeared in the early 1940s, more than two centuries after the language had emerged. It was devised by a Northern Irish Methodist pastor, Ormonde McConnell, who received advice and support from the noted American literacy expert Frank Laubach. McConnell developed the spelling within the context of a program to develop literacy among monolingual speakers of HC. His starting point was a phonological transcription of HC in IPA (the International Phonetic

Table 4.2. Correspondences Between the Three Systematic Representations of Consonants

IPA	McConnell-Laubach	Faublas-Pressoir	IPN (official)
p	p	p	p
b	b	b	b
t	t	t	t
d	d	d	d
k	k	k	k
f	f	f	f
v	v	v	v
s	s	s	s
z	z	z	z
ʃ	ch	ch	ch
ʒ	j	j	j
tʃ	tch	tch	tch
dʒ	dj	dj	dj
m	m	m	m
n	n	n	n
ɲ	gn	gn	y
ŋ	ng	ng	ng
l	l	l	l
r	r	r	r/w

118   Toward a Systematic Autonomous Spelling

Alphabet) contained in the first expert description of the language (S. Sylvain 1936). Wherever possible, McConnell adopted French phoneme-to-letter correspondences, provided the symbols selected were monographic, i.e., at first, he rejected digraphs such as *ou* for the representation of /u/. The representation of consonants posed few problems (see Table 4.2). The major obstacle was the representation of /k/. In French, there are a variety of ways to write /k/: *c* (*cour*), *qu* (*qui*), *q* (*coq*), *ch* (*chrétien*), *k* (*kilo*), *cc* (*accord*), *cq* (*acquis*). McConnell selected the IPA symbol *k*. To represent the palatal fricative /ʃ/ he first opted for *sh* but, upon the wise advice of Laubach, adopted the French representation *ch*.[16]

McConnell also adopted French spelling conventions to represent oral vowel contrasts. Nasal vowels posed difficulties since, as we have seen in Chapter 2, unlike French, HC has combinations of nasal vowels followed by the nasal consonants, as well as sequences of oral vowels followed by these consonants. Straightforward representations using the French convention of a vowel letter plus *n* or *m* do not always yield unambiguous correspondences. For example, the letter sequence *on* could be read /ɔ̃/ or /on/, and there is no way to distinguish between the potential contrasts /ũ/ vs. /un/. Accordingly, on the model of the IPA transcription, McConnell decided to note nasal vowels with the corresponding vowel letter plus a diacritic, the tilde. Unfortunately, printers in Haiti did not have that symbol, so instead he chose the most similar standard diacritic, the circumflex accent (see Table 4.3). An argument to justify the use of the circumflex accent is that it resembles a sort of pincer, well known to all Haitians, termed *bwa nan nen* 'wood in the nose', that losers in a round of cards or dominoes must put on their nose.

Table 4.3. Distribution of Nasal Vowels and Sequences of Oral Vowel and Nasal Consonants in HC and Their Representation in the McConnell-Laubach orthography

Nasal vowel	Oral vowel + n	Nasal vowel + nasal consonant.
/sã/ blood *sâ*	/pan/ breakdown *pan*	/pãn/ to hang *pân*
/nũ/ 1st person pl. inclusive pronoun *nû*	—	/mũn/ person *moûn*
	/maʃin/ machine *machin*	/sĩj/ sign *sîng*
/pɔ̃/ bridge *pô*	/mɔn/ mountain *mòn*	/pɔ̃n/ to lay (eggs) *pôn*
/ʃẽ/ dog *chê*	/rɛn/ queen *rèn*	/ʃẽn/ chain *chên*

To represent the semivowels /j/ and /w/ McConnell opted for *y* and *w*, respectively, although he hesitated in the case of /j/. In later texts, he accommodated French spelling conventions by using *i* before a vowel and *y* elsewhere: *Dié* 'God', *viân* 'meat' vs. *gêyê* 'to have', *yo* 'they'.

4.4.2 The Faublas-Pressoir orthography

The McConnell-Laubach orthography marked a signal step in language planning in Haiti: for the first time it provided a simple and unambiguous way to write the language. Initially, the spelling elicited great interest and was used in a translation of the New Testament, in a bi-weekly magazine featuring only HC called *Limiè, Fòs, Progès* ('Light, Strength, Progress') published between 1943 and 1946, and in a literacy project linked to a major rural development program in the Marbial valley (southern Haiti) sponsored by UNESCO in 1949 (U. Fleischmann 2010).

However, during this time, Haiti was in the midst of a nationalistic cultural movement which stressed at the same time the colonial French and African roots of the country. This was a direct reaction to a nineteen-year US occupation that ended in 1934 (see Section 1.2.2). It was to be expected that any cultural and educational innovation introduced by Anglo-Saxons would be met with deep suspicion. Such was the case with the McConnell-Laubach spelling; indeed, the letters *y* and *w* first chosen to note the semivowels were dubbed 'Anglo-Saxon' letters! Some Haitians, involved in the movement to promote HC and to give the monolingual masses access to education, felt that any systematic orthography for the language should nonetheless take into account the special relationship between the vernacular and its lexical-base language: French. For these opponents, the most objectionable feature of the spelling was the choice of the circumflex accent to represent nasal vowels, a striking departure from its use in French. As the Haitian writer Charles-Fernand Pressoir (1947: 67) remarked:[17]

> This McConnell-Laubach alphabet would be perfect, even with the circumflex accent, if it were used for the Australian aborigines or in some lost corner of the world. It fails because Creole is a mixed language, in a country with French traditions.

In 1947, Pressoir and the then minister of education, L. Faublas, proposed another phonologically based systematic orthography that made use of more French spelling conventions in two critical areas, the semivowels and the nasal vowels. For the latter, Faublas and Pressoir decided to represent the three primary nasal vowels /ẽ, ã, õ / by using vowel + *n* sequences: *in*, *an*, and *on*, respectively. This choice, involving a departure from strict bi-uniqueness, led to some minor problems that were solved in an ad hoc manner. The choice of *in* to note /ẽ/ made it impossible to use that combination for /in/. This problem was solved by inserting a hyphen to differentiate combinations of vowels plus *n* from the corresponding nasal vowels: *machi-n* /maʃin/ 'car' vs. *chin* /ʃẽ/ 'dog', *pa-n* /pan/ 'breakdown' vs. *pan* /pã/ 'section of a wall'. No special representations were provided for the marginal nasal vowels /ĩ/ and /ũ/; they were written as *i* or *in* and *ou* or *oun* respectively: *sign* /sĩj/ 'sign', *pinga* /pĩnga/ 'watch out', *nou* /nũ/ 'we, us', *moun* /mũn/ 'person', *ounfò* [ũfɔ] 'altar'. However, we saw in Chapter 2 that the phonological status of these two high nasal vowels is indeterminate.

In the case of the semivowels, /w/ was represented with the same symbol used for /u/, the combination *ou*. This was workable since the sound value of *ou* can be determined by the context: *ou* is read /w/ when it occurs before a vowel and /u/ elsewhere: *ouanga* /wãga/ 'Vodou charm', *zouazo* /zwazo/ 'bird', *mouin* /mwẽ/ 'I, me' but *lou* /lu/ 'wolf', *bouyi* /buji/ 'to boil'. In the case of initial /w/ before rounded vowels, the use of etymological *r* was retained: /wuʒ/ *rouj* 'red'. Two symbols were chosen to represent /j/: *y* in word-initial position and between vowels and *i* between a consonant and a vowel: *pié* /pje/ 'foot', *viann* /vjãn/ 'meat' vs. *yo* /jo/ 'they, them', *binyin* /bẽjẽ/ 'to bathe'. This choice, together with the use of *in* for /ẽ/, led to awkward sequences, such as *biin* for /bjẽ/ 'good'. These were eliminated in an ad hoc manner by using *y*: *byin*.

The Faublas-Pressoir spelling, perceived as a national response to foreign cultural imperialism, enjoyed great favor and rapidly superseded the McConnell-Laubach orthography. It was adopted by the government's adult literacy organizations, ONEC (Office national d'éducation communautaire) and its successor, ONAAC (Office national d'alphabétisation et d'action communautaire), and was unchallenged until 1975.[18] Ironically, a spelling nearly identical to the Faublas-Pressoir system had been devised in 1872 by a French judge established in French Guiana (Auguste de Saint-Quentin 1872). He believed firmly that, as a language in its own right, Guianese French Creole should be written with a systematic autonomous orthography (see Section 1.4.3). His pioneering effort did come to the attention of Pressoir, who acknowledged his debt, but not to that of McConnell. Had the latter been better read in the area of French-based creoles, surely he would not have tried to re-invent the wheel, as it were. His worthy attempt would not then have provoked adverse reactions on the part of the bilingual élite, and the energy and time invested in polemics, pro or con, about the two orthographical proposals could have been better channeled toward other aspects of the establishment of a standard written norm.

4.4.3 The IPN officialized orthography

In addition to the ill-conceived neo-etymological spelling devised by Paul Berry, several minor revisions were proposed after 1947, to solve some of the infelicities of the Faublas-Pressoir orthography. In teaching materials designed for American learners of HC, I used the sequence *en* for /ẽ/ to avoid the ad hoc use of the hyphen in words such as *machi-n*; the combination /in/ would be written *in* and the nasal vowel /ẽ/, *en* (Valdman 1968). There were also attempts, following Berry, to revert to etymological notations, for example, by Pompilus (1973). A so-called Pan-Creole spelling was put forward in 1975 by the Francophone development agency, the Agence de Coopération Culturelle et Technique (AGECOP), in which /k/ was written *c* before a back vowel and *qu* elsewhere (*cabann* /kabãn/ 'bed', *couman* /kumã/ 'how' vs. *qui moun* /kimun/ 'who', *quinbé* /kẽbe/ 'to hold on'). Also, /wa/ was spelled *oi* (*zoizo* /zwazo/ 'bird').[19] The assumption underlying the Pan-Creole orthography, namely, that the various FBCs constituted dialects of a single language, was challenged on linguistic and nationalistic grounds, and this orthographic proposal met with indifference. This was not surprising, given the Haitian government's relative inefficiency and lack of interest in concerted language-planning endeavors; it had failed to officialize the Faublas-Pressoir writing system used for more than twenty years by its agencies, ONEC and ONAAC.

A more durable impact was made by another proposal for a writing system put forward by the Groupe de recherches et d'expérimentation en alphabétisation (GREAL) and French consultants to the French-supported National Pedagogical Institute of Port-au-Prince (IPN), led by Alain Bentolila, a linguist from the University of Paris V-René Descartes. This minor modification of the Faublas-Pressoir system launched in 1975 received official government support in 1979. It was adopted in the materials prepared by the IPN in conjunction with an educational reform program that had instituted the vernacular as the main classroom vehicle for the first four years of primary schooling (see Section 12.5.2) and it was used progressively by all groups in Haiti and the diaspora that produce materials in HC. Today, it is the orthography used by all individuals both in Haiti and in the diaspora communities.[20]

The IPN orthography introduces five changes in the sound-to-letter conventions of the Faublas-Pressoir system (see Table 4.4).

1. *é* was changed to e. This eliminates the diacritic in a combination that occurs with relatively high frequency; it also provides a symmetrical treatment for the oral vowels:

    e   *pe* 'quiet'   o   *mo* 'word'
    è   *pè* 'priest'   ò   *mò* 'dead person'

However, this is a very ill-advised change in the context of the educational reform program according to which children were supposed to switch to French as a pedagogical vehicle after four years of instruction in HC. In French, the letter *e* by itself, versus its use with accents for the vowels /e/ and /ɛ/, represents the so-called mute e, which stands for zero or a vowel intermediate between the vowels /œ/ and /ø/ or one or the other of these two vowels. Thus, with the use of the letter *e* without the acute accent, a Haitian child would be led to pronounce the phrase *je ne le ferai pas* 'I won't do it' as /ʒe ne le fe re pa/ instead of /ʒø nlø fø re pa/.

2. *in* /ẽ/ is written *en*. This avoids recourse to the ad hoc use of the hyphen, e.g., *vi-n*.
3. The so-called Anglo-Saxon letters are reinstated to write the semi-vowels. This restores bi-uniqueness in the representation of both /y/ and /w/ and simplifies letter-to-sound correspondences.
4. It is 'suggested' that /w/ be written *w* instead of *r* before rounded vowels and, in the case of speakers who show this pronunciation, after labial consonants (/p/ and /b/). This also extends bi-uniqueness where the two other previous systematic spellings had departed from it. The letter *r* is used only to represent the velar resonant: *diri* /diri/ 'rice', *rete* /rete/ 'to remain' vs. *wouj* /wuʒ / 'red', *wòb* /wɔb/ 'dress', *wont* /wõt/ 'shame', *pwan* 'to take' (which alternates with /prã/).
5. The grave accent is used instead of the hyphen for the sequence /an/: /pan/ is written *pàn* instead of *pa-n*. This eliminates completely the need for the hyphen in the representation of phonemes.

Within the context of transitional literacy and bilingual education programs in which learners were to be first taught to read and write their native language, HC, and then have their literacy skills transferred to French, the IPN orthography shows several weaknesses. The first, pointed out above, is the replacement of *é* by *e* for the representation of /e/. The second is the use of *y* to represent /j/ in pre-vocalic position instead of using *y* and *i* in complementary distribution: *y* in initial and final position (*yo* 'they', *bagay* 'thing') and *i* before a vowel (*pie* 'foot'). This convention would differ slightly from French where: (1) *y* appears initially, mostly in foreign loan words: *yaourt* 'yoghurt', *yole* 'skiff', *yacht* 'yacht'; (2) *i* is used pre-vocalically (*pied* 'foot'); and (3) where final /j/ shows a variety of spellings: *travail* 'work', *bille* 'marble', *cobaye* 'guinea pig'. Third, the use of *w* to replace *r* before rounded vowels is ill-advised because: (1) particularly in Northern HC, it is often difficult to distinguish between /r/ and /w/, even with the use of instrumental acoustic analysis (see Chapter 2);

4.4 Systematic Autonomous Orthographies

Table 4.4. Correspondences Between the Three Systematic Representations of HC Vowels and Semivowels[21]

IPA oral vowels	McConnell-Laubach	Faublas-Pressoir	IPN-officiel
i	i	i	i
u	ou	ou	ou
e	é	é	*e
ɛ	é	é	é
o	o	o	o
ɔ	ò	ò/ô	ò
Nasal vowels and sequences of nasal/oral vowels plus n			
ẽ	ê	in	*en
in	in	i-n	*in
ẽn	ên	inn	enn
ɛn	èn	èn	èn
ã	â	an	an
ãn	ân	ann	ann
an	an	a-n	*àn
õ	ô	on	on
õn	ôn	onn	onn
ɔn	òn	òn	òn
ĩ	î	in	in
ũ	ûn	oun	oun
Semivowels and combinations of semivowel + vowel			
w	w	ou	*w
wa	wa	oua	wa
j	y	y	y
pje	pyé/pié	pié	*pye
r	r	r	r
wou (French *roue*)	rou	rou	*wou

(2) the two phonemes alternate after labial consonants: *vrè* /vrɛ/ or /vwɛ/, again especially in Northern HC.

To summarize this section on autonomous phonologically based orthographies for HC, the McConnell-Laubach system proved to be the most effective one in the unambiguous conversion of letters to sound. The other two systems encounter problems with sequences of nasal vowels + n + vowel or y: *vanyan* /vãyã/ 'brave' or *bakonye* /bakonye/ 'trickster, schemer', which could be read also as /vanyã/ or /bakõye/, respectively. The spelling of these words is unambiguous with the use of the circumflex accent diacritic, namely, *vâyâ* and *bakonyé,* respectively. The error of proponents of a strict bi-unique system is to define reading skills narrowly as the conversion of letters to sound, whereas in fact, as pointed out in Section 4.1.1, they involve principally extracting meaning from written texts. On the other hand, bi-uniqueness does facilitate the conversion of sound to letters, although some level of abstractness is inevitable given the existence of the morphophonological processes described in Chapter 3 and the sociolinguistic and dialectal variation to be presented in Chapter 11.

4.5 Normalization

4.5.1 The concept of normalization

The choice of a suitable alphabet and the elaboration of a systematic set of phoneme-to-letter correspondences constitute only one part of the development of a writing system. Other conventions must be set up: those dealing with the segmentation of linguistic units, that is, the insertion of spaces between words or related units; those dealing with choices among variant forms; those dealing with the demarcation of syntactic units, such as phrases and sentences (Vernet 1980; Valdman 1999, 2005).

The orthographies of such languages as English or French are highly standardized, but total uniformity is not a prerequisite for an efficient orthography. It is possible to receive and transmit written messages while allowing individual scriptors some leeway. **Standardization** refers to higher-level choices among linguistic variants linked to geographical areas or social classes, for example, in English the choice among words referring to the same concept (*bag* or *sack*, *bucket* or *pail*, *elevator* or *lift*) or among grammatical features serving the same function (*isn't* or *ain't*; *you*, *y'all* or *you'uns*; *it is I* or *it is me*). Underlying standardization is the acceptance by a linguistic community of a variety to be used in writing and, as a corollary, for administrative, educational, and other purposes, the **standard** variety (**norm**). **Normalization** involves lower-level choices among variant forms used by the same speaker but correlating with differences of style or tempo of speech or phonological environment. In this section, I will deal with the latter type of variation.

The difference between these two concepts and their implications for the elaboration of a systematic orthography for HC is illustrated by the treatment of the word for 'with' in HC. It occurs in four variants: *avèk*, *avè*, *ak*, and *ak*e. In HC texts, *ake* is rejected because it is a marked feature of the speech of the Cape Haitian area. That decision falls under the heading of standardization. Normalization would involve deciding whether one would choose only one form that would stand for the other three variants that are part of the standardized variety of HC, presumably the fullest variant *avèk*, or whether all of the three variants would be used. It is the extensive nature of morphophonemic variation of HC that forces language planners to make decisions about normalization.

Normalization also involves the complex issue of the demarcation of the word, particularly in compound words. Consider the English word *bookworm* 'someone who reads a lot'. It is written as one word because, although derived from *book worm* 'a worm that attacks books', it has become a metaphor whose meaning cannot be deduced from its constituent parts. The representation of compound words varies greatly in the English-speaking world. Clear-cut criteria are not always available to decide whether a compound should be written as a single word (*grasshopper*), as a hyphenated combination (*grass-roots*) or as a group of words (*grass tree* 'a woody stemmed Australian plant'). In fact, whereas the *American Heritage Dictionary* lists the latter compounds as two words, the *Cambridge International Dictionary of English* prefers the one-word spelling. It appears that the single-word representation for idiomatic compounds, that is, those whose meaning cannot be easily derived from their constituent parts, is gaining ground. It can be expected that this issue will be particularly thorny in HC, a language for which there exist neither standard dictionaries nor official agencies charged with language-planning initiatives.

Language planning in Haiti, including the elaboration of orthographies, the choice of varieties to be used (standardization), and normalization, was first undertaken by religious groups whose objectives were, on the one hand, to proselytize or minister to the needs of the faithful and, on the other, within the framework of humanitarian assistance, to provide the illiterate and downtrodden masses access to information as part of cultural, economic, and social development by means of adult literacy programs. We have seen that the first effort in language planning in Haiti, the elaboration of a systematic orthography, was undertaken by Ormonde McConnell, a Methodist minister. He followed that initiative by the preparation of school readers, because an orthography without suitable reading material would be useless. Following his lead, a group of local Protestant ministers launched a monthly publication, *Boukan*, which contained only HC material. A Belgian-based Catholic order, the Fathers of Scheut, created a similar monthly, *Bon Nouvèl*. Today, it is the only regular publication in HC and its circulation of about 30,000 copies reaches the largest number of potential readers. Arguably the next most widely read text is the HC adaptation of the Old and New Testament, *Bib la*. Except for officializing the IPN orthography, the Haitian government has had a minor impact on language planning (see Chapter 12).

Because their objective was to reach monolingual speakers and to provide those who had been taught literacy with reading material reflecting their native speech, these religious groups opted for a norm based on the usual speech of these speakers. They eschewed a norm based on their own speech, that characteristic of literate bilingual speakers belonging to the higher levels of Haitian society; see Chapter 11.4 for a detailed discussion of the differences between the HC of monolingual and that of bilingual speakers, *kreyòl swa*.

4.5.2 Two models for normalization

Variations in the speech of individual speakers, that is, alternations that do not reflect dialect or social class differences, may be handled in orthographies in either a concrete or an abstract fashion. An **abstract** or **normalized** representation involves setting up a single written form that subsumes variant forms. In English, for example, there are numerous phonological variants that are not directly represented by the spelling. In normal style, within close-knit syntactic units *t*, *d*, *s*, and *z* assimilate to a following *y*: *I'll hit you, they'll aid you, we'll pass you, he'll buzz you*. These consonants are palatalized; for example, in *hit you* the combination of *t* and *y* sounds like the *ch* /tʃ/ of *chew*. This type of variation is not represented in the spelling, which shows the unassimilated variant only. Also, variation in vowel quality correlating with the placement of main stress is not reflected in English spelling: compare the pronunciation of the vowels shown in bold face: *I c**a**n* vs. *I c**a**n do it*; *democr**a**t* vs. *democr**a**cy*. In French, forms that undergo liaison are represented by the full form, for example, the final *s* of the pronoun *nous* stands for /z/ that is pronounced before a vowel but never before a consonant or a pause: *nous allons* 'we go' vs. *nous lavons* 'we wash', *avec nous* 'with us'. There is much to recommend about this abstract representation of forms which are subject to variations that are so automatic that native users are not usually aware of them.

There are, however, instances where variations that are as automatic as those cited above are reflected by different spellings. English spelling opposes the pre-vowel and the pre-consonant forms of the indefinite determiner: *an apple* vs. *a pear*. Contractions, which are optional, may or may not appear: *I cannot* or *I can't*, *I will* or *I'll*, *I am* or *I'm*. In French, whereas some masculine adjectives have a single abstract form subsuming differing pre-vocalic and pre-consonantal forms: *un grand* /grãt/ *arbre* 'a big tree' vs. *un grand* /grã/ *jardin* 'a large garden', others show distinct written forms: *un bel oiseau* 'a beautiful bird' vs. *un beau chat* 'a beautiful cat'.

4.5.3 Abstract representation in HC

In practice, most Haitian scriptors follow the advice of Dejean (1974: 33): '*Lè ou ezité pou yon mo, kalkile kouman ou di-l vré, lè ou di-l dousman dousman, lè ou séparé chak moso ladan*' (When you hesitate for [noting] a word, think of how you say it when you separate each of the words). M.-C. Hazël-Massieux (1993: 82) gives complementary advice when she recommends the use of the longer form wherever there exist morphological variants. The major cases of morphophonological variation (see Chapter 3) are handled in the IPN spelling as follows:

1. The indefinite determiner is given a single form, *yon*, in the official orthography. Usually, the form is pronounced without the initial semivowel and it alternates between /ɔ̃/ and /ũ/.
2. Vowel blends (assimilations) are not shown. Forms involved in vowel blending are represented in their isolation form: the blend /avòw/ appears in the full form of its two constituent words, *avè ou* 'with you', /sɔ̃/ (*mouch*) as *se yon (mouch)* 'it's a fly', (*m ap*) /duw/ as *m ap di ou* 'I'm telling you', /papòw/ as *papa ou* or *papa w* 'your father'.
3. The intervocalic semivowel /j/ that is inserted between a high or high-mid vowel and the definite determinant variant is not represented in the spelling: [pyeʲa] *pye a* 'the foot' or [zutiʲa] *zouti a* 'the tool'. Similarly, the intervocalic semivowel /w/ inserted between a high or high-mid back vowel is not indicated: [wuʷa] *wou a* 'the wheel', [dloʷa] *dlo a* 'the water'.

4.5.4 Concrete representations in HC

Variants determined by phonological factors, as well as those that involve what we might term free variation, that is, where no apparent factors seem to determine the use of a particular variant, are usually given a concrete representation: the actual occurring form, that is, the one the scriptor thinks of as she or he writes.

1. **Definite determiner.** The variants of the definite determiner *la*, *a*, *an*, *nan* or *lan*, whose form is determined by the preceding phonological environment, are given a concrete representation: *tab la* 'the table', *kre a* 'the chalk', *kreyon an* 'the pencil', *gonm nan* 'the eraser', *mont nan/lan* 'the watch'. In the case of *-nan* and *-lan*, where some free variation occurs, either of the two variants

may be used. The nasalization after non-nasal segments that are more frequent (see Section 3.4.1) is usually not indicated; compare *mont lan* and the variant *chat la* /ʃatlã/ 'the cat'. However, as this linguistic change gains ground, there is a tendency to write the nasal variant forms (allomorphs) of the definite determiner, especially after the vowel /i/. In an open letter from the prime minister of Haiti, Michèle Duvivier Pierre-Louis, dated April 9, 2000, and reprinted in the weekly periodical *Haïti en Marche*, produced in Miami, there were the following numerous cases of 'misspellings' involving the use of nasalized variants after non-nasal segments: *Jodi an* 'today', *nan Primati an* 'in the Prime Minister's office', *nan wotè li te swete l lan* 'at the level she had wished', *sou Ayiti an* 'about Haiti', *sitiyasyon peyi an* 'the situation of the country', *Kounye an* 'now', *Dezyèm kategori pwojè an* 'the second category of the project', *ekstansyon rezo an* 'the extension of the network'.

2. **Cardinal numbers.** Unlike the corresponding forms in French, HC cardinal numbers show no general variation linked to the phonological environment. But before the words *an* 'year' and *è* 'hour' they do appear in a variant form. Rather than indicating the variation in the isolation form of the number, the general practice is to agglutinate it to the following noun (see Table 4.5).

1. **Elision in pronouns.** We have seen that except for the fact that the full forms occur obligatorily after a consonant and elided forms before the progressive and definite future makers, elided and full forms of personal pronouns are in free variation. In the Faublas-Pressoir spelling elided forms were written with a hyphen; in the official orthography, the government guidelines recommended the

Table 4.5. Isolation and Agglutinated Forms of Cardinal Numbers

	Isolation form			Agglutinated form			
2	*de*	*de fwa*	two times	*dezan*	two years	*dezè*	two o'clock
3	*twa*	*twa chat*	three cats	*twazan*	three years	*twazè*	three o'clock
4	*kat*	*kat jou*	four days	*katran*	four years	*katrè*	four o'clock
6	*sis*	*sis alimèt*	six matches	*sizan*	six years	*sizè*	six o'clock
9	*nèf*	*nèf pye*	nine feet	*nevan*	nine years	*nevè*	nine o'clock
10	*dis*	*dis ekip*	ten teams	*dizan*	ten years	*dizè*	ten o'clock

Table 4.6. Distribution of 3rd Person Singular Pronoun Variants in an Oral Corpus*

Pre-posed (subject)				Post-posed					
						Object		Possessive	
		[l]	[li]			[l]	[li]	[l]	[li]
V ---V	epi *li/l* ale	9	1	V---V	*y ap fè li/l ale papa li/l antre*	2	0	2	0
#---V	*Li/l* ale	15	1	V---#	*Yo va delivre li/l nan mizè li/l*	10	3	8	1
C---C	*donk li* pati	0	3	V---C	*yo touye li/l vre frè li/l mouri*	24	3	5	0
		24	5			36	6	15	1
V ---C	*epi li/l* pati	44	13						
#--- C	*Li/l* chante	1	101						
C---C	*Fòk li sòti*	0	4						
		45	118						

* # stands for phrase-initial or final, C for consonant, V for vowel; sample phrases are provided to illustrate the phonological environment.

use of an apostrophe, a convention adopted from French:[22] compare *Lè-l rive lakay li, Bouki mande-l* … vs. *Lè l'rive lakay li, Bouki mande l* 'When she arrived at his house, Bouki asked her…'. Current practice has eliminated both the hyphen and the apostrophe: *Lè l rive lakay li, Bouki mande l.*[23]

It is useful to observe actual current practice. Table 4.6 offers an analysis of the distribution of variant forms for the 3rd person singular pronoun that occurred in a representative oral sample collected in Haiti from monolingual speakers. It reveals the following tendencies: (1) pre-posed, as a subject, the pronoun is very likely to occur in its elided form in the context of a vowel, and more often if a vowel follows; it occurs in its full form after a phrase boundary and before a consonant; (2) post-posed, as an object of a verb or preposition and after a vowel, its elided form is favored; a following phrase boundary or consonant constitutes a factor favoring retention of the vowel; (3) as a possessive after a vowel, it generally occurs in its elided form.

Unlike the obligatory occurrence of full forms after a consonant, these tendencies are variable and cannot be converted into hard-and-fast rules that could serve as a rigorous guide for normalization. To complicate the situation, the alternation of elided and full forms is not parallel across the three pronouns subject to elision. The 1st/2nd person plural pronouns *nou* and *ou* are less frequently elided but the 1st person singular pronoun *mwen* and the 3rd person singular pronoun *li* are more subject to elision, even when serving as a subject and occurring between a phrase boundary and a consonant, for example, **M** *pa bliye ou* 'I didn't forget you'; **L** *pa bliye ou* 'She didn't forget you' or **N** *pa bliye ou* 'We didn't forget you' would be much rarer than the use of the full forms *li* and *nou*, respectively.

The tendencies discussed above do inform scriptural practice, as the two sample texts (13 and 14) illustrate. Text 13 is taken from an article in the monthly magazine *Bon Nouvèl* that deals with various brutalities hawkers endure at the hands of the Port-au-Prince police.

Text 13

M te konn vann chanpou, savon, eksetera. **M** konn ranje yo pa ti kivèt, **m** sere kès la anba yon galri, paske **ou** pa ka soti avè **l**: lè gen kouri, afè **ou** vin kraze.

I used to sell shampoo, soap, etc. I used to arrange them in small pans, I stored the box under a gallery, because you can't leave with it: when people start running, your things get crushed.

... **nou** konnen lè y ap pran afè **nou** yo se nan machin yo konn vini.

... You [plural] know that when they take our things, it's with cars they usually come.

Note that *mwen* is systematically elided when it serves as a subject, even after a phrase boundary but that the plural pronouns *nou* and *ou* occur in their full forms.

Text 14 is an excerpt from a *Bouki ak Malis* folktale, related to the Brer Bear and Brer Rabbit tales of the American South, contained in a primary school reader produced by the most prestigious educational group in Haiti, the Frères de l'Instruction Chrétienne (Brothers of Christian Instruction). This primer, *N ap li ak kè kontan II* (We're Reading with Joy), represents an alternative to materials prepared by the IPN (National Pedagogical Institute) within the framework of the Educational Reform Project of 1979. In this part of the story Bouki's daughter Boukinèt has come back from Malis' place with some food which her gluttonous father would like to enjoy.

Text 14

Bonjou, pitit **mwen**, ban m nouvèl Bouki, konpè **m**.	Hello, my child, how's Bouki, my compadre [Malis is Boukinèt's godfather].
Li pa pi mal, non, men **li** pa gen alimèt pou **l** limen yon ti dife.	He's fine, but he doesn't have any matches to light a little fire.
Li t ap manje ze fri a. Manje a te santi bon. Boukinèt ta anvi jwenn ti moso ladan **n**. Chans pou **li**, Ti-Malis ba **li** on bon moso nan men **l**.	He was eating a fried egg. The food smelled good. Boukinèt would have wanted to get a little piece of it. Fortunately for her Malis handed her a good piece of it.
Lè **l** rive lakay **li**, Bouki mande **l** « Sa k pase konsa? **M** twouve ou pran anpil tan pou jwenn dife a! »	When she arrived home, Bouki asked her, 'So what happened? I find that you took a long time to get the fire.'
Ala chans ou genyen pou manje ze! Kote ou jwenn tout ze sa yo? **Mwen** menm, afè **m** pa bon.	What luck you have to eat eggs! Where do you find all these eggs? As for myself, things are not so good.

This excerpt again shows that, as a subject after a phrase boundary, *mwen* is elided more frequently than *li*. Also noteworthy is the nasalization of *li* after a nasal consonant (*ladan n*); the full form also undergoes optional nasalization: *madanm ni* 'his wife'. Also, the indefinite determiner appears in its full and short forms: *yon ti dife* versus *on bon moso*. However, it appears that the use of full or short forms of the personal pronouns may be influenced by stylistic considerations. Text 15 contrasts two types of text taken from *Bon Nouvèl* (Number 498, June 2004). The first is an expository text that deals with the role of HC in Haitian society; the second is a joke. Note that the short form *l* is much more frequent in the more informal text.

Text 15

Yon Ayisyen ap pale franse lè **l** al nan yon biwo oswa avèk yon etranje pou **li** fè enpòtan, pou montre **li** konn **li**, **li** pa «sòt», men lang kreyòl la rete lang pou **li** esprime tout rèv **li**, emosyon **li**, santiman **li**. Lang pou **li** revandike identite **l**.	Haitians usually speak French when they go to an office or with a stranger to show off, to show that they can read, that they're not stupid, but the Creole language remains the language in which they express all their dreams, their aspirations, their emotions, their feelings. A language in which to affirm their identity.

Premye jou lekòl nan yon kindègadenn, pandan premye rekreyasyon, gen yon ti fi ki mande matmwazèl la èske **l** kapab retounen lakay li pou wè maman **l**. Matmwazèl la mande **l** : « Pou ki sa? » **Li** reponn: « Se premye fwa mwen kite **l** pou kont **li,** lakay la. »	On the first day of school in kindergarten, at the first recess, there was a little girl who asked the teacher whether she could return home to see her mother, The teacher asked: 'Why?' She answered: 'It's the first time that I have left her by herself at home.'

In the course of the last few years, some scriptors, eschewing the abstract representation of the 2nd person singular pronoun *ou* that occurs as three variants /u/, /uw/ and /w/, have chosen to provide a special spelling for the latter variant. As is the case for the pronouns *mwen, li*, and *nou, ou* appears in a 'short' form in the context of a vowel. Compare: /w ap rãse/ 'you're talking nonsense', /avɛw/ 'with you', /liv u/ 'your book', /l ap bat u/ 'she's going to beat you'. Because *ou* does not have, strictly speaking, an elided form, it is argued that in fact /w/ is equivalent to the elided form of the other personal pronouns. Just as one would write *avè l*, one should write *w* whenever one 'thinks' of the short form. Thus /w ap rãse/ and /avɛw/ should be represented as *w ap ranse* and *avè w*, respectively, in contrast to *liv ou* and *l ap bat ou*.

1. **Elision in other forms**. Concrete representations are also preferred in the other cases of elision: loss of the final vowel in modal verbs and elision of the vowel in monosyllabic function words, such as the verb marker *te* (past, anterior) and the relative pronoun *ki*. In the case of *te,* elision is obligatory before the verb markers *ap* 'progressive, definite future' and *a* 'indefinite future'. In the latter case, there is agglutination: *ta*. In the case of modal verbs like *fin(i)* and *sot(i)* 'to have just', *vin(i)*, 'to become', *konn(en)* 'habitual', *ka(p) (ab)* 'to be able to', the form showing elision is obligatory. Strictly speaking, there is no elision since only these short forms occur when these verbs function as modals.
2. **Nasalization**. The nasalization of *ba* 'to give' before pronouns containing nasal vowels is usually indicated: *ban mwen* vs. *ba li*.

4.6 Demarcation of Word Boundaries

The aspect of HC spelling that is least standardized is the demarcation of word boundaries. As in English, the most productive means for lexical enrichment in HC is compounding. As we have seen, this is a thorny issue even for a well-standardized language like English. The treatment of the interrogative pronouns and adverbs of HC formed with the constituent *ki* is particularly revealing. The governmental recommendations accompanying the document promulgating the official orthography of HC suggested writing as a single unit *kilès* 'which', presumably because *lès* does not occur independently, but as two-word phrases other interrogatives whose second element occurs with an autonomous meaning: *ki jan* 'how' (*jan* = manner), *ki moun* 'who' (*moun* = person), *ki lè* 'when, what time' (*lè* = time, hour). Compound cardinal numbers are written as single units (*disèt* '17', *swasantdouz* '72'), as are combinations of numbers and certain nouns where there occurs a variant form of the number containing a final consonant not found in the isolated form (see Section 4.4.2).

As one might suspect, practice in this area varies greatly among scriptors. A knowledge of French would prompt them to isolate morphemes whose meaning can be derived from French. For example, *àlèkile* 'currently, at present' is derived from French *à l'heure qu'il est* 'at present; literally, at the hour that it is [now]', but the ordinary speaker, even a bilingual one, is not conscious of the etymological meaning any more than a French speaker analyzes *aujourd'hui* 'today', etymologically 'at the day of today', into its constituent morphemes: *au + jour + de + hui*. What complicates matters is that many idiomatic compound words show great variation in pronunciation and, ultimately, in spelling, for example, 'whatever, whichever, any old, etc.', formed on the French etymon *quel qu'il en soit* appears as *kèlkanswa, kèlkelanswa, kèlkilanswa, kèlswa*, to list only half of the attested variants.

Summary

HC has progressed considerably on the road to standardization. As I will discuss in detail in Chapter 11, first, a geographical and social variety has been selected early in the process of providing the language with a relatively uniform norm. Second, as detailed in this chapter, three systematic, autonomous orthographies were developed, one of which – that of the IPN – though not substantially different from its predecessor, the Faublas-Pressoir spelling, was recognized as official in a rare governmental action in language planning. The problem of the representation of elided and reduced forms seems to progress toward a general consensus: the use of hyphens and apostrophes appears to have been rejected, and idiomatic compound words are represented as single words rather than as a series of morphemes reflecting French etyma.

In the context of literacy programs in particular, many of the discussions about spelling and the elaboration of orthographies for languages that have not been previously endowed with a standardized spelling start from the wrong premises about the nature of writing and the objectives of reducing language to writing. As the French creolist Marie-Christine Hazaël-Massieux, who has authored a detailed discussion of these questions (1993: 84), reminds us:

> *N'oublions pas que généralement l'écriture ne vise pas à donner des indications pour une prononciation, mais à permettre d'identifier des mots pour comprendre le sens d'un texte ...*

> Let us not forget that in general writing does not aim to provide indications for a particular pronunciation, but to allow the identification of words in order to understand a text ...

Concerning the issue of the representation of the elision of personal pronouns in Guadeloupean Creole, which is more variable than in HC, she points out that the advantage of a unitary (abstract) representation is that it facilitates the identification of the particular pronoun. In the reading aloud of texts, individual readers are free to select a particular variant to affect the desired stylistic. This implies a rigorous normalization according to which the personal pronouns of HC would also be represented in their full form. At the very least, Hazaël-Massieux's view should be heeded by those scriptors who have departed from a twenty-year-old practice of writing the 2nd person pronoun as *ou* in all environments, no matter how readers might choose to pronounce it in particular contexts.

One feature of the IPN spelling that does merit re-examination is the decision to change the representation of /e/ from *é* to *e*. As I have argued, this choice renders the transition to French spelling difficult within the framework of the educational reform program, whose objectives were, on the one hand, to valorize the vernacular and facilitate the acquisition of learning skills and, on the other hand, to provide monolingual children access to the still-prestigious language: French. However, such language-planning issues are always complex and problematic, to paraphrase the Haitian proverb that warns of the difficulty of leading complex endeavors to a successful resolution: *Mennen koulèv lekòl se pa anyen, se fè l chita sou tab ki tout!* 'To get the snake to school is quite a feat but the real accomplishment is to make it sit up straight on the school bench!' In other words, to provide a systematic orthography for HC is necessary but not sufficient. There remains the task of normalizing the written form of the language. Still, as Yves Dejean (1974) aptly points out, the priority in Haiti is to teach monolingual speakers – adults and children – to read and write so that they can more fully participate in the economic, social, and political spheres. In the face of this challenge, the minor issues that remain in the use of IPN spelling lose their urgency. In the absence of any institutions that can guide insightful and reasonable policies for the normalization of the writing system, it is best to let an informal – concrete rather than abstract – normalization run its course. In other words, it is best to adopt a *laissez faire* rather than a purist attitude toward the representation of variant forms by spelling conventions that respect the autonomy of the exclusive mother tongue of about 90% of the population of Haiti.

Notes

1. Yves Dejean (1980) offers the most detailed discussion concerning the elaboration of writing systems for HC.
2. For an extensive anthology and detailed discussion of early texts in French-based creoles of the Caribbean, see M.-C. Hazaël-Massieux (2008).
3. My translation reflects the approximative pidginized nature of the French original.
4. For a detailed discussion of the linguistic aspects of this text, see G. Hazaël-Massieux (1994), Fattier (1996), Prudent (1989), and especially, M.-C. Hazaël-Massieux (2008).
5. One question that the *Passion* raises is whether, in the early part of the eighteenth century, distinct geographical varieties of French-based creoles had emerged in the Caribbean basin (including Louisiana and Cayenne – present-day French Guiana), or whether there was a relatively uniform variety used in all regions. In addition to features that are found today in HC, this excerpt shows typical features of Lesser Antilles creoles: the progressive verb marker *ka* (as versus HC *ap/pé/apé*) and *tini* 'to have' (as versus HC *gengnen/gen*). Absent from the *Passion* are some other marked Lesser Antillean features such as the future verb *ke* and the pre-posed plural marker *sé* combined with post-posed *la*, e.g., *sé bèf la* 'the cows'.
6. As I pointed out in Chapter 2, the weakening and/or absence of final and post-vocalic *r* was a phonological particularity of vernacular and some regional varieties of French. It was no doubt a phenomenon present in the target speech of the creators of SDC. It happens to be a feature of diaspora varieties, for example, Louisiana French.
7. Still today the syllable nucleus /we/ is found in the vernacular French spoken in Picardy.
8. Except for the 3rd person singular pronoun *li*, derived from French *lui*, all the forms in the text are identical to corresponding French forms (cognates).
9. Note in particular the use of the comparative construction 'more than' expressed with the verb *passé* 'to pass'. Another grammatical feature that is typical of current HC is the topicalization and reduplication of the verb or adjective found in other verses, for example: *c'est charié vous vlé charié* 'you're really joking'.
10. For a detailed discussion of the linguistic features of the *Manuel*, see Fattier (1994).

11. The conventional etymologizing spelling is also found in a post-independence collection of texts published in France in 1852 by a French observer (Gustave d'Alaux 1860). This author, who curiously claimed that Haitian independence had brought an end of the beneficial influence of French rule on the creole and that the latter had become impoverished, is the source for the description of the notable gathering of slaves and the subsequent uprising in the Cape Haitian region that constituted the prelude to the slave revolt. Below is the opening of the reported sacramental oath pronounced by the Vodou priest (*houngan*) and leader of the uprising, Boukman.

   Bon Dié qui fait soleil, qui clairé nous en haut,
   Qui soulévé la mer, qui fait grondé l'orage,
   Bon Dié la, zot tendé? Caché dans youn nuage,
   Est là qui gadé nous, li vouai tout ça blancs faits!

   God who made the sun, who provides us with light from above,
   Who makes the sea rise, who makes the storm rumble.
   That God, do you hear? Hidden in a cloud,
   He is there who watches us; he sees what the Whites do [cruelties]!

   Noteworthy in this excerpt are the accurate representations of the indefinite determiner *youn* (*yon* in the current official orthography) and the absence of the post-vocalic *r* in *gadé*. Finally, there are passages in SDC in Victor Hugo's novel *Bug-Jargal* (1826 [1985]), which is set during the slave revolt. The following brief excerpt shows that Hugo's source provided both accurate and erroneous renditions of the pronunciation.

   Zoté (*sic*) /zɔt/ coné /konẽ/ bon Giu /dʒe/; ce /se/ li mo fe zoté voer. Blan touyé li, touyé blan yo toute.
   'You know God, it is he that I am making you see. The Whites killed him, kill all the Whites.'

12. For a discussion and examples of these spellings, see Pompilus (1973).
13. Berry is also the author of *Introductory Exercices in Haitian Creole*. Philadelphia: American Friends Service Committee, 1962. His orthographical system starts with a bi-unique phonemically based notation to which are added forty-four 'Teacher Rules' that render HC words closer to their French cognates. For a detailed critique of Berry's orthographic system, see Dejean (1976).
14. Pompilus (1973) also proposed an etymological spelling. His attempt, characterized as a compromise between etymological spellings and the autonomous phonologically based systems described in Section 4.4, is merely suggestive and mentions only a few conventions, for example, the use of *c* for /k/ in medial and final position and of the digraph *oi* for /wa/.
15. In creating a written standard, proponents of maximal differentiation create neologisms that differ as much as possible from French equivalents. For example, for the word *jansiv* 'gums' (French *gencives*) they propose the neologism *jenndan* (French *gaine des dents*, literally, 'sheath of the teeth').

16. Underlying McConnell's original orthography is not only strict adherence to bi-uniqueness but also the exclusion of digraphs. Originally, he had proposed *h* for /ʃ/. The Haitian educator F. Lofficial (1979) goes further in eliminating digraphs. He proposes the use of *w* or *ü* for /u/, *h* or *c* for /ʃ/, as well as *î* for what he recognizes as the nasalized variant of *i*, in *lign* [lĩy] 'line'. Curiously, he would use *w* for both /u/ and /w/: *bwt* /but/ 'end', *bwat* /bwat/ 'box'. He claims, without providing empirical evidence, that orthographic systems using monographs are more easily learned. For other proposals for radical rejection of digraphs, see Churchill (1957).

17. Original quote: 'Cet alphabet McConnell-Laubach serait parfait, même avec l'accent circonflexe, si on l'employait avec les sauvages de l'Australie ou de quelque point perdu. Il est mis en échec par le fait que le créole est une langue mixte, dans un pays à traditions françaises.'

18. These governmental agencies launched during the Duvalier regime were involved in rural community development and literacy training that included a heavy pro-regime propaganda apparatus. Beginning in 1966, they published a monthly mimeographed newsletter, *Solèy leve* 'rising sun', that used HC exclusively and had adopted the Faublas-Pressoir orthography. In 1976, the publication of *Solèy leve* was taken over by a newly created body, GREAL (Groupe de recherches et d'expérimentation en alphabétisation), associated with the Institut pédagogique national and supported by a French educational mission. It launched a modification of the Faublas-Pressoir orthography that is described below (Section 4.4.3). See Section 12.5.1 for a discussion of literacy programs in Haiti.

19. A 17-page booklet, undated but presumably published in the late 1940s or early 1950s, illustrates an etymological spelling designed expressly to facilitate the transition to French spelling. That orthography very much resembles the AGECOP proposal. Interestingly, it adopts a somewhat purist tone in favoring the use of front rounded vowels and some post-vocalic /r/'s (*lumiè* 'light', *eur* 'hour'): 'Utiliser eur ... sans adopter la déformation: lè, pour l'heure (Use eur ... without adopting the corruption: lè for l'heure)'[i.e., spelling 'when' *leur* not *lè*].

20. These changes were implemented gradually in the context of rural development and literacy programs in the region of Côtes-de-Fer (in Southern Haiti) by GREAL and disseminated through the periodical *Solèy leve*. The major initial change was the use of *e* for /e/ and the use of the grave accent to distinguish sequences of vowel + /n/ from nasal vowels in digraphs representing the latter vowels: *pàn* /pan/ 'breakdown', *vìn* /vin/ 'to come', *mòn* /mòn/ 'hill'. Also, the digraph *in* was retained to represent /ẽ/ instead of the IPN *en*, as was *r* before rounded vowels: *rouj* instead of the IPN *wouj*.

21. Boldface indicates changes from the McConnell-Laubach system and an * changes from the Faublas-Pressoir orthography.

22. The use of the apostrophe for short forms of the personal pronouns has been retained in the page devoted to HC texts in the weekly periodical *Haïti en Marche*, published in Miami and in Port-au-Prince. As shown below, it is

used when pronouns occur before the predicate. When short forms of pronouns occur in post-position, as objects, they are linked to the preceding word with a hyphen. The apostrophe is also used for the short forms of other function words, e.g., the relative pronoun *ki* and the modal verb *pou*. The hyphen is also used between the definite determiner and the preceding word.

> *Yo **fè-m** konnen se toulejou yo wè, swa youn machann lèt ki vin touche oun lajan li pa janm ka touche, osnon youn machann chabon **k'ape fè** eskandal, k'ape fè youn lòbèy pou oun kapay yo **dwe-l**. Ou konnen, **teledyòl-la ap** fonksyone. Gen flannè sou galri **kwafè-a** ki pa **p'fè** anyen, se chomè yo ye, yo la toutlasent jounen, yo wè, yo konnen tout sa **k'ap** pase. Devenn pou machann **chabon-an**, Madan Prevo pa te la lè **sa-a**, se li ki **pratik-la**, machann chabon-an jwenn ak Bòs Prevo, se sa l'bliye li pa **di-l**.*

They informed me that it's every day that they see either a milk vendor who comes to collect some money that she never received, or a charcoal vendor who is creating a scene for a large straw bag they owe her. You know that the rumor mill is functioning. There are loafers on the barber's porch who aren't doing anything, they are there all blessed day, they see, they know everything that takes place. Unfortunately for the charcoal vendor Ms. Prévos wasn't there at that time, she's the one who is the customer, the charcoal vendor found Mr. Prévos, the artisan, that's what she forgot that she didn't tell him.

23. Most scriptors have abandoned the use of hyphens and apostrophes, except those who contribute to the HC page of *Haïti en Marche*.

5 The Structure of the Haitian Creole Lexicon

In this chapter, I will describe the structure of HC lexical items and show how new words are created to enable speakers to deal with the various uses to which the language is put.

5.1 The Problem of the Definition of the Word

The lexicon of a language is made up of **words**, and one assesses its lexical richness in terms of the number of words it contains. In fact, it is very difficult in some languages, including HC, to identify individual words in fluid speech. A word is generally defined as that part of a written string delimited by spaces. However, this criterion is inoperative in speech. Indeed, we have seen that one of the problems in the elaboration of a writing system for HC was the delimitation of words.

There are several problems in the delimitation of words. First, some languages do not have phonetic features that delimit what the layman considered a word. In English, for example, phrases are distinguished from words by differences in stress and intonation. Compare, for example, the following pairs: *the white house* 'any house that is white' versus *the White House* 'the residence of the president of the United States'; *the night-rate* vs. *the nitrate*. In the first pair, the words are demarcated by different stress patterns; in the second, by differences in the pronunciation of the consonants /t/ and /r/. These phonetic features do not operate the same way in HC; for example, the word *malanga* 'taro' and the two-word construction *mayi moulen* 'cornmeal' have the same stress pattern. As is the case for French, there are no stress differences within isolated words. Generally, stress falls on the last syllable of a word or group of words, such as compounds and short phrases. However, in noun phrases containing a post-posed determiner consisting of a full syllable, the stress still falls on the last syllable of the noun, not on the post-posed determiner: *malanga, malanga a*.

A second problem in the identification of individual words is that it is difficult to distinguish between cases of **homophony** and **polysemy**. Homophones

140   *The Structure of the Haitian Creole Lexicon*

are words with different meanings that are pronounced alike: *fair*, adjective (*she's fair*) vs. *fair*, noun (*she went to the county fair*), and *fare*, noun (*she paid the fare and boarded the bus*). In a dictionary, homophones are listed as separate entries.[1] A polysemous word is one that has a wide range of meanings, and its various senses would be listed under the same entry. Consider the verb *to break*; each of the following examples reflects a different meaning, yet we would still agree that all should be listed under the same entry for the verb *to break*: *He broke his back by falling down the stairs*, *He broke her heart*, *Can you break this twenty-dollar bill?*, *The thick bushes broke her fall*. Sometimes it is difficult to decide whether to classify words as homophones or polysemes. For instance, with regard to the following sentences, not all English speakers would agree that they exemplify the same verb *to join*: *This bridge joins two islands*, *John joins our club*. The difficulty in distinguishing between homophones and polysemous words explains why lexicographers prefer to call the items listed in dictionaries **entries** rather than words. HC presents analogous problems. In the following sentences, the phonological sequences *kou* represents four homophones: *Li koupe* **kou** *poul la* 'He cut the chicken's **neck**'; *Yo ba l de* **kou** *d baton* 'They hit him twice [with two **blows**] with a stick'; ***Kou*** *ou fini, ou mèt ale* '**When** you've finished, you may go'; *Li lèd* **kou** *koukou douvan jou* 'He's as ugly **as** a cuckoo at dawn'. However, we would probably want to group the instances of *kou* in the two following sentences as two senses of the same word: *Kounye a se* **kou** *mwen* 'Now it's my **turn**'; *Manje a desann nan vant li yon sèl kou* 'The food went down his stomach in one **swallow**'.

A third problem is that words defined as strings of letters between blank spaces vary greatly in their structure. Some words contain a single meaningful element, a **morpheme**, others are combinations of several morphemes, for example, *ball* vs. *basketball*; *to play softball* vs. a *soft ball*.

5.2   Morphemes and Lexemes

It is more useful to describe the units of a lexicon in terms of morphemes, defined as the smallest meaningful units of a language with relatively stable form, and **lexemes**, syntactic units with relatively cohesive meaning. Lexemes may be composed of a single morpheme, as in *iron*, or of several, as in *basketball* or *indivisibility*.

5.2.1   Types of lexemes

There are three types of lexemes: (1) simple lexemes, (2) compound lexemes, and (3) idioms. Simple lexemes contain a single morpheme; the following HC sentence has nine simple lexemes: *Li bwè yon grenn pou l pa fè pitit* 'She took a pill so as not to have children'. On the other hand, *dwèt jouda* 'index finger' and *madichonnen* 'to curse' are compound lexemes. Each contains two morphemes: *dwèt* 'finger' + *jouda* 'Judas' (the apostle who betrayed Jesus by presumably pointing him out to his enemies with his index finger) and *madichon* 'curse' + *en* 'verb-forming suffix', respectively. These two compound lexemes differ from each other in that the latter is composed of two bound morphemes and the former of a combination of two free morphemes; it is a **compound** (see below). Idioms are phrase-length lexemes whose meanings differ from that of their constituent parts. For example, in English the expression *to look a gift horse in the mouth* is an idiom meaning 'one should not be choosy about gifts'. It is impossible to derive the total meaning of this idiom from that of its individual constituents. In a sense, compounds resemble idioms since, usually, their total meaning is not the sum of the meaning of their individual constituents, as is the case for HC *dwèt jouda*. In the English sentence *I can't come over tonight but I'll take a rain check*, that is, *I'll do it some other time if you invite me again*, the meaning of the compound *rain check* is only remotely related to that of its two constituents *rain* and *check*.

5.2.2 Types of morphemes

Morphemes may be classified on the basis of several criteria. The first criterion is the role they play in a language: **content** versus **functional** morphemes. Content morphemes refer to some thing or concept, whereas functional morphemes are semantically empty, as it were, and carry mainly grammatical meaning. Compare the following Spanish, French, English, and HC examples that bear the same meaning: *hablaran, ils parleront, they'll speak, yo va pale*. In all four languages, the only morphemes that carry a clear-cut meaning are *habl-, parl-, speak*, and *pale*. The other morphemes *-ar, -an*; *ils, -er, -ont*; *they, -'ll*; *yo, va* are **functional**: they express various modalities of the action of speaking (specifically, the future), in the case of Spanish *-ar-*, French *-er-*, English *-'ll*, and HC *va*, or they indicate the **agent** (the initiator of the action, specifically, the 3rd person plural), *-an* and *-ont*, in the case of Spanish and French, respectively; *they* and *yo*, in the case of English and HC, respectively. Note that the indication of the **agent** is marked redundantly in French by the free morpheme *ils* and the bound morpheme *-ont*.[2]

Morphemes may occur independently as **free**, in the case of English *-'ll* or HC *va*, or as **bound**, in the case of French *-ont* in the above examples. Bound functional morphemes such as French *-ont* are also termed

inflectional. However, there are also bound content morphemes. These are **derivational** affixes (prefixes or suffixes). For example, in HC the addition of the suffix *-en* to the noun *madichon* 'curse' converts it to the corresponding verb *madichonnen* 'to curse'. The affixation of the suffix *-mann*, which denotes an agent, to the noun *kawoutchou* 'tire' produces the noun, *kowoutchoumann* 'tire repairman'. Unlike English, French, or Spanish, HC does not have bound functional morphemes; all functional morphemes are free forms. On the other hand, it does possess bound derivational morphemes that have some semantic content.

5.2.3 Identification of morphemes

Some morphemes occur with variable phonological forms; for example, in English the plural of nouns is pronounced either /z/ (*dogs*), /s/ (*cats*), or /əz/ (*horses*), depending on the nature of the last phoneme of the noun (see Chapter 2). Generally, variation is patterned and affects large sets of morphemes; for example, in English, vowel quality is determined by stress level. The unstressed vowel is usually the central vowel /ə/; compare the pronunciation of *you* in *Did you?* (/uʷ/) versus *Did you* /ə/ *do it?* That central vowel is usually written as *a* in eye dialect:[3] *didja* (did you), *gonna* (going to). In HC, however, variation in the form of morphemes is fairly idiosyncratic, affecting individual morphemes or small sets of related morphemes. One example of the latter is the alternation between the full and elided form of personal pronouns (see Chapter 3). To be grouped under a single morpheme, variant forms must show some phonetic similarity. For example, in HC one would group together the following sets of variant forms *ak*, *avèk*, and *avè* 'with'; *dis* 'ten' and *diz*, occurring in *dizan* 'ten years'; *lè* 'hour' (*ki lè*) 'what time' and *è* occurring in *inè* 'one o'clock', *dezè* 'two o'clock', and *katrè* 'four o'clock'.

5.2.4 Identification of lexemes

Two criteria may be used to determine whether a lexeme can be divided into constituent lexemes or whether it forms an indivisible whole: **syntactic separability** and **semantic cohesion**. Unless syntactic permutations can be effected or other material inserted within a lexeme without any change in meaning, that lexeme is an indivisible whole. For example, with regard to syntactic separability, in English one may say *I pulled off the tape* or *I pulled the tape off*; consequently, *to pull off* can be segmented into two lexemes *to pull* and *off*. In HC, *fòkseli* 'cornmeal' constitutes a single lexeme because no material may be inserted within it without modifying the meaning: *fòk se nou* means 'it must be us', *fòk nou ale* means 'we must go'; the meaning of these two combinations bears no similarity to *fòkseli*.[4]

In the application of the criterion of semantic cohesion, a complex lexeme whose meaning parallels that of simple lexemes may be assumed to constitute an indivisible whole: *bout digo* 'sickle' parallels such simple lexemes as *manchèt* 'machete' or *wou* 'hoe', as, for example, in *li pran yon bout digo (yon manchèt)* 'she takes a sickle (a machete)'. It contrasts with the homophonous *bout digo* 'a piece of indigo', in which the homonym *bout* 'piece' has a different meaning and parallels other quantifiers: *yon bout digo* 'a piece of indigo', *anpil digo* 'a lot of indigo'. Consequently, *bout digo* 'sickle' is analyzed as a single lexeme: a compound word.

5.2.5 Identification of lexical material and spelling

The question of the identification of lexemes bears on some of the issues I discussed with regard to spelling in Chapter 4. One of the aspects of HC orthography that has not yet received sufficient attention is how to treat words that appear to be composed of several lexemes, as is the case of *poukisa* 'why': *pou ki sa* 'for + interrogative maker + that'. Because one variant of this word is *pouki sa* and another *pouki*, should not the spelling reflect the existence of the variant, that is, be *pouki sa*?

For HC, it is also important that decisions about delimitation of lexemes be made on the basis of autonomous structural facts about the language itself, not on the basis of etymology. For example, as was pointed out in Chapter 4, although *alèkilè* 'currently, at present' is derived from the French *à l'heure qu'il est* 'literally, at the hour that it is [now]', the ordinary HC speaker, even a bilingual one, is not conscious of its etymological meaning any more than a French speaker analyzes *aujourd'hui* 'today' (etymologically 'at the day of today') into its constituent morphemes: *au, jour, de, hui*. Exceptional cases involve some of the cardinal numbers that, although they can be segmented into distinct lexemes, are written as simplexes, e.g., *diznèvan (dis + nèf + an)*, because their constituents appear in a different phonological form from their isolation one.

5.3 Creative Processes in the HC Lexicon

In all living natural languages, the lexicon is in constant flux, because, more than any other aspect of language, it reflects changes in culture, society, and technology. As certain cultural practices are given up and certain techniques, practices, and artifacts, as well as beliefs, become obsolete, the lexemes that denote them fade from general knowledge. On the other hand, as cultural and technological innovations arise and spread, new lexemes are needed to refer to them. In the course of the last five decades, the use of HC has extended to new areas: education, administration, rural development, and family planning. For HC to be used in these newly acquired domains of language use, new terms have had to be coined from existing processes in HC or borrowed from French or other languages, notably English and Spanish. In addition, languages undergo normal lexical renewal as established terms get used up, as it were, either because they lose their expressive force or because they no longer remain fashionable. An example is the current replacement in US English of *goodbye* by *have a nice day* or *have a good one*.

The lexicon of a language may be expanded in two ways: existing morphemes may be combined to yield novel lexemes or morphemes may be 'borrowed' from other languages. Words taken from other languages are termed **loanwords**, despite the fact that they are rarely given back to the 'lending' language. Borrowed morphemes or lexemes may also be combined with items from the native stock. Linguistic communities differ with regard to the freedom with which speakers may form new lexemes. These differences do not reflect inherent structural features of particular languages but the attitude of speakers and the degree to which formally established institutions control the development of the lexicon. For example, Americans freely coin new terms, and there are no governmental or other agencies that assume an official function in the development of the lexicon. In France and in Quebec Province, on the other hand, laws have been passed giving government agencies or other bodies certain powers in charting the course of lexical development. For example, in the Province of Quebec, the Office de la Langue Française is charged with proposing appropriate terminology; in France business firms that use foreign terms in public announcements may be subject to fines. In contrast, in Haiti, the government assumes a low profile in linguistic matters. I have shown in Chapter 4 that its only official act was to rule in favor of one of the alternative systematic spellings put forward by individuals or groups. There are no government or other official agencies involved in the management of lexical development. In this section, I distinguish between internal and external sources for new lexical items. Internal sources are the processes of derivation, compounding, and onomatopoeia; external sources consist of borrowing.

5.3.1 Derivation

Derivation involves the creation of new lexemes by combining bound content morphemes with free content morphemes. Content (derivational) bound morphemes (prefixes and suffixes) differ from functional (inflectional) bound morphemes in that they produce new combinations whose meaning and grammatical function may differ from that of the free content morpheme (base) to which they are affixed. For example, in English the affixation of the inflectional morpheme 'plural' does not change the basic meaning and function of the noun to which that suffix is attached: the plural form *boys* functions syntactically very much like the corresponding singular form. However, the addition of the suffix *-al* to the noun *nation*, for example, produces an adjective meaning 'pertaining to a nation'. In HC, there are a sizeable number of relatively productive derivational morphemes (**affixes**).

For those scholars who considered them as evolved from rudimentary contact languages, pidgins and creole languages have restricted derivational capabilities:

> ... in the European-based pidgins and creoles, derivational affixes and suffixes seem to have lost their original conceptual content and become fossilized. Obviously, there are other devices for word formation [e.g. periphrases] ... but what cannot be generated very successfully by the combination of concrete words are abstract terms, in which it is notorious that pidgins and creoles are deficient. (Whinnom 1971: 109)

As will be shown in this section, to the contrary, HC does not lack derivational power. Also, with the 30,000 single lexeme entries, 70,000 individual senses, and 35,000 compound lexemes and idioms contained in the most authoritative dictionary for the language (Valdman *et al.* 2007), HC is not lacking in abstract terms. Furthermore, as I argue in Chapter 13, it is clear that HC was generated without a passage through a pidgin stage.

When an affix is productive, speakers can readily create new lexemes. In addition, the meaning of these lexemes generally can be derived from that of the base and from that carried by a particular affix. In other words, the resulting complex lexemes are semantically transparent. For example, in the English lexemes *deregulate* and *de-emphasize*, the prefix *de* carries an **inversive** meaning, and the complex lexeme denotes an action that is the opposite of that of the base morpheme: *deregulate* means the contrary of 'to regulate'. Likewise, *de-emphasize* means 'not to emphasize'. However, there are cases where the complex lexemes formed by the affixation of derivational bound morphemes are semantically opaque. Even though an affix can be readily identified, it no longer carries its base meaning. For example, in English *to depose* 'to remove from a position of power' cannot be claimed to be the straightforward inversive of *to pose* 'to cause to sit or stand in a particular position'. The absence of a clear semantic relationship is even more pronounced in the pair *to demean/to mean*. These two compound lexemes are best analyzed as simple lexemes and the *de* as an integral constituent part and not a prefix. As will be seen below, the corresponding HC prefix *de-* poses the same problems.

In a description of the derivational potential of HC, it is important to distinguish between the lexical stock inherited from French, including nonstandard varieties of the language, its major lexical source (see Chapter 6), and the native stock, i.e., those words newly created since the emergence of the language. For example, the lexeme *planche* 'floor' appears on the surface to be derived from *planch* 'board, plank' and a suffix *-e*. However, it is clearly inherited from the French cognates *plancher* and *planche*, both with the same meaning. In addition, the putative suffix *-e* is totally opaque (unlike the verb-forming suffix *-e* mentioned below). Speakers of HC do not interpret *planche* as something necessarily composed of planks. Accordingly, there is no justification to treat this word as anything but a simple lexeme. On the other hand, the verb *klete*[5] 'to open with a key', derived from *kle* 'key' (French *clef*) and the verb-forming suffix *-e*, offers a clear-cut example of the operation of a lexical process that contributes to the expansion of HC's native stock.

However, any attempt to distinguish between the inherited stock of HC and newly created lexemes (**neologisms**) presents several difficulties. For instance, one must assess the degree of freedom individual speakers have to create new lexemes by combining affixes and lexical bases. Also, a significant part of the lexical stock of HC is derived not from Standard French but from other varieties. Thus, the consultation of current dictionaries of French must be supplemented by reference to those that provide etymological sources, the *FEW* and the *TLF*,[6] as well as lexical inventories of regional varieties of the language, including those outside of France. For example, *demare* 'to untie', derived from *mare* 'to tie', although it does not occur with that sense in Standard French, is attested widely in regional varieties, including those of Louisiana (Valdman *et al.* 2010) and Réunion (Chaudenson 1974). Opinions vary widely about the stock of productive affixes of HC. R. A. Hall (1953) lists more than seventy of them, whereas Suzanne Sylvain (1936) recognizes only five. Hall's estimation is grossly exaggerated because many of the affixes he posits are dubious, for example, the prefix *sis-* 'sus-' in *sispann* 'to suspend' (from *pann* 'to hang') and *pro-* 'pre-' in *propoze* 'to propose' (from *poze* 'to put'). Both of these lexemes are clearly derived from French cognates with the same meaning: *suspendre* and *proposer*. In fact, it is doubtful from a semantic perspective that even the French cognates are complex rather than simple lexemes. The discussion of the derivational system of HC proposed below reflects a position intermediate between those of these two scholars.

In the remaining part of this section, I list the various affixes I recognize, and I illustrate each one with neologisms, that is, combinations not attested in Standard French or other varieties of French.[7] HC neologisms are defined in regard to their relationship to the lexical stock inherited from French or other languages. There are three types of neologisms: (1) the combination of an affix to a new base: *wanga* 'Vodou charm' + agentive *-tè* → *wangatè* 'someone who prepares or devises such charms'; *kawoutchou* 'tire' + agentive *-mann* → *kawoutchoumann* 'tire repairman'; (2) the novel combination of an affix with a pre-existing base: *pasyante* 'to wait patiently' + inversive *de-* → *depasyante* 'to become impatient' (such a combination does not exist in French, in which nonetheless both the prefix and the base occur); (3) the derivative shows semantic drift with respect to the corresponding etymological form: *bwa* 'woods' + *(z) e* → *bwaze* 'to escape into the woods' (the French corresponding form *boiser*, built on the base *bois-*, means 'to plant trees'). It is important to bear in mind that, just as there are homophonous lexemes, there are homophonous affixes; for example, I will show below that there are several prefixes realized as *de-*. I list suffixes first and the shorter set of prefixes second. Suffixes will be ordered with regard to the grammatical class of the output of the derivational process: noun-forming, verb-forming, and adjective-forming.

5.3.1.1 Noun-forming suffixes

1. Multifunctionality or deverbal nouns with zero suffix. One of the striking features of the HC lexicon involves the use of the same content morpheme with different syntactic functions. This derivational process also occurs in English, for example, the shift of the verb *to run* to nominal functions: *I went for a run*. This process may be interpreted as either the conversion of one word-form class into another, for example, a verb used as a noun, that is, **multifunctionality**, or the addition of a 'zero', or null, suffix to verbs. In HC, multifunctionality usually takes the form of using verb bases as nouns. Nouns formed by this process are called **deverbal** nouns, i.e., nouns derived from a verb base. For example, one could convert the HC verb *mòde* 'to bite' to a noun, *Mòde a fè m mal* 'The bite hurt me'. Verbs that may undergo this process are transitive verbs that can also be used intransitively, that is, without a direct object: *chen an mòde vole a* 'the dog bit the thief', *chat kap mòde* 'cats may bite'. Verbs that may be used only transitively, such as *achte* 'to buy', or that take both a direct and an indirect object, such as *bay* 'to give' or *voye* 'to send', cannot be converted to nouns. Thus, one could not say **m fè yon ti achte* 'I did a little buying' or *Voye li a te bèl 'Her sending something was beautiful'. Two other groups of verbs to which conversion cannot be applied include those that are derived from nouns (**denominal** verbs) by the adjunction of the suffix -e/-en, for example, *kariyonnen* 'to chime, to ring', derived from the noun *kariyon* 'chime', and those that yield deverbals by the adjunction of the suffix -ay. For example, *fri* 'to fry', from which *fritay* 'fried food' is derived, cannot be converted to a noun. One cannot say **yon fri* 'a fried food'. Although it does end in -en, the verb *goumen* 'to fight' is not a denominal formed on a hypothetical **goum,* but a simple lexeme. Nouns produced by conversion behave like other nouns in most respects. Notably, they may be combined with the various determiners and they assume all the syntactic functions of that word class: for example, *pwoche* 'to draw near', *li fè yon ti pwoche* 'he drew near progressively'; *danse* 'to dance', *danse a te bèl anpil* 'the way they danced was very beautiful'; *rive* 'to arrive'; *m pa wè ou depi rive ou a* 'I haven't seen you since your arrival'.

Multifunctionality is also a feature of certain lexemes that behave like adjectives in that they may occur as predicates of sentences, although they never enter into attributive constructions, as do true adjectives like *bèl* 'beautiful': *Li bèl* 'She's pretty' and *Se yon bèl chat* 'It's a beautiful cat'. These lexemes include *swèf* 'thirst, thirsty' and *grangou* 'hunger, hungry', which function as both nouns and predicates: *Grangou touye m* 'Hunger is killing me', *M grangou* 'I'm hungry'.

Apart from a small group of forms that, like their French cognates, function as attributes and occur before the noun they modify (*bèl* 'beautiful', *gwo* 'big', *ti* 'small', etc.), in HC it is difficult to draw a sharp line between adjectives and verbs (see Chapter 7). Verbs may assume adjectival functions, namely, in predicative as well as attributive constructions, for example: *bale* 'to sweep', *lakou a bale* 'the yard is swept' (compared to the full-fledged adjective *pwòp*: *lakou a pwòp* 'the yard is clean'); *glise* 'to slide, to slip', *yon chimen glise* 'a slippery road'; *konnen* 'to know', *yon pitit konnen* 'a sly child'.

While conversion usually operates unidirectionally, from verbs to deverbal nouns and adjectives, there are some indeterminate cases. For example, *pwòpte* may function as noun, verb, and adjective: *Ki kalite pwòpte sa a ye la?* 'What kind of cleaning is this?'; *Fòk nou siveye pwòpte timoun yo* 'We have to control the cleanliness of the children'; *Fòk ou pwòpte kay la* 'You have to clean the house'; *Plat la pwòpte deja* 'The plate has already been cleaned'. Note that in its attributive role *pwòpte* contrasts with *pwòp*. The latter, unlike *pwòpte*, does not necessarily have a passive meaning. This fact supports the directionality of verb → adjective in this type of conversion. However, no directionality can be postulated between the nominal and verbal usage. All these facts support the interpretation of these lexical relations in terms of a general process, conversion, rather than the adjunction of a zero suffix.

2. -è/-èz. This agentive suffix is relatively productive and forms derivatives describing a person habitually involved in the action denoted by the base noun; *-è* refers to a man and *-èz* to a woman: *djòl* 'mouth' (of animals, pejorative for humans) → *djòlè/djòlèz* 'talker'; *eskandal* 'uproar' → *eskandelè/-èz* 'rowdy person'; *rans* 'nonsense, joke'→ *ransè/-èz* 'joker'; *woulib* 'free ride'→ *woulibè/-èz* 'someone who takes advantage of others'. In the pair *lang* 'tongue' → *landjzè/-èz* 'gossip', the final consonant of the base changes. In the case of *piyay/piyaj* 'looting, bargain', the derived lexeme is formed on the variant ending in *-j*: *piyajè/-èz* 'looter'.

3. -adò/-adòl. This deverbal and de-adjectival agentive suffix originates in Spanish loanwords transmitted to HC by the intermediary of contacts with the Dominican Republic: *babye* 'to complain' → *babyadò* 'chronic complainer'; *fouye* 'to harass with questions' → *fouyadò* 'nosy, busybody'; *mize* 'to dawdle' → *mizadò* 'dawdler, idler, slowpoke'. *Chichadò* 'miser' is derived from the adjective *chich* 'miserly'.

4. -mann. This other agentive suffix has its source in English *man* that appears in loanwords: *fòmann* 'foreman', *bamann* 'bartender', and *watchmann* 'watchman'. It is adjoined to noun bases to form novel derivatives denoting an agent, none of which are English loanwords: *aza/daza* 'chance' → *azamann/dazamann* 'gambler'; *batri* 'percussion' → *batrimann* 'drummer'; *gwòg* 'drink' → *gwògmann* 'drunkard'; *bolèt* 'lottery' → *bolètmann* 'lottery operator'; *kad* 'frame' → *kadmann* 'maker of frames'; *djaz* 'band' → *djazmann* 'musician in a band'; *douko* 'metal paint' → *doukomann* 'painter in a body shop'. *Dasomann* 'gatecrasher' is based on the second part of the compound *pran daso* 'to gatecrash'. *Pakèmann* 'someone who memorizes things' starts from the expression *pa kè* 'by heart'.

5. -ay/-aj (a). This suffix produces deverbal nouns that express the general meaning 'result of the action' of the verb base to which it is adjoined. It follows that it can only attach to transitive verbs: *brigande* 'to misbehave' → *briganday* 'disorder, carousing'; *kalbende* 'to flatter, deceive' → *kalbenday* 'flattery, deception'; *swenyen* 'to take care of, treat medically' → *swenyaj* 'care, medical treatment'; *parye* 'to bet' → *paryay* 'bet'; *fri* 'to fry' → *fritay* 'fried food'. In some cases, the verbs that yield these derivatives are themselves the result of a derivational process. For example, *swenyen* is derived from the noun *swen* 'care, treatment'. Suffixation usually operates on the verb base if it ends in a consonant, as is the case of *brigande*, for instance (*brigand-e + ay/aj*). In the case of *fritay*, a consonant is inserted to avoid a sequence of two vowels: **friay*. There is a verb *frite* 'to wander around, to loiter' (in the hopes of getting food) but it is semantically unrelated to *fritay*. Excluded are intransitive verbs like *manti* 'to lie' (**mantay). Also, verbs to which this suffix may be adjoined cannot be converted to nouns, that is, there is no derivative **yon parye* matching *paryay* 'bet' *-ay/-aj* **(b)**. This suffix also expresses the meaning 'totality of Xs': *bèt* 'animal' → *betày* 'all the animals'; *kouzen/kouzin* 'cousin' → *kouzinay* 'the totality of cousins'. In the case of the last derivative, it is formed on the noun with feminine reference, *kouzin,* rather than that with masculine reference, *kouzen*. When the base noun ends in a vowel, *r* is inserted before the suffix to avoid a two-vowel sequence: *fanmi* 'family' → *fanmiray* 'all of one's family members'; *zanmi* 'friend' → *zanmiray* 'all of one's friends'. Although *langay* 'mystical language used in Vodou rites' may be similarly derived from *lang* 'language, tongue', it does not fit the semantic pattern of these derived nouns, and it is therefore best analyzed as a simple lexeme, especially with the existence of the French cognate *langage*. This is a simple case of semantic extension.

6. -*syon/-asyon*. This deverbal suffix forms derivatives whose meaning is 'action or result of the action' of the base verb. If the base verb ends in a consonant or a vowel other than *-e*, the suffix allomorph *-syon* or *-asyon* is added directly: *viv* 'to live' → *vivasyon* 'subsistence'. If the verb base ends in *-e*, the vowel is deleted before the adjunction of the suffix: *eklere* 'to provide light, illuminate; enlighten' → *eklerasyon* 'lighting; education'; *panse* 'to think' → *pansayon* 'anxiety'.[8] The semantic link between the verb and its deverbal derivative is more tenuous in *dekoupe* 'to carve' → *dekoupasyon* 'separation wall, screen'; *leve* 'to educate, raise' → *levasyon* 'education'; *pèdi* 'to lose' → *pèdisyon* 'false pregnancy'. In the case of the pair, *deside* 'to decide' → *desidasyon* 'decision', the derivative appears to be a more expressive synonym of the more common *disizyon* 'decision, judgment'.

7. -*ri*. This denominal suffix forms derivatives referring to actions characteristic of the noun base to which it is adjoined. It also conveys a pejorative connotation: *bouzen* 'prostitute, slut' → *bouzendri* 'sluttish behavior'; *brigan* 'thug' → *brigandri* 'thuggish act'; *makak* 'monkey' → *makakri* 'monkeyshines'. Note that *-ri* can only attach directly to stems ending in a consonant. If that condition is not met, a supporting consonant *d* is inserted. This productive suffix must be distinguished from its inherited homonym to which R. A. Hall (1953: 37) assigns the meaning of 'collective', e.g., *lajantri* 'silverware' (collection of silver items), a simple lexeme clearly inherited from French *argenterie* with the same meaning.

8. -te. The de-adjectival suffix is abundantly represented in the lexicon inherited from French, for example, *mechan* 'wicked' → *mechanste* 'wickedness'. But it appears also in such neologisms as *bèl* 'beautiful' → *bèlte* 'beauty'; *brav* 'brave' → *bravte* 'bravery'; *saf* 'gluttonous' → *safte* 'gluttony'; *frekan* 'insolent' → *frekanste* 'insolence'; *mal* 'bad' → *malsite* 'wickedness'. In the case of the last two derivatives, phonemes are inserted prior to the affixation of the suffix.

9. -man. Suffixed to verb bases, -*man* forms deverbals that refer to the result of the action of the base verb, as in: *koze* 'to speak' → *kozman* 'gossip'; *chagrinen* 'to cause sorrow' → *chagrinman* 'sorrow, grief'; *koze* 'to speak, to chat' → *kozman* 'chat'. In *fini* 'to finish, to complete' → *finisman* 'completion', an *s* is inserted between the base and the suffix. The derivative *chagrinman* is related to *chagren*, a noun with more or less the same meaning and to the adjective *chagren* 'sorrowful'.

10. -èt. This suffix is a diminutive added to noun bases that is not particularly productive and where the semantic link between the derivative and the base is seldom transparent: *chouk* 'tree stump' yields five derivatives: *choukèt* 'tree stump used as a stool, support under a woman's hips during childbirth, tooth stump, milepost, short person'. The following are additional derivatives formed with this suffix: *louch* 'ladle' → *louchèt* 'crowbar, hole-digger'; *ponm* 'apple' → *ponmkèt* 'muffin'. In the latter form, the *k* is inserted by analogy with other derivatives that contain this consonant.

11. -zon. The derivatives produced by this relatively rare suffix generally refer to states: *soule* 'to get drunk' → *soulezon* 'drunkenness'; *goumen* 'to fight' → *goumezon* 'fight'.

12. -i/-is. This suffix indicates either partisans of a particular political party or group, or the beliefs and/or behavior of that party or group: *makout* 'thug that served as militia during the Duvalier dictatorships' and, by extension, 'beliefs or behavior of that group' → *makoutis* 'member of that group; state violence, corrupt or lawless rule'; *Divalye* 'Duvalier' → *divalyeris* 'Duvalierist'.

5.3.1.2 Verb-forming suffixes

1. -e/-en. This denominal suffix is the most productive of HC suffixes. Sample derivatives, formed by the adjunction of this suffix, include: *bourik* 'donkey' → *bourike* 'to work like a horse'; *flay* 'missed kick' (in soccer) → *flaye* 'to miss the ball'; *rans* 'nonsense' → *ranse* 'to talk nonsense'.

After bases ending in a nasal vowel, an *n* and the allomorph with the nasal vowel *-en* are affixed: *madichon* 'curse' → *madichonnen* 'to curse', *estasyon* 'station' → *estasyonnen* 'to park'. The allomorph *-en* is also affixed after noun bases ending in a nasal consonant: *makòn/makonn* 'paired items, bunch, group' → *makonnen* 'to tie together, to bunch, to entangle'. In some cases, when the base ends with a vowel, a consonant is inserted; the particular consonant used is not predictable: *kab* 'a dribble' → *kabre* 'to dribble'; *kle* 'key'→ *klete* 'to open with a key'; *bwa* 'wood'→ *bwaze* 'to run away, to run to the woods'. The vitality of this suffix is reflected by the fact that it may be affixed to loanwords, especially those borrowed from English: *djak* 'jack' → *djake* 'to jack up'; *flach* 'flashlight' → *flache* 'to light with a flashlight'; *plòg* 'plug'→ *plòge* 'to plug'; *tep* 'recording tape' → *tepe* 'to tape record'.

2. *-aye*. This suffix produces deverbal verbs that express repetition and continuation that have a negative connotation: *drive* 'to drift' → *drivaye* 'to keep drifting, to hang around in streets'; *trennen* 'to loaf, to lie around' → *trennaye* 'to dawdle, to loiter'. In the case of *wode* 'to prowl'→ *wodaye* 'to keep prowling', its origin is undoubtedly in the regional *rôdailler*, attested in Louisiana French (Valdman et al. 2010).

5.3.1.3 Adverb-forming suffix
The only adverb-forming suffix is *-man*, which occurs widely in lexemes inherited from French and in some neologisms. It is adjoined to adjectives: *angran* 'haughty' → *angranman* 'haughtily'; *banda* 'elegant' → *bandaman* 'elegantly'; *fen* 'fine' → *finman* 'completely, finally'(in this derivation, the noun changes from *fen* to *fin*, perhaps because of the influence of the French cognate *finement* /finmã/). When added to adverbial bases, it serves as an intensifier: *souvan* 'often' → *souvanman* 'really often'; *toujou* 'always' → *toujouman* 'absolutely always'.

5.3.1.4 Miscellaneous suffixes
The following are derivationally related pairs showing virtually unique instances of a particular suffix. In view of the low productivity of these suffixes, the derivatives are best analyzed as simple lexemes: *biyèt* 'lottery ticket' → *biyetèl* 'lottery ticket vendor'; *chik* 'chigger' → *chikata* 'person infested with chiggers'; *pawòl* 'speech' → *pawoli* 'parable, proverb'; *pyan* 'yaws' → *pyannis* 'afflicted with yaws'; *kabouya* 'quarrel' → *kabouyatif* 'quarrelsome'; *vèy/veye* 'watch, vigil'/ *veye* 'to pay attention, watch over' → *veyatif* 'wary, vigilant'; *kout*e 'to listen' → *enkoutan* 'stubborn' → *enkoutab* 'stubborn', that is, 'one who does not listen'; *makout* 'straw bag' → *makouti* 'small straw bag'.

5.3.1.5 Prefixes

There are three productive prefixes in HC, two of which are verb-forming: *de-* and *re-*, and one, *ti-*, noun-forming. The first of these is polysemous. A close analysis of the semantic relationship between the base and the derivative, as well as the word class to which *de-* is attached, suggests that, semantically, it represents, in fact, three semantically different prefixes. An indication of the productive nature of *de-* is that it enters into more than half of the derivatives occurring in Franketienne's *Dézafi* (The Challenge), the first novel written in HC.

1. Inversive *de-*. This prefix is an inversive, that is, it produces derivatives whose meaning is the opposite of the base form: *griji* 'to wrinkle' → *degriji* 'to smooth out wrinkles'; *kore* 'to block' → *dekore* 'to set loose'; *makonnen* 'to tie' → *demakonnen* 'to untie'; *pasyante* 'to be patient' → *depasyante* 'to become impatient'; *plòge* 'to plug in' → *deplòge* 'to unplug'. In the case of *apiye* 'to lean' → *dezapiye* 'to stop leaning', a *z* is inserted to avoid two successive vowels. For *respekte* 'to respect' → *derespekte* 'to insult, show lack of respect', as pointed out by DeGraff (2001: 79) and Damoiseau (1991: 33), the derivative is not, properly speaking, an inversive. The two verbs are not precise opposites of each other (McWhorter 1998). Damoiseau notes that *respekte* refers to a static psychological stage whereas *derespekte* refers to an action.

2. Privative *de-*. This prefix, which produces derivatives many of which yield the meaning 'to take off a part of the body or to inflict injury', is adjoined to many verbs that refer to a part of the body. For example, *desabote* 'to remove the hooves from a horse' is derived from *sabo* 'hoof of a horse'.[9] Starting with *fresi* 'liver', an intermediate non-occurring verb is constructed with the adjunction of the verb-forming suffix *-e*: **fresiye*. The privative prefix *de-* added to this constructed verb yields the derivative *defresiye* 'to disembowel, to beat up'. These derivatives, which involve the derivation of non-occurring bases as an intermediate step, are termed **parasynthetic**, as opposed to **synthetic**, which are derivatives built, at each step, on occurring derivatives, such as *plòg* → *plogé* → *deploge* or *brigan* → *brigande* → *briganday*. Table 5.1 shows the derivational steps in synthetic versus parasynthetic derivation.

In the following derivatives produced by the adjunction of privative *de-*, the meaning of the derivative may be literal or metaphorical: *gagann* 'throat'→ *degagannen* 'to slit the throat'; *mwèl* 'marrow'→ *demwèle* 'to weaken' (i.e., to remove the marrow); *trip* 'intestines'→ *detripe* 'to disembowel'; *vant* 'belly' → *devantre* 'to slit the belly'. Some derivatives are not

154   *The Structure of the Haitian Creole Lexicon*

Table 5.1. Comparison between Synthetic and Parasynthetic Derivation

Synthetic derivation	Parasynthetic derivation
plòg 'plug'	*fresi* 'liver'
plog-e 'to plug'	**fresi(y)-e* 'to insert liver'
de-plog-e 'to unplug'	*de-fresi(y)-e* 'to disembowel, to beat up' (literally, 'to remove the liver')

based on a body part, as in: *prestij* 'reputation' → *deprestije* 'to tarnish a reputation'. An interesting case is the contrast between inversive and privative *de-* adjoined to the same base: *grès* 'fat'→ *degrese* 'to lose weight' (inversive with respect to *grese* 'to fatten up') and *degrese* 'to remove fat' (privative with respect to *grese* 'to add fat').[10]

There are many words beginning with *de-* whose meaning is clearly privative but whose remaining morphological material cannot be assigned to any attested base. For example, for *dekire* 'to skin' there is no **kire* 'to add skin', for *depifre* 'to unravel, pull off thread' and its homonymous adjective 'rumpled' (of clothing) no **pifre* 'to sew' or 'to straighten out clothing' exists. An interesting case is polysemous *detoufe* 'to remove the lid from a pot in which food is cooking' and 'to take clothes off', which can only be linked to *toufe* 'to stew, let steam' (as of rice). In the final analysis, these forms are best analyzed as simple lexemes.

3. Intensifier *de-*. This prefix enters in derivations whose outputs show little to no semantic differences from the base. In some cases, the adjunction of *de-* adds an expressive connotation, for example, in *chire* 'to rip, tear' → *dechire; refize* 'to refuse' → *derefize*. In the pair *kale* 'to peel' → *dekale* 'to scrape, to scale', the prefix denotes a slightly different action. It should be pointed out that *kale* is extremely polysemous and that *dekale* reflects only two of its numerous senses; in addition to 'to peel' there are at least the following senses: 'to hull, shuck; to shell; to skin; to beat up; to abuse'. In addition, as is the case with privative *de-*, there are cases where there is little, if any, semantic link between the base and the derivative, or where the identity of the base is not obvious: *degrije* 'to mess up, put in disarray' (compare to the homonymous inversive derivative *degrije* 'to unwrinkle' ← '*griji* 'to wrinkle'); *degonfler* 'to disperse, remove one's self' (compared to inversive *degonfle* 'to let air out' ← *gonfle* 'to inflate' as a balloon, a tire). In such cases, an alternative analysis is to consider these forms not as derivatives constructed with *de-* but as simple lexemes. These cases differ from those where *de-* constitutes part of simple lexemes, such as *dechifre*

5.3 Creative Processes 155

'to decipher', for which no base **chifre* exists. This is analogous to English forms such as *detach* or *demote* which, as compared to *deconstruct*, cannot be analyzed as the prefix *de-* plus a base.

4. Duplicative *re-*. The duplicative suffix *re-* forms derivatives of which most are not neologisms but parallel corresponding French forms: *moute/ monte* 'to go up' → *remoute/remonte* 'to go up again'; *tranpe* 'to immerse' → *retranpe* 'to immerse again'; *sòti* 'to go out' → *resòti* 'to go out again'. Some neologisms involve the adjunction of *re-* to bases borrowed from English: *ploge* 'to plug in' → *reploge* 'to plug in again'; *tepe* 'to tape record' → *retepe* 'to record again'.

5. Diminutive *ti-*. This affix poses a problem for morphological analysis. Specifically, is it to be considered as a proper diminutive prefix, as an adjective entering in compound lexemes, or as a syntactic construction of the type Adjective + Noun? From a semantic perspective there are two sets of combinations in which *ti* enters: (1) with animate nouns, in which case it bears the meaning of 'young of the particular species'; and (2) with nouns whose meaning varies widely, in which case it bears the meaning 'small'. In the latter usage, it parallels the French suffix *-ette*: *maison* 'house' → *maisonnette* 'cute little house' and the HC suffix *-èt* appearing in *louchèt* 'crowbar, hole-digger' (as was indicated above, the derivatives in which that suffix enter are semantically opaque: a hole-digger is anything but a small ladle, although it does have its general concave shape). When it functions as an antonym of *gran* 'large, big', it is best analyzed as a variant of the adjective *piti* 'small', for it cannot occur with that variant nor with *gran*: *ti flè* 'small flower' (**yon gran ti flè* 'a big small flower'), *ti kay* 'little house', *ti chante* 'small song'. On the other hand, in combinations of the type in (1), because (a) its meaning is not 'small' but 'young' and (b) because it can combine with *piti*, e.g., *yon piti ti chat* 'a small kitten', it is best viewed as a prefix: *tichat* 'kitten'; *tichwal* 'colt'; *timoun* 'child'; *tifi* '(young) girl'. The case of *ti wòch* 'pebble' is intermediate because of a slight semantic drift; a pebble is a particular type of small stone. As a prefix, *ti-* also occurs with proper names, in which case it takes on a hypocoristic connotation: *Ti-Jo/ Tijo, Ti-Mari*.

5.3.2 Productivity and semantic transparency in derivation

To assess the degree to which native speakers of a language can produce new words by combining bases and affixes, one applies two criteria: productivity and semantic transparency. The productivity of an affix may be measured by the number of derivatives resulting from its combinations with bases.[11] For example, the denominal verb-forming suffix *e-/en-* is extremely frequent. In addition, it is semantically transparent. On the basis of their knowledge of the meaning of the base, speakers can predict the meaning of the derivative. For example, if they know that *flay* means 'a missed kick' (in soccer), they can infer that *flaye* means 'to miss the ball', and if they know that *rans* means 'nonsense', they can predict that *ranse* means 'to talk nonsense'. Note that these two bases are neologisms in HC; they are neither part of the lexicon inherited from the original French variety targeted by the creators of HC nor adapted from current Standard French, from which much of the lexicon of HC used in newly gained domains is borrowed. The application of this suffix to bases borrowed from English and the semantic transparency of the resulting derivatives attests to the availability of this suffix to speakers and, consequently, to its productivity: *flach* 'flashlight' → *flache* 'to shine a flashlight', *patch* 'patch' → *patche* 'to patch an inner tube or an article of clothing'.

On the other hand, with regard to suffixes such as agentive *-mann* and diminutive *-èt*, as well as the inversive prefix *de-*, none enter in a large number of derivatives nor do they evidence great semantic transparency. Although *-mann* does indeed denote an agent, the relationship between the action and the agent is not always clear. For example, from its constituents *kawoutchou* 'tire' and *-mann* 'person', it is not readily predictable that a *kawoutchoumann* repairs rather than produces tires. The relationship between *gwòg* 'alcoholic beverage' and *gwògmann* 'heavy drinker, drunkard' is even more tenuous; the derivative could just as well be interpreted as someone who produces alcoholic beverages. But because of the agentive nature of *-mann*, there is sufficient motivation to consider the derivatives in which it enters as complex rather than as simple lexemes.

Such is not the case for the suffix *-èt*. The semantic link between *chouk* 'tree stump' and the various senses of *choukèt*: 'tree stump used as a stool, support under a woman's hips during childbirth, tooth stump, milepost' is not evident. In addition, in *ponm* 'apple' and *ponmkèt* 'muffin', the consonantal insert *k* renders the relationship between the putative base and the derivative even more opaque. It is more justified to consider these words as simple lexemes.

5.3.3 Compounding

Compounding involves the juxtaposition of two simple lexemes to create a new lexeme whose exact meaning cannot be derived from that of its constituents. In a sense, a compound constitutes an idiom, and it results from the metaphoric use of combinations of simple lexemes. For example, in English the term *curve ball* started out in baseball's specialized jargon with the rather straightforward, non-metaphoric meaning of 'a ball thrown so that it assumes a curved trajectory'. Because in baseball a curve ball is hard for a batter to hit, the expression was extended from the specialized baseball vocabulary to general use with the idiomatic meaning 'unexpected difficulty, unfair challenge', as in *During cross-examination, he threw me a curve ball*.

In English, compounds may be distinguished from non-idiomatic sequences of two simple lexemes by phonological differences, mainly stress patterns. For example, compounds composed of Adjective + Noun show reduced stress on the noun: compare *the big house* 'a house that is big' vs. *the big house* 'jail', *the white house* vs. *the White House* 'the official residence of the president of the United States'. In HC, there are no grammatical or phonological signals that differentiate compounds from non-idiomatic sequences. For example, *yon tichat* 'kitten', whether it is analyzed as a phrase consisting of Adjective + Noun or as a complex morpheme formed with a prefix + base (see above), may be considered non-idiomatic since the total meaning of the combination is readily derived from that of its constituents, as are *ti chen* 'puppy', *ti kabrit* 'baby goat', *tigason* 'young boy'. However, *ti chat* 'honey, dear', *ti gason* 'servant', or *ti dife* 'provocative statement' (not 'little fire') are genuine compounds containing the reduced variant of the adjective *piti*. As was indicated in Section 5.1, in HC, in the absence of phonological signals and grammatical markers, it is difficult to draw a distinction between homonymous compounds and syntactic combinations.

Most compounds in HC are nouns composed of combinations of adjectives, nouns, and verbs. Below, illustrative samples of compounds are grouped in seven categories. In the first column, I list the compound, in the second the 'literal' meaning of the corresponding syntactic combination, and in the third the actual, idiomatic meaning. As was indicated in Chapter 4, practice varies widely in the orthographic representation of compounds as single words or phrases.

1. Adjective + noun, or noun + adjective

je fò	strong eye	bold
fo tèt	false head	crook
granmoun	big person	adult
gwo nèg	big guy	big shot
gwo zotèy	big toe	bumpkin
gwo gòj	large throat	trachea
gwo moso	big piece	important man
kretyen vivan	living Christian	human being

2. Noun + noun

bouch kabrit	goat mouth	Cassandra
non jwèt	play name	nickname
chwal Bondye	horse of God	ladybug
manman lajan	mother money	capital
pitit lajan	child money	interest
nèg mòn	guy of the mountains	bumpkin
wòch kwen	corner rock	cornerstone
nannan tèt	nucleus of the head	brain
dlo je	water of eye	tear

3. Adjective + adjective

totalkapital	total and important	complete
natifnatal	native, native	genuinely native

Related to these two terms is the lexeme *fondalnatal* 'fundamental', whose first part does not occur independently.

4. Verb + noun

bay tèt	to give head	to be financially independent; to head (toward)
potemak	to bear a mark	coward
dekole mabouya	to loosen the lizard	to whet the whistle, i.e., have an early drink

5. Verb + adjective

fèklè	make light	dawn
fènwa	make dark	obscurity

6. Verb + verb

mòdesoufle	to bite and to blow (on a wound to relieve pain)	to act as an hypocrite
sousetire	to suck and to pull	to act as a parasite
retepran	to remain and to take	to tolerate

The above verb combinations contrast with one of the important syntactic structural features of HC: serial verbs (see Chapter 8).

7. Preposition + noun

anbachal	under the shawl	on the sly
anfòm	in shape	O.K.
anflèch	form of an arrow	in good shape
anjwèt	in play	in jest
ansante	in health	in good health
sou moun	on top of a person	brazen

I have not considered as compounds apparently complex idiomatic expressions whose individual constituents do not occur as independent morphemes. Most of these, in fact, correspond to and are derived from French phrases: *angiz* (*en guise de*) 'instead', *an katamini* (*en catimini*) 'on the sly', *ansoudin* (*en sourdine*) 'in soft-pedaled fashion', *sizoka* (*si au cas où*) 'in case', *poukisa* (*pour qui ça*) 'why', *koulyea* = *kou li ye a* (*le coup il est là*, literally, 'the time that is') 'now'; the interpretation of the latter term as a simplex is supported by variant pronunciations that deviate from the etymological form: *kounyea, konnya*.

There are also in HC certain set patterns of compounding whose products are semantically transparent. For example, as was indicated above in denoting animals, *ti* placed before the species name refers to the young. Whether it is a prefix or the reduced form of the adjective *piti* is a moot issue, as I discussed above. However, *manman* or *fimèl* referring to the female, and *mal* to the male are clearly constituents of compounds: *fimèl chat* 'female cat', *manman bourik* 'female donkey' vs. *mal kodenn* 'tom turkey'. In the case of *makou chat* 'tomcat' and *bouk kabrit* 'billygoat', the French etymological term for the male (*makou, bouk*) is used instead of the more semantically transparent qualifier *mal*. Except for the last two, these combinations are best analyzed as syntactic combinations since the overall meaning is fully predictable.

Intermediate between the fully semantically transparent syntactic constructions and semantically opaque compounds, such as those listed above, are semi-transparent combinations of two nouns whose meaning becomes apparent if one takes into account the extension of the meaning of the **headword**. I label as headword the noun whose basic meaning remains constant and which, modified by the second, accounts for the meaning of the compound. In Table 5.2, the words *dlo* and *bwa* bear a meaning broader than simply 'water' and 'tree, wood', respectively. *Dlo* refers to any liquid and *bwa* to a rigid and straight object. The table also lists compounds whose headword *je* 'eye' is modified by nouns whose basic meaning is shifted so that the resulting compound refers to the various parts of the eye. Note that, except for 'pupil', 'tear', 'optic matter', and 'cerum', the English equivalents are constructed in the same way as their corresponding HC term.

160   The Structure of the Haitian Creole Lexicon

Table 5.2. Semi-transparent Noun + Noun Compounds

Bwa + noun		Noun + *je*	
bwa	'tree, wood, forest, stick'	je	'eye'
bwa dife (fire)	'torch'	dlo je grenn/nanan je (kernel/core, nucleus)	'tear, tear-drop' pupil'
bwa drapo (flag)	'flag-pole'	kaka je (dirt)	'eye matter', 'cerum'
bwa linèt (eyeglasses)	'frame' (of eyeglasses)	kalalou je (stew)	'optic matter'
bwa pip (pipe)	'pipe-stem'	plim/pwal je (hair)	'eyelash'
bwa pi wo (taller)	'bean pole' (i.e., tall person)	po je (skin) pòch je (pocket)	'eyelid' 'eye-socket'

5.3.4 Reduplication

Reduplication constitutes another word-creation process in HC, although it could be considered a type of compounding in which the base morpheme is reduplicated. The meaning of reduplicated forms varies widely. Many convey an augmentative meaning: *bèl* 'pretty' → *bèlbèl* 'extremely pretty'; *sale* 'salty' → *salesale* 'very salty'; *mache* 'to walk' → *machemache* 'to walk a lot'. In some cases, an attenuative sense is conveyed: *blan* 'white' → *blanchblanch* 'whitish' (where the form *blanch* means 'blank').

5.3.5 Onomatopoeia

One of the means of lexical creation in HC, often neglected in descriptions of the language, is the rich stock of onomatopoeic expressions. These are exclamations forming set patterns that bear some phonetic resemblance to the action portrayed. English has fewer of these, for example, *wham bam* to represent the action of hitting. In HC, there exist numerous such expressions and the list, though subject to certain constraints linking the sound and the action depicted, is open, allowing speakers a certain amount of creativity. These onomatopoeic lexemes function as predicates. I provide an illustrative sample of this linguistic resource. In the absence of corresponding conventional English equivalents, I have preferred simply to add '...' to the English rendition: *li **ra** li kouri* 'he ran ...'; *li **voup** li vole* 'it flew away ...'; *li tonbe **vip*** 'he fell ...'; *limyè a file **yan*** 'the light streamed across ...'; *kè a te **bipbip*** 'his heart beat erratically ...'; *m **pan**, li rele anmwe* 'I whacked him ...', 'he shouted out in pain'; *li kase **kow*** 'it broke suddenly ...'; *kou a pati **daw*** 'the shot went off ...'; *li **pèchpèch** nan figi li a* 'he struck a hard blow in the other guy's face ...'.[12]

These onomatopoeias, or **ideophones**, fall into general classes determined by their constituent vowels and consonants. For example, a loud, resonant noise is represented by a stop consonant followed by a grave vowel *o, ou, a*: *pow, taw, kaw;* note that *w* is the semivowel related to *ou*. A muffled sound is symbolized by a stop plus the high-pitched vowel *i* and a final stop, usually *p: pip, vip, kip*. Rapid movements causing surprise are represented by CVC expressions ending in *p* and containing a rounded vowel: *toup, zoup, pop, pap*. Hard blows, like jabs, are depicted by a vowel, often high-pitch *i*, contained in a syllable beginning with a stop and ending in *p, t, ch: bich, pich, kip* ; sometimes *r* and the vowel *è* may follow the initial consonant: *brèt, prèt*.

Related to these onomatopoeic patterns is reduplication. Various types of noises are depicted by *toptop, ploplop, bangbang, chanmchanm, djoukdjouk, wounouwounou, kèjèkèjèk*. Some of these combinations are used as lexemes, often as verbs: *Y ap chwichwichwi nan kwen an* 'They're whispering secrets in the corner'; *L ap wounouwounou nan zorèy mwen* 'She's muttering in my ear'. This rich system of onomatopoeic devices probably reflects African influence. Some of these expressions are found in areas of the West Indies, from Jamaica to Trinidad, where English-based creoles are used, as well as in African-American Vernacular English (Black English). For example, the expression *tchwip* refers to a scornful sucking in of the lips to produce a slight hissing sound. It has been lexicalized in HC as *tchwipe*: *Li tchwipe m* 'She treated me with scorn'. The HC variants *en-en, an-an, enhen*, produced with various intonational patterns, are negative expressions whose corresponding English forms are widely attested in the United States.

5.4 Gender in Haitian Creole

As is the case in English, HC does not have grammatical gender, i.e., differentiated noun classes, such as French masculine and feminine. Except for the morphophonological alternations, described in Chapter 3, determiners are invariable, as are adjectives. Some nouns referring to humans have matching masculine and feminine forms, but these do not reflect any grammatical gender differentiation; they are simply corresponding forms analogous to English *tailor/seamstress* or *aviator/aviatrix*. One set of these corresponding nouns is derivationally related, the male-reference form containing the -è suffix and the female-reference form containing the corresponding suffix -èz, as well as the matched pair -en/-èn denoting nationality: dansè 'male dancer' vs. dansèz 'female dancer'; eskandalè 'noisy man' vs. eskandalèz 'noisy woman'; kanadyen/kanadyèn 'Canadian'. Some adjectives derived from nouns ending in -e have matching female-referencing derivatives formed by deleting the final -e and then adding the suffix -èz: yon malere 'a poor man', yon malerèz 'a poor woman'; yon visye 'a gluttonous and crafty man', yon visyèz 'a gluttonous and crafty woman'.[13] Another group of matching nouns does not show clear derivational patterns: nèg/nègès 'Black person'; milat/milatrès 'Mulatto'; chaben/chabin 'type of Mulatto with reddish kinky hair'; grimo/grimèl 'Black person with lighter skin'; chèmèt/chèmètrès 'master'; Kapwa 'man from Cap Haitian' and Kapwaz 'woman from Cape Haitian'.

Even when two matched forms are available, the male-referencing form assumes the status of an undifferentiated form, and may be used for female reference: Tifi a visye anpil 'That girl is gluttonous'. In some cases, the etymologically distinct masculine and feminine forms assume different meanings; for example, the etymological masculine form vè means 'green', yon fèy vè 'a green leaf', and the etymological feminine form means 'unripe', yon zannanna vèt 'an unripe pineapple'. Undifferentiated adjective forms may derive from French masculine or feminine forms: sòt (sotte) 'stupid', las (lasse) 'tired'. In fact, in French itself, so-called feminine forms like belle/bel /bel/ 'beautiful' constitute pre-vocalic variants that occur before both masculine and feminine nouns: un bel homme 'a handsome man', une belle femme 'a beautiful woman'; the HC form is the non-differentiated bèl.

Some HC nouns referring to human beings contain the elements ma-, mon-, lan-, or la-, corresponding to French determiners. In French, these determiners (definite articles, possessive adjectives) are differentiated for gender: ma and la are used with feminine nouns and mon and le with masculine nouns. In HC, these elements have been agglutinated and constitute an integral part of the noun. Thus, matant means 'aunt', monnonk 'uncle', lafimen 'smoke', lanmè 'sea'. Some other nouns contain the element me/mez-, which, although it denotes plural, does not function as a plural determiner. The noun mezanmi, related to zanmi 'friend', is used only as an exclamation: Mezanmi, m bouke, wi! 'Man, am I tired!' The element la- functions marginally to differentiate nouns from related verbal forms (verbs and adjectives): fimen 'to smoke'/lafimen 'smoke', swèf 'to be thirsty'/laswèf 'thirst', mò 'dead'/lanmò 'death'. In most cases, a form containing la- alternates freely with one without: ladousè/dousè 'sweetness', lafrèch/frèch 'coolness', lafwa/fwa 'faith', lajounen/jounen 'day', lafyè/fyèv 'fever'.

5.5 Borrowing

The main source for lexical enrichment, in the domains of language use newly gained by HC, remains borrowing, mainly from French. Indeed, it is sometimes difficult to distinguish between the lexicons of the two languages since any French term is a potential loanword. Massive borrowing from French does not reflect any inherent inadequacy of HC but simply the fact that, without any group or agency able to assume the responsibility of coining new terminology from native resources, it is more expedient to adapt French terms. The examination of any text in the administrative, educational, or technical fields reveals a wide variety of French loanwords. Most of these are individual lexemes: *izin idwo-elektrik* (*hydro-électrique*) 'hydro-electric plant'; *afè pati inik* (*unique*) 'the matter of a single (political) party'; *sa sa vle di ekiminis?* (*œcuméniste*) 'what does ecumenical mean?'; *enjistis ak esplwatasyon* (*injustice et exploitation*) 'injustice and exploitation'; *pou n rekonstwi machin nan* (*reconstruire*) 'so that we may rebuild the car'. More insidious than straightforward borrowing is **calquing** or **loan translation**, the cloaking of a semantic concept from another language with native lexemes. What is borrowed is the concept but the phonological form is that of the borrowing language. For example, the English compound *cornerstone* has been adapted in HC as *wòchkwen* (literally, 'stone corner'). In other words, in creating this **calque**, one simply provides a literal translation of the English lexemes to create a new term that is opaque for speakers of HC. What is transferred, into HC, is the new concept. Calques may be viewed as disembodied loanwords: only the meaning is borrowed, not the phonological form. Only an HC speaker familiar with English would be able to detect the term's English origin. The semi-transparent compounds illustrated in Table 5.2 undoubtedly derive from African **calques**. English and Spanish are also rich sources for expanding the lexicon (see Section 6.4).

Frequently, loanwords consist of phrases: *isit aletranje* (*à l'étranger*) 'here abroad' (compare the HC corresponding expressions for 'abroad': *lotbò, nan peyi blan*), *se yo ki alabaz tout richès peyi a* (*à la base de*) 'they're the basis of all wealth', *deklarasyon dwa lòm, lig ayisyen pou dwadlòm* (*les droits de l'homme*) 'the declaration of human rights, the Haitian League for human rights'. As indicated by the last example, borrowing combinations of lexemes may lead to grammatical changes. In HC, no syntactic markers, such as prepositions, are required to relate two nouns; they are simply juxtaposed: *papa timoun yo* 'the children's father', *se tout chapant sosyete a* 'it's the entire structure of society'. The introduction of such grammatical devices as the preposition *d/de* with French loanwords has serious consequences for the structure of HC and for the maintenance of a clear line of demarcation between HC and French.

Summary

This survey of the lexical resources of HC demonstrates that, *pace* those scholars who assumed it originated in an impoverished pidgin and, consequently, lacks creative lexical generative processes, the language is capable of meeting all the communicative needs of its primary speakers. The most comprehensive dictionary of HC (Valdman *et al.* 2007) shows the breadth of is lexicon: 30,000 separate entries, 26,000 sub-entries, 35,000 idioms and compounds, and 70,000 individual senses. Like all properly formed natural languages, it possesses a variety of mechanisms for lexical renewal: a derivational system with about two dozen productive affixes (prefixes and suffixes), a robust component for the creation of compounds, and a rich stock of ideophones particularly suited for expressive needs. Exposed to close contact with Spanish from the Dominican Republic, with which it shares the island of Hispaniola, and with English through diaspora communities in the United States and the Bahamas, speakers of HC will, as is natural, borrow from these two languages. However, the main source of loanwords remains French, the language that it is gradually replacing in domains from which it had been excluded for more than two centuries: education, administration, governance, and the media. Admittedly, this development renders the line of demarcation fuzzy between the two languages but only at the level of the lexicon, inasmuch as the grammatical system of HC remains impermeable to French influence.

Notes

1. In fact, the homophonous form *fair* is listed in at least five separate entries in most dictionaries: (1) adj. just, reasonable, equitable; (2) adj. pale (of skin); (3) adj. generally, a large amount; (4) adj. pleasant and dry (of weather); (5) n. large public event.
2. In English, the agent is also marked redundantly in the case of the 3rd person singular of verbs, by the pronoun (*he, she, it*) and the endings *-s/-es*, e.g., *he speaks, she hisses, it rains*.
3. The term 'eye dialect' refers to the use by authors of a non-standard spelling to draw attention to characters' pronunciation which reflects dialectal, uneducated, or foreign deviation from standard educated speech.
4. The analysis of the three constituents of this word, *fòk se li*, yields the meaning 'it must be it'. Because cornmeal is considered the least-expensive food available, the name given to it implies 'if you can't afford anything else, that's it'.
5. As will be pointed out in 5.3.1.1 below, the *t* is inserted to prevent two-vowel sequences: **kle e*.

6. Von Warburg's *Französisches Etymologisches Wörterbuch* (*FEW*) and the *Trésor de la langue française* (*TLF*), especially the former work, are the standard references for etymological research on French language varieties.
7. Whereas the existence of Standard French cognates can readily be verified by consulting authoritative dictionaries, such as the *Robert* or the *Larousse*, eliminating cognates derived from lexemes occurring in vernacular or regional varieties of the language is more arduous. Consequently, some of the neologisms I posit may actually occur in non-standard varieties of French.
8. Most likely, *imigrasyon, inskripsyon,* and *diskisyon* are not formed by derivation but form part of the lexicon inherited or borrowed from French.
9. *Desabote* has undergone metaphorical semantic drift to 'amputate arms and/or legs'; human limbs are compared to the hooves of horses.
10. A.-M. Brousseau, of the University of Toronto, pointed out to me (via personal communication) that privative *de-* could, in fact, be assigned inversive meaning. In the case of *defresiye*, as Table 5.1 shows, if one posits a potential unattested verb **fresiye* 'to insert the liver', the derivative can be assigned an inversive sense. My analysis of privative *de-* as a separate prefix has the advantage of concreteness and simplicity.
11. For HC, because of the non-availability of large computerized corpora, productivity can only be measured by counting particular derivatives in dictionaries, the most extensive of which is Valdman *et al.* (2007). However, only the assessment of the occurrence of derivatives in corpora provides an indication of the actual production of derivatives in natural linguistic communication.
12. Some examples like *li **pèchpèch** nan figi li a* have onomatopoeic equivalents in English – 'He biffed/bopped/whacked him in the face' – yet these examples in English are far outnumbered by those in HC.
13. These nouns may also be used as adjectives and form the predicate: *Li visye* 'He's gluttonous and crafty', *Li visyèz* 'She's gluttonous and crafty'. It is difficult to determine whether these are nouns converted to adjectives or vice versa.

6 The Origin of the Haitian Creole Lexicon

Chapter 5 focused on the mechanisms by which the lexical resources of HC are expanded. This chapter will deal with the origins of the HC vocabulary; I will discuss some of the problems encountered in determining exact origins. Where possible, I will identify the source of certain words: in French, African languages, native Amerindian languages, Spanish, and English. Additionally, I will provide correspondence rules that account for differences between the form of HC words of French origin and the corresponding forms (**cognates**) in Standard French and I will categorize the various types of semantic changes that have affected the lexicon of French origin.

The lexicon of HC comprises three main parts. First, like its congeners in the Caribbean, Louisiana, French Guiana, and the Indian Ocean islands, it consists of an older stratum of terms associated with the plantation society that Chaudenson (1974) labels '*le vocabulaire des Isles*'. Second, at its core are terms derived from the target language that the slave population of French plantation colonies attempted to acquire and eventually restructured. That core comprises lexemes that are identical in form and meaning to Standard French equivalents but also a large component that differs at both levels and that reflects what I term Colonial French (see Sections 1.2.3 and 6.3 below). This core also includes lexemes from various external languages that have been adopted over three centuries, some of which have undergone changes in form and meaning. Third, as Chaudenson (2008) aptly observes, and as has been mentioned in Chapter 5, in all French-based creoles that co-exist with their source language, any French word can be incorporated into the lexicon of these languages, with or without phonological and/or semantic modifications. As a result, the lexicon of HC is infinitely expandable as the language is used in domains that were previously reserved to French: administration, education, the media, scientific discourse, etc.

6.1 On the Perils of Etymological Research

The above considerations make it clear that it is misguided to attempt to derive HC forms directly from those of any present-day speech varieties in France, except of course recent borrowings from French. Caution should also guide attempts to link them to other sources, in particular current forms of African languages. Determining the exact origin (**etymology**) of a particular HC word is fraught with great risks that can be avoided only by careful comparative and reconstructive research. Unfortunately, most individuals fascinated by the exciting field of etymology tend to jump to conclusions on the basis of superficial similarities of form and then proceed to formulate ingenious scenarios to account for semantic differences. For example, Jules Faine (1936), a pioneer in the study of HC, derived the word *bèkèkè* 'to remain speechless, left out in the cold, holding the bag' from the English expression 'back-aching' by invoking the curious argument that someone left holding the bag is in the painful posture of someone who received a kick in the posterior. At first, Faine never asked himself whether the expression 'to be left back-aching' occurs in any variety of English. In fact, in revising the etymology, he found a more plausible source: the expression *bec sec* 'high and dry', which he attributed to Normand French, modified by a process of reduplication of the final sequence *-ec* plus the inversion of the last two phonemes. The latter, presumably, is a well-attested stylistic process in HC. The final result, *bèkèkè*, provides a well-justified account of the derivation of this term.

Amateur etymologists tend to seize upon the first available form in a contemporary speech variety and forget that the basic vocabulary of HC was formed three centuries ago. Faine derives *atò* (with a variant form *astò*) 'now, presently' from Spanish *a esta hora* 'at this time'. In so doing he passes over a more probable origin in the dialectal word *asteur* (*à cette heure*) found with the exact meaning 'at this time, now' in overseas varieties of French, for example, in Québec French and Louisiana French, as well as under the variant form *aste* in Réunion. Of course, *atò* is not derived from LF *asteur* or Réunion Creole *aste;* it reflects a Colonial French form, evidenced by survivals in several overseas varieties of French, as well as in French regional dialects.

As would be expected, some HC forms are derived from the convergence of multiple sources. For example, *moun* 'person', occurring in compounds like *timoun* 'child', *granmoun* 'adult', *vye moun* 'oldster', resembles the word *mun-tu* 'human being' in Kikongo, a Bantu language. A more plausible origin is the French *monde*, widely attested in regional dialects of France and in Louisiana as an isolated form meaning 'person' and 'people' or in a wide range of combinations: *jeune monde* 'young people', *les vieux monde* 'older people', *le monde blanc* 'White people', and pronounced /mõn/. As we will see below, any current French word ending in a nasal vowel plus a voiced stop corresponds to a HC form ending in a nasal vowel and a nasal consonant with the same place of articulation as the voiced stop. In the latter form, there is assimilation of the voiced stop to the preceding nasal vowel, for example: [mɔ̃d] → [mɔ̃n]. The evidence that this phonological change was not initiated in Haiti but reflects the target form to which the creators of HC were exposed is the widespread presence of that feature in regional and vernacular varieties of French. Witness its occurrence in present-day 'ordinary' French, for example, in the variant pronunciation of '22': *vingt-deux* [vɛ̃ndø] instead of more formal [vɛ̃tədø]. Another case of a form of French origin whose incorporation in HC was reinforced by a coincidently related African form is that of the verb *ba/ban/bay* 'to give'. It reflects the verb *bailler*, the standard form for 'to give' in the seventeenth and eighteenth centuries, and the forms *bayes* and *ba* attested in the African languages Hausa and Wolof. The structure in which *ba* is equivalent to the English preposition 'to', for example, *pote sa ba mwen* 'bring me that' (literally, 'carry that give me'), probably reflects a syntactic structure found widely among West African languages. Consultation of regional dialects in France also reveals other convergences with African languages, for example, the polysemic word *bakoulou* 'rotten, crooked, dishonest, unscrupulous; cunning, crafty; con man, deceiver, double-dealer (esp. toward women); crook' may reasonably be linked to Kikongo *bakoukou* 'someone who tries to seize, to gain something' and Picard *bacoulou* 'despicable person'. A form fully inherited from an African language is *masisi* 'homosexual' that corresponds to Ewe *masisa* 'eunuch'.

The first step in establishing the etymology of HC words that bear some similarity of form and meaning with those of languages other than French is to check an authoritative historical or etymological dictionary of French, in particular, the *Trésor de la langue française* (TLF) or the monumental etymology of French compiled by Walter von Wartburg (1922–28), *Französisches Etymologisches Wörterbuch* (FEW). Pierre Anglade (1998) traces the verb *teke* 'to hit someone else's marbles, to strike, to hit' to West African languages distributed over a very wide area: Bambara *tégé* ('the hand'), Mandingo *tekè* ('to tap'), Sango *kètèkètè* ('tiny'), and Swahili *teke* ('sharp kick or blow'). Only the Swahili form bears any semantic relationship with HC *teke*. Checking the FEW suggests a more likely origin in French *taquer* 'to strike', attested in France since 1460 and occurring in several regional dialects.

For words whose pronunciation or meaning cannot be traced to varieties of French, the next step is to consult Bollée (1993), an etymological dictionary containing words of non-French or unknown origin. This invaluable resource, however, deals only with Indian Ocean French-based creoles. Because of the limitations of this important source, consultation of other putative sources (African, Amerindian, and the two languages with which Haitians have had contact since the emergence of HC, namely, English and Spanish) is suggested. An interesting case in point is *doukoulou*, which refers to a dessert made of sweetened sweet potato paste cooked in a banana leaf or corn pudding. An African origin proposed by Anglade (1998) is convincing because he links it to Ashanti, a language spoken in Ghana, where he finds *dõkõnõ* 'corn mush cooked in a banana tree leaf'. Any convincing etymology must meet the twin criteria of both phonological and semantic similarity.

6.2 *Le Vocabulaire des Isles*

Because their settlement and economic development antedates the Indian Ocean plantation colonies of Isle de France (Réunion), Bourbon Island (Mauritius), and the Seychelles, it was in the French colonies of the American zone that an older stratum of the lexicon of French-based creoles, termed *vocabulaire des Isles* ('vocabulary of the islands') by Chaudenson (1974), was first constituted and then exported to French plantation colonies in the Indian Ocean. It consists of lexemes referring to flora, fauna, and artifacts borrowed mostly from Amerindian languages, as well as terms reflecting the regional and vernacular speech of French settlers, who mostly hailed from northern and western France. Many of these terms first appeared in Spanish sources published in the early sixteenth century and were then adopted by French navigators, travelers, and missionary priests – to whom we owe the first descriptions of the New World French settlements. A telling example of the *vocabulaire des Isles* is the term *créole*, first coined by the Portuguese, then adapted by the Spaniards. It initially referred to persons of European origin born in the colonies, and was then extended to characterize persons, as well as animals, native to the plantation colonies. Note, for example, HC *kochon kreyòl* 'a variety of hogs native to Haiti' (see Section 1.1.1).

Table 6.1 offers a sample of lexical stock of words of Amerindian provenance, with an indication of the probable Amerindian source language. Most of these words, although they were transmitted by the Caribs in the Lesser Antilles or the Tainos in Saint-Domingue, originated in the coastal areas of central and northern South America.

170   *The Origin of the Haitian Creole Lexicon*

Table 6.1. Sample of *Vocabulaire des Isles* Terms of Amerindian Origin

HC word	English gloss	Amerindian source language
anmak/ranmak	'hammock'	Taino
igwann/gwàn	'iguana'	Taino
joupa/ajoupa	'hut made of foliage'	Tupi
kayiman	'caiman' (S. American alligator)	Carib
mabouya	'small lizard' (larger than a gecko)	Carib
manyòk	'manioc' (yucca)	Tupi
papay	'papaya'	Taino
sapoti/sapotiy	'sapotilla'	Taino
woukou	'annatto' (used to produce red dye), 'lipstick brush'	Galibi
zandolit	'gecko'	Carib

Most of the lexemes of the *vocabulaire des Isles* of French origin constitute lexical particularities, i.e., lexemes that are either absent from current dictionaries of Standard French (SF) or whose meanings differ significantly from that of their SF cognates. For example, the sense that HC *rete* shares with other French-based creoles 'to live, inhabit, reside' differs markedly from that of its French etymon *rester* 'to stay', *mare* 'to tie' has a much broader sense than the nautical term *amarrer* 'to tie up a boat', and *abitan* whose SF etymon simply means 'dweller, inhabitant' is first attested in the Americas in 1645 with the sense of 'farmer'. However, in HC, its meaning has been extended to refer to a country dweller in contrast to a city dweller and also bears the connotation of 'country bumpkin, hick'.

6.3   Colonial French

The core vocabulary of HC was constituted during the second half of the seventeenth century and throughout the course of the eighteenth century. French indentured laborers, soldiers, artisans, and adventurers who served as models for the first group of slaves brought to the West Indian colonies did not speak in the graceful cadences of the Versailles courtiers. Indeed, most did not even speak Standard French (SF), the prestige variety of the language, originating in the Parisian area and in use among cultivated upper and middle classes throughout the country. Many of these settlers spoke vernacular varieties of SF and, in many cases, local dialects grouped under the term **Oïl** (geographical varieties of northern French, now seriously endangered, spoken in such areas as eastern Brittany, Normandy, Picardy, the Loire valley, the Atlantic coastal regions south of Brittany, the Paris area, and other eastern regions). This term is used to contrast with the **Oc** (Occitan) dialects, which in the seventeenth and eighteenth centuries were the exclusive speech forms for 90% of the population in southern France. We have little written evidence for the speech in use in the French colonies of the period, so we must base our conjectures on extrapolation from current varieties of French found today in the Americas – in Quebec province, the Maritime Provinces of Canada, Louisiana, and the small island of Saint-Barthélemy (St. Barts) in the French West Indies – as well as other French-based creoles, in particular, those more remote in the Indian Ocean (the overseas French department of Réunion, Mauritius and its dependency, the island of Rodrigues, and the Seychelles). Comparative research involving the latter creoles is particularly relevant because most of the slave populations there were not imported from West Africa.

In all likelihood, the slaves heard a highly variable linguistic common denominator, a **koinè**, based on the speech of the lower classes of Paris and the cities and towns of northern and western France, which was termed **français populaire** (plebian French), with admixtures from regional Oïl dialects and geographical varieties of SF influenced by local dialects. Freed from the normative pressures of the standard variety, Colonial French showed, in a more advanced form, some of the deep-level dynamic tendencies of the language (Chaudenson 1992), for example, the reduction of verbal inflection in favor of the use of auxiliary and modal verbs, as well as a small number of invariant verb stems.

6.4 Vocabulary of French Origin

Lexical items of French origin fall into three main classes: (1) those that correspond to SF cognates but which differ slightly with respect to form and meaning, (2) survivals from older stages of the language or regional dialects, but which do not necessarily have a modern-day counterpart, and (3) neologisms, that is, items that have either shown considerable semantic drift from an original form or been created by recombining existing material.[1]

6.4.1 Systematic phonological correspondences between HC and SF

Many HC words are easily relatable to corresponding French forms by means of systematic rules of language change. These rules do not pretend to reflect historical changes, seeing as the SF form may show as much change from a postulated common form as the matching item in HC. These are simply correspondence rules that make it possible to deduce SF cognates from HC forms or vice versa. It should be kept in mind that in many cases the differences between an HC form and its French cognate are traceable to forms in regional varieties of SF and Oïl dialects or current vernacular varieties of French that deviate from the standard variety, as in the case of *moun* 'person', derived from dialectal /mɔ̃n/, not SF /mɔ̃d/, as pointed out above.

1. Simplification of final consonant clusters. Final consonant clusters composed of stop consonants (/p t k b d g/) or labiodental fricatives (/f v/) plus a liquid (/r/ or /l/) are simplified by the loss of the liquid (French forms are given in standard orthography, in which the *e* is silent in the isolated form; HC forms are listed in the official IPN orthography):

> *table* 'table' *tab*   *propre* 'clean' *pwòp*
> *livre* 'book'   *liv*   *sucre* 'sugar'   *sik*

Note that in everyday spoken French, in France and in other areas, such as Quebec province, where French is the indigenous language, this type of consonant cluster is generally simplified. One is more likely to hear *une tab'ronde* [yn tab ʁɔ̃d] 'a round table', *quat'fois* [kat fwa] 'four times', *ouv' la porte* [uv la pɔʁt] 'open the door', than *une table ronde* [yn tablə ʁɔ̃d], *quatre fois* [katʁə fwa], and *ouvre la porte* [uvʁə la pɔʁt], respectively. The retention of the consonant cluster will trigger the pronunciation of the final so-called **mute e**, a vowel usually represented in phonetic transcriptions as [ə] but in fact intermediate in quality between the phonemes /ø/ or /œ/, or as one or the other of these two phonemes. Words containing a nasal vowel followed by a consonant cluster consisting of one of the voiced stops /b d g/ plus a liquid correspond to HC words that end with a nasal consonant characterized by the same point of articulation as the voiced stop:

> *chambre* 'room' *chanm*/ʃãm/   *pendre* 'to hang' *pan*/pãn/
> *ongle* 'nail'   *zong*/zɔ̃ŋ/

2. Loss of post-vocalic r. In the standard variety of HC the resonant /ʁ/ does not occur after a vowel, at the end of a word, or at the close of a syllable.[2]

word-final:

> *sœur* 'sister' *sè*   *corps* 'body' *kò*

syllable-final:

> *porter* 'carry' *pòte*   *chercher* 'look for' *chèche*

before a consonant in final syllable:

> *porte* 'door' *pòt*   *charme* 'charm' *cham*

3. R plus rounded vowel. The French resonant /ʁ/ does not occur before a rounded vowel; it corresponds to /w/ in HC:

se promener 'to walk'   *pwomenen*   *gros* 'fat'   *gwo*
rouge 'red'   *wouj*   *rond* 'round'   *won*

4. Absence of front-rounded vowels. In most varieties of HC spoken by monolingual speakers the front-rounded vowels /y ø œ/ do not generally occur.[3] As a rule, they correspond to their matching front unrounded vowel counterparts /i e ɛ/, respectively.

l'heure 'hour'   *lè* [lɛ]   *voleur* 'thief'   *vole* [vɔlɛ]
des oeufs 'eggs'   *ze* [ze]   *deux* 'two'   *de* [de]
jus 'juice'   *ji* [ʒi]   *du riz* 'some rice'   *diri* [diɣi]

In some cases, HC shows a back-rounded vowel instead:

brûler 'to burn'   *boule* [bule]   *sucer* 'to suck'   *souse* [suse]
voleur 'thief'   *vòlò* [vɔlɔ]   *l'heure* 'hour'   *lò* [lɔ]
                       (variant)   (variant)

The mute *e* of French, when it is pronounced, shows the same correspondences as /ø/ or /œ/:

genou 'knee'   *jenou* (also jinou, jounou) [ʒenu]
cheveu 'hair'   *cheve* (also chive) [ʃeve]

5. Regressive nasal assimilation. Oral vowels occurring before a nasal consonant often correspond to a matching nasal vowel:

lame 'blade'   *lanm* [lãm]   *graine* 'seed'   *grenn* [gɣẽn]
la mer 'the sea'   *lanmè* [lãmɛ]   *fourmi* 'ant'   *fwonmi* [fwɔ̃mi]
connaître 'to know' *konnen* [kɔ̃nẽ]   *commerce* 'trade'   *konmès* [kɔ̃mɛs]

However, there are numerous cases of free alternation between forms with or without nasalization:[4]

commettre 'to commit'   *konmèt* [kɔ̃mɛt] / *kòmet* [kɔmɛt]
connaissance 'knowledge'   *konnesans* [kɔ̃nesãs] / *kònesans* [kɔnesãs]
canard 'duck'   *kanna* [kãna] / *kana* [kana]

Comparative evidence from overseas varieties of French clearly indicates that this nasalization does not represent an evolution from French etyma without the nasal vowel. Consider the following data from St. Barts Patois (SBP) (see Section 1.4.2). The HC form is listed first, followed by the English gloss, then the St. Barts cognate with its variant forms (separated by a slash where relevant) is represented using the French-based spelling provided in G. Lefebvre (n.d.); the corresponding SF form appears within parentheses: *zonyon* 'onion' *angnon/ongnon/zongnon* (*oignon*); *kannòt* 'small boat, rowboat', *kannote* (*canot*); *kanna* 'duck' *cannard* (*canard*). Nasal assimilation also occurs widely in LF. Sample forms are provided in the spelling of entries in Valdman *et al.* (2010). This spelling, which mirrors conventional SF orthography, has been chosen by local activists for the maintenance and revitalization of the language. Again, the English gloss and then LF follow the HC form or forms,: *anmè/amè* 'bitter' *amer, amère* [ɑ̃mɛr, omɛr, ɔ̃mɛr]; *kann* 'sugar cane' *canne* [kɑ̃n].

French verbs of the *-er* group that contain a nasal consonant in their final syllable correspond to verbs that end with *-en* in HC:

    mener 'to lead' *mennen* *fumer* 'to smoke' *fimen*

In some cases, HC shows an oral vowel preceding or following a nasal consonant:

    dodine 'rocking chair' *dodin* *panne* 'breakdown' *pàn*
    novembre 'November' *novanm* *mauvais* 'bad' *move*

No nasal vowel occurs in HC items whose corresponding French form contains a vowel separated from the following nasal consonant by *r*:

    corne 'horn' *kòn* *charme* 'charm' *cham*

We have to assume that at some earlier stage of HC, or in the Colonial French form from which the HC form is derived, the presence of an actual *r* blocked the nasal assimilation. However, there is no trace of this *r* in present-day standard HC. Note also that there are contrasts between such forms as *cham* 'Vodou charm' and corresponding ones that contain a nasal vowel like *chanm* 'room'.

6. Replacement of the nasal vowel *un* (/œ̃/). The nasal vowel /œ̃/ corresponds to HC *en*. Note that the merger of /œ̃/ with /ɛ̃/ also characterizes the speech of Parisian speakers of SF.

    lundi 'Monday' *lendi* *brun* 'brown' *bren*

7. Reduction of *ui*. In many cases, but not all, the sequence /ɥi/ shows loss of the semivowel:

    la pluie 'the rain' *lapli* *bruit* 'noise' *bri*

In the case of combinations of /ɥ/ + other vowels, the semivowel corresponds to /w/:

    nuage 'cloud' *nwaj* *suer* 'to sweat' *swe*

This semivowel does occur, however, in the sequence *ui*, although it is subject to alternation with *w*:

    huit 'eight' *uit/wit* *la nuit* 'the night' *lannuit/lanwit*

8. Final /j/. HC words that correspond to SF words that end in *-age* /aʒ/ or *-ange* /ɑ̃ʒ/ show the replacement of /ʒ/ by /j/, spelled *y*:

    pillage 'looting' *piyay* 'bargain' *bagage* 'baggage' *bagay* 'thing'[5]
    charge 'load' *chay* *orange* 'orange' *zorany*

6.4 Vocabulary of French Origin   175

9. Retention of final consonants. Some words ending in silent -*s* and/or -*t* have cognates in which these are pronounced; note that in French final -*x* also represents silent -*s*:

>   *rat* 'rat'   *rat* /rat/   *chat* 'cat'   *chat* /ʃat/
>   *moins* 'minus'   *mwens* /mwãs/   *doux* 'sweet'   *dous* /dus/

The pronunciation of these final written consonants also characterizes SBP: *chate, rate*.

10. Correspondence *oi* /wa/ → *wè*. Some HC forms show the older sequence /wɛ/ that was progressively changed to /wa/ in SF during the eighteenth century:

>   *poisson* 'fish'   *pwèson*   *doigt* 'finger'   *dwèt*
>   *boîte* 'box'   *bwèt*   *voir* 'to see'   *wè*

However, forms exhibiting the SF change from /wɛ/ to /wa/ do occur, and in fact are dominant, e.g., *bwa* (bois) 'wood', *wa* (roi) 'king', *lwa* (loi) 'law'. In addition, generally, there is variation between *wa* and *wè* (see Chapters 5 and 11).

11. Modification of syllable structure. The favored syllable type in HC is consonant (C) + vowel (V); consequently, many words have the structure CVCV. French words with the structure VCV (CV) have HC-matching words in which the initial vowel has been lost (apheraesis). The result is to maximize the syllabic structure CVCV:

>   *oublier* 'to forget'   *bliye*   *arriver* 'to arrive'   *rive*

Another way by which this syllabic structure is maximized is by **agglutination**, or the incorporation of the liaison consonant of the French word's determiner (articles, demonstrative and possessive adjectives) into the noun itself:

>   *les os* 'bones'   *zo* 'bone'   *les yeux* 'the eyes'   *zye* or *je* 'eye'
>   *les ongles* 'nails'   *zong* 'nails'   *les oreilles* 'ears'   *zorèy* 'ear'
>   *l'église* 'the church'   *legliz* 'church' *l'école* 'the school'   *lekòl* 'school'
>   *un homme* 'the man'   *nonm* 'man'   *une âme* 'a soul'   *nanm* 'soul'
>   *mon oncle* 'my uncle'   *monnon* 'uncle'   *de l'eau* 'some water'   *dlo* 'water'

Agglutination may extend to the full determiner of words with the structure CV or CVC:

>   *du riz* 'some rice'   *diri* 'rice'   *du vin* 'some wine'   *diven* 'wine'
>   *la lune* 'the moon'   *lalin* 'moon'   *la mer* 'the sea'   *lanmè* 'sea'
>   *ma tante* 'my aunt'   *matant* 'aunt'
>   *des égards* 'some consideration'   *mank dèzega* 'lack of consideration'

6.4.2 Survivals from older stages of French or from regional dialects

These are words of HC that have a cognate attested in some regional variety of metropolitan French that shows phonological similarity and shared semantic make-up. Many of these words occur in broad areas of France rather than in geographically restricted dialects. For example, the words *mare* 'to tie', *rale* 'to pull' (related to *haler*), and *rad* 'clothes' (related to *hardes*) have been thought to belong to a nautical vocabulary used by sailors and other persons engaged in activities related to maritime trade. In fact, they occur far inland: *mare* in Normandy and most of the western provinces, *haler* in Normandy and eastern Brittany, *harde* in an extensive area in western and central France. Also, some terms which are today restricted geographically were at one time forms of SF in use throughout the Oïl territory, for example, *zen* 'baiting hook'(today replaced by *hameçon*) and *grafiyen* (*grafigner*) 'to scratch' (today pushed out by *gratigner*). It is important to bear in mind that the conduit for these survivals was not a particular Oïl dialect but the Colonial French to which the slaves were exposed. This accounts for the fact that many of these terms are also found in other former French colonies, such as Quebec, Louisiana, the French West Indies, and in the Indian Ocean islands.

To be sure, some lexemes of HC may be traced to a particular regional variety of SF and eventually to a corresponding Oïl dialect. Such is the case for the following terms originating in Normandy (Chauveau 2012). The original meaning is indicated with the SF term(s) in parentheses: *raje* 'undergrowth, scrub, thicket; woods, backwoods' (*buisson* 'bush', *brousailles* 'scrub, brushwood'); *lak* 'fish trap, fish bait' (*appât pour la pêche* 'fish bait'). The verb *digonnen* 'to goad' is particularly interesting. In the Norman dialect, it means 'to pick, prick continuously' but as the term spread to other parts of France, it assumed the metaphoric senses of 'to tease, to complain continuously, to grumble' that are related to the sense of the HC word.[6]

In the speech of French-speaking areas in North America and St. Barts, these lexemes constitute linguistic particularities with respect to SF, i.e., lexemes that have either disappeared from that variety of the language or that have some senses that are no longer current in French. Table 6.2 presents a sample list of these lexical particularities that correspond to HC forms with similar pronunciation and shared meaning. The table lists the HC word with its meaning, the corresponding LF word that bears the same or closely related meaning, and the meaning for the SF etymon in cases where such a corresponding SF word exists (I use ---- to indicate the absence of a cognate in Standard French).[7]

6.4 Vocabulary of French Origin

Table 6.2. Lexical Correspondences between Haitian Creole and Louisiana French

HC form	Meaning	LF form	SF usual meaning
abitan, n.	farmer	*habitant*	inhabitant
atò, adv.	now, at present	*asteur*	(*à cette heure*) at this hour
ap/ape, v. marker	progressive marker	*après*	after
lavalas, n.	downpour	*avalasse*	-------
babye, v.	to complain	*babiller*	to babble
bo, n.	kiss	*bo*	-------
bokit, n.	bucket, pail	*baquet/bokette*	
bawòk, adj.	crude, coarse, vulgar	*baroque*	odd, bizarre, whimsical
bonm, n.	pot, saucepan	*bombe*	bomb
boukan, n.	bonfire	*boucan* 'smoke'	------
brigan, n.	unruly (of a child)	*brigand*	brigand, robber
kabarè, n.	tray	*cabaret*	bar
kagou, adj.	sad, dejected	*cagou* 'out of sorts'	-------
kenbe, v.	to hold	*tchambo*	-------
cheran, adj.	expensive	*chérant*	-------
klete, v.	to lock	*cléter*	-------
kwoke/koke, v.	to have sex	*coquer*	-------
dal, n.	drainpipe, gutter	*dalle* 'drain'	flagstone, slab
demare, v.	to untie	*démarrer*	to start (a car, machine)
anpil, adv.	a lot	*en pile*	in stacks, piles
goud, n.	basic monetary unit	*gourde* 'dollar'	gourd
grèg, n.	coffee strainer	*coffee pot*	breeches
joure, v.	to curse, insult	*jurer*	-------
makonnen, v.	to tie, join together	*macorner*	-------
maladi sik, n.	diabetes	*maladie de/du sucre*	-------
mayi moulen, n.	ground corn	*maïs moulé*	-------
nenenn, n.	godmother	*nénaine*	-------
pare, v.	to make ready	*paré*	to make ready for a maneuver (maritime)
rete, v.	to live, reside	*rester*	to stay
saf, adj.	gluttonous	*safre*	-------
yo, pron.	they	*yeux*	3rd person plural (*eux*)

Particularly noteworthy is the term *bawòk*. Below, I provide the full range of meanings of this word in HC and its corresponding congener in LF, as well as an indication of the distribution of these terms across French-based creoles. This word illustrates a change of meaning in HC from both the SF etymon and Colonial French. According to the TLF (IV, 200–2), the

SF etymon is ultimately derived from a loanword from Portuguese, *barroco* 'a rock of irregular shape'. As a loanword its sense was a technical one, in the domain of jewelry, used to describe a pearl of irregular shape. In the eighteenth century, it took on the sense 'unusual, bizarre' to describe an architectural style that departs from the rules of Renaissance architecture, and was then subsequently applied to art and music. In current SF, in addition to these senses, it describes things and behaviors that are bizarre, odd, unusual, peculiar, or whimsical. But the TLF cites a sentence from a work of the late-nineteenth/early-twentieth-century writer, Anatole France: '*Où ces militaires, demandait-on, étaient-ils allés chercher des phrases si baroques et ridicules?*' (Where did these army people go to look for these sentences that are so odd and ridiculous?). This sentence provides a link to a presumably older sense associated with language whose presence in Colonial French can be inferred from an attestation in LF and in the French-based creoles of the Indian Ocean. Whereas in LF *baroque* assumes a very specific sense, a broken variety of French with a heavy admixture of English, in the Indian Ocean varieties (Réunion, Mauritius, and the Seychelles), it refers to a bizarre sort of language. Specifically, in the case of Mauritius, it refers to child-like language;[8] in the Seychelles, the expression *nõ barok* designates a nickname; and in Réunion, it also means 'unbalanced', as for example a toy top, *toupi barok* (Bollée 2000). In HC, the senses of *bawòk* have become more generalized and clearly pejorative, as indicated in the entry from Valdman *et al.* (2007):

> **bawòk** adj./n. 1 coarse, vulgar, crude *Moun bawòk konsa ka fè ou wont nan lasosyete.* Such a vulgar person can embarrass you in society. **cf.** gwo soulye, mastòk 2 slipshod, slovenly *Ala nèg bawòk se ou, ou mache nenpòt jan al kay moun.* What a slovenly oaf you are, you go to people's houses dressed improperly.

6.4.3 Semantic differences between HC and SF cognates

In this section, I treat semantic differences between HC words and SF cognates. As was pointed out earlier in this chapter, our understanding of the linguistic situation in the overseas French colonies during the formative years of the seventeenth and eighteenth centuries remains sketchy. Furthermore, we have only partial knowledge about earlier stages of SF and imperfect descriptions of regional dialects, most of which are now on the verge of extinction. For that reason one cannot always determine whether differences in meaning between HC items and SF cognates reflect survivals or neologisms. Semantic changes may be classed in four main groups: (1) restriction of meaning, (2) extension of meaning, (3) change of word class, and (4) general semantic change. Finally, I will introduce the notion of the semantic potential, which is a theoretical construct put forward to account for semantic change (Picoche 1977).

1. **Restriction of meaning.** There are few instances of absolute restriction of meaning. One such case is *lestomak*, which only refers to the chest, whereas in LF, and presumably in Colonial French, it refers to the stomach as well. Another is *kabann* 'bed', whose French cognate means 'shack, hut' but is related to the verb *cabaner* 'to spend the night', noted in Louisiana in 1727 by a French traveler and attested in Louisiana and Old Mines, Missouri[9] (Rézeau 1997: 317). More generally, the HC term takes on, in addition to some of the meanings of its SF cognate, a more restricted sense. In the following sentence, *kabinè* and *jete* undergo some restriction or, more accurately, specialization of meaning: *Doktè a mande pou wè kabinè pitit la pou wè si l ap jete vè* 'The doctor asked to see the child's stools to see if he's excreting worms.' In Standard French, *cabinet* only means 'toilet' and *jeter* never has the restricted sense of excreting.

2. **Extension of meaning.** Instances of this type of semantic drift are numerous. For example, the term *blan* (from *blanc*) no longer refers exclusively to a White person but to any foreigner, so that American Blacks may be referred to as *blan*. The term *fyèl* (*fiel*) 'bile' refers to the gall bladder as well. *Jennen* (*gêner*) 'to bother, to make uncomfortable' extends its meaning to include the adjective 'narrow' (*Wout la te jennen, machin nan pa te kapab pase fasil* 'The road was narrow; the car couldn't pass easily') and 'to trap' (*Yo jennen rat la dèyè bifèt la* 'They trapped the rat behind the kitchen cabinet'). A more complex type of semantic extension is the use of *myèl* (*miel*) 'honey' for 'bee'. The word is derived by ellipsis from *mouche à miel* ('honey fly'), found in several Oïl-speaking regions of France. The term also means 'upset, irritated', as in *Ou pa fouti pale avè l maten an, msye myèl* 'You can't speak with him this morning, he's irritated.' Incidentally, in HC 'honey' is *siwo myèl* 'bee syrup'.

3. **Change of word class.** This type of change is more properly grammatical than semantic, although a semantic shift often accompanies a change in word class: adjective from noun, noun from verb, etc. In Section 5.3.1, I pointed out that, in HC, the grammatical class membership of words is relatively fluid. By conversion, verbs may take a nominal function. In this way, individual words of the language have a greater potential semantic range than their SF cognates. In this respect, HC functions more like Eng-

lish, as the following examples attest: *Li **gade** bèf la* 'He looked at the cow', *Fò ou fè on ti **gade*** 'You have to have a little look'. The verb *debòde* (*déborder*) illustrates both change of word class and semantic extension. The French cognate is a verb meaning 'to flow over' but in HC *debòde* functions as a verb with broader meaning: *rivyè a debòde* 'the river flowed over its banks', *Men lapriyè sa a dwe debòde sou sa n ap fè sou jan n ap viv* 'But religious devotion must extend to our actions and our way of life'. It also functions as an adjective whose meaning has drifted considerably from that of the corresponding verb: *Lè m sou, m fin debòde* 'When I'm drunk, I get really exuberant', *Debòde kou debòde, fò ou peye m* 'As shameless as you might be, you still have to pay me', *Msye a fin debòde sou tout moun jodi a* 'He's really furious at everybody today'. The following are other instances of combined word-class change and semantic shift: *gou* 'taste' → 'tasty'; *manman* 'mother' → 'female', *manman chat* 'female cat' → 'really large': *Msye gentan genyen on manman vant* 'he's gotten a real big belly'; *kolonn* 'column' →'a lot': *Gen on kolonn moun k ap vini* 'a lot of people are coming'.

4. **Miscellaneous change.** The following are examples of semantic shifts that do not necessarily involve extension or restriction of meaning, although in many cases some metaphoric extension seems to be involved. *Fyèl* 'bile' takes on the meaning of 'stamina, endurance': *Foutbolè yo ap fè fyèl* 'The soccer players are building up their endurance'; this semantic shift appears to be based on the belief that the production of bile leads to the build-up of strength and endurance. The meaning of *frèt* 'cold' (SF *froid* 'cold, cool') is extended to include 'quiet'; *jaden* (SF *jardin* 'garden') means any cultivated piece of land; *frekan* (SF *fréquent* 'frequent') has shifted to 'impertinent, insolent, rude, bold or forward'.

5. **The notion of semantic potential**. The meaning of a given word is not static. Words may be viewed as characterized by a semantic core that has the potential of being expanded or restricted. The semantic core usually refers to something that is concrete but has the potential to apply to more abstract notions. For example, in English the semantic core of 'to iron' refers to the concrete action of using a heated instrument (an iron) to flatten and make a textile substance smooth: 'I'm ironing the creases in my skirt'. But by metaphoric extension, it can refer to the straightening out of problems: 'Let's iron out our misunderstandings'. Metaphors involve comparison; in this case, misunderstandings are compared to wrinkled clothes and ironing them out results in 'flattening them out',

Table 6.3. Expansion of the Semantic Potential in Haitian Creole

SF etymon	SF semantic range	HC semantic range
barrer	1. to bar (a door) 2. to block, close (of road, etc.)	1. to bar, lock 2. to lock (close with bar) 3. to fence in, enclose 4. to exclude 5. to give s.o. a hard time 6. to put in a difficult condition 7. to surprise, catch red-handed 8. to conceal, hide
casser	1. to break 2. to overturn (as in a judicial decision) 3. to turn and break	1. to break 2. to tear down, eliminate 3. to cancel, annul, overturn 4. to break into, burglarize 5. to stop growing, developing 6. to change (a currency; break bill) 7. to pick, shell, shuck 8. to shake hands on a deal 9. to turn 10. to bow (while bending the knees) *kase koub* – to turn a corner *kase pye* – to stumble

just as ironing flattens out wrinkles. This semantic movement extends from the concrete (clothes) to the abstract (misunderstandings). The comparison of some HC words to their SF cognates suggests that an aspect of its lexical development is the extension of the semantic potential of the French etymon. Table 6.3 shows how the meaning of two sample verbs has expanded from French to HC.

Barrer originally meant to close a door with a bar, but in HC its meaning has broadened in two directions, the dominant one of which encompasses all actions that involve putting up any kind of obstacle, both concrete and abstract. The HC sense 'to surprise, to catch red-handed' is accountable in terms of that notion, for to surprise people in the process of doing something illicit or reprehensible is, in a figurative sense, to put obstacles in front of them. The sense 'to hide' appears to involve a more radical semantic shift that might lead to a split and the formation of a homonymous lexeme. In a sense, 'to hide' might be conceived as putting up obstacles so the hidden person cannot be seen.

In the case of the semantic development of *casser* in HC, two directions are discernible. The first direction yields the new metaphorical meanings of interrupting normal growth and of breaking a large bill by replacing it with lower-denomination bills or coins. The second direction, which occurred in Colonial French, as attested by the presence of that sense in LF (Valdman *et al.* 2010) and Réunion Creole (Chaudenson 1974: 724–6), spreads in the form of a metonymic development 'to pick, i.e., to break off part of a plant in order to harvest'. A further progression in that direction has led to more abstract senses, such as interrupting a forward movement by turning and breaking the vertical position of one's body by bowing.

6.5 The Contribution of Other Languages

In the second half of the eighteenth century, the population of colonial Saint-Domingue was predominantly of African origin. Slaves imported from West Africa, many of them recently arrived and referred to as *bosal*, outnumbered Whites and Mulattoes by a proportion of nearly 8 to 1. Yet the direct effect of African languages on the overall lexicon of HC in terms of transferred lexemes is relatively small. A more accurate evaluation of the impact of these languages is gained when we consider more indirect influences, such as calques and ideophones (see Chapter 5). The first external (non-French) influence on the developing vernacular of Saint-Domingue was that of the indigenous Amerindian languages, Taino in Hispaniola and neighboring islands, and Carib in the Lesser Antilles. In more recent periods, English and Spanish have profoundly influenced the lexical development of HC. Finally, French continues to be the main source for lexical enrichment. The special sociolinguistic relationship between the two languages and the linguistic influence of bilingual speakers make it inappropriate to consider transfer of lexical material from contemporary SF as borrowing; this issue will be discussed in Chapter 11.

6.5.1 Amerindian influence

Amerindian words, referring to local flora and fauna, came to constitute part of a specialized vocabulary connected with colonial economic life that is reflected in the French-based creole languages of the New World and the Indian Ocean. This source of the HC lexicon has been discussed in Section 6.2 (*Le Vocabulaire des Isles*); see Maginat (2006), Bollée (2012) and Jansen (2012).

6.5.2 African influence

In light of the fact that at the end of the colonial period people of African origin constituted nearly 90% of the population of Saint-Domingue, one would expect there to be a major influence of African languages on the lexicon of HC. In fact, the number of terms that can be traced directly to African sources is surprisingly small, yet significant. This is probably because the communicative needs of newly arrived slaves could only be met by the language shared by all subgroups in the plantation setting. Yet, as was pointed out in Chapter 1, African languages survived well into the post-colonial period even though on most plantations, and certainly in towns, the slaves had diverse ethnic origins and spoke different languages. However, African languages had low prestige and probably were not transmitted to new generations of locally born individuals: the creoles.

On the other hand, because the slaves who toiled in the fields and in the sugar mills had little contact with speakers of French, some terms associated with African culture and the domestic domain did survive. Indeed, most of the terminology associated with the Vodou religion and magic practices originates in Ewe and Fongbe. These were languages spoken in areas bordering the Guinea coast, whose speakers had a major role in the introduction and preservation of Vodou practices: *Vodou* 'Vodou', *kanzo* 'initiatory fire ordeal to reach a certain degree in Vodou', *manbo* 'Vodou priestess', *oungan* 'Vodou priest', *oungenikon* 'leader of chants in Vodou ceremonies', *ounsi* 'Vodou initiate'. Another large group of Africanisms refers to food: see Table 6.4 for a sample of words of African origin, with an indication of the probable West African source. The first African slaves imported to Saint-Domingue came from Senegambia and spoke such languages as Wolof, Bambara, and Mandingo. More numerous were later importations, from the Guinea Coast ports, of speakers of Yoruba, Ibo, and languages of the Kwa group (Ewe and Fongbe), and from regions south of the Equator who spoke Bantu languages, for example, Kikongo (Bollée 2012) and (Manigat 2006).

As was mentioned in Section 5.3.2, the relatively meager stock of lexemes of African origin belies the African influence in the HC lexicon. More important is the large number of calques in which African concepts are clothed in words of French origin. For example, the terms for the various parts of the eye (*po je* 'skin of the eye', *plim je* 'hair of the eye', etc.) are based on semantically transparent compounds in the Kwa languages. Another major African lexical influence are onomatopoeic expressions (onomatopoeia/ideophones), for which see Section 5.3.5.

Table 6.4. Words of African Origin in Haitian Creole

HC word	English gloss	African source language
aganman	chameleon	Ewe/Fongbe
akasan	corn-based, milky gruel	Fongbe
akra	malanga fritter	Fongbe
bakoulou	dishonest, crafty, sly person	Kikongo
banza	one-string guitar	Kimbundu
bègwè	dimwit, dummy	Fongbe
bo	kiss	Ewe
bòkò	Vodou priest who has not undergone full initiation	Ewe
bounda	rear-end, butt	Bambara
degi	extra measure, bonus, supplement, a little extra for good measure	Ewe
foufou	dish made from mashed manioc, plantain, sweet potato, breadfruit	Kikongo
gonbo	okra	Ewe/Fongbe
kalalou	dish prepared with okra, meat and spices	Fongbe
koko	vagina	Kikongo
kore	to prop up, hold in place	Mandingo
lota	rash, heat rash, skin disease, skin spots	Kikongo
madansara	woman who transports and sells goods	Bambara
manba	peanut butter	Kikongo
masisi	homosexual	Gun, Ewe
rara	musical group parading before Carnival	Yoruba
tchentchen	finely ground corn	Twi
wanga	Vodou charm	Kikongo
zonbi	zombie	Kikongo

6.5.3 English influence

The first contacts between Haiti and the English-speaking world date back to the Revolutionary period, when an English expeditionary corps conducted several campaigns against the French in Saint-Domingue (1790–1800). After the Declaration of Independence, King Henri Christophe, who ruled northern Haiti, established strong commercial and cultural links with England to insure protection against any attempt by France to regain the lost colony. Christophe also had an especially good rapport with British abolitionists such as William Wilberforce. Indeed, for some time the Haitian ruler contemplated the replacement of French by English as his country's official language. American traders were also present from the first years of the creation of the Black Republic. Some English loanwords can be dated back to this early period of English contact. For example, there still exists in the north the term *djal* 'girlfriend' (cognate with *gal*). The initial affricate of that word also occurs in the West Indian cognate *gyal* and identifies it as an early loanword.

The nineteen-year US occupation (1915–34) was accompanied by massive lexical saturation that has continued unabated since that period. The most active agents for the transmission of English loanwords have been the growing number of young Haitians who elect to study at US universities and, especially, members of the diaspora living in the United States and the Bahamas, whose number exceeds one million. These individuals can be considered the conduits for a growing number of English loanwords in the varieties of HC spoken in these communities, which are then brought in during their visits or returns to the mother country, or by the intermediary of exchanged communications. Many of these loanwords refer to technology: *gedj* 'gauge', *bouldozè* 'bulldozer', *djak* 'jack', *estatè* 'choke', *gaz* 'gasoline', *kontenè* 'container', *plòg* 'plug', *tep* 'tape recorder'. Many others denote everyday items: *bamann* 'bartender', *bebidòl* 'babydoll nightdress', *chany* 'shoeshine boy', *dayiva* 'diver, excellent swimmer', *kanistè* (canister) 'tin box', *tcheke* 'to check', *yès* 'yes'. We have seen, in Section 5.3.1, that by way of loanwords containing the English suffix -*man* (*bamann, wachman* 'watchman') this suffix has been adopted in HC and has become moderately productive by being adjoined to native bases, for example, *dasomann* 'gatecrasher'. On the other hand, English loanwords may become the base for derivation, for example, *plòg* → *plòge* 'to plug', *klips* 'paper-clip' → *klipse* 'to staple'.

One of the most interesting English loanwords is *konbèlann*, from Cumberland. Originally, it referred to the trade name of a type of copper wire used to illegally tap electric current. Its meaning has been generalized to include 'siphon' and any makeshift device: *M pa jwenn pyès la pou machin nan men mekanisyen an fè yon konbèlann pou m ka sèvi avè l konsa* 'I couldn't find the part for the car but the mechanic managed to make some makeshift device to enable me to use it like that'.

With the massive international involvement in reconstruction of the Haitian infrastructure after the devastating earthquake of January 12, 2010, and with the presence of the UN multinational stabilization force (MINUSTAH), the influence of English as a language of wider international communication can be expected to expand. A phenomenon that has both social and linguistic implications is the popularity of rap and its most famous group, B.C. (pronounced as in English [bi si], not as HC [be se]): Barricade (Barikad Crew). Nowadays, rap has become a major vector for the introduction of English loanwords among young Haitians.

6.5.4 Spanish influence

In their trading contacts with Dominicans, Haitians who live in border regions use numerous Spanish loanwords, some of which have been incorporated in HC. Another important vector for the transmission of Spanish loanwords is the *zafra*, the recruitment of seasonal cane-cutters for the large sugar plantations in the Dominican Republic. In the early twentieth century, Haitians migrated to Cuba to seek work in sugar plantations and brought back loanwords. Some sample Spanish loanwords are *bobo/bobòy* (*bobo*) 'fool', *bolèt* (*boleta*) 'lottery', *kabés* (*cabeza*) 'head', *kabicha* (*cabecear*) 'to doze', *kako* (*caco*) 'guerrilla fighter during the American occupation', *mantèg* (*manteca*) 'lard', *matcho* (*macho*) 'womanizer', *vyewo* (*viejo*) 'cane-cutter returned from Cuba'. Two Spanish loanwords, *mòn* (*morro*) 'hill, mountain' and *mawon* (*cimarron*) 'maroon (escaped slave)' date back to the colonial period and form part of the *vocabulaire des Isles*. In the case of *kaba* (*acabar*) 'done for', which is also attested in colonial texts, it may represent a convergence between Spanish and African influences. Dyola shows a form that shares both the form and the meaning of the HC word: *kaba* 'to be finished, completed'.

Summary

Table 6.5 provides some indication of the provenance of the HC lexicon as determined by Annegret Bollée, a creolist from the University of Bamberg, Germany, who is compiling the first etymological dictionary for French-based creoles. The table lists the origin of words beginning with the letter (also phoneme) *k* taken from the *Ti Diksyonnè Kreyòl-Franse* (A. Bentolila *et al.* 1976).[10] The 5,000 entries of that HC–SF bilingual dictionary are based on the analysis of a specific corpus collected in the Saint-Marc region, north of Port-au-Prince.

Table 6.5. Origin of the Lexicon of French-based Creoles

Origin	Entries	Percentage
Contemporary French	244	60.2
Survivals (dialect and Old French)	67	16.5
Neologisms	63	15.6
French origin total		**92.3**
Vocabulaire des Isles	4	0.4
Spanish/Portuguese	5	1.2
English	1	0.3
Other European origin total		**1.9**
African	11	2.7
Amerindian	4	1.0
Other sources or unknown	10	2.5
Non-European origin total		**6.2**

Notes

1. Neologisms involving the affixation of suffixes and prefixes were discussed in Chapter 5.
2. But, as we pointed out in Chapter 2, post-vocalic *r* does occur variably in NHC (Capois); see also Chapter 11.
3. As indicated in Chapters 2 and 11, these vowels occur widely in *kreyòl swa*, spoken by bilinguals and, variably, in Capois.
4. There is widespread alternation in the verb bases derived from French *-er* verbs in which final *e* is followed by a nasal consonant, e.g., *pwomene/pwomenen* 'to stroll', *fime/fimen* 'to smoke'. Generally, the absence of progressive nasal assimilation characterizes *kreyòl swa*.
5. Note that there is a semantic shift from Standard French.
6. One of the two Haitian pioneers in the description of HC, Jules Faine, hypothesized that French-based creoles reflected an origin in regional varieties of French and dialects of France: '... *elles* [French-based creoles] *accusent uniformément le caractère de langue néo-romane, les différences entre elles étant une fonction de l'apport même des dialectes ou des patois d'origine*' (...they uniformly show the nature of a neo-Romance language, the differences among them being a function of the direct contribution of the original regional varieties or dialects; 1939: xix–xxii). In his 1936 book, he posited a direct influence of the Norman dialect but, after looking at other French-based creoles, in particular Mauritian, in 1939 he proposed the existence of a sort of nautical lingua franca (*un patois nautique*) in use in the French harbors of the English Channel and the Atlantic Ocean that sailors carried to the seventeenth- and eighteenth-century French colonies.

7. The choice of Louisiana French (LF) rather than other varieties of the language that emerged in the French overseas colonies of the seventeenth and eighteenth centuries stems from my recent and simultaneous editing of dictionaries of HC and LF (Valdman et al. 2007, 2010). Most of the senses found in Louisiana also occur in the other North American regions: Quebec Province, Acadia, St. Barts.

8. In LF, *baroque* occurs both as an adjective and as an adverb. Although the adjective is polysemous, like the adverb, it bears on a variety of the language heavily affected by English (Valdman et al. 2010):

> **baroque**[1] [barɔk] *adj.* **1** foolish, silly *Toute cette famille est manière baroque.* 'That whole family is sort of foolish'. **2** strange, bizarre *Une histoire baroque.* 'A bizarre story'. **3** broken, mixed (of speech) *Avec ma mère je parle en français avec elle tout le temps, mais alle parle moitié en anglais. On appelle ça baroque, c'est mêlé, quelques mots français, anglais.* 'With my mother I speak French all the time, but she speaks half in English. We call that broken, it's mixed, some words in French, [others] English.' *Et comme mon garçon qui reste en haut là, tu peux voir, lui il parle plein français, mais il parle pas comme nous-autres. Tu peux voir qu'il était pas habitué à parler français. T'appelles ça 'baroque'.* 'And like my son who lives up in the bayou, he speaks French, but he doesn't talk like us. You can tell he was not used to speaking French. They call that "baroque".'

> **baroque**[2] [barɔk] *adv.* in a broken, mixed way (of speech) *Il comprend tout et il peut dire quelques affaires, mais il parle pas bien en français. C'est pour ça on dit qu'il parle baroque. Parce que il dit quelques mots en anglais et quelques mots en français.* 'He understands everything and he can say a few things, but he doesn't speak French well. That's why we say he speaks "baroque". Because he says some words in English and some words in French'.

9. Old Mines (La Vieille Mine) is a community located in southeast Missouri founded, in the early eighteenth century, by French settlers who mined for lead. As part of the Illinois region of New France, located close to the Mississippi river, it had close contact with Louisiana. Few fluent speakers of the original French variety remain today.

10. The data are adapted from a table comparing the provenance of samples of vocabulary from HC and Seychellois Creole listed in Stein (1984: 34). That author's source of the data was a presentation made by Bollée at the Third Colloque International des Etudes Créoles in St. Lucia, in May 1981.

7 Basic Sentence Structure

7.1 Introduction

Chapters 7 through 10 will deal with the syntactic structure of HC. The present chapter describes the structure of simple sentences. Chapter 8 focuses on the verb system, in particular, verb markers that express tense, mood, and aspect (TMA markers). It also discusses one important type of verbal construction in HC: serial verbs. Chapter 9 examines the structure of noun phrases. Chapter 10 covers processes that characterize complex sentences, such as interrogation, coordination, embedding of relative clauses, and permutation of sentence elements (focalization and topicalization), all of which affect the order of sentential constituents.

Simple sentences are defined as declarative sentences containing a single predicate. The core of a sentence is the predicate that structures[1] the information contained in an utterance. Some sentences contain only a predicate: *Come on! Well! John? What rain!*, but generally the predicate is accompanied by a subject. It may also be followed by one or more adverbial complements:

Subject	Predicate	Adverbial complement
the boy	broke the glass	last night

By and large simple sentences in HC follow the same general structure as those in English:

(1)
Subject	Predicate	Adverbial complement
Mari ak manman l	*t ap lave rad*	*bò larivyè a*
'Mary and her mother'	'were washing clothes'	'by the river'

Nouns and verbs are the two basic or **prototypical** classes of words. In many languages of the world, these are the types of words that first appear in child-language (G. Hazaël-Massieux 1983; Ludwig 1992). Prototypically, verbs denote actions and nouns are the **agents** of actions. Adjectives and adverbs are, in a sense, secondary: the latter modify verbs and the former modify nouns. For many languages, verbs, but not adjectives, occur as the core of predicates. A major difference between English and HC, however, lies in the structure of the predicate. In English, all predicates must contain a verb. In (2a), the action verb *to trim* forms the core of the predicate, while the noun *John* is the agent. Sentences (2b) and (2c) differ significantly from (2a) in that the cores of the predicates are not action verbs, and the subjects *it* and *the magnolia tree* do not function as agents. The function of the verb *to be* is simply to link the subject and the nominal predicate in (2b) and the adjectival predicate in (2c).

(2a) John *trimmed* the magnolia tree.
(2b) It *is* a magnolia tree.
(2c) The magnolia tree *was* red.

In contrast, HC adjectives and nouns, as well as verbs, may by themselves constitute predicates:

(3a) Li   bèl.
     3SG   pretty (ADJECTIVE)
     'She's pretty.'

(3b) Ou   pa   gason.
     2SG   NEG   man (NOUN)
     'You're not manly.'

Some may be adverbial complements:

(3c) Yo   nan   jaden   an.
     3PL   in   garden   the
     'They're in the garden.'

7.2 Multifunctionality of Words in HC

Three features characterize the syntax of simple sentences in HC: (1) the important role of linear order to signal syntactic function, (2) the relative lack of clear marking on word classes, and (3) the multifunctionality of words, as was stressed in Chapter 5. For example, *manje* can serve as both noun ('food') and verb ('to eat'):[2]

(4a) Li   manje   ze   a.
     3SG   to eat   egg   DET
     'She ate the egg.'

(4b) Li   renmen   manje   kreyòl.
     3SG   like (VERB)   food (NOUN)   creole (ADJ)
     'He likes creole food.'

Other multifunctional words, *bosal*, for example, can function equally as an adjective (5a), a noun (5b), an adverb (5c), and a predicate (5d) (Damoiseau 1996: 161):

(5a) Sanon *se yon nèg bosal*. 'Sanon is a brutal guy.'
(5b) Se *yon bosal*. 'He's a brute.'
(5c) Li jwe *bosal*. 'He plays dirty.'
(5d) Li *bosal* twòp. 'He's too brutal.'

HC lacks inflectional affixes like the plural morpheme attached to nouns in English, nor does it have separate morphemes corresponding to English 3rd person singular or past tense inflectional endings affixed to verbs. In HC, nouns may be pluralized or modified by determiners, but the plural marker, the free morpheme *yo*, and various other determiners like the definite determiner *LA*[3] do not necessarily occur alongside the noun. For example, in (6) the plural marker *yo* (which also carries the semantic notion 'specific or presupposed') has scope over the entire noun phrase rather than only its head noun (see Chapter 9):

(6) Timoun (ki rete ak Avina) *yo* ...
    Children who to live with (PROPER NOUN) 3PL
    'The children who lived with Avina ...'

While verbs are often preceded by TMA markers (7a, 7b) and auxiliary verbs (7c),[4] these elements are not obligatory; in fact, they are more properly described as predicate markers since they may also occur with nouns and adjectives.

(7a) Yo   *t*   *ap*   lave   rad.
     3PL   TMA MARKER   TMA MARKER   to wash clothes
            [+PAST]   [+PROG]
     'They were washing clothes.'

(7b) Yo   *te*   bouke.
     3PL   TMA MARKER   tired (ADJ)
            [+PAST]
     'They were tired.'

(7c) Li   *va*   gason.
     3SG   TMA MARKER   man (NOUN)
            [+FUTURE]
     'He'll become manly.'

192 Basic Sentence Structure

7.3 Predicate Types in HC

The grammatical machinery of HC consists of function words and word order. Accordingly, the focus of a grammatical description for the language must be to identify various possible combinations of function words, constraints on word order, and the semantic content of function words. In this section I describe various types of predicates that ultimately determine sentence structure.

7.3.1 Introducers

These are adverbs or verbs that introduce predicates in subjectless sentences. They are analogous to *there*, *here*, or *that* in English or *voici*, *voilà*, and *il y a* in French. In this section, I treat only those adverbs that serve this function, as well as the verb *gen* (the short form of *genyen*) and *se*. Other verbs that function as introducers will be presented in Section 8.4. The most common introducer in HC is *se*, which is homonymous with the verbal linking element, the overt **copula** *se*:

(8) *Se* yon bèl kannot. 'That's a nice rowboat.'

Gen 'to have' also serves frequently as a predicate introducer:

(9) *Gen* anpil moun nan lakou a. 'There are a lot of people in the yard.'

Both *gen* and *se* may occur with TMA markers, for example, the past marker *te* and the conditional marker *ta* (see Section 8.2), and more rarely auxiliary verbs like *vin* (Section 8.3).

(10a) *Se te* pou veye. 'It was for the wake.'
(10b) *Se ta* pi gwo peche. 'It would be a bigger sin.'
(10c) *Vin gen* yon branch lanmè 'An arm of the sea appeared that blocked
 a ki bare l. her.'

Other frequently used introducers are *men* 'here is', *nanpwen* 'there isn't', and the polysemic exclamation *apa*:

(11a) *Men* lajan an. 'Here's the money.'
(11b) *Nanpwen* mal nan sa. 'There's no harm in that.'
(11c) *Apa* ou vini? 'It's true that you came?'
(11d) *Apa* ou sa! 'Here you are (finally)!'
(11e) Bondye papa! *Apa* volè 'My God! Thieves broke into the house!'
 kase kay la!

7.3.2 The copula

In English and French, predicates containing an adjective or noun require the use of an overt copula, a form of the verb *to be* (*être*). These predicates typically assign a quality to the subject in a descriptive sentence (12a), situate the subject either spatially or temporally in locative and temporal sentences (12b) and (12c), respectively, or identify the subject in equational sentences (12d):

(12a)	'Her cheeks *are* red.'	'Ses joues *sont* rouges.'
(12b)	'We *were* in Haiti.'	'Nous *étions* en Haïti.'
(12c)	'It *is* two o'clock.'	'Il *est* deux heures.'
(12d)	'We *are* lawyers.'	'Nous *sommes* avocats.'

HC does not always display an element equivalent of *to be* in these types of sentences. The absence of the overt copula often forms the basis for the claim that HC is a 'simple' language. It is arbitrary to use such a specific and relatively minor feature as the presence or absence of a copula in descriptive, locative, or equational sentences as the criterion for the relative simplicity or complexity of a language. Furthermore, the absence of an overt copula turns out to be a feature widely shared among the world's languages. For instance, Russian has a **zero copula** in some instances: *on soldat* 'he's a soldier'. In any case, because HC does have two elements corresponding to the English *to be* or the French *être*, *se* and *ye*, one must look at particular sentence types. As a general statement, though, one might say that zero copula is the rule in HC; *se* and *ye* are introduced only in certain cases.

Descriptive and locative sentences

No copula appears in neutral descriptive sentences whose predicates consist of adjectives or adverbial expressions:

(13a)	Dlo a *sale*.	'The water is salty.'
(13b)	Tifi a *bèl*.	'The girl's pretty.'
(13c)	M *byen*.	'I'm fine.'
(13d)	Li *avèk lafyèv*.	'She has fever (literally, she is with fever).'

Zero copula also characterizes predicates containing the expressions *grangou* 'hunger', *pè* 'fear', *swèf* 'thirst', etc., which function as verbs (14a) or nouns (14b):

(14a)	Ou *swèf*?	'Are you thirsty?'
(14b)	M gen yon *swèf* k ap touye m.	'I'm dying of thirst (literally, I have a thirst that's killing me).'

Both *grangou* and *swèf* may occur as post-nominal adjectives. Compare the position and the meaning of these two forms with the pre-posed adjective *bèl*:

(15a) Li *bèl*. 'She's beautiful.'
(15b) Se yon *bèl* moun. 'She's a beautiful person.'
(15c) Se yon moun *swèf*. 'He's a man who is always thirsty.'
(15d) Se yon moun *grangou*. 'He's a man who is always hungry.'

Also *pè* 'fear', for example, patterns like many verbs that accept verbal complements:

(16a) Li *bezwen* dòmi. 'He needs to sleep.'
(16b) Li *renmen* dòmi. 'He likes to sleep.'
(16c) Li *pè* dòmi. 'He's afraid to sleep.'

Locative and temporal sentences are constructed with zero copula as well:

(17a) Bèf yo *nan lakou a*. 'The cows are in the yard.'
(17b) Mwen *lekòl kounye a*. 'I'm at school now.'

The copula se

The copula *se*, to be distinguished from the introducer *se* discussed in Section 7.3.1 above, characterizes equational sentences whose predicate is composed of a noun or **noun phrase (NP):**

(18a) Li se *ayisyen*. 'She's Haitian.'
(18b) Sa se *yon chwal*. 'That's a horse.'
(18c) Jodi a se *dimanch*. 'Today is Sunday.'
(18d) Li se *yon nèg kare*. 'He's a solid guy.'

There are sentences, however, in which the predicate contains a noun phrase in which either *se* or zero copula appears. Jules Faine (1936) noted the possibility of a contrast between *se* and zero copula when he stated that the latter reflected 'temporary, accidental qualities, or a transitional state, essentially mobile or changing', whereas the former expressed 'fixed, essential qualities, inseparable from the subject, or a permanent state.' In setting up this distinction, Faine may have been influenced by the contrast in Spanish between the two copula verbs *estar* 'temporary state copula' and *ser* 'permanent state copula.'

In fact, in HC the possible contrasts between zero copula and the presence of *se* involve descriptive rather than equational sentences. In (19a), the speaker is identifying the subject *yo* as 'men' in opposition to 'women'; in (19b) she is making a descriptive statement and ascribing a quality: *gason* means 'manly, virile' rather than the classificatory feature 'man'. Similarly,

7.3 Predicate Types 195

in (19c) an identification is made, whereas (19d) involves a value judgment, ascribing in effect a temporary rather than an essential quality, as Faine perceptively observed.

(19a) Yo *se* gason. 'They're men.' (equational)
(19b) Ou gason. 'You're a man (i.e., you act in a manly fashion, you're not impotent).' (descriptive)
(19c) Li *se* yon kretyen. 'She's a Christian (versus a Vodou practitioner).' (equational)
(19d) Ou kwe yo bon kretyen? 'Do you think they're good Christians (i.e., that they behave like good Christians)?' (descriptive)

As a linking element in equational sentences *se* is freely replaced by the introducer *se*; the latter, occurring without an NP subject, begins sentences:

(20a) Li *se* yon bon gason. 'He's a good boy.'
(20b) *Se* yon bon gason. 'It's a good boy.'

(21a) Sa *se* chèlbè. 'That's pretense, for show.'
(21b) *Se* chèlbè. 'It's pretense, for show.'

(22a) Sa ou di la *se* bobin. 'What you say here is nonsense.'
(22b) *Se* bobin. 'It's nonsense.'

Copular *se* is deleted in negative sentences. Compare (23a) and (23b):[5]

(23a) Yo *se* gason. 'They're men.'
(23b) Yo pa gason. 'They're not men.'

Thus, in the case of negative sentences, the distinction between the descriptive and the equational interpretation is neutralized.

The copula *ye*
Compare the following paired sentences:

(24a) Li avèk lafyèv. 'She has fever.'   (24b) Se avèk lafyèv li *ye*.
(25a) Bèf yo nan lakou a. 'The cows are in the yard.'   (25b) Se nan lakou a bèf yo *ye*.
(26a) Li se ayisyen. 'He is Haitian.'   (26b) Se ayisyen li *ye*.

The paired sentences are synonymous, except that in the (b) versions the complement (*avèk lafyèv, nan lakou a, ayisyen*) are **focalized**, i.e., the stress is on the **focus** of the sentence. **Focalization** refers to a syntactic transformation that involves the fronting of the focus (or **comment** or **rheme**), the part of the sentence that contains the new or most important information, as opposed to the part of the sentence that contains the **topic** (or **theme**) (see Section 9.2.7 and Chapter 10). In HC, as is the case in English and French, focalization involves shifting the focus – adverbial complements in (24b) and (26b) and the noun in (25b) – to the front of the sentence. In effect, the focalized element is moved to the front of the sentence (**fronting**), it is introduced by *se* and is then embedded in a complex sentence. However, this fronting has the consequence of **stranding** the subject in final position. *Ye* is inserted to avoid this stranding. Schematically, (24b) is derived by the application of the following hypothetical steps:

Step 1 – Focalization: Li *avèk lafyèv*.
Step 2 – Fronting: *avèk lafyèv* li –
Step 3 – Embedding in a clause introduced by *se*:   Se (*avèk lafyèv*) li –
Step 4 – *Ye* insertion: Se (*avèk lafyèv*) li *ye*.
Actual transformed sentence: *Se avèk lafyèv li ye.*

Thus *ye* does not constitute another copula but a sort of grammatical operator triggered by the presence of semantic or textual elements in a sentence that cause syntactic permutations; it replaces both zero copula and *se*.

Ye typically appears in *wh*-questions, which, like focalization, involve the fronting of a syntactic element, specifically, the question element. In *wh*-questions, the interrogation refers to a particular syntactic element (subject, direct object, adverbial complement, etc.) rather than to the entire predicate. *Wh*-questions are so termed because the questioned element is replaced by an interrogative pronoun or adverb, which in English usually begins with *wh*; in HC they would be more appropriately labeled *ki*-questions (see Section 9.3.2). In (27a–d), interrogative sentences that open with the interrogative marker *ki* are shown, together with the responses they might elicit:[6]

(27a)   *Ki jan* ou ye? – M *byen*.   'How are you?' – 'I'm well.'
(27b)   *Ki lè* li ye? – Se *inè*.   'What time is it?'– 'It's one o'clock.'
(27c)   *Ki kote* li ye? – Li *nan lakou a*. 'Where is she?' – 'She's in the yard.'
(27d)   (*Ki*) *sa* li ye? – Se *yon bèf*. 'What is it?' – 'It's a cow.'

The copula, TMA markers, and auxiliary verbs

Predicates linked to the subject by zero copula, *se* or *ye* behave like any predicate in that they may include the presence of TMA markers and auxiliary verbs that express the various predicative semantic notions (see Section 8.1). Generally, the nominal, adjectival, and adverbial complements that form the core of copula predicates are **statives**, that is, they refer to states rather than processes or events. As a result they are unlikely to actualize the progressive meaning which, together with definite (certain) futurity, constitutes the semantic potential of the marker *ap*. When it occurs with these types of predicates, *ap* expresses futurity:

(28)   Kè mwen *ap* nan men ou.   'My heart will be in your hands.'

The adjective *malad* 'ill', on the other hand, is a **non-stative** that refers to a possible process and it may take on a progressive as well as future meaning (Damoiseau 1996: 252).[7]

(29)   L ap malad.   'She'll be ill; she's becoming ill.'

TMA markers are placed before predicates containing zero copula. In (30a), *va* expresses the future; in (31b) *te*, the past.

(30a)   Zafè a *va* gate.   'That business is going to fail.' (literally, is going to be spoiled)
(30b)   Li *te* geri.   'She was healed.'

As is the case with the negative, for example, (23b) above, the presence of TMA markers causes the copula (*se*) to be deleted:

(31a)   Li *te* jandam.   'He was a policeman.'
(31b)   Li *t av ap* ti bway.   'He would probably be a big boy.'

The deletion of *se* with the negative and TMA markers shown in (23b) and in (31a) and (31b) supports the claim made in Section 7.3.2 that in HC zero copula constitutes the general rule and that *se* and *ye* appear under special circumstances.

7.3.3   Auxiliary verbs

These verbs generally impart a specific meaning of some sort of process, in addition to linking the predicate to the subject. Most auxiliary verbs correspond to verbs that may independently constitute predicates (lexical verbs), but they differ in meaning from them (see Table 7.1). Some do not have corresponding lexical verbs, for example, *fèk* 'to have just', *kapab/kap/kab/ka* 'to be able to', and *mèt* 'to be allowed to'. In a sense, most auxiliary verbs may be considered the short form of verbs that constitute full predicates. Generally, there is some semantic relationship between the lexical verb and the corresponding auxiliary.[8] For example, *rive* 'to succeed' may be viewed as 'to have arrived' or 'to have met a goal'. The completive *fin* is closely

198   Basic Sentence Structure

Table 7.1. Auxiliary Verbs and Corresponding Lexical Verbs

Lexical verb	Auxiliary verb
konnen 'to know'	*konn* 'habitual'
mete 'to put, place, put on'	*mete* 'to begin'
pran 'to take'	*pran* 'to begin'
rann 'to give back, return'	*rann* 'to make, render'
rive 'to arrive'	*rive* 'to succeed'
sanble 'to resemble'	*sanble* 'to appear, seem'
soti 'to go out'	*sot* 'to have just'
tonbe 'to fall'	*tonbe* 'to become, start to'
tounen 'to make a turn, return'	*tounen* 'to become'
vini 'to come'	*vin* 'to become, turn'
fini 'to finish'	*fin* 'to have just'
dwe 'to owe'	*dwe* 'to have to'

related to the sense 'to finish' of the corresponding lexical verb. However, auxiliaries are best viewed as separate verbs because of the significant difference in meaning, and their different functional and syntactic properties.

Verbs of this type enter into constructions with adjectives, for example, *Ou sanble malad* 'you seem ill' and *Li vin nwè* 'it turned black'. In the latter example, the verb *vin* does more than ascribe the quality of blackness to the subject; it expresses that it has acquired this quality. Auxiliary verbs also enter into more complex constructions in which they assign a quality to a noun phrase; this construction is termed **predicate** or **object complement** since an adjective complements the meaning of the direct object NP, which together with the verb constitutes the predicate:

(32)   Li rann Pyè *fou.*   'She made Peter crazy.'

The difference between matched auxiliaries and lexical verbs may be demonstrated by questioning the complements. For example, to question the adjective *fou* that serves as second complement of (32), one could not use that auxiliary verb; most native speakers question the grammaticality of (33a):

(33a)   ?Ki jan li rann Pyè?   Literally, 'How did she make Peter?'

One would have to say:

(33b)   Ki sa li fè Pyè?   'What did she do to Peter?'

On the other hand, to question the noun phrase *liv la* that serves as second complement of (34), one would use the interrogative pronoun *ki sa* 'what':

(34) Li rann Pyè *liv la*.   'She gave the book back to Peter.'

(35) Ki sa li rann Pyè?   'What did she give back to Peter?'

Kapab, *mèt*, and *dwe* form a separate subclass of auxiliary verbs, not only because they do not have corresponding lexical verbs, but also because they have particular syntactic properties. As shown in (36) and (37), *kapab* and *dwe* are also polysemic. In (36a), the latter is a deontic (expressing obligation) and an epistemic (expressing eventuality):

(36a) Li *dwe* ale.   'She has to go away.'
(36b) M *dwe* bliye chapo mwen an lekòl la.   'I must have forgotten my hat at the school.'

Kapab expresses both ability and possibility:

(37a) Yo pa *kapab* mache.   'They can't walk.'
(37b) M pa *ka* vini.   'I won't be able to come.'

Auxiliary verbs will be treated in greater detail in Section 8.3.

7.3.4 Transitive verbs

These verbs, which comprise the largest group in HC, may be followed by a NP object. Generally, the object follows the verb directly:

(38) Li mare *konpè Makak* nan paravan.   'He tied Brer Monkey to the screen.'

Transitive verbs vary greatly with regard to their semantic features. These features are reflected by the types of subjects and objects with which these verbs may co-occur and, ultimately, by the semantic relationship between the subject and the object. For example, subject NPs whose **heads** (main words) are animate nouns may be **agents** that cause a change in animate or inanimate **patients**:

(39a) Li kage *chèz la*.   'She made the chair lean.'
(39b) Chasè a touye *pentad yo*.   'The hunter killed the guinea hens.'

Other subject NPs contain animate nouns that are not truly agents, for they have no effect on the object NP; we may speak here of the

200   *Basic Sentence Structure*

nominative-accusative relationship to underscore the relative neutrality of the link. Note that, semantically, these verbs do not denote actions, as do *kage* and *touye* in (39):

(40a) Ti gason an gade *liv mwen*.   'The boy looked at my book.'
(40b) Anayiz vle *wòb la*.   'Anayiz wants the dress.'

Inanimate subject NPs may be an **instrument**, effecting a change by a named or unnamed agent or an independent **force** that acts directly upon a patient:

(41a) Kouto a kap koupe *zo*.   'The knife can cut bones.'
(41b) Klou sa a pete *kawoutchou a*.   'This nail punctured the tire.'

Some transitive verbs select agents that act upon themselves. They do not show any special structural characteristics. The **reflexive** relationship between the agent and the patient or between the nominative and the accusative is indicated by the special NPs *kò* 'body' + Pronoun or *tèt* 'head' + Pronoun:

(42a) Mari l touye *tèt li*.   'Her husband killed himself.'
(42b) Souke *kò ou*.   'Hurry up.' (literally, shake yourself)

However, the reflexive relationship may also be expressed by a direct-object pronoun, as well as the equivalent of English *self*, namely, *kò* or *tèt* (Carden and Stewart 1988):[9]

(43a) Li blese *l*.   'He hurt himself.'
(43b) Li blese *tèt li*.   'He hurt himself.'

The use of the object pronoun instead of *tèt/kò* + Pronoun appears limited to the 3rd person (the use with 1st or 2nd person is doubtful):

(44a) M blese *tèt mwen*,   'I hurt myself.'
(44b) ?M blese *m*.
(44c) Ou blese *tèt ou*.   'You hurt yourself.'
(44d) ?Ou blese *ou*.

As was pointed out in Section 7.2, HC is characterized by the multifunctionality of words. In the examples below, in the same sentence *chante* and *dòmi* function as a verb and as a noun serving as an object:

(45a) Li *chante* yon bèl ti *chante*.   'She sang a nice little song.'
(45b) M *dòmi* yon bon jan *dòmi*.   'I had a good sleep.' (literally, I slept a good sleep.)

Fè 'to do' readily takes nominalized verbs as an NP object:

(46a) Li *chita*. Li *fè yon chita*.   'She sat down.'
(46b) Li *rantre*. Li *fè yon lòt rantre*.   'She came in. She came in another time.'

Transitive verbs fall into two groups, depending on whether or not they also occur in intransitive predicates, i.e., without any NP complement. Some transitive verbs that may occur without object NPs are: *bwè* 'to drink', *manje* 'to eat', *rele* 'to call', and *santi* 'to feel, to smell'.

(47a) Li *bwè* toujou.[10]   'He always drinks.'
(47b) Li *bwè* anpil tafya.   'He drinks a lot of raw rum.'

Among the transitive verbs that cannot occur as intransitives are *jwenn* 'to find', *limen* 'to light', *rekonnèt* 'to recognize', *twouve* 'to think'.

(48a) Ou *twouve* sa bon?   'Do you think that's good?'
(48b) Yo *jwenn* bag sa a nan chemen an.   'They found this ring on the road.'

7.3.5 The passive and middle verbs

In English or French, focus may be placed on patient NPs through passivation: moving the object NP to the subject position and, optionally, inserting the agent in a prepositional phrase introduced by *by* or *par*:

(49a) The truck destroyed the house.   *Le camion a détruit la maison.*
(49b) The house was destroyed by the truck.   *La maison a été détruite par le camion.*

In both languages the passive transformation produces past participles that assume adjectival functions. For instance, in English they occur as predicates in descriptive sentences constructed with the verb *to be* – *the house is destroyed* – or as modifiers in NPs – *the broken toys*. In HC, patients are shifted to the subject position without additional grammatical machinery, such as the use of a copula:

(50a) *Lanp lan* klere kay la.   'The lamp lights the house.'
(50b) *Kay la* klere.   'The house is lit.'
(50c) *Ak lanp lan* kay la klere.   'The house is lit with the lamp.'

As shown in (50c), the instrument may be mentioned explicitly by inserting the subject NP with the aid of the preposition *ak* 'with' (or its variants *avèk/avè/ake*). Generally, the adverbial complement that is created is placed at the front of the sentence. Only patient NPs can be shifted to the subject slot, so verbs that permit this typically have agent subjects and patient objects. Accusatives are unlikely to be shifted to the subject slot:

(51a)   Ti gason an gade liv la.   'The boy kept the book.'
(51b)   *Liv la gade.

In HC, the agent may be indeterminate in passive sentences: the focus is on the patient. For example, the agent is specified in (52a), but not in (52b). The focus is on the fact that food is being cooked, and who is doing the cooking is not viewed as relevant (Damoiseau 2005a: 83). *Manje* is shifted to the front of the sentence and there is no mention of the agent. To focus on the agent one would need to focalize it and front it in a clause introduced by *se* (52c):

(52a)   Mari ap kuit *manje*.   'Mary is cooking food.'
(52b)   *Manje* ap kuit.   'Food is being cooked.'
(52c)   Se *Mari* k ap kuit manje.   'It's Mary who is cooking the food.'

A small set of verbs that behave superficially like transitive verbs do not permit the shifting of the object. For these verbs, termed **middle verbs**, their object NP is neither a patient nor an accusative:

(53a)   Kolye a koute *san goud*.   'The necklace costs 100 gourdes.'
(53b)   *San goud* koute.

Other verbs belonging to this class are *genyen/gen* 'to have', *estime* 'to estimate', *vo* 'to be worth'.

At the surface-structure level the verbs in sentences whose patient has been shifted to the subject slot cannot be distinguished from adjectival predicates. In (54b), *bale*, derived from the verb 'to sweep', does not differ from an adjective like *pwòp* 'clean':

(54a)   Nou *bale* lakou a.   'We swept the yard.'
(54b)   Lakou a *bale*.   'The yard is swept.'
(54c)   Lakou a *pwòp*.   'The yard is clean.'

In the case of deverbal adjectives (adjectives derived from verbs, for example, *bale*) they may undergo copying as part of focalization:

(55)   Se *bale* lakou a *bale*.   'So far as sweeping is concerned, the yard was indeed swept.'

As seen above, this type of copying involves embedding in a higher clause introduced by *se* (56a). Another way to focalize an adjective is to use the introducer *ala* followed by a numeral (*de* 'two' or *kat* 'four'), or *ti* 'little' and the negativizer *pa* may be used with adjectives, but not verbs (see Chapter 10):

(56a)　*Se pwòp* lakou a *pwòp*.　　'The yard is really clean. / So far as cleanliness is concerned the yard is clean.'

(56b)　*Ala pwòp* lakou a *pwòp*.　　―――――――

(56c)　*Se pa de (kat) pwòp* lakou a *pwòp*.　　―――――――

(56d)　*Se pa ti pwòp* lakou a *pwòp*.　　―――――――

7.3.6　Ditransitive (double-object) verbs

In HC, as in English or French, some transitive verbs may take a second object, either following directly or linked by a preposition. According to traditional terminology, the first object is labeled the **direct object** and the second, the **indirect object**:[11]

(57a)　Mary gave the *book* (direct object) to *John* (indirect object).
(57b)　Mary gave *John* the *book*.

Note that in (57b) without the preposition *to* the indirect object immediately follows the verb and thus precedes the direct object. In these double-object constructions, the direct object usually refers to an inanimate noun functioning semantically as an accusative, i.e., it is fairly neutral with regard to effect by the agent. The indirect object NP usually (but not exclusively) contains an animate noun that functions as **beneficiary** or patient. The subject noun is best analyzed semantically as the **source**, since double-object sentences generally refer to some sort of transaction, real or metaphorical. Compare (58) and (59):

(58)　Konpè Kabrit fè pantalon pou *konpè chen*.　　'Brer Goat made trousers for Brer Dog.'

(59)　Matant mwen mande *misye a* de goud.　　'My aunt asked the man for two gourds.'

In (58), the indirect object *konpè chen* introduced by the preposition *pou* is the beneficiary, whereas the subject *Kabrit* is more properly a source than an agent. The direct object, *pantalon,* as the item involved in the transaction, is not a patient but the more neutral accusative. In (59), the direct object *misye a* is the source and the subject NP *matant mwen* is the potential beneficiary.

As is the case in English (see 57b), when no linking preposition is used, the indirect object (patient or beneficiary) occurs immediately after the verb, followed directly by the direct object (accusative):

(60)   Li pase *misye* yon koutfwèt.   'He gave him a lashing.'

Ditransitive verbs comprise transaction verbs: *bay* 'to give', *fè* 'to make', *pase* 'to give', e.g., like a blow, *prete* 'to lend, to borrow', *rann* 'to return', and *remèt* 'to return'. They also comprise discourse verbs: *di* 'to say, to tell', *mande* 'to ask for', *montre* 'to show', and *voye* 'to send':

(61)   Prete *m* bisiklèt ou a.   'Lend me your bicycle.'
(62)   Li voye bagay sa a *pou mwen*. 'He sent me that thing.'

The use of the same form for 'to lend' and 'to borrow' leads to a potential ambiguity:

(63)   Li prete *m* machin nan.   'He lent me/borrowed the car from me.'

The ambiguity is lifted by using the expression *nan men yon moun* 'from somebody' to express 'to borrow':

(64)   Li prete machin nan *nan men mwen*.   'He borrowed the car from me.' (literally, from my hand)

The expression *nan men yon moun* 'from/in someone's hand' also serves to emphasize the orientation of the transaction toward the beneficiary:

(65)   Remèt li *nan men l pou mwen*.   'Return it to her for me.' (literally, return it in her hand for me)

In effect, in (65) there are two beneficiaries. The person mentioned, namely, *l* 'her' (elided form of *li*) is the ultimate beneficiary in that she is to receive the item in the transaction (*li* 'it'); the speaker also benefits because the addressee would be doing her a favor.

In double-object constructions, the direct object may be identified not only by the linear order, but also by the fact that it is the only object that may be fronted in focalization (66b):

(66a) Li ba tifi a *yon ze*.   'He gave the girl an egg.'
(66b) Se *yon ze* li ba tifi a.   'It was an egg he gave the girl.'
(66c) *Se *tifi a* li ba yon ze.

Finally, the ditransitive verb *bay* differs from a homonymous form derived from it that functions as a preposition (see also Chapter 8) and is synonymous with the preposition *pou*:

(67a) Chante l *ban* mwen. 'Sing it for me.'
(67b) Chante l *pou* mwen. _____

The meaning of 'to give' for *bay*, excluded in sentences like (67a), is potentially present in (68a and b):[12]

(68a) Al chache l *ba* sò Meli. 'Go fetch it to bring (to give) to Sister Meli.'
(68b) M ouvri kè m *ba* ou. 'I open up my heart to you (to give to you).'

7.3.7 Intransitive verbs

The number of HC verbs that do not allow any object is limited. A large number of candidates for admission to that group includes verbs of movement such as *ale* 'to go', *antre* 'to enter', *derape* 'to start, take off', *parèt* 'to appear, seem', *rive* 'to arrive'. These verbs typically take adverbial complements of place or time. Note that locative adverbial complements need not be preceded by a preposition:

(69a) L ale *nan jaden*. 'She went into the garden.'
(69b) Yo rive *yè*. 'They arrived yesterday.'
(69c) L ale *lavil*. 'She went to town.'

In addition to adverbial complements, *parèt* may be followed by adjectives:

(70) Li parèt *bèl* nan foto a. 'She looks pretty in the photograph.'

Finally, *derape* bearing the sense 'to start, initiate something' takes a direct object. Compare the meaning of the verbs in (71a) and (71b):

(71a) Avyon an derape *vè sizè*. 'The plane took off at six o'clock.'
(71b) Li derape *yon ti bizniz*. 'She launched a little business.'

Other intransitive verbs include *dekontrole* (to lose one's self-control), *etonnen* 'to be surprised', *kanpe* 'to stand up', *mouri* 'to die', *peri* 'to perish', and *sezi* 'to be surprised':

(72a) Yo *sezi* lè yo tande nouvèl la. 'They were surprised when they heard the news.'
(72b) Li *kanpe* douvan kay la. 'She stood in front of the house.'

A possible candidate for intransitive verb status, *soufri* 'to suffer', does take direct objects, in which case its meaning shifts to 'to be ill':

(73) L ap *soufri* maladi sida. 'He has AIDS.'

206   Basic Sentence Structure

We have seen in Section 7.3.4 that *dòmi* 'to sleep' may take its nominal copy as object. This constitutes a productive process for intransitive verbs; for a full discussion of reduplication and clefting, see Section 10.3.

(74)   M *dòmi y*on bon *dòmi*.   'I had a good sleep.'

7.3.8 Verbal complements

Many transitive verbs may be expanded by complements consisting of predicates. Verbal complements may consist of a verb only (75a) or of a verb plus object(s) and adverbial complements, as in (75b) and (75c):

(75a)   Li ede tig la *sòti*.   'She helped the tiger come out.'
(75b)   Li te blije *pran anpil masay*   'She had to get a lot of massages and
        ak pansman pou l ta ka geri.   dressings to get well.'
(75c)   Li ta renmen *goute nan ti*   'She would like to taste a little of that
        manje sa a   food.'

Adjectival predicates may also be expanded by verbal complements:

(76)   Li pa te cho *reponn*.   'He wasn't eager to answer.'

7.4 Phrase-final Emphatic Markers

To signal emphasis on the semantic content of a sentence HC speakers use monosyllabic markers of emphasis or, as Claire Lefebvre (1998: 213) labels them, markers of the speaker's point of view: *non* and *wi*. There is no pause between these markers and the rest of the sentence, although they are produced with a sentence-final rise in intonation. *Non*, homonymous with the negative adverb, serves several pragmatic functions. First, it reinforces a negative statement:

(77)   M pa ka fè travay sa a *non!*   'I really can't do this job!'

Second, with imperatives, it softens commands:

(78a)   Ann ale *non*, nou deja an reta.   'Let's go, we're already late.'
(78b)   Ann manje *non!*   'Come on, let's eat!'

Lefebvre suggests that the use of the marker indicates that the speaker disagrees with the addressee. In (79), presumably the addressee was not willing to go:

(79)   Ale *non!*   'Go!'

It also signifies impatience or, on the other hand, signals that permission is granted:

(80) Pote manje a vini *non*! 'Bring the food already!'
(81) Chante *non*! 'Why don't you sing!'

Wi, whose homonym is the adverb meaning 'yes', also has several pragmatic functions. It provides emphasis:

(82a) M byen *wi*! 'I'm FINE!'
(82b) Se mwen ki Jak *wi*! 'I'm the one whose name is Jack!'

Or it adds a tone of insistence or reminder:

(83a) Mache ak lajan *wi*! 'Make sure you bring money with you!'
(83b) Fèmen pòt la *wi*! 'Don't forget to shut the door!'

Summary

There are several signal features of HC predicates. First, because of the multifunctional nature of words, the fact that a given word may assume various syntactic functions, nouns and adjectives as well as verbs may constitute predicates. Second, word classes, such as nouns, adjectives, adverbs, and verbs are not marked morphologically either by inflection, such as the plural of English nouns, or by specific derivational affixes like English *-ly* or French *-ment* that identify adverbs. Third, predicates consisting of nouns, adjectives, adverbs, or adverbial phrases do not generally require an overt copula. Such forms are syntactic operators in the case of *ye*, or a form, *se*, occurring in very specific contexts, for example, in descriptive rather than equational sentences that refer to inherent qualities or states. Fourth, reflexivity is not affected by the use of a special set of reflexive pronouns as in English or French, but lexically with terms referring to the body (*tèt, kò, kadav*); otherwise it is unmarked. Fifth, in passive sentences there is no focus on the agent and no passive transformation. There is no overt agent and the focus is on the patient. Finally, most auxiliary verbs are matched by corresponding lexical verbs, from which they appear to be derived semantically.

Notes

1. As in English (and generally in French), Subject + Verb + Object (SVO) is the basic sentence order in HC.
2. ADJ = adjective, DET = determiner (article), here the definite determiner, NEG = negative, 3SG = 3rd singular personal pronoun, 3PL = 3rd person plural pronoun.

3. Because the form of the definite determiner varies according to the nature of the last phonemes of the preceding word (see Chapter 3), I will use the abstract form *LA* to refer to it in discussion of Haitian Creole syntax.
4. For a discussion and list of these linguistic units, see Chapter 8.
5. However, the introducer cannot be deleted in a negative sentence: *Sa se chèlbè* 'That's pretense', *Sa se pa chèlbè* 'That's not pretense'.
6. In the interrogative pronoun *ki sa*, the interrogative marker is optional.
7. That author contrasts dynamic adjectives like *cho* 'hot', *fou* 'crazy', *mètdam* 'clever, cunning', and *ayisyen* 'Haitian' to static ones like *kri* 'raw': *Dlo a ap cho* 'The water is heating', *Apa ou a cho* 'Now you're acting crazily', *Pitit Pyè ap mètdam* 'Peter's child is becoming clever', *Blan sa a ap ayisyen* 'That foreigner is taking on Haitian manners' versus *Vyann nan kri* 'The meat is raw' (*Vyann nan ap kri).
8. *Kapab* in its lexical form also functions as an adjective. It may modify nouns or serve as a predicate adjective: *Se yon moun kapab* 'She's a competent person', *Li kapab anpil* 'He's very competent'.
9. For a detailed discussion of the use of object pronoun versus the marked reflexive forms *tèt* or *kò* + pronoun at various historical stages and in various dialects of HC, see Carden and Stewart (1988).

   (43c) M blese tèt mwen. (?M blese m.) 'I hurt myself.'

  Note, however, that with the use of the pronoun (43a) is ambiguous; it could also mean 'He hurt him'.

10. Note that *bwè* also functions as a noun in copular sentences: *Li toujou bwè* 'He's a drunkard'.
11. In French, an NP indirect object must follow the direct object and the preposition cannot be deleted: *Marie donne le livre à Jean*; **Marie donne Jean le livre*. (Note that the asterisk indicates that the sentence is not grammatical.) As in English and HC, pronominal indirect objects precede the direct object and the preposition is deleted: *Marie lui donne le livre* 'Mary gives him the book', *Mari ba li liv la*.
12. Whereas *ba* as a preposition always occurs as the single form *ba*, the verb shows three phonological variants: *bay*, which varies freely with *ba* and *ban* before the 1st person pronoun *m(wen)*. It is also quite polysemous:

  (a) Konben yo *bay* pou travay sa a? 'How much do they give for this work?'

  (b) Yo *ba(y)* lapolis kriminèl la. 'They handed over the criminal to the police.'

  (c) Li *ban* m pase. 'He let me go by.'

8 The Verbal System

In this chapter, I describe the semantic information that, in addition to lexical information, is carried by the predicate. This chapter consists of five parts. Section 8.1 discusses the semantic distinctions carried by the verb and lays out the general overall structure of the predicate. It stresses the fact that, as is somewhat the case for English, semantic distinctions are expressed not by inflection, which is the case generally in Romance languages, but by various combinations of free morphemes: pre-posed verb markers, auxiliary verbs, and sentence introducers. Section 8.2 describes the verb markers that carry the semantic categories of tense, mood, and aspect (TMA). Section 8.3 provides an inventory of aspectual and modal auxiliary verbs, many of which are derived from semantically related verbs. Section 8.4 describes sentence introducers, which are closely related to auxiliary verbs, and Section 8.5 deals with the intensely debated particle *pou*. Finally, Section 8.6 treats an aspect of the predicate structure of HC that differs greatly from that of French: serial verbs.

8.1 Semantic Structures and Structural Mechanisms

8.1.1 Verbal categories of HC

HC provides grammatical machinery to indicate three types of semantic information about states and events: tense, mood, and aspect. **Tense** situates states and events on a timeline with reference to the moment of speech (enunciation) or with reference to some other point. For example, in English, *The cat ate the rat* is located in the past by the change in form of *eat*; *the cat had eaten the rat (by the time I came into the barn)* situates the event *to eat* in the past with reference to the event *to come*. In addition to tense, there are other semantic categories that characterize states and events: was an event completed or in progress (e.g., *I have filled the bottle* versus *I was filling the bottle*)? Is it about to begin or end (*they started excavating* versus *they've just excavated*)? These categories, covered by the term **aspect**, provide information not directly related to a timeline. Compare: *I filled the bottle* with *I was filling the bottle* and *I have filled the bottle*. The first utterance simply situates the event in the past; the other two, in addition to past tense, provide aspectual information: progressive versus completive. Finally, **mood** provides information about the attitude of the speaker toward a state or event. In *John left*, the speaker assumes a neutral stance: the event is only stated as having occurred. However, in the following statements the speaker adds psychological involvement: *John could leave, John might have left.*

On a different plane, one may place **focus** or emphasis on the information carried by the other parts of an utterance rather than the predicate. For example, *John climbed easily* does not place special emphasis on the information conveyed, but various permutations of sentence elements highlight the new information presented: *It was easy for John to climb; Climbing, John did that easily; So far as John was concerned, he climbed with ease.* Focus and emphasis are not features carried by the predicate and will be presented in Chapter 10, devoted to sentence transformations.

8.1.2 Structural mechanisms

It is important to distinguish between semantic categories carried by the predicate and the structural mechanisms used to express these categories. We have assigned a semantic value to the term 'tense' but often it is used to refer to specific structural features of particular languages. For example, in English the past tense is an inflectional mechanism that serves as a means – not the only one – to situate an event in the past; witness the contrasting forms *I filled, I have filled, I was filling*. Tense is often used to refer to an inflectional set – a lexical base and various endings – that may express several types of verbal semantic features.

It will be useful to review the structural mechanisms available in English to express tense, mood, and aspect so that those of HC may be placed in proper perspective. Unlike those of such languages as Latin, Spanish, and to a lesser extent French, the English verb system has little inflectional machinery. Most English verbs show only four or five distinct forms, for example, *walk, walked, walking, walks* or *freeze, froze, frozen, freezing, freezes*. Thus, the English verb system does not have extensive inflectional sets (conjugations), and to 'conjugate' a verb would be just as useless an exercise as to 'decline' a noun. One would simply be repeating the same form with different pronouns or function words. In comparison, Spanish verbs constitute large sets of forms sharing the same base but distinguished by endings that signal different persons and tense-mood-aspect distinctions. In contrast to the five forms of the English irregular verb *sing* (*sing, sings, singing, sang, sung*),[1] the Spanish verb *cantar* 'to sing' consists of numerous forms organized on two axes: grammatical persons versus tenses:

8.1 Structural Mechanisms

	Present Ind.	**Pres. Subj.**	**Preterit**	**Imperfect**	**Future**	**Conditional**
1st SG	*canto*	*cante*	*canté*	*cantaba*	*cantaré*	*cantaría*
2nd SG	*cantas*	*cantes*	*cantaste*	*cantabas*	*cantarás*	*cantarías*
3rd SG	*canta*	*cante*	*canto*	*cantaba*	*cantará*	*cantaría*
1st PL	*cantamos*	*cantemos*	*cantamos*	*cantábamos*	*cantaremos*	*cantaríamos*
2nd PL	*cantáis*	*cantéis*	*cantasteis*	*cantabais*	*cantaréis*	*cantaríais*
3rd PL	*cantan*	*canten*	*cantaron*	*cantaban*	*cantarán*	*cantarían*

Note that in Spanish, unlike English, subject pronouns are not obligatory: *canto* versus *I sing*. Pronouns are used only for emphasis: *Sí, yo puedo* 'Yes, I can', whereas in English the equivalent of the Spanish use of the subject pronoun is spoken stress on the pronoun *I*.

In English, verbal semantic categories are expressed primarily by choice of function words rather than by inflection. Except for inflectional forms marked for past tense and 3rd person singular present tense, e.g., *walked, walks*, respectively, English verbs consist of combinations of three forms with various function words; the particular meaning is expressed by the choice of the form and the function word. English verbs have a base form, the infinitive (listed in dictionaries with a preceding *to*), a present participle consisting of the base form + *-ing*, and a past participle consisting of the base form + *-ed* for regular verbs and various other formations for irregular or 'strong' verbs. Some combinations and the semantic categories these forms express are:

Progressive: form of *be* + *-ing* form: *I'm walking, I was walking*

Completive: form of *have* + past participle: *I've walked, I had walked, I would have walked, I might have walked*

Deontic:[2]   *must, ought to, should* + base: *you must walk, you ought to walk, you should walk*

Futurity: *will ('ll)* + base, *going to* + base: *I'll walk, I'm going to walk*

Epistemic: *may* + base: *I may walk, I might walk, I might have walked*

HC behaves like English insofar as it favors the use of function words to express tense, aspect, and mood. In fact, HC has no inflection and goes further than English in relying exclusively on combinations of various function words and an invariable base. Such variations of the lexical form carrying the base meaning that do occur are free variants; we have seen in Chapter 7 that some frequently occurring verbs have shortened forms: *vini/vin, mete/met,* etc. For example, to express **progressivity** (an event in progress) or definite futurity, one combines the invariant base form of a particular verb with the marker *ap*: *m ap manje kounye a* 'I'm eating now', *m ap manje aswè a* 'I'll eat tonight'. As these examples show, in HC there is no obligatory one-to-one relationship between function words and semantic categories: a function word may express several semantic categories and, conversely, a particular semantic category may be expressed by different function words. But, in this regard, HC does not differ from other languages. In English, futurity is expressed by *will,* '*ll,* and *going to,* and the so-called present tense forms may be used in conjunction with various adverbial expressions or the general situational context to express different timeline references: *I leave, I leave tomorrow, I leave my house at eight o'clock every day.* In HC, various tense-mood-aspect semantic categories are expressed by a combination of function words and an invariable lexical base that interacts with the meaning of the lexical base and the linguistic context: the presence of other sentential elements and the general situational context.

The absence of inflection does not necessarily make HC a 'simpler' language. To be sure, it is perhaps easier for a foreign learner to learn to combine an invariant form with a set of four tense-mood-aspect markers (see Section 8.2) and a set of about two dozen auxiliary verbs (Section 8.3) and introducers (Section 8.4). But this absence of inflection is offset by the need to memorize possible combinations of a base and various markers and other verbal elements, to take into account restrictions on combinations, and to use complex devices termed serial verbs (Section 8.6). Like English, HC favors **analytic** grammatical machinery (combinations of lexical bases and function words) over the **synthetic** machinery (combinations of lexical bases and bound morphemes) that characterizes Latin and Spanish, for example. French, particularly vernacular spoken French, occupies an intermediate position in this regard:

synthetic – – – – – – – – – – – – – – – – – – analytic
Latin   Spanish   French   English   HC

We may say that HC is an analytic language, not that it is a simple language.

This being the case, it is important not to carry over terminology appropriate for synthetic languages in describing HC. Its verbs have no conjugations, no 'tenses' in the sense of sets of inflectionally different forms (paradigms). In the sections that follow, I will inventory the various function words used in HC to express tense, mood, and aspect, using labels that describe the semantic features expressed. For example, *te* will be termed an anterior and past tense marker, *ap* a progressivity and certain futurity marker, and *konn* an auxiliary verb expressing habitual action, an **iterative** auxiliary verb.

8.1.3 The tense-mood-aspect marker system

In HC tense, mood, and aspect features are expressed by the use of a set of four free morphemes that precede the predicate and are termed tense-mood-aspect (TMA) markers. The presence of one or more of the TMA markers (*ap, apral, a, te*) contrasts with the absence of any marker. Since the absence of markers by itself carries specific meaning, I consider the zero marker (Ø) as an integral element in the system.

The TMA marker *a* is derived from the present singular forms of the French auxiliary verb *aller* 'to go'. In fact, it is one of three variant forms: *a, ava, va*, the last one coinciding with the present singular forms of the French verb: *vais, vas, va*.³ In French, the verb *aller* functions as an auxiliary verb expressing definite future, as in, for example, *il va manger* 'he is going to eat' in contrast to the indefinite inflected future, *il mangera* 'he'll eat'. The origin of the anterior and past marker *te*, alternating with *t*, is problematic. Superficially, it would seem to originate in the past forms of the verb *être* 'to be': *été, étais, était*, or *étaient*, all of which are pronounced alike by most French speakers. It is tempting to derive the verb marker *te* from the first of these forms. The problem, as Chaudenson (2003: 248–51) points out, is that in vernacular French varieties there are not and never were periphrastic constructions consisting of the verb *être* + infinitive. There exists, however, the progressive construction *être à* + infinitive, synonymous with *être après* + infinitive: *je suis à manger, je suis après manger* 'I'm eating'. The corresponding past-tense forms would be *j'étais à/après manger* 'I was eating'. According to Chaudenson *te* would be derived from the imperfect tense forms *étais, était, étaient* but assigned a general past-tense meaning in French-based creoles. However, it may be that the use of *te* might have been influenced by the past participle *été* that occurs in passive constructions: *la souris a été dévorée par le chat* 'the mouse was devoured by the cat'.

Ap, alternating with *ape* and *pe* in southern Haiti and *ape* in northern Haiti, is derived from French *après*, a constituent of one of the periphrastic constructions with progressive meaning: *je suis après manger* 'I'm eating', which, although supplanted in present-day Standard French by *être en train de* (*je suis en train de manger*), occurred widely in French regional dialects and is widely attested today in North American varieties of French, notably

214   *The Verbal System*

Louisiana French. However, whatever their origin in French, the HC TMA markers have developed functions that differ markedly from those of their French cognates and form an independent system. The fourth TMA, *apral* (with variant *pral*), a combination of *ap* and the verb *ale* 'to go', serves to express an action or process about to be initiated and is therefore described as an **inceptive**.

8.1.4 Semantic classification of TMA markers

An understanding of the function of the TMA system of HC rests on the fundamental difference between the two basic types of verbs and other constituents of verbal predicates: **stative** versus **dynamic** (**non-stative**).[4] Examples of stative verbs in English are *to have, to know, to love, to wish, to owe*. Dynamic verbs refer to actions: *to buy, to hit, to run, to try, to walk*, etc. Unlike dynamic verbs, stative verbs have no clear beginning or end point. Generally, they do not occur with the progressive.

(1a)   He is walking home.   (1b)   *He is knowing the answer.

In zero copula constructions, adjectives and nouns like *pè* 'fear' or *swaf/swèf* 'thirst' (see Chapter 7) are generally statives. Whether the constituent of a predicate is dynamic or stative determines the meaning provided by a particular TMA marker. In Section 8.3, I treat separately the TMA markers occurring with stative and dynamic verbs.

In his influential theory about the genesis of creoles based on European languages, Derek Bickerton (1981) claimed that these languages, including HC, share the same basic verb marker system for the expression of tense, mood, and aspect – what may be referred to as the classic TMA marker system (Spears 1993b). In Bickerton's system, three TMA markers and Ø, either individually or in combinations, express three semantic category contrasts: punctual versus durative, realis versus irrealis, anterior versus non-anterior. **Punctuality** involves clear beginning and end points whereas **durativity** expresses progressivity and habituality (Spears 1993a: 251). Bickerton characterizes **irrealis** as subsuming futurity, conditionality, and subjectivity as opposed to what is real and concrete (**realis**). **Anteriority** refers to the past with respect to a past event or state. Table 8.1 represents the application of the classic model of the relationship between the HC TMA markers and the semantic categories posited by that model. As will be shown in Section 8.2, the classic model does not hold for HC.

Table 8.1. Semantics of the TMA Classic System[5]

	Punctual	Durative	
	Ø	ap/apral	**Non-anterior**
Realis			
	te	t ap	**Anterior**
	va	av ap	**Non-anterior**
Irrealis			
	ta	t av ap	**Anterior**

8.2 The HC TMA System

For the sake of convenience and greater clarity, I will discuss the semantics of the TMA system in two parts. In Section 8.2.1, I describe the tense and aspect systems, because these are intertwined. I will first treat the tense and aspect system of stative verbs (Section 8.2.1), then that of non-stative verbs (Section 8.2.2). In Section 8.2.3, I deal with the mood system, specifically the semantic categories of the TMA markers *a* and *ta*.[6]

8.2.1 The tense-aspect marker system with statives

The semantic categories carried by the TMA markers, of which the bare stem (Ø) is an integral member, more clearly emerge in statives, that is, stative verbs such as *bezwen* 'to need', *genyen* 'to have', *konnen* 'to know', *renmen* 'to love', as well as adjectives and nouns that pattern like adjectives, such as *pè* 'fear' and *grangou* 'hunger'. With statives, Ø, *ap*, and *te* express the present, certain future (prospective), and past tenses, respectively. The bare stem (Ø) confers a present reading:

(2a) Ti sourit *pè* chat. 'The little mouse is afraid of cats.'
(2b) Li *bouke*. 'He's tired.'
(2c) Li *genyen* di goud. 'She has ten gourdes.'
(2d) Yo *renmen* diri ak pwa. 'They like rice and beans.'

As pointed out by Comrie (1976), there is an internal contradiction between the stativity of a verb and the non-stativity essential to the progressive. Consequently, with statives, *ap* carries only the futurity meaning:

(3a) N *ap* bouke. 'We'll be tired.'
(3b) L *ap* koute anpil kòb. 'That will cost a lot of money.'
(3c) Rekòt la *ap* anpil. 'The crop will be plentiful.'

As pointed out in Chapter 7 (footnote 4), adjectives that carry a dynamic meaning, such as *cho* 'hot', behave like non-statives; with these, *ap* conveys progressivity as well as futurity (Damoiseau 2005a: 106). This semantic variation of *ap* underscores the fact that in HC the linguistic context plays a determinant part in the interpretation of utterances (Lainy 2010: 170–240).

(4a) Dlo a *ap* cho. 'The water is heating.'
(4b) Dlo a *ap* cho a twazè. 'The water will be hot at three o'clock.'

To indicate past tense with statives the use of *te* is obligatory:

(5a) Ze a *te* gen anpil grès. 'The egg had a lot of grease.'
(5b) M *te* lekòl. 'I was at school.'

In general, statives constitute *background* events: they describe the situation that obtains as processes take place:

(6a) *Abitan yo te deja nan jaden* 'The farmers were already in the field,
     an lè m rive. when I arrived.'

Note that with statives the use of *te* corresponds to that of the imperfect in French:

(6b) M *te* bouke. 'I was tired.'
     'J'*étais* fatigué(e).'

8.2.2 Tense-aspect markers and non-stative verbs

As Damoiseau (1988) stresses, in HC there are two types of non-stative verbs: **processives** and **resultatives**. The latter, such as *echwe* 'to fail', *konprann* 'to understand', and *wè* 'to see', like statives, refer to a process that has no clear beginning or end points. Understanding is not viewed as a continuous process, such as beating; it is inherently a holistic process. Accordingly, such verbs refer to the result of a process that is completed, hence the use of the term 'resultative'. On the other hand, most processive verbs, for example, *chire* 'to tear', *kenbe* 'to catch', or *tonbe* 'to fall', may be viewed as continuous process events. As will be shown below, in combination with TMA markers resultative verbs behave in some respects like statives and in other respects like processives. I will begin by describing combinations of tense and aspect markers with processives.

Tense-aspect markers with processive verbs
With processive verbs, *apral* refers to an event that is about to happen:

(7a) M konnen sa k *apral* pase. 'I know what's going to occur.'
(7b) W *apral* ban m sa fen. 'You're going to give me all the details.'

Alternatively, this TMA marker may be analyzed as the combination of *ap* and the verb *ale* 'to go'. This combination carries a prospective meaning inherent in the verb 'to go', which indicates motion forward, not only spatially but temporally as well:

(8a) Bon, m *prale*. 'OK, I'm going.'
(8b) Sa ou *pral* fè aswè a? 'What are you going to do tonight?'
(8c) N *apral* lakay nou. 'We're going home (now).'
(8d) Li kòmanse ta, m *aprale* talè. 'It's getting late, I'm going soon.'

The specific meaning carried by Ø and *ap* depends on the context expressed by syntactic elements in the sentence, as well as on the overall contextual situation. In other words, these two TMA markers carry a fairly abstract meaning that is narrowed down by the linguistic and extralinguistic context in which an utterance is produced. This is a situation typical of spoken discourse in all languages, but, since HC is still primarily a spoken language, the interaction between linguistic elements and the context of the situation is more salient than in the written version of such languages as English and French. No doubt, as HC increasingly becomes a more widely used written medium, it might develop more grammatical machinery independent of context.

The TMA marker Ø
With statives, Ø takes on the contextual meaning of general truth or universal present and habituality:

(9a) Digo ble. 'Indigo is blue.'
(9b) M toujou lakay mwen. 'I'm always at home.'

In (9a), the absence of a determiner indicates that the noun *digo* is considered in its generic sense and that the attribute expressed by the adjective applies universally. In (9b), the adverb *toujou* carries the notion of habituality. Thus, the semantic category of habituality does not reside in Ø itself but, instead, stems from the interaction between the basic meaning carried by that TMA marker and the linguistic and extralinguistic context in which the utterance appears. The same contextually derived meaning of habituality obtains for processive verbs:

218   *The Verbal System*

(10a) Lapli tonbe isit.   'Rain (usually) falls here.'
(10b) Pòl fimen.   'Paul (habitually) smokes.'
(10c) Li travay lematen.   'She works (generally) in the morning.'

However, the following contrastive examples demonstrate that, with processive verbs, present tense and habitual aspect are not the only meanings of Ø:

(11a) Mayi bay nou bon garanti.   'Corn provides us a good income.'
(11b) Mayi **a** bay nou bon garanti.   'That corn provided us a good income.' (Bentolila 1987: 107)
(11c) Ebenis la wete grenn bwa ak papye sable.   'The cabinet-maker removes rough spots on boards with sandpaper.'
(11d) Ebenis la wete grenn bwa *yo* ak papye sable.   'The cabinet-maker removed the rough spots on the boards with sandpaper.'

The TMA marker Ø is neutral with regard to tense. It refers to the present: (1) with statives; (2) with processives when the context suggests a generic or habitual interpretation. In (11a) and (11c), the non-particularized nouns (see Chapter 9) *mayi* and *bwa* carry a generic meaning and require the matching semantic category of habituality. In contrast, in (11b) and (11d) the nouns are particularized by the definite determiners *a* and *yo*, respectively. This excludes the habituality interpretation and points instead to the semantic categories past and completive. Indeed, with processive verbs past tense is usually expressed by Ø rather than by *te*, as is the case for statives. The following short passage, featuring verbs marked by Ø, illustrates the indication of past and completive events in narratives. Note that in (12) *twouve* bears a stative sense equivalent to 'to think' rather than 'to discover', which implies a process:

(12) Lè l *rive* lakay li, Bouki *mande* l: 'Sa k *pase* konsa? M *twouve* ou *pran* anpil tan pou jwenn dife a!' Boukinèt *ba* li bwa chandèl la.   'When she arrived at her house, Bouki asked her: "What really happened? I find that you took a lot of time to find the fire!" Bouquinette gave him the piece of candlewood.'

In the following examples note the contrast between the absence of *te* with processives and its use with statives:

(13a) Poukisa li *ban* mwen konsèy sa?   'Why did she give me that advice?'
(13b) Pou ki sa l *te bezwen* mande konsèy sou sa?   'Why did she have to ask advice about that?'
(13c) Se konsa tou je m *tonbe* sou yon bagay ki *te* atè a … Se *te* papye, e papye sa a, se *te* testaman an.   'And it was how both of my eyes fell upon a thing that was on the ground … It was a document, and that document was the will.'

The TMA *ap*

With processive verbs *ap* imparts either a future or a progressive reading equivalent to the English *be … -ing* construction. The progressive reading stems from the basic prospective meaning of this TMA marker. For example, in (14) the action 'to paint' begins in the present and proceeds forward in time.

(14) Sa w ap fè koulye a?   'What are you doing now?
– M ap pentire baryè a.   – I'm painting the fence.'

Future-time readings are triggered by a linguistic element with future reference or by the situational context (Lainy 2010: 210–18). In the following examples, (15a) and (15b) contain adverbial complements *demen* and *talè a* indicating futurity and (16a) and (16b) contain verbs with prospective reference:

(15a) M ap rache l **demen**.   'I'll pull it out tomorrow.'
(15b) Y ap voye moun nan **talè**.   'They'll send that person soon.'

(16a) Y ap **vini** ak nou.   'They're coming with us.'
(16b) N ap **pati** si ou vle.   'We'll leave if you want.'

Thus, with processives, like Ø the TMA marker *ap* straddles a temporal spectrum, in this case ranging from the here and now to the future.

The TMA *te*

We have seen that, when combined with processive verbs, the TMA marker Ø may express completed past events. It is in fact the primary grammatical means for narratives, as shown by the short text in (12) above. The TMA marker *te* provides an overt mark of past time, and it may be used in many cases in free variation with Ø. However, there are instances when its use is obligatory. First, it provides a clear reference to past time. Compare (17a) and (17b):

220   The Verbal System

(17a) Yè m boule boukan nan jaden m.   'Yesterday I lit a fire in my field.'
(17b) **Se yè** m **te** boule boukan nan jaden m.   'It was yesterday (and not some other time) that I lit a fire in my field.'

Example (17a) does not highlight the comment (new information) contained, namely, the time reference *yè*. On the other hand, (17b) does this in two ways: by extraposing (see Chapter 7) the temporal complement and by clearly marking past time with *te*.

Spears (1993b) characterized *te* as an **anti-perfect** because, unlike perfect verb forms, it does not link a past action to the present, as does, for example, the English construction *have* + past participle:

(18a) She went home.   (18b) 'She has gone home.'

For this author, *te* functions to negate a given situation's connection to the present or to some posterior reference time. He illustrates that function with the following excerpt, among others:

(19)   Mizik sa yo i *te* voye chèche Ayiti a yo?[7]   '(What about) those records he ordered from Haiti?'

In (19), the speaker wants to stress that the records should have arrived by the moment of the speech act, that they should not still be on order; the pragmatic implication is that they should have arrived.

In (20a), the speaker, a farmer from Thibeau, a village in the vicinity of Cape Haitian, explains that in the past their elders were able to cultivate crops that are no longer profitable because the land is now less fertile. He goes on to point out that school fees were lower in the past.

(20a)   ... *tout bagay granmounannou yo **te** konn fè lontan an, tèren yo pa fè l ankò ... E lontan lekòl **te** konn peye yon goud ... degouden. Gen moun ki pa **te** mete timoun lekòl ... Men se degouden yon goud lekòl **te** konn peye.*[8] *(NSF1)*   '... all the things that our elders used to be able to do, the fields no longer can produce it anymore ... And for a long time you would pay a gourde and a half for school. There were people who did not send their children to school ... But it's a gourde and a half you used to pay for school.'

For Lainy (2010: 227), the marker *te* indicates that a past action is viewed as separated from the moment of production of an utterance. He offers, among other examples, (20b) to support this view. Note that the example, in which *lontan* introduces distance between the event and the moment of speech production, patterns very much like that in (20a):

(20b) **Lontan**, timoun **te** konn manje mango vèt.   'A long time ago, children used to eat unripe mangoes.'

Typically, *te* is used to situate narratives in the past. Generally, it occurs in the opening of folktales, as in (21):

(21) Se **te** yon manman ki **te genyen** yon pitit fi ak yon pitit gaso. Chak kou pitit fi a **ale** nan dlo, li **pòte** dlo pwòp. Chak kou ti gason an **ale** nan dlo, li **pòte** dlo sal. Manman l **mande** ti gason an pouki li **pòte** dlo sal. ... Ti gason an **ale**, li **plen** kalbas li, li **retounen** ... li **pran kouri** ... li **vire** dèyè yon pye bwa.   'Once upon a time, there was a mother who had a daughter and a son. Every time the daughter went to fetch water, she brought back clean water. Every time the son went to fetch water, he brought back dirty water. His mother asked the boy why he brought back dirty water ... The boy went, he filled his gourd, he came back ... he started to run ... he ducked behind a tree.'

After the ritual opening of the folktale with *se, te*, and the stative verb *genyen* that requires the obligatory use of *te* to mark past tense, all the processive verbs occur in their bare form, i.e., with the Ø marker.

Another major function of *te* is to express anteriority, that is, it situates a past event occurring before another past event; in this regard, it corresponds to the English **pluperfect** (*had* + past participle) construction. In the complex sentence in (22), the main clause *m te rive lakay mwen* foregrounds the event, whereas the subordinate clause *lè li rele m* provides the background

(22) M **te** rive lakay mwen lè l rele m.   'I had arrived at my house when he called me.'

In the short dialogues illustrated by (23a) and (23b), the response expresses that the action requested by the initial statement had been carried out. In this example, *te* corresponds to the English present perfect:

(23a) Al benyen!
 – M **te** benyen yè aprèmidi.   'Go take a bath!'
' – I've already taken a bath yesterday afternoon.'

(23b) Nou bezwen achte pen.
 – Jan **te** achte pen an deja.   'We have to buy bread.'
' – John has already bought the bread.'

222 The Verbal System

In the news item in (24), the current Haitian president Michel Martelly decided to intervene in the administrative affairs of Cape Haitian after he had already assumed office, and when opposition to him was voiced:

(24) *Martelly deja **foure** pye l nan koze lakomin yo, lè li **deside mete** yon nouvo konsèy nan tèt lakomin Okap. Se nan vil Okap yo **te voye** toya sou Martelly, kèk tan apre li **te fin monte** prezidan.*   'Martelly got involved in the matters of town councils, when he decided to appoint a new council head of the city of Cape Haitian. It's in the city of Cape Haitian that they disparaged Martelly, a short time after he had acceded to the presidency.'

As was noted in Section 8.2.1, stative predicates referring to past time require the use of *te*. In the following examples presented earlier in (13), note the contrast between the absence of *te* with non-statives and its use with statives:

(25a) Poukisa li **ban** mwen konsèy li fèk m ban m la?   'Why did she give me the advice she has just given me?'
(25b) Poukisa l **te bezwen** mande konsèy sou sa?   'Why did she have to ask advice about that?'
(25c) Se konsa tou je m **tonbe** sou yon bagay ki **te atè a** ... **Se te papye**, e papye sa a, **se te testaman an**.   'And it was how my eyes fell on a thing that was on the ground ... It was a document, and that document was the will.'

The TMA *a(v)(a)*

When used as a prospective – with statives and in certain linguistic and situational contexts with non-stative verbs – *ap* refers to future events that are likely to be completed, as it signifies definite futurity. In contrast, the TMA *a*, which also occurs in the variant forms *va* and *ava*, signifies indefiniteness, as shown by comparing (26a) and (26b):

(26a) Aswè a m **ap** rete lakay mwen.   'Tonight, I'll stay home.'
(26b) Dimanch, m **a** sakle mayi a.   'Sunday, I'll hoe the corn.'

The example in (26a) suggests that the critical difference between the two sentences is not near versus remote future. It is the case that less-remote prospective events are more likely to be realized, but the distinctive features between the two markers are definiteness and certainty versus indefiniteness. Compare (27a) and (27b), neither of which contains a temporal adverb:

(27a) L **ap** gen yon timoun; li ansent. 'She'll have a child; she's pregnant.'
(27b) M **a** genyen sèlman de, twa timoun. 'I'll have only two or three children.'

The certainty of child-bearing is evident in (27a) but hypothetical in (27b). The next two examples illustrate the use of variant forms:

(28a) Ou **va** vin leve m. 'You'll come to wake me.'
(28b) Li di: 'Demen ou **prale** nan mache.' 'He said: "Tomorrow you'll go to the market" (i.e., I expect you to go to the market).'
– Wi, papa, m **ava** ale. '– Yes, father, I'll go.'

Note that, in her reply, the second interlocutor hedges by not responding with *ap* but with *ava*, which implies that she may or may not go to the market. For Lainy (2010: 228), *ap* conveys a somewhat modal force:

> *L'emploi de **ap**, avec ou sans adverbial circonstanciel, traduit une sorte d'engagement de la part du locuteur de présenter l'événement envisagé comme certain, alors que **a**, **va** ou **ava**, utilisés sans «morphème circonstanciel temporel», déterminent la dimension éventuelle de l'action.*

> The use of *ap*, with or without a temporal adverb, indicates a sort of commitment on the part of the speaker to present the event as considered as certain, whereas *a*, *va*, or *ava* used without a 'temporal adverbial morpheme' limit the action as possible.

The close link, in fact the near-complementarity, between *ap* and *a* is underscored by the fact that the latter is excluded from negative sentences. Semantically, the negative implies certainty, i.e., a negative statement about the likelihood of an event implies that it is certain not to be realized:

(29a) M **a** ba ou anpil lajan. 'I'll give you a lot of money.'
(29b) M p **ap** ba ou anpil lajan. 'I won't give you a lot of money.'

Resultative verbs

As mentioned in Section 8.2.2, resultative verbs share syntactic features with both stative and processive verbs. Compare *gade* 'to look at' in (30a) to *wè* 'to see' in (30b) and (30c):

(30a) L **ap** gade avyon an. 'She's looking at the plane.'
(30b) L **ap** wè avyon an (lè l ale ayewopò a). 'She'll see the plane (when she goes to the airport).'
(30c) Li wè avyon an. 'She sees/saw the plane.'

Unlike a processive verb such as *gade*, *wè* cannot be perceived as the action progresses. As Damoiseau and Saint-Louis (1986) and Damoiseau (1988: 54) point out, the event to which a resultative verb refers cannot be dissociated from its process. One only perceives its end point, its result. Consequently, like stative verbs, with the resultative verb *wè*, *ap* can only take on a futurity meaning. On the other hand, as is the case for processive verbs, bare stems of resultative verbs may refer to either the present or past tense. This semantic class of verbs includes: *blese* 'to wound', *bliye* 'to forget', *chire* 'to tear', *dechouke* 'to overthrow', *defann* 'to forbid', *fache* 'to lose one's temper', *geri* 'to be healed', *jwenn* 'to find', *kondanen* 'to condemn', *konprann* 'to understand', *manke* 'to miss', *pèmèt* 'to allow', *pini* 'to punish', *rann* 'to give back', *refize* 'to refuse', *santi* 'to feel', *sonje* 'to remember', *twouve* 'to find', *vag* 'to ignore someone'.[9]

Many resultative verbs are polysemous, or if one prefers, there are two homonymous verbs, one of which is processive and the other resultative, for example, *klere* 'to light up, to provide light', *grate* 'to itch, to scratch', *defann* 'to defend, to forbid', *dechouke* 'to uproot, to overthrow'.

(31a) Lanp la ap klere n. 'The lamp is providing light for us.'
(31b) Lanp la klere chanm nan. 'The lamp lights up the room.'

(32a) L ap grate pye li. 'He's scratching his foot.'
(32b) Pye m grate m. 'My foot itches.'

(33a) Y ap defann vil la. 'They're defending the city.'
(33b) Yo defann mwen ranje machin mwen. 'They forbid me to park my car.'

(34a) N ap dechouke pye bwa yo. 'We're uprooting the trees.'
(34b) Nou dechouke dwayen an. 'We overthrew the dean.'

Summary of the tense and aspect system

In describing grammatical phenomena, the temptation is great to seek a one-to-one relationship between a particular morpheme and a single semantic notion whose function that morpheme is supposed to express. This approach falls short in the analysis of the TMA system of HC, even if one decomposes the meaning of the various markers into a relatively abstract basic meaning and a contextually derived secondary meaning.

It is possible to assign a specific tense reference to each TMA marker only with stative predicates, and then only at the cost of assigning future reference to both *ap* and *a*. With non-stative predicates, the situation is more complex. The five TMA markers express both tense and aspect. When there are linguistic or situational elements indicating definiteness, Ø signals past tense and completive aspect; when these are absent, it signals present tense and habitual aspect. *Apral* refers to an action about to be undertaken. Although it is always prospective, *ap* is equally ambivalent from a semantic point of view: it refers to future tense when accompanied by appropriate linguistic and situational cues but to the progressive aspect in the absence of specific contextual information. Only *te*, which always refers to past events, and *a*, which refers to future events, provide independent tense marking.

8.2.3 Mood

Mood distinctions enable speakers to express their attitude toward what they are saying. For Spears (1990: 128), 'the indicative mood in HC refers to the communication by a speaker of a situation as one which is normal or unremarkable'. It refers to facts that are simply asserted and presupposed and, accordingly, psychologically neutral. The tense and aspect semantic notions (progressive, habitual, completive, perfective, and so on) covered in Section 8.2.2 all fit under the rubric 'indicative mood'. In this section, I deal with the expression in HC of the subjunctive and conditional moods. I am using the term 'subjunctive' not to refer to particular sets of forms, such as the subjunctive tense forms of French. For example, in French the present subjunctive forms of the verb *aller* 'to go' differ from the corresponding forms of the present indicative: *j'aille, tu ailles, il/elle/on aille, ils/elles aillent, vous alliez, nous allions* versus *je vais, tu vas, il/elle/on va, ils/elles vont, vous allez, nous allons*. Instead, I am referring to a set of semantic notions.[10]

It is important to stress the fact that in HC there are no subjunctive or conditional tenses. These two moods, like the indicative mood, are expressed by pre-verbal markers. In addition, it will be illustrated that the same pre-verbal markers, for example, *a* (recall that this marker occurs in three variants, *ava, va, a*), may express different moods. In addition, in HC, most modal notions – desire, permission, volition, and so on – are also expressed by auxiliary verbs (see Section 8.3. below).

Subjunctive mood

The subjunctive mood is non-factual. It is used to express commands, desires, opinions, requests, wishes, and other states labeled as irrealis. It usually occurs in dependent clauses of complex sentences. In languages like French and Spanish, the subjunctive is marked by particular verb endings or changes in the verb stems (as shown above). In English, it is expressed in a variety of ways. For example, desire may be expressed by the subjunctive that involves the use of the plural past tense form *were* instead of the corresponding singular form *was*: *I wish my wife were here* instead of *I wish my wife was here*. Necessity may be expressed by the use of the unmarked (bare) form instead of the present form: *It's necessary that he go in now* versus *... that he goes in now*.

In HC, the subjunctive may be expressed with *a*, *ap*, or *ta* (Spears 1990: 133–6). In (35), *a* is used to express desire or hope.

(35) M espere ke pitit mwen an **a** vin doktè.   'I hope that my child will become a doctor.'

In (36), it conveys surprise:

(36) Kounye a m tande i di m l **a** ban m venn senk goud.   'Now he tells me that he'll give me (a raise to) twenty-five gourdes (an hour).'

In (37a), *a* is used to attenuate the command. It is perceived as more of a suggestion, as opposed to the imperative in (37b). Note that here, unlike the examples in (35) and (36), *a* occurs in simple sentences.

(37a) W **a** rele m, w *a* telefonnen m.   'You call me, you telephone me.'
(37b) Rele m, telefonnen m.   'Call me, telephone me.'

However, the subjunctive mood may also be expressed with *ap*, as shown in (38), excerpted from the folktale 'Adelina':[11]

(38) Wa a fè sèman l **ap** bay Malis yon pa wayom nan ...   'The king promised he would give Malice part of the kingdom ...'

Ta is another marker that expresses subjunctive modalities. Superficially, this marker appears to be a combination of the past anterior marker *te* and *a*. *Ta* functions as a deontic in expressing necessity in (39a) and (39b) and desire in (39c) and (39d):

(39a) I nesesè pou ou **ta** rive demen.   'You have to arrive tomorrow.'
(39b) Fo ou **ta** wè sa.   'You should see that.'
(39c) M **ta** renmen vin pastè.   'I'd like to become a Protestant minister.'
(39d) M **ta** renmen yon bon ti ji kowosòl.   'I'd like a nice little (glass of) soursop juice.'

As is the case with the English modal verb *would, ta* may be used to soften commands or requests:

(40) Ou **ta** vle pote panyen an ban mwen?   'Would you want to carry the basket for me?'

Spears (1990: 133) interprets (41) as expressing an anterior subjunctive because the verb *di* 'to say' refers to the past:

(41) Men, m pa **t** bay okazyon pou l **ta** di sa.   'But I didn't give her any reason to say that.'

Note that the elided form of **te** occurs in the first clause.

Conditional mood

The conditional mood is used to express hypothetical events or actions, both past and future. Its primary linguistic means is **ta**, which occurs in both simple and complex sentences. Compare the semantic distinctions effected by *ap, a,* and *ta*.

(42a) Li di l **ap** jwe domino.   'He said he'll play dominoes.' (definite)
(42b) Li di l **a** jwe domino.   'He said he'll play dominoes.' (indefinite)
(42c) Li di l **ta** jwe domino.   'He said he would play dominoes.'

In complex sentences, *ta* may occur in both clauses:[12]

(43) Se **ta** pi gwo lachte pou m **ta** renmen yon fi ki fin kite m ale.   'It would be the biggest cowardice for me to love a woman who just jilted me.'

8.3 Auxiliary Verbs

The TMA markers constitute pure function morphemes. They do not occur independently and do not carry any lexical meaning. Indeed, their inherent semantic features are relatively abstract: they are best viewed as a meaning potential whose precise value depends on the linguistic and situational context of the predicate. From a phonological point of view, TMA markers are monosyllabic elements that fuse with contiguous grammatical and lexical materials. There exists in HC another set of free morphemes whose function is to express aspectual and modal distinctions. By and large, these are lexical verbs reduced in phonological form in which meaning has shifted toward abstraction. Following general grammatical tradition, I will label these free morphemes **auxiliary verbs**, abbreviated as AUX.

As pointed out for the list in Section 7.3.3, many AUX have corresponding lexical verbs. Consider, for example, the lexical verb *fini* 'to finish' and its corresponding AUX *fin* 'completive aspect', referring to actions that have been completed:

(44a) Yo poko **fini** travay la.   'They haven't finished the work yet.'
(44b) Kou a **fini**?   'Is the class over (finished)?'
(44c) Li **fin** kuit diri a.   'He just cooked the rice.'

From a phonological perspective *fin* is clearly derived from the verb *fini*. The semantic link is also quite transparent. To underscore the completive sense of this AUX, Suzanne Sylvain (1936: 92) uses the adverb *complètement* as she provides a two-step translation for examples she offers to illustrate its use: *Ou te fin bwè (vous aviez bu complètement, vous aviez fini de boire)* 'you had drunk completely, you had just finished drinking'. The illustrative examples which that author provides for *fin* cover a wide range of senses. Note the abstract nature of the meaning that *fin* adds to the main verb, which accounts for the polysemy that derives from the nuclear meaning 'to finish'. In a sense, the meaning that *fin* adds interacts with that of the main verb. For example, in (45c) to have finished knowing is to know everything.

(45a) Ou **fin renmen** pitit sa a.   'You really like this child.'
(45b) M **fin pale**.   'I've spoken. (That's it.)'
(45c) Li **fin konnen**.   'He knows everything.'
(45d) Ou kwè l a **fin pare**?   'Do you think he's quite ready?'
(45e) N t apral **fin mèt kouri**.   'We were just about to start running.'

Compared to the lexical verbs from which they are derived some AUX undergo **truncation**, i.e., they lose their final vowel, for example, *fini > fin*, *sòti > sòt*, and *vini > vin*. Some show more extensive phonological reduction: *konnen> kon*, *kapab>kap, kab, ka*. However, that is not a defining criterion. For example, the lexical verb *vini* may undergo truncation when it is followed by a verbal complement: *Yo vin manje* 'they came to eat'.

It is primarily syntactic criteria that distinguish AUX from lexical verbs. First, unlike lexical verbs that enter into verbal complement constructions, AUX do not occur independently in predicates, as in the ungrammatical (46b). Compare the syntactic properties of the AUX *konn* 'habitual' (46a) and the lexical verb *bliye* 'to forget' (46d):

(46a) Yo **konn** remèt kòb yo prete.   'They usually pay back the money that they borrow.'
(46b) *Sa yo **konn**?
(46c) Pa bliye **remèt** pyas la.   'Don't forget to pay back the gourde.'
(46d) Pa **bliye**!   'Don't forget!'

Only *vle* behaves exceptionally in this regard. It might be termed a **semi-auxiliary verb** since it shares with lexical verbs the possibility of independent occurrence in predicates. Note the important fact that the meaning of *vle* in (47a) and (47b) is the same:

(47a) M **vle** manje.   'I want to eat.'
(47b) Sa ou **vle**?   'What do you want?'

Sequences of lexical verb + verb complement may be interrupted by TMA markers:

(48) Konpè sourit koumase **ap** tranble.   'Brer Mouse began to tremble.'

In contrast, AUX form a tight-knit syntactic structure with lexical verbs before which TMA markers are placed.

(49a) Li **te** tonbe kriye.   'She began to cry.'
(49b) Poukisa l **t ap** tonbe kriye?   'Why did she begin to cry?'

Compared to TMA markers, AUX do not combine freely with all types of predicates. They occur generally only with non-stative verbs, although there are instances of their use with adjectival or nominal predicates.

(50) Lè m **vin** granmoun, m ap lese bouk mwen.   'When I become an adult, I'll leave my village.'

In this syntactic context, AUX may be preceded by TMA markers (S. Sylvain 1936: 93), as is the case with non-stative verbs, as shown in (49a,b) above:

(51a) Yo **ta** fin grangou si m pa te bay yo kasav.   'They would have been hungry had I not given them cassava.'
(51b) Bagay **te** vin dous la.   'That thing had become sweet.'

230   The Verbal System

In some cases, AUX combine with each other, although the combinations are limited. These include the **completives** *fèk* and *sòt* that refer to initial stages of an action, the **deontic** (obligation) *dwe*, the epistemic (possibility) *sa*, the completive *fin*, the **attenuative** (reducing the effect of an action) *manyen* and *manke* ('almost') that refer to actions at the point of being initiated but that are not completed. As shown in (52e), there are combinations of three and even four AUX (S. Sylvain 1936: 90–105):

(52a) Jan **dwe fèk** sòti.   'John must have just gone out.'
(52b) M te **fèk sòt** kontre l.   'I had just met him.' (at that very moment)
(52c) N apral **fin mete** kouri.   'We were about to start running.'
(52d) Ou ta **sa manyen** vin kote m.   'You could have come to me for a while.'
(52e) Nèg sa a **ka fèk sòt fin** manje.   'It's possible that this man could have just finished eating.'

In the sections that follow, I classify AUX according to their semantic properties in two groups: **aspectual** versus **modal**. Some AUX do not derive from lexical verbs: *fèk*, *fouti*, *sa*, and *kapab* (*kap*, *kab*, *ka*), which is derived from the adjective *kapab* 'able'. For AUX that are matched by a lexical verb, the examples will include one illustrating the meaning of the lexical verb.

8.3.1 Aspectual AUX

Completive: *fin, fèk, sòt*
These three AUX refer to an action that has just been completed. Accordingly, they also carry the sense of recent past. As pointed out above, *fèk* does not have a corresponding lexical verb.

(53a) M **fin kale** zoranj lan.   'I've just peeled the orange.'
(53b) Li **fini** chèz yo.   'He's finished the chairs.'

(54a) M **sòt achte** jwèt la epi pitit mwen **sòt** kase l.   'I've just bought the toy and my child has just now broken it.'
(54b) Msye a **fèk soti**.   'He has just gone out.'
(54c) A ki lè yo **soti**?   'At what time did they go out?'

To emphasize the completive state of an action, it is not unusual that several AUX of this subclass may be used (S. Sylvain 1936: 93). In (52e), repeated below, the immediacy of the completion of the event is emphasized with the use of four completive AUX:

(55) M **fèk sòt** manje.   'I have just eaten.'
(52e) Nèg sa a **ka fèk sòt fin** manje.   'It's possible that this man could have just finished eating.'

Habitual: *konn*
This habitual AUX is derived from the lexical verb *konnen* 'to know':

(56a) Yo te **konn leve** bonè.   'They used to get up early.'
(56b) L **konn manyen ride** m.   'He has the habit of helping me a bit.'
(56c) Sa ou **konnen**?   'What do you know?'

Inchoative: *pete, pran, met(e), tonbe*
The term **inchoative** refers to the beginning stage of an action or event. In English, it is usually expressed by the verb *to get*: *Let's get moving*. Except for *met*, whose lexical counterpart *mete/met* also displays optional vowel truncation, these AUX are phonologically identical to their corresponding lexical verbs. The semantic distance between *met* and its corresponding lexical verb *mete* is somewhat greater than between the other three inchoative AUX and their respective lexical verbs, as shown by the examples (57) to (60) below:

(57a) Li **pete kriye**.   'He began to cry.'
(57b) Si li antre nan je ou, l ap **pete** l.   'If it enters your eye, it will make it burst.'

(58a) Chen an **pran jape** fò.   'The dog began to bark loudly.'
(58b) Yon gran chagrinman **pran** li.   'She was taken by a deep grief.' (i.e. She was grief-stricken.)

(59a) Yo **tonbe kodase**.   'They began to cackle.'
(59b) Lapli ap **tonbe**.   'Rain is falling.'

(60a) Tout moun **met(e) danse**.   'Everyone began to dance.'
(60b) **Met(e)** epis nan manje a.   'Put some spices in the food.'
(60c) Yo fèk **mete** yon nouvo direktè.   'They just appointed a new director.'
(60d) Konben tan ou **mete** pou ale lakay ou?   'How long do you take to go to your house?'

The verbs *koumanse* and *tanmen*, both of which mean 'to begin', share an inchoative sense with *pete*, *pran*, and *tonbe*. However, when they combine with verbal complements, their meaning does not differ substantially from the one they bear when they occur individually. For example, although they share the same meaning, the difference between the AUX *tonbe* and the lexical verb *koumanse* is that the latter's meaning does not differ whether it occurs as a lexical verb with or without a verbal complement. This is not the case for *tonbe*, as demonstrated by the pair of examples (59a) and (59b).

(61a) A ki lè kou a **koumanse**? 'At what time does the class begin?'
(61b) Li **koumanse chante**. 'She began to sing.'

Completive-inchoative: *vin*
As the examples below show, *vin* has a meaning intermediate between that of completives, such as *fin,* and inchoatives, such as *sòt*. It underscores the gradual progression of an action or state from beginning to completion. Note, too, that *vin* may also represent the short form of the lexical verb *vini* used in verbal complement constructions such as (62e):

(62a) Li **vin** midi. 'It turned noon.'
(62b) Tifi a **vin renmen** l. 'The young girl came to fall in love with him.'
(62c) Tifi a **vin leve**. 'The girl got up.'
(62d) Li **vini** jodi a. 'She came today.'
(62e) Ou **vin rele** m two bonè. 'You came to call (on) me too early.'

Somewhat related to *vin* is *twouve* 'to happen':

(63a) Li **twouve mouri**. 'It came to pass that he died.'
(63b) Nou **twouve** yon mò. 'We found a dead person.'

Two aspectual AUX, the meanings of which do not fall squarely into the usual semantic categories such as completive or inchoative, are *manke* and *prese*. The latter, derived from 'to hurry', bears the sense of immediacy. *Manke*, whose corresponding lexical verb means 'to miss', has the sense of near-completion.

(64a) M **manke glise**. 'I almost slipped.'
(64b) Chasè a **manke** pentad yo. 'The hunter missed the guinea hens.'
(64c) Zarenyen an **prese reponn**. 'The spider answered immediately.'
(64d) **Prese**, non! Li lè pou n ale. 'Hurry up! It's time for us to go.'

Intensifier: *peze*
Peze, derived from the lexical polysemous verb 'to weigh, to press', extracts from these two basic meanings overtones of immediacy and urgency. The

semantic link with the lexical verb appears clearly in (65a).

(65a) Li **peze disann** sou li.[13]   'He rushed at him suddenly with strength (literally, descended upon him).'
(65b) Li **peze** vyann nan.   'She weighed the meat.'
(65c) **Peze desann**, nou an reta.   'Hurry getting down, we're late.'
(65d) **Peze** bouton sa a.   'Press that button.'

Attenuative: *manyen*

The pioneer Haitian linguists, Jules Faine and Suzanne Sylvain, differ somewhat in their analysis of *manyen*. In his dictionary, Faine (1974: 289) classifies it as an adverb to which he assigns the English meaning 'kind of' and the French *d'une certaine manière* 'in a certain manner, a little, somewhat'. He also notes it as *mangniè*, presumably pronounced as *manyè* [mãɲɛ]:

(66a) **Manyè** vanse.   'Come forward a little.'
(66b) Kouman malad la ye?   'How is the patient?
  – Li **manyè** miyò.   – He's a little better.'

Suzanne Sylvain (1936: 92–3) transcribes it as [mãɲẽ] and views it as an AUX with the same meaning as that listed by her compatriot:

(67a) Li **manyen** manje.   'He ate a little.'
(67b) M **manyen** grangou.   'I'm a little hungry.'
(67c) Talè n a **manyen** sòti.   'We'll go out for a while in a little while.'

However, she also recognizes an adverbial function for the word, although in the example she provides, in which *manyen* occurs with adjectival predicates, it does not seem to differ substantially from that in (67b), which contains a nominal predicate:

(68) Bagay **manyen** dous la.   'The thing is somewhat sweet.'

The corresponding lexical verb *manyen* is quite polysemic: 'to touch, feel, handle, massage, set (bones), handle, use; to cause difficulties, harm by slander or supernatural forces', for example: *Si ou manyen chodyè a, w ap boule ou.* 'If you touch the pot, you'll burn yourself', *Se medsen fèy la ki te manyen bra ki kase a.* 'It's the folk healer who was able to set the arm that was broken'; *Y ap manyen mwen serye pou m p ap jwen djòb la.* 'They're causing me a lot of difficulty keeping me from getting the job'. From these examples and those below from Valdman *et al.* (2007: 463), the semantic link between *manyen* as AUX and its corresponding lexical verb is somewhat tenuous:

(69a) Li **manyen mache** pou manje a ka desann.   'She's taking a small walk to digest the food.'
(69b) Fò ou n **manyè** reprimande pitit ou wi paske li twò maledve.   'You should at least reprimand your child because he's too impolite.'
(69c) Pinga ou **manyen** chodyè.   'Be careful not to touch the cooking pot.'

8.3.2 Modal AUX

Some modal AUX may express several modalities, for example, depending on the linguistic context *mèt* is **epistemic** or **deontic**. An epistemic form refers to eventuality, possibility or probability, as in English *might*: *It might snow tonight*. A deontic form refers to a variety of modalities: commands, wishes, desires, threats, etc., for example: *I wish you were here, could you help me, may I try*.

Capacity: *kapab (kap, kab, ka), fouti*

The AUX *kap* 'capability', occurring in four variants, *kapab, kap, kab*, and *ka*, is derived from the adjective *kapab* from which it does not differ significantly in meaning. However, the adjective never occurs in reduced form. It also expresses eventuality and obligation, and it may be used with adjectival predicates, as in (70c).

(70a) Li pa **ka** dòmi.   'She couldn't sleep.'
(70b) M pa **kapab**.   'I'm not able (to do it).'
(70c) Ti gason an **kap** malad ki fè l pa vini.   'The boy might be sick; that's why he didn't come.'

The following examples (Dejean n.d.: 34) contrast the senses of capacity versus permission borne out by *kapab*:

(71a) Manman m di ... m a **kapab** leve yon sak 100 liv lè m a gen 15 an.   'My mother said that I'll be able to lift a 100 pound bag when I'm 15 years old.'
(71b) Manman m di m **kapab** met sik nan lèt mwen.   'My mother said that I could (be allowed to) put sugar in my milk.'

Fouti is always used in the negative:

(72a) Yo pa **fouti fè** l. 'They're not able to do it.'
(72b) M gen mal dan. M pa **fouti manje** anyen. 'I've got a toothache. I can't eat anything.'

It should be distinguished from the exclamation *fout!* 'damn!' as well the lexical verb *fout(e)* 'to deliver, punch, wallop; hand over':

(73) M **fout** di ou pa met men nan sa! 'I damn well told you not to put your hand into that!'
(74) M a **fout** ou yon kout pwen. 'I'll give you a punch.'

Eventuality and probability: *sa*

Sa bears the senses of eventuality as well as probability. It does not have a corresponding lexical verb. Note that in (75a) the negative *pa* precedes both the lexical verb *parèt* and *sa*.

(75a) Mwen pa **sa** pa **parèt**. 'It's not possible for me not to appear.'
(75b) Ouvè pòt la pou m **sa sòti**. 'Open the door so that I can go out.'
(75c) Nou pa t sonje m pa ta **sa fin pran** l. 'You didn't remember that I couldn't have taken all of it.' (S. Sylvain 1936: 100)[14]

Permission: *mèt*

Like *vle*, *mèt* may occur as a lexical verb with the same meaning as in its role as AUX. Thus, on the basis of this criterion it may be classified as a semi-auxiliary. It is to be distinguished from the polysemous verb *mete* 'to put, to insert, to set, to appoint, to take (time)', whose corresponding AUX is the inceptive *met* (see Section 8.3.1).

(76) Eske m kap pran kribich sa yo? 'May I take these shrimps?
– Ou **mèt**. – You may.'

However, Dejean (n.d.: 39), starting from the example (77) excerpted from Faine (1936: 138), points out that, as a lexical verb, *mèt* conveys defiance, and he provides additional examples to stress the pragmatics of this use:

(77) M a pale manman ou pou ou. 'I'll tell your mother the bad thing you did.'
– Ou **mèt**! '(Go ahead.) Do it!'[15]

(78) M bouke ak ou. M ap divòse. 'I'm tired of you. I am going to divorce (you).'
– Ou **mèt**. 'Go ahead.'

236 The Verbal System

Dejean also questions the grammaticality of (76). For him *mèt* cannot occur with a permissive meaning as a lexical verb in utterance final position. He offers the following example, parallel to (76), where *mèt* occurs obligatorily as AUX:

(79) Manman, eske m **mèt** jwe?   'Mother, may I play?'
      – Ou **mèt** jwe.   'You may play.'

Mèt also conveys obligation or advice as well as eventuality.

(80a) Ou **mèt kache** kò ou.   'You had better hide yourself.'
(80b) Li **mèt touye** m.   'He could kill me.'
(80c) Ou **mèt malad**, ou pral lekòl.   'Sick as you might be, you're going to school.'
(80d) N a **mèt pran ri**, m p ap pe.   'You (pl.) may begin to laugh, I won't stay quiet.'

Lefebvre *et al.* (1982: 109) claim that when *mèt* is preceded by the negative adverb *pa*, it conveys a deontic reading, whereas if the negative follows, *mèt* bears both an epistemic and a deontic meaning, i.e., it is ambiguous.

(81a) Li **pa** mèt vini.   'He can't come.'
                               (not allowed to come)
(81b) Li mèt **pa** vini.   'He can't come.'
                               (not allowed/not able to come)

Dejean (n.d.: 32–3) views (81b) as ungrammatical, or at least questionable. He points out that a negative obligative meaning can only be conveyed with the use of the AUX *dwe*:

(82a) Jak **mèt** al jwe deyò a.   'Jack can play outside.'
       *Jak **pa mèt** al jwe deyò a.
(82b) Jak **pa dwe mèt** al jwe deyò a.   'Jack can't go to play outside.'

Obligation: *dwe*
Dwe, also realized as *do*, shares the same form with its corresponding lexical verb but it differs considerably semantically. It is useful to compare it to *blije*, a verb with the same general obligative meaning that never occurs in final position. The reason I analyze *dwe* as AUX but *blije* as a lexical verb that occurs obligatorily with verbal complements is precisely the semantic difference that exists between *dwe* as AUX and its corresponding lexical verb. An alternative would be to posit two lexical verbs *dwe*: a transitive one meaning 'to owe' and an intransitive one that occurs obligatorily with verbal complements bearing obligative mean-

ing. Another reason, of course, is phonological, namely, the fact that AUX occurs as *dwe* and *do* whereas its lexical counterpart only occurs as *dwe*.[16]

(83a) M **blije vann** ti tak tè m nan.   'I have to sell this small piece of land of mine.'
(83b) Papa l te **blije l ale** lekòl.   'His father forced him to go to school.'

(84a) Ou **dwe ale** wè Jezila.   'You should go see Jezila.'
(84b) Ou **dwe** m dis goud.   'You owe me ten gourdes.'

The epistemic sense (eventuality) of *dwe* is illustrated clearly by (85):

(85) M pèdi chapo m; m **dwe bliye** l lekòl la.   'I lost my hat; I must have forgotten it at the school.'

Dwe also behaves exceptionally in allowing a following TMA:

(86a) M te dwe **te** vini.   'It was necessary for me to have come.'
(86b) Jan dwe **te** vini.   'John might have come.'

Volition: *vle*

As we have seen, *vle* is the only AUX that occurs independently as a lexical verb bearing the same meaning:

(87a) Li **vle fè** l.   'He wants to do it.'
(87b) Poukisa ou pa **vle**?   'Why don't you want to?'
(87c) Li pa **vle** pitit yo soti.   'He doesn't want his children to go out.'

Dominique Fattier (2003: 4) reports the use of *vle* as a future TMA marker in isolated localities: *Yo vle mouri* 'They are going to die'. She points out that there existed in Latin a periphrastic future constructed with the verb 'to want' whose reflexes are attested in regional varieties of French and that are listed in reference grammars of Standard French, such as Grevisse (1969: 599), for example, *il veut pleuvoir* 'it's going to rain'.

8.4 Modal Introducers

In Section 7.3.1, I presented introducers, verbal forms that occur in initial position in sentences: *se, gen, apa, men, nanpwen*. These forms function like English *there is/are* or French *voici* and *voilà* and share their general meaning. In this section, I deal with introducers with a modal meaning. With regard to their modality and their syntactic characteristics, they share similarities with English *let*: *Let's think this over, Let him have some milk*. Like AUX some of these introducers, namely, *kite, pito,* and *sanble* correspond to lexical verbs. In this section, they will be classified according to their meaning.

8.4.1 Exhortative: *annou/ann*

Exhortative forms are meant to encourage or urge:

(88a) **Annou** sòti aswè a. 'Let's go out tonight.'
(88b) **Ann** wè si n a pase anba filfè a. 'Let's see if we'll go under the wire fence.'

8.4.2 Permission: *kite/te*

Kite/te functions as a modal AUX but always with a direct object. As a lexical verb it means 'to leave'; in this regard, it parallels English 'to leave' and Haitian French *laisser*, which takes on that meaning.[17]

(89a) **Kite** m lave pwason an pou ou. 'Let me wash the fish for you.'
       – Ou mèt lave pwason an. – You may wash the fish.'
(89b) **Te** m kouri pou lapli pa bare m. 'I'd better run so the rain doesn't catch me on the way.'

(90a) Eske ou ap **kite m sòti** aswè a? 'Will you let me go out tonight?'
(90b) Madanm ni **kite** l poutèt li vakabon. 'His wife left him no doubt because he's too dissolute.'

8.4.3 Preference: *pito*

As both introducer and main verb *pito* expresses preference:

(91a) **Pito** n ap voye Manno. 'It's better that we send Manno.'
(91b) **Pito** m pile zepis yo. 'I'd better pound the spices.'
(91c) M **pito** bwè dlo. 'I'd prefer to drink water.'
(91d) Sa ou **pito**: ji chadèk oswa ji granadin ? 'What would you prefer: grapefruit juice or grenadilla juice?'

Pito also functions as an adverb:

(92) M pa vle vyann, ban m legim **pito**.   'I don't want meat, give me vegetables instead.'

8.4.4 Necessity: fòk/fò

(93a) **Fòk** ou rete.   'You have to stay.'
(93b) **Fò** m ta wè.   'I have to see (that).'

8.4.5 Prohibition: *piga/ pinga*

Like *fò*, *pinga* functions exclusively as an introducer:

(94a) **Pinga** ou janbe l.   'Don't cross it.'
(94b) **Pinga** nou boule vyann nan.   'Don't let the meat burn.'
(94c) **Pinga** m wè nou jwe nan rivyè a.   'I'd better not see you play in the river.'

8.4.6 Appearance: *sanble*[18]

In addition to the modal meaning 'to appear, to seem', this introducer's corresponding lexical verb also means 'to resemble':

(95a) **Sanble** se pwason karang k ap kouri dèyè l pou manje l.   'It seems that's the common jackfish that's running after it to eat it.'
(95b) Li **sanble** li pa vini.   'Looks like she's not coming.'
(95c) Ala tifi a **sanble** manman l, papa!   'Boy, does that girl look like her mother!'

8.5 The Case of *pou*

There is significant disagreement among scholars about the analysis of the form *pou*: see Koopman amd Lefebvre (1981, 1982), Sterlin (1988), and Spears (1989). As summarized by Spears, this form serves five functions in HC: (1) preposition: *Fè sa pou mwen* 'Do that for me'; (2) marker of purposive clauses: *Li vini pou l etidye* 'He came in order to study'; (3) predicate complementizer: *M vle pou pitit mwen an ka mache byen lè l vin gran*, 'I want my child to be able to walk well when he becomes an adult'; (4) relative complementizer: *Men i te ka jwenn fason pou i ta lwe oun chanm kay pase epòk sa yo* ... 'But, he could have found a way to have rented something like a studio because at that time ...'; (5) preverbal modal auxiliary: *Li pou vini demen* 'He's supposed to come tomorrow'.

With regard to the putative AUX in (5), Koopman and Lefebvre (1981, 1982) and Sterlin (1988) refer to Suzanne Sylvain (1936: 90–1) to support their claim that *pou* functions as preverbal AUX. The examples listed by Sylvain include:

(96a) Ou kwè l **pou mouri**? 'Do you think he's about to die?'
(96b) M te **pou ale** lò l rive. 'I was about to leave when he arrived.'
(96c) Li pa ta **pou peye** m, m ta vann li toujou. 'Even if he would not pay me, I would always sell to him.'

Koopman and Lefebvre (1982: 76–80) support positing *pou* as a modal AUX with the examples (97a) and (97b) and Sterlin (1988: 143) puts forward example (97c):[19]

(97a) M te **pou** vini. 'I had to come.'
(97b) M **pou** ale lekòl. 'I have to go to school.'
(97c) Tout moun **pou** vin lan fèt la. 'Everyone must come to the party.'

On the basis of data he collected from a large set of HC speakers and the opinion of two native-speaker linguists, notably, Yves Dejean,[20] Spears (1991) casts doubt on the analysis of *pou* as a preverbal deontic modal presented by Koopman and Lefebvre and Serlin. In an unpublished critical evaluation of Lefebvre *et al.* (1982), Dejean (n.d.: 27–33) offers other deontic constructions in which *pou* appears following another non-lexical verb, especially *sa pou, gen(yen) pou, dwe pou*:

(98a) Sa **pou** nou fè. 'What we have to do.'
(98b) Nou **gen pou** di sa. 'We have to say that.'
(98c) Li montre nou tou sa nou **dwe pou** konnen. 'He teaches everything that we must know.'

He also cites the mention of *genyen pou* in Faine (1974: 52):

(99) Mwen **genyen pou** m travay. 'I have to work.'

Pou also occurs in a pre-subject position in sentences introduced by *se*:

(100a) **Se pou** ou ede l. 'You have to help her.'
(100b) **Se pou** ede l. 'He has to be helped.'

8.6 Serial Verbs

8.6.1 What is a serial verb?

In addition to the use of TMA markers and auxiliary verbs, aspectual and modal semantic features may be expressed by a type of verbal compounding: **serial verbs**. As is the case for compounding in general (see Section 5.3.3), serial verb combinations generally are idiomatic. The overall meaning of a particular combination differs from the total meaning of the constituent verbs. For example, in *Vwazen yo **bwote vini** yè swa*, the constituent verbs *bwote* and *vini* mean, respectively, 'to carry, haul' and 'to come', but the meaning of the sentence is: 'The neighbors moved in yesterday evening'. The interpretation of the sentence is highly dependent on the context: the fact that it is the neighbors who come carrying things suggests that they are moving in.

Like Givòn (1991: 137), it is tempting to define serial verbs in terms of cross-linguistic comparison:

> An event/state that one language codes as a single clause with a single verb, is coded in another language as a complex clause with two or more verbs.

A more useful definition is provided by Collins (1997: 462):

> A serial verb construction is a succession of verbs and their complements (if any) with one subject and one tense value that are not separated by any overt marker of coordination or subordination.[21]

Consider the verb sequence *voye* 'to send' + *jete* 'to throw': *Li **voye jete** rad sa yo*. This two-verb combination does not mean 'She sent and threw those clothes' but 'She threw away those clothes'. Serial verbs thus contrast with simple verb complements where the complementary verb retains its base meaning. Compare (101a), which illustrates a verbal complement construction in which the verbs *ale* 'to go' and *pote* 'to carry, bring' retain their basic meaning and the serial verb *pote ale* in (101b), where the order of the verbs is reversed to convey an idiomatic meaning:

(101a) Li **ale pote** bannann yo nan mache a.   'She went to bring the plantains to the market.'
(101b) Li **pote ale** bannann yo.   'She brought back the plantains.'

Note that the serial verb construction (102d) differs semantically from the sequences of coordinated clauses (102a–c):

(102a) Li **pote** rad sa yo.   'She carried those clothes.'
(102b) Li **voye** rad sa yo.   'She sent those clothes.'
(102c) Li **pote** rad sa yo epi li **voye** rad sa yo.   'She carried those clothes and she sent these clothes.'
(102d) Li **pote** rad sa yo **voye**.   'She took those clothes away.'

As is the case for *pote* ... *voye* in (102d) and *pote ale* in (101b), the second verb functions like the English preposition *back* and the adverb *away*, indicating motion away from the speaker.

8.6.2 Serial verbs in early descriptions of HC

Jules Faine (1936: 149) considered serial verbs, which he termed **compound verbs**, to constitute one of the salient traits of the language. For him, verb serialization is a process that 'consists in fusing together two verbs so that one complements and reinforces the meaning of the other'.[22] Indeed, at the semantic level, serial verbs may be analyzed as the modification of the meaning of a verb by the addition of some of the semantic features of another. However, except for listing several pairs of serial verbs, Faine does not provide any contextual examples or analysis.

Suzanne Sylvain's treatment is more extensive (1936: 128–35), although somewhat confused. She discusses serial verbs first briefly as compounds, without providing contextual examples, then more fully as equivalents to French combinations of verbs + prepositions or adverbs:

(103)   **Kouri   vin   rive**   mache   pou   li.
         run   come   arrive   market   for   her
        'Go quickly to the market for her.'

Here, *kouri* adds a sense of urgency to the request. For Sylvain, *vini* signals movement toward the speaker – in fact, she generally translates this directional verb with the French adverb *ici* 'here', as in (104c) – whereas *ale* indicates movement away. These interpretations account for the other examples she provides, (104a) and (104b); however, the use of *vin* in (103) seems puzzling since presumably the person giving the order is not at the market.

(104a) **Bwote** barik **vini** isit.   'Bring the barrel here.' (carry–come)
(104b) Li **mennen** pitit yo **ale**.   'He took the children away.' (lead–go)
(104c) Li **rale** chèz la **vini**.   'He pulled the chair toward here.' (pull–come)

How to distinguish serial verbs, on the one hand, from sequences of AUX + lexical verb and, on the other, from verbal complement constructions is problematic. In (105a), presented above as (65b), and (105b) Sylvain analyzes *peze* and *manyen* as participating in serial verb combinations in which they occur as the first verb. However, she had previously listed them as AUX (see Section 8.3.1 above). She does not provide new examples for *peze*. Instead, she states that it imparts on a movement verb the senses of 'with force' and 'with liveliness' (*entrain*).

(105a)   Li **peze disann** sou li.[23]   'He rushed suddenly at him with force.'

For *manyen* she provides (105b):

(105b)   Li **manyen kouri**.   'He runs a little.'

Robert Hall (1953: 55) considers serial verbs to be verbal complement constructions: 'several verbs occur in a series, each as a complement to the preceding one':

(106a)   Manman m **vin rive sòt** lavil.   'My mother came home from town.'
                                             (literally, came [to] arrived [after] leaving town)
(106b)   L ap **mennen** l **ale jwenn**   'He was to take him to his mother.'
         manman li.   (literally, he was going to take to go to find his mother)

In (106b), *jwenn* is not part of the serial verb; the sentence could be rephrased with a prepositional complement as *L ap mennen ale **pou** jwenn manman li*.

8.6.3 Types of serial verbs

Serial verbs fall into two main groups. In the first group, the second verb (**deictic verb**) situates the first verb (**focal verb**) spatially with respect to the speaker. The focal verb bears the central semantic content of the combination. A **deictic element** in a language is one whose function is to 'point', to situate an element with respect to the speaker: *here, there, yonder, this, that*, etc. Serial verbs consisting of a verb of movement as second constituent are clearly distinguished from both AUX + main verb and verbal complement constructions.

In the second group of serial verbs, as is the case for combinations of focal plus deictic verb, the focal verb carries the primary meaning of the combination. The second, or **modifying**, verb does not situate the focal verb spatially relative to the speaker. It modifies its meaning in a variety of ways. In a certain sense, it often functions semantically as an adverb.

Focal verb + deictic verb

Deictic verbs generally pair off, one referring to a location away or forward, the other back to the deictic center, usually the speaker: *ale* 'to go' vs. *vini* 'to come back', *vanse* 'to go forward' vs. *rekile* 'to return', *monte* 'to go up' vs. *desann* 'to go down'. The direction with respect to the speaker is implicit in the base meaning of the verb: note that in English one would say *go there* but never *come there*, or *come here*, but never *go here*; similarly, the expression *downtown* suggests centrality or nearness whereas *uptown* suggests remoteness or the periphery. Thus, deictic verbs function very much like prepositions in English:

(107a)	Li **janbe ale** Fisi.	'He crossed over to Furcy.'
	cross over/go	
(107b)	Tidjo **kouri ale** lakay li.	'Tidjo ran over to his house.'
	run/go	
(107c)	Yo toujou **monte desann**.	'They keep going up and down.'
	go up/go down	
(107d)	Lè msye fache, li **ale vini**.	'When he's angry, he walks back and forth.'
	go/come	

Other deictic verbs that do not pair off with an antonym, as is the case of *ale* and *vini*, include *jete* 'to throw away', *kite* 'to leave', *soti* 'to leave, go out', *tounen* 'to turn', and *rive* 'to arrive'. In some cases, the first verb functions as an adverbial (108a, b), in other cases, the second one does (108c–e):

(108a)	Li **vole kite** peyi a.	'She hurriedly fled the country.'
	fly/leave	
(108b)	Fòk ou **voye** vye soulye sa yo **jete**.	'You have to throw away those old shoes.'
	send/throw	
(108c)	Ti pa ti pa, n ap **vanse rive** kote n prale a.	'Little by little, we're getting where we're going.'
	move forward/arrive	
(108d)	Mato a **vole soti** nan men m.	'The hammer flew out of my hand.'
	fly/go out	
(108e)	Yo **pote** lajan an **tounen** ba l.	'They returned the money to her.'
	carry/return	

Focal verb + modifying verb

As pointed out in Section 8.6.3, in focal plus modifying serial verbs, the modifying verb is semantically subordinate to the focal verb. It amplifies, restricts, or otherwise modifies its meaning. In the following example, the verb *tenyen* stresses the unsteady nature of the light provided by the light bulb, as if it were being lit and going off at the same time:

(109)   Anpoul la **limen tenyen**.   'The light bulb is flickering.' (is
           turn on/turn off   providing light in a flickering manner)

In the following example, containing the focal verb *mache* 'to walk', *mache bwete* 'to limp' (*Jwè a te mache bwete apre match la* 'The player was limping after the game'), the modifying verb provides a finer tuned meaning and specifies the exact nature of the action. Note that rendering the meaning of these serial verbs into English often requires the use of a more specialized term. In some cases, the HC structure is more economical from a lexical perspective: it reduces the lexical burden and makes the meaning more transparent. It evokes the lexical transparency achieved in German by the use of native compounds for medical specialties versus the English and French resort to Greco-Latin borrowings: *Frauenarzt* (women doctor) 'gynecologist, *gynécologue*', *Kinderarzt* (children doctor) 'pediatrician, *pédiatre*'. This is the case of *mache bwòde* 'to walk + to embroider' = 'to strut' or *mete kanpe* 'to put + to stop' = 'to park' as in *Ou mal mete machin ou an kanpe* 'You parked your car badly'. In some cases, the modifying verb serves to emphasize the focal verb, as in *jakase ranse* 'to chatter, prattle + to talk nonsense' = 'to really talk nonsense while prattling' or *mache bwete* 'to walk + to limp' = 'to limp badly'.

Some serial verbs are quite idiomatic and require reference to the extra-linguistic or situational context for their precise meaning, for example, those in which the focal verb is *mete* 'to put' or *pote* 'to carry':

(110a)   Se Vilè ki **mete** lekòl la **kanpe**.   'It is Vilaire who established the
             put/set up   school.'
(110b)   M depanse anpil kòb pou m   'I spend a lot of money to have the
             mete pitit la **kanpe**.   child fully recover.'
             put/stand up
(111a)   Fòk nou **pote boure** ak zanmi   'We have to back up our friends.'
             nou yo.
             carry/stuff
(111b)   Ann **pote kole** ak otorite   'Let's cooperate with the health
             lasante yo.   services.'
             carry/attach

The idiosyncratic nature of some focal + modifying serial verb combinations make them extremely opaque. Note that in (113), the modifying verb *plede* 'to do something continuously' precedes the focal verb, whose sense in that context, 'to vomit', is an extension of the sense 'to spill'.

(112) Koutiryèz **kole pyese** pantalon an.
glue/piece together
'The seamstress sewed up the pants.'

(113) Li ansent, se pou sa li **plede ranvèse** konsa.
act continuously/turn over
'She's pregnant, that's why she keeps vomiting like that.'

8.6.4 Multiple serial verb constructions

In (114a), only the first two verbs constitute a serial verb construction; *al wè* is a complex verb complement consisting of *ale*, itself complemented by *wè*, i.e.: *kouri desann ((al) wè)*. It could be glossed as (114b).

(114a) M **kouri desann** al wè sa l t ap fè.
'I ran down to see what he was doing.'[24]

(114b) M **kouri desann** pou al epi pou wè sa l t ap fè
'I run go down to go and to see what he PAST PROG do.'

The apparent four-verb serial verb *pwomennen mache monte desann* ('to stroll + to walk + to go up + to go down') = 'to wander around', in fact, consists of a series of two serial verbs: *pwomennen mache* 'to stroll' + *monte desann* 'to go up and down'.

On the other hand, the three-verb series *vole sove kite* 'to fly, rush + to flee, escape + to leave' constitutes an inseparable unit. In the following examples, it appears that the emphasis is placed on fleeing from a dangerous or bad situation, as expressed by *vole*.

(115a) Li **vole sove kite** machin nan k ap pran dife a.
'She quickly rushed out of the burning car.'

(115b) Restavèk la **vole sove kite** kay la.[25]
'The child servant scampered away from the house.'

8.6.5 Placement of direct objects in serial verb constructions

In combinations of focal verb + deictic verb, the direct object generally follows the focal verb:

(116a) Yo **pote** machinakoud la **vini**.
carry/come
'They carried off the sewing machine.'

(116b) **Pote** si a **ale**.
carry/go
'Take the saw away.'

(116c) **Mennen** Tidjo **ale** lekòl.   'Take Tidjo over to school.'
       lead/go
(116d) Lavalas la **bwote** tout bon tè a 'The torrential rain carried off all of the
       desann.   good soil.'
       carry/go down

The placement of the direct object in sentences (116a–d) underscores the dependency relationship between the deictic verb and the preceding focal verb.[26] On the other hand, in combinations of focal verb + modifying verb the direct object usually follows the two-verb combination:

(117a) Pa **voye jete** liv mwen an.   'Don't throw away my book.'
       send/throw
(117b) Pa **tounen vire** tout lide sa yo 'Don't keep turning all these thoughts
       nan tèt ou.   over in your mind.'
       turn/turn around

The placement of the direct object after the first verb is not excluded, however:

(118) Li te toujou wè papa l **antre** 'She always saw her father bring in
       danre **sòti** nan jaden an.   cash crops from the field.'
       bring in/take out

8.6.6 The verb *bay* in serial verb constructions

The verb *bay*, also realized as two other variants, *ba* and *ban*, occurs with the basic meaning 'to give' but its senses extend to 'to hand over, to denounce, to give off, to permit' and so on:

(119a) Li **ban** m twa zoranj.   'She gave me three oranges.'
(119b) Konben yo **bay** pou travay   'How much do they give for this work?'
       sa a?
(119c) Yo **ba** l pase.   'They let him go.' (gave him
                                          permission to pass)
(119d) Fimen **bay** kansè poumon.   'Smoking causes lung cancer.'

In its shortest form *ba*, *bay* may occur with a prepositional function comprising a benefactive meaning, translated by either 'for' or 'to':

(120a) Fè travay la **ban** mwen.   'Do the work for me.'
(120b) Li voye anpil kob **ba** sè l.   'She sent a lot of money to her sister.'

But this short form also occurs in serial verb constructions, in which case the question arises whether it participates in these constructions as a verb or functions as a preposition:

(121)   **Pote** liv a **vini ban** mwen.   'Bring this book (back) to me.'
        to carry   to return

Summary

One general observation that emerges from the description of the verb system of HC is that it has continued the evolution toward analytic structure evident in vernacular French, the language from which it has inherited most of its lexicon and the major part of its grammatical structure. As pointed out in Gougenheim's description of periphrastic structures in French (1929), the use of auxiliary verbs provided grammatical means to code aspectual and modal distinctions in a language that gave the priority to the marking of tense distinctions by inflection. In addition to the use of verb markers – *ap(e), (a)(v)a, te* – most of them derived from French periphrastic constructions – *être après* (progressive) → *ap(e)*, *aller* + infinitive (definite future) → *(a)(v)a*, *être pour* (progressive) → *pou* – HC displays a wide variety of aspectual and modal auxiliaries.

Two central features characterize the HC verbal system: first, the absence of a bi-unique (one-to-one) correspondence between semantic categories, such as past or future, and structural mechanisms, such as verb markers or auxiliaries. For example, with non-stative verbs *ap* may express both the progressive and the future. Second, there is a sharp distinction between stative and non-stative verbs. With the former, the relationship between semantic categories and verb markers is straightforward: bare stems (Ø) express present, *te* past, and *ap* future. On the other hand, with non-statives bare stems carry past or present meaning and *ap* progressive aspect or futurity. Consequently, to carry over the notion of verb conjugation, itself questionable for vernacular spoken French (Valdman 1976), to HC leads to a failure to properly interpret the nature of the HC verbal system. Thus, independently of context, the following phrase, containing the bare stem of the non-stative verb *bwè*, *li bwè wonm*, may mean either 'she drinks rhum' or 'she drank rhum'.

Non-stative verbs themselves are subdivided into two classes: processives and resultatives. Like statives, resultative verbs are incompatible with the progressive aspect. Thus, *ap* only expresses futurity when combined with resultative verbs such as *wè* 'to see' (see the contrast in sentences (30a) and (30b) between the resultative verb *wè* and the processive verb *gade* 'to look at'). On the other hand, as is the case for processive verbs, the bare stem expresses both present and past, as in (30c). Some non-stative verbs are polysemous: they are both processive and resultative, for example, *grate* means 'to scratch' as a processive verb (32a) but 'to itch' as a resultative verb (32b).

Another aspect of the analytic nature of the HC verb system is the large number of auxiliary verbs, many of which are derived from lexical verbs that occur independently in predicates. Auxiliaries express a wide range of aspectual and modal meanings: completive, habitual, inchoative (referring to the onset of an action or event), intensifying, and attenuative in the case of aspectual auxiliaries; epistemic (eventuality, probability, capability) and deontic (permission, volition, obligation) in the case of modal auxiliaries. Related to auxiliaries are introducers, some of which correspond to lexical verbs (*pito, kite, sanble*) and others that occur only in sentence-initial position (*annou, fòk/fò, pinga*). Although it serves a variety of other functions in HC and its status is the subject of diverse opinions, *pou* takes its place among AUX, as exemplified in (96).[27]

Serial verbs constitute a signal feature of the HC verb system. As shown in example (102), they differ from coordinated clauses. I have analyzed them as being composed of a main verb (focal verb) and a subordinate one and I have distinguished two groups. In the first group, the subordinate verb (deictic verb) orients the action or event spatially, often either toward or away from the speaker; it functions somewhat like the English prepositions and adverbs *back* and *away* or *down* and *up*. In (117), *jete* 'to throw' is equivalent to English *away* and in fact it reinforces the polysemous verb *voye*, one of whose senses is 'to throw', as in *pa voye wòch* 'don't throw stones'. In the case of combinations of focal and modifying verbs, which may either precede or follow, there is a semantic interaction between the two verbs that makes these combinations of verbs highly idiomatic and highly dependent on the pragmatic context.

Notes

1. *Sing* is irregular because its past-tense form is not formed by the addition of *-ed* to the base *sing* (**singed*) but has a different vowel: *sang*.
2. The term *deontic* refers to obligation and *epistemic* to possibility.
3. French dialects and older varieties of the language show *vas* (*je vas*) as the 1st person singular present form instead of SF *je vais*.
4. Claire Lefebvre (1998: 110–40) proposes an initial three-way semantic classification of HC verbs: dynamic, resultative, and stative rather than

250 The Verbal System

Damoiseau's (1988) initial two-way distinction: dynamic (processive vs. resultative) and stative.

5. Before *ap*, *a* is realized as *av*. This is the result of elision of the final vowel of the variant *ava* before a vowel. The meaning of the combinations of TMA markers will be discussed in Section 8.2.

6. As pointed out in footnote 5 above, the irrealis marker occurs in three morphophonological variants: *ava, va, a*. The last variant is the most frequent, and it combines with *te* as *ta*. In the description of the HC mood system, I will cite the actually occurring variants.

7. The speaker quoted by Spears is from northern Haiti and uses the variant *i* instead of *li* for the 3rd person singular personal pronoun. This is also the case for the speaker quoted in the next example. See Chapter 11 for a detailed discussion of the speech of speakers from that area.

8. In SHC, the equivalent of Capois *granmounannou* (*granmoun a nou*) is *granmoun nou*. A *gouden* is one-fourth of a gourde. These excerpts are part of a corpus collected in June 2007. They can be accessed online from the Indiana University Creole Institute website (http://www.indiana.edu/~creole/).

9. For a more extensive list of resultative verbs, see Damoiseau (1988: 60–1).

10. Earlier descriptions of HC did not identify the subjunctive as a mood; see Suzanne Sylvain (1936), R. A. Hall (1953), d'Ans (1968), and Valdman (1978). However, Faine (1936: 138) recognized that there is no specific subjunctive marker in the language. He refers to the subjunctive as 'purement conventionnel' because for him it is expressed with the same marker as the indicative, namely, *ap*, although usually preceded by the conjunction *ke*. He exemplifies the use of the subjunctive with *Li dit (ou li dit con ça ou li dit que) lap-vine faire ous explication – Que l vini! (que l vini non!) m'pare pou li*, translated with a French subjunctive form, *vienne: Il dit qu'il vient exiger de vous des explications – Qu'il vienne, je suis prêt pour lui*. 'He says that he's coming to insist that you give him explanations – Let him come, I'm ready for him.'

11. There is a clear link between the subjunctive mood and futurity. Fleischman (1982) suggests that in Romance languages the future tense grew out of deontic modalities: obligation, volition. The French future tense that expresses indefinite futurity developed from the Latin infinitive + *to have*, e.g., *cantare habeo* 'I have to sing' to French *je chanterai* 'I will sing'. In a sense, obligation or volition are prospective (looking forward) semantic notions. In English, the future often implies deontic notions: command (*You will study tonight, I insist*) or intention (*I will study tonight*).

12. A more detailed treatment of conditional complex sentences is provided in Section 10.1.

13. The verb 'to go down' has two variants: *desann* and *disann*. The example in (65a), with the latter variant, is cited by Suzanne Sylvain (1936: 94); the variant *desann* occurring in (65c) is listed as the standard variant in Valdman et al. (2007) and was elicited by one of the native speaker collaborators of that dictionary.

14. Sylvain translates this example as: *Vous ne vous rappeliez pas que je n'aurais pas pu le prendre en entier.* The completive AUX *fin* is rendered by *en entier* 'as a whole'.
15. From Faine's French rendition: *Que vous le fassiez (faites-le, je m'en moque)* 'Whether you do it or not, I couldn't care less about it'. The defiant overtone of the rejoinder is quite clear.
16. Lefebvre *et al.* (1982: 141–3) consistently represent this AUX as *do*, whereas Dejean opts for *dwe*. In Valdman *et al.* (2007), the entry is listed under *dwe* because it was found to be the most frequent variant by far.
17. In Standard French, 'to leave a place' is expressed by *quitter*. Compare: 'I left Haiti' in Haitian French, *J'ai laissé Haïti* and Standard French *J'ai quitté Haïti*. That sense of *laissé* derives from Colonial French as it is attested in Louisiana French: *Ils ont laissé la France dans les seize cents* 'They left France in the 1600s' (Valdman *et al.* 2010: 359).
18. Fattier's list of auxiliaries or introducers includes *annik*: *Annik m rive m retounen* 'I had barely arrived before I went back' (2003: 5). But in Valdman *et al.* (2007), it is listed as an adverb with variable meaning, 'just, merely, only, simply, as soon as': *M ap annik repose jodi a* 'I'm only relaxing today'; *Mwen annik rive, li ba nouvèl la* 'As soon as I arrived, he gave me the news'.
19. Koopman and Lefebvre (1982: 146) state that they found twenty occurrences of modal *pou*, out of 246 other instances of the form, in the large written corpus compiled in R. A. Hall (1953). However, they fail to provide these examples. In a ten-hour sample of the corpus I collected in the Cape Haitian region in 2007, not a single instance occurs of preverbal modal *pou*. Most are of the preposition *pou*.
20. Spears analyzes *pou* as a preverbal marker. The issue of the status of this form as a preverbal marker or a preverbal AUX is beyond the scope of this presentation and will not be discussed here.
21. Some creolists operate with a less-constrained definition of a serial verb. Syea (2013) includes two verb sequences, each containing a subject, as is the case for the following example from Mauritian Creole:

li	pran	lakle	li	uver	bwat
he	take	key	he	open	box

'he opens the box with a key'

22. '*souder ensemble deux verbes de manière que l'un complète et renforce le sens de l'autre*'.
23. The other two examples Sylvain provides – *Ou manyen wo* 'You are a little tall' and *M manyen douvan* 'I'm a little in front' – raise the issue of whether *manyen* might be an adverb. In the first of these examples, *manyen* may be interpreted as an AUX preceding an adjectival predicate, as I did in (75b) and (76b) above. However, in the second it precedes an adverbial predicate.
24. *Al(e)* like *vin(i)* is subject to truncation when it occurs in non-final position.

25. The word *restavèk* is derived from the French *rester avec* 'to stay with'. In Haiti, *restavèk* are young children, usually under the age of fifteen, whose parents are too poor to care for them. Typically rural children, they are sent to live with a more affluent relative or a host family in an urban area who are expected to feed them and send them to school in exchange for housework. However, *restavèk* are often abused and treated as slaves.
26. In (116d), some speakers would accept the placement of the direct object after the second verb. It may be that *disann* does carry the same deictic strength as *ale* and *vini*.
27. Chaudenson (2003: 360) notes that *pou*'s French etymon, the preposition *pour*, occurs as part of periphrastic constructions in different parts of France: as an inchoative in western France (*j'étions pour partir* 'I was about to leave') and with futurity meaning in the Franco-Provençal area in eastern France (*j'étais pour construire* 'I planned to build').

9 The Structure of Noun Phrases

9.1 The General Structure of Noun Phrases (NPs)

9.1.1 The syntactic functions of nouns

Nouns play a variety of roles in HC. As we have seen in Chapter 7, they may constitute the full predicate: *ou pa gason* 'you're not a man, i.e., manly'; they serve as primary or as secondary objects in predicates: *ti bòn lan prete Alisya lanp tèt bobèch li a* 'the little maid lent Alicia her oil lamp'; as object complements: *yo rele jako a Kòkòt* 'they named the parrot Kòkòt'; and as subjects and adverbial complements: *moun sik yo te pase kèk jou nan peyi a* 'the circus people spent a few days in the country'. One of the salient traits of HC is that the line that separates nouns and verbs is not clear. Certain emphatic constructions involve using verbs and adjectives in nominal functions, for example, *li dòmi yon bon ti dòmi* 'she had a nice little sleep'; *se pa yon ti bèl li te bèl* 'she was more than a little beautiful' = 'she was really beautiful'. Conversely, nouns may serve a verbal function: *yo bèf li* 'they changed him into a cow'. Note that in *li dòmi yon bon ti dòmi*, *dòmi* remains a verb. This fact is made clearer by the following related sentences:

(1a) *Pradèl bwè yon bwason.*   'Pradel drinks a drink.'
(1b) *Se pa ti kras bwè Pradel bwè.* 'Pradel really did some serious drinking.'

In (1a), *bwason,* a noun, serves a typical nominal function, namely, as direct object, but in (1b) the focus is not on what is being drunk but on the action of drinking itself. In assuming the various nominal functions nouns enter into, constructions of varying complexity are built around a **head noun**. We label these **noun phrases** (**NPs**). In this chapter I will describe the structure of these constructions.

9.1.2 Constituents of NPs

The core of an NP consists of a noun. In HC, it is not unusual for a noun to form an NP by itself. The first level of expansion of an NP involves the specification of the abstract semantic features that characterize the

Table 9.1. Structure of HC Noun Phrases

Pre-determiners*			Adj₁	N	Adj₂	Inner det	Det
A	B	C					
tout	Quantifiers			N		Possessive Demonstrative	Definite Plural
chak	Ordinals	lòt		NP			
	Cardinals	menm		S			
	anpil						
	kèk						
	okenn						
	plizyé						
	Indefinite						

*Although, for the sake of convenience, I show Possessive Demonstrative in the Inner Determiner slot, personal pronouns functioning as possessives are not strictly speaking determiners, as will be shown in Section 9.3. However, they do function like determiners.

particular use of a noun. These features, on the axes specific–non-specific and pre-supposed–non-pre-supposed, are expressed by **determiners** (**Det**) including the absence of any determiner, which we represent as zero (Ø).

Although they set the inner semantic parameters of nouns, determiners occur at the outer core of NPs, before the outermost component of NPs, the plural marker *yo*. Two sets of determiners need to be recognized in HC: the outer Det (indefinite vs. definite) and the inner Det (demonstrative). As will be shown in Section 9.4, personal pronouns, which serve to express possession and correspond to the possessive determiners (adjectives) of English or French (*my book, mon livre*), are not, strictly speaking, determiners. Another set of elements, the **pre-determiners**, related to Det, also occurs at the periphery of NPs.

Proceeding toward the inner core we find **quantifiers** (**Quant**), which can be subdivided into indefinites and numbers (cardinal and ordinal) followed by adjectives. These (**Adj₁**) are generally placed to the right of the head noun, although a few precede it on the left (**Adj₂**). The inner core of an NP consists of the head noun, optionally expanded by a modifying noun, NP, a preposition phrase (**PrepNP**), or a clause (**S**). The various expansions of the core head noun are shown in Table 9.1 and illustrated in Section 9.1.3 below. All expansion elements are optional, since a noun can constitute an NP by itself; such is the case, for instance, for proper nouns.

9.1.3 Types of NPs

I illustrate below the various types of NP expansion. The kinds of nouns and the structure of Det will be treated in detail in a separate section, as will adjectives and personal pronouns.

1. Noun (N) only

    Tijo rive. 'Tijo has arrived.'
    Pentad se bèt ki malen. 'Guinea hens are clever animals.'
    Joumou pa janm bay ***kalba***s. 'Pumpkins never produce calabashes.'
    Ba l ***diven***. 'Give him wine.'

2. Det + N/N + Det

    Yon ***chat*** mete ***rat*** *la* nan bouch li. 'A cat put the rat in its mouth.'

3. N + pronoun

    Li lave ***wòb*** *li*. 'She washed her dress.'

4. *Tout, chak, okenn, pyès* + N

    Tout ***moun*** se moun. 'Every person is a person.' = Every human being has his/her own dignity.

    Chak ***mwa*** li bay *chak* ***moun*** san goud. 'Every month she gave each person a hundred gourdes.'

    Pa gen *okenn* ***moun*** nan lari a. 'There wasn't anyone in the street.'

    Pa te gen *pyès* ***mango*** ki rete. 'There wasn't a single mango that remained.'

5. Quant + N

    Nou wè *de* ***zwazo***. 'We saw two birds.'
    Li voye *dènye* ***grenn*** nan ki rete. 'She threw the last seed that remained.'
    Twa ka mas ***pèp*** ayisyen pa konn li. 'Three-quarters of the Haitian masses can't read.'
    Yo konn manje *anpil* ***diri***. 'They usually eat a lot of rice.'
    Li achte *plizyè* ***milèt***. 'He bought several mules.
    Se dwe *kèk* ***moun*** ki di l sa. 'It must have been someone who told her that.'

256 The Structure of Noun Phrases

6. *lòt, menm* + N

    M desann lavil ak kèk *lòt **machann***.   'I went downtown with a few other hawkers.'

    *Menm **timoun*** yo li pa bay anyen.   'He didn't even give anything to the children.'

7. Adj_1 + N

    Gen yon *ti **pyebwa*** douvan kay la.   'There's a small tree in front of the house.'

    Li pa renmen *vye **nèg*** sa a.   'She didn't like that old guy.'

8. N + Adj_2

    Se yon ***nèg*** *visye*.   'He's a crafty guy.'

    Li toujou jwenn yon *bon **dlo*** pwòp.   'She always found nice clean water.'

9. N + N

    Li vini yon ***jou*** *dimanch*.   'He arrived on a fine Sunday.'

10. N + NP

    M ap tann ou douvan ***kay*** *bòs ebenis la*.   'I'll wait for you in front of the house of the cabinetmaker.'

    Se ***manman*** *ti kouzen mwen*.   'She's the mother of my little cousin.'

11. N + Prep NP

    Sèvi m ***lèt*** *ak patat*.   'Serve me some milk and potatoes.'

    Yo fè ***resepsyon*** *pou mesye a*.   'They gave a reception for the man.'

12. N + S

    M ap rakonte nou *yon **istwa*** *ki pase nan gagè*.   'I'll tell you a story that took place in a cockfight pit.'

    Ou-menm ki konn fè *bèl **fig*** *ki dous*.   'You who know how to produce nice bananas that are sweet.'

13. N + Det

> ***Kay** la* boule. 'The house burned down.'
> Li vole gwo ***bèf*** *mwen*. 'He stole that big cow/steer of mine.'
> Fò nou swiv ***konsèy*** *yo*. 'You must follow the advice.'

14. N + Det + Det

> Ki lès moun ki fouye ***tou*** *sa a*? 'Who dug this hole?'
> Li manje *ze sa yo*. 'She ate those eggs.'
> ***Pitit*** *sila a* pral Pòtoprens. 'This child is going to Port-au-Prince.'

9.2 The Determiner System

9.2.1 The inherent semantic features of nouns

In addition to their specific lexical meaning, e.g., *cat* 'feline, domestic animal', nouns carry semantic features characteristic of whole subsets: *milk* refers to an indivisible mass (**mass noun**) that cannot be enumerated in terms of individual units; *books*, on the other hand, can be so enumerated (**count noun**). It is, however, possible to view mass nouns as individualized units. For example, *I'll take one milk and two ice creams*, in which case what is understood is a glass of milk and two servings of ice cream. Unlike mass nouns or count nouns, nouns such as *liberty* do not refer to something concrete; they are **abstract nouns**. These three classes of nouns are **common nouns**. They do not refer to a person, a thing, or a concept that is viewed as unique, as do such proper nouns as *John*, *Haiti,* the *Caribbean*, etc. Furthermore, there are semantic features that nouns take on in certain contexts. In *Where is the book?*, the noun refers to a previously mentioned (pre-supposed) and specific member of the class *book* or one whose identity is known to the speaker and the hearer. In *I don't have any books*, reference is made to a member of the class that is neither specific nor pre-supposed. In *I like books*, reference is made to the entire class referred to by the noun *book*; it is the **generic** meaning of the noun. In languages, there are various constraints in the combination of these four classes of nouns (proper, count, mass, abstract) and constituents of the NP. The semantic features +/– specific and +/– pre-supposed are generally indicated by the absence or presence of various types of Det.

In English, to refer to the entire class of a count noun, that is, the generic (–specific and –pre-supposed), one may use either the plural or the indefinite article: *books are precious things; a book is a precious thing.* On the other hand, for mass nouns and abstract nouns that semantic feature is expressed by the absence of any determiner (zero): *milk is good for your health, liberty is never obtained without great sacrifices.* The features +specific and +pre-supposed are expressed by the definite determiner for all classes of common nouns: *I lost the book, the milk is sour, the liberty we fought for.* In each case, reference is made to a specific thing or concept that the speaker assumes is known to the interlocutor. Because proper nouns are inherently specific and pre-supposed in English, they are generally not accompanied by determiners: *Haiti shares the island of Hispaniola with the Dominican Republic.* In the latter proper noun, *the* is an integral part of the proper noun and does not strictly function as a determiner.

The expression of the nominal semantic features of specificity and pre-supposition is much more straightforward in HC. The combination of +specific and +pre-supposed is indicated by the definite determiner *LA*: *Kote liv la?* 'Where is the book?', *Lèt la bon* 'The milk is good'.[1] Nouns that are specific but not pre-supposed are indicated by the indefinite determiner: *m gen yon liv* 'I have a book', *se yon lèt ki bon* 'It's a milk that's good'. The generic is indicated by the absence of any determiner (Ø): *m renmen liv* 'I like books', *se bèf ki ban nou lèt* 'It's cows that give us milk'. The negative is also expressed by Ø: *m pa gen chat* 'I don't have cats, I don't have any cat', *m pa vle lèt* 'I don't want any milk'. The above statements represent a sort of first approximation; a more detailed discussion of the expression of nominal semantic features will be provided in the sections of this chapter that deal with particular determiners.

Mass nouns such as *lèt* may carry the features +specific and +pre-supposed, *Kote lèt la?* 'Where is the milk (the one that we know about)?', +specific and –pre-supposed, *Sa se yon bon lèt* 'That's a good kind of milk', or –specific and –pre-supposed: generic *M renmen lèt* 'I like milk', negative *M pa renmen lèt* 'I don't like milk'. The various combinations of the semantic features (pre-supposed) (+/–) and (specific) (+/–) define four domains (see Table 9.2).

Table 9.2. The Marking of Inherent Semantic Features in HC

	+pre-supposed		–pre-supposed	
+specific	LA	lèt la	yon	yon bon lèt
–specific			generic	M renmen lèt.
			negative	M pa renmen lèt.

The inherent semantic features of nouns are expressed by the outer Det, the definite determiner, noted as the abstract form, *LA*, the indefinite determiner *yon*, and the absence of determiner, Ø. In the next section, I will discuss and illustrate the link between Det and the expression of the semantic features of nouns.

9.2.2 The definite determiner

The term 'definite' used to characterize *LA* is somewhat misleading, and it is important to bear in mind that neither its meaning nor its scope of use is identical to those of either its English near-equivalent *the* or its French equivalent *le* (which for the sake of convenience here represents all variant forms: *le, l', la, les*). First, *LA* occurs at the end of the noun phrase, not necessarily contiguous to the noun:

(2a) Kote **liv** la?   'Where is the book [that we all know about]?'
(2b) Ou wè **liv** m te achte yè *a*?   'Have you seen the book I bought yesterday [and that you know about]?'

Except for its placement at the end of NPs, *LA* patterns very much like the English definite article. In the examples (3) to (5), observe the contrast between the positive and negative values of presupposition and specificity expressed in HC by Ø vs. *LA*:

(3a) M t achte diri nan mache a.   'I bought rice at the market.'
(3b) Diri *a* pa te gou menm.   'The rice didn't taste good at all.'

(4a) Li lave dra.   'She washes sheets [that's her profession].'
(4b) Li lave dra *a*.   'She washed the sheet [that we are talking about].'

(5a) Poukisa l te bezwen mande *konsèy* sou sa ?   'Why did she have to ask advice about that?'
(5b) Poukisa l ban mwen *konsèy* li fèk ban m *la* ?   'Why did she give me the [specific piece of] advice she just has given me?'

Note that the absence of *LA* in (4a) indicates that the noun is asserted as being –specific (sheets in general) and, therefore, this triggers the interpretation of the invariable verb base as the progressive and habitual verbal aspects (see Section 8.2). On the other hand, in (4b) the presence of the definite determiner *a* indicates the +specific value of the noun, which assigns a completive reading to the predicate containing the verb base. *LA* is used, then:

1. Anaphorically, that is, to refer to something previously introduced in the discourse, as in (6):

(6) Yon jou *yon mesye* vin konfese.   One day a man came for confession.
     Li di: 'Monpè, padonnen m   He said: 'Father, forgive me because
     paske mwen fèk sòt vole *yon*   I have just stolen a watch.'
     mont.'
     Pè a di: 'Se pa pou mande padon   The priest said: 'Not only must you
     sèlman, fò ou renmèt *mont lan*   ask forgiveness, you must also return
     tou ...'   the watch ...'
     Nèg la reponn: 'Enben, m ofri l   The man answered: 'Well, I offered
     men li pa vle l.'   it but he didn't want it.'

The noun *mont* is first introduced with the indefinite determiner, and then, having been identified, on the second occurrence it is marked with *LA* because it is [+specific] and [+pre-supposed].[2]

2. Anaphorically, but in a more general way, to mark a noun whose semantic equivalent has been previously introduced in the discourse. This is the case in (6), in which *mesye* and *nèg* are co-referential, that is, they refer to the same person (these two words are in fact near-synonyms), so that *nèg* being specific and pre-supposed is marked with *LA*. The same applies to *pè a*, which refers back to the title *Monpè*. The reference may be quite general and the specified noun may be greatly separated from the original mention. For instance, in (7), taken from a folk tale, we find reference to a spring, *sous,* and three mentions of *dlo* in the opening segment, which has two senses: 'water' in *pran dlo nan sous* and 'source, stream, body of water' *bon dlo* in the final occurrence. In its first two occurrences, *dlo* is a mass noun, that is, –specific and –pre-supposed. Accordingly, no determiners are used. But in the third occurrence it is marked with *LA* because it is co-referential with *sous* and thus both +specific and +pre-supposed.

(7) Se yon manman ki gen de pitit: 'Once upon a time a mother had
     yon pitit fi ak yon pitit gason.   two children: a girl and a boy. But
     Men lè manman an voye pitit   whenever the mother sent the girl to

fi a pran *dlo* nan *sous*, li toujou pote bon *dlo* pwòp ... Kounye a lè ou rive nan *dlo a*, ou jwenn de pwason: se tifi a ak mari li.

fetch water at the spring, she always brought back water that was nice and clean ... And now when you get to the [body of] water, you find two fish: it's the girl and her husband.' [4]

3. To refer to a noun whose existence is assumed to be known to the hearer. For instance, in a report on a protest demonstration in the town of Gonaives, reference is made to the people and to the customs and tax office:

(8) *Pèp la* manke met dife nan biwo *ladwann nan* ak *kontribisyon an*.   'The people almost set fire to the customs and tax office.'

The existence of a single customs and tax office in Gonaives is assumed as knowledge shared by the writer and his readers. Note that in the specific event narrated in (8) the use of *LA* with the nouns contributes to the completive reading of the verb *manke*. In (9), on the other hand, the absence of *LA* with nouns referring to well-known entities signifies the habitual aspect:

(9) Lajounen gen solèy, leswa gen lalin.   'In the daytime there's the sun and the moon at night.'

4. Deictically, the definiteness of the noun may stem not from previous mention in the context or general awareness but from the immediate situational context, that is, the hearer or reader must visualize the here-and-now natures of the noun mentioned. For instance, in an Anansi (spider) story, that character manages to eliminate its creditors by having them trapped in a back room and devoured by their natural enemy. In persuading his creditors to hide in the room, one assumes that Brer Spider points to it:

(10) Ou mèt kache ko ou nan *pyès dèyè a*.   'You may hide in the back room.'

Suzanne Sylvain (1936: 55) contrasts the simple use of *LA* with that of the combination *LA* + *LA* (realized as *la a*): *jwèt la* 'the toy (in question)' versus *jwèt la a* 'the toy (precisely in question)'.[4] This raises a question, that will appear again in Sections 9.2.3 and 9.2.4, of the semantic value of the second *LA*. It appears that the first *LA* (*LA¹*) carries a meaning intermediate between the English definite and demonstrative determiners: when referring to something that, from the perspective of the extra-linguistic context, is +pre-supposed and +specific, it is **deictic**. The second *LA (LA²)* increases the level of presupposition. One might describe it as a marker of presupposition, as do Lefebvre *et al.* (1982) and Jean-Baptiste (1992), who uses the French term *micro-opérateur de pré-supposition* (MOP).

9.2.3 The demonstrative determiner

The HC demonstrative determiner is a strong deictic; it corresponds to both *this* and *that* in English, that is, the language does not use a determiner to localize a noun with reference to psychological distance from the speaker. This demonstrative determiner consists of *sa* followed by *LA* (in its variant *a*) in the singular and *yo* in the plural. As pointed out in Section 8.2.4, some speakers reduce *sa a* to *sa* by shortening the long vowel a [a:].

(11a) Kote ou jwenn ze *sa a*?   'Where did you find this/that egg?'
(11b) Kote ou jwenn ze *sa yo*? 'Where did you find these/ those eggs?'

Another form (*sila a/ sila yo*), with variants *sit* (*sit la/sit yo*), appears to vary freely with *sa a/sa yo*. The distinction 'remote' (distal) versus 'near' (proximal) effected in English by *this/that* is provided by the use of *sa a* for remote or the combination of adverbs for 'place' *kote*, or *bò* and *sit la*:

(12a) jaden *sa a*   'this/that garden'
(12b) jaden kote *sila a* 'this garden'

Jules Faine (1936: 114) cites the use of *se* preceding the noun and *la yo* following it. I will return to this construction in Section 9.4.

(13) *se* mesye *la yo*   'these men'

9.2.4 The marking of plural

Compared to English or French, one of the striking features of HC is the fact that the plural need not be obligatorily marked. In fact, HC shares this feature with many other languages, and it is indeed the obligatory overt indication of plural that constitutes a salient feature. Be that as it may, in HC the marked plural carries the feature [+pre-supposed, +specific]. The plural marker in HC is the form *yo* occurring at the end of NPs; the form is identical to the 3rd person plural pronoun.

(14a) Kote liv *la*?   'Where is the book?'
(14b) Kote liv *yo*?   'Where are the books?'
(14c) Kote liv *yo*?   'Where are their book(s)?'

As an expression of the semantic features [+ specific] and [+pre-supposed], *yo* does not appear with the negative or with quantifiers, or when the head noun is not specific, as in (15e):

(15a) *Pa* gen liv. 'There aren't any books.'
(15b) Ban m *de* zoranj. 'Give me two oranges.'
(15c) Yon *bann* vye manti. 'A pack of bad lies.'
(15d) Yo touye *anpil* moun. 'They killed a lot of people.'
(15e) Gen poul nan lakou a. 'There are chickens in the yard.'

Yo appears in all instances where *LA* would appear in the singular: definite reference to nouns (16a), anaphoric recall (16b), underscoring of the here-and-now nature of the reference, or shared knowledge (16c).

(16a) Li te gen yon pati **grenn** ... Li pran twa *grenn yo*. 'She had a quantity of seeds ... She took three of the seeds [previously mentioned].'
(16b) 'M pral chache **zanmi** m pou yo fè konesans ak ou.' L al chache *kanmarad* li *yo*. '"I'm going to get my friends so that they may meet you." He went to get his friends.'
(16c) *Fi yo* m konnen an se bon moun yo ye. 'The women I know [and of whose acquaintance with me you are aware] are nice people.'

Yo parallels the distribution of *LA*, that is, any pluralized NP marked by *LA* would also be marked by *yo*.

(17a) Kote timoun *nan*? 'Where is the child [that we have been talking about]?'
(17b) Kote timoun *yo*? 'Where are the children [that we have been talking about]?'

In this regard, *yo* is the expression of two sets of features: plurality and definiteness: *LA* + plural = *yo*. There is one significant difference between the two markers: *yo* functions exclusively as an NP determiner. It does not characterize parts of speech other than nouns or NPs headed by a noun. This difference appears clearly in the following set of contrastive examples:

(18a) Li poze *plim nan*. 'She put down the pen.'
(18b) Li poze *plim* (m te prete l) *la*. 'She put down the pen I lent her.'
(18c) Li poze plim *nan* (m te prete l *la*). 'She put down the pen I lent her [a fact that you know about].'
(18d) Li poze *plim yo*. 'She put down the pens.'
(18e) Li poze *plim* (m te prete l) *yo*. 'She put down the pens I lent her.'
(18f) Li poze *plim yo* (m te prete l *la*). 'She put down the pens I lent her [a fact that you know about].'

In (18a) and (18d) *LA* and *yo* mark the definiteness of the noun *plim*. In (18b) and (18e), *LA* and *yo* still only mark the definiteness of *plim* but in the expanded NP of which it is the head. In (18c) and (18f), however, the head noun *plim* and the expanded NP are determined separately. In (18c), the singular noun is determined by *LA* and in (18f) the plural noun by *yo*. In both sentences the full NP, consisting of N + S, is characterized separately by the clause determiner *LA*. I will return to the use of *LA* to stress pre-supposed facts presented in full clauses in Section 9.2.7.

As pointed out in Section 9.2.2 (4) above, Suzanne Sylvain (1936) cites cases of NPs containing the form *la yo* (*chat la* 'the cat' vs. *chat la yo* 'the cats') and also the combination *la a* (*chat la a* 'the cat'). The latter NP could also be interpreted as the combination of the noun plus the locative adverb *la* + *LA*: 'the cat there'. As we shall see below, locatives may be marked by *LA*. However, the combination *la yo* may well be a survival from an earlier stage of the language in which definiteness and plural were marked separately, the combination definite + plural (*LA* + *yo*) subsequently being reduced to *yo*. That this may be the case is suggested by rare forms containing that combination plus a second plural marker *se* preceding the noun, which are found in early descriptions of HC. For example, Jules Faine (1936: 114) cites:

(19a)   *se* mesye *la yo*   'these men'
(19b)   *se* diskou monpèr *la yo*   'these speeches of priests'

Faine qualifies these instances as 'pompous sentences' and 'frenchified structures'. Interestingly, in Lesser Antilles French creoles such as those of Dominica, Guadeloupe, Martinique, and St. Lucia definiteness and plural are marked separately, the plural by a pre-posed marker, *se*, derived from the French plural demonstrative determiner *ces: ces messieurs* 'these gentlemen' and definiteness by the post-posed determiner *la: chat la* 'the cat' vs. *se chat la* 'the cats'.[5]

The fact that the plural marker is not obligatory and that only one overt realization of the definite determiner may occur in a NP leads to numerous cases of ambiguity. In sentence (20a), *pye* could be either singular or plural but *tab* can be interpreted only as singular. Sentence (20b) is also ambiguous; *tab* could be plural or singular because one cannot mark the dependent noun *pye* for plural. Sentences (20c) and (20d) are not grammatical. Figure 9.1 shows diagrams of the two possible interpretations of (20a) and the sole interpretation of (20b).

(20a)   Li kase pye tab *la*.   'She broke the foot of the table.'
(20b)   Li kase pye tab *yo*.   'She broke the feet of the table.'
(20c)   *Li kase pye *a* tab *la*.   'She broke the feet of the tables.'
(20d)   *Li kase pye *yo* tab *la*. 'She broke the feet of the table.'

9.2 Determiner System

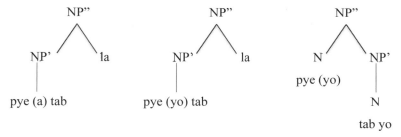

'foot of the table' (20a)   'feet of the table' (20b)   'feet of the tables' (20c)

Figure 9.1. Interpretations of NPs with nouns

In (21), as pointed out by Joseph (1988: 214), the NPs containing three nouns headed by *lajan* 'money' lead to a four-fold ambiguity:

(21) Sil kenbe **lajan** tè frè nèg *yo*.   a) Sil kept the money of the land of the brothers of these men.
b) Sil kept the money of the lands of the brothers of these men.
c) Sil kept the money of the lands of the brother of these men.
d) Sil kept the money of the land of the brother of these men.

9.2.5 Changes of noun class

Although proper nouns inherently connote uniqueness, and thus need not be specified with the definite determiner, it is possible, as it were, to decompose them into non-unique entities. For example, in the context of criticism of the handling of tests for the toxicity of prescription drugs, an employee of the FDA (Federal Drugs Administration) exclaimed: 'That's not the FDA I know.' He was implying that the FDA formerly had strict standards but that under its present administration it had changed into a different institution. In effect, for him there were two FDAs, the former one versus the present one. The same distinction can be made in HC:

(22a) Alse se yon mèt gason.   'Alse is a nice guy.'
(22b) Menm Alse fache, *yon* Alse ki si   'Even Alse got angry, an Alse who
       dous.   usually is so calm.'
(22c) Ala gade *yon* Alse !   'What a guy this Alse! [literally,
                                            Wow, look at an Alse!]'

In (22b), Alse is viewed as two individuals, the usual one who never loses his cool and the one who surprisingly got angry. In (22c), the speaker, as it were, converts Alse to a common noun by the use of the definite determiner in order to stress the quality that makes Alse such a great guy, and this reinforces the force of the exclamation. This change affects all types of proper nouns, place names as well as first names of persons, for example, the use of *LA* in *Jakmèl **la** bèl vre!* 'This Jacmel is really beautiful' adds emphasis to the statement. In *Jakmèl ou te konnen **an**, se pa menm Jakmèl la k gen konnye **a*** 'The Jacmel you knew is not the same as the Jacmel that exists now', the speaker stresses the major transformation of the city from a previous state (Jean-Baptiste 1992: 200). Mass nouns may also be used as count nouns:

(23a) N ap plante diri.   'We're planting rice.'
(23b) N ap plante twa kalite diri.   'We're planting three types of rice.'
(23c) N ap plante twa diri.   'We're planting three [types] of rice.'

In (23c), *diri* is construed not as the mass noun referring to rice in general but as a specific type of rice. This in effect involves switching it from a mass to a count noun.

9.2.6 Other uses of *LA*

There is one significant difference between the two definite markers *LA* and *yo*. The latter functions exclusively as an NP determiner overtly marking plurality. It does not characterize parts of speech other than nouns or NPs. On the other hand, *LA* extends to other word classes.

First, it occurs with some temporal and locative adverbs:

(24a) M pa wè Asefi jis jounen jodi.   'I didn't see Asefi until today.'
(24b) Jodi *a* m wè Asefi.   'Today, I saw Asefi.'

(25a) Li pa moun isit, li se moun Okap. 'She isn't someone from here, she's from Cape Haitian.'
(25b) Isit *la* anpil moun grangou.   'Right here, a lot of people are hungry.'

The addition of *LA* to the adverbs *jodi* and *isit* reinforces their deictic force. In (24a), the speaker is focusing on the fact that she hasn't seen Asefi for some time prior to the discourse situation, but in (24b) she stresses that it is today that she saw her. In (25a), *isit* serves to contrast the current location of the interlocutors with a distant one, whereas in (25b) it emphasizes their present location. Note that it would be possible to add *LA* to (24a) and (25a) to reinforce the deixis. On the other hand, it would not be possible to delete *LA* from (24b) and (25b) because of the strong deixis implied by the situation. The differences in meaning created by the presence and absence of *LA* with locative adverbs are brought out more clearly by the translations of the following examples.

(26a) Li te isit.   'She was here.'
(26b) Li te isit *la*.   'She was right here.'

(27a) Yo chita dèyò.   'They sat outside.'
(27b) Yo chita dèyò *a*.   'They sat right outside.'

The use of *LA* in (26b) underscores the presence of the speaker and hearer at the place referred to: 'right here where we are now'. In (27b), the use of *LA* suggests the close presence of the persons referred to. The use of *LA* has become fixed in certain locative and temporal expressions whose meaning incorporates the notion of here-and-now: *la a* 'here', *kounye a* (also pronounced *koulye a* or *kounya*) 'now', *jodi a* 'today'.

9.2.7 Sentential *LA*

More complex is the use of *LA* to impart the notion of shared knowledge to whole clauses.

(28a) Pyè te bòs chapant?   'Was Peter a carpenter?'
(28b) Pyè te bòs chapant *la*? 'Was Peter a carpenter (as I think he was)?'
(28c) Pyè te pati *a*?   'Had Peter left [as I was told he did]?'

In (28b) the determiner does not refer to *Pyè* but to the entire sentence. The question is not intended to find out whether he was a carpenter but to verify previously held knowledge. Note that this use of the determiner is parallel to (28c), where there is no doubt that it bears on the full sentence since it follows the verb.

The sentence determiner *LA* is often used in the embedded clauses of complex sentences:

(29a) Kay *la* boule.   'The house burned down.'
(29b) [Kay (ki boule *a*)] te bèl. 'The house that burned down was beautiful.'

(29c) Kay *la* (ki boule *a*) te bèl.   'The house that burned down was beautiful. [We are speaking about the fact that the house burned down.]'

In (29b), *kay* is modified by a relative clause and, as it is head of the NP, the determiner occurs at the end of the NP. In contrast, in (29c) the focus is not on the house that burned down but on the event itself, the fact that the house burned down. Several native speaker consultants offered a different interpretation of (29c): 'The house that people knew was beautiful burned down'. In (30b) sentential *LA* is also used after the copy of the duplicated verb is **clefted** and fronted. As shown in (31b), sentential *LA* reinforces the emphasis provided by clefting (see Section 10.4).

(30a) Vini l neve m.   'Her coming made me nervous.'
(30b) (Vini l vini *an*) neve m.   'The fact that she came made me nervous.'

(31a) Kè m koumanse pran dèy ak tout verite sa a ou blayi devan m.   'I'm beginning to feel sad with the entire truth you are exposing before me.'
(31b) (Ak tout verite sa a ou ap blayi devan *m* nan) kè m koumanse pran dèy.   'With all the entire truth [that is now apparent to me] you are exposing before me, I'm beginning to feel sad.'

The following pair of sentences contrasts the absence versus the presence of *LA* with verbs only. In (32b), the focus is on the fact of leaving, whereas (32a) is a neutral question:

(32a) Pyè te pati?   'Had Pierre left?'
(32b) Pyè te pati a?   'Had Pierre really left?'

9.3 Pronouns

The term **pronoun**, interpreted as 'pro-noun', is misleading because it suggests that it always replaces nouns. Indeed, some pronouns have a clearly anaphoric function: third personal pronouns do function in general as substitutes for nouns:

(33) M ba *Alse[1] mato a[2]*; *li[1]* pran *ni[2]*.   'I gave Alse the hammer; he took it.'

The two uses of *li* (the second undergoes nasal assimilation) are both anaphoric, each referring to a singular head noun in the first clause, as indicated by the subscript numbers, *li* to *Alse* and *ni* to *mato a*. In (34a), the pronoun *li* (occurring in the form *l*) is not only anaphoric but also **co-referential**, that is, it refers to the same individual mentioned:

(34a) Ou te wè *frè m* ? 'Did you see my brother?'
 – Wi, m te wè *l*. ' – Yes, I saw him.'
(34b) *Ki moun* ou te wè ? 'Whom did you see?'
 – M wè *frè ou*. ' – I saw your brother.'

Because of the change of speakers *l* does not replace *frè m* but *frè ou* 'your brother.' First and 2nd person pronouns are not anaphoric but deictic: they refer to the speaker and the hearer in the here-and-now situation of speech production. Interrogative pronouns such as *ki moun* 'who' do more than replace a syntactic element, the subject in the case of *ki moun*; they also serve to request information. With these clarifications about the nature of pronouns we proceed to describe personal and interrogative pronouns in HC.

9.3.1 Personal pronouns

General system

The system of personal pronouns in HC differs from that of English in two main ways. First, there are only five person distinctions and profound differences in the referential value of the corresponding pronouns. In the 3rd person singular there is no sex differentiation corresponding to *he* versus *she* nor any difference between human animates versus non-human animates and inanimates, *he/she* versus *it*. The form *li* refers to all types of nouns. In addition the 3rd person singular pronoun is used in impersonal constructions: *Li jou* 'It's daylight', *Li frèt* 'It's cold'. To effect gender distinction, the substitutes *madanm* 'Mrs', *manmzèl* 'miss', and *misye/msye* 'mister' are used: *Manzèl bèl anpil* 'She is very beautiful', *Mwen annik fin pale ak li, msye tonbe kriye* 'I had just finished speaking with him, he started to cry'. Unlike French, HC does not distinguish between formal and informal address. As opposed to English and French, there is a single form covering both 1st and 2nd person plural: *Kote nou prale ?* may mean 'Where are we going?', 'Where are you (all) going?' and 'Where are we and you (singular or plural) going?' However, there is a distinction between 2nd person singular and 2nd person plural. Variations in form, namely, long versus short forms, are determined by the phonological environment and many are free variants (see Section 3.3.1).

Table 9.3. Personal Pronouns in HC

Person	Singular	Plural
1	mwen/m	nou/n
2	ou/ (w)	nou/n
3	li/l	yo/y

Second, HC pronouns assume all syntactic functions; there are no differentiated forms for subject, direct object, indirect object, object of preposition, or possessive:

(35a) *Subject*: *M* voye l kèk goud.   'I sent him some gourdes.'
(35b) *Direct object*: Li peye *m*.   'He paid me.'
(35c) *Indirect object*: Li ban *m* kèk goud.   'He gave me some gourdes.'
(35d) *Possessive*: Frè *m* voye m chache dlo.   'My brother sent me to fetch water.'
(35e) *Object of preposition*: Li pa vle vini avè *m*.   'She didn't want to go with me.'

Variant forms
In northern Haiti, a variant form, *zòt*, is attested, covering 2nd person plural and 3rd person plural (Fattier 1996: 214), although its low occurrence suggests that it is a residual survival from an earlier stage of the language.[6] It is derived from French dialect forms *vous autres* 'you all' and *eux autres* 'they'. In present-day vernacular French and North American varieties of the language, for example, Louisiana French, one still finds the set: *nous autres, vous autres, eux autres*. Such compound forms appear to still be used, for example, *ak nou zòt* 'with us' (Desmarattes 1983: 7).

(36a) M a boule *zòt*.   'I'll burn you [all].'
(36b) L a pòte i a *zòt*.[7]   'He'll bring it to them.'

Older forms of HC, as reflected by the first written texts (see Chapter 4), show a system distinguishing three persons in the singular and the plural. There existed a form *to/twe* for the 2nd person singular informal, opposed to formal *vou*, as well as the 2nd person plural form *zòt*. These texts also show two functionally differentiated sets: a subject set (*mo/m, to*) contrasting with another that assumes all other syntactic functions (*mwe/mwen, twe*). Faine (1974: 444, 457) lists *toué* and *to*: *Qui ça to di ?* 'What are you saying?'

Northern HC shows another particularity: the form of the 3rd person singular pronoun. The sociolinguistic study to be discussed in Section 11.3.2

revealed retention rates of nearly 90% of the local variant that occurs mainly as *i* or *y*, largely depending on the phonological context. The semivowel *y* is favored after a vowel and the vowel *i* in initial position: *I bon*. 'It's good', *Le maten y mare y* 'Mornings, he ties it'. Another variant, *li*, homophonous with Standard HC *li/l*, has a more restricted role. It occurs in focalized and emphatic constructions:

(37) Se *li* ki chèf a yo. 'It's **him** that is their leader.'
(38) Men lòt *li* i di l ap vini.[8] 'But the other **he** [guy] said he's coming.'

As an emphatic marker, *li* refers to other grammatical persons, as well to forms other than pronouns (Fattier 1996: 229):

(39) Pwason sa yo *li*, se yo ki pi gwo. 'So far as these fish are concerned, they're the ones that are the largest.'
(40) Lontan *li*, yo pa gen sewòm. 'So far as long ago is concerned, there was no serum.'

Ditransitive verbs represent another syntactic context where *li* appears frequently as a direct object:

(41) Konnya, i bèy i *li*.[9] 'Now, he gave it to her.'

Personal pronoun modifiers

Personal pronouns may be modified by a variety of grammatical forms—adjectives, quantifiers, or adverbs (Fattier 1996: 223–8). The adjective *sèl* 'alone', optionally combined with the introducer *se*, precedes pronouns:

(42a) *Sèl* li ki te sove. 'She's the only one who was saved.'
(42b) *Se sèl* mwen ki ka ede nou. 'It's only I who can help you [plural].'

The adverb *menm* 'self' and various types of quantifiers may follow pronouns:

(43a) Yo kapab fè sa yo *menm*. 'They can do that themselves.'
(43b) Nou *de* mèt ansanm pou fè l. 'The two of us get together to do it.'
(43c) Manman m gen nou *twa* zanfan. 'My mother has the three of us as children.'
(43d) M te nan yon bwa mwen *youn*. 'I was alone in the woods, me by myself.'
(43e) Yo *tout* chèch. 'All of them are dry.'

Finally, the 3rd person singular pronoun may occur with a copy:

(44) Men m kite manman *li sèl li*.   'But I leave Mother, her all alone.'

Position of personal pronouns

As indicated in Section 7.3.6, with ditransitive verbs, the indirect object precedes the direct object:

(45) Prete *m* bisiklèt ou a.   'Lend me your bicycle.'

This also applies to sequences of two pronouns:

(46a) Yo konn vann *mwen* li.   'They used to sell it to me.'
(46b) Liv yo? Li pral prete *ou* yo.   'The books? She'll lend them to you.'

The same order of pronouns follows *bay* 'to give':

(47) L ava ba *ou* yo.[10]   'He will give them to you.'

In these double-object constructions with *bay*, the indirect object refers to the beneficiary of the transaction. The ditransitive verb *ba* differs from a homonymous form derived from it that functions as a preposition (see also Section 8.5) and is synonymous to the preposition *pou*:

(48a) Chante l *ba* mwen.   'Sing it for me.'
(48b) Chante l *pou* mwen.

With these two prepositions, the prepositional phrase referring to the beneficiary occurs after the direct object.

9.3.2 Interrogative pronouns and adverbs

The salient feature of this system is its symmetrical nature. Generally, interrogative pronouns consist of an interrogative marker *ki* followed by a form derived from a corresponding generic noun (Table 9.4).

Table 9.4. Interrogative Pronouns and Adverbs in HC

Place	*ki* + *bò, kote* ('place')	where
Manner	*ki* + *jan* ('manner, way')	how
Time	*ki* + *lè* ('time, hour')	when
Person	*ki* + *moun* ('person')	who, whom

Only the interrogative pronoun questioning non-person subjects and objects departs from this symmetrical pattern. It is composed of *ki* plus the indefinite pronoun *sa* 'what'; the use of *ki* is optional:[11]

(49a) *Sa* ou ap manje la a?   'What are you eating here [in front of me]?'
(49b) *Ki sa* l ap di?   'What is he saying?'

Ki also serves by itself as an interrogative pronoun but it conveys an exclamatory overtone, and it may in fact be related to the homonymous exclamatory pronoun in (49b):

(50a) *Ki* mele m si li kite ou!   'What do I care that she left you!'
(50b) *Ki* bagay! M sezi!   'What a story! I'm shocked!'

There are also monomorphemic interrogative words: *kouman* 'how', *konbe* 'how much'. Note also *pou ki sa* 'why'.

9.3.3 Other pronouns

The demonstrative pronoun is *sa*, which is homophonous with the first part of the demonstrative determiner *sa a* (see Section 9.2.3 above). That pronoun may be pluralized by the adjunction of *yo*:

(51a) Tou *sa* yo fè, se bobin.   'All that they did is nonsense.'
(51b) *Sa* se yon fig.   'That's a banana.'
(51c) M pa vle ou fè *sa*.   'I don't want you to do that.'
(51d) M vle, *sa yo*.   'I want those/these.'
(51e) *Sa* k vle kola se pou di l kounye a.   'Those who want cola should say so now.'

Deictic force is provided by adding *LA* to *sa* (in the post-vocalic variant *a*). Note that in this case, *sa a* is equivalent to 'this one':

(52a) Nan de mango sa yo, m vle *sa a*.   'Of these two mangoes, I want that/this one.'
(52b) Se *sa a* w ap ban mwen an.   'That's what you gave me.' (Fattier 1998: Map no. 2005)

As was the case with the demonstrative determiner (see Section 9.2.3), *sila a* alternates with *sa a*:

(52c) M ta vle *sila a*, m pa vle *sila yo*.   'I want this one, I don't want those.'

The distinction between the function of *sa (a)* as demonstrative pronoun and as indefinite pronoun appears somewhat fuzzy. In some cases the sense imparted by this pronoun depends on the context, for example, in the expression *sou sa*, literally, 'above, on that'.

(52d) Ou ka fè *sa* ou vle?   'You may do whatever you want.'
(52e) Di *sila a* ki vin anvan an li gen pou tann mwen.   'Tell the one who came before to wait for me.'
(52f) Chak *sa* m fè, nou fè l tou.   'Everything that I do, you [all] also do it.' (Fattier 1998: Map no. 2005)
(52g) Li kapab ranje machine nan, men li pas *sou sa*.   'He is capable of fixing the car, but he isn't willing to do that.'
(52h) Sa l di a se *sa*.   'What she said is true.'

There are no reflexive pronouns in HC. As was pointed out in Section 7.2.4, when the primary object is co-referential with the subject the constructions *tèt* 'head' or *kò, kadav* 'body' + pronoun are also used:

(53a) Li touye *tèt li*.   'He killed himself.'
(53b) Yo renmen *kadav yo*.   'They like themselves.'
(53c) M te gade *kò m* nan glas.   'I was looking at myself in the mirror.'

However, reflexivity may also be expressed by the use of personal pronouns:

(54a) Li lave *l*.   'He/she washes him/herself.'
(54b) Ou a degaje *ou* ak sa.   'You'll get along with that.'
(54c) M tronpe *m*.   'I made a mistake.'

9.4 Possession

9.4.1 Attribution and possession in NPs

In English, attribution, indicating in NPs that a noun attributes some property to the head noun, is effected by simple juxtaposition of the noun complement to the head noun. The noun complement, the one that provides attributes, follows the head noun. This can also be effected with a prepositional phrase that precedes the head noun:

(55a) the door *of* the house
(55b) the house door

On the other hand, possession cannot be expressed by simple juxtaposition. It requires some syntactic machinery, either recourse to the preposition *of* or the possessive marker *'s*:

(56a) the owner of the dog
(56b) the dog's owner

In French NPs, both attribution and possession are indicated in a manner parallel to the (a) examples above, namely, by a prepositional phrase:

(57a) la porte *de* la maison   'the door of the house'
(57b) le maître *du* [= *de* + le] chien   'the dog's master/the master of the dog'

But when the head noun is a proper noun, possession differs from attribution:

(58a) la maison *de* Jean   'John's house/the house of John'
(58b) la maison *à* Jean[12] 'John's house/the house of John'

Example (58b) is characteristic of vernacular French, the variety of the language that probably constituted the target for African slaves involved in the creation of Saint-Domingue Creole. This construction served as a model for the possessive construction in that creole and it is reflected in Capois. Possession is indicated by the use of the preposition *a* preceding the personal pronoun:

(59a) kay *a* Pradèl   'Pradel's house'
(59b) mari *a* Anita   'Anita's husband'

Note that, in this geographical variety of HC, attribution and possession pattern somewhat like the English construction in that attribution usually involves simple juxtaposition but possession requires the use of a preposition:

(60a) pòt kay   'the house door'
(60b) kay *a* Alse   'Alse's house/the house of Alse'

In standard HC (SHC), both attribution and possession are indicated by simple juxtaposition:

(61a) pòt kay la   ---
(61b) kay Alse   ---
(61c) wòb koton an   'the cotton dress'
(61d) wòb Mari a   'Mary's dress'

9.4.2 Possession with pronoun complements

Possession may also be expressed with pronominal complements. The head noun is replaced by a personal pronoun:

(62a) Sa sè chwal *Alse*.   'That's Alse's horse.'
(62b) Sa se chwal *li*.   'That's his horse.'
(62c) C'est son cheval.   'That's his horse.'

Unlike English or the French of (62c), in HC possession is expressed not with a possessive determiner but by a pronoun which functions as a complement and parallels the noun complement structure, as is shown in (62a) and (62b). When used as a complement, pronouns are subject to elision according to the same set of phonological rules affecting them in other contexts (see Section 3.3).

(63a) Kote sè *m*?   'Where is my sister?'
(63b) Manman *w* ap rele ou.   'Your mother's calling you.'
(63c) Marenn *ni* renmen li anpil.   'His godmother loved him very much.'
(63d) Sa se poul *nou*.   'That's our/your (plural) chicken.'
(63e) Ou ranje machin *yo*?   'Have you repaired their car?'

As is the case for the nominal possessive construction, in the Cape Haitian variety the pronoun is linked to the NP by the preposition *a*.

(64a) Se chat mwen.   Se chat *a* mwen.
(64b) Kote papa m?   Kote papa *a* mwen?

As noted in Section 3.5, in that geographical variety of HC there are several morphophonological processes that in ordinary conversational style render the combination of noun + *a* + personal pronoun opaque. In sentences (65a) to (65c), compare the usual pronunciation of the Capois variants to the corresponding SHC forms:

(65a) kayanm   (kay a m(wen)) 'my house'   Kay mwen
(65b) maròw   (mari a w (ou)) 'your husband'   Mari ou/mari w
(65c) sèrayo   (sè a yo) 'their sister'   Sè yo

9.4.3 Pronominal possessive complement plus LA

The definite determiner *LA* may follow pronominal possessive complements. In this case, *LA* adds the semantic feature **pre-supposed** to the specific feature already carried by the pronoun. In *chat mwen*, for example, reference is made to a specific cat owned by the speaker but one that is not assumed to be known to the hearer. This latter meaning is added by the insertion of *LA*. Compare:

9.4 Possession

(66a) Kote manje mwen?   'Where is my food?' [i.e., the food given to me, as versus to some other person]

(66b) Kote manje mwen *an*?   'Where is my food?' [i.e., the food given to me, a fact that you know]

The following situations illustrate the difference between the presence and the absence of *LA* in (66a) versus (66b). Tidjo is invited to a meal, he arrives late, and all the persons present have a plate of food but there is none for him. He would ask: *Kote manje mwen*? Food is served to him but he has to leave before finishing it. When he returns, the plate and the food are gone. He then asks: *Kote manje mwen an*? Another example: Tidjo and his wife have been invited to a party but he arrives alone. His host, who knows his wife, would ask:

(66c) Kote madanm ou an?   'Where is your wife? [I know you are married and I know your wife.]'

rather than:

(66d) Kote madanm ou?

This use of *LA* adds the notion of strong pre-supposition that is found with its sentential use, as in (30b):

(30b) Vini l vini *an* neve m.   'The fact that she came made me nervous.'

The precise meaning added by *LA* is subtle and is determined by the context. It also depends on the inherent semantic features of the head noun. In general, nouns that convey inalienable possession, for example, parts of the body or items uniquely possessed, do not take *LA*.

(67a) *Sante m* pa bon menm.   'My health isn't good at all.'
(67b) *Tèt li* fè mal.   'She has a headache.'

However, with strong pre-supposition *LA* may be used to express inalienable possession:

(68a) Lave figi ou! Li sal.   'Wash your face. It's dirty.'
(68b) Lave figi ou *a*!   'Why don't you wash your face [as I already told you to do]?'
(68c) Kote frè nou *an* ye?   'Where is that brother of yours [2nd person plural]?'

Example (68c) carries a strong pejorative connotation, and (68b) conveys impatience.

Since possessive pronouns vary in form, the variant of the definite determiner occurring in a particular case will depend on the last phoneme of the pronoun:

(69a)   Kote manje *mwen an*?   'Where is my food?'
(69b)   Kote manje *m nan*?

In (69a) the use of the full form of the pronoun (*mwen*) that ends in the nasal vowel *en* triggers the post-vocalic nasal variant of *LA: an*. In (69b), the short form (*m*) triggers the post-consonantal nasal variant *nan*. In the case of the pronoun *ou*, when the last element of the NP ends with a vowel (70b, 70c), it is pronounced with the glide variant *w*. Like consonants, glides require the post-consonantal variant of *LA* rather than the post-vocalic variant *a*:

(70a)   chat *ou* a   'the cat of yours'
(70b)   chen *w* la   'that dog of yours'
(70c)   chat visye *w* la   'that sly cat of yours'

9.4.4 Plural of possessive construction

The possessive construction may be pluralized by the addition of *yo*:

(71a)   Li pa vle ban m jwèt li.   'He didn't want to give me his toy.'
(71b)   Li pa vle ban m jwèt li *yo*. 'He didn't want to give me his toys.'

Devoid of linguistic or pragmatic context, (71a) is ambiguous. It also means 'He doesn't want to give me his toys', and only the addition of *LA* would lead to a singular reading: *Li pa vle ban m jwèt li a*.

The homonymy of *yo* (plural marker and 3rd person plural pronoun) and the fact that the combination *yo yo* is excluded leads to additional potential ambiguities. Sentence (72) conveys three meanings:

(72)   Kote tifi yo ?   'Where are the daughters?'
                                 'Where is their daughter?'
                                 'Where are their daughters?'

9.4.5 Other possessive constructions

Adjunction of the demonstrative determiner
In addition to *LA*, pronoun complements in possessive constructions may be followed by the demonstrative determiner *sa a/sa yo*:

(73a) Pitit mwen *sa a* frekan.   'This child of mine is insolent.'
(73b) Istwa fanm ni *sa yo* ap mennen li lwen.   'These women stories of his can lead him far (into trouble).'

Verbs as heads of possessive constructions
We have seen in Section 9.1.1 that verbs may be used in nominal functions, as in *li dòmi yon bon ti dòmi* 'she had a nice little sleep'. In this case, they also take a pronoun complement in possessive constructions:

(74a) Kite mwen *dòmi dòmi m.*   'Let me sleep my sleep [that is, let me sleep as much as I want to].'
(74b) Ou pa gen anyen pou wè nan *sòti l.*   'You have nothing to say in her going out [that's her affair].'

Possessive pronoun
The equivalent of the English possessive pronouns (mine, yours, etc.) consists of the use of the term *pa* 'part' and a personal pronoun. The Cape Haitian variant *kin* is linked to the pronoun with the preposition *a*:

(75a) Sa se pa *pa* ou se *pa m*.   'That's not yours, it's mine.'
(75b) Sa se *kin a ou*.   'That's yours.'

The definite determiner may also be used with this construction:

(76) Machin Iv la nèf men *pa m nan* kraze.   'Yves' car is new but mine is wrecked.'

Agglutinated French possessive determiners
Finally, some kinship terms and titles contain fused elements derived from French possessive determiners: *masè* 'nun', *matant* 'aunt', *monnonk* 'uncle', *monpè* 'Father' (when addressing a Catholic priest). These elements are an integral part of the noun and do not carry any possessive meaning, as is demonstrated by their combination with pronoun complements in possessive constructions: *matant mwen, masè m, monnonk li*. See Section 5.4 for other examples of agglutination of French articles.

280   The Structure of Noun Phrases

9.5 Summary of Post-posed Determiners

The various combinations of post-posed determiners and the possessive construction are summarized in Table 9.5.

Table 9.5. Summary of Post-posed Determiners and Possessives

Determiner type	Singular	Plural
Definite	*LA*	*yo (la yo)*
Demonstrative	*sa-a, sila (a)*	*sa yo, sila yo*
Possessive	*mwen/ m*	*mwen yo/ m yo*
	ou	*ou yo*
	li/ l	*li yo*
	nou/ n	*nou yo*
	yo	*yo*
Possessive + Definite	*mwen an/ m nan*	*mwen yo/ m yo*
	ou a/ ou la	*ou yo*
	li a/ l la	*li yo/ l yo*
	nou a/ n nan	*nou yo/ n yo*
	yo a	*yo*

9.6 Pre-posed NP Elements

9.6.1 The indefinite determiner

The indefinite determiner expresses the semantic features –specific and +pre-supposed. It occurs at the beginning of NPs; only the pre-Det *tout* may precede it:

(77)   Yo manje tout *yon* sak diri.   'They ate a whole sack of rice.'

In the plural the indefinite is expressed by Ø. Compare:

(78a)   M gen *yon* chen.   'I have a dog.'
(78b)   M gen chen.   'I have dogs.'

Although we follow the general practice in representing the indefinite article by its long form *yon*, it occurs most frequently in the short form *on*. It also has the variant forms [ũ], *oun*, and, when it occurs after a vowel, *w*. That glide is also the usual variant of the 2nd person singular pronoun *ou* in the environment of vowels.

(79a) Y ap bare *yon /w/* vòlè nan lakou a.   'They trapped a thief in the yard.'

(79b) M ap ekri w *yon /w/* on lèt.   'I'm writing you a letter.'

9.7 Adjectives

9.7.1 Pre-nominal adjectives

Except for a small set, in HC adjectives occur immediately following the head of an NP. The exceptional pre-posed adjectives that are placed immediately before the head noun include those listed in Table 9.6.

Table 9.6. Pre-posed Adjectives in HC

bèl	beautiful, pretty
kout	short
gwo	big
jenn	young
joli	pretty
move	bad
nouvèl	new
vye	old

This list is not exhaustive since adjectives may be inserted in pre-nominal position for stylistic effect, for example:

(80) Ou konnen *sal* men kwochi sa a?   'Do you know that dirty miser?'

Pov 'unfortunate', occurring in the reduced form *po*, and *sèl* 'lone' occur only in idioms: *po dyab* 'poor fellow' and *sèl kòk chante* 'ruler of the roost'. The expression *kokennchenn* 'enormous' also functions as a pre-nominal adjective:

(81) M te wè yon *kokennchenn* koulèv.   'I saw an enormous snake.'

Finally, *ti* has linguistic status intermediate between that of a prefix and an adjective. It occurs in fixed combinations such as *timoun* 'child' (from *ti* + *moun*) and *tifi* 'girl' (from *ti* + *fi*). Its meaning differs from that of the post-nominal adjective *piti* 'small' in that it often takes hypocoristic connotations:

282 The Structure of Noun Phrases

(82a) Yo achte on bèl *ti* kay.   'They bought a nice little house.'
(82b) Kay yo te *piti*.   'Their house was small.'

Syntactically, *ti, pòv, sèl*, and *kokennchenn* behave differently from other pre-nominal adjectives in not allowing focalization. For this structural feature, see Section 10.4.

(83a) Yon gwo koulèv.   'a big snake'
(83b) Se *gwo* koulèv te ye.   'There was a really big snake.'
(83c) *Se *kokennchenn* koulèv te ye.   '*There was an enormous snake.'

9.7.2 Post-nominal adjectives

Post-nominal adjectives form a large heterogeneous class in HC. In addition to words that function only as adjectives, as in (84a) and (84b), the class includes de-verbals, derived from verbs (85 b, c).

(84a) Yo achte yon ti kanmyon *jòn*.   'They bought a little yellow truck.'
(84b) Yon flanm *wouj* kouvri syèl la.   'A red flame covered the sky.'

(85a) Yo *moulen* mayi-a.   'They ground the corn.'
(85b) Mayi-a *moulen*.   'The corn is ground.'
(85c) Yo vle mayi *moulen*.   'They want ground corn.'

Another set of post-nominal adjectives originates in prepositional phrases and embedded relative clauses:

(86a) yon ti chen *ki gen plim frize*   'a little dog that has curly hair'
(86b) yon ti chen *ak plim frize*   'a little dog with curly hair'
(86c) Nou pa wè yon ti chen kouri pase la? Yon ti chen *plim frize*.   'Haven't you seen a little dog running through here? A little dog with curly hair.'

(87a) Ti gason an *gen sizan*.   'The boy is six years old.'
(87b) yon ti gason *ki gen sizan*   'a six-year-old boy'
(87c) yon ti gason *sizan*   'a boy who is six years old'

(88a) Li gen vant *ki fè l mal*.   'She has a belly that hurts her (i.e. her belly hurts).'
(88b) Li gen vant *fè mal*.   'She has a sore belly.'

(89a) M gen lafyèv *ak frison*.   'I have a fever and the shivers.'

(89b) M gen lafyèv *frison*.

Focalization separates lexical adjectives from derived ones:

(90a) Se *jòn* ti kamyon an ye. 'It's yellow that the little truck is.'
(90b) *Se plim frize ti chen an ye.
       (Se plim frize ti chen an gen.) 'It's curly hair that the puppy has.'
(90c) *Se sizan ti gason an ye.
       (Se sizan ti gason an gen.) 'It's six years that the boy has.'
(90d) *Se fè mal vant mwen ye.
       (Se ak vant fè mal mwen ye.) 'It's with a belly ache that I find myself.'

9.7.3 Emphatic constructions

Adjectives may be emphasized by reduplication or the adjoining of *menm*:

(91a) yon *bèl bèl* fi 'a very beautiful woman'
(91b) Vyann nan *sale sale*. 'This meat is very salty.'
(91c) Se moun *sòt menm*! 'He's a really stupid person!'

9.7.4 Comparison of adjectives

Equality in adjective constructions is expressed by *tankou* or its variant form *kou*:

(92a) Dan li blan *tankou* lèt. 'Her teeth are as white as milk.'
(92b) Li sòt *kou* Bouki. 'He is as stupid as Bouqui.'

Superiority is expressed by the use of *pase* 'past' following the adjective, to which may be adjoined *pi* preceding the adjective:

(93a) Li rich *pase* m. 'He's richer than me.'
(93b) Li *pi* rich *pase* m.
(94a) M miyò *pase* l. 'I'm better than her.'
(94b) M *pi* miyò *pase* l.

Inferiority is expressed by *mwen* preceding the adjective and *pase* following it:

(95a) Yon kabrit *mwen* gras *pase* yon kochon. 'A goat is less fat than a pig.'

However, instead of the comparison of inferiority, the comparison of superiority may be used with the antonym of the adjective (S. Sylvain 1936: 44):

(95b) Mwen rich *pase* yo.   'I'm richer than them.' (i.e. They are poorer than me.)

Kilès followed by *ki* is used for questions requesting comparison:

(96a) Kilès ki *pi* gwo: yon chadèk oswa yon zoranj?   'Which is bigger: a grapefruit or an orange?'
– Chadèk *pi* gwo. Li *pi* gwo *pase* zoranj.   'A grapefruit is bigger. It's bigger than an orange.'
(96b) Kilès ki *mwen* move: yon chat oswa yon towo?   'Which is less mean: a cat or a bull?'
– Yon chat *mwen* move. Li *mwen* move *pase yon* towo.   'A cat is less mean. It's less mean than a bull.'

9.7.5 Superlative of adjectives

In making comparisons the superlative is formed by inserting *pi* 'more', either singly or preceded by *ki* before an adjective, and *pa*se following it:

(97a) Anemiz *pi* bèl pase *tout* lòt fi.   'Annémise is the prettiest of all the girls.'
(97b) Se kay mwen an *ki pi* gran *pase* yo tout.   'It's my house that's the biggest of all of them.'

When expressing the superlative outside the context of a comparison, *pi* stands alone before the adjective. In embedding a superlative phrase into a sentence introduced by *se*, the relative pronoun *ki* is used. The phrase could also be clefted, as in (98d).

(98a) **Pi gwo kay** se pa m nan.   'Mine is the biggest house.'
(98b) Se Pòl **ki pi fò**.   'Paul is the strongest.'
(98c) Se bèf *ki* **pi gwo bèt**.   'Cows are the biggest animals.'
(98d) **Pi gwo bèt** se bèf.   'The biggest animals are cows.'

Note the following use of the superlative in temporal clauses introduced by *se* (S. Sylvain 1936: 45); note that *la* represents the locative adverb, not the determiner LA:

(99a) Se *lò* yo griyen yo pi lèd la.   'It's when they make faces that they are the ugliest.'
(99b) Se te *jou sa yo* nou te pi gwo la.   'It was in these days that you (all) were the fattest.'

Additional superlative constructions involving various types of clefting will be presented in Chapter 10.

The augmentative meaning is expressed with post-posed *menm* and *kont* + a co-referential pronoun (S. Sylvain 1936: 45). This scholar translates *kont kò nou* in (100c) as *le compte de votre corps* 'up to the amount of your body'.

(100a) Nou sèvyab *menm*.   'You're very helpful.'
(100b) Li vole *kont li*.   'He's very thievish.'
(100c) Nou parese *kont kò nou*.   'You (all) are extremely lazy.'

9.8 Sex Reference

Unlike French, and as is the case for English, there is no gender distinction for nouns in HC. There are matched pairs, one member referring to a male and another to a female: *yon ayisyen* 'a Haitian man' versus *yon ayisyèn* 'a Haitian woman' but that does not constitute gender. Sex distinctions are made within animal species by the use of the generic terms *mal, makou* for males and *manman, fimèl* for females:

(101a) yon manman bourik   'a jenny'
(101b) yon makou chat   'a tomcat'
(101c) yon fimèl rat   'a female rat'
(101d) yon mal kodenn   'a tom turkey'

Summary

From the point of view of semantics, the HC noun phrase system resembles that of English. The definite article indicates +specific and +pre-supposed, the indefinite article –specific and +pre-supposed, and absence of any determiner –specific and –pre-supposed (generic).

(102a) M renmen lèt ou te sèvi *a*.   'I like the milk you served.'
(102b) Se *yon* bon lèt.   'It is a good [kind of] milk.'
(102c) Lèt bon pou ou.   'Milk is good for you.'

Like English but unlike French, HC has no gender distinction, so determiners and adjectives show only free variation or variation determined by phonological factors.

The signal feature that differentiates the noun-phrase structure of HC from that of these two languages is the post-position of all determiners except the indefinite one: *yon liv* vs. *liv la, liv sa a, liv mwen, liv mwen an*. Plural is marked only with definiteness: *M gen liv* 'I have books' vs. *M gen liv yo* 'I have the books'.

Another marked feature of HC is the fact that the use of post-posed *LA* allows for the clear indication of pre-supposition, that is, previously known information. That distinction may be made with both noun phrases and full sentences.

(103a)	pitit mwen	'my child, my children'
(103b)	pitit mwen *an*	'my child [the one that you know or the one you know about]'
(103c)	kay ki boule *a*	'the house that burned'
(103d)	kay *la* ki boule *a*	'the house that burned [a fact that is generally known]'

HC personal pronouns do not vary with syntactic function; they show only phonologically based or free variations, and there is no gender-based distinction in the 3rd person:

(104a)	Li envite m (mwen).	'She invited me.'
(104b)	M (mwen) envite l (li).	'I invited her./him.'

A marked feature of the pronominal system is the absence of distinction between the 1st and 2nd person plural: *Kote nou prale?* 'Where are we going? Where are you (all) going?'

Notes

1. Recall that *LA* (here the abstract term that subsumes all variants) is subject to variation determined by the final phonemes of the preceding word: *tab la* 'the table', *dlo a* 'the water', *mòn nan* 'the hill', *van an* 'the wind', *mont lan* 'the watch'. Henceforth, I will use *LA* to refer to this determiner to subsume all phonological variants. The indefinite determiner shows variants – *yon, on, oun, w* – which are not generally determined by phonological factors but by style. Because it occurs in this chapter less frequently than *LA*, I will list it as *yon*. Of course, in examples derived from cited sources or from material I collected the actually occurring variant will be provided.

2. In anaphoric relationships, after a noun has been introduced, although presupposed and specific on the second mention, it may not be marked with *LA*. It is the extralinguistic context that indicates its specific nature. This is characteristic of the opening of folk tales (F. Joseph 1988: 254): *Vwala gen **yon** wa ki te gen yon bèl fiy, epi **wa** voye fi a fè etid nan yon peyi etranje* 'Once upon a time there was a king who had a beautiful daughter, and then the king sent the girl to study in a foreign country'.

3. In this folk tale, when the girl goes to fetch water at the spring, a magical fish clarifies the water for her. This is not the case with her brother. The parents catch and eat the fish. As she grieves its loss, the girl sinks into the ground that is turned to mud by her tears and is herself transformed into a fish. She is then reunited with the magical fish.

4. Sylvain does not list *jwèt la* but provides a list of nouns followed by *LA* that she translates as the gloss plus a deictic reference, e.g., *rad la* 'le costume (dont il s'agit) (the suit in question)'. For *jwèt la a* she provides the translation 'le jouet (dont il s'agit précisément) (the toy in question precisely)'.

5. A similar fusion of the definite determiner and the plural marker appears to have occurred in Guianese Creole. The earliest lengthy text in that language, the novel *Atipa* (Parépou 1882: 100) contains the combination /ye la/ *ça zoseau yé la* 'these birds'; note the preposed demonstrative determiner *ça* /sa/, which makes this example equivalent to present-day HC *zozo sa yo*. The current plural marker of Guianese Creole shows the same fusion as HC: *zozo ya* 'these birds' (HC *zozo yo*). *Atipa* is in fact the first novel written in an FBC. The author's name, Alfred Parépou, is a pseudonym (see Section 1.4.3).

7. Fattier points out that *zòt* (3rd person plural) is used in Desmarattes's adaptation of Molière's play *Le Tartuffe, Mouché Défas: Ou pansé sa sifi pou fè zòt fè silans* 'You think that's enough to force them to keep it quiet' (Desmarattes 1983: 5).

8. The form *i* is the Northern HC (Capois) variant for *li*.

9. As pointed out in Section 11.3.2, Capois speakers alternate between the Standard HC variant and their own. Before *ap*, the Standard HC variant *l* is often likely to be used instead of *y*.

10. In Northern HC, /a/ is often raised to /è/ before /y/: *bay* 'to give' > *bèy*, *bagay* 'thing' > *bagèy*.

11. As a verb, rather than a preposition, *bay* has three variant forms: the general form *bay* that alternates freely with *ba* and *ban* before the 1st person singular pronoun: *Li ban m li* 'she gives it to me'. As a preposition it is realized as *ba* (as in 48a).

12. *Ki* may also be deleted in *ki kote*: *Kote ou prale?* 'Where are you going?'

13. In Old French, *à* and *de* varied freely: *li filz à/de Marie* 'Mary's son', and it is, as it were, only by chance that *de* became generalized.

10 Complex Sentences: Coordination, Subordination, and Clefting

This chapter covers processes that characterize complex sentences in HC and that affect the order of sentence constituents in various ways. These processes include coordination and the embedding of various types of subordinate clauses: completive, conjunctive, relative, and conditional clauses. It also treats the permutation of the sentential elements focalization and topicalization.

10.1 Coordination

Clauses are conjoined with the conjunction *epi*, which has the variants *enpi* and *anpi*:

(1a) Wozlò achte poul la.
Mari kuit poul la.
(1b) Wozlò achte poul la **epi** Mari kuit li.   'Rose-Laure bought the chicken and Mary cooked it.'

(2a) Mis dezabiye malad la.
Doktè konsilte malad la.
(2b) Mis dezabiye malad la **epi** doktè konsilte l.   'The nurse undressed the patient and the doctor examined her.'

Less frequently, the conjunction *e* may be used:

(3a) Li bèl **e** li gen bon jan.   'She's pretty and she's easy-going.'
(3b) E ou menm?   'And you?'

Epi may also link several coordinated clauses:

(4) Li vini yon dimanch maten, li abiye m **epi** li mete ti soulye yo nan pye m.   'She came on a Sunday morning, she dressed me, and she put the little shoes on my feet.'

However, *epi* should not be confused with *ak* (occurring with the variant *avèk*) that serves to coordinate constituents within a single clause:[1]

(5) Papa m **ak** manman m vini. 'My father and my mother came.'
(6) Jodi a m wè Tijo **avèk** Pradèl. 'Today I saw Tijo and Pradel.'
(7) Tande **ak** wè se de. 'Hearing and seeing are two different things.'

Alternative choice in coordinated clauses is expressed by the following correlative conjunctions occurring singly or in pairs: *osnon* (*osinon*, *ousnon*, *ousinon*), *swa* (*oswa*, *ouswa*) ... *osnon* or *swa* ... *swa*:

(8) Kale m kòb mwen **osnon** m ap rele ou nan leta. 'Cough up my money or I'll sue you.'
(9) **Swa** l revoke m **osnon** l respekte m. 'Either he fires me or he respects me.'
(10) **Swa** ou ale **swa** ou rete. 'Either you go or you stay.'

Swa may also be used to express an alternative within a clause:

(11a) **Swa** Jan ou Mak ki pran kòb la. 'Either John or Marc took the money.'

The combination *ni* ... *ni* is used to convey either negative or positive alternatives:[2]

(11b) M pa kapab **ni** vann **ni** lwe l. 'I can neither sell nor rent it.'
(11c) Li pèdi **ni** papa l **ni** manman l. 'She lost both her father and her mother.'

Connecting two statements, in which the second disagrees with the first, is achieved by *men* 'but':

(12) Li ta achte machin nan **men** li pa gen lajan. 'She would buy the car but she doesn't have any money.'

10.2 Embedding

There are four types of embedding of a subordinate clause within a **main** or **matrix** clause in HC complex sentences: (1) **completive** clauses, where the **embedded** or **subordinate** clause serves as the complement of the verb of the main clause; (2) **conjunctive** clauses, where the embedded clause, introduced by a conjunction, serves as an adverbial complement of the verb of the main clause; (3) **relative** clauses, where the embedded clause modifies a noun phrase that serves as a subject, object, or prepositional complement of the verb of the main clause; (4) **conditional** clauses, which are characterized by various restrictions on the use of verb markers of the irrealis type, namely, *ap*, *a(va)*, and *ta*.[3] I shall discuss these types of embedding in the order in which they have been listed here.

10.2.1 Completive clauses

Completive clauses assume the same role as verbal complements in simple sentences. Compare (13a) that illustrates a verb complement construction and (13b) that contains a completive clause:

(13a)   Yo vle **manje**.   'They want to eat.'
(13b)   Yo vle **m ba yo diri**.   'They want me to give them rice.'

Note that in French completive clauses require the insertion of the complementizer *que*: *Elles veulent que je leur donne du riz*, whereas in English there are several ways to insert embedded completive clauses: the use of the preposition *to*, the complementizer *that*, or a null complementizer. The latter two constructions can vary freely: *they asked us to give them some rice, they demanded that we give them some rice, they demanded we give them some rice*.

Typically in HC, completive clauses are dominated by verbs of perception, e.g., *wè* 'to see', *tande* 'to hear', of cognition, e.g., *konnen* 'to know', *kwè* 'to believe', or communication, e.g., *di* 'to say', *mande* 'to ask', *reponn* 'to answer'. However, other verbs may also assume this function.

(14a)   Ou tande **klòch legliz la k ap sonnen**?   'Do you hear the church bells ringing?'
(14b)   M pa kwè **yo kap fè l**.   'I don't think (that) they can do it.'
(14c)   Yo di **y ap chante**.   'They say (that) they'll sing.'
(14d)   Li tann **n a rive**.   'She waited for us to come.'

Note that in French the subjunctive is required for the equivalent of (14b): *Je ne pense pas qu'ils puissent le faire*.

Completive clauses may be embedded in sentences whose predicate contains the zero copula:

(15a)   Li fasil **repare machin nan**.   'It's easy to fix the car.'
(15b)   Yo pè **li bat yo**.   'They're afraid (that) he will beat them.'

Note that in (15b) the completive clause functions like the nominal predicate in (16):

(16)   Yo pè **dlo**.   'They're afraid of water.'

10.2.2 Conjunctive clauses

Conjunctive clauses serve as adverbial complements of main clauses. They may precede or follow the main clause. In the following list, conjunctive clauses are classified according to the adverbial type: cause, condition, manner, time, etc. Examples are derived from S. Sylvain (1936) and Valdman *et al.* (2007). Some conjunctions are polysemous, for example, *depi/denpi* 'because, if, as soon as' and *tank* 'as soon as, as much'.

Cause: *afòs, davwa, dapre, daprezavwa, depi/denpi, dèske, difòs, etan, konm/kòm, paske/pask, poutèt*

(17a)   *Afòs* **li kouri** li pèdi souf.   'Because she ran, she was out of breath.'
(17b)   *Daprezavwa* **bèf mwen an kraze jaden li**, li fè m peye.   'Since my cow trampled his field, he made me pay.'
(17c)   Li fache *paske* **m pa vini nan kay li**.   'She's angry because I didn't come to her house.'
(17d)   *Difòs* **l ap travay**, l ap gen plis esperyans.   'Since she's working, she'll have more experience.'
(17e)   Li fache *davwa* **m pa vini nan fèt la**.   'She's angry because I didn't come to the party.'
(17f)   Moun yo rayi l *poutèt* **li pretansye twòp**.   'People hate her because she's too pretentious.'

Condition: *a sipoze, anka(ke), depi/denpi, pase, si, sizanka*:

(18a)   *Si* **li la**, rele l pou mwen.   'If he's there, call him for me.'
(18b)   *Ankake* **ou pa ta la**, kite kòb la pou mwen.   'Just in case you're not here, leave the money for me.'
(18c)   *Anka* **gen dife**, pase nan eskalye a.   'In case of a fire, take the stairs.'
(18d)   Mache ak parapli ou *sizanka* **ta gen lapli**.   'Take your umbrella just in case it rains.'

Consequence or result: *alèkilè, alòs, donk, dizondi, konsa, kidonk, poutèt, sekife*

Note that in (19d), the sentence contains three clauses; the third one is a conjunctive complement of the second, which complements the first. In (19e), the third clause serves as the direct object of the main clause, itself preceded by a conjunctive clause:

(19a) Ba sa a fè m kenz jou, ***dizondi*** **l bon**. — 'This stocking lasted me two weeks; thus it is good.'
(19b) Ou pa vle travay, ***alèkilè*** **ou p ap touche**. — 'You don't want to work, therefore you don't get paid.'
(19c) M ba yo manje, ***konsa*** **yo rete trankil**. — 'I gave them food so that they stayed quiet.'
(19d) M sòti bonè, ***alòs*** **m pa konn si li vin dèyè m nan**. — 'I left early, so I don't know if she came after I left.'
(19e) Se Ayisyen ou ye, ***donk*** **ou pa ka di m ou pa konn pale kreyòl**. — 'You're Haitian, so you can't tell me you don't know how to speak Creole.'

Goal or purpose: *asèlfen, dekwa*

(20a) Li bay manti a ***asèlfen*** **pou l chape poul li**. — 'She lied only in order to save herself.'
(20b) Li vini ***dekwa*** **pou l pale avè m**. — 'He came in order to talk to me.'

Manner: *ansòt, demànyè, kòmsi/konsi/konsi, kòmsidire, kouwè, tankou(wè)*

(21a) Fè manje a plis ***ansòt*** **pou tout moun jwenn**. — 'Make more food so that everybody will have some.'
(21b) Nou ede yo ***demànyè*** **pou yo ede tèt yo**. — 'We're helping them so that they may learn to help themselves.'
(21c) Lè li wè m, li fè ***kòmsi*** **li pa konnen m**. — 'When she saw me, she pretended she didn't know me.'
(21d) Msye ap tranble ***kouwè*** **l te wè yon mò**. — 'He shook as if he had seen a dead person.'
(21e) Li fè ***tankou*** **li pa wè m**. — 'She acted as if she hadn't seen me.'

Restriction: *alòke, atout(sa), dizondi, kanfèti, kanmenm, ke ... ke, kit ... kit, kwak, sèlman, swadizan, tank, tansèlman, malgre, toutfwa*

To express a double restriction (*either ... or*) one uses *ke ... ke* or *kit ... kit*. The latter conjunction also occurs alone with the sense of 'even if', see (22d):

(22a)	*Atout* **li malad**, li vin kanmenm.	'Although he's sick, he came anyway.'
(22b)	*Kanbyenmèm* **li ta vini**, m p ap resevwa l.	'Even if she were to come, I wouldn't receive her.'
(22c)	*Ke* **ou pati** *ke* **ou rete**, sa pa deranje m.	'Whether you leave or stay, it doesn't matter to me.'
(22d)	*Kit* **ou pati m**, m ap toujou renmen ou.	'Even if you leave me, I'll always love you.'
(22e)	*Swadizan* **li rich,** l ap woule yon bogota.	'Although he's rich, he drives an old jalopy.'
(22f)	Ou mize kont ou nan wout *alòke* **m te di ou pa fè reta.**	'You dawdled on the way so much whereas I told you not to delay.'
(22g)	*Tank* **nou pale l**, li fè menm bagay.	'As much as we talked to her, she keeps doing the same thing.'
(22h)	Mèt la pa move moun, *dizondi* **kèk fwa li ka manke ou pawòl.**	'The boss isn't a bad person, however, sometimes he doesn't keep his promise to you.'
(22i)	Gen mizè, *malgre* **sa moun yo ap viv.**	'There's poverty, nevertheless people are carrying on with their lives.'

Time: *anvan, annatandan, annik, apre, atan, dèke, depi, dirantan, kom, kou, sito, tan, tandisje, toutotan*

Annik 'as soon as' occurs following the subject of the conjunctive clause:[4]

(23a)	**Mwen** *annik* **rive**, li ban m nouvèl yo.	'As soon as I arrived, he gave me the news.'
(23b)	*Depi* **l vini an**, li pa fè anyen.	'Since he arrived, he hasn't done anything.'
(23c)	*Annatandan* **paran m rantre,** rete avè m.	'Until my parents return, stay with me.'
(23d)	M gen yon bagay pou m di ou *anvan* **m ale.**	'I have something to tell you before I go.'
(23e)	Mwen rankontre Jak yè *apre* **m fin kite ou a.**	'I met Jacques yesterday after I had just left you.'
(23f)	*Dèke* **ou gen nouvèl li**, fè m konnen.	'As soon as you receive news from her, let me know.'

10.2.3 Relative clauses

Relative clauses modify noun phrases of the main clause. In the following examples, English and French relative clauses are introduced by a **relative pronoun** that is a substitute for the head of the noun phrase (NP) that is modified by the relative clause. The rather detailed discussion of the structure of relative clauses is provided, first, to exemplify the notion of relative clauses and, second, to underscore the differences and similarities in structure between English, French, and HC.

(24a) I saw **the man** (**the man** stole the bike).   J'ai vu **l'homme** (**l'homme** a volé le vélo).
(24b) I saw the man **who** stole the bike.   J'ai vu l'homme **qui** a volé le vélo.

Whereas in French a relative pronoun is always required to introduce a relative clause, in English it is optional when the relativized NP serves as direct object, as is the case in sentences (25b) to (25d):

(25a) I know the man. They arrested **the man**.   Je connais **l'homme**. Ils ont arrêté **l'homme**.
(25b) I know the man (**who(m)** they arrested).   Je connais l'homme **qu**'ils ont arrêté.
(25c) I know the man (**that** they arrested).
(25d) I know the man (they arrested).

In English, the relative pronoun varies depending on the animacy of the head of the NP modified: for animate nouns, *who* or *that* for subject of the relative clause or *whom, who, that* or zero (Ø) for the direct object:

(26a) The man (**who/that** took the bike) is a known thief.
(26b) They arrested the man (**whom/who/that/Ø** I know).

For inanimate nouns *which* or *that* are used for the subject and *which, that* or Ø for the direct object of the relative clause:

(27a) I lived in the house **which/that** burned down.
(27b) John built the house **which/that/Ø** you liked.

For the possessive, *whose* is used for both animate and inanimate NPs:

(28a) The man (his dog ran away) called yesterday.   The man **whose** dog ran away called yesterday.
(28b) The house (its owner is away) burned down.   The house **whose** owner is away burned down.

10.2 Embedding

For NPs that serve as prepositional complements of the main clause, there are two options in English. One may use a relative pronoun with the preposition placed before it (**pied-piping**) or delete the relative pronoun and leave the preposition *in situ*, that is, in place (**stranding**):

(29a) John is the man **with whom** I work. John is the man I work **with**.
(29b) This is the knife **with which** I carve my roasts. This is the knife I carve my roasts **with**.
(29c) Do you know the student **to whom** I gave the book? Do you know the student I gave the book **to**?

For locative prepositional complements **where** is used:

(30) They sold the house (I lived in that house). They sold the house **where** I lived.

Relativized subject

The structure of HC relative clauses closely resembles those of English: the relative pronoun *ki* is required for the subject of the relative clause:

(31a) Yo kontre yon moun *ki* **pale panyòl**. 'They met the person who speaks Spanish.'
(31b) Li mete wou ki **bon an** nan machin ni.[5] 'He put the wheel that's good on his car.'

The relative pronoun *ki* may undergo final vowel elision:

(32a) Se sèl Mari **k ale**. 'It's only Mary who went.'
(32b) Li wè demon an **k t ap kouri**. 'She saw the ogre who was running.'

As pointed out in Section 9.2.7, the definite determiner of a noun modified by a relative clause usually occurs at the end of that clause. Also, when it is the content of the relative clause that is being asserted, as in (33b), the sentential *LA* is inserted at the end of that clause:

(33a) Kay (**ki boule** *a*) te bèl. 'The house that burned down was beautiful.'
(33b) Kay *la* (**ki boule** *a*) te bèl. 'We are speaking about the fact that the house burned down.'

Relativized direct object

As is the case in English, relativized direct objects are usually subordinated with Ø:

(34a) Se pwason sa a **yo ban mwen**. 'That's the fish (that) they gave me.'
(34b) Li mete chemiz **ou te lave a**. 'He put on the shirt (that) you washed.'

The complementizer *ke* may also be inserted. Although it characterizes the Frenchified variety of HC (*kreyòl swa*) (see Section 8.4), it may appear in the speech of monolingual speakers as well. In the speech of bilingual speakers, *ke* may be pronounced with a front rounded vowel [ø] but it remains spelled *ke*:

(35a) Tab **la *ke* m te achte a** bèl. 'The table (that) I bought is pretty.'
(35b) Ayiti se yon peyi ***ke* mwen renmen anpil**. 'Haiti is a country (that) I love a lot.'

As pointed out in Section 9.5, *pou* may serve as a direct-object complementizer. But it carries obligative meaning:

(36a) Gen yon bagay ***pou* m fè**. 'I have a thing (that) I must do.'
(36b) M gen timoun ***pou* m bay manje a**. 'I have children (that) I have to feed.'

Relativized possessive

Recall that, in English, a relativized possessive clause requires the use of the complementizer *whose*. The equivalent HC complex sentence combines the two sentences in (37a) into (37b):

(37a) Msye rele yè. Chen li bwaze. 'The man called yesterday. His dog ran away.'
(37b) Msye **chen li bwaze** rele yè. 'The man whose dog ran away called yesterday.'

No complementizer is required and the relativized clause containing the pronoun, which functions as a possessive determiner, occurs after the possessor NP, as is the case in the English equivalent. However, in HC the possessive pronoun must be retained.

(37c) M te wè madanm **pitit *li* yo malad**. 'I saw the woman whose children are sick. [literally, I saw the woman; her children are sick.]'
(37d) **Nèg m pale ou a** se yon blan. 'The guy I'm speaking of is a foreigner.'
(37e) Chen **m kase pat li a** te mode m. 'The dog whose leg I broke bit me' (Koopman 1982: 175).

Relativized prepositional complements

In HC, the structure of relativized adverbial complements parallels that of English. In some cases, the adverb or preposition may be followed by the complementizer *ki* or the preposition may be stranded and no complementizer is used. But in most cases *ki* introduces the embedded prepositional phrase.

(38a) Moun **ak ki** ou rive se yon bòkò. 'The man with whom you came is a sorcerer.'
(38b) Moun ou rive **ak li** se yon bòkò. 'The man you came with is a sorcerer.'
(38c) Kay **nan ki** m te rete a boule. 'The house in which I lived burned down.'
(38d) M konnen **patron pou ki** ou travay. 'I know the boss for whom you work.'

In the case of locative relativized clauses, the adverb *kote* occurs without the complementizer *ki*:

(39a) Yo vòlè makout **kote** m mete kòb mwen. 'They stole the straw bag in which I put my money.'
(39b) Yo te tounen soti nan peyi **kote** yo te depote yo a. 'They came back to the country from which they deported them.'
(39c) Eske ou konnen machann **pou ki** m te bay kòb la? 'Do you know the seller to whom I gave the money?'

Conditional complex sentences

The conjunction *si* is used to express conditions. If the action or event expressed by the conditional clause is connected to the moment of speech, its verb is preceded by either Ø or *ap*. In such cases the event or action of the main clause refers to the future and *a(va)* precedes the verb:

(40a) Si kasav **bon**, m **a achte** yo. 'If the cassavas are good, I'll buy one.'
(40b) M **ap ba** ou san goud si ou **a mennen** bèf mwen yo desann nan bouk. 'I'll give you a hundred gourdes if you take my cattle down to the village.'

If the main clause expresses a command or request that is connected to the moment of speech, its verb is preceded by Ø:

(41) Si l **ap limen** dife a, **pote** chabon ba li. 'If she's lighting the fire, bring her some coal.'

Ta generally occurs in the resultative clause of conditional hypothetical sentences. However, *a* or *ap* may also be used. The verb of the clause indicating the condition is preceded by *te* or *ta*. As is the case in (42a) and (42b), the combination of the markers *te* in the conditional clause and *ta/t ap* in the resultative clause leads to an ambiguous interpretation. These sentences may refer to either a hypothetical event in the past or one referring to the moment of speech.

(42a) Si chemiz la **te** sal, yo **ta** lave l.   'If the shirt were dirty, they'd wash it.'
'If the shirt had been dirty, they would have washed it.'

(42b) Si m **te gen** lajan, m **ta achte** yon kamyon.   'If I had money, I'd buy a truck.'
'If I had had money, I would have bought a truck.'

The use of *ta* in both the conditional and the resultative clause situates the hypothetical action in the past.

(42c) M pa bezwen di n sa pou n **ta** fè si n **ta** kontre youn.   'I don't have to tell you [plural] what we would have done if we had met one.'

Note that, in (42d), there occurs the elided variant of *te* (*t*) and *a* appears as the *ava* variant.

(42d) Si sa **ta** rive fèt tout bon vre, se **t ava** yon bèl jefò.   'If it were really done, it would be a great effort.'

In (42e), the use of *ap* in the two resultative clauses reflects the certainty of the outcome:

(42e) Menm si l **ta** mouv, gwoup la pa **t ap** tonbe non, gwoup la **ap** toujou mache.   'Even if he were to move, the group wouldn't dissolve; the group will always keep going on'(Spears 1990: 133).

If the event of the resultative clause is one ongoing at the moment of speech, a combination of all three TMA markers is used:

(43) Si m **te** pati yè, m **t av ap** kabicha nan kabann mwen kounye a.   'If I had left yesterday, I would now be taking a little nap in my bed.'

Suzanne Sylvain (1936: 87) claims that *t ava* characterizes the speech of southern Haitian speakers. She also mentions that these speakers use *ta* for the present and *t ava* only for emphasis. However, whereas (44a) involves a future hypothetical event with regard to a present situation, (44b) clearly involves one that is located in the past. In addition, there appears to be a typographical error. Sylvain's original example, *M t ava renmen l chita*, that she translates as *Je l'aurais tant aimé!* 'I would have loved him so much!' actually means 'I would have liked for him to sit'.

(44a) Ou **ta** lage m!   '(You mean) you would abandon me!'
(44b) M **t ava** renmen l chita.   'I would have liked for him to sit.'

Expressing a hypothetical future event from the perspective of a situation in the past is another function of the conditional *ta*. Often the statement of the past situation involves the use of verbs of communication or thought preceded by the past/anterior marker *te*:

(45a) Jozèf **te** di l **ta** tounen.   'Joseph said he would return.'
(45b) Nou **te** kwè ou **ta** vini.   'We thought you would come.'

Lainy (2010: 84–6) observes that *ta, t ap, t apral, t ava* all may be used to refer to counterfactual hypothetical events or situations, that is, those that might have happened or obtained but never did:[6]

(46a) San nèg sa, vi w **t ap** toujou tris.   'Without that man, your life would always have been sad.'
(46b) San kout volan sa, mwen **t apral** antre nan mi a.   'Without a sharp turn of the steering wheel I would have hit the wall.'

10.2.4 Temporal relations in complex sentences

In Standard French and English, there are strict rules about expressing temporal relations between the main and dependent clauses of complex sentences, as shown by (47a), versus (47b) and (47c):

(47a) Elle dit qu'elle partira.   'She says (that) she'll leave.'
(47b) Elle a dit qu'elle partirait.   'She said (that) she would leave.'
(47c) Elle disait qu'elle partirait.   'She was saying (that) she would leave.'

In both of these languages, to indicate that a future action will take place with reference to the moment of speech one uses the present tense in the main clause and the future tense in the subordinate clause. On the other hand, to refer to a future action that will take place with regard to the past, one uses a past-tense form in the main clause, in French the conditional tense, and in English the modal verb *would* in the subordinate clause. In HC, to refer to a future action with regard to the moment of speech, one uses the bare stem in the main clause and either *ap* or *a* in the subordinate clause depending on the degree of certainty of the future action.

(48a) Li di l ap vini. 'She says she'll come.'
(48b) Li di l ava vini. 'She said she would come.'

To refer to a future action with respect to the past, one uses *te* or Ø in the main clause and either *ap* or *a* in the subordinate clause. However, the use of *ap* does not specify whether the action will be certain or hypothetical (49a). It also may refer to an event that is concurrent with that of the main clause, as in (49b). The particular temporal reference is determined by the situational context (Lainy 2010: 86).

(49a) Li **(te)** di m l **ap** vini. 'She told me she'll come.'
 'She told me she'd come.'
(49b) Li **(te)** di m l **ap** travay labank. 'She told me she was working at the bank.'

To refer to an action that occurs concurrently or after a future situation, one uses *a* and *ap* or *apral*:

(50a) Lè ou rive, l **av ap** manje. 'When you arrive, he will be eating.'
(50b) Lè ou rive, l **apral** mande ou ki sa ou **te** ban m nan. 'When you arrive, he will ask you what you had given me.'

In (51), *apral*, preceded by *te* (here the elided variant *t*), is used to express a progressive action in the past concurrent with another one.

(51) Lè ou **t apral** marye ak manman m nan, m pa te di ou se manman m li ye non. 'When you were in the process of thinking about marrying my mother, I didn't tell you that she was my mother' (Spears 1990: 133).

10.3 Reduplication and Clefting: Topicalization and Focalization

In Chapter 7, in connection with the insertion of *ye* in copulative sentences (Section 7.3.2), I introduced the notions of **topicalization** and **focalization**.

I indicated that these terms refer to syntactic transformations that involve primarily isolating the part of a sentence that contains either the **topic** (or **theme**) – what or whom is talked about – or the **focus** (or **comment** or **rheme**) – the part of the sentence that contains the new or most important information. As is the case in English and French, the basic component of these operations is the clefting (extraction) and fronting of the focalized element of a sentence and, in some cases, the embedding of the sentence element in a higher-level clause introduced by *se*. This two-step operation was illustrated with a copulative sentence containing a prepositional predicate:

(52a) Li **ak lafyèv**. 'She has fever.'
(52b) Clefting and fronting: *[**ak lafyèv**] li.
(52c) Embedding with the introducer *se [**ak lafyèv**] li
      se:

Because this operation leaves the pronoun stranded, *ye* is inserted.

(52d) **Se ak lafyèv** li *ye*. 'She really has fever.'

Note that *se* is derived from the French *c'est* that also serves as introducer for focalized elements: *Elle a de la fièvre* > *C'est de la fièvre qu'elle a*, *Il est français, pas un étranger*> *C'est un Français qu'il est, pas un étranger*.[7] At the semantic level focalization by clefting and insertion in a higher clause adds the notion of intensification reflected by the English gloss 'really'.

This section is divided into four parts: (1) the topicalization and focalization of NPs; (2) the focalization of nonverbal predicates in copulative sentences; (3) the focalization of verbal predicates; and (4) adverbial topicalization and focalization.

10.3.1 Topicalization and Focalization

Topicalization of subject NPs
The topicalization of subject NPs follows the pattern of French left dislocation (*détachement*). The topicalized NP is extracted, clefted to the head of the sentence, and replaced by the corresponding pronoun copy. In (53a), the subject *madanm lan* is extracted from the base-generated sentence (53b), and then reinforced by the 3SG *li*.

(53a) **Madanm lan** bèl. The woman is beautiful.
(53b) * [**madanm lan**] ----bèl
(53c) **Madanm lan** *li* bèl. The woman, she's beautiful.

Suzanne Sylvain (1936: 172) offers a variant of (53c) in which the exclamation *o* follows the clefted subject NP. She translates it as *Elle est belle, la femme (dont nous parlons)* 'She's beautiful, the woman (we're talking about)', in which case the parenthesized clause serves to indicate the deictic force of the definite determiner.[8]

    (53c)   **Madanm lan *o*** li bèl.

The pragmatic force of clefting is borne out by the other example she provides:

    (54a)   **Pitit la *li*** manje.   *Il mange, l'enfant.*

which I would paraphrase as 'Speaking of the child, (s)he's eating'. Sylvain provides an intensified version of this topicalized sentence:

    (54b)   **Pitit la *o li*** manje.   *Eh! bien, il mange l'enfant.* ('Well, he's eating, the child.')

Topicalized, pronominalized NPs leave behind a copy (S. Sylvain 1936: 172). However, (55b), the topicalized version of (55a), is more complex than it appears on the surface; her translation is provided:

    (55a)   **Ou** rive.   'You've arrived.'
    (55b)   **Ou menm menm o ou** rive.   *Quant à vous, vous êtes arrivé.* ('So far as you are concerned, you've arrived.')

This sentence involves resumptive emphasis on the pronoun by the adjunction of *menm*, as is the case in (56a). In the English translation, the pronoun would receive stress. In (56b), clefting of *ou menm* involves non-resumptive emphasis and the sentence reflects an interdiction of the action:

    (56a)   Kote ou prale la a **ou menm**?   'Where are **you** going?'
    (56b)   **Ou menm**, kote ou prale la a?   'You there, where are you going? [You're not supposed to go there.]'

According to Suzanne Sylvain (1936: 170), the adverbial *o* assumes the same function in (57a) and it can reinforce a reduplicated **menm**, as in (57b). The same function appears to be served by the locative adverb *la*, distinct from the definite determiner *LA* (57c):

10.3 Reduplication and Clefting 303

(57a)   **Ki sa o** k vini?   *Qui donc est venu?* ('Who is it in fact who came?')
(57b)   yo **menm menm** o   *quant à eux* ('with regard to them')
(57c)   nou **menm** la   *nous mêmes précisément* ('we, precisely')

To recapitulate the generative process of (55b), *Ou menm menm o ou rive*:

(1) Base sentence: *Ou rive*.
(2) Adjunction of **menm**: Ou **menm** rive.
(3) Reduplication of **menm**: Ou **menm menm** rive.
(4) Clefting of **ou** and its modifiers: [**Ou menm menm**] rive.
(5) Adjunction of **o**: *[**Ou menm menm o**] rive.
(6) Insertion of the resumptive pronoun **ou**: *Ou menm menm o* **ou** rive.

As will be shown below, reduplication is a fundamental process in HC focalization.

Focalization of other NPs

Focalization involves focus on new information. As is the case for subject NPs, the focalized object and adverbial complements are sometimes clefted. However, more generally, after being clefted the NP is embedded in a higher clause introduced by *se*, particularly with direct-object and indirect (dative) NPs. The meaning of the (b) and (c) sentences in the sets below does not differ:

(58a)   Nou rive **nan yon raje**.   'We arrived at a thicket.'
(58b)   **Nan yon raje** nou rive.   'It's at a thicket that we arrived.'
(58c)   **Se nan yon raje** nou rive.

(59a)   M souse zo kodenn.   'I sucked on turkey bones' (S. Sylvain 1936: 172).
(59b)   Zo kodenn m souse.   'What I sucked on are turkey bones.'
(59c)   Se zo kodenn m souse.

(60a)   M achte rad sa yo pou pitit mwen an.   'I bought these clothes for my child.'
(60b)   Pou pitit mwen an m achte rad sa yo.   'It's for my child that I bought these clothes.'
(60c)   Se pou pitit mwen an m achte rad sa yo.

In Frenchified varieties of HC, the complementizer *ke* may be inserted after clefted NPs embedded in a **se** clause: *Se zo kodenn **ke** m souse*. Also, as is

304 *Complex Sentences*

the case for topicalized subject NPs, the intensifiers *menm* and *o* may be inserted to extraposed NPs (S. Sylvain 1936: 172):

(61)   Ayè **menm** *o* m te vini.   *C'est hier exactement que j'étais venu.* ('It's precisely yesterday that I came.')

10.3.2 Focalization of non-verbal predicates in copulative sentences

As presented in Section 7.3.2, when predicates in copulative sentences are focalized, they are embedded in a higher clause and *ye* is inserted to fill the gap left by the clefted predicate:

(62a)   Li **nan lakou a**.   'She's in the yard.'
(62b)   Se **nan lakou a** li *ye*.   'It's in the yard that she is.'
(63a)   M se **yon dòktè**.   'I'm a doctor.'
(63b)   Se **yon dòktè** m *ye*.   'What I am I is a doctor.'

In (63a), *se* is not the introducer but the copula. Since it cannot be stranded as in **Se yon dòktè m se,* it is replaced by *ye*.

Although focalized adjectival predicates may also be clefted and embedded in a higher clause, intensification of the meaning conveyed by adjectives may be amplified by reduplication, twice or more times:

(64a)   Li **bèl**.   'She's beautiful.'
(64b)   Se **bèl** li *ye*.   'She's really beautiful.'

(65a)   Li **blanch blanch**.   'It's very white (or a little white, i.e., whitish)'[9] (S. Sylvain 1936: 42).
(65b)   Boukinèt **bèl, bèl, bèl, bèl** …   'Boukinet is really beautiful' (Harbour 2008: 864).

In addition, a cognate noun of the adjective may be clefted and intensified with the numerals *de* or *kat*, as well as the adjective *ti* indicating quantity. This is analogous to English *to jump a (high) jump*, where a cognate noun to the verb *jump* is inserted in place of the clefted verb and preceded by an adjective. From a point of view of pragmatics, this is equivalent to *to jump very high*.

(66a)   Se *de* **bèl** li bèl.   'She's really very beautiful.'
(66b)   Se *kat* **dous** li dous.   'She's very sweet' (S. Sylvain 1936: 46).

10.3 Reduplication and Clefting 305

The negative *pa* may be optionally added in front of the number but it is required for *ti*. For example, (66c) literally means: 'He's not four times more fresh but much more.'

(66c) Se *pa kat* **frekan** ti gason an frekan.   'The boy is really very insolent.'
(66d) Se *pa ti* **mouye** yo mouye.   'They're really very wet.'

A cognate noun may be inserted in place of the clefted adjective and it may be preceded by the indefinite determiner *yon*:

(67a) Li **move** *yon* **move**.   'He is exceedingly bad' (S. Sylvain 1936: 46).

Another way to focalize adjectives is to embed them in higher clauses introduced by *ala*:

(67b) *Ala* **banda** li banda!   'How elegant he is!'

But post-adjectival modifiers cannot be clefted and embedded in a *se* clause with the adjective head, as (68b) shows; only simple clefting applies, as in (68c). This is because in the latter case the entire adjectival clause *ble fonse* 'dark blue' is intensified, whereas in (68d) the focus bears only on the color *ble* as distinct from another color (Jason Siegel 2011):

(68a) Li ble fonse.   'It's dark blue.'
(68b) *Se **ble fonse** li ble fonse.
(68c) Se **ble fonse** li ye.   'It's really dark blue.'
(68d) Se **ble** li ble fonse.   'It's dark blue [not green].'

10.3.3 Focalization of verbal predicates

Constraints on reduplication and clefting
The focalization of verbal predicates patterns very much like that of adjectival predicates. However, there are various restrictions on which dependent elements of these predicates may be clefted with a given verb. Like adjectives, verbs may undergo reduplication:

(69) Yo **kouri, kouri, kouri**.   'They ran, ran, ran.'

Generally, focalization of verbs involves clefting and embedding in a higher *se* clause:

(70)   *Se* **manje** mwen manje.   'What I did is eat.'

TMA pre-verbal markers as well as the subjects cannot be clefted to accompany the duplicated copy of the verb. This is at least in part because the emphasis is on the verb itself, not the full predicate, as is made clear below by the translations. For example, in (71c) the speaker is focusing on the act of eating itself.

(71a)   M ap manje.   'I'm eating.'
(71b)   *Se *m ap* manje m ap manje.
(71c)   **Se manje** m ap manje.   'What I'm doing is eating.'

Concerning the movement of auxiliary verbs with the clefted duplicated verb, Piou (1982a) deals with six auxiliaries that she divides into two groups on the basis of their putative behavior in this syntactic operation: the **semi-auxiliaries** *fin*, *fèk*, *sòt*, which I labeled aspectual completive auxiliaries, and the modals *dwe* (*do*), *ka*, *mèt*, which I labeled modal auxiliaries (see Section 8.3).

Piou, a native Haitian linguist, deals with two questions posed by auxiliaries with regard to clefting. First, unlike TMA markers, can they be moved from the base clause? Second, are they retained in the base clause if a copy of them is moved? From the evidence provided by Suzanne Sylvain (1936: 173), Piou's semi-auxiliaries may be clefted:

(72a)   Se **fèk rive** moun yo te **fèk rive**.   *Ces gens viennent d'arriver.* ('These people have just arrived.')
(72b)   Kanta **sòt tonbe** madanm lan **manke sòt tonbe**.   *Cette dame a failli tomber tout à l'heure.* ('This lady almost fell down a while ago.')

What is interesting about these examples is that (72a) shows, as one would expect, that the TMA marker *te* is not clefted, but then neither is the first auxiliary *manke* in (72b). What is puzzling, though, is that Sylvain's translations do not reflect semantic focalization: they do not show the difference between these sentences and their base counterparts: *Moun yo fèk rive* and *Madanm lan sòt manke tonbe*, respectively. In (72b), it is the introducer *kanta* 'as far as' that indicates focus of the clefted verb phrase: *sòt tonbe*. I would translate that sentence as: 'As far as almost falling, that lady almost fell a short while ago', since what is stressed is that the event is very recent.

Concerning the two questions she addresses, Piou's treatment appears somewhat muddled. On the one hand, she states that, as is the case with TMA markers, modals cannot be clefted (1982a: 139); on the other hand,

10.3 Reduplication and Clefting 307

as shown by footnote 10, she adds that modals *ka* and *dwe* occur only in the clefted clause but not in the base clause (ibid.: 140–5).[10] Her examples (36), (39) and (40a) show different positions of the deontic modal *dwe* (*do*) in clefted sentences.

(73a) (36) Se travay li **do** fin travay. 'He must have finished working.'
(73b) (39) Se **do** desann larivyè a **do** desann. 'Perhaps the river is in its flood stage.'
(73c) (40a) Se **do** malad pitit la malad. 'The child may be sick.'

In Piou's other examples, *ka* patterns like *do* but a third of the modals she posits cannot be clefted:[11]

(73d) (40b) Se **ka** vini li vini. *C'est pouvoir venir il venir.* ('He can come.')
(73e) (40c) *Se **mèt** pati li pati. *C'est pouvoir partir il partir.* ('He can leave.')

Clearly, constraints on auxiliaries in clefting constitute an aspect of verbal focalization that requires further research.

In clefted sentences, the negative adverb *pa* may occur either only in the base clause or in both clauses, depending on the scope of the negation. Examples (74a) and (74c) are from Piou (1982a: 135–6) but (74b) has been added to show the exact difference of scope between the two sentences:

(74a) Se travay Mari **pa vle travay**. *Marie ne veut pas travailler.* ('Mary doesn't want to work.')
(74b) Se **pa travay** Mari pa vle travay. 'It's not that Mary doesn't want to work.'
(74c) **Se pa renmen Nuyòk** Mari pa renmen Nuyòk. *Ce n'est pas que Marie aime New York.* ('It's not that Mary likes New York.')

In (74a), it is the fact that Mary doesn't want to work that is negated. Piou's translation fails to show the focalizing force of clefting. I would modify it with 'really': 'Mary really doesn't want to work', as does Damoiseau (2005a: 145) in (74d):

(74d) Se **pa** vante mwen **pa** vante. *Vraiment, je ne me vante pas.* ('Really, I'm not bragging.')

His second example translated with initial *ce n'est pas* adds support to Piou's analysis of the focalizing force of clefting *pa*:

(74e) Se **pa peye** nou p ap peye. *Ce n'est pas que nous ne paierons pas.* ('It's not that we won't pay.')

Whereas pre-adjectival modifiers may be clefted with the adjective head, this is not possible for verb complements (Jason Siegel 2011):[12]

(75) Se **twò bèl** li twò bèl. 'She's so pretty.'

(76a) Jan **manje pòm nan**. 'John ate the apple.'
(76b) *Se **manje pòm nan** Jan manje pòm nan.
(76c) Jan **pale vit**. 'John spoke quickly.'
(76d) *Se **pale vit** Jan te pale vit.

Siegel also points out that conjoined verbal predicates, as in (77b) and (77c), cannot be clefted:

(77a) N **ap chante ak danse**. 'We're singing and dancing.'
(77b) *Se chante n ap chante ak danse.
(77c) *Se danse n ap chante ak danse.
(77d) *Se chante ak danse n ap chante ak danse.

Clefting in serial verbs

According to Piou (1982a: 145–8), any of the verbs of serial verb constructions may be clefted. However, she only treats the focal + deictic subtype of serial verbs where the deictic verb assumes a clearly semantically subordinate role.[13] In addition, the translations she provides for the examples used to support her analysis do not highlight the directional sense of the various deictic verbs provided. There does not seem to be any difference between absence of clefting, in what I assume is the base sentence (78a), and the clefted version she provides: (78b). Native speakers I have consulted translate (78b) instead by 'Mary carried the dress away'. For (78c), Piou provides only glosses and not a translation – that would presumably be 'What John did was to lead Mary back' – since, as a deictic verb, *tounen* is equivalent to the English preposition 'back'.

(78a) Mari pote rad la ale. 'Mary took the dress.'
(78b) Se **pote** Mari pote rad la ale. *Marie a apporté la robe.* ('Mary brought the dress.')
(78c) Se **mennen** Jak mennen Mari tounen. *C'est amener Jacques amener Marie retourner.*

10.3 Reduplication and Clefting

Harbour (2008: 866) better elucidates the pragmatic function of focalization in this type of serial verb construction by adding a clause to show that the stress is on the direction specified by the deictic verb. Starting with the base sentence (79a), where the deictic verb is not focalized, he suggests that (79b) is not grammatical. He states that predicate clefting is permitted, but only with a contrastive interpretation. In (79c), he contrasts two deictic verbs, *tounen* 'to return = back' and *ale* 'to go = away'. In this case, the first deictic verb, *tounen* 'back' can be clefted.

(79a) Jan mennen bèt yo tounen.   'John led the animals back.'
(79b) *Se mennen Jan mennen bèt yo tounen.
(79c) Se tounen Jan mennen bèt yo **tounen,** li pa mennen yo **ale**.   'John led the animals back, he didn't lead them **away**.'

Clefting in complex sentences

In complex sentences, the verb of the dependent clause may be clefted and the copy moved to the front of the main clause. The moved copy then becomes the verb of the main clause introduced by *se*:

(80a) [Li vle [pou Jan **ale** avè l]].   'She wants John to go with her.'
(80b) [Se **ale** [[li vle pou Jan **ale** avè l]]].   '[Question of going] She wants John to go with her.'

In complex sentences containing dependent clauses embedded at several levels, the clefted verb can be moved in front of any of the higher-level clauses. Starting with the complex sentence (81a), whose main clause dominates another containing a dependent clause, the copy of the duplicated and clefted verb *ale* may be moved into either of the two higher-level clauses (Harbour 2008: 855). Presumably, there is no pragmatic difference between (82a) and (82b).

(81a) [Li di [li vle [pou Jan ale avè l]]].   'He said that she wanted John to go with her.'
(81b) *[Li di [li vle [pou Jan **ale ale** avè l]]].
(82a) Li di li vle se **ale** pou Jan **ale** avè li.   'He said that so far as going is concerned, she wanted John to go with her.'
(82b) Se **ale** li di li vle pou Jan **ale** avè l.

310   *Complex Sentences*

According to Piou (1982a: 132), the further the clefted verb is moved from its original position, the higher the degree of focus. Thus, there would be a pragmatic difference between (82a) and (82b).

There are various constraints on verb clefting (Piou 1982a: 132–3); for example, verbs in interrogative clauses cannot be clefted:

(83a) M ap mande m **ki sa pou m kuit**.   'I'm thinking about what I should cook.'
(83b) *Se **kuit** m ap mande m **ki sa pou m kuit**.

Nor can verbs occurring in relative or conjunctive clauses be clefted:

(84a) Madanm **ki te te konn vann mwen kokoye** mouri.   'The woman who used to sell me coconuts died.'
(84b) *Se **vann** madanm **ki te konn vann mwen kokoye** mouri.

(85a) M an reta **paske mwen t ap ede yon gran moun**.   'I'm late because I was helping an older person.'
(85b) *Se **ede** m an reta **paske mwen t ape ede yon gran moun**.

Clefting and nominalization

In Section 7.3.4, I pointed out that nouns may be derived from verbs and used in predicates with the verb *fè* 'to do' as equivalent to the verb from which they are derived:

(86a) Li chita.   'She sat down.'
(86b) Li fè **yon chita**.   'She sat down.' [literally, 'She did an act of sitting.']
(86c) Li rantre. Li fè **yon lòt rantre**.   'She came in. She came in another time.'

Jason Siegel (2011) points out that clefting applies to intransitive verbs with cognate objects (i.e., nouns derived from them):

(87a) Jan dòmi dòmi l.   'John slept fully. [John slept 'his sleep'.]'
(87b) Se **dòmi** Jan dòmi dòmi l.   'John really had a good sleep.'
(87c) Se chita m chita chita m.   'I'm just sitting.'[14]

Instances of clefting accompanied by an intensifier (see (66) above) question the part of speech of the clefted element: is it a nominalized cognate of a verb or the verb itself?

(88a) Mwen manje manje m.   'I ate my food.'
(88b) Se **pa kat manje** yo manje.   'They ate for four.'

10.3.4 Adverbial topicalization and focalization

Clefting may be used instead of various adverbial complements. In this case, it cannot be accompanied by embedding in a higher clause introduced by *se*. In (89b), the clefted verb replaces the temporal adverbial complement *lè* 'when':

(89a) **Lè** li rive lakay li, l al dòmi.   'When she arrived home, she went to sleep.'
(89b) **Rive li rive lakay li**, l al dòmi.

In general, clefting may be used to express the simultaneity of two events or actions, and it is thus equivalent to *kou* 'as soon as' as well as *lè*. Note that when an auxiliary verb with a short variant is clefted the full form occurs obligatorily, as in (90b).

(90a) **Moute** mwen **moute**, Jilbè desann.   'As soon as I went up, Gilbert came down.'
(90b) **Fini** Pòl **fin manje mango l la**, li kite sal la.   'As soon as he finished eating his mango, Paul left the room.' (Lainy 2010: 264)
(90c) Li vle pou ou fenmen pòt la, **sòti l sòti**.   'He wants you to close the door as soon as he goes out.' (Piou 1982b: 162)

Harbour (2008: 868) offers an interesting example of temporal meaning affected by clefting that involves a nominalized copy of the verb:

(91) **Touse l touse yon ti touse**, kouri!   'As soon as he gives a little sneeze [sic], run!'[15]

Suzanne Sylvain (1936: 171) identifies another case of clefting that involves all types of parts of speech: nouns, pronouns, adjectives, verbs, etc. This requires, in addition to reduplication and clefting of the copy of the element in focus, insertion of the relative pronoun. This structure serves as an equivalent to the adverb *menm* 'even'. I show the derivation of the first example in (92a) and (92b), and then provide others illustrating other parts of speech.

(92a) Bèt pa mache kon ou. 'Animals don't walk as much as you do.'
(92b) **Bèt** ki **bèt** pa mache kon ou. 'Even animals don't walk as much as you do.' (i.e., ' You walk more than animals do.)

(93a) **Mwen** ki **mwen** yo pale m mal. 'They speak ill even of me.'
(93b) **Bwè** ki **bwè** mwen pa kapab. 'I can't even drink.'
(93c) **Pwòp** ki **pwòp** li pa te pwòp ankò. 'It wasn't even cleaner.'

Sentence (94c) differs somewhat from the preceding examples in that it involves prior reduplication and clefting of the verb. For that reason, I have modified Sylvain's translation to show the pragmatic effect of the previous clefting.

(94a) Bèt la pa t sa chante. 'That animal couldn't sing.'
(94b) Se **chante** bèt la pa t sa **chante**. 'So far as singing is concerned, that animal couldn't sing.'
(94c) **Chante** ki **chante** bèt la pa t sa **chante**. *Cette bête ne pouvait plus chanter.* ('So far as singing is concerned, that animal couldn't even sing.')

Sylvain also identifies a restrictive use of clefting particular to NPs. It is equivalent to the use of the adverbial phrase pronoun + *sèl* 'only, alone' combined with relativization and embedding in a sentence introduced by *se*. It consists of the use of the phrase *yon grenn* 'single unit or piece of anything' following the NP in focus. In the case of the pronoun *menm* 'self', it is used in addition.

(95a) **Li sèl** sa rache l. 'Only he could tear it out.'
(95b) Se **li sèl** ki sa rache l. 'It's only he that could tear it out.'
(95c) **Li menm yon grenn** sa rach l. *Lui seul pourrait l'arracher.* 'It's only he himself that could tear it out.'

(96a) **Ou menm yon grenn** m vini wè. 'It's only you yourself that I came to see.'
(96b) Fi a bwote yo **li menm yon grenn**. 'The girl carried them by herself alone.'
(96c) **Kannari yon grenn** pitit la pòte. 'The child brought only one earthenware jar.'

Summary

In HC, the formation of complex sentences by coordination is quite straightforward. There are a wide variety of conjunctions that can be used to form conjunctive clauses. With regard to the formation of complex sentences by subordination, in many respects HC resembles English. The use of a relative pronoun is required only for relative clauses that expand subject NPs. For relative clauses that modify direct and indirect NPs, no complementizer is necessary. A major difference is in possessive (genitive) complements, where English requires the complementizer *whose* but HC only the appropriate pronoun functioning as possessive determiner: e.g., (37c) *M te wè madanm **pitit li yo malad***. 'I saw the woman whose children are sick.'

HC possesses a wide variety of syntactic means to emphasize and individualize sentence constituents. They involve clefting and in many cases prior reduplication. These syntactic features allow speakers a wide expressive scope and they belie the misconceived view that HC is a simple language lacking suitable linguistic resources for precise expression of meaning and flexible pragmatic effect.

Notes

1. This conjunction has the Northern Haiti (Capois) variant *ake*. A homonymous form functions as a preposition 'with': *Li rete ak matant li* 'He lives with his aunt'.
2. The idiom *ni Pyè ni Jak, ni Jak ni Pyè* means 'no one': *Eske ou pase bò kay la? – Wi, men ni Pyè ni Jak, ni Jak ni Pyè te la non*. 'Did you stop by the house? – Yes, but no one was there.'
3. The last verb marker, presumably, is the result of an evolution in which *te* combined with the *a* variant *ava*.
4. *Annik* also functions as an adverb: *M annik repose m jodi a* 'I'm only resting today'. It also occurs with the variants: *annèk*, *nik*.
5. As pointed out in Section 3.3.6, after a nasal consonant *ni* is the variant of the 3rd person singular pronoun (3SG) *LI*.
6. Lainy lists the demonstrative determiner variant as *sa*. The standard norm opts for *sa a* realized with a long /a/ [sa:]. It appears that a growing number of speakers shorten the vowel and use this variant form.
7. There are in French other types of syntactic operation for focalization and topicalization: left and right dislocation, in which the focalized or topicalized element is moved from its position in the sentence and reinforced by a pronominal copy: *Jean est parti* 'John left'> *Jean, il est parti* or *Il est parti, Jean*; *J'aime Jean* 'I love John'> *Jean, je l'aime*, *Je l'aime, Jean*. 'I really love John'.

8. The HC exclamation *o!* is highly polysemous. It expresses surprise, wonderment, disapproval, etc. For example: *Asefi o! Men manman m ap rele ou.* 'Yoo-hoo, Asefi! My mother is calling you.' *Pitit o! Sa w ap fè la?* 'Hey, son! What are you doing?' (surprise, disapproval) *O! Apa ou chire liv la?* 'Hey! Why are you tearing up the book?'
9. Sylvain indicates that the difference in degree is conveyed by a tonal difference, 'very often' with a falling tone on the repeated adjective and 'slightly' by an even tone.
10. 'Généralement, les modaux, pas plus que les particules verbales, ne subissent le clivage du prédicat ... les modaux *ka* et *do* ne sont présents que devant le verbe clivé (In general, modals do not undergo predicate clefting anymore than verbal markers ... the modals *ka* and *do* occur only before the clefted verb).'
11. The problem with these examples is that neither is provided with a proper translation; only the constituent morphemes are glossed. As pointed out in Section 8.3.2, *ka* and *mèt* differ semantically. The former refers to capability 'to be able' and the latter to permission 'to be allowed'. The contextual translations offered in (73d) and (73e) are mine.
12. Examples (76a–d) are taken from Harbour 2008 (856–7).
13. See Section 8.6.3 for the analysis of serial verbs.
14. An interesting case is that of the noun *grangou* 'hunger', which like *swèf* 'thirst' may by itself constitute a predicate, i.e., serve as a verb (see Section 7.3.2). Siegel (2011) shows that it can occur as both verb and noun in the same sentence and undergo clefting: *Se grangou m grangou grangou m.* 'I'm just hungry.'
15. Actually, *touse* means 'to cough', not 'to sneeze'.

11 Variation in Haitian Creole

11.1 Types of Variation

As stressed in Section 1.3.1, Haitian Creole (HC) is arguably the best-described creole language. The vast literature listed in that chapter contrasts with the paucity of studies dealing with variation in HC and the very few descriptive works based on genuinely empirical data, that is, collected in specified locations from speakers with clearly identified social characteristics. The few exceptions in the last category are Spears (1990, 1993a, 1993b) and Bentolila *et al.* (1976). The latter work is an HC–French dictionary derived entirely from a geographically identified corpus of which the nomenclature and examples in the microstructure are based on sixty hours of speech recorded in the vicinity of the town of Saint-Marc, in the central region of Haiti. However, neither the actual recordings nor the transcription of this corpus are available.

Research on geographical variation constitutes a signal exception to the near-lack of empirical anchoring of descriptive studies. Dialect geography studies by Orjala (1970) and Fattier (1998) have grounded the study of geographical variation on solid empirical bases. The monumental Fattier study provides data on more than two thousand variables representing phonological, grammatical, and lexical features. It is at the same time the more comprehensive and the more trustworthy of these two works. However, both of these important studies are somewhat dated and do not provide a full description of linguistic variation in present-day Haiti. Orjala's data were collected nearly forty years ago, and the relatively recent publication date of the Fattier linguistic atlas is misleading since the data were collected in the early 1980s. Because her much-awaited work was conceived within the scope of a French *doctorat d'état* dissertation, the analysis of geographical variation that constitutes one of the truly original and highly significant aspects of her work could not be published until after her doctoral defense at the University of Provence (Aix–Marseille I) in 1998. But the most serious gap in the study of variation in Haitian Creole is the lack of research on sociolinguistic (**diastratic**) variation and stylistic or register (**diaphasic**) variation. The former type of variation is related to social factors (social class or group, age group, sex) and the latter to the context of speech production (nature of interlocutors, level of formality of the situation, purpose or function of the

316 Variation in Haitian Creole

linguistic interaction). In this chapter, in Section 11.2, I review the two geographical (**topolectal**) variation studies, namely, those of Orjala (1970) and Fattier (1998). In Section 11.3, I describe the only two major existing studies of sociolinguistic variation (Valdman 1991, 2008) and I discuss the continuum that exists between the variety of HC characteristic of monolingual speakers from the central region around Port-au-Prince and that spoken by bilingual Haitians, termed *kreyòl swa*. In the absence of any studies devoted to stylistic variation in the speech of individual speakers, little can be said about diaphasic variation. In most sociolinguistic studies that deal with that type of variation, data are generally obtained by comparing conversational speech to that produced in less-natural circumstances, for example, by the reading of texts. Because many monolingual speakers of HC are illiterate, it is difficult to sample their formal register in the latter manner.

11.2 Geographical Variation

11.2.1 Dialect geography

The study of **geographical variation**, the variation of language across geographical areas, has a long tradition that reached its apogee during the first half of the twentieth century. Scholars in Europe who focused mainly on the speech of rural dialects were the first to launch this branch of linguistics, termed dialect geography, which involves representing variable features of a language on maps. To prepare for the spatial representation of variation, investigators consult representative speakers in a number of areas in a country or region, generally adults who are fluent speakers of the local speech and who are relatively geographically sedentary. In most studies, they are asked to provide the names of objects or notions that the investigators know in advance are likely to be designated by different terms in different places: words in which pronunciation may differ or morphosyntactic features are likely to vary. The variant features are then represented on maps; for example, Figure 11.1, taken from Hans Kurath's *A Word Geography of the Eastern United States* (1949), maps the terms used to designate a container used to carry water: either *pail* or *bucket*. The study underlying this map involves a dense network of points where investigation was conducted in the eastern United States. It shows that both *pail* and *bucket* generally coexist in the same area but that *bucket* dominates in the southern part of the area and *pail* in the north. Studies such as this one, that focus on the designation of objects or concepts (**onomasiological** studies), are the most frequent. The black triangles in Figure 11.1 show the points where *pail* refers to a wooden container rather than a metal one. Studies that focus on the meaning of par-

that extends westward from Port-au-Prince and includes the main towns of Jacmel, Les Cayes, and Jérémie). Hyppolite's pioneering study was followed by two surveys that do meet the basic canons of dialect geography.

The first systematic investigation of geographical variation in HC to follow the methodology of linguistic geography was 'A Dialect Survey of Haitian Creole', a doctoral study undertaken between 1956 and 1964 by P. R. Orjala (1970), an American missionary who had resided in Haiti for about a dozen years. He collected data at 62 geographical points from 84 speakers, half of whom were monolingual in HC and half of whom were bilingual in French and HC. They ranged in age from twelve to seventy-five, with about two-thirds between the ages of twenty-one and forty, of whom the majority were men. The study focused on 238 variables; about half of these were represented on maps, but only 57 appear in the book. About 75% of the variables represented on maps are phonological in nature, for example, the alternation between the vowels *a* and *è* in such words as *pwav/pwèv* 'pepper', *swaf/swèf* 'thirst', or *bwat/bwèt* 'box'. Information about onomasiological variants is provided in the book but without precise localization on maps. Figure 11.3, adapted from Orjala's maps 35 and 52, depicts the diffusion of variants for 'garlic', French *l'ail*, and 'box', French *boîte*, into the northern and southern regions.[2] The black symbols represent local variants and the white ones the corresponding invading variants from the central area.

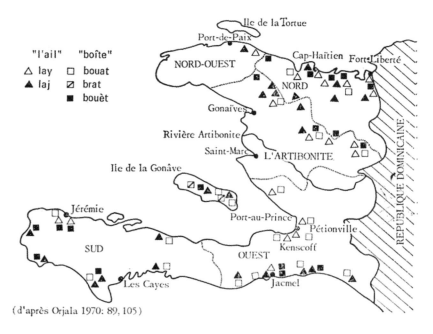

Figure 11.3. Variants of 'garlic' and 'box' as represented by Orjala (1970)

Orjala's dialect survey suggests that Hyppolite's division of Haiti into three primary dialect areas is somewhat reductionist. Accordingly, the author posits in addition six transitional zones: the Northwest, two areas of the central plateau (Hinche and St. Michel de l'Attalaye), Gonaïves, Ile de la Gonâve, and Jacmel. As will become clear when I present more detailed data on geographical variation, this proposed modification is not altogether satisfactory.

The second dialect geography survey, 'L'Atlas linguistique d'Haïti' (1998), subsequently referred to as ALH, was undertaken by the French linguist Dominique Fattier and is a remarkable piece of research in terms of its scope and its sophistication. It was launched in the early 1980s, with support from the then-francophone intergovernmental agency, Agence de coopération culturelle et technique (ACCT),[3] under the aegis of the prominent French creolist Robert Chaudenson. At that time, the latter was collaborating in a dialect survey of Réunion (Carayol et al. 1984–95). Fattier's survey was conducted in twenty localities (see Figure 11.4) and involved a questionnaire bearing on more than 2,200 variables, most of which are represented on individual maps. The collection of data was entrusted to two native speakers of HC, students at the Centre de Linguistique Appliquée of Port-au-Prince (CLA, now the Faculté de Linguistique Appliquée of the State University of Haiti), where Fattier taught from 1979 to 1985. The consultants selected, on average a dozen for each locality, were rural monolingual speakers of HC with at most two years of primary education and with as little contact with French as possible. All interviews were recorded and yielded a corpus of more than 200 hours. Fattier started without any preconceived theory of dialect differentiation in the country and she made no attempt to trace isoglosses: the distribution of variants across the twenty points selected was left to speak for itself. Compared to Orjala's study, Fattier sacrificed density of geographical coverage in favor of a broader coverage of variables and more reliable information for each locality. For example, no information is provided for many regions, including Ile de la Gonâve, which, given its relative isolation, might contain archaic forms. In addition, the essentially monolingual consultants, several at each point of investigation, were less likely to be influenced by French than the bilinguals among Orjala's population. Figure 11.4 shows the location of these twenty points.

The overall picture of geographical variation in HC that emerges from the Orjala and Fattier surveys is that there exist few clear major isoglosses delineating the three generally assumed dialect regions (Bollée and Nembach 2006). Except for the variant *pe* instead of *ape/ap* for the progressive verb marker that characterizes speakers of Standard HC (SHC), the variety used in the west, especially the Port-au-Prince area and in written texts, and the Northern HC particularities *i/y* instead of Central or SHC *li/l* for the

11.2 Geographical Variation

Table 11.1. Northern HC Lexical Variants

English	Northern variant	SHC
to go	ay/èy	ale/al
possessive pronoun	kin/ken + pronoun	pa + pronoun
1st person singular pronoun (1SG)	mwen/m/wen	mwen/m
3rd person singular pronoun (3SG)	i/y/li	li/l
with	ake	avèk, avè, ak
altar for Vodou	badji	ounfò
ankle	boulèt (pye)	je pye
ceremony for *loa* (Vodou spirit)	gonbo	sèvis lwa/djab/satan/mò
cooking pot	kanistè	mamit
gate	pòtal	baryè
kettle	kaderik	bonm
lay person serving as Catholic priest	lèktè	pè savann
peanut	amizman	pistach
sesame seed	jijiri	wowoli
throat	gòjèt	gangann
to hang, hung	pann, pandye	kwoke
to lock	kadnase, take	klete
twins	jimo	marasa

Table 11.2. Southern HC Lexical Variants

English	Southern variants	SHC
progressive verb marker	pe	ap
bat (animal)	chòtchòt	chòv/chat souri(t)
dwarf, short person	choukèt	kout, babèt
godmother	nennenn	marèn
nickname	non badnay	non jwèt
night	leswa	lanwit/lanüit
tarantula	krab (b)anbara	zarenyen krab
to give up (in guessing riddles)	bwè pwa	bwè + 3SG pronoun
to joke	badinen	jwe
winnowing tray	bichèt	laye/layo
wooden block (used as a stool and as a birthing aid)	choukèt	biyòt

Highly localized lexical variants

Some onomasiological variables are narrowly localized, although in many cases the general variant co-occurs with the regionally marked one. For example, Figure 11.5 shows that the variant *bichèt* is localized in the south but it co-occurs with the general variant *laye* in all localities. This occurrence of the two variants and the fact that *bichèt* is attested in the north at point 2 suggests that it may constitute an archaism that was progressively displaced by the corresponding SHC term.

Figure 11.5. Geographical distribution of *bichèt* in southern Haiti with co-occurrence with *laye*

Another Southern HC particularity is the word for 'wood block' *choukèt* (used for various functions, see Table 11.2), which occurs exclusively at all points. On the other hand, the local particularity for 'nickname' *non badnay* coexists with the general term *non jwèt* or some other variant at those points where it is used (points 16, 17, 18, 20; see Figure 11.6). The terms *badji* for 'Vodou temple' and *pòtal* for 'gate' are distinct Northern HC particularities, although at some points they co-exist with the central variant (Figure 11.7).

In some cases, localized variants do occur in other areas but with a different meaning. For example, the variant *nennenn* for 'godmother' is a marked southern variant, but in SHC it appears to alternate with *marèn* as the form for direct address: *Nennenn, nennnen! Sa ou pot pou mwen?* 'Godmother, godmother! What did you bring me?' The general variant for 'to hang', *kwoke*, is taboo in Northern HC because there it is the vulgar term for 'to have sex'.

11.2 Geographical Variation

Figure 11.6. Distribution of the SHC variants for 'nickname'

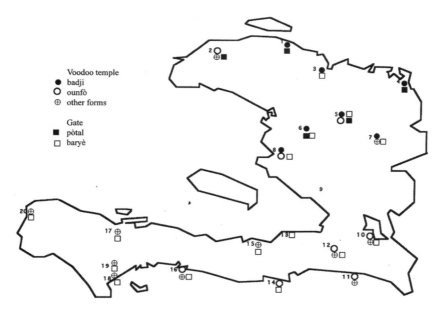

Figure 11.7. Distribution of the terms for 'Vodou temple' and 'gate'

An interesting northern particularity is the expression to describe rain when the sun is shining. The SHC expression is *dyab/zonbi ap bat/kale madanm ni* 'the devil/zombie is beating his wife'; the corresponding northern variants are more morbid: *yon moun k apray mouri* 'someone is dying', *yon madanm marye k ap mouri obyen on msye marye* 'a married woman who is dying or a married man', or *lapli moun mouri* 'rain of a dying person'.

Peripheral versus standard lexical variants

Many lexical variants involve minor phonological differences. The most frequent changes involve alternations between the vowels *a* and *è* (*bwat/bwèt*) and *e* and *i* (*cheve/chive*), and between the final consonants *j* and *y* (*zoranj/zorany*). For these variables, the variants are not localized in the north or south, but a general variant radiating from the center co-occurs with another that is found in the north and in the south. The co-occurrence of these peripheral particularities and SHC counterparts is illustrated by Table 11.3, which indicates that the local variants for 'garlic', *laj* and 'box', *bwèt* occur in both the north and the south together with the SHC variant.

Table 11.3. Peripheral and General Lexical Variants

English	Peripheral variant	General variant
box	bwèt	bwat
thirst	swèf	swaf
pepper	pwèv	pwav
finger	dwèt	dwat
cloth	twèl	twal
already	deja	dija
hair	chive	cheve/cheveu/cheuveu
to sow	simen	semen
need	bizwen	bezwen
to go down	disann	desann
orange	zorany	zoranj
cloud	nway/nüay	nwaj/nüaj
wise	say	saj
garlic	laj	lay
water	dyo	dlo
wasp	djèp	gèp
crest of chicken	krèp	krèt/krèk
belly-button	lonbrik	lonbrit
mourning period	even	nevèn, levèn
eye	zyeu, zye, jye, jeu	je

Figure 11.8. Distribution of variants for 'eye'

For most of the variants listed in Table 11.3, the general form is closer to the French etymon. The salient exceptions are the variants for 'eye', where the peripheral form *zyeu* corresponds to the plural form of the French etymon *les yeux* /lezjø/. In Figure 11.8, although the ALH lists *janm* for 'my eye' in the Cape Haitian region (point 2), most of the subjects in the study described in Section 11.4 provide *zyeu* as the isolation form.

Concerning the variants for 'garlic', *lay* and *laj*, that show an alternation between final *y* and *j*, and those for 'box', *bwat* and *bwèt*, that show an alternation between the vocalic nuclei *wa* and *wè*,[4] their distribution indicates that the general variants, *lay* and *bwat*, respectively, are replacing the peripheral variants. At most points, except in the extreme southwest, both variants co-exist (see Figure 11.3). It is a well-known dictum in dialect geography that every word has its own history. This is exemplified by the alternation between *y* and *j* in the terms for 'sour orange' and 'cloud' (see Figure 11.9). Note that retention of the older forms with final *y* is more frequent with the latter word than with the former.

328 *Variation in Haitian Creole*

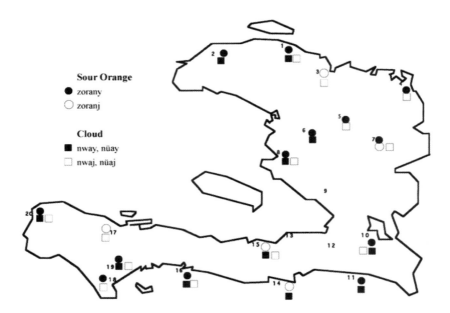

Figure 11.9. Distribution of the terms for 'cloud' and 'sour orange'

The general form *bokit* refers to all types of containers used to carry liquids. In the north, *syo* refers usually to a container to fetch water from a well. It shares a lexical field with *kin*, a container used to carry liquids, and *bokit*; the latter is used only for excretion, as a sort of chamber pot, as is demonstrated by the following statement from a consultant: *Gen moun pipi nan bokit … fè twalèt nan bokit* 'There are people who urinate in a *bokit* … they have bowel movements in a *bokit*'. Obviously, this container is not used to carry water! The ALH lists *syo* (with a variant *so*) as the most widespread variant, attested at all points except 9 and 12, where only *bokit* is indicated. No indication of the precise meaning is given, except for a contextual example at point 2 (*M pran syo a pou m rale dlo nan pi, rale dlo a monte* 'I take the *syo* to get water from the well, to bring up water'). This concurs with my own observations in the Cape Haitian area (point 3 of the ALH). I suspect that a semiologically oriented survey might show that the term *syo* has that restricted meaning wherever it occurs.

11.2.4 Phonological variation

Most phonological variants in Haiti involved the variable pronunciation of some words rather than the presence or absence of particular phonemic distinctions. With regard to the latter, there are a few words that in their southern variant contain an initial /h/: *hanch* vs. *ranch* 'hip' and *had* vs. *rad* 'clothing'. Northern HC is marked by three major phonological particularities. First, post-vocalic *r* occurs, both in final position, e.g., *figir* vs. *figi* 'face', *sèr* vs. *sè* 'sister', and within words, e.g., *pèrdi* vs. *pèdi* 'lost'. The *r* is weakly articulated (an approximant rather than a fricative), and it is often difficult to distinguish it from the lengthening of the preceding vowel. Second, *r* is replaced by *w* when it follows a labial consonant: *bwa* vs. *bra* 'arm', *apwè* vs. *aprè* 'after', *apwann* vs. *aprann* 'to learn'. However, Fattier lists the form *bwa* in two southern points (11, 20) in her map no. 276, which suggests that this feature might constitute an archaism. As was mentioned in Chapter 2, it is difficult to hear the difference between HC *w* and *r*. Also, the latter functions like a glide (semivowel) in the morphophonological alternations of the definite determiner *LA*: the consonantal allomorph expected after *r* does not occur in Northern HC: *mèr a bèl* 'the sea is beautiful' instead of **mèr la bèl*. In addition, as a result of hypercorrection resulting from their perception of this feature as incorrect, some speakers perform the reverse replacement in words containing *w*, e.g., *bwa* >*bra* 'wood', *bwat*>*brat* 'box'. Recall that in SHC *r* does not occur before rounded vowels. There it has been replaced by *w*: *wouj* 'red', *won* 'round'. In Northern HC, there appear to be cases where *r* does occur in this context, although the difference between these two phonemes is not readily perceptible in that environment. Third, a frequently occurring particularity, identified neither in the dialect surveys nor in the literature on HC, is the raising of the vowel *a* before the glide *y*, e.g., *travèy* vs. *travay* 'work', *bagèy* vs. *bagay* 'thing, stuff', and *èy*, a variant of the Northern HC particularity *ay* (SHC *ale*) 'to go'.

As was discussed in Section 2.3, the occurrence of front rounded vowels in the speech of monolingual speakers constitutes the thorniest issue in the phonology of HC. As will be pointed out in Section 11.4, these vowels are the most salient feature of the variety of HC spoken by bilinguals (**kreyòl swa**). Orjala (1970: 123) concurs with Valdman (1969)'s assumption that the vowels *u*, *eu*, *èu* might constitute survivals from Saint-Domingue Creole (see Section 2.5), but he ascribes them to what he terms Urban Creole. Fattier lists many occurrences of these vowels, but she points out that they are intermediate in pronunciation between full rounding and non-rounding. She notes these vowels with a superscript symbol of rounding above that of non-rounding, e.g., zye^{α} 'eye', an observation that concords with my own. On the other hand, the view that these vowels are part of the inventory of monolingual speakers and may constitute archaisms independent of the direct influence of *kreyòl swa* is supported by their occurrences in

330 *Variation in Haitian Creole*

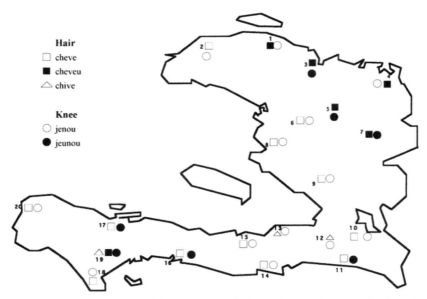

Figure 11.10. Occurrence of the front rounded vowel *eu* in the terms for 'knee' and 'hair'

peripheral locations. Figure 11.10, which maps the occurrence of terms for 'knee' and 'hair', shows the occurrence of variants containing *eu* in northern and southern locations. Recall that Fattier's subjects were all monolinguals, so that the presence of that vowel cannot be attributed wholly to *kreyòl swa*.

In Section 2.5, I cited data from the recent sociolinguistic study in the Cape Haitian area described in Section 11.3 that documents the presence of front rounded vowels. They are most frequent in the speech of urban schoolchildren but they also occur in the speech of their rural counterparts and older rural speakers. These observations are backed by data from the ALH. This survey also indicates the presence of these vowels in other peripheral regions of Haiti. Figure 11.11 shows the occurrence, in both the north and the south, of the vowel *u* in *lin/lun*. Note that the symbol u^i in the key represents a sound intermediate between /i/ and /y/. The distinction between front rounded vowels and their unrounded equivalents is unstable and there are frequent cases of hypercorrection. One such instance involves the word for 'wheat' being pronounced as *bleu* instead of *ble*. This hypercorrection masks the distinction between this word and that for 'blue', whose pronunciation in the *kreyòl swa* of bilingual speakers is *bleu*, but which most monolingual speakers produce as *ble*.

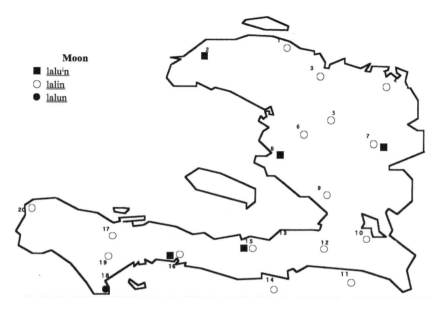

Figure 11.11. Distribution of the front rounded vowel *u* and the front rounded semivowel *ü*

11.3 Sociolinguistic Variation

A strength of the ALH, in addition to numerous lexical and grammatical variables investigated, is the large number of speakers consulted at each of the twenty areas throughout Haiti. In addition, they represented a fairly uniform social group: monolingual speakers with little schooling and little contact with French who had not traveled extensively within Haiti. From a geographical perspective these represent, as Fattier remarks (1998, Vol. II), 'ideal speakers', although not for the purposes of sociolinguistic inquiry. For the latter purpose, the investigator needs to analyze variations correlating with social variables, such as gender, age group, social status, and so forth. To my knowledge, no wide-scale study focusing on sociolinguistic variation has been published to date except my pilot study on the extension of the nasalization of the definite determiner *LA* (Valdman 1991; and see Section 3.4) and the study of the diffusion of SHC into the Cape Haitian region from which I will provide preliminary data in Section 11.3.2 below (Valdman 2008; Valdman *et al.* 2015).

11.3.1 Spread of nasalization in the definite determiner

I reproduce in this section the data from Section 3.4 that show that, in the speech of younger bilingual speakers from the Port-au-Prince region, by the mid-1980s the nasalization of the definite determiner *LA* had spread to a preceding non-nasal environment (Table 11.4).

Table 11.4. Nasalization in the Definite Determiner among Middle-class Port-au-Prince Speakers

Speaker			Post-vowel frequency	%	Post-consonant frequency	%	Total frequency	%
Juniors								
13	M	2+	13/21	61.9	49/52	94.2	62/73	84.9
14	F	2+	13/20	6.4	42/47	89.7	55/67	82.1
16	F	2+	23/31	74.2	28/42	66.17	5/73	69.9
18	M	1	21/43	48.8	39/47	83	60/90	66.7
3	F	2	18/60	30	39/60	65	57/120	47.5
1	M	1	27/105	25.7	69/103	67	96/208	46.1
4	F	1	8/57	14	6/57	10.5	14/114	12.3
2	M	2	2/105	2	13/105	12.4	15/120	7.1
			125/442	28.3	285/513	55.5	410/955	42.9
Seniors								
17	F	1	5/18	27.8	4/25	16.3	9/4	20.9
12	F	2	1/11	9.1	3/29	10.3	4/40	10
15	M	1	1/21	4.8	3/35	8.6	4/56*	7.1
8	M	1	0/44	0	3/44	6.8	3/88	3.4
7	F	2	1/78	1.3	4/79	5.1	5/158	3.2
5	F	2	1/91	1.1	1/91	1.1	2/182	1.1
6	M	2	0/91	0	1/91	1.1	1/182	.5
11	M	2	0/2	0	0/25	0	0/27	0
			9/357	2.5	19/419	4.5	28/776	3.6

The first three columns (under the heading 'Speaker') provide information about the speaker identification (1 to 18), the sex (male or female), and the estimated social-class level: 1 for lower-middle class, 2 for middle class, and 2+ for upper-middle class.

Interestingly, it does not appear that the speakers consulted modeled their production on that of the interviewers, as is illustrated by the following two exchanges in which the subject produces the nasalized equivalent of the variant occurring in the interviewer's question (I = interviewer; S3 = one of the junior subjects).

I: Ou pa konn fè vakans lòt **bò a**?
'You don't usually spend your vacation elsewhere (i.e., outside of Port-au-Prince)?'
S3: M fè yon vakans lòt **bò an**, sa m fè nan lanmè a.
'I once spent a vacation elsewhere, what I did, I went to the beach.'

I: **Lavi a** bèl lòt **bò a**.
'Life is nice elsewhere.'
S3: Ou pa ka konte sou **sinema a** pou di ke **lavi an** bèl.
'You can't depend on the movies to say that life is nice.'

It is very puzzling why younger urban bilingual Haitians would begin producing such forms as *dlo an* instead of *dlo a* and *chat lan* instead of *chat la*. Compared to their French cognate, many HC words have undergone nasal assimilation. Generally, any vowel occurring in the immediate vicinity of a nasal consonant is nasalized; compare, for example, French *canard* /kanar/ vs. HC *kanna*; Fr. *panier* /panje/ vs. HC *panyen*; Fr. *même* /mɛm/ vs. HC *menm*. For these words, all speakers of HC generally show a nasalized vowel, but other words are subject to variation. The bilingual speakers of the study tended to use a non-nasalized vowel where monolingual speakers evidence the corresponding nasalized vowel, for example, *chèn/chenn* 'chain', *abandone/abandonnen* 'to abandon', *demen/denmen* 'tomorrow', *lamizè/lanmizè* 'hardship', *telefòn/telefonn* 'telephone'. Superficially, it would appear that in the case of the definite determiner younger bilingual speakers are transposing a marked feature of monolingual speech to a different context. Perhaps this reinforcement of nasalization distinguishes them from members of the intermediate group of speakers with some knowledge of French who adopt the various Frenchified features that mark bilingual HC. In a random sampling of current young monolingual speakers in a rural district near Port-au-Prince, no evidence was found of this linguistic change in progress.

That this change is spreading was demonstrated to me in 2002, when, at a conference devoted to the use of creole in education in Port-au-Prince, sponsored by the Agence universitaire de la francophonie (AUF), I was asked to organize a workshop on sociolinguistic research. When I asked the participants what they wanted to discuss, they overwhelmingly responded that they wanted to discuss a feature of 'bad' HC that was spreading, precisely, the nasalization of *LA*. This feature, of which speakers were not generally aware twenty years prior, had reached the level of a **stereotype**, a linguistic variant of which speakers are highly conscious and which is the topic of public discussion.[5]

So far, no extensive empirical studies exist to determine whether this feature has spread to monolingual speakers in the central area or in peripheral areas. It does occur in the speech of the Cape Haitian area consultants of the study described in Section 11.4 below, but with very low frequency. One consultant, an adult male from Cape Haitian, showed a relatively high number of cases of diffusion of nasality in non-nasal contexts, but interestingly only after syllables containing the high vowels *i* and *ou*: *peyi an* 'the country', *isi an* 'here', *Vodou an* 'the Vodou', *gwoup lan* 'the group'. In this oral corpus, the only case of frequent nasalization is *chemiz lan* 'the shirt'. A tentative hypothesis, which requires empirical validation, is that nasalization first spread to the context of nasal consonant plus high vowel, e.g., *seremoni an* 'the ceremony', *jenou an* 'the knee', a case that is now obligatory in HC (see Section 3.4), and then to these two vowels outside of the context of a nasal consonant. This generalization is borne out by 'errors' in spelling, i.e., the use of nasal allomorphs of *LA* in non-nasal contexts, that crept into the written text of a speech by the prime minister of Haiti, Michèle Duvivier Pierre-Louis, dated April 9, 2009, and published in the April 10, 2009, free-access internet service Alterpresse: *jodi an* 'today', *Primati an* 'the office of the prime minister', *peyi an* 'the country', *avni an* 'the future', *Ayiti an* 'Haiti'. Vowels other than *i* also are affected: *rezo an* 'the network', *pwojè an* 'the project', *nan wotè li swete l lan* 'to the level that it [the government] wanted it'. This case of nasalization still remains variable; for example, of the two words that recur, there are only three cases of nasalization out of five for *jodi* and two cases out of twelve for *peyi*.

11.3.2 Social factors in the retention of local particularities

As indicated in Section 11.2 the variety of HC spoken in the north of Haiti, particularly in the region of Cape Haitian, the nation's second largest city, is marked by many particularities. In addition to the frequent localized particularities noted in Section 11.3.1, the most salient one is the possessive construction corresponding to the English possessive determiners. In the Northern HC (Capois) dialect, as opposed to SHC, the preposition *a*

11.3 Sociolinguistic Variation   339

Table 11.7. Retention of Capois Variants for (3SG), (POSS), (WITH), and (TO GO) Variables (percentage of retention)

	Total	Rural	Urban	Senior	Junior	Male	Female
(3SG)							
A	86	91**	83	84	87	87*	84
B	90	90	90	89	92	90	89
(POSS)							
A	85	93**	78	90**	79	84	85
B	91	90	93	87	92	89	92
(WITH)							
A	59	83**	48	74*	46	65	56
B	70	66	74	73	63	64	75*
(TO GO)							
A	49	57*	44	59**	44	55*	44
B	53	57	48	61**	37	59*	48

Table 11.8. Social Factors Affecting Capois (3SG) in Pair (A) and Individual (B) Interviews (percentage of retention)

	All speakers		Rural		Urban	
Factors	A	B	A	B	A	B
Overall	86	90	91	90	83	90
Age						
juniors	87	92	92	92	85	86
seniors	84	86	90	88	80	90
Sex						
males	87	90	92	90	84	90
females	84	89	89	89	82	90
Locality						
rural	91	90				
urban	83	90				

With regard to the social factors, in the case of paired interviews (A) the difference in retention of Capois features on the part of rural versus urban speakers is highly significant for all four variables but somewhat less so in the case of (TO GO). Age also proved to be a highly determining factor for (POSS) and (TO GO), less so for (WITH) but not at all for (3SG). Differences between female and male speakers were not generally significant.

Linguistic factors in the use of Capois (3SG)

Linguistic factors, for example, the phonological environment (whether a form is followed by a vowel, a consonant, or a pause), are often a greater determining factor in linguistic change than social ones. For example, the Capois variant *ake* [WITH] is used exclusively with the Capois variants of the (3SG) variable (see Table 11.9). Another notable characteristic is the low occurrence of *ake* before vowels, as shown in Table 11.9.

Table 11.9. Linguistic Factors Affecting Capois (WITH) in Individual Interviews

Factors	All speakers %	N	p	Rural %	N	p	Urban %	N	p
Following (3SG) variant			$\leq .001$			$\leq .01$			N/A
Local (*y / i*)	90	77		82	33		95	44	
Standard (*li / l*)	0	3		0	3		—	—	
Following segment			$\leq .001$			$\leq .001$			$\leq .001$
Consonant	68	153		70	91		65	62	
Vowel	16	25		11	18		40	7	
Glide	86	112		80	51		90	61	

Table 11.10. Construction Type and Capois (POSS) in Pair Interviews

	All speakers			Rural			Urban		
Factor	%	N	p	%	N	p	%	N	p
Possessive construction			≤ .001			≤ .001			≤ .001
NP + (a) + NP	62	69		74	19		58	50	
NP + (a) + PRON	88	504		95	231		82	273	

We have seen (in Section 11.3.2) that there are two types of possessive construction: (Noun + *a* + Noun) and (Noun + *a* + Pronoun). As shown in Table 11.10, the latter variant is significantly more frequent than the former. This means that the preposition is more likely to be dropped before a noun than before a pronoun.

An analysis of linguistic constraints (Table 11.11) raises the issue of the status of the variant *li*. A superficial view would classify *i* and *y* as Capois variants and *li* and *l* as their SHC counterparts. However, the fact that *li* appears to be used categorically in focalizing and contrastive constructions (Fattier 2003) suggests that it also functions as one of three Capois variants, as was observed by Gérard Etienne (1974). When used to focalize and emphasize (3SG) never occurs as *i* or *y* but always as *li* and occurs in highly restricted morphosyntactic contexts from which *i* and *y* generally are excluded, e.g., *Se li ki chèfayo*[9] 'He's the one who is their leader', *Kanaval la ki plis fete isi, rara li se Leyogàn* 'Carnival is celebrated more here; as for *rara*, it's in Léogâne', *Men, lòt la **li** i di denmen l ap vini* 'But, the other, HE said that he's coming tomorrow', *Nou **li** nou ka pale pi byen pase yo* 'Us, WE speak better than them', ***Li** menm li di 'kwoke sa pou **li**'* 'HIM, he said "hang that for him" '. Ditransitive verbs, in particular the verb *bay* 'to give', constitute another syntactic context where *li* is preponderant, although its use is not categorical, e.g., *Konnya, i bèy **li**,*[10] 'Now, he gives it to her', *yo moutren wen **y***[11] 'they showed it to me', *Alò pwason sa yo **li**, se yo k pi gwo.* 'So, as far as these fish are concerned, they're the ones that are the largest.' These syntactic contexts might evidence the retention of an earlier form of *li*. Indeed, in one of the more extensive Saint-Domingue Creole texts, an eighteenth-century play given in colonial Cape Haitian (Cap-Français), the playwright uses only *li*: *parole a li verser moi gage* 'his words give me a guarantee', *c'est li qui capitaine* 'he's the captain', *li metté li* 'she puts it' (M.-C. Hazaël-Massieux 2008: 131–48).[12] It appears, then, that in northern Haiti the original form *li* was replaced by *i/y* in certain contexts but retained in others. Thus, there are in Capois three allo-

342 *Variation in Haitian Creole*

morphs of (3SG): *li, i,* and *y*. Consequently, if this variant is counted as part of the Capois variant, the retention rate of the local (3SG) is even higher than indicated in Table 11.11.

There is nearly free variation between the variants *i* and *y* but the syllabic variant tends to occur more frequently in utterance-initial position and the glide after a vowel, e.g., *I bon* 'It's good', *Le maten y mare y* 'Mornings, he ties it'. The phrase *kwoke sa pou li* in the example above shows the near-categorical occurrence of *li* after the preposition *pou* 'for'. The Capois variant for (WITH), *ake*, is followed categorically by *y*. Also, urban speakers use *y* categorically with *avè*, one of the three SHC variants of that preposition (see Table 11.12).

Table 11.11. Linguistic Factors Affecting Capois (3SG) in Individual Interviews

	All speakers			Rural			Urban		
Linguistic factor	%	N	p	%	N	p	%	N	p
Syntactic context			≤.001			≤.001			≤.001
__ *gen* 'there is' (impersonal)	100	127		100	75		100	52	
Se X __ *ye*	85	60		76	17		88	43	
__V (subject)	90	1060		95	392		87	668	
V__ (object)	91	437		89	161		92	276	
Prep__	77	97		76	34		75	63	
*Se*__*ki*/focal./contrastive	5	87		11	18		3	69	
Preceding segment			≤.01			≤.01			≤.05
Consonant	78	189		83	71		75	118	
Vowel	87	1539		93	544		84	995	
Glide	86	118		82	60		90	58	
Following segment			≤.001			≤.001			≤.001
Consonant	92	1405		94	532		90	873	
Vowel	63	333		80	123		53	210	
Glide	85	104		82	33		86	71	

Table 11.12. Prepositions Affecting Capois (3SG) in Pair Interviews

Factor	All speakers % N p	Rural % N p	Urban % N p
Preposition	≤ .001	≤ .001	≤ .001
ake Capois)	100 35	100 15	100 20
avè (SHC)	73 11	0 3	100 8
pou	6 18	17 6	0 12
Other	88 33	100 10	83 23

11.3.3 Epilinguistic aspects of variation

Sociolinguistically oriented research on linguistic variation also needs to include an epilinguistic component, that is, inquiry about speaker attitudes toward and representations of the variants of linguistic variables. For example, in HC the variant *pe* of the progressive/definite future verb marker (vs. *ap* and *ape* used elsewhere) constitutes a particularity of the speech of speakers from the western part of the southern peninsula of Haiti that has reached the level of stereotype. It is the one feature that speakers from other areas of the country consider the most characteristic feature of that region. Interestingly, comments made by several younger speakers interviewed in the Les Cayes area, in which *pe* was declared to be a HC form and *ap* a corresponding French equivalent, suggest that, first, these variants have at the same time diatopic and diastratic status, and, second, these speakers view *pe* as less prestigious than *ap*. On the other hand, they may retain it precisely because it is emblematic of their regional identity.

Identification of variables

In the sociolinguistic study conducted on Capois described in Section 11.3.2 above, the variable mentioned most frequently by all types of speakers is intonation, expressed by comparing the expression of surprise as *o o* with rising intonation attributed to SHC speakers and the Capois *ò ò* with falling intonation. As one might expect, speakers from all social categories tended to mention the most typical stereotype, the possessive construction *kin/ken* + *a* + pronoun compared to SHC *pa* + pronoun, e.g., *se kinanm* vs. *se pa m* 'it's mine'. In some cases they contrasted the latter to their own *pou* 'for' + pronoun, *se pou m*. Speakers also consistently referred to (WITH), with *avè* selected as the most salient SHC variant as opposed to Capois *ake*. Another frequently mentioned variable that functions as a stereotype is the verb 'to hang', *pandye* or *pann* vs. SHC *kwoke*. The salience of this variable stems from the vulgar sense the term has in Capois, namely, 'to have sex'. The frequently mentioned lexical variables include (with the Capois variant mentioned first): 'bucket' *kin* vs. *bokit*, 'iron (for ironing)' *fè/fèr* vs. *kawo*, 'tin can for measuring rice' *gode* vs. *mamit*, 'okra' *kalalou* vs. *gonbo*, 'type of plantain' *bòzbòt* vs. *poban*. One schoolboy in Thibeau noted the difference in pronunciation of the verb 'to give' and that of (3SG): *Yo konn di m* **ba li** *manje a. Moun nan nò di m* **bèy** *manje*. 'They [SHC speakers] usually say, "I give it food." People from the north say, "I give it food."' He raised the vowel *a* before *èy* in the verb 'to give', whose form alternates between *ba* and *bay* in SHC but between *bay* and *bèy* in Capois. Because he usually would use the local variant *i/y* for (3SG), he appeared to view *li* as the typical SHC corresponding variant.

To determine the level of awareness of (POSS), interviewers elicited the use of the construction with parts of the body. In many cases, consultants produced the SHC variant even though in the rest of the guided conversation the Capois variant occurred preponderantly, as is the case for R, a rural senior speaker, who in the rest of the A interview used the Capois variant in 83% of the cases, somewhat below the 93% average of rural male speakers. In contrast, his conversation partner S alternated between the two variants.

Text 6

S: Bon, nou di. Sa se **zorèyannou** ... Nou rele sa **plim je nou** ... sa se anba **gojètannou**, se **kwannou**. Nou di sa se **dèyè kou**. Nou di sa se de **zepòlannou** ... sa se **men nou**, de **men nou**.
R: Mwen menm ... **figi mwen**, **je mwen**, **sousi**, **tèt mwen**, **ne mwen**, **vant mwen**, **pye mwen**.

S: O.K., we say. That's our ear ... We call that our eyelashes ... that's the lower part of our throat it's our neck. We say that's the nape of our neck. We say these are our two shoulders, ... that's our hand, these are our two hands. Myself ... my face, my eye, eyebrow, my head, my nose, my belly, my foot.

Attitudes toward SHC

About half of the younger speakers expressed valorizing attitudes toward SHC, although they did not generally denigrate their own speech. The higher status assigned to SHC rests on its origin in the capital of the country and its use in written texts, as expressed by an urban schoolboy: *Sa yo pale nan kapital la, se li ki ekri nan liv ... Sa Okap la se li nou pi renmen, men lè n ap ekri, kòm sa ekri nan liv, se sa Pòtoprens lan nou ekri*. 'That which they speak in the capital, it's the one that is written in books ... The one of Cape Haitian is the one we like more, but when we write since it's the one written in books, it's that of Port-au-Prince that we write.' Indeed, in the epilinguistic part of the B interview, when asked to take a dictation containing Capois variants, youngsters often exclaimed that they couldn't write these down; they had never seen them represented with the official IPN spelling. Another youngster stressed the fact that it is in the capital that books are produced and where the major industries are located.

Another feature younger speakers, especially urban ones, associated with SHC is its more formal nature, specifically, the use of fuller variants and absence of vowel deletion: *Moun Okap pale avèk yon kontraksyon. Moun Pòwoprens di konsa: 'm **genyen** yon maladi'. Moun Okap la di: 'M g on maladi'.*[13] 'Cape Haitian people speak with a contraction. Port-au-Prince people say it like this: "I have a sickness". People in Cape Haitian say: "I've got a sickness". In fact, the use of reduced forms resulting from apocope extends to all varieties of HC.

Another positive feature assigned to SHC is rapidity. Port-au-Prince speakers are said to *pale vit* or *pale brèf* 'to speak fast' versus *pale trennen* 'to speak by dragging syllables', a term that is used to compare the speech of remote rural areas in the north, as contrasted to the speech of Cape Haitian or a speaker's own locality.

As was the case for the older farmer quoted in Text 2 above, many consultants view using SHC as a way to *fè chèlbè*, 'put on airs, be pretentious and affected'. The following excerpt from an individual interview with an urban schoolgirl additionally stresses the fact that Capois is the authentic variety of HC.[14]

Text 7

Mwen lè m moute Pòwoprens, m wè moun yo pal on jan, tankou yo pa pale menm jan ansanm avèk moun Okap la. M pa konn si se pou **fè chèlbè** tou, men lang lan nou pale nan Okap la, se li menm ki vwè lang ayisyen an. Tankou *o o* sa pa pa m. Mwen m pa wè poukisa y ap **fè chèlbè**. Sa se gaspiye salivayo.	When I went up [down] to Port-au-Prince, I saw that people spoke in a manner, in such a way that they don't speak the same way as people in Cape Haitian. I don't know if it is also to be **pretentious**, but the language we speak in Cape Haitian, it's the one that's the real Haitian language. Like, *o o*, that's not mine, I don't see why they are acting **pretentiously**. That's wasting their saliva.

Another urban schoolgirl went so far as to characterize SHC as involving a contortion of the mouth, as compared to a natural way of speaking, as is the case with Capois speech: ... *ou pi alèz ak bouchòw. Ou pa nan kwochi bouch aprèy fè o o, pou ay fè makak* '... you're more relaxed with your mouth. You're not into twisting your mouth, in saying **o o**, to go acting like an ape.' Capois speakers who have visited or stayed in Port-au-Prince report that their speech is the subject of derision or amusement, with the use of the verb and expressions *chare* 'to tease, mimic', *fawouche* 'to mock, make fun', *pase nan risib* 'to mock', *ri* 'to laugh, make fun'. Often, the teasing is viewed as well intentioned, and Capois variants considered pleasant by SHC interlocutors, as reported by a rural speaker in Text 8.

Text 8

| ... moun Pòtopwens konn menm ap ri nou pase lè nou konn ale, yo di yo renmen tande pal a moun Okap | ... Port-au-Prince people often even make fun of us because when we used to go [there], they said that they liked to hear the speech of Cape Haitian people. |

An urban schoolboy even specifies Capois features that Port-au-Prince friends singled out for gentle mockery: (POSS), e.g., *afèranm* 'my things', (WITH), *wen* '1SG variant', and vowel raising as in *bagèy*.

Consultants who have resided in the capital for an extensive period of time report that they accommodated to the SHC, so much so that their own native speech had become, as they say, corrupted: *Pòwoprens gate m* 'Port au-Prince spoiled me [my speech]'. When they return home, they become the subject of derision by fellow Capois, and they attempt to recover their native speech: *lè m vini moun isi ap chare m epi m change pale a* 'when I came (back) here people made fun of me and I changed my speech'. As the speaker quoted in Text 2, who uses SHC variants for the primary Capois linguistic particularities, attests, recovering the native dialect proves difficult for them. That speaker was importing features from an external variety into his native dialect even as he affirmed linguistic loyalty toward that dialect.

The high level of retention of Capois variants by the speakers in the sample analyzed in the preceding section reflects the existence of a strong sentiment of loyalty toward the local dialect. This sentiment is corroborated by the statement in Text 7 made by a schoolgirl from the Cape Haitian subgroup. Although she uses the SHC variant of (WITH) *avèk* and the

SHC possessive pronoun construction *pa* + pronoun, she does produce the local variant *vwe* 'true' instead of SHC *vre* – Capois speakers variably replaced *r* by *w* in contexts after a labial consonant – and *Pòwoprens* 'Port-au-Prince' instead of SHC *Pòtoprens*. In Text 9, an older farmer stresses the link between his dialect and the transmission of his cultural heritage. Yet he uses the SHC possessive construction headed by *pa*, but, on the other hand, the Capois (POSS) N + *a* + PRO *granmoun an nou*. Note also the front rounded vowel in *kultive*.

Text 9

Enben, lang **pa granmoun an nou** te kultive, se **li** nou kultive e nou menm nou pa janm di ke yo pa byen pale. E nou menm ... kreyòl la **granmoun an nou** te moutre nou an, se **li** nou kultive.	Well, the language of our elders that [was] preserved, that's the one that we preserve and us, we never say that they [our elders] didn't speak well, And us ... the Creole that our elders taught us, that's the one we preserve.

11.3.4 Graphic representation of Capois particularities

The strong grassroots sentiment of loyalty toward Capois that these statements reflect has not yet been translated into its graphic representation. The scholar Max Manigat, a Cape Haitian native to whom we owe a partial lexical inventory of Capois (2006), deplores the fact that the region has been treated as a poor relative by authors. Indeed, I have been able to find only one text that attempts to represent Capois features, chapters of a forthcoming book that Jacques J. Garçon has published in issues of the weekly periodical *Haïti en Marche*, published in Miami.[15] Interestingly, this author's indication of Capois features does not fully reflect the data from our study. In the first excerpt from Garçon's texts (Text 10), the following Capois features are represented categorically: (WITH), (POSS), and the replacement of *r* by *w* after a labial consonant; the last feature has relatively low frequency in our interviews. Noteworthy, although variable, are the use of the variant *wen* of the 1st person singular pronoun and the alternation between the variants of (3SG): *i, y, l. Wen* is used generally as complement and after the introducer *se; i* and *l* alternate as subject and *y* as complement. Another variant found in this text is *ape* instead of *ap* for the progressive tense-aspect marker.

348 *Variation in Haitian Creole*

Text 10

M ape *pale* **ake** youn **zanmi an wen**, youn nonm save. **L** ap etidye tout tan; **I** pa janm bouke. Men **y ape** tripote **cheve a y**; konmsi pandanstan **l ape** mete kònèsans **nan kabòch a y**, **l ape** wete cheve yo **bwanch** pa **bwanch**; kounouye a, **i pwèt** fin chòv wi. **i** di **wen**, an **fwanse**: 'Un vieillard qui meurt est une bibliothèque qui brûle'.

I'm speaking with my friend, a scholar. He's studying all the time; he's never tired, but he keeps pulling at his hair as if by doing this he's putting knowledge into his noggin. He's pulling out his hairs one by one; at present he's really almost bald. He told me in French: 'An old man who dies is a library that burns down'.

A! **M** rank a **kò an m** pou **m** dirije koze a; pase lang pa pou **wen**. San pèdi tan, **i** ride **wen konpwann** : lè youn dife pase, boule denyè fèy papye, **lu**v [sic][16] elatriye; anseyman ki te make nan yo, pèdi. Menm nan, lè youn grandèt fini fè tan **y**, **i** mouri; **l** ale **ake** tout sa **i** te konnen, tout **eksperyans a y**.

Ah! I wrack my brains to get the sense of this saying; because that language is not mine. Without wasting time, he helps me understand: when a fire goes through, burning the last sheet of paper, books, etc., the lessons that were contained in them are lost. Similarly, when an ancestor's time is up, she dies, she goes with all that she knew, all of her experience.

Menm kote a, m vin chonje grann Mari te toujou ap rakonte **wen** labitid, koutim, bagay ki te konn pase denpi **i** menm te ti katkat. Onètman, fò m di si **wen** pa te nèglijan osnon **lamemwa an m** pa te faya, de san gwo **lu**v [sic] pa t ape ase pou kenbe koze sa yo …

On the same topic, I began to think that Grandmother Mary was always telling me habits, customs, things that used to take place ever since she was a small child. To tell the truth, I must say if I were not negligent or if my memory did not fail, two hundred big books would not be sufficient to store all these talks …

A comparison of Texts 10 and 11 reveals in the latter the categorical use of post-vocalic *r*, whereas that feature is absent in the former excerpt, notably in *pale, make,* and *pèdi*. Note, too the apparent hypercorrection in *luv* (*liv*).

Text 11

Lèr yon moùn mouri jenn, yo konn di **i** mouri **alaflèrdelaj**. Konsa yon ti demwazèl dizwit an mouri. Timoùn fin chape wi, **i** resi **bakaloreyay**; te pare

When a person dies young, they say that she dies in the full bloom of youth. It is in this way that a young girl eighteen years old died. That child was really

pou leve **tèt a fanmiy y an**. **Pèrsonn** nan katye ya[17] pa te tande **i** te malad ni fè aksidan; kidon yo di **i** mouri sibit. Gan tou ki di se **zonbi a** y yo **pwan** osnon yo manje y. Yon fanm yo rele Idalya parèt **ake** yon terin dite fèy **vèrvenn** vyòlèt, pote bay manman pitit la pou ride **y** anba sezisman. **i** menm tou, **i** mete po fig mi de bò **letanp a y fwiksyonnen ake swif a bèf**. Yon twèl mouye **ake** kafe **anmèr** soutni renmèd sa a kòm oun **konpwès** anwo **tèt a y**.

doing well; she passed her baccalaureate exam: she was ready to make her family proud of her. No one in the neighborhood had heard that she was ill nor that she had an accident; thus they said that she died suddenly. There are some who said that they turned her into a zombie or that they cast a spell on her. A woman that they called Idalya appeared with an earthen pan filled with a purple verbena tea, she brought the mother of that child to help her when she [the girl] had fainting spells, she also put banana skins on both her temples and rubbed them with beef tallow. A cloth soaked in plain coffee supported this remedy like a compress on her head.

A comparison of the frequencies of Capois variants in our study and Garçon's texts show that, whereas those of (3SG) and (POSS) are comparable, those of (WITH) and (TO GO) are far greater; indeed, these two variants are nearly categorical (see Table 11.13). Another interesting aspect of Garçon's textual representation of Capois is the preponderance of the variant *wen* of (1SG) as a complement (see Table 11.14). There is near-complementary distribution between the short form *m* as subject and *wen* as complement; the form *mwen* is rare. In our corpus, the form *wen* has a very low frequency of occurrence, and it is found more often in the speech of older rural speakers than in that of those belonging to other social categories.

Table 11.13. Comparison of the Frequency of Occurrence of the Four Primary Variables in the Sociolinguistic Study and the Garçon Text

Variable	Corpus A	Corpus B	Garçon texts
(3SG)	86%	90%	85%
(POSS)	85%	91%	88%
(WITH)	59%	70%	98%
(TO GO)	47%	44%	98%

350   *Variation in Haitian Creole*

Table 11.14. Distribution of (1SG) in the Garçon Text

	m	*wen*	*mwen*
Subject	43	2	4
Complement-predicate	0	17	1
Complement-preposition	0	3	0
Possessive	0	3	0
Other	0	0	1
Total	43	25	6

Another interesting aspect of Garçon's idealized representation of Capois consists in his use of peripheral variants that are viewed as reflecting rural speech; see Table 11.15 (compare also with Table 11.3). It seems that for him these peripheral lexical variants represent an older, more authentic form of his dialect and are more suitable for the evocation of memories of his grandmother's conversation than the corresponding current Capois variants, which are viewed as closer to Port-au-Prince speech.

That Garçon's innovative representation of his Capois dialect reflects an affirmation of linguistic loyalty as part of regional identity is supported by the following comments by the author in the course of an e-mail exchange in French (Text 12). Interestingly, he ascribes the linguistic particularities of Capois to West African languages spoken by the slaves imported into Saint-Domingue. In fact, in many respects, some of these particularities, e.g.,

Table 11.15. Rural/Peripheral Lexical Variants Used by Garçon

English	**Rural/peripheral**	**Central**
cloth	*twèl*	*twal*
chair	*chèy*	*chèz*
slavery	*esklavay*	*esklavaj*
fever	*lafyèb*	*lafyèv*
positive	*positib*	*positiv*
to follow	*sib*	*swiv*
hole	*tou*	*twou*
to show	*moutre*	*montre*
calm	*kal*	*kalm*
really	*reyèlteman*	*reyèlman*
to help	*ride*	*ede*

post-vocalic *r* and (POSS) are closer to French than corresponding features of SHC. These Capois particularities better reflect the earlier formative stages of HC documented in the early Saint-Domingue texts (see Chapter 4).

Text 12

| Notre créole nous différencie des Haïtiens du reste du pays. C'est un héritage de nos bisaïeux africains. S'il a vécu jusqu'à nos jours, il vivra certainement très longtemps encore … Cette variété non-standard restera la signature du Capois. | Our Creole differentiates us from Haitians in the rest of the country. It's a heritage from our African ancestors. If it has survived up to the present day, it will certainly still live for a long while … This non-standard variety will remain the hallmark of the Capois people. |

11.4 The Sociolinguistic Continuum

Certain sociolinguistic variants, which often overlap with geographical ones, appear to be ordered on a bipolar continuum that, erroneously, has been linked to the decreolization continuum. This continuum ranks varieties according to their similarity to the putative original target language, termed the **acrolect**, especially with regard to grammatical features. Varieties closer to the target are labeled **acrolectal**, those most distant **basilectal**, and those in between **mesolectal**. Because HC does not really undergo decreolization, these labels are not altogether suitable. It is indeed the case, however, that the variety of HC typically spoken by bilingual speakers, referred to as *kreyòl swa* (Fattier-Thomas 1984),[18] is closer to French. For example, it regularly features front rounded vowels in such words as *duri* for *diri* 'rice', *zeu* for *ze* 'egg', or *kèu* for *kè* 'heart', post-vocalic *r*, fewer nasal vowels in nasal environments, e.g., *kana* for *kanna* 'duck' or *goume* for *goumen* 'to fight', the use of the complementizer *ke/keu* in clausal complements and relative clauses (*Si ou wè ke sa pa vre* 'if you see that it is not true') and of the preposition *de/deu* in attributive constructions (*mwen fyè de pitit mwen yo* 'I'm proud of my children'), and extensive code switching to French and nonce loanwords from the language (Zéphir 1990). No generally recognized term is used to refer to the opposite pole of the sociolinguistic continuum, although the term *kreyòl rèk* is used to refer to the speech of rural, unschooled, monolingual masses. Many Haitians who write about language variation prefer the term *kreyòl pèp la* 'the Creole of the people' to the somewhat pejorative term *kreyòl rèk*.[19] For the sake of convenience, henceforth, I will refer to *kreyòl swa* as KS. As was pointed out in Section 4.5.1, the implementation of a systematic phonologically based orthography for HC was accompanied by the choice of the speech of monolingual speakers of the central region of Haiti, in particular, that around the capital Port-au-Prince. In effect, the written norm, from which some features have spread to the Cape Haitian area, as was documented in Section 11.3.2, and which has been labeled SHC in this book, coincides, in fact, with what is termed *kreyòl pèp la*.

In Text 13, I provide a sample of KS. It is an excerpt from a conversation I held in the early 1980s with Franketienne, the author of the first novel in HC: *Dezafi*. During the conversation, held in HC, he stressed that this signal work reflected the speech of the common folk. Raised in a rural milieu in the vicinity of Saint-Marc, part of the central region of Haiti, he felt he had absorbed, as he put it, '*la langue des mornes*' (the language of the hills/mountains'), i.e., rural speech. In addition, as director of a school in the lower-class area of Bel Air in Port-au-Prince, he routinely asked his pupils to collect and share with him interesting words and expressions they heard in their surroundings. The excerpt, which deals with that topic, illustrates the systematic use of front rounded vowels that characterizes KS and contains one code switch to French (underlined in the text).

Text 13

Ki kote m jwenn mo?… Pr**eu**myerman, m komanse jwenn mo yo andan m … Tout anfans mwen m fè l an pwovens, m fè l sou Bèlè [Bel Air], m fè l nan p**èu**p … Se nan rapò m te genyen depi lè m te piti avèk p**èu**p mwen, piske se nan p**èu**p la mwen leve … D**eu**zyèm bagay la kounye a. Mwen vin fè yon veritab konpilasyon. <u>Au moment où</u> m ap ekri *Dezafi*, non s**èu**lman – piske pa bliye m se yon dirèkt**èu** lekòl – non s**èu**lman mwen menm pèsònèlman m t ap pwonmennen tout kote ranmase mo, men m gen elèv mwen sistematikman, chak jou, gen ki te pòte di, kenz, ven mo ban mwen. M itilize yo pou sa, yo pot mo ban mwen.

Where do I find words? … First, I found words within myself … My entire childhood was spent in the provinces [outside of Port-au-Prince], I spent it in Bel Air. I spent it with the people … It's in the relationship that I had with my people ever since I was a child, since I was raised with the people … The second thing now. I went about making a veritable compilation. When I was writing *Dezafi*, not only – since don't forget that I am the principal of a school – not only I personally, I walked around everywhere collecting words, but I had my pupils systematically, each day, there were some who brought me ten, twenty words. I used them for that, they brought words to me.

Even more representative as a sample of KS is Text 14, an extract of a recorded radio interview from 1989 between a journalist and the former president of Haiti, Jean-Bertrand Aristide, prior to his accession to the presidency (Howe 1990). In addition to front rounded vowels and the post-

11.4 The Sociolinguistic Continuum

vocalic *r*, he produces the complementizer *keu/ke* and the preposition *deu/de* and a code switch to French (underlined in the text).

Text 14

Esk**eu** m gen <u>dè</u> bagay <u>keu</u> m r**eu**grèt? Wi! M r**eu**grèt … <u>keu</u> legliz la trayi … legliz la <u>jusqu'à ce point là.</u> M r**eu**grèt … <u>keu</u> tèt legliz la pa bay temwanyaj d**eu** kretyen vanyan menm jan anpil evèk dan <u>leu</u> tan te konn bay. M r**eu**grèt k**eu** nons apostolik la rive red**u**i monsenyè nou yo tankou timoun nan men l, nou menm, yon p**eù**p ki gen ero, ero ki genyen … <u>deu</u> pe**r**sonalite ve**r**tikal dwat, ki pa t kite blan trennen yo atè e <u>keu</u> jodi a, mil n**eù**f san kat**reu**ven n**èu**f, ou santi se blan k ap trennen ou atè, k ap mache sou ou … e se a kòb … li … mennen n anpil … nan nou. Se avèk … pouvwa … <u>keu</u> nou ba li k**eu** l mennen anpil nan nou. Sa se r**eu**grè sa yo, s**u**rtou, <u>keu</u> m genyen pask**eu** yo gen konsekans grav.	Are there things that I regret? Yes, I regret … that the Church betrayed … the Church up to that point. I regret … that the heads of the Church didn't give an example of brave Christians like many bishops used to give formerly. I regret that the apostolic nuncio was able to reduce our monsignors to the role of children, us, a people that has heroes … heroes who stood up straight, that didn't let foreigners drag them down and that today, in 1989, you feel that foreigners drag you down, that they are walking on you … and it's with money … he …leads a lot … of us. It's with … the power … that we gave him that he leads many of us. These are the regrets, especially, that I have because these have grave consequences.

What complicates the description of sociolinguistic variation in HC is that some of the features characteristic of KS appear in the speech of monolingual speakers in peripheral areas of Haiti, namely, beyond the central Port-au-Prince area. For example, the two morphosyntactic features illustrated above were found in the speech of a monolingual rural speaker who, however, had spent some time in Port-au-Prince (Valdman 2004). The Capois speaker who affirmed the superiority of his native dialect while using mostly SHC (cited in Text 2 above) also demonstrated that even illiterate monolingual speakers like him have access to features characteristic of KS: for example, the complementizer *ke*: *Si ou wè **ke** sa pa vre* 'If you see that's not true', *Isit miyò **ke** Pòtoprens* 'Here it's better than in Port-au-Prince' (instead of *Isit pi bon pase Pòtoprens*); the preposition *de*: *Mwen fyè **de** pitit mwen yo* 'I'm proud of my children'. He also dips into the French lexicon, since the line of demarcation between the two languages is very permeable: *avrèdi* (*à vrai dire*) 'really', *onivo de lakilti* (*au niveau de la culture*) 'at the level of agriculture', *ifo ke* (*il faut que*) *m respekte grandèt* 'I have to respect my elders'.

Summary

Compared to the wide range and quantity of descriptive and theoretical studies of HC, research on variation in the language is limited, particularly with regard to variation correlated with social, stylistic, and pragmatic factors. The Fattier linguistic atlas of Haiti (1998), which provides information on more than 2,000 variable words and grammatical structures, offers an excellent view of geographical variation. Nonetheless, this impressive study is somewhat dated, since the fieldwork underlying it was conducted in the early 1980s. What it shows is: first, the geographical varieties of HC are mutually intelligible; second, variation affects mostly the lexicon and a few morphological and phonological features but does not significantly affect syntax; third, rather than clear geolectal boundaries, geographical variation often involves the coexistence in the same areas of alternation between variants. Thus, the earlier division of Haiti into three clearly demarcated dialect zones turns out to be clearly reductionist.

The speech of northern Haiti, notably the area around Cape Haitian, shows many differences from that of monolingual speakers of the central area of the country where the capital, Port-au-Prince, is located, which forms the basis for the standardized variety of the language represented with the IPN spelling: SHC. The study of the effect of SHC on Northern HC (Capois) described in this chapter shows retention of local features, particularly 3SG and the possessive construction marked by the use of the preposition *a* (*mari a mwen*, realized as *maranm* vs. SHC *mari mwen/m*). The part of the study that elicits attitudes toward Northern HC and SHC reveals generally positive attitudes toward local variants, a reflection of the existence of a significant sense of local identity, as does the only attempt to represent Capois features in literature.

Sociolinguistic (diastratic) and diaphasic (style, register) variation remains seriously understudied. One small-scale pilot study (Valdman 1991) identified a phonological change in progress among younger bilingual speakers (the surprising generalization of the nasalization of the definite determiner *LA*) that currently has spread widely and reached the level of stereotype.

The most significant sociolinguistic variation is KS, the Frenchified variety of the language used by a minority of bilingual speakers, estimated at 10% of the population, who constitute the upper stratum of Haitian society. Its most salient features are the use of front rounded vowels and the function words *de* and *ke* (instead of zero) and frequent code switching. However, precisely because KS is associated with the economically, socially, and politically dominant group, it constitutes a target of imitation for the monolingual majority.

Notes

1. These are the variant forms for 'yes', and the line separating the varieties that use each is itself an isogloss.
2. This map, showing the data from two of Orjala's maps, is reproduced from Valdman (1978: 289).
3. This agency has now been replaced by the Organisation intergouvernementale de la Francophonie (OIF), which assumed the same functions as the ACCT.
4. There is another variant that shows the alternations between *w* and *r*, namely, *bwat* vs. *brat*. According to Orjala (1970), it occurs only on Ile de la Gonâve, although I have observed it as a sporadic variant elsewhere. For that particular alternation, see Section 11.2.4. Concerning the alternations *wa/wè*, the forms with the latter sequence reflect a pronunciation that was the norm in France until it was replaced by *wa* from the seventeenth century on.
5. What led me to conduct the pilot study on the spread of nasalization in the definite determiner was a random observation in 1982 at a summer institute for teachers in bilingual school programs in the USA. In a class where non-native speakers were taught HC, the bilingual, upper-middle-class Haitian instructor pronounced *chat la* 'the cat' as *chat lan*. A student pointed out that she had not pronounced it as it was written in the book, namely, *chat la*. The instructor answered that she had pronounced it that way and repeated the form with the nasal vowel: *chat lan*. I noted that two other bilingual instructors were also nasalizing *LA* in non-nasal contexts without being aware of it.
6. The original group of thirty urban juniors we were able to recruit were not fully comparable to their rural counterparts: they tended to be one to three years older and had two to three years of additional schooling; the rural youngsters were completing their sixth year of elementary schooling. In 2008, we then recruited a second group of urban juniors comparable in age and years of schooling (specifically, six years of elementary school) to rural teenagers.
7. Individual interviews with this group of ten younger urban youngsters were conducted by the Port-au-Prince area Haitian who had conducted similar interviews with Thibeau youngsters. Pair interviews with this group were conducted by one of the Capois teachers who had interviewed urban adults in 2007.
8. Ironically, this speaker, who resided in Port-au-Prince for a dozen years, evidences SHC variants for 'with' (*avè*), the possessive pronoun (*pa m*), some of the POSS, and the unraised vowel in *bagay* (instead of Capois *bagèy*). Capois variants are shown in boldface and SHC in boldface italic.
9. The actually occurring normal conversational Capois style combinations of (noun + *a* + personal pronoun), unlike their SHC counterparts, are represented as single sequences, for example, Capois *maranm* vs. SHC *mari m(wen)*. Because of the effect of the various morphophonemic processes discussed, one would have to represent truncated or modified versions of the noun with artificial word boundaries, for example, *maranm* > *mar an m* (*mari a m(wen)*, *dwanm* > *dw a m* (*do a mwen*).

10. Here, it is the Capois variant with vowel raising before *y* that is used.
11. Note the local variant *wen* for the 1st person singular pronoun.
12. This play, *Jeannot et Thérèse*, labeled '*Parodie nègre du Devin de village*', written by Clément, has survived in two versions, of 1758 and 1783. As M.-C. Hazaël-Massieux (2008) indicates, this musical comedy is more probably directly inspired by an earlier northern French dialect adaptation of the Jean-Jacques Rousseau original play of 1752, namely, *Les Amours de Bastien et Bastienne* (1753) by Mme Favart and Harny de Guerville (Darlow 1999); see Chapter 4 for more detail.
13. The verb 'to have', derived from the French verb *gagner*, occurs in a long verb *genyen* and in a short form *gen*. Generally, in all varieties of HC, the final vowel of the short verb is deleted before the indefinite determiner (*y*)*on*. Apocope occurred frequently in our corpus, in nearly half of the cases.
14. It is interesting to note that this speaker uses the following SHC variants *avèk* instead of *ak*, *pa m* instead of *kinanm* but Capois *salivayo*.
15. *Haiti en Marche* contains material in French, except for one page in HC devoted to linguistic and literary matters.
16. *Luv* is a hypercorrection for *liv* 'book'.
17. Note the representation of the intervocalic glide [j] in *katye a > katye ya*.
18. The term *swa* 'silk, silky' usually refers to the fine hair typical of individuals of Caucasian ethnicity: *cheve swa* 'smooth, silky hair'.
19. The adjective *rèk/hèk* is highly polysemous; depending on the lexical context it means 'almost ripe, too far gone, older than he seems, experienced, well' (Valdman *et al.* 2007).

12 Language Planning and Language Choice in Education

12.1 Introduction

Shortly after the devastating January 12, 2010 earthquake, more than fifty organizations, representing grassroots civil society in Haiti, met several times in Port-au-Prince to develop their political, economic, and social priorities, and to make their voices heard. A declaration at the first meeting on February 13 read in part:

> We have decided to launch a national and international campaign to bring forth another vision of how to redevelop this country, a vision based on people-to-people solidarity to develop the opportunity now facing this country to raise up another Haiti. We want to build a social force which can establish a reconstruction plan where the fundamental problems of the people take first priority. These include: housing, environment, food, **education, literacy** [*emphasis mine*], work, and health for all; a plan to wipe out exploitation, poverty, and social and economic inequality; and a plan to construct a society which is based on social justice.

Central to the long-term reconstruction of Haiti, which has proceeded very slowly since January 12, 2010, is the formation of human capital, an endeavor in which basic education for children and adult literacy play a crucial role. Accordingly, this chapter on language planning and language choice in education will focus on these two basic functions for which the government of Haiti must assume primary responsibility. But before I deal with how and to what extent the Haitian government has been involved in basic education and adult literacy, in Section 12.2 I will first discuss two aspects of language planning: status planning and corpus planning. Section 12.3 will focus on linguistic ecology, specifically, the access of Haiti's two languages to different parts of the population. Section 12.4 will review attitudes toward the two languages. Section 12.5 will deal with initiatives by the Haitian government and non-governmental organizations (NGOs) to extend literacy and promote the acquisition of language skills in the educational system.

12.2 Language Planning in Haiti

Decisions about the role that language plays in a state, region, locality, etc. fall into two categories: status planning, on the one hand, and corpus planning, on the other. Status planning deals with defining and modifying the **status** of a language, and corpus planning with its **corpus**, that is, increasing its domains of use and equipping it with the means of satisfactorily covering these domains. Status planning refers to decisions about the functions that will be assigned to the various languages or language varieties used in a given community and the linguistic rights of citizens. For example, which language or languages will be used in drafting and disseminating laws, or which language will be used in judicial proceedings. Once specific functions are assigned to a given language, it must be equipped with the means of carrying them out: endowed with a systematic written representation, a relatively invariant norm, and provided with sufficient lexical means, i.e., a vocabulary, adequate for the functions and domains for which it is employed (administration, education, technology, etc.).

12.2.1 Status planning

At the dawn of Haitian independence, although the number of speakers of French had been reduced by the flight of Europeans or their eventual elimination, the Act of Independence was drafted in French, a language that still monopolizes the official domain.[1] This was so despite the fact that some of the military leaders, in particular Jean-Jacques Dessalines, who became the country's first absolute ruler, were primarily speakers of HC. It was not until 1918, during the American occupation, that the country's constitution, for the drafting of which Franklin D. Roosevelt, then Secretary of the Navy, presumably claimed credit, contained an article referring to the official language (see Section 1.2.2):

> *Le français est la langue officielle. Son emploi est obligatoire en matière administrative et judiciaire.* (Article 24)
>
> French is the official language. Its use is mandatory in administrative and judicial matters.

The exclusive official role of French was maintained in the numerous constitutions that followed: in 1932, 1946, 1950, and 1956. But in 1964, during the presidency of François 'Papa Doc' Duvalier, a clause was added that, for the first time, mentioned HC:

> *Le français est la langue officielle. Son emploi est obligatoire dans les services publics. Néanmoins, la loi détermine les cas et conditions dans lesquels l'usage du créole est permis et même recommandé pour la sauvegarde des intérêts matériels et moraux des citoyens qui ne connaissent pas suffisamment la langue française.* (Article 35)

> French is the official language. Its use is mandatory in public services. Nevertheless, the law determines the cases and conditions in which Creole is permitted and even recommended for the preservation of the moral and material interests of citizens who do not know the French language sufficiently well.

It is not clear to what extent during Papa Doc's rule HC was used in judicial proceedings and in informal administrative matters. There is no evidence that it was ever used in legal or official documents.

Under the reign of Papa Doc's son Jean-Claude Duvalier ('Baby Doc'), the 1983 constitution signaled a major shift in language policy: HC acceded to the status of co-national language equal to French but was still not granted official status:

> *Les langues nationales sont le français et le créole. Le français tient lieu de langue officielle de la république d'Haïti.* (Article 62)

> The national languages are French and Creole. French serves as official language of the Republic of Haiti.

In 1987, a year after the overthrow of the Duvalier regime, a new constitution was promulgated in which HC was finally granted official status. That clause appeared in one of the first articles of the constitution and was preceded by one that stressed it was HC, not French, that all citizens of Haiti shared. Implicitly, it established HC as the national language of the country:

> *Tous les Haïtiens sont unis par une langue commune: le créole.* (Article 5.1)

> All Haitians are united by a common language: Creole.

> *Le créole et le français sont les langues officielles de la République.* (Article 5.2)

> Creole and French are the official languages of the Republic.

Another article stipulated that all of the country's official acts and decrees should be made public in both languages:

> *Obligation est faite à l'État de donner publicité par voie de presse parlée, écrite et télévisée, en langues créole et française aux lois, arrêtés, décrets, accords internationaux, traités, conventions, à tout ce qui touche la vie nationale* ... (Article 40)
>
> The State is required to publish by means of oral, written, and televised press in the Creole and French languages all laws, rulings, decrees, international agreements, treaties, accords, everything that impacts on national life ...

If this article were to be implemented, all official documents, administrative decisions, and announcements would be available in both languages which the constitution recognized as official. This is far from being the case nearly thirty years after the promulgation of the 1987 constitution.

Since Haiti's independence, the role of the Haitian government in language planning has remained practically non-existent. In Section 4.4, I pointed out that the government did officialize the IPN spelling (devised primarily by French experts), although for more than thirty years its agencies for adult literacy had used the one proposed by Haitians, the Faublas-Pressoir orthography. In addition, the standard norm of the language, based on the speech of monolingual speakers of the Port-au-Prince regions rather than that of the dominant bilingual élite, was developed by religious groups not affiliated with the government (see Section 4.5).

Corpus planning

It is significant that no official HC version of the 1987 constitution was commissioned, as required by Article 40. An unofficial one was prepared later by Paul and Yves Dejean.[2] That version of Article 5 differs from the original French phrasing of the first clause by stressing the solidarity of the nation's population affected by HC: The only language that binds (*simante*) all Haitians together is Creole:

> *Sèl lang ki simante tout Ayisyen nèt ansanm, se kreyòl la.*

In spite of the intent of Article 40, the presence of HC in the administrative and political spheres, as well as in education and the media, pales before that of French, as shown in Table 12.1 (Coriolan 2010). The vernacular's presence is limited to the religious sphere where it is much more dominant than indicated by the table because Coriolan's survey no doubt did not take into account HC's exclusive role in Vodou. In the media, HC has a dominant place on the numerous radio stations, many of which broadcast only in HC.

Table 12.1. Use of Languages in Various Linguistic Domains

	French	Creole	English
Official status /12	6	6	0
Use in administration /20	17.5	2.5	0
Official texts /4	4	0	0
Administrative texts /4	3.5	0.5	0
Justice /4	4	0	0
Local administration /4	4	0	0
Religion /4	2	2	0
Language of education /30	25.5	2.5	2
Primary /10	7	2	1
Secondary /10	9	0.5	0.5
Post-secondary /10	9.5	0	0.5
Media /25	17	4.2	2.7
Press /5	3.8	0.2	0
Radio /5	1.7	2.5	0.7
Television /5	2	1	2
Cinema /5	5	0	0
Publication /5	4.5	0.5	0
Potential for economic and social advancement /20	18	0	2
Total STATUS /107	84	15.2	6.7

The 1987 constitution provided for the creation of an institution, patterned after the Académie française, that would take a leading role in the development of HC: elaboration of a standard norm, terminological innovation, etc.:

> *Une Académie haïtienne est instituée en vue de fixer la langue créole et de permettre son développement scientifique et harmonieux.* (Article 213)
>
> A Creole Academy is instituted with a view to standardizing the Creole language and to allow for its scientific and harmonious development.

In October 2011, under the auspices of the State University of Haiti, a colloquium entitled *Academi kreyòl ayisyen: Ki avantaj? Ki pwoblèm? Ki defi? Ki avni?* 'The Haitian Creole Academy: What advantages? What problems? What challenges? What future?' was organized to discuss the creation of such an academy. The widely representative committee, formed to organize the colloquium and to pursue the various steps necessary for formal approval of the Academy by the government, proposed the following ambitious goals[3] (Alterpresse 2013):

362 *Language Planning and Language Choice in Education*

> *... faire le nécessaire pour encourager la production dans la langue créole; encourager les expériences populaires dans la découverte, la création, la production tant orale qu'écrite en créole; travailler et veiller à des relations équilibrées dans l'utilisation des langues par les institutions dans la société; travailler pour la publication des documents officiels en créole par les institutions étatiques ... Cette institution a la mission également de proposer des canevas d'utilisation de la langue créole en communication publique, d'encourager des travaux de développement d'outils linguistiques tels grammaires, dictionnaires, lexiques en créole dans tous les domaines ... L'administration publique, la justice, l'Etat en général et la science doivent parler créole.*

> ... to do what is necessary to encourage creations in the Creole language; to encourage experiments by the people in discovery, creativity, production in Creole, oral as well as written; to work toward and to insure balanced relations in the use of the languages [French and Creole] by societal institutions; to strive for the publication of official documents in Creole by state institutions ... This institution also has as its mission to propose models of use of the Creole language in public communication, to encourage the development of linguistic tools in Creole such as grammars, dictionaries, lexicons in all domains ... Public administration, the judicial system, the State in general and science must speak Creole.

The committee formulated a proposal which served as the basis of a law establishing the Academy. The law was approved by both chambers of the Haitian Parliament in April 2013. However, when it was presented for approval to the country's president, Michel Martelly, he objected on the grounds that no French translation of the law had been provided, which constituted a violation of Article 40 of the 1987 Constitution, according to which all of the country's official documents were to be drafted in both French and HC. Finally, he yielded and the decree establishing the Academy was promulgated a year later.

12.3 The Linguistic Ecology of Haiti

Any language-planning initiative requires taking into account the linguistic environment of the segment of the population that is its putative beneficiary, in the case of Haiti, the extent to which monolingual speakers are exposed to the socially dominant language – French. It also requires information about the attitude of these speakers toward that language and their own speech. In this section, I discuss access to French on the part of the monolingual creolophone majority.

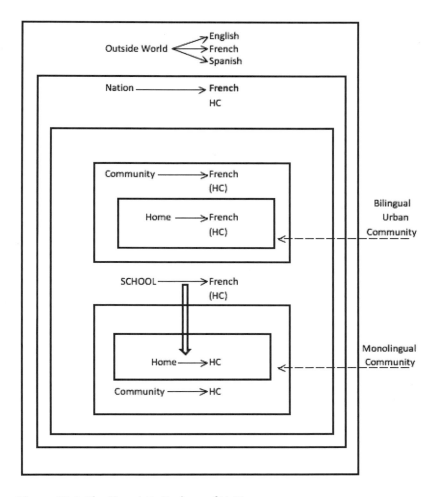

Figure 12.1. The Linguistic Ecology of Haiti

Haiti may be characterized as a nation composed of two linguistic communities: a small urban bilingual élite, on the one hand, and, on the other hand, the monolingual rural population and urban lumpenproletariat, which is rapidly increasing as a proportion of the population due to accelerating urbanization.[4] As shown in Figure 12.1, the élite use French and HC at home. Parents generally interact with each other in HC but address their children in French to insure that they master the language that guarantees them social dominance. Outside of the home their choice of language will depend on a variety of factors: the situational context, the social status of interlocutors, the purpose of the linguistic interaction, etc. As pointed out in Section 1.2.3, the Haitian urban élite bilingual speakers are diglossic. For them, French serves as the formal register and HC as the informal one. On the other hand, for the monolingual community HC necessarily serves all communicative needs. Yet French remains the primary language of instruction even in most primary schools. Although the vast majority of Haitians are monolingual speakers of HC, a language that has been declared as a co-official language with French, the latter language still maintains social dominance.

Y. Joseph (1980) interviewed fifty schoolchildren in Port-de-Paix, in northwest Haiti, to determine their degree of exposure to French. As can be observed in Table 12.2, schools and radio broadcasts were the primary sources of French input for these children. If anything, the number of radio stations that broadcast today exclusively in HC has increased. Whereas, predictably, teachers and clergymen are considered the only persons who are likely to speak French, doctors are perceived as unlikely to use this language. Clearly, in the medical sphere, communication between health workers and patients is essential, and it can only be successful in the language shared by both parties of the interaction.

Table 12.2. Exposure to French on the Part of Haitian Primary School Students

In what situation do you hear French spoken?				
	Never	Sometimes	Often	Always
At the market	50			
Your home	45	5		
In the streets	39	11		
At church	26	24		
On the radio	10	26	17	
School		38	5	
Who speaks French?				
Teachers		26	18	6
Nuns		26	17	7
Priests	3	34	8	5
Foreigners (*blan*)	11	29	8	2
Ministers	23	12		
People from Port-au-Prince	35	15		
Your friends	44	6		
Doctors	38			

Table 12.3. Evaluation of Languages used in the Classroom

	HC	French	Both languages
Student evaluation	21.7%	26.1%	52.2%
Teacher evaluation	69.2%	7.7%	23.1%

In a more recent study, P. M. Laguerre (2010) asked students and teachers in sixteen rural primary schools to evaluate the use of HC and French in the classroom. Interestingly, Table 12.3 shows that students tend to overestimate the use of French. Assuming that the teachers' evaluations are more reliable, and on the basis of Yves Joseph's study, the obvious conclusion to be drawn is that, at least in rural Haiti, even schools do not provide adequate access to the socially dominant language.

As the results of a questionnaire eliciting urban teachers' self-reported use of language show (Table 12.4), for bilingual speakers, HC remains the language of everyday communicative interactions (Jean-François 2006). There are few situations where the use of HC, alone or with French, is excluded, although French dominates in formal situations. Interestingly, courtship is viewed as a formal domain where French is preferred.

In the three decades since Yves Joseph's (1980) study, there has been an increase in the use of HC by radio stations, which means that exposure to French has decreased considerably. In addition, the use of HC has increased in political debates and all domains where French was predominant at the earlier time. Although, except for the monthly *Bon Nouvèl* (see Section 4.5.1), there do not exist in Haiti any periodicals that exclusively offer texts in HC. However, the language is extensively present in internet and social media communication. An interesting extension of the use of HC in the media consists of written comments made about individual articles published by the daily newspaper *Le Matin*. For example, in response to a May 5, 2012, editorial by a certain Daly Valet entitled 'Souillures' (stains), which discussed allegations of bribes paid to President Michel Martelly and his opponent in the presidential election, Mirlande Manigat, by a politician from the Dominican Republic, a reader commented (spelling errors are indicated in boldface, followed by the correct spelling within brackets):

> *Mwen pa dako ak tèks sa. Ou pa ankète, ou pa genyen okenn dosye, ou pa genyen okenn pwèv, epi **wap**[w ap] manke **estitisyon** [enstitisyon] ak lidè peyi dayiti dega pou yon jounalis dominikani*

Table 12.4. Language Preference of Urban Teachers

Which languages do you prefer in the following situations?	Always HC	Often HC	HC/ French	French often	French always
	%	%	%	%	%
Family	35.2	20	39.2	4.8	0.8
Neighborhood	33.6	35.2	26.4	3.9	0.9
Courting a girl	1.6	2.4	35.2	27.2	19.2
University conversation	1.6	22.4	28.8	31.2	16
Lectures on literature	1.6	1.6	34.4	25.6	24.8
Mass	11.2	9.6	56.8	10.4	5.6
Sermon	5.6	13.6	49.6	15.2	10.4
Official evaluation	0.8	1.6	21.6	28.8	42.4
Job interview	0.8	2.4	20	29.6	41.6
Court	2.4	0.8	34.4	20	29.6

ki bezwen PRD genyen eleksyon? ... **Tampr***i* [*tanpri*] *Daly respekte règ jwèt jounalis, respekte* **reg** [*règ*] **jwet** [*jwèt*] *laprès. Respekte moun.*

I don't agree with this text. You haven't investigated, you don't have any files, you don't have any proof, and you don't show respect toward the institutions and the leaders of the country of Haiti in favor of a journalist of the Dominican Republic who needs to have the PRD [political party of the Dominican Republic] win the election ... Please, Daly respect the rules of the role of journalists, respect the role of the press. Show respect for people.

12.4 Attitudes toward French and HC

12.4.1 Attitudes toward French and HC on the part of monolingual speakers

For a large proportion of the Haitian population, French – despite its socially dominant status – plays no major role in daily life. Monolingual creolophones do not need it to solve day-to-day problems or to deal with the immediate social environment. According to Bentolila and Ganni (1981), French is viewed by monolingual speakers primarily as a means of social and economic advancement. For Lundahl (1979), it serves as a filtering device that the élite uses to exclude the masses from the political process and to deny them economic opportunities. Bilingual speakers' use of French as a social barrier was perceived by a peasant I interviewed in the Les Cayes region in 1982:

Text 1

> *Gen moun ki pale franse pa ogèy, l ap eseye ba yon lòt moun baryè ... Lè yon enjenyè pale franse avè ou, se pou dekonsidere ou ...*

> There are people who speak French to show off, they try to set up barriers between themselves and other people ... When an agricultural agent speaks French with you, it's to put you down ...

Another rural speaker expressed deep alienation toward the socially dominant language:

Text 2

> *Fransè se pa lang pa n, se lang achte ... Ti moun fèt pou konn kreyòl paske se lang ni, li pa achte l.*

> French is not our language, it's a 'bought' language ... A child is born to know Creole because it's her language, she didn't 'buy' it.

The speaker was making an analogy with *loas*, Vodou spirits. Like *loas* that are bought from Vodou priests – and are more capricious and demand more expensive offerings – French is viewed as alien and not inherited as part of one's lineage. For rural Haitians, HC is the only authentic language. During the interview, the speaker continued to grant that French is necessary to acquire knowledge but he viewed its adoption as the written language of the newly established country rather than HC, after the overthrow of French rule, as a key strategic error on the part of the nation's founders:

Text 3

Aprann franse itil, Pou devlope lespri ou plis epi sitou paske ann Ayiti apre lendependans se franse ki gen premye plas ... Nous poko pran endepandans nou paske apre endepandans nou se kreyòl pou nou ta li ekri a. Nous pa dwe sèvi ak lang blan.

To learn French is useful. To further develop your mind and especially because in Haiti after independence, it's French that had the first place ... We haven't yet gained our independence because after our independence, it's Creole that we should have written and read. We shouldn't have used the Whites' [foreigners'] language.

Table 12.5 displays the results of a survey I conducted in 1982 among parents of children enrolled in rural primary schools in the Les Cayes region. Clearly, for these speakers their mother tongue is their national language, sufficient for all of their communicative needs, including learning artisans' technical skills. It is only in dealing with the outside world – obtaining employment and dealing with officialdom – that French becomes a useful tool, although HC is also viewed as adequate for these domains of language use. Interestingly, knowledge of English is viewed as nearly as useful for children to learn as French, no doubt as an exit strategy for securing a better life in what the individuals consulted referred to as *Miyami*, the USA.

Table 12.5. Attitudes toward Languages and Perceptions of Their Usefulness by Monolingual Creolophones

	French	HC	FR/HC	English	Spanish
What is the language of Haiti?	1	23			
In which language can you say anything you wish?	0	28			
Which language is the most beautiful?	8	16	2	2	1
Which language is best to learn a trade or to deal with technical matters?	9	25			
Which language is most useful for children?	7	8	10	9	1
Which language is most useful in the following situations?					
To get a job	20	17			
In an administrative office	18	11			
To make a speech	17	12			
To interact with educated people	16	9			

My rural consultants seemed keenly aware of the fact that schools remain the sole means of acquiring French (see Table 12.6). They also realize that attaining a useful level of competence in this language requires an extensive period of study. When the Réforme Bernard that introduced HC as instructional vehicle was being launched (see Section 12.5.2 below), rural parents did not oppose this innovation, provided that it would not lessen the possibility for their children to acquire French.

Table 12.6. French and Schooling

Where does one learn French?					
At school	23	Elsewhere	1		
Why is it important to learn French?					
Most widely spoken language	12	To get work	10	Social standing	5
Why do some schoolchildren not acquire fluency in French?					
Insufficient schooling	17	Lack of intelligence	6	Insufficient practice	4
Objectives of schooling					
To learn French	14	To learn good health habits	13		
To acquire literacy skills	14	Others	10		
Should HC be used in the schools?					
Yes 17 No 6 No response 4					

A study conducted among students enrolled in courses in French at the French Institute of Haiti, (Damoiseau and Guimbretière 1994), also revealed the ambivalence of Haitians toward French. Nevertheless, these students did recognize the primary role of French in education and in administrative services. As was the case with some of the teachers interviewed by Jean-François (2006), many of them felt that French facilitates communication at the international level. However, Haitians' external contacts involve mainly the use of Spanish or English. More than two million people of Haitian origin live in the neighboring (Spanish-speaking) Dominican Republic, and many Haitians attend universities in that country. In addition to the massive presence of Cuban doctors at home, many Haitians are enrolled in Cuban medical schools, as well as at universities in Mexico and Venezuela. The migration of Haitians to the French overseas departments of Guadeloupe, Martinique, and French Guiana pales in comparison to migration to the Bahamas and the United States. The American economic, political, and cultural dominance in the Caribbean guarantees English an uncontested role as a regional vehicular language. The increased presence of international non-governmental agencies (NGOs) following the 2010 earthquake has bolstered the presence of English in Haiti. In addition to a Haitian diaspora community estimated at more than one million persons, there are certainly many more Haitian students attending American than French or francophone universities. As Chaudenson and Vernet (1983: 45) rightly noted, when they compared the role of English and French in Haiti:

> *L'anglais est perçu comme un moyen permettant d'aboutir à un mieux-être économique. Le français, en revanche, est vécu comme un élément à valeur symbolique doué d'un pouvoir de valorisation et dont la maîtrise assure l'ascension économique mais surtout sociale et culturelle.*

English is perceived as a means leading to economic improvement. In contrast, French is experienced as something with symbolic value endowed with a power to lead to a higher status and whose mastery insures not only economic but especially social and cultural advancement.

12.4.2 Attitudes toward HC varieties

It is reductionist to view the linguistic situation of Haiti only in terms of the dichotomy: French versus HC. There exist regional varieties of the vernacular, notably, that of northern Haiti, Capois. As was indicated in Chapter 11, this variety constitutes an important marker of regional identity, although it is being eroded under the influence of the standard variety of HC and does not enjoy the support of written texts or a tradition of graphic representation. More important is the existence of the sociolinguistic variety spoken by the élite, *kreyòl swa* (see Sections 2.5 and 11.4). Two studies by Jean-Charles (1987) and Jean-François (2006) explored the attitudes of teachers in the Port-au-Prince area toward French and these two varieties of HC: on the one hand, what Jean-Charles termed urban versus rural Creole, and what Jean-François labeled mesolectal versus basilectal Creole, i.e., *kreyòl swa*, and, on the other hand, the speech of monolingual speakers, respectively. Both of these authors administered the matched-guise test[5] in which teachers were to express their preference toward voices of the same persons speaking in French and in the two socially differentiated varieties of HC. In Jean-Charles's study, in their *kreyòl swa* 'guise', the voices elicited much more favorable reactions than in their monolingual 'guise' across all three types of potential listeners posited by the test: friends, persons related by marriage, and neighbors (Table 12.7).[6]

12.5 Language and Education in Haiti

Table 12.7. Teachers' Rating of French, Urban Creole, and Rural Creole

Teachers' curriculum	Speakers								
	Friendship			Relative by marriage			As a neighbor		
	Yes	No	NP*	Yes	No	NP	Yes	No	NP
French								
Reform	84.1	5.3	10.6	46.2	12.9	40.9	75.6	1.5	22.9
Not Reform	72.1	7.0	20.9	40.2	10.4	49.4	67.3	7.0	25.7
Urban Creole								
Reform	73.5	8.3	18.2	25.4	21.5	53.1	66.2	6.2	27.7
Not Reform	64.9	9.7	25.5	32.0	14.3	53.7	59.5	9.7	30.9
Rural Creole								
Reform	51.5	25.8	22.7	12.1	37.9	50.0	47.7	20.5	31.8
Not Reform	50.8	23.8	25.4	10.8	35.4	53.8	43.4	20.9	35.7

*NP, no opinion

The reactions of bilingual speakers suggest that monolingual creolophones are doubly disadvantaged from a sociolinguistic perspective. On the one hand, they do not have the competence in the language that confers social and political prestige, and on the other, they speak a variety of HC that is depreciated by bilinguals.

12.5 Language and Education in Haiti

12.5.1 Adult literacy education programs

The history of literacy training in Haiti is characterized more by the number of governmental agencies created to launch programs and their declared and ambitious objectives than by the number of illiterates taught to read and write. Between 1947 and the present day nine different governmental institutions have been founded:

- 1943: Bureau haïtien de l'éducation des adultes 'Haitian Bureau of Adult Education'
- 1947: Direction générale de l'éducation des adultes 'General Office of Adult Education'
- 1948: Programme d'éducation ouvrière 'Workers' Educational Program'
- 1957: Office national de développement communautaire 'National Office of Community Development'
- 1961: Office national d'éducation communautaire (ONEC) 'National

Office of Community Education'
- 1969: Office national d'alphabétisation et d'action communautaire (ONAAC) 'National Office of Literacy and Community Action'
- 1986: Office national de participation et d'éducation populaire (ONPEP) 'National Office of Collective Action and People's Education'
- 1989: Office national d'éducation communautaire et d'alphabétisation 'National Office of Community Education and Literacy'
- 1995: Secrétairerie d'État à l'alphabétisation (SEA) 'State Secretariat for Literacy'

As is the case in many developing countries, in Haiti the first adult literacy courses were the result of proselytizing efforts by religious groups. When Ormonde H. McConnell, a minister from Northern Ireland, was sent to Haiti as a missionary by the English Methodist church in 1937, he soon realized that literacy could only be imparted to most of the population of the country through the intermediary of the only language they spoke: HC (McConnell n.d.: 30). As a start, he devised the first phonologically based orthography for the language (see Section 4.4). Then, in 1940, with the approval of the Ministry of Education, he tried out an approach used widely throughout the world by the famous American literacy specialist Frank Laubach. The approach, with the slogan 'Each one teach one', was first applied with country folk in the Cul de Sac plain, near Port-au-Prince. McConnell wisely realized that teaching people to read must be followed by providing them with suitable reading material. He launched a weekly newsletter in HC, *Zétwal Métodis* 'Methodist Star', which, in addition to religious material, provided national and world news. 'The first newspaper of the country people has come into being' proclaimed the local newspaper, *Haïti Journal* (McConnell n.d.: 35).

In 1943, the Haitian government organized centers for literacy education in HC under the aegis of the Bureau haïtien de l'éducation des adultes (Belloncle 1981). But the first well-documented and highly publicized governmental program that linked literacy to rural development was not launched until 1947 by UNESCO at the request of the Haitian government in a valley named Marbial near the southern port town of Jacmel. The area was chosen because it illustrated all the rural development problems in Haiti: erosion, deforestation, small landholdings, extreme overpopulation, social disorganization, etc. The Marbial pilot project opted to use the McConnell-Laubach orthography instead of the Faublas-Pressoir system espoused by Haitian intellectuals[7]. For a variety of reasons, including mismanagement, corruption, etc., this linkage of adult literacy education with community development – which was to become the favored model for governmental literacy training over the next fifty years – proved a dismal failure and was abandoned (Fleischmann 1984, 2010).

The first fairly well-structured governmental agency capable of launching large-scale adult literacy programs was the ONEC, created during the Papa Doc dictatorship. As its name indicates, the Office national d'éducation communautaire (National Office of Community Education) aimed to assist peasants in community development through the intermediary of teaching them to read and write while they undertook community-wide projects: building roads, schools, and irrigation canals that would ultimately improve the life of the participants. As described by a flyer that in 1967 celebrated the seventh anniversary of ONEC:[8]

> Cet aspect du travail de l'ONEC se traduit par nombre d'écoles, de systèmes d'irrigation, de centres sociaux, de routes de pénétration construites avec le pic, la bonne volonté et la sueur du paysan soucieux de son mieux être.
>
> This aspect of the work of the ONEC translates into a number of schools, irrigation systems, community centers, secondary roads built with the pickaxe, the good will, and the sweat of the peasant concerned with improving his life.

By the ONEC's own evaluation, its results in achieving literacy were rather modest. Its actions extended over 40% of the area of the country, with a population of about 765,000 adults of whom 294,667 attended sessions but only 65,628 of whom achieved literacy, a success rate of only 22%.[9] The launching of a literacy program in a particular area and the awarding of diplomas were accompanied by pomp and circumstance and a visit by national dignitaries, during which the personal interest and generosity of the Lifelong President were duly stressed. It is clear that one of the undeclared major objectives of ONEC and its successor agency, ONAAC, was propaganda for the Duvalier regime and a means to extend governmental control over the rural population.

The UNESCO Teheran International Conference on Literacy Education signaled a shift from a focus on the simple acquisition of reading and writing skills on the part of illiterates to the use of these skills to improve their standard of living through their own resources. In 1969, the Haitian government decided to move to what became known internationally as **functional** literacy training, although, as we have seen, in Haiti, beginning with the UNESCO Marbial project, this type of education had always been closely linked to community development. The major change under ONAAC was the creation of community councils (*conseils communautaires*) that would be provided with literacy training but were expected to apply their newly acquired skills to various development activities using, in large part, their own resources. Plagued by endemic corruption, ONAAC's efforts were no more successful than those of ONEC in providing Haitian illiterates with literacy skills. A dozen years after the agency's creation the rate of illiteracy in Haiti still stood at 65.3% overall, according to the 1982 census (Hadjadj 2000). Today, it is estimated at 57%, not significantly lower.

To bolster the ONAAC program, with support from the French government, a unit was created to improve pedagogical methodology and to institute a post-literacy phase, the Groupe de recherches et d'expérimentation en alphabétisation (GREAL) (Research and Experimental Group in Literacy). Led by Alain Bentolila of the University of Paris V (René Descartes), GREAL tried out the new approach in the Côtes-de-Fer region in southern Haiti. One of its innovations was to teach the sound–letter relationships with the use of key sentences that dealt with important aspects of improving the economic development of peasants. For example, the sound [õ] was linked to the sentence *bon rekòt se bon tè ak konnin travay* 'a good harvest is good soil and expertise'. One of the dubious accomplishments of the GREAL experiment was a modification of the orthography used by both ONEC and the ONAAC that ultimately led to the IPN spelling (see Chapter 4). It also highlighted the fact that few of the participants were older adults. Of the initial 1,200 persons enrolled, only 6% were older than thirty-five and 80% were younger than twenty-four (Belloncle 1981: 63), hardly the most influential members of rural communities.

Unlike Ormonde McConnell, the governmental agencies failed to provide reading materials to new literates. It was not until 1976 that ONAAC published the monthly periodical *Solèy Leve* 'Rising Sun'. Following McConnell's *Zétwal métodis*, several religious groups launched monthlies written exclusively in HC: in 1944, a Protestant group involved in literacy, Comité de diffusion de l'enseignement par le créole (Committee for Spreading Education by the Use of Creole), published the short-lived *Fòs-Limiè-Progrè* 'Strength-Light-Progress'; the Protestant Committee for Literacy and Literature followed with *Boukan* 'Bonfire' in 1964; and the Scheut Catholic order brought out *Bon Nouvèl* 'Good Tidings' in 1967. The latter is the only surviving regularly published periodical written exclusively in HC, with a circulation of about 30,000.[10] The founding editor of *Boukan*, Carrié Paultre, wrote several edifying novels, and the staff of *Bon Nouvèl* has produced a wide variety of books in HC covering a broad range of fields. In comparison, except for teaching materials, for example, *N ap li* 'We're reading', the ONEC–ONAAC production of reading materials was rather meager.

In the last days of the Duvalier regime, a sort of grassroots movement arose in Port-au-Prince that aimed to increase adult literacy and to improve both economic and social conditions. This led to the creation in 1985 by the Catholic Church of Mission Alpha (Longuefosse 1996). Concerned about the populist trend of the movement, the hierarchy of the Church terminated its support in 1988. During the politically troubled period between the eviction of Jean-Claude Duvalier in 1986 and the election of Jean-Bertrand Aristide in 1991, two short-lived agencies were created: the Office national de participation et d'éducation populaire (National Office of Literacy and Community Action) and the Office national d'éducation communautaire et d'alphabétisation (National Office of Community Education and Literacy). Upon his return to the presidency in 1995,[11] Jean-Bertrand Aristide created the Secrétairerie à l'alphabétisation (State Secretariat for Literacy) and appointed Paul Dejean, a noted advocate for adult literacy (Y. Dejean 1993) and brother of the linguist Yves Dejean, as head of the agency. Although it continued after the exiling of Aristide in 2004, in its fifteen years of operation, the Secrétairerie does not appear to have been much more successful than ONEC and the ONAAC in significantly reducing adult illiteracy in Haiti.

In 2007, at a projected cost of 186 million dollars, the Secrétairerie launched a new campaign, the objective of which was to eliminate illiteracy in Haiti in two years by reaching three million people and creating 100,000 new jobs. With technical support and a contribution of 7.7 million dollars from Cuba, it planned to adapt the very successful *Yo si puedo* approach devised by the Cuban Instituto Pedagógico de Latina America y del Caribe.[12] Labeled *Wi mwen kapab* 'Yes, I can', the program used televised material and consisted of 65 lessons to be spread over three months; it was to be offered in 7,500 instructional centers. In an article published on October 29, 2009, the daily Port-au-Prince newspaper *Le Matin* cited the then head of the secretariat, Carol Joseph, as reporting that only 117,000 people had successfully completed the course, a mere 4% of the target population. Joseph stressed that with only 0.9% of the annual national budget allotted to his agency, it would be difficult even to attain the revised goal of reaching 1,500,000 illiterates. The dismal results of the various literacy programs implemented by the Haitian government are due not only to insufficient funding but, more importantly, they reflect a lack of political will and support.

12.5.2 Basic education

The early period
During the colonial period, education was a privilege reserved for some members of the free population. It was strictly prohibited for the slave population. A certain M. Villaret declared (Fouchard 1988):

Le gouvernement français a reconnu que la nécessité d'étendre et de généraliser l'instruction – convenable sans doute à un peuple libre – est incompatible avec l'existence de nos colonies qui reposent sur l'esclavage et la distinction de couleur ... Ce serait donc imprudence bien dangereuse de tolérer des écoles pour les nègres et les gens de couleur.

The French government has recognized that the need to extend and to generalize instruction – no doubt suitable for a free people – is incompatible with the existence of our colonies that are based on slavery and color distinction ... Therefore it would be a very dangerous imprudence to tolerate schools for Negroes and people of color.

Even for freemen, who constituted less than 20% of the population, there were few educational establishments. The sons of the élite – Whites and Mulattoes – were sent to France to study, as was the case, for example, of Alexandre Pétion, son of a Black mother and wealthy French father, who became one of the leaders of the Haitian revolutionary forces and subsequently president of the southern part of the newly created independent state. Education for slaves was limited to religious instruction imparted by missionary priests of various Catholic orders or professional training for the artisans needed for the colonial economy (Joint 2006: 48).

After independence, the founder of the nation, Jean-Jacques Dessalines, inserted in the country's first constitution (1801, article 19) a clause that required the establishment of a public school in each of the six administrative divisions of the newly founded nation: *Dans chaque division militaire une école publique sera établie pour l'instruction de la jeunesse* 'In each military district a public school shall be established for the education of young people'. After the division of the country into northern and southern parts in 1807, the two rulers, Henri Christophe in the north and Alexandre Pétion in the south, established a few schools, located mostly in the main towns. Christophe appealed for support to the British and Foreign School Society, which practiced the Lancastarian or monitorial didactic approach, in which more advanced students taught less advanced ones under the tutelage of a single teacher for each school (Joint 2006: 50–5). Pétion founded the first secondary school of the country in Port-au-Prince, the Lycée Pétion. However, by 1820, there were still only nineteen primary and three secondary schools nationwide. Pétion's secretary, General Gélin, advocated the preparation of a grammar for the vernacular language and its use in education. Under the presidency of Fabre Geffrard (1857–67), efforts were made to extend education to the poorer members of the population and several secondary schools were created under the aegis of religious groups, for example, the Frères de l'Instruction Chrétienne (Tardieu 1990; Hadjadj 2000).

Nonetheless, the proportion of Haitian children attending school remained low throughout the nineteenth and the first half of the twentieth centuries, particularly in rural areas. In 1844, during Jean-Pierre Boyer's term of office as president, the longest in the country's history (see Section 1.2.2), there existed only four national and four municipal primary schools, together with sixteen private ones, attended by a total of only 1,821 students, approximately 4% of Haiti's school-age child population. By 1894, that proportion had only doubled (Joint 2006: 70–5).

The situation improved gradually in the second half of the twentieth century. Still, a statistical analysis conducted by the Haitian Institute of Statistics and Information (IHSI) indicated that in 1971 the percentage of pupils who had completed six years of primary education was only 24% of the school-age population overall, with a disproportionate rural versus urban breakdown, 14% versus 62%, respectively (Wiesler 1978). In addition, the average entering age of rural pupils was ten years. By 1981, the number of children schooled had increased to 38% but with a continued rural versus urban disproportion of 30% versus 74%, respectively. The last available statistics compiled by the IHSI show that, in 2008, 23.2% of the 4,462,154 Haitian children and youths up to the age of 24 had not attended school. For the age group 5 to 9, the percentage was 36.8%. Uli Locher (2010: 191) cites a sample taken in 2000 of 16,500 children and youths aged 5 to 17 that set the school attendance figures much higher: 90% in urban schools and 78% in rural schools for children age 5 to 17, and 92% in urban schools, and 86% in rural schools for children aged 5 to 13. These differences suggest that the broader the age range, the lower the school enrollment, and that the percentages cited by Locher provide a more accurate perspective. The picture that emerges of school attendance is that it has increased dramatically since 1894. As will be pointed out in the next section, low school attendance is not the primary problem in the Haitian educational system; it is the inefficiency of the system itself and weak governmental control.

A dysfunctional educational system

Although the 1987 constitution stipulates that primary and secondary education is compulsory and free, schooling is far from free, even in public schools. It constitutes an onerous financial burden for the Haitian population, 80% of whom struggle with an income of less than $3 per day. According to statistics provided by the IHSI for 2003, less than one-third of schools were administered by the government (Table 12.8). More recent estimates place the proportion of schools not administered by the Ministry of Education and Professional Training (MENFP) even higher, at about 80%.

Table 12.8. Types of Schools in Haiti (IHSI statistics, 2008)

	Type of school			
	Public	Private secular	Private religious	Other
Pre-school	23.6%	65.3%	3.7%	
Primary	28.2%	60.9%	5%	7.4%
Secondary	27.3%	68.8%	2%	1.9%

Shortly after the 2010 earthquake, at a conference at George Washington University (Washington, DC), Elisabeth Préval, the wife of the then president of Haiti, gave the following somber assessment of the dismal educational infrastructure of her country: 77% of all educational institutions had no access to electric power, 65% no running water, 74% no library, 31% were located in churches, 16% in private homes, and 29% in inadequate buildings, *lieux précaires*. Many of the private schools are proprietary, i.e., operated for profit, and the designation of many of them as 'écoles borlettes', after the name of the most popular lottery in Haiti, is an apt characterization of their inferior quality.[13] Tuition costs in private schools vary greatly. Fees are as high as $250 per year in the better urban schools. Although it is generally much lower in the rudimentary rural ones, they are still beyond the financial capability of most families.

Another aspect of the dysfunctional state of Haitian schools is the low level of education and training of the teaching corps. In an empirical study of sixteen rural schools in Furcy, a mountainous area close to Port-au-Prince, Laguerre (2010: 79) indicates that 15% of teachers had only completed primary school, 55% had begun studies at the secondary level, and only 30% had completed that level. Few, if any, had professional training. Teacher salaries, often paid irregularly, were as low as $50 per month in these rural primary schools. The generally low educational level of rural teachers is often accompanied by a lack of mastery of French. Laguerre reports that on average teachers used French only 10% of the time, HC 20%, and both languages 70% of the time. In addition, their self-evaluation of competence in French was relatively low: 47% speaking, 48% comprehension, 52% writing, and 57% reading. A more recent general survey of the level of training of the Haitian teachers corps, contained in the report submitted in August 2010 by a committee appointed by the then president, René Préval (Groupe de travail sur l'éducation et la formation), is no more encouraging: of the 60,261 teachers in the nine-year basic educational cycle, 79% had not completed the secondary level and had not undergone pedagogical training; only about 15% had post-secondary education and only about 6% had obtained a teaching certificate (Daudier 2011).

The most serious problem Haiti faces in basic education is not the low proportion of children attending primary school – as pointed out above, the percentage is relatively high for a developing country – but the high dropout rate and the large proportion of over-age students. Citing surveys conducted by FONHEP (Fondation haïtienne de l'enseignement primaire 'Haitian Foundation for Private Education') and other sources, Locher (2010: 186) estimates that of the 100 children who start primary school, at any time between the ages of five and seventeen, only about ten obtain the CEP (Certificat d'études primaires 'Certificate of Primary Education') administered at the end of the six-year primary cycle. During the past twenty to thirty years, the internal efficiency of the educational system has deteriorated. In the 1980s, it took ten student-years to get one student who completed the first six-year school cycle. At present, it takes twenty-three student-years.

Another indication of the inefficiency of the educational system is the large proportion of over-age children. According to a survey conducted by FONHEP in 1999–2000, about 80% of children entering the first grade of primary school were over age. By the sixth grade the percentage had increased to about 94%. This creates serious pedagogical problems because young children and teenagers who are in the same class have different learning styles, and there is a risk that older learners will bully or abuse younger ones.

The linguistic issue in basic education

Despite the fact that the 1843 and 1867 constitutions stipulated that '*Les langues usitées dans le pays seront enseignées dans les école*s (The languages used in the country will be taught in schools)', there was opposition up to the 1970s, both from the élite and at the governmental level, over the use of HC as the language of instruction. After the signing in 1860 of the Concordat, an agreement between the state and the Holy See of the Catholic Church specifying certain privileges accorded to the Church and, in return, certain responsibilities of the Church to the state, religious orders had a profound influence on education in Haiti. The most prestigious schools in Haiti, generally founded by religious orders, such as the Catholic Frères de l'Instruction Chrétienne and Sœurs de Saint Joseph de Cluny, were largely staffed by foreign personnel up to the middle of the twentieth century. Schools administered by these orders were attended mainly by children of the Mulatto élite and their mission was to train them according to the standards of the French educational system of the nineteenth and early twentieth centuries. Foreign teachers, primarily from France, applied the traditional methods of French instruction, stressing memorization of material that monolingual students often did not fully understand. The Haitian primary and secondary systems followed the organization of their French counterparts. Even if the political break with France was total, the French language and French culture exerted a large influence on the Haitian bilingual élite, whose sons were sent to study at French schools and universities, as was the case for such influential writers as Jacques Stephen Alexis, Jacques Roumain, and Dany Laferrière (Berrouët-Oriol *et al.* 2011: 107).

During the nineteen-year US occupation (1915–34), invoking the principle of separation of church and state, the US officials who had effective control of the administration and finances of Haiti attempted a radical transformation of its educational system. While they maintained the traditional church-dominated schools, aimed at the élite, which followed the classical French-influenced curriculum, they introduced new ones administered by the Department of Agriculture rather than the Department of Education. These schools, under the supervision of the Service Technique (see Section 1.2.2), were designed to provide literacy in French as well as vocational training to rural children, as part of the occupiers' controversial belief that this innovation would significantly contribute to the country's economic development and political stability. Although the Service Technique schools enrolled only one-sixth of students, they received twice the funds allotted to primary and secondary education (Joint 2006: 85–90).

In a widely cited experiment on bilingual education in Montreal, Lambert and Tucker (1972) concluded that no adverse effects resulted from educating children in a language other than their mother tongue. However, these authors pointed out that this was a special case, where the mother tongue was the community's dominant language and the children found strong support for it in the home. This situation does not obtain for Haitian monolingual children whose home language, HC, has a lower status than that of French. Also, as pointed out in 12.3 above, French is relatively absent in their social environment. More generally, mastery of school subjects and second-language learning progress more effectively if early education is conducted in the first language (Thomas and Collier 1997).

In the late 1970s, the label 'dysfunctional' accurately applied to a Haitian educational system that left many children unschooled and that was plagued by high drop-out rates and low academic achievement (De Regt 1984). Following a UNESCO conference in Addis Ababa, there was a push for the use of vernacular languages, particularly in sub-Saharan Africa in which some Haitians teaching there participated (Locher 2010: 178). According to Locher, groups inside and outside the Jean-Claude Duvalier regime saw an opportunity to reform the dysfunctional Haitian educational system, in part because it was believed that generalized literacy might lead to economic development. Massive external aid from international sources became

12.5 Language and Education in Haiti 381

available to implement major changes in education, notably, extension of the use of children's mother tongue following the African model. The government decided to embark on a major restructuring effort. The first step was to bring rural education, previously entrusted to the Ministry of Agriculture, under the administration of the Ministry of National Education. International donors, in particular the World Bank, provided major funding and technical assistance for a large-scale program. In 1972, the French government sponsored an educational task force, the Mission pédagogique française, whose objectives were to improve the teaching of French and to modify pedagogical methodology at the primary school level. Personnel of that organization also provided technical assistance for the GREAL adult literacy program. This organization morphed into the Institut pédagogique national (IPN), provided with a new building and staffed by 63 local specialists and 23 French experts who eventually assisted in the implementation of the reform of the educational system.

The educational reform initiated in 1979, termed Réforme Bernard, after the Minister of National Education, Joseph C. Bernard, set itself an array of ambitious objectives: the extension of primary and secondary education to a wider population base, the introduction of technical and vocational education at the secondary level, the improvement of management and physical infrastructure in both the public and private spheres, new pedagogical approaches that superseded the traditional memorization of material, an increase in the number and improvement of the training of teachers, etc. But its boldest and most controversial aspect was the replacement of French by HC as the instructional language during the first four years of primary education and the associated teaching of French as a second language.

The adult literacy programs discussed in Section 12.5.1 had triggered a long-term debate about the appropriate instructional language that spread to basic education in the 1970s. In addition, in 1975 even though their target readership remained the bilingual élite, some writers began to publish in HC, notably, Franketienne (Frank Etienne) and Célestin-Mégie, authors of the first novels in HC, *Dezafi* 'The Challenge' (1975) and *Lanmou pa gin baryè* 'Love Has No Barriers' (1975, 1977), respectively. From a linguistic point of view, the reform program did not constitute a major break with the traditional curriculum. It set up a transitional bilingual program (Craig 1980), in which HC would be used as the primary instructional medium in the early stages of schooling only until French could take over. A new nine-year basic educational system was established, divided into three cycles: a four-year initial primary cycle followed by a two-year primary and a three-year secondary cycle. During the first four years, instruction was to be conducted in HC and French taught as a second language. During the next two years French would gradually take over as instructional medium. Then, in the last three years of the proposed fundamental cycle, French would serve as both subject matter and instructional medium.

In 1974, the Centre Haïtien d'investigations en sciences sociales (CHISS), headed by Hubert de Ronceray, Under Secretary in the Ministry of National Education, tested the effectiveness and feasibility of the proposed transitional bilingual approach (Ronceray and Petit-Frère 1975). Funded by the Inter-American Foundation, this experimental trial involved three first-year classes of fifty pupils each from three different schools in the area of Léogane, a town west of Port-au-Prince. The experiment benefited from the support of two leading foreign specialists: the social psychologist Richard Tucker, then at McGill University, and the late educational linguist Denis Craig of the University of the West Indies-Jamaica. The results of the innovation proved very encouraging for the use of HC as initial instructional language (Table 12.9).

The two control groups followed the traditional curriculum in which French serves as the instructional language; the experimental group was exposed to the transitional bilingual approach in which literacy was first imparted in HC. The latter group's performance in HC reading and mathematical reasoning and computing proved superior to that of both control groups. Not surprisingly, the two control groups demonstrated a higher competence in French, but the differences compared with that of the experi-

Table 12.9. The CHISS Experiment

	Experimental group	Control group I	Control group II
Parental background			
Professional qualification	6%	23%	3%
Literate	36%	44%	39%
Secondary school	0%	8%	7%
Results			
HC reading (sentences)	**49%**	32%	28%
HC reading (global)	**52%**	31%	17%
Math reasoning	**4.145**	2.893	1.020
Math computing	**3.00**	1.617	.395
French vocabulary	17%	**19%**	18%
French comprehension	9%	**14%**	10%

mental group were relatively small. Although there was no control of the level of training or pedagogical effectiveness of the teachers, what the experiment demonstrated was that in a well-administered program a bilingual approach that recognizes that basic educational skills and knowledge are best imparted in a child's mother tongue leads to better cognitive achievement. The experimental group's overall better cognitive performance over that of Control group I was somewhat surprising in view of the higher socioeconomic and educational levels of the parents of the children in that group, an important factor in the Haitian educational system (Locher 2010: 181). In addition, the teachers of Control group I received pedagogical support from the IPN.

Given the high drop-out rates in Haitian schools, another important factor in assessing the success of the reform program would be to what extent it improved retention rates and secured parental approval. From that perspective, there were two major limitations in the CHISS experiment. First, surprisingly, it was conducted for only one school year, and thus retention rates could not be assessed. Second, no information could be obtained about parental reactions to the new approach. Had it been extended to several years and involved new groups each year, it would have been possible to observe whether parents would have continued to enroll their children in the experimental program. In 1979, on the eve of the launching of the Réforme Bernard, with funding from the United States International Development (USAID) Haiti program, the Indiana University Creole Institute organized a symposium, 'Créole et enseignement primaire en Haïti' (Creole and primary education in Haiti), at the National Pedagogical Institute, with the participation of the Minister of National Education, Joseph Bernard (Valdman and Joseph 1980). The symposium provided an opportunity for several religious groups to show that, prior to the launching of the reform program, they had begun to use HC as the instructional language in their primary schools. One of these schools, located in Laborde, a village near Les Cayes in southwest Haiti, had applied the transitional bilingual approach beginning in 1974. Although, unlike the CHISS experiment, there was no evaluation of cognitive achievement, because that innovative approach had been undertaken several years before the launch of the Reform, it was possible to provide information about retention rates and parental reactions.[14] The retention rate of 60% over four years compares favorably with that of a sample of schools following the traditional curriculum (Table 12.10). In addition, the increase of 98% in total enrollment after four years of the introduction of the bilingual program indicates strong parental support.

Table 12.10. Laborde (Cayes) Experiment

Year	1erA	CP I	CP II	E1.I	E1.II	Moy I	Moy II
1974	**182**	136	127	55	42	28	--
1975	209	**156**	107	88	41	28	23
1976	229	164	**131**	97	76	35	25
1977	239	206	115	**116**	81	36	23
1978	**360**	247	177	102	**109**	71	32

The progression of the initial cohort enrolled in 1974 through the first five years is indicated in boldface type, as is the number of pupils enrolled in 1978.

With regard to the linguistic issue, the evaluation of the Réforme Bernard centered on cognitive aspects, namely, did the use of HC as the initial language of instruction result in superior acquisition of instructional content – literacy skills, math, general science, and social studies? Another central criterion was whether the initial teaching of French as a second language would enable pupils to acquire sufficient competence in that language and to use it subsequently for the acquisition of academic content. It is not surprising that the introduction of HC as the language of instruction faced strong opposition from both the bilingual élite and its presumed beneficiaries: the economically disadvantaged monolingual masses. For all families, the role of education is to provide their children with the means of economic and social advancement, as well as access to cultural and scientific knowledge and an opening to the outside world. In view of the social, political, and economic dominance of the bilingual élite, all segments of the Haitian population are fully aware that knowledge of French opens the way to a better life. The bilingual élite, whose children master French at home,[15] know that HC does not lead to social advancement and look to schools to increase competence in French. For the monolingual majority of the population, for whom sending their children to school entails a heavy financial burden, the mastery of French constitutes a necessary step toward economic and social advancement. They must be convinced that the proposed transitional bilingual program characterized by the initial use of HC as the instructional medium will not reduce the possibility of their children acquiring some mastery of French (Pompilus 1980).

Joseph Bernard knew that he needed to implement the educational reform before the élite could be mobilized to oppose it – in fact it did mobilize, and he was dismissed in 1982. The result was a hasty and poorly prepared launch of the reform on a nationwide scale without a prior, carefully controlled experimental trial for at least the full four-year basic first

Table 12.11. Comparison of Achievement in Academic Content and French between Students Enrolled in the Reform and the Traditional Programs

	French	**Math**	**General studies**
Traditional			
4th year	66	55.7	58.3
6th year	66	50.3	62.2
Reform			
4th year	63.5	47.3	52.8
6th year	63.5	49.2	54.5

primary school cycle. In addition, the campaign to inform the population about the various aspects of the reform was launched too late, in 1982. Surprisingly the promising cognitive results of the CHISS experiment in Léogane and of the successful retention rates of the Laborde initiative were never publicized.

The only thorough evaluation of the Réforme Bernard commissioned by its major international funding source, the World Bank, concluded that the transitional bilingual approach yielded unsatisfactory results (Locher *et al.* 1987; see also Wiesler 1978). The study provided information about achievement in a large number of schools, in all parts of Haiti, after four and six years of schooling. As Table 12.11 shows, students enrolled in the traditional program performed much better in math at the end of the fourth year but not at the end of the sixth year. As was the case for the CHISS experiment, the traditional program led to only to a slightly superior achievement in French. Regrettably, reading and writing skills in HC were not evaluated. In addition, the study revealed a great difference in retention rates after the full six years: 2,539 (57%) of the 4,445 students of the traditional cohort who completed the sixth year versus 687 (31%) of the 2,225 students enrolled in the Reform classes. From a methodological perspective, this evaluative study leaves much to be desired: there does not seem to have been any control of such important factors as class size and experience and competence of teachers. In addition, the traditional sample was twice as large as the Reform one and no measure of statistical reliability of differences was provided. Given this lack of controls, it would be too hasty to conclude that the relatively poor results shown for the transitional bilingual approach are due to the use of HC as an instructional medium. However, it did provide opponents of the Reform with justification for opposing the innovation.

The current situation

Locher accurately describes the post-1979 follow-up of the Réforme Bernard: 'A score of education ministers ... have tried to variously promote, modify, or sabotage the reform ... Probably not a single student in Haiti has ever been taught exclusively according to reform plans' (2010: 179). Nonetheless, today there seems to be greater use of HC in primary schools, more production of educational materials in HC, but not wholesale application of all the components of the Reform.

A signal improvement in the educational system was the introduction of a testing program. In 1993, a battery of tests was devised to be administered to primary school students, the first at the end of the second fundamental cycle (sixth year or *certificat* level), and the second at the end of the third year of the third cycle (ninth year).Tests were developed to evaluate HC and French language skills – reading and writing – as well as knowledge of the structure of these two languages and knowledge of three subject-matter areas: math, social sciences (geography and history), and experimental sciences (biology, chemistry, physics). However, although there are HC and French versions of these tests, most teachers opt for the French versions. Thus, it is difficult to determine to what extent student performance depends on knowledge of that language or on mastery of the academic content. One would have expected that parts of these tests would be administered in HC. It is noteworthy that the test battery does not include an evaluation of oral proficiency in French.

Yves Dejean (2006, 2010) argues for the exclusive use of HC as instructional medium in basic education, with French being relegated to a foreign language. As Chaudenson points out (2008: 23), this position is both legitimate and reasonable but it has the inconvenience of being politically unrealistic. Members of the bilingual minority, for whom competence in French acquired in the home constitutes a linguistic capital that it is loath to give up, would oppose it. In addition, this competence is viewed by the monolingual majority as a means for social and economic advancement which they do not want denied to their children. On the other hand, given the dysfunctional and chaotic nature of the Haitian education system and the restricted availability of French outside of the school environment to most children, it is problematic whether under present pedagogical approaches the fundamental nine-year school curriculum can lead monolingual children to competence in French. One promising step toward the attainment of that goal is a pedagogical approach that stresses the similarities rather than the differences between HC and French, thereby facilitating the acquisition of the latter language. This approach, starting from a contrastive analysis of the two languages in contact, was first delineated by Pressoir (1954) but perfected by Pompilus (1973, 1976). It involves the identification of differences in the structure of the two languages that could lead to possible acquisitional difficulties and, conversely, of similarities that could lead to potential positive transfers that would facilitate learning. The ultimate objective of Pompilus's contrastive analysis was the improvement of the teaching of French. It stemmed from the author's realization that French is an alien language for all but a tiny majority of his compatriots. As a sort of foreign language, Pompilus argued, French must be taught by appropriate methodologies, namely, by the application of contrastive analysis. The approach of these two Haitian pioneers has been extended and refined by a project headed by Chaudenson (2008) and sponsored by the francophone agency, the Organisation internationale de la Francophonie (OIF). The convergent approach proposed by Chaudenson (2008) consists in taking into account the local context, teaching a French lexicon that refers to artifacts and concepts familiar to the learners, and focusing first on phonological and grammatical features common to the local French-based creoles and French, or that are closely related.

Because HC serves as the vernacular for bilingual Haitians, the variety of French they speak tends to be much closer to formal written French than the colloquial speech of speakers from France. It is also more distant from HC than colloquial French and, consequently, more difficult to acquire. For example, in producing interrogative structures bilingual Haitians favor inversion (*Où vas-tu?* 'Where are you going?'), whereas in ordinary speech the French will generally use simple fronting or stranding of the interrogative form (*Où tu vas?*, *Tu vas où?*) or use the interrogative marker *est-ce que* (*Où est-ce que tu vas?*). In France, the usage of inversion is infrequent in speech and marked as very formal. It turns out that the corresponding HC structure parallels French colloquial usage:

ki kote	*ou*	*prale*
où	*tu*	*vas*
where	you	go
Where are you going?		

Thus, the fronting construction, rather than inversion, should be the one first taught to Haitian children. Other examples of grammatical similarities between HC and French are: (a) yes–no questions: *Selina kontan*? > *Selina est contente*? 'Selina is happy?' instead of *Selina est-elle contente?*; (b) periphrastic future: *N a(va) travay demen.* > *On va travailler demain.* 'We'll work tomorrow', instead of the inflected future *Nous travaillerons demain.*

The expression of possession constitutes a major difference between HC and French. In the latter language, possessive adjectives are pre-posed, whereas in HC possession is expressed by post-posed pronouns: *mon chat* vs. *chat mwen* 'my cat'. However, in colloquial speech in France there exists a possessive construction in which possession is also expressed with a post-posed pronoun, albeit with the use of the preposition *à*: *le chat à moi*. As pointed out in Chapter 11, the Northern HC (Capois) variant of HC *chat mwen* is *chat a mwen*, which matches the structure of the vernacular variety of the language spoken in France. In teaching the Standard French construction *mon chat*, one might begin with *chat a mwen*, then provide *le chat à moi*, and then move to *mon chat*.

A major obstacle in the implementation of such a policy is a purist attitude toward French evidenced by many bilingual Haitians. This attitude is fueled in part by the more formal nature of Haitian French, as compared to that of metropolitan France. Precisely because the élite master both their variety of HC and French, they do not show the wide range of variation within that latter language evidenced by their French counterparts. In particular, they do not have the equivalent of metropolitan French vernacular speech. Thus, for example with regard to interrogative structure, whereas the fronting WH-question structure exemplified by *Où tu vas?* 'Where are you going?' constitutes the overwhelming majority of instances of this structure in vernacular French, it is considered 'incorrect' by Haitian bilinguals who typically use the inversion *Où vas-tu?*, which occurs in less than 10% of cases in the colloquial conversation style of speakers in France. For example, in a pedagogical guide for primary education (Ministère de l'Education Nationale 2010: 37) the authors recommend the following verse for oral communication practice in French:

Le chien et le chat	'The dog and the cat'
Irai-je où tu iras?	'Will I go where you'll go?'
Disait le chien au chat.	'Said the dog to the cat.'
Rirai-je où tu riras?	'Will I laugh where you laugh?'
Lui demanda le chien.	'The dog asked it.'

Note that, in addition to the use of the inversion structure with the first person, which is extremely rare in spoken French, this text contains the inflected future and the preterite (passé simple), both of which are features of formal, written French.

In 1987, the Ministry of Education reviewed the state of the country's educational situation and formulated the Plan national d'éducation et de formation (PNEF; National plan for education and training). This master plan correctly identified the fundamental problems of the Haitian educational system: inadequate governmental funding that negates the article of the 1987 constitution that mandates that basic schooling be obligatory and free, high drop-out rates, over-age students, inadequate infrastructure, a lack of qualified teachers, and the preponderant role of the private sector.

The chaotic political situation that followed the demise of the Duvalier regime, the *dechoukaj* 'uprooting', did not permit immediate implementation of the plan and it was not until 1993 that any attempt was made. An article on the internet news site, Alterpresse (January 28, 1998), bemoaned the fact that even then there was no evidence that the Haitian educational situation had significantly improved. Only 8% of the nation's budget was allocated to education, and the private sector's presence had increased. The article concluded that there was still a lack of:

> ... une éducation haïtienne de qualité, accessible à tous les citoyens, pilier de la démocratie et du développement national et d'un Ministère de l'Éducation qui exerce pleinement son rôle de garant de la démocratisation et de la qualité de l'éducation à tous ses niveaux, dans les secteurs publics et privés, à travers tout le territoire national.
>
> ... a Haitian quality education, accessible to all citizens, the pillar of democracy and national development, and a Ministry of Education that fully exercises its role as guarantor of the democratic extension and quality of education at all levels, in public and private spheres, throughout the national territory.

After the 2010 earthquake, a presidential commission drafted a five-year plan to improve all aspects of education from kindergarten to university (*Vers la Refondation du Système Educatif Haïtien. Plan opérationnel 2010–2015* 'Toward the Rebuilding of the Haitian Educational System. Operational Plan 2010–2015'). This ambitious plan is expected to cost 4.3 billion dollars, of which 500 million has been allocated by the Interamerican Development Bank (IDB). The salient features of the plan include the institution of free primary and secondary education and a more rigorous control of private schools by the Ministry of National Education and Professional Training (MENFP). It remains to be seen how the MENFP will integrate all denominational and private schools, especially the for-profit ones (*écoles borlettes* 'lottery schools'), which constitute an overwhelming part of basic education in Haiti, and, particularly, to what degree it will generalize the transitional bilingual approach and extend the use of the language of the majority of the population upward in the education system. It is of some concern, however, that the 294-page document that details the plan does not deal explicitly with the linguistic situation, which, as I have tried to demonstrate in this section, remains the most important factor in the elaboration of an effective educational system for Haiti.

The plan to reconstruct the Haitian educational system focuses on the construction of new schools provided with solar power, computers, and information technology. About 70% of the IDB contribution would be allocated to infrastructure. Students would be provided with school kits comprising school supplies and books (8% of the funds) and an equal proportion for subsidies to schools so that instruction is free. That only 4% is budgeted for teacher training constitutes a signal weakness of the plan, given the fact that the Haitian teacher corps is largely untrained and, as was noted in Section 12.5.2, possesses low competence in French, which presumably will remain the main instructional language.[16] In May 2011 the newly elected president of Haiti, Michel Martelly, proposed a national educational fund (Fond national pour l'éducation, FNE), to be financed by taxing incoming international telephone calls and money transfers, most of which originate in the diaspora communities. The fund, estimated to yield $114,000,000 over the five years of his presidential term, was designed to support a massive educational campaign to be launched in the fall of 2011. According to the program labeled Programme de scolarisation universelle gratuite et obligatoire (PSUGO; Program for universal obligatory and free schooling), a total of 772,000 children were to be provided with free schooling, 490,000 of whom were to be enrolled in public schools.

However, this bold program ran into difficulties during the openings of the 2011–12, 2012–13, and 2013–14 school years. The opening of schools was postponed for one month, initial attendance was low, and there were several teacher strikes because of a delay in providing back pay. The coordinator of UNNHOH (Union Nationale des Normaliens Haïtiens), a teacher union to which belong graduates of teacher colleges, the best-qualified pedagogical corps in the country, evoked serious doubt about the success of the president's bold program (*Le Matin*, October 4, 2011). He pointed out that with only 10% of students enrolled in schools controlled by the state, private school tuitions ranging from $375 to $625, and no specific provisions for teacher training and remuneration, providing free education of quality to all Haitian schoolchildren was fraught with serious difficulties. It is noteworthy that under the PSUGO program public schools receive about $6 per pupil, whereas the subsidy for private schools reaches $90. Not surprisingly, according to an article in the major Haitian newspaper, the *Nouvelliste,* this has led to massive fraud. The article reports that 766 fictitious private schools were receiving PSUGO funding.[17]

Of equal concern is that the extensive discussions in the Haitian media and in the *Vers la Refondation du Système Educatif Haïtien* document (see above) fail to mention the issue of the choice of instructional language in primary education. It is doubtful that a significant increase in the effectiveness of the Haitian educational system can be attained without the emergence of a national consensus on the fundamental linguistic issue: what respective roles should be assigned to HC, the exclusive means of linguistic communication for an estimated 90% of the population, and Haitian French, at present the exclusive privilege of the bilingual minority but still perceived by the entire population as the way toward economic, social, and political advancement (Y. Dejean 2006, 2011; Berrouët-Oriol et al. 2011; Berrouët-Oriol 2011)? On the other hand, there has been a significant increase in the use of HC at all educational levels, even in the Catholic schools attended by children of the élite (Joint 2006: 415–22). HC also has a dominant role in the media: whereas there is only one television station, Télévision National d'Haïti (TNH) that broadcasts programs in HC, as opposed to eighteen other channels, most of which relay US programming in English, there are about eighty radio stations, a quarter of them in Port-au-Prince, that use mainly HC. Although the monthly *Bon Nouvèl* remains the only periodical written in HC, texts in the language appear more frequently.

Summary

It was not until more than two centuries after it had emerged and become the language spoken by the entire population of the republic of Haiti that HC was promulgated, in 1987, as the national language of the country and given co-official status with French. The article of the most recent constitution adopted in 1987 that stipulates that HC should appear in all administrative and legal documents has never been implemented. There is not even an official HC version of the constitution.

Although it is the country's co-official language and is endowed with an officially recognized orthography, HC is by and large relegated to vernacular usage. Except for the monthly newsletter *Bon Nouvèl*, which has limited distribution, HC is absent from the written media and, generally, literary and other works in which it appears are destined for the nation's bilingual élite. It has a dominant role only in the religious domain and in radio broadcasts.

For monolingual HC speakers, who constitute about 90% of the population of Haiti, HC is viewed positively as the language of their ethnic origin, although they do realize that competence in French constitutes the means to social and economic promotion. Because it is generally absent from their immediate environment, they firmly believe that it is the role of schooling to provide access to it. As it is, they tend to view with suspicion the educational reform (Réforme Bernard), launched in 1979 and poorly implemented since its inception. Because nearly 80% of schools in Haiti are private, operated by religious groups or proprietary, the Haitian government has limited control of educational institutions. With regard to attitudes toward French and HC studies, teachers evidence a clear preference for French as well as the bilingual variety of HC, *kreyòl swa*.

Since the launching of the Réforme Bernard, the use of HC in education and Haitian society in general has grown but it still plays a limited role in the educational system. A promising approach to the teaching of French focuses on similarities between HC and French. But since these similarities obtain when HC is compared to vernacular varieties of French spoken in France and North American varieties of French, they run counter to the highly formal nature of the variety of that language used by the Haitian bilingual élite. The institution of a program for free and obligatory education following the 2010 earthquake promises to broaden access to education for the monolingual masses. But it remains to be seen how effectively that program will be implemented and how free from corruption it will remain. Finally, the fact that a law establishing the Académie créole was first drafted in HC might signal a radical change of attitude among all Haitians toward the only language they all share: HC.

Notes

1. This document and its translation are available in the *Journal of Haitian Studies*. As was pointed out in Chapter 4, during the French colonial period written representations of Saint-Domingue Creole appeared only in religious works, descriptions of the social life of the period, and some plays, poems, and songs. This situation endured for a long time after Haiti gained its independence.
2. The two Dejean brothers were pioneers in the use of HC by the Catholic Church in Haiti. Forced into exile by Papa Doc, they eventually returned to their native land after the fall of the Duvalier regime. Paul Dejean served as minister in charge of diaspora affairs (the Tenth Department) and briefly as the first head of the Secrétairerie d'état à l'alphabétisation (State Secretariat for Literacy) during the Aristide presidency before parting with that regime. Yves Dejean also served in that agency. He holds strong views about the extension of the use of HC at all levels of the educational system (Dejean 2006, 2011).
3. In addition to the State University of Haiti, the following institutions were represented on the committee: the monthly publication *Bon Nouvèl* (the only Haitian periodical written entirely in HC), the National Presses of Haiti, the Secretariat for Literacy, and the National Confederation of Vodou Practitioners.
4. According to figures released in 2008 by the Institut Haïtien de Statistiques et d'Informatique (IHSI), the urban population, estimated at about 377,000

in 1950 (12% of the total population), had grown to nearly 3,400,000 (40% of the total population) by 2008.

5. The matched-guise test is a sociolinguistic technique originally designed by the Canadian social psychologist Wallace Lambert to determine attitudes toward language or language varieties (Lambert et al.1967). Individuals living in Montreal listened to bilinguals speaking in two linguistic 'guises', Quebec French and English. They were then asked to make evaluative judgments about each of the guises. The subject of the study rated the English guise more favorably than the Quebec French guise. The application of the matched-guise test in Jean-Charles's study is flawed by the choice of only two voices. This fails to eliminate the confounding variable of voice quality and possible personality factors reflected in the voices' elocution in the three linguistic varieties.

6. Note that there does not appear to be any significant difference in the responses of teachers who were following the Réforme Bernard curriculum and those who were not. For the Réforme Bernard, see Section 12.5.2.

7. There was a religious overtone to the quarrel about a suitable orthography for HC. The Haitian intellectuals and educators who supported the Faublas-Pressoir spelling were Catholics, whereas McConnell and Laubach were Protestants, as were Robert A. Hall, Jr. (an ardent defender of the 'Anglo-Saxon' spelling) and Alfred Métraux, the eminent specialist on Vodou and first director of the Marbial project.

8. Although instituted in September 1961, it did not begin to operate until 1962.

9. The results of the pilot program launched in late 1961 and early 1962 in Port-au-Prince and its vicinity under optimal conditions in 97 centers are equally unimpressive. Of the 8,399 adults involved (5,805 urban and 2,594 rural) about half completed the course and only 2,017 (24%) were certified (undated unpublished official report signed by Edouard C. Paul, the technical director of ONEC). The report does not provide separate results for urban and rural certified learners.

10. In 1979, ONAAC published a short-lived monthly HC newsletter, *Bwa cbandèl* (the term for any pinewood- or candelabra-shaped cactus). The subtitle, *Twonpèt Janklodis* 'Jean-Claudism trumpet', transparently reflects the periodical's propagandist objective. Between 1970 and 1995 there were several non-governmental HC monthlies, none of which attained the longevity of *Bon Nouvèl*: *Gindòl*, *Libète*, as well as the educational materials distributed by the Catholic Church's radio station, *Radyo Solèy* 'Sun Radio'.

11. Unseated by a military coup, Aristide took refuge in the United States. He was returned to power in 1994 with American intervention and later exiled, with presumed US and French intervention, in 2004.

12. This method, used successfully in several Latin American countries, notably Venezuela, Mexico, and Brazil, was awarded the UNESCO prize for literacy in 2006.

13. In its USAID-funded 1984 project (Incentives to Improve Education) the Improving the Efficiency of Educational Systems Consortium (IEES) char-

acterized proprietary schools as having a short and financially troubled lifespan (IEES: Annex 9). This document also indicates the following breakdown of private schools: 49% Protestant (mostly funded by US religious groups), 20% Catholic (local and foreign support), 31% proprietary. An earlier 1982 inventory (Luxana 1997) concords generally with these figures: 49% Protestant, 26% Catholic, 25% proprietary. In that inventory, public schools, controlled by the government, account for only 26% of the total. This suggests that the IHSI figures for secular versus religious schools are questionable.

14. What remains puzzling in the CHISS experiment is its limitation to a single year, far too short a period of time. In addition, although De Ronceray attended the 1979 symposium as a representative of the Ministry of Education, he did not report on the experiment at that important event.

15. Members of the bilingual élite who speak HC among themselves at home generally address their children in French.

16. The January 2010 earthquake caused the collapse of the Faculté de Linguistic Appliquée and the death of about 200 students, most of whom would have served as the cadres of educational reform.

17. See Frantz Duval, '766 fausses écoles, combien de vraies?', *Le Nouvelliste*, March 11, 2013.

13 The Genesis and Development of Haitian Creole

13.1 Theories about Creole Genesis

Theories about the genesis of creole languages fall into two major categories. The first comprises those theories that view these languages as exceptional in that they differ markedly from other natural languages from the perspective of their linguistic structure or the language-acquisition process that triggered their original development.[1] This category may be subdivided into three subgroups: the first, the **Creole Prototype**, posits particular typological features specific to creole languages (McWhorter 1998, 2005, 2013); the second posits the instantiation of the human language faculty, the **Bioprogram** (Bickerton 1981), to which children had to resort when their primary linguistic input for first-language acquisition was a supposedly impoverished and unlearnable pidgin; the third, **Relexification**, assumes an atypical language-acquisition process involving the total transfer of the morphosyntactic and semantic structures of the language of learners onto the lexicon of the primary linguistic input, the **lexifier language** (C. Lefebvre 1988, 1998).

In contrast to these three approaches, the other theoretical perspective is the so-called Superstratist Theory, which views creoles as nonexceptional from structural and language-acquisition perspectives (Valdman 1971, 1978; Chaudenson 1974, 1979, 1992, 2003; Mufwene 2001, 2008; DeGraff 2003). Rather, it views them as the result of unguided second-language acquisition under particular sociohistorical conditions, namely, the context of the plantation-based European colonies of the seventeenth and eighteenth centuries. This model applies especially to French-based creoles (FBCs), and will be presented in Section 13.2.

13.1.1 The Creole Prototype

A long tradition views creoles as forming a distinct class among natural languages. Going back to the end of the nineteenth century, linguists such as the American Addison Van Name (1869–70), the Portuguese Adolfo Coelho

(1880), the German Hugo Schuchardt (1882), the French Lucien Adam (1883), and the Dutch Dirk Christiaan Hesseling (1897) all observed that creole languages differed in some manner from other natural languages. The most specific and radical proposal, however, has been put forward relatively recently by John McWhorter (1998). This scholar claims that creoles are uniquely characterized by the combination of only three traits: (1) little or no inflectional affixation; (2) a lack of tonal distinctions to contrast monosyllables or to encode syntax; and (3) semantically transparent and regular derivational affixes. Interestingly, after listing these linguistic traits McWhorter does make reference to the sociohistorical context of creole genesis (1998: 799):

> Because there exist no languages combining these traits other than those with the creole sociohistorical profile, we can conclude that creole is indeed a linguistic, typologically identifiable class as well as a sociohistorical one.

We have seen in Section 7.2 that HC indeed has no inflectional affixes. Tense and aspect distinctions in the verbal system of the language are expressed by free preverbal markers (*ap, te, ava*, etc.) and plurality in nouns is marked by the free post-posed form *yo*. In establishing the third criterion, McWhorter cites the case of the exclusively inversive meaning of the HC prefix *de-*, which he exemplifies with, among other instances, *degrese* 'to lose weight' from *grese* 'to gain weight'. However, Section 5.3.1 shows that in fact *de-* subsumes three semantically distinctive prefixes: inversive, privative, and intensifying. *Degrese* 'to lose weight' is a homonym whose co-constituent contains the privative *de-*: *grese* 'to add fat' versus *degrese* 'to remove fat'. Thus, *degrese* is in no way transparent, nor can *dekale* 'to scrape, to scale' constitute the privative derivative of *kale* 'to peel' whose meaning is inherently privative. In Chapter 5, this derivative was analyzed as containing the intensifier *de-*. As this chapter shows, and DeGraff (2005) points out, HC evidences considerable derivational morphology. Note that McWhorter hedges somewhat by suggesting that some creoles might show 'a little' inflection and 'a little' use of tone.[2]

13.1.2 The Bioprogram Hypothesis

The Portuguese historical linguist Adolfo Coelho, who became interested in those creole languages spawned by the spread of Portuguese in African and Asian colonies, was the first scholar to suggest that creoles demonstrate the operation of universal linguistic principles (1880: 193ff, cited by Holm 1988: 27):

> They [Indo-Portuguese and other Portuguese-based creoles] owe their origin to the operation of psychological or physiological laws that are everywhere the same, and not to the influence of former languages of the peoples among whom these dialects are found.

Later, the Danish linguist Otto Jespersen more specifically invoked further detailed language-acquisition principles to account for the development of pidgins akin to those for young children acquiring their first language, 'as if their mind were just as innocent of grammar as those of very small babies' (1922: 225).

Derek Bickerton, who had done considerable research on Guyanese (English-based) Creole (1975), joined the University of Hawaii in the mid-1970s. There exists in Hawaii an English-based creole based on a Hawaiian Pidgin English (HPE) that had supplanted the previously existing, unrelated Hawaiian Pidgin used on the islands' plantations. Presumably it was used for interlinguistic communication by speakers of Chinese, Japanese, Filipino languages, and Portuguese, among others. Bickerton (1981: 5) characterized HPI as:

> ... quite unfit to serve as anyone's primary tongue, which, by reason of its variability, does not present even the little it offers in a form that would permit anyone to learn it ... here, if the child is to have an adequate language, he must speedily outstrip the knowledge of the parent.

According to Bickerton, children confronted with this highly defective primary linguistic input, an unlearnable target language, resorted to a construct related to the Chomskian Innate Language Faculty, which he termed the Language Bioprogram, to create Hawaiian Creole English (HCE). To prove the universality of the Bioprogram, he argued that:

> ...if all creoles could be shown to exhibit an identity far beyond the scope of chance, this would constitute strong evidence that some genetic program common to all members of the species was decisively shaping the result. (ibid.: 42)

Bickerton then proposed eight features of HCE that are either shared by all creoles or that show minor differences in some. The eight features he identifies are: movement rules, the TMA system, realized and unrealized complements, relativization and subject-copying, the definite article, existential/possessives, adjectives as verbs, and passive equivalents (ibid.: 72). Bickerton also proposed a scale of **radicalness** of creoles. The most radical creoles show the majority of these morphosyntactic features and, thus, differ most from the language or languages from which their lexicon is derived.[3] He specifically lists HC as belonging to this category of creoles.

However, we have seen in Sections 8.1.1 and 8.2 that the Bioprogrammatic TMA system posited by Bickerton does not account for the corresponding TMA system of HC. In HCE, there is an exclusive durative (progressive) verb marker *stei.* Its corresponding HC form *ap,* carries both durative and irrealis (future) meanings: *y ap travay* 'they're working'; *l ap vini* 'she'll come'. Nonetheless, it is indeed striking that such widely geographically distant creoles based on different lexifiers such as HCE and the Indian Ocean French-based Mauritian Creole share several central linguistic features.

Bimorphic question words are among the features where Bickerton concedes that various creoles differ. Generally, in most creoles, question words are composed of a target-language question word followed by a form derived from a generic noun. This does in fact describe most HC interrogative words: *ki kote/bò* 'where'; *ki moun* 'who'; *ki jan* 'how'; *ki sa* 'what'. But Bickerton (ibid.: 71) does admit, as is attested in HC, that 'often a creole has doublets, a superstrate [lexifier language] adaptation and a bimorphemic creole form *(ki) sa l ap di* "what does he say?", *(ki) kote ou prale* "where are you going?"' (see Section 9.3.2). However, HC also diverges from HCE by showing monomorphemic interrogative words: *kouman* 'how' and *konbe* 'how much'.[4] Invoking decreolization for such divergences from the Bioprogram is questionable, unless data from the early stages of the development of those creoles that evidence exceptions fully conform to the pattern assumed by the Bioprogram hypothesis.

Sociohistorical facts do not support Bickerton's scenario for the development of Hawaiian Creole. Sarah Roberts (1998, 2000, 2005) points out that the purported Hawaiian pidgin developed over two generations. Children growing up on plantations were bilingual in the language of their parents and the pidgin, and some children were schooled and had access to the local varieties of English.

Interestingly, in addition to defining creole languages on the basis of general or quasi-general linguistic features, both the Creole Prototype and the Bioprogram hypotheses assume that creoles stem from an earlier pidgin. However, in an article focused on FBCs (McWhorter and Parkvall 2002), these authors suggest that the differences between these creoles and SF may be accounted for without recourse to an intermediate pidgin stage (2002: 182). Indeed, it was pointed out in Section 1.4.2 that Antillean creoles (Guadeloupean, Martinican, and Saint-Domingue) were more likely to have been preceded by a pidginized foreigner talk based on Colonial French (CF). In the Indian Ocean, Chaudenson stresses that the first communicative medium used by the slave population, which he labels Bourbonnais, was not a creole but rather a pidginized variety of vernacular French (see Section 1.4.4). Although there is no evidence for the presence of a true French-based pidgin during the homestead phase of the development of French plantation colonies, it is most unlikely that, as second-language acquirers, the speech of members of the slave population would not show traces of pidginization. As Jeff Siegel (2006: 176, cited by McWhorter 2013: 411) suggests, the source of some creoles might not have been conventionalized pidgins but pidginized interlanguages. Finally, McWhorter and Parkvall (2002: 182) grant that one may account for the genesis of FBCs without recourse to an intermediate pidgin stage.[5]

13.1.3 Relexification and substrate influence

The view that in their attempt to acquire the language of the European population of plantation colonies, the slaves massively transferred linguistic features from their native language dominated early theorizing on the genesis of creoles.

The French philologist Lucien Adam, after examining descriptions of French-based Indian Ocean and Atlantic creoles (Mauritian, by Baissac 1880; Guyanese, by Saint-Quentin 1872; Trinidadian, by Thomas 1869), concluded (1883: 3–5):

> [...] les nègres guinéens, transportés dans ces colonies, ont pris au français ses mots, mais qu'ayant conservé, dans la mesure possible, leur phonétique et leur grammaire maternelles, ils ont fait du tout des idiomes sui generis ne présentant aucun des caractères propres à nos patois de France.

> [...] the Guinea Negroes, transported to those [Caribbean] colonies, took from French its words but, having retained as much as possible their native phonology and grammar, they made from all that sui generis languages showing none of the particular features of our French dialects.

Although the father of creole studies, Hugo Schuchardt, in his numerous publications did not share Adam's extreme view of the influence of the creole creators' mother tongue, he did recognize the importance of this influence.

In hypotheses about the genesis of European-based creoles, a traditional distinction is made between the **substrate**, the language of the subordinate learners, and the **superstrate**, the European language-learning target and the source of the primary linguistic input. These two terms, adapted from historical linguistics, are somewhat misleading. For example, in studies of the development of French from vernacular Latin varieties, the language of the indigenous Celtic-speaking population of Gaul was termed the substrate of the emerging Gallo-Romance speech. No term is given to the target language, vernacular Latin. In fact, it constitutes the stratum.[6] It is the speech of the Germanic tribes who later gained political control of Gaul and influenced the development of Gallo-Romance that is referred to as the **superstrate**. Thus, to label as superstrate the speech of the previously established European population of plantation colonies and as substrate that of the incoming slave population is misleading. Proposals to redefine these two terms in sociopolitical terms may be more useful. For DeGraff (2009: 892) the superstrate is the language of the socially dominant segment of the population and the substrate is that of the subordinate slave element. From a language-acquisition perspective the superstrate refers to the learning target, the source of primary linguistic data, and the substrate to the language(s) of the incoming slave population. But application of the model used to account for the genesis of French from Vulgar Latin yields a different scenario. Vernacular French, the acquisitional target for the slaves, constitutes the stratum. The languages that the slaves brought to colonial plantation societies may be characterized as the substrate. In the case of HC, the superstrate refers to languages introduced into Haiti after the development of HC – English and Spanish.

The dominance in creole studies of the belief in the major contribution of substrate languages to creole genesis extended into the 1960s. In the case of Atlantic creoles, earlier proposals tended to pick and choose specific linguistic features from the variety of African languages spoken by the incoming slaves. This practice is pejoratively referred to as the **cafeteria principle** (Dillard 1970). However, several decades earlier, the Haitian linguist Suzanne Sylvain (1936: 178) departed sharply from this approach when she identified a single African language, Ewe, belonging to the Kwa group spoken in the Gulf of Guinea region, as the source of the entire grammar of HC. She defined the language as:

> ... un français coulé dans le moule de la syntaxe africaine ou, comme on classe généralement les langues d'après leur parenté syntaxique, d'une langue éwé à vocabulaire français.

> ... a type of French cast in the mold of African syntax or, as one generally classifies languages on the basis of their syntactic relationship, an Ewe language with French vocabulary.

More recently, for the putative substrate of HC, Claire Lefebvre (1986, 1998) opted for Fongbe, a language, like Ewe, belonging to the Kwa language group.[7] This scholar and her associates at the Université du Québec à Montréal have the merit of providing a theoretical basis for the wholesale transfer of the syntax of one language onto the lexicon of another, namely, the notion of **Relexification**. This theory was first put forward by Muysken (1981) in the context of the acquisition of Spanish by speakers of Quechua in Ecuador, and the subsequent creation of a new variety of Spanish termed Media Lengua. This cognitive process involves, on the one hand, the retention on the part of second-language learners of their entire grammar plus the links between grammatical structures and their semantic properties and. on the other hand, the substitution of the lexical items of the acquisitional target with nearly their full phonological representation for corresponding lexical items of their mother tongue or primary language.

The term 'Relexification' was previously used to refer to the purported emergence of European-based pidgins on the coast of West Africa from an earlier pidgin developed by Portuguese traders. Whinnom (1965) suggested a possible link between this Portuguese pidgin and Lingua Franca, a trade language used in the Mediterranean region from at least the thirteenth century to the early nineteenth century. With the arrival of sailors and traders from other European nations (the Netherlands, England, France) this postulated Portuguese-based pidgin would have been relexified, that is, its grammatical structure was maintained but its lexicon replaced by that of these newly arrived languages. Ian Hancock (1979: 7) proposed that English-based creoles spoken on the African coast, in the Caribbean, and North and Central America derived from a 'single early pidgin spoken probably with local variants along the West African coast from the early sixteenth century'. However, the French Africanist Gabriel Manessy casts doubt on this hypothesis and favors the existence of an indigenous interethnic language of communication such as those that exist currently in sub-Saharan Africa (1995: 163). Presumably, current English-based creoles like West African Pidgin English have their source in the contact between such a vehicular language and English. As far as French is concerned, there is no attestation of any pidgin based on an indigenous contact vernacular language in coastal West Africa (see Section 13.2.1).

13.1.4 Basic problems of the exceptional hypotheses for Creole genesis

The three hypotheses that view creole genesis as exceptional face several fundamental problems. The Bioprogram and the Relexification hypotheses assume unattested second-language acquisition scenarios. With regard to the latter hypothesis, while transfer of first language (L1) features is widely attested at all linguistic levels in second-language acquisition, there are no reported cases of the global transfer of the total semantic and grammatical structures as posited by the Relexification Hypothesis (Jeff Siegel 2008: 273). DeGraff (2009: 939) aptly cites Bickerton's criticism of the hypothesis (1987: 235):

> You can't abstract words from the framework you meet them in and the properties that, in consequence, they trail with them. Those properties may be sharply reduced, as in early L^2 acquisition or pidginization, but they are always there, and you cannot just peel them off like you would the rind from an orange.

Concerning the development of HCE, doubts have been raised about the linguistic situation assumed by Bickerton, in particular, the multilingual nature of the indentured laborer population. According to Mufwene (2008: 189) it was not generally multiethnic. Hawaiian plantations tended to have laborers who shared the same L1: Chinese, Japanese, Korean, etc. Also, S. Roberts (1998: 34) pointed out that the majority of the foreign-born laborers lived where speakers of English were more numerous. It is questionable, then, that the primary linguistic input of the creators of HCE was so unlearnable that they had to resort to the innate Bioprogram. Finally, there is no evidence that adults were not involved in the creation of HCE, and that the children who presumably created the creole had no contact with fluent speakers of English.

With regard to French-based creoles (FBCs) at least, none of the three exceptional hypotheses concord with the sociohistorical setting of plantation colonies. Both the Bioprogram and the Relexification Hypotheses assume an initial disproportion between the slave and dominant populations. For example, Bickerton first claimed that 'not more than 20 percent [of the population] were native speakers of the dominant language' (1981: 4). As will be discussed in Section 13.1.5, this type of assertion flies in the face of all documented historical evidence. In the case of the Creole Prototype Hypothesis, there is no absolute evidence of the prior existence of an established pidgin that could have served as the primary linguistic input for the development of any French-based creole. However, as pointed out above (Section 13.1.2), its proponents do point out that the initial stage of FBCs could be a pidginized interlanguage. Importantly, the Creole Prototype hypothesis does allow for significant substratal transfer (see McWhorter and Parkvall 2002: 195–204 for specific features).

13.1.5 The Superstratist hypothesis

Most specialists in French-based creoles propose a setting for the genesis of creoles in which the usual processes of unguided second-language acquisition operated, and where it is the speakers of the varieties of the target language who first provided the primary linguistic input. The **Superstratist Hypothesis** was first put forward most explicitly by Robert Chaudenson (1974, 1992, 2001, 2003). He distinguishes two phases in the establishment of the seventeenth- and eighteenth-century French plantation colonies: the *société d'habitation* (homestead phase) and the *société de plantation* (proper plantation phase). The term *habitation* refers to small landholdings, where the farming settlers, the *habitants* 'residents', existed in precarious conditions as a particular colony underwent its initial settlement phase, building the infrastructure for its later development. Those Europeans who were *habitants* possessed very few slaves and lived in hardly better material conditions than them. Chaudenson (2003: 97) indicates that in Bourbon (currently Réunion), forty years after the initial settlement, *habitants* possessed an average of only four slaves, and in Martinique in 1664, a generation after the founding of the colony, of the 684 homesteads, 529 *habitants* held fewer than six slaves. During that initial phase of European settlement, there was relatively close social contact between masters and slaves, as well as between the latter and European indentured laborers who formed the initial labor pool. Consequently, African slaves had relatively full access to the Europeans' speech. Most young children of the slave population, like their free peers, were *creoles*, that is, born in the colony, and did not have to resort to the Bioprogram to communicate. They acquired the ambient speech as a first language under normal circumstances. It may well be that during initial contacts with slaves the Europeans made use, not of a pidgin, but of the pidginized foreigner talk described in Section 13.2 below. The speech of foreign-born adult slaves reflected more the processes of unguided second-language acquisition.

A central tenet of the Superstratist Hypothesis is that the variety of French to which the slave acquirers were exposed was not the standard variety but a vernacular koinè (Chaudenson 1974, 1979, 1992, 2003; Valdman, 1969, 1971, 1978). The linguistic heterogeneity of the European component of plantocratic colonies is reflected by an early census (1665–1715) taken in Bourbon, which is cited by Chaudenson (1974: 462). Of the 164 White heads of household, 60% came from west of a line between Bordeaux and Paris and no doubt spoke varieties of French influenced by a variety of dialects. Interestingly, 23% were foreigners, speakers of Dutch, English, Portuguese, etc., who undoubtedly had acquired French as a second language, if they spoke the language at all.

In Saint-Domingue, France's chief plantation colony, during the homestead phase, which extended from about 1640 to 1700, the main products for export were leather, from the wild cattle abundant in Hispaniola, tobacco, and indigo. The population was preponderantly White: buccaneers, small-scale *habitants*, and indentured laborers (Exmelin 1980). It was the introduction of the sugar-based agro-industry, requiring massive injections of capital and a large workforce, that marked the beginning of the plantation phase. It was not until France had formally acquired Saint-Domingue from Spain, following the treaty of Ryswik (1697), that imported African slaves became more numerous than the Whites. As shown in Table 13.1, slaves constituted nearly 90% of the population on the eve of the Haitian Revolution, which marked the end of the French colonial period (Frostin 1975: 2).

Table 13.1. Population Evolution in Saint-Domingue

	Whites	Freed Slaves and Mulattoes	Slaves
1681	4,336	210	2,101
1687	4,441	224	3,358
1700	5,509	500	9,082
1739	11,699	2,527	109,780
1789	30,826	27,548	465,429

In the linguistic context of the plantation phase, the newly arriving slaves, the *Bozals* (French *bossal*; see Section 1.2.2 for the origin of the term), condemned to the hard labor of the cane fields or the sugar mills, had little, if any, contact with fluent speakers of French, particularly Europeans. Their primary linguistic input was limited to the evolving speech of the creole or **seasoned** slaves, that is, locally born slaves or African slaves who had arrived earlier and were already acculturated. These slaves also spoke closer approximations of the target language. As the development of the export-based economy producing sugar, coffee, and indigo steadily increased, so did the numbers of new arrivals, increasing from an annual average of 300 in 1741 to 29,000 between 1784 and 1791 (Cornevin, 1982: 24).[8] By this time a French-based creole specific to Saint-Domingue had been fully established, as demonstrated by the *Passion de Notre Seigneur selon Saint-Jean en Langage Nègre,* estimated to have been written between 1720 and 1740 (see Section 4.3.2).

13.2 The Genesis of French-based Creoles

13.2.1 Monogensis versus polygenesis

Striking similarities, primarily at the lexical but also at the morphosyntactic level, have led some authors to assume a common origin for all French-based creoles (FBCs), a theory known as monogenesis:

Only by positing a single origin for Creole can one account for this historical connection, and its place of origin can scarcely have been other than West Africa, from which it was transported to the various parts of the world where Creole is now found. (Goodman 1964: 130ff.)

Like the general monogenetic theory advanced to account for all European-based creoles (see the discussion in Section 13.1 above), Goodman posits a 'slaver jargon of some sort'. Alexander Hull (1979: 176) is more categorical and specific: '*Il ne peut y avoir aucun doute qu'un pidgin français s'est formé sur la côte de l'Afrique* (There can be no doubt that a French pidgin was formed on the African coast)'. Following Hancock (1969), Hull locates the trading post of Whydah (Ouidah) in present-day Benin as the birthplace of this assumed French-based pidgin.

This hypothesis runs into several problems. First, there is no textual evidence for the existence of this pidgin, which, according to Hull, would have been learned by the slaves as they were being prepared for shipment to the Atlantic and Indian Ocean plantation colonies. Second, the first main French trading post in West Africa was not Whydah but further north at Saint-Louis in present-day Senegal and at the mouth of the Gambia river. As pointed out in Section 1.1.1, the French navigator Le Courbe, who had sailed into these ports, is cited as saying that the Senegalese, in addition to their own language, spoke a 'corrupted' Portuguese which they called a creole (Chaudenson 1979: 9; Holm 1988: 15). As shown in Figure 13.1, Hull assumes that this presumed pidgin developed from the contact between a vernacular variety of French used by sailors (*français maritime*) and the Portuguese-based pidgin that most creolists who favor monogenesis posit as the ancestor of all European-based creoles.[9] Furthermore, Hull does not provide any evidence for the evolution of the original French-based pidgin (*pidgin français primitif*) into the more complex one (*pidgin français avancé*) he posits. Nor does he indicate why, curiously enough, the latter led to HC, Louisiana Creole, and Mauritian Creole, whereas the former was the ancestor of the Lesser Antilles creoles, Réunion Creole, and Guianese Creole.[10]

Philip Baker and Chris Corne (1982) opt for a polygenetic hypothesis, according to which an FBC developed independently in each plantation colony when social conditions were propitious. They applied their model specifically to Mauritius. Operating within Bickerton's Bioprogram framework and his radicalness scale for Creole languages (see Section 13.1.2 above), they account for Mauritian Creole's greater **radicalness** from Réunion Creole (i.e., its greater linguistic divergence from French) on the basis of crucial chronological points in the development of plantation colonies. Their model comprises three such crucial points, termed Events: Event

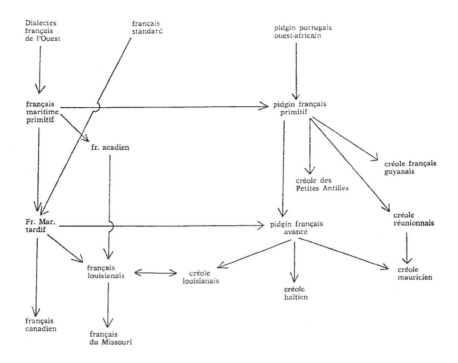

Figure 13.1. Links between a Presumed Maritime French and French-based Creoles

1, the date when the number of imported slaves became greater than French speakers; Event 2, the date when the creole slaves (i.e., those born in the colony) outnumbered French speakers; Event 3, the date when the importation of slaves ceased. In Réunion, Event 1 occurred about fifty years later than in Mauritius, thus explaining why Réunion Creole diverges less from French (has less radicalness) than Mauritian Creole because the contact of the slaves with the dominant language was more intensive and the hypothesized Bioprogram had a lesser effect. Similarly, the time interval between Event 1 and Event 2 in Réunion was greater than in Mauritius. According to this model, newly imported slaves still had contact with native speakers of French, whereas in Mauritius creole slaves, who as children would have resorted to the Bioprogram to 'create' a creole distinct from the approximative French continuum, more often provided newly imported slaves with a target speech consisting of the crystallized creole. Furthermore, in Mauritius, unlike in Réunion, the importation of slaves continued for two generations after the creole slaves constituted the majority of the population.

13.2 Genesis of French-based Creoles

However, there is evidence that suggests that, in both zones where FBCs arose, earlier settlements constituted focal centers for the diffusion of the colonial model for social and economic organization. The speech associated with these focal centers may well have been transported with the organizational model. On the basis of historical records, Robert Chaudenson (1992: 59ff) shows that Mauritian Creole did not develop independently, but that, instead, there was initial input from the previously settled neighboring island, Bourbon (the original name of Réunion Island). He indicates that in 1721 the French East India Company ordered the governor of the island to take steps to promote the establishment of a plantation economy in Mauritius. He obliged by sending three Europeans and thirty slaves, who presumably spoke Bourbonnais, the speech variety that had developed on Bourbon Island more than a half-century after the initial settlement. Chaudenson cautions that he does not suggest that the speech variety he labels Bourbonnais was a creole, since he states: '*à cette date un créole, il n'existe pas* (at that date a creole did not yet exist)' (2003: 84). The term Bourbonnais refers to a pidginized, approximative variety of CF that developed during the homestead phase of Réunion.

On the basis of this case, Chaudenson accounts for the geographical spread of FBCs in terms of **generations** (1992: 38, 45–46), a modified polygenetic model.[11] Following this model, Mauritian Creole is a second-generation FBC, and those of the other two Indian Ocean islands, settled mostly from Mauritius, namely, Rodrigues Island and the Seychelles archipelago, are third-generation creoles.

An argument that could be put forward for the monogenesis of FBCs rests on the existence of a core lexicon, labeled by Chaudenson (1974: 591ff.) as a *vocabulaire des Isles* 'insular lexicon' (see Section 6.4), regrouping terms attested in both the Indian Ocean and Atlantic FBCs, for example: *habitation* 'homestead, landholding', agricultural property settled by *habitants* 'settlers engaged in farming'; *engagé* 'indentured servant'; *boucaner* 'to smoke' (meat); *cabanne* 'bed'; *corossol* 'soursop' (*Annona muricata*); *manoque* 'small bunch of tobacco leaves'; *maron* 'fugitive slave, also wild animal or uncultivated plant'; *pistache* 'peanut' (versus Standard French *arachide or cacahuète*); *patate* 'sweet potato' (*Convolvulus batatas*).

There did exist administrative and commercial links between the two zones as well. Some of the sailors, traders, and settlers who landed in Bourbon and Isle de France had gained previous colonial experience in the earlier-settled Atlantic colonies; indeed, some had been recruited by the Compagnie des Indes that oversaw Réunion during the early phase of its settlement (Chaudenson 1974: 594).

408   *The Genesis and Development of Haitian Creole*

According to the proposed modified polygenetic model, although they share many features at all linguistic levels without being mutually intelligible, Indian Ocean and Atlantic creoles do not derive from a common creole ancestor. As put forward below, both sets of FBCs have their origin in vernacular koinè varieties of French, Colonial French (CF), spoken by the first settlers, rather than, as Hull (1979) assumes, a pidginized variety of vernacular French (a **maritime** French) spread by sailors.

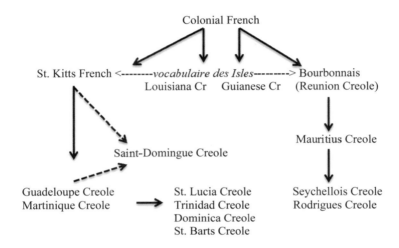

Figure 13.2. The Origin of French-based Creoles

As pointed out in Section 1.4.2, the island of St. Kitts (in French, Saint-Christophe) became the first French settlement in the Antilles. A first attempt was made by Huguenots in 1538, and a more permanent one in 1626 with the official approval of Cardinal Richelieu under the leadership of the Norman privateer and trader Pierre Bélain d'Estambuc (see Section 1.4.2). In 1635, d'Estambuc recruited a hundred experienced settlers from St. Kitts and established a new settlement in Martinique (Chaudenson 1992: 59).

That same year, another Norman settler from St. Kitts, Charles Liénard, and an associate, Jean du Plessis, obtained a commission to establish a settlement in Guadeloupe. It is unlikely that an FBC developed during the twelve years that separate d'Estambuc's original settlement in St. Kitts, and his founding of the new settlement in Martinique. Most likely what was transported at that time was an early adaptation to the homestead setting and an approximative variety of French.

Martinican and Guadeloupean creoles may be considered **second-generation** creoles because of their link to the earlier-settled St. Kitts, just as Mauritian Creole is a second-generation creo[...]. Although there were fewer contacts between St. Ki[tts...] the FBC that developed in the latter colony may also be consi[dered a second-] generation one (Parkvall 1995). Subsequently, the FBCs that deve[loped in] Martinique and Guadeloupe were transported to others of the Leeward islands, St. Barts, Dominica, St. Lucia, Grenada, and Trinidad, where they spawned **third-generation** creoles. There might also have been some influence on Saint-Domingue from Martinique and Guadeloupe, which had been settled earlier.

Guy Hazaël-Massieux (1991), in suggesting a monogenetic model for Atlantic creoles, identifies St. Kitts as the focal point for the spread of all Atlantic FBCs. Applying Bartoli's stratigraphic dialectological model (1945), he postulates that Guadeloupe, Martinique, and Saint-Domingue constituted the central zone in the formation and diffusion of Atlantic FBCs (see Figure 13.2). Accordingly, it is in these colonies that one would expect to find the most innovative FBC features. Louisiana, Grenada, and French Guyana are peripheral zones where one would expect to find forms reflecting older stages of the initial creole. Indeed, Louisiana Creole and Guianese Creole differ from the presumedly more innovative FBCs in sharing with Indian Ocean FBCs pre-posed possessive determiners rather than post-posed constructions with post-posed personal pronouns (see Table 13.2). Hazaël-Massieux postulates the fossilized possessive construction attested in Louisiana, *no vyé paron a nou zòt* (SF *nos vieux parents à nous autres* 'our older relatives') (I. Neumann 1985: 13), as a possible source of both forms in the peripheral and the central zones. The example, an emphatic variant of SF *nos vieux parents*, was presumably restructured differently in the two zones. In the case of the innovative central zone, the possessive pronoun is post-posed, as exemplified by Northern HC (Capois) *paran an nou* and Standard HC *paran nou*.

With regard to Saint-Domingue Creole, when France ceded St. Kitts to England by the Treaty of Utrecht (1713) – an island it previously had shared with its rival – planters moved to the newly developed colony. D'Ans (1987: 122) also mentions the transfer of sugar plantation owners from Guadeloupe and Martinique to the more economically promising Saint-Domingue territory. It is most likely, though, that Guianese and Louisiana Creoles had an independent development. For Louisiana, Klingler (2003: 50–4) shows that a major influence from earlier established Caribbean French-based creoles is questionable because, in the early stages of settlement, most of the slaves shipped there arrived directly from Africa. However, as indicated in Section 1.4.1, the arrival of about 10,000 Saint-Domingue refugees (Whites, freemen, and slaves) in the early stage of the development of Louisiana may have led to a subsequent influence of Saint-Domingue Creole.

In the final analysis, by the time the *Passion* was composed, there no doubt existed, prior to Saint-Domingue Creole, local varieties of FBCs that had formed in the central Atlantic zone: St. Kitts, Martinique, and Guadeloupe. In addition, there was ongoing contact between all of these colonies resulting in the diffusion of linguistic forms. This might account for the use of *qu'a* in the *Passion*, a form found today in all the Antillean FBCs and Guianese Creole.

As illustrated by Figure 13.2, the following scenario is proposed for the development of French-based creoles. As argued above, they have their origins in CF, perhaps modified by its speakers to facilitate its acquisition by the slave population. FBCs developed separately in the Atlantic and Indian Oceans. In the latter region, an FBC or a somewhat homogeneous approximative variety of CF first developed on Réunion and yielded a second-generation one in Mauritius. Speakers of Mauritian Creole then carried the latter to the later-settled island of Rodrigues and the Seychelles archipelago, although there also were contacts between Bourbon and the Seychelles.

In the Atlantic zone, Louisiana Creole and Guianese Creole probably developed independently from those in the Caribbean. As noted in Chapter 1, although the French first attempted to establish a colony in Cayenne in 1604, French Guyana's main town, it was not until the 1660s that a permanent small-scale settlement was established. An FBC did not develop in Louisiana until the early years of the eighteenth century. In the Caribbean, it may be that an approximative variety of CF that first developed in St. Kitts was exported to the later settled colonies in Martinique, Guadeloupe, and Saint-Domingue. There may have been some influence from Martinique and Guadeloupe on the creole that arose in the Saint-Domingue colony, where the plantation economy developed later. From Guadeloupe and Martinique, FBCs were transmitted to the southern Caribbean, namely, Dominica, St. Lucia, Grenada, and Trinidad, with some influence on Guianese Creole as well. Finally, there were links to the Indian Ocean, mostly at the lexical level (*vocabulaire des Isles*), from the colonies settled earlier in the Caribbean.

13.2.2 From Colonial French to HC

The central tenet of the Superstratist theory of creolization is that the learning target of the creators of FBCs was not the standard variety of French, reflected in written texts, but rather the vernacular varieties. As suggested in Valdman (1971: 205):

as Mauritian Creole is a second-generation creole based on Bourbonnais. Although there were fewer contacts between St. Kitts and Saint-Domingue, the FBC that developed in the latter colony may also be considered a second-generation one (Parkvall 1995). Subsequently, the FBCs that developed in Martinique and Guadeloupe were transported to others of the Leeward islands: St. Barts, Dominica, St. Lucia, Grenada, and Trinidad, where they spawned **third-generation** creoles. There might also have been some influence on Saint-Domingue from Martinique and Guadeloupe, which had been settled earlier.

Guy Hazaël-Massieux (1991), in suggesting a monogenetic model for Atlantic creoles, identifies St. Kitts as the focal point for the spread of all Atlantic FBCs. Applying Bartoli's stratigraphic dialectological model (1945), he postulates that Guadeloupe, Martinique, and Saint-Domingue constituted the central zone in the formation and diffusion of Atlantic FBCs (see Figure 13.2). Accordingly, it is in these colonies that one would expect to find the most innovative FBC features. Louisiana, Grenada, and French Guyana are peripheral zones where one would expect to find forms reflecting older stages of the initial creole. Indeed, Louisiana Creole and Guianese Creole differ from the presumably more innovative FBCs in sharing with Indian Ocean FBCs pre-posed possessive determiners rather than possessive constructions with post-posed personal pronouns (see Table 13.2). Hazaël-Massieux postulates the fossilized possessive construction attested in Louisiana, *no vyé paron a nou zòt* (SF *nos vieux parents à nous autres* 'our older relatives') (I. Neumann 1985: 13), as a possible source of both forms in the peripheral and the central zones. The example, an emphatic variant of SF *nos vieux parents*, was presumably restructured differently in the two zones. In the case of the innovative central zone, the possessive pronoun is post-posed, as exemplified by Northern HC (Capois) *paran an nou* and Standard HC *paran nou*.

With regard to Saint-Domingue Creole, when France ceded St. Kitts to England by the Treaty of Utrecht (1713) – an island it previously had shared with its rival – planters moved to the newly developed colony. D'Ans (1987: 122) also mentions the transfer of sugar plantation owners from Guadeloupe and Martinique to the more economically promising Saint-Domingue territory. It is most likely, though, that Guianese and Louisiana Creoles had an independent development. For Louisiana, Klingler (2003: 50–4) shows that a major influence from earlier established Caribbean French-based creoles is questionable because, in the early stages of settlement, most of the slaves shipped there arrived directly from Africa. However, as indicated in Section 1.4.1, the arrival of about 10,000 Saint-Domingue refugees (Whites, freemen, and slaves) in the early stage of the development of Louisiana may have led to a subsequent influence of Saint-Domingue Creole.

The only available texts from the period of French colonization in St. Kitts consist of short passages from missionary priests' accounts. They contain what appears to be a pidginized variety of French, reflecting foreigner talk, and African slaves' approximative attempts at reproducing the French vernacular koinè spoken by early settlers – recall that the early settlers originated in Normandy. As pointed out in Section 4.3.1, the first attested texts from the Atlantic zone document a French-based pidgin developed in contact with Caribs (Chevillard 1659), reproduced as Text 1.

Text 1

Toy sçavoir qu'il y a UN DIEU: luy grand Capitou: luy sçavoir tout faire sans autre pour l'ayder: luy donner à tous patates: luy mouche manigat pour tout faire, non point autre comme luy.

'You know that there is a God: him big Chief: him know do everything without other to help him; him give to all sweet potatoes: him very powerful to do all, none like him'[12]

In one of the letters dated 1689 he sent to an acquaintance in France, Father Louis Mongin, who was based in Martinique but travelled to St. Kitts, described the salient features of the pidginized French used to communicate with the newly arrived slaves (Chatillon 1984: 134–5). Presumably it was a modification of an earlier contact variety of French (see Text 2):

Text 2

Les nègres ont appris en peu de temps un certain jargon français que les missionnaires savent et avec lequel ils les instruisent, par l'infinitif du verbe, sans jamais le conjuguer, en y ajoutant quelques mots qui font connaître le temps et la personne de qui l'on parle. Par exemple, s'ils veulent dire: je veux prier Dieu demain, ils diront moi prier Dieu demain, moi manger hier, toi donner manger à moi, et ainsi en toutes sortes de choses. Ce jargon est fort aisé à apprendre aux nègres et aux missionnaires aussi pour les instruire, et ainsi ils le donnent à entendre pour toutes choses.

'The negroes have in a short time learned a kind of French jargon that missionaries know and with which they instruct them, which is with the infinitive of the verb without conjugating it, and by adding a few words that indicate the tense and the person about whom one speaks. For example, if they wish to say: I want to pray to God tomorrow, they'll say me pray to God tomorrow, me eat yesterday, you give eat to me, and so on and so forth. This pidgin is very easy to teach to negroes and to missionaries, as well as to instruct them [in religious matters], and thus they use it to communicate about everything.'

In fact, other forms of the verb were occasionally used in this pidginized French. For example, another missionary priest, Pierre Pelleprat, cites a prayer by a fourteen-year-old slave boy from St. Kitts whose brother was gravely ill (Pelleprat 1655: 63, cited by Calvet and Chaudenson 1998: 55). Note in Text 3 the use of the second person plural form *voulé* (voulez) 'to want' together with the infinitives *mentir* 'to lie', *iurer* (*jurer*) 'to swear', *dérober* 'to steal', *demander* 'to ask', *aller* 'to go', and *faire* 'to do'.

Text 3

Seigneur, toi bien sçave que mon frère luy point mentir, point luy iurer, point dérober, point aller luy à femme d'autre, point luy méchant, pourquoi toy le voulé faire mourir?	'Lord, you know well that my brother him not lie, not swear, not steal, not go with woman of another, not him bad, why you want make him die?'

Perhaps, in addition to Colonial French (CF), the initial linguistic input of the creators of Atlantic FBCs was this approximative variety of CF, most likely based on French foreigner talk that developed into the individual Atlantic FBCs. Text 3 and three other texts Mongin provided show, for example, the primary use of the infinitive and stressed pronouns rather than clitic forms (French *je/j'*, *me/m'*, *il/l'*, etc.). They do not support Jennings's claim (1995) that these prove the existence of a St. Kitts FBC.

The first attested text that provides incontrovertible evidence for the existence of a genuine FBC is a Saint-Domingue text, *La Passion de Notre Seigneur selon Saint-Jean en Langage Nègre* attributed to one Father Boutin, and estimated to have been written between 1720 and 1740 (see Section 4.3.2). This period coincides with the launching of a robust agro-industrial economy grounded in sugar production in Saint-Domingue. By that time, there certainly were creole slaves (i.e., locally born slaves) in the colony. A fully constituted tense-aspect system with three verb markers appears in this text: durative *qu'a*, equivalent to HC *ap(e)*, past *té*, and future *va*, as well as the post-posed determiner *LA*, the plural marker *io* and the possessive construction consisting of the optional preposition *a* plus pronoun. The *Passion* also displays a wide variety of verb forms in addition to the infinitive, including the plural imperative and the past participle.[13]

Text 4

... tous pères jouifs **la ïo** ... pendant ïo **té qu'a** *mangé*, Jesi *prend* pain, *cassé* li, *séparé ba* ïo tous; di ïo ... '*prend* li, *mangé*, cila sé corps **moé**, vous *tende* ?' ... li **té** *metté* di vin ... li *dire* ïo ; 'boire ça, c'est sang **a moé**...'	'... all the Jewish priests ... while they were eating, Jesus took some bread, he broke it, divided it for all of them. He said to them ... "take it, eat, this is my body, you hear?"... He put some wine ... he said to them, "drink this, it is my blood ..."'

In the final analysis, by the time the *Passion* was composed, there no doubt existed, prior to Saint-Domingue Creole, local varieties of FBCs that had formed in the central Atlantic zone: St. Kitts, Martinique, and Guadeloupe. In addition, there was ongoing contact between all of these colonies resulting in the diffusion of linguistic forms. This might account for the use of *qu'a* in the *Passion,* a form found today in all the Antillean FBCs and Guianese Creole.

As illustrated by Figure 13.2, the following scenario is proposed for the development of French-based creoles. As argued above, they have their origins in CF, perhaps modified by its speakers to facilitate its acquisition by the slave population. FBCs developed separately in the Atlantic and Indian Oceans. In the latter region, an FBC or a somewhat homogeneous approximative variety of CF first developed on Réunion and yielded a second-generation one in Mauritius. Speakers of Mauritian Creole then carried the latter to the later-settled island of Rodrigues and the Seychelles archipelago, although there also were contacts between Bourbon and the Seychelles.

In the Atlantic zone, Louisiana Creole and Guianese Creole probably developed independently from those in the Caribbean. As noted in Chapter 1, although the French first attempted to establish a colony in Cayenne in 1604, French Guyana's main town, it was not until the 1660s that a permanent small-scale settlement was established. An FBC did not develop in Louisiana until the early years of the eighteenth century. In the Caribbean, it may be that an approximative variety of CF that first developed in St. Kitts was exported to the later settled colonies in Martinique, Guadeloupe, and Saint-Domingue. There may have been some influence from Martinique and Guadeloupe on the creole that arose in the Saint-Domingue colony, where the plantation economy developed later. From Guadeloupe and Martinique, FBCs were transmitted to the southern Caribbean, namely, Dominica, St. Lucia, Grenada, and Trinidad, with some influence on Guianese Creole as well. Finally, there were links to the Indian Ocean, mostly at the lexical level (*vocabulaire des Isles*), from the colonies settled earlier in the Caribbean.

13.2.2 From Colonial French to HC

The central tenet of the Superstratist theory of creolization is that the learning target of the creators of FBCs was not the standard variety of French, reflected in written texts, but rather the vernacular varieties. As suggested in Valdman (1971: 205):

13.2 Genesis of French-based Creoles 413

Many of the phonological and syntactic features of HC are shared by non-standard varieties of 17th and 18th century French which still survive today in North American French dialects and, of course, in vernacular metropolitan varieties. The speech to which African slaves were exposed was not French 'baby-talk' but the untutored speech of the lower classes of colonial society.

This view, adopted by all superstratists, has been extended to all European-based creoles by Mufwene (2008: 84):

The connection between, on the one hand, creoles, and on the other, the relevant European and substrate languages is unmistakable once one compares them not so much with the standard varieties of European languages but with the nonstandard vernaculars actually spoken by the European yeomen and indentured servants with whom the non-European labor interacted regularly.

Thus, with regard to FBCs of the Atlantic zone, the learning target of the imported slaves was not SF but CF, a koinè of vernacular varieties of the language, about which we can gain insights by examining varieties of the language exported to the French colonies in the seventeenth and eighteenth centuries that had evolved in a different social context from the plantation colonies. Particularly useful in understanding the genesis and development of Haitian Creole (in fact, of all FBCs) is the examination of French varieties spoken in Quebec, Nova Scotia, and New Brunswick (formerly Acadia), Newfoundland, Louisiana, French-speaking isolates in Old Mines (Missouri), Red Lake Falls (Minnesota), as well as by part of the indigenous white population of the small islet of St. Barts (Saint-Barthélemy) in the French Antilles.

Below, I show links at the morphosyntactic and lexical levels between these American varieties of French, particularly Louisiana French (LF) and the French dialect of St. Barts, St. Barts Patois (SBP), and the FBCs. These two varieties are particularly noteworthy, because they have evolved with less contact with Standard French (SF) than the other American varieties of the language.

Morphosyntax verb forms

Pelleprat (see Section 13.2.1 above) attributes the use of the infinitive to slaves' reanalysis of a wide variety of French verb forms. Also, inasmuch as the development of FBCs involved the approximative acquisition of CF, it is useful to seek insights from present-day unguided second-language acquisition of vernacular French and first-language acquisition by French children.

With regard to the latter, Clark (1985: 722) suggests that situational salience in communicative interactions guides the learners' reanalysis. Many interactions of children with adults involve orders, and indeed imperative forms are among the first produced:

> Children's first verb forms appear to be the singular and the plural of the imperative, e.g. donne, donnez. However, the singular imperative coincides with the three singular forms of the indicative, while the plural one coincides with the infinitive in pronunciation, for most verbs.

No doubt, orders and directives, varying in directness and pragmatic context, occurred with great frequency in communicative interactions between the various social categories of Europeans and slaves, as well as between more seasoned slaves and the Bozal slaves, newly imported from Africa. In view of Clark's observation, it is pertinent to note that the past participle of verbs like *manger* and *casser* is also homophonous with their plural imperative form.

Descriptions of North American varieties of French show numerous cases of what would be considered verb 'errors' in SF. Neumann-Holzschuh (2003) provides an inventory of the use of infinitives in Louisiana, Acadia, and Newfoundland French, citing, among others, Guilbeau (1950) and Rottet (1995) for LF and Brasseur (1997) for the other two varieties. The following examples from Rottet (page numbers in parentheses) illustrate instances of the use of the infinitive in main and subordinate clauses instead of the subjunctive and the imperfect; SF 'correct' forms are provided in parentheses.

(1) Elizabeth veut **mon aller** (que j'aille) avant les autes. (R 271) 'Elizabeth wants me to go before the others.'

(2) Je veux que **eusse aoir** (ils aient) eine bonne vie. (R 267) 'I want them to have a good life.'

(3) Je vous ai amenés ici pour **vous autres s'amuser** (pour que vous (pl.) vous amusiez). (R 26) 'I brought you here so that you would have fun.'

In demonstrating the use of invariable verb forms in North American French, Neumann-Holzschuh (2003) cites instances of the replacement of plural forms of the present by corresponding singular ones, taken from Rottet (1995: 156):

(4) Les enfants dans l'église **comprend** (comprennent) pas le français. 'Children in church don't understand French.'

13.2 Genesis of French-based Creoles 415

And Guilbeau (1950: 168):

(5)   Qui vous-autres **fait** (faites) ici?   'What are y'all doing here?'

However, like the 'advanced' varieties of French described in particular by Henri Frei (1929), in Louisiana French, in the present indicative, grammatical person is marked by the exclusive use of the personal pronouns. Concomitantly, verb endings are eliminated. This trend manifests itself in vernacular SF by the replacement of *nous* by *on* for first person plural. For the foremost and only productive verb class in French, *-er* verbs, there are only two oral forms in the present indicative: *je chante, tu chantes, i(l)/elle chante, on chante, i(l)s/elles chantent* /ʃãt/ versus *vous chantez* /ʃãte/. In LF, the use of the plural marker *aut(res)* following the personal pronoun renders verbs of this class invariable in the present tense: *je chante, tu chante, i(l)/elle chante, nous aut' chante, vous aut' chante, eux-aut'/eusse/ça chante* /ʃãt/. The invariability of the present indicative is even more extensive in SBP. Only two verbs, 'to be' and 'to have', have more than one present indicative form: *j'è* vs. *t'a, i/al a, on a, vous aut'a*; *eu sont* vs. *t'è, vous-aut'è* (Highfield 1979: 85). Thus, the slaves often heard only one present indicative form, that is, they did not replace plural forms by corresponding singular ones but simply reproduced those they heard. Except in the Indian Ocean FBCs and Louisiana (see Section 1.4) where there is a long form (based on the infinitive, the past participle or the plural imperative) alternating with a short form based on the present stem, the Caribbean FBCs and Guianese Creole show a single invariable verb form, either long or short. For example, in Haitian Creole, one finds a long basic form like *chante* 'sing' as well as a short one like *travay* 'work'.

To conclude this section on verb forms, it is no doubt the case that the widespread presence in FBCs of forms derived from the French infinitives does constitute a trace of a pidginized interlanguage stage, as has been proposed by proponents of the Creole Prototype (McWhorter and Parkvall 2002: 184).

The possessive construction

Table 13.2 shows that Louisiana (LC) and Guianese (GuyC) Creoles are outliers among Atlantic FBCs. In these two FBCs, possession is expressed by a pre-posed possessive determiner (adjective), just as it is in the Indian Ocean creoles. The other Atlantic FBCs, including HC, have a post-posed construction consisting of the personal pronoun and, in the case of Guadeloupean Creole and Northern HC (see Chapter 3), preceded by the preposition *a*.

416 The Genesis and Development of Haitian Creole

Table 13.2. Possessive Determiners in French-based Creoles

Creole	1SG	2SG	3SG	1PL	2PL	3PL
Mar.	N + *mwen*	N + *ou, w*	N + *li*	N + *nou*	N + *zòt*	N + *yo*
Gua.	N + *an-mwen*	N + *a-w*, N + *a-vou*	N + *a-y*	N + *an-nou*	N + *a-zòt*	N + *a-yo*
Hai.	N + *mwen, m*[14]	N + *ou*	N + *li, i*	N + *nou*	N + *nou*	N + *yo*
Gui.	*mo* + N	*to* + N *ou* + N (polite)	*li* + N	*nou* + N	*zòt* + N	*yé* + N
Lou.	*mo* + N	*to* + N	*so* + N	*nou*, *nouzot* + N	*vou* *vouzòt* + N	*ye* + N
Reu.	*mon* + N	*out*, *ton* + N	*son* + N	*nou*, *not* + N	*out*, *zot* + N	*zot* + N
Mau.	*mo* + N	*to* + N *vou* + N (polite)	*so* + N	*nou* + N	*zot* + N	*zot* + N
Sey.	*mon* + N	*ou* + N	*son* + N	*nou* + N	*zot* + N	*zot* + N

SBP provides support for Guy Hazaël-Massieux' hypothesis that CF constitutes the source of the fossilized possessive construction attested in Louisiana Creole; recall *no vyé paron a nou zòt* (SF *nos vieux parents à nous autres*) 'our older relatives'; see also Chaudenson (2003: 303–11). As is the case in some present-day varieties of vernacular French, in noun phrases where the possessor is expressed as a proper noun, possession is usually indicated with the preposition *à* rather than *de*: *les enfants à Alphonse est bien élevé* 'Alphonse's children are well-behaved' versus *les nasses de mon mari* 'my husband's fishing traps' (Highfield 1979: 63), *les familles du mort* 'the families of the deceased' (Calvet and Chaudenson 1998: 93). Highfield also notes that the preposition *à* may be deleted: *les livres Alphonse* 'Alphonse's books'. In addition, although SBP, like SF, has pre-posed possessive adjectives, for example, *mes nasses* 'my fishing traps', these are often reinforced with the post-posed possessive construction consisting of *à* + the stressed personal pronoun: *dans mon temps à mouin* (SF *moi*) 'in my days'.[15]

The definite and demonstrative determiners

The Atlantic FBCs part with Réunion and Seychellois Creoles in the position of the definite determiner (see Table 13.3). The variation in form of this part of speech triggered by gender and number distinction leads to a low level of saliency in SF. It has five phonetically short oral forms determined by the gender and number of the noun and its initial phoneme: /lə/ *le chien*, masc. 'the dog'; /l/ *l'oiseau*, masc. 'the bird'; *l'oie*, fem. 'the goose';

13.2 Genesis of French-based Creoles

Table 13.3. Definite Determiners in French-based Creoles

Creole	Definite determiners	
	Singular	Plural
Mar.	N + *la*	*sé* + N + *la*
Gua.	N + *la*	*sé* + N + *la*
Hai.	N + *la*	N + *(la) yo*[16]
Gui.	N + *a*	N + *ya*
Lou.	N + *la*	N + *ye, le* + N
Reu.	*la/le/* + N	*(le) bann* + N
Mau.	N + *la*	*bann* + N + *la*
Sey.	*sa* + N	*bann* + N

/la/ *la poule*, fem. 'the hen'; /lez/ *les oiseaux*; /le/ *les chiens*. Consequently, unguided foreign learners are likely to look for a more salient marking of definiteness and deixis. They find it in the locative adverb *là* that encodes two semantic values or pragmatic functions.

First, *là* expresses the deictic function of the demonstrative determiner *ce/ cet/ cette/ces*. This is widely attested in North American varieties of French: Old Mines *blé sèc-là* 'this dry wheat', *liv-là* 'this book', *chose blanc-là* 'this white thing' (Thogmartin, 1979: 115). In LF and SBP, *là* is used obligatorily to reinforce the deictic force of the demonstrative determiner: LF, *il s'a accroché une des ces vignes-là* 'he caught onto one of those vines' (Valdman *et al.* 2010: 9); SBP *c't enfant-là* 'this child', *ce chien-là* 'this dog', *ces hommes-là* 'these men' (Highfield 1979: 63). In fact, this construction occurs widely in present-day vernacular French: *Tu connais c'type là?* 'You know this guy?' Among French first-language learners, *là* occurs with the definite article. In his classic study, A. Grégoire (1947) reports his children producing *i est mésant, le môsieur là* 'he is mean, this man'. They also produced a post-posed *là* by itself, *c'est pou(r) papa, liv-là* 'it's for daddy, this book', and a post-posed *ça*, reinforcing the pre-posed definite determiner, *un mésant, le garçon ça* 'a mean one, this boy'.

Second, in vernacular French the adverb *là* serves a wide range of pragmatic functions in addition to its primary spatial meaning. Compare (6a) and (6b):

(6a) Mets le crayon **là**. 'Put the pencil here.'
(6b) Tu sais le prof de l'année dernière **là**. 'You know last year's teacher [the one that gave a lot of homework].' (Ludwig 1988: 38)

In (6a), *là* has its canonical spatial meaning but in (6b) the speaker presupposes prior knowledge on the part of the interlocutor about the past situation to which she refers. In this regard, it is analogous to the use of the HC sentential *LA* presented in Sections 9.6 and 9.7, where it expresses pre-supposition on the part of the speaker. As Ludwig and Pfänder (2003: 273ff) suggest and illustrate with examples from English-influenced Canadian French, *là* also serves to structure discourse.

(7)   ... c'est peut être ben pas/   ... it's maybe not really in fashion
       à la mode **là** / tout le monde   / not everyone still wears it (you
       n'en porte pas encore **là** ...   know) ... (Perrot 1992: 100)

These two authors cite an example from LF that, for them, shows that *là* serves as a 'deictico-temporal' marker. It seems that the first occurrence of *là* is indeed temporal (equivalent to 'then') but the second one is more deictic, stressing the instrument:

(8)   ... il touchait éyou il était et pis **là**   ... he touched where he was and
       il l'enveloppait avec la seine **là** ...   then he covered it with the draw-
                                                    net ... (Stäbler 1995: 66)

These various examples illustrate that the adverb *là* has a wide range of meaning and discourse functions in vernacular varieties of French in and outside of France (Chaudenson 2003: 280–5). No doubt, it had a high frequency of occurrence in the CF that constituted the speech target for the slaves in the plantation colonies. It formed a salient target for re-analysis as a deictic marker, the same function that the post-posed definite serves in the Atlantic creoles.

The verb marker system

In Section 8.1.2, it was pointed out that vernacular French occupies an intermediate position in the synthetic (use of inflections) < – > analytic or periphrastic (use of function words) verb morphology continuum. Unlike the standard variety used in writing and formal speech, vernacular varieties show relatively few inflected forms. The Standard French (SF) verb system, inherited from Latin, favors the expression of tense rather than aspect; therefore, vernacular varieties developed periphrastic means to express this semantic category. In documenting the diachronic development of French periphrastic constructions, Gougenheim (1929) indicates that, for example, an action in process (durative or progressive) was expressed successively by several constructions prior to the adoption of the current SF one: the auxiliary verb *être* and the adverbial expression *en train de* 'in the process of'. These constructions included:

- into the eighteenth century, *être* + *à* + the infinitive: *j'étais sur le balcon à travailler au frais* 'I was on the balcony working in the cool air';
- up to the beginning of the nineteenth century, the verb *aller* 'to go' + the present participle: *il s'en va nageant* 'he's swimming';
- up to the nineteenth century, the verb *être* 'to be'+ the present participle: *la femme est au logis, cousant les vieilles toiles* 'the wife is in the house sewing old cloth';
- still attested in local speech in several parts of France, as well as in North American dialects of French, the source of HC *ape*, *pe*, and *ap*, the verb *être* 'to be' + *après* 'after', *elle est après écrire* 'she's writing'.

These various periphrastic durative constructions no doubt coexisted in CF. Thus, they offered salient targets for the developing periphrastic system of FBCs.[17] The most widely distributed construction appears to have been *après* + infinitive, found in the Indian Ocean FBCs, Louisiana, and Haiti. For example, LF *Ça c'est les padnas que t'après parler avec sus le TELEPHONE?*[18] 'Are they the friends that you were talking to on the phone?' (Rottet 2001: 233–4). SBP shows a more complex structure consisting of *être* 'to be' + *qui* + verb: *je suis qui pars* 'I'm leaving', *j'étais qui partais* 'I was leaving',[19] as well as *être à*: *chus à manger* 'I'm eating' (Chaudenson 2003: 350). The latter author also cites a 1799 source from Réunion that provides evidence for the presence of this construction in CF: *Mon frère qui était à veiller le chien* 'My brother was watching over the dog' (ibid.: 345).

In the first Saint-Domingue Creole text, the *Passion*, the progressive aspect marker appears as *ka*, a form that occurs in all Lesser Antilles FBCs. Various unconvincing hypotheses have attempted to account for that feature in terms of an African substratum. After reviewing all the evidence, Chaudenson (2003: 351) concludes that the source of this verb marker lies in the CF expression *n'a qu'à*, as first suggested by Guy Hazaël-Massieux (1992: 656) and refined by Fattier (1996: 11). He notes the high frequency in Saint-Domingue Creole texts of the expression *necq* 'only, just', derived from CF *il n'est qu'à* 'he is only about to'. For example, *li boir necqu diau* 'he drinks only water'. Presumably, the slave acquirers reinterpreted the first part of the expression as *necq* with the adverbial meaning or the second part *qu'à* as a marker of progressive aspect. In Saint-Domingue, *être >ap(e)* rapidly replaced *ka*.

The periphrastic construction *aller* 'to go' + infinitive stands as the default expression of futurity in vernacular French. The question is whether it marks the definite future, whereas its synthetic counterpart expresses indefiniteness. For example, *Moi, j'aurai trois enfants* 'I'll have three children' (non-definite) versus *Elle va avoir un enfant* 'She's going to have a child' (definite: presumably she's pregnant). Alternatively, the distinction might be one of level of formality; the periphrastic construction being viewed as more informal and vernacular. In addition, in overseas varieties of French, the singular form *va* occurs with all singular grammatical persons, as does the reduced form *a*: *je va fèr* 'I'll do', *m a ki va le fèr* 'I'll do it', *t é ki va le fèr* 'you'll do it' (Highfield 1979: 90). In addition to *va*, Ducœurjoly's 1802 *Manuel des habitants de Saint-Domingue* lists *ava*: *M va ale, m ava alé nan tout maché* 'I'll go, I'll go to all the markets' (Chaudenson 2003: 357). This variant, which has been preserved in present-day HC, may have as its origin the construction *en* + *aller* found in the seventeenth-century playwright Corneille, *Rome s'en va renaître* 'Rome will be reborn', and in the northern French Picard dialect *tu t'en vas tomber* 'you're going to fall', as well as in a 1793 text in Réunion, *Moi s'en va foutre le camp dans bois* 'I'm going to take off to the woods' (Chaudenson 2003: 357). Finally, the widespread use in vernacular French of the periphrastic *aller* + infinitive construction stems from the morphological complexities of the inflected future. As Chaudenson remarked about the use of *aller* + infinitive (personal communication, 2013):

> Il y a là une stratégie commode pour éviter la conjugaison des futurs qui échappent à beaucoup de Français en particulier pour un certain nombre de verbes courants en -*ir* comme *mourir, bouillir* ou *courir*.
>
> We're dealing with a convenient strategy to avoid the conjugation of future forms that many French speakers are not familiar with, in particular a certain number of frequently used -*ir* verbs like *mourir, bouillir* or *courir*.

Indeed, in some verbs of this class the future is formed regularly by adding the personal endings to the infinitive, *bouillir* → *je bouillirai* 'I'll boil', whereas for others the stem extension is added to the present stem: *mourir* → *je mourrai* 'I'll die', *courrir* → *je courrai* 'I'll run'.

In Section 8.2.2, it was pointed out that in HC *a*, which expresses indefiniteness in the future, does not occur in negative sentences, but *ap*, which marks definiteness, does: *M a ba ou anpil lajan* 'I am going to give you a lot of money' versus *M p ap ba ou anpil lajan* 'I won't give you a lot of money'. Curiously, in overseas varieties of French the situation is reversed: the synthetic future occurs in negative sentences, as reported by Phillips in his 1936 study of Evangeline Parish, Louisiana (Byers 1988: 49). To be sure, synthetic forms occur in these varieties, particularly those of the conditional tense of irregular verbs: *tu voudrais* 'you would want', *j'irais* 'I would go', *je serais* 'I would be', *je ferais* 'I would do'. These are reflected marginally in some FBCs: Louisiana Creole *sa*, presumably from 3SG future tense *sera* /sra/ in SF, *Li **sa** la pou nev è* 'He'll be there at nine o'clock' (Klingler 2003: 259); Réunion Creole *sa* and the suffix *-ra* that occurs in negative sentences: *M i sa sant en romans* 'I'll sing a song', *mi santra pa* 'I won't sing' (Papen 1978: 379–80).

13.2.3 Lexicon

The lexicons of North American varieties of French and St. Barts Patois (SBP)[20] exhibit two types of differences from that of SF: words that do not exist in the latter variety, and those whose form and especially meaning differ from that of SF cognates. It is the latter type of lexical particularities that are of interest in the reconstitution of the lexicon of CF.

This section provides a comparison of the form and meaning of selected North American differential terms for cognate items in FBCs, focusing as I did in Section 6.4 on Louisiana French and HC.

Agglutination

As pointed out in Section 6.4.1 (11), a signal feature of HC words derived from vowel-initial French words is the agglutination of the final consonant of the French definite and possessive determiner. Table 13.4 compares HC words containing an agglutinated consonant with LF cognates and those of SBP. In both LF and SBP, there is alternation between the form with and without agglutination. The following contextual example shows that alternation and the fact that the singular agglutinated form *noncle* constitutes the base for the plural. That is, it supersedes the agglutination of the plural marker /z/, **zoncl* [zõk]: *oncle (n-oncle, noncle, nonc)* [ɔ̃k(l), nɔ̃k(l)] *Je devais parler pour mes tantes et mes noncles.* 'I had to speak for my aunts and my uncles.' (Valdman *et al.* 2010: 427).

Table 13.4. Agglutination in HC, Louisiana French and SBP

English	SF	HC	LF	SBP
eye	œil/yeux	zye/je	zyeux	
bird	oiseau	zwazo	zwazo	zózyó
nail	ongle	zong	*ongle	zõg
friend	ami	zanmi	*ami	zãmi
onion	oignon	zonyon	z-oignon	*õyõ
uncle	oncle	nonk/mononk	nonc/noncle	
they	eux	yo	y'eu	

The asterisk denotes the absence of agglutinated /z/.

422 The Genesis and Development of Haitian Creole

Although agglutination in the development of the lexicon of HC resulted from the slave learners' re-analysis of combinations of French pre-posed determiners and possessive adjectives, the evidence presented in Table 13.4 suggests that some agglutinated forms were already present in the input: namely, CF.

Shared differential terms (lexical particularities)

Section 6.4.2 focused on HC words that constitute survivals from earlier stages of French or regional dialects. More accurately, they are derived from CF, some of whose offshoots in the former overseas French colonies, such as LF, have preserved words or senses of words that have disappeared from the former homeland. Table 13.5, a modified version of Table 6.2, presents a comparison of matching LF and HC survivals from CF.

Table 13.5. Lexical Correspondences between Haitian Creole and Louisiana French

HC form	Meaning in HC/LF	LF form	SF usual meaning
abitan, n.	farmer	*habitant*	inhabitant
atò, adv.	now, at present	*asteur*	(*à cette heure*) 'at this hour'
ap/ape, v. marker	progressive marker	*après*	after
lavalas, n.	downpour	*avalasse*	-------
babye, v.	to complain	*babiller*	to babble
bo, n.	kiss	*bo*	-------
bokit, n.	bucket, pail	*baquet/bokette*	
bawòk, adj.	crude, coarse, vulgar	*baroque*	odd, bizarre, whimsical
bonm, n.	pot, saucepan	*bombe*	bomb
boukan, n.	bonfire	*boucan* 'smoke'	------
brigan, n.	unruly (of a child)	*brigand*	brigand, robber
kagou, adj.	sad, dejected	*cagou* 'out of sorts'	-------
kenbe, v.	to hold	*tchambo*	(*tiens bien*) 'hold firm'
cheran, adj.	expensive	*chérant*	-------
klete, v.	to lock	*cléter*	-------
dal, n.	drainpipe, gutter	*dalle* 'drain'	flagstone, slab
demare, v.	to untie	*démarrer*	to start (a car, machine)
anpil, adv.	a lot	*en pile*	in stacks, piles

goud, n.	basic monetary unit	*gourde* 'dollar'		gourd
joure, v.	to curse, insult	*jurer*		to swear (intransitively)
makonnen, v.	to tie, join together	*macorner*		-------
mayi moulen, n.	ground corn	*maïs moulé*		-------
nenenn, n.	godmother	*nénaine*		-------
pare, v.	to make ready	*paré*		to make ready for a maneuver (maritime)
rete, v.	to live, reside	*rester*		to stay
yo, pron.	they	*yeux*		(eux)

Section 6.4.2 also provides a detailed presentation of the semantic evolution of *baroque* from its earliest attested technical meaning in jewelry, namely, a precious stone of irregular shape, to its different outcomes in LF and the FBCs. Below are discussed three other words attested in LF and other North American varieties of French, and the FBCs. It will be noted that these varieties generally share the basic sense of their CF source.

grègue [grɛg, greg]
This word, attested in LF with the senses 'drip coffee-pot, coffeemaker', occurs with more or less the same meaning in all FBCs. It is derived from the cognate in SF *grègues* 'breeches', currently of rare usage, having been replaced by *haut-de-chausses*. Presumably, coffee was originally filtered using this garment. However, there is evidence that it was replaced by some coffee-filtering utensil that continued to bear the original name.

> FBCs: **Lou**[21] *greg/lagrèg/grèg* 'coffee-pot', *greg kafe* 'coffee-pot'; **Haïti** *grèg/grèk/grèp* 'cloth, coffee filter', *anba grèg* 'first batch of filtered coffee'; **Gua** *grèg* 'coffee-pot'; **Guy** *grek-kafé* 'coffee-pot'; **Réu** *grègue* 'coffee-pot, *greg/grek* 'coffee filter'; **Maur** *lagrek* 'coffee filter', *lagrèg* 'coffee-pot'; **Rod** *lagrek* 'coffee filter', *lagreg* 'coffee-pot'; **Seych** *lagrèg* 'coffee-pot'

bougre [bug(r), buk]
In LF, this word has a wide range of senses: 'man, fellow, guy, chap', generally with a positive connotation, for example, *bon bougre* 'good guy', *vaillant bougre* 'nice, sympathetic chap'. In Acadia, it is more pejorative: 'idiot'. It is considered vernacular and obsolescent in SF and it is usually restricted to expressions with a condescending connotation such as *un bon bougre* 'good ole boy', *pauvre bougre* 'unfortunate person'. It appears to have followed an ameliorative path from an earlier discourteous term. In

CF and subsequently in the FBCs, its sense broadened and became a more generic term for 'man' but conserved a positive connotation.

> **Lou** *boug* 'guy, fellow, chap', *jèn/jenn boug* 'young man', *ti boug* 'boy'; **Haï** *boug* 'chap'; **Gua** (Lud 82) *boug* 'man, chap, person', 'fellow, buddy, friend'; **Mart** *boug* 'person, chap, man'; **St-Luc** *boug* 'guy, chap', *bon boug* 'good guy', *move boug* 'bad guy'; **Guy** *boug* 'person, someone'; **Dom** *boug* 'guy, chap'; **Kar** *bug* 'fellow, kid', 'chap'; **Réu** *bug* 'man, person (sometimes pejorative)', 'lover, live-in lover', *bel/gro bug* 'tough guy', *bõ bug* 'good man', *mõ bug* 'my husband', *ti bug* 'boy'; **Maur** 'chap, person, man', *maleñ boug* 'shrewd guy'; **Rod** *boug* 'chap, person, man'; **Seych** *boug* 'chap, person, man'

safre [saf(r)]
In North American varieties of French – LF, Acadia and Quebec – this adjective characterizes a gluttonous and greedy person. It has long since disappeared from SF but is attested in earlier periods, when it also referred to revelers and gastronomes. It is widely attested in northern regional dialects of the language (patois) in France with the sense it bears in North American varieties of French and the FBCs. Hence, undoubtedly, it bore that sense in CF: **Lou** *safre/saf/zaf* 'to gorge oneself, to binge, to stuff oneself'; **Haï** *saf* 'gluttonous'.

13.3 The Role of Substrate Transfers in the Genesis and Development of Haitian Creole

13.3.1 Second-language acquisition and creolization

The Creole Prototype, Relexification, and Superstratist accounts of HC all view unguided second-language acquisition as a fundamental process in the genesis and development of HC. This raises the issue of the applicability of the vast corpus of second-language-acquisition (SLA) research to the field of creole studies.[22] However, Salikoko Mufwene, associated with the Superstratist camp, has stressed the inapplicability of most SLA research to creolization. In publications dealing specifically with SLA and creolistics, he underscores two signal differences between these two fields. First:

> It should be remembered that the literature on SLA has typically focused on individual language acquisition experiences with no account of how communal norms arise, whereas that on the emergence of creoles and language evolution has generally focused on changes at the communal-norm level. (Mufwene 2010: 371)

Second:

> ... the interlanguages on which research on SLA has focused are transitional idiolectal varieties toward closer approximations of the target language (TL), whereas creoles are communal evolutions in the opposite direction, away from the 'lexifier' ... (Mufwene 2008: 133)

In his appraisal of the degree of inclusion of SLA theoretical models in fundamental works by authors he considers to be leading exponents of the three main theoretical strands in creole studies, namely, the Bioprogram (Bickerton 1981), Relexification (C. Lefebvre 1988), and Superstratism (Mufwene 2001), Rex Sprouse concludes that none of these major works contain any relevant discussion of theoretical issues in SLA research:

> I cannot say that any of the three books surveyed offers anything like a serious discussion of a model of second language acquisition, let alone a discussion (or even an awareness of the existence) of competing models of second language acquisition. I do not believe that these three books are unique. I am unaware of any introductory textbook for creole or contact linguistics that includes even a short section on major issues or models of second language acquisition. Considering the presumed centrality of the cognitive mechanisms underlying second language acquisition for the investigation of creole genesis and contact phenomena, this would appear to be a serious gap. (2006: 276)

To this blanket negative evaluation, no doubt Mufwene would respond that indeed the objects of study of SLA researchers and creolists are fundamentally incompatible. Creolization differs not only from the typical carefully controlled studies of SLA researchers, but also from the more naturalistic acquisition of the language of host communities by migrant workers investigated, for example, by the long-term longitudinal studies funded by the European Foundation of Science (Perdue 1991). In fact, Mufwene does discuss this particular situation. He points out that in plantation societies that spawned FBCs, substrate speakers used the version of the superstrate language they were acquiring as their primary intercommunity language. In contrast, this is not the case for migrant workers:

> Unlike the populations that developed creoles, foreign workers use their approximations of the host country's language primarily, if not exclusively, to communicate with the host population – that is, the majority in which they are hardly integrated. In other words, the host country's language functions as a lingua franca, not as a vernacular, for the adult immigrants. (2006: 380)

Migrant workers, most of whom form linguistically homogeneous communities, generally use their first language (L1) for communications with their fellow immigrant compatriots.

The Relexification theory appears to operate within the Full Transfer/Full Access (FT/FA) framework (Schwartz and Sprouse 1996). According to this hypothesis, upon first contact with second-language (L2) input data, learners carry over the principles and parameter values of their L1. In this regard, this does not differ substantially from the older model put forward by Krashen, according to which 'the L1 may "substitute" for the acquired L2 as an utterance initiator when the performer has to produce target language but has not acquired enough of it …' (1988: 67). Apparently, the Relexification Hypothesis places greater emphasis on FT in as much as it assumes that the creators of HC transferred the entire morphosyntactic and semantic systems and relabeled them with the L2 lexicon. According to Lumsden (1999), a major figure in the Relexification camp, relabeling constitutes a subtype of transfer.

Although they reject the total transfer of substrate morphosyntax and semantics, superstratists do recognize some transfer in the genesis of FBCs (Chaudenson 1974, 2003; DeGraff 2003; Mufwene 2008, 2010; Valdman 1977, 1978). However, the major differences between these creolists and proponents of Relexification reside, first, in the social context of the acquisition of the superstrate language, second, in the nature of the target language input, and, third, on the development of these creoles.

13.3.2 The diachronic development of HC: basilectalization

Claire Lefebvre and her collaborators assume that HC arose from the initial contact between a slave population that outnumbered speakers of the superstrate: 'During the period of creolization, the African population of Haiti was much larger than the French population' (Lumsden 1999: 134). Consequently, speakers of the substrate had few opportunities to interact with speakers of the superstrate. However, as pointed out in 13.5.1 above, in colonial Saint-Domingue it was not until about thirty or forty years after initial French settlement that the slave population greatly outnumbered the highly socially differentiated population that spoke an undoubtedly variable Colonial French (CF). Importantly, that variety differed significantly from seventeenth- and eighteenth-century standard speech, which, according to the first French linguistic survey (Grégoire 1794), was spoken fluently by only one-sixth of the population of France. The slaves who arrived in Saint-Domingue during the homestead phase benefited from closer contact with speakers of CF, and had more opportunities to interact with them than the masses of Bozal slaves who would be imported as the plantation economy took root in Saint-Domingue. As Mufwene points out, 'Africans were generally integrated minorities (although discriminated against) ... In fact the Europeans depended on the Africans to survive in the new, tropical ecologies' (2010: 372).

Krashen (1988: 102ff) notes that in naturalistic SLA the acquirers' task is facilitated if target language speakers modify the primary linguistic data, just as do caretakers in L1 acquisition (Snow and Ferguson 1977). Intake of primary linguistic data is facilitated by: (1) focusing on the immediate here-and-now environment, (2) keeping the syntax simple, and (3) making sure that the input is comprehensible. Krashen pursues this line of thought by invoking simple codes: foreigner talk, teacher talk, and interlanguage:

> Simple codes are of tremendous help to acquirers at early and intermediate stages, child and adult, first and second language. (1988: 136)

Apparently, this is precisely the path followed by missionary priests such as Mongin and Pelleprat, who evangelized newly arriving slaves, as evidenced by the excerpts cited in Section 13.2.1.

A fundamental difference between the Superstratist and Relexification accounts of the genesis of HC resides in the nature of the development of the language. Proponents of Relexification assume that upon their first contact with the target input (the CF koinè) African slaves restructured it and created HC as it appears in the first detailed descriptions of the language in the early twentieth century (Faine 1936, 1939; S. Sylvain 1936). The Superstratist view of the development of HC is much more nuanced. Unlike the interlanguage of second-language acquirers, as HC developed, it moved away rather than toward the target language, CF, in a process that Chaudenson (1992, 2001, 2003) and Mufwene (2001, 2006, 2008) label **basilectalization**. During the homestead phase of the French settlement of Saint-Domingue, the slaves, less numerous than the European colonists, interacted primarily with speakers of CF. Consequently, they acquired an approximative version of CF. However, during the plantation phase, the slaves greatly outnumbered the European colonists and they appropriated and progressively modified that approximative version (Mufwene 2008).

The narrow stylistic range of the colonial Saint-Domingue texts cited in Section 4.3.2 renders difficult a comparison with the data on which current linguistic analyses of HC are based. Except for the *Passion,* a religious text, Ducœurjoly's *Manuel des habitants de Saint-Domingue,* a sort of guide for apprentice planters, and the proclamations posted by French officials (the commissioner Santhonax and General Leclerc) during the uprising against

French rule, surviving texts consist of poems or plays destined for speakers of the superstrate language with variable competence in a variety of Saint-Domingue Creole that no doubt differed from that of the slave population. With regard to the proclamations, they were no doubt drafted by French-dominant bilinguals.[23] Undoubtedly by the mid-eighteenth century, the period during which the *Passion* was written, Saint-Domingue Creole showed diastratic and diaphasic variation. Nonetheless, all these texts reflect a language that differs significantly from current-day HC and that was closer to CF. In other words, it had not yet undergone the basilectalization that has made it the most radical of the FBCs.

The merger of the 1st and 2nd person plural personal pronouns, both expressed by *nou* in present-day HC, provides support for the basilectalization hypothesis. Early texts consistently display a distinction between the 1st and 2nd person plural pronouns, *nou* versus *zòt*, spelled variously *zautres* and *zote* (see the early Saint-Domingue texts in Section 4.3.2). As was pointed out in Section 9.3.1, *zòt* as 2nd and 3rd person plural pronoun was noted by Fattier's field interviewers (Fattier 2000: 214) and earlier by Suzanne Sylvain (1936). This form is clearly derived from French *vous autres*, as is attested, for example, in Louisiana French where *autres* follows all three plural pronouns; *nous-autres*, *vous-autres*, *eux-autres* (Valdman et al. 2010). Currently, the pronoun form *zòt* has by and large been lost. Claire Lefebvre attributes the merger of the 1st and 2nd person pronouns into the pronoun *nou* to a transfer from Fongbe, where 1st and 2nd person plural pronouns are distinguished only by a tonal difference over a shared segmental sequence *mi*. However, as noted in the next section, comparison of Indian Ocean and Atlantic FBCs raises some doubts about this claim.

It is likely that most transfers from the substrate languages took place when early Saint-Domingue Creole became progressively more different from its CF target, as it became the community language of the mass of field and sugar mill slaves. Also, at that stage, it replaced CF as the new acquisitional target for the massive arrivals of Bozal slaves. According to Manessy (1995: 98), as a language becomes a means of social integration rather than exclusively a means of communication, it undergoes complexification. The apparent free variation between the presence and absence of the preposition *à* in the post-posed possessive construction reflected in the *Passion* text gives way to a geographical difference between Capois (NHC) and the varieties spoken in other regions of Haiti. In addition, in Capois the sandhi phenomena triggered by the vocalic sequences in the language further distinguish speakers of that variety from their compatriots. For instance, utterances such as *sèranm* 'my sister' or *dwanm* 'my back' become opaque for speakers who pronounce them as *sè m* and *do m*, respectively (see Sections

3.5 and 11.3.2 for a detailed discussion of these differences). As pointed out above, early colonial texts such as the *Passion* show monomorphemic WH forms, for example, *outi* instead of bimorphemic *ki kote* or *ki bò* 'where'.

Most of the creolists who have invoked massive transfers from African languages have failed to apply an initial step advocated by Chaudenson (2003: 262–9), namely, checking whether a claimed transfer occurs only in the zone (be it the Indian Ocean or the Atlantic) where slaves spoke the substrate language or languages that exhibit the claimed transferred feature. For example, in the case of massive agglutination involving the incorporation of whole French determiners, *le, la, les, l', du*, as opposed to only the liaison consonant evidenced in the words cited in 13.2.3, the preponderance of these agglutinated forms in Mauritian Creole, as compared to the Atlantic FBCs, does point to the possible influence of the Bantu languages spoken by slaves imported from East Africa (Baker 1984; Grant 1995). Although such agglutinated forms occur frequently in HC, for example, *lalin* (*la lune*) 'moon', *lanmè* (*la mer*) 'sea', *lank* (*l'ancre*) 'anchor', *lezo* (*le os*) 'bone', *diri* (*du riz*) 'rice', their total of 156 pales before those of Mauritian Creole (637) and Seychellois Creole (646).[24]

To return to the merger of the 1st and 2nd person plural pronouns that Claire Lefebvre credits to transfer from Fongbe, where the two forms are distinguished only by tone (see above). Comparative evidence suggests that transfer from African substrate languages may not be the sole source of this merger. Damoiseau (1987: 91) observes that the interpretation of that pronoun is highly context dependent. For example, if when witnessing a car breakdown involving several persons, a passerby says *Ki sa n apral fè?* 'What are you going to do?', it is clear that *nou* (of which *n* is the truncated variant) bears the meaning 'you (all)', whereas if it is the driver of the vehicle who utters that sentence *nou* is clearly interpreted as 'we'. Damoiseau points out that in that same situation the vernacular French polysemous subject pronoun *on* carries the same ambiguity as *nou*: *Qu'est-ce qu'on fait?* Thus, speakers of substrate languages where there is no distinction between 1st and 2nd person plural in the pronominal system would find in the input data a pragmatic-semantic feature that corresponded to their native language usage.

As has been suggested most recently by Corne (1999), Chaudenson (2001, 2003), Mufwene (2001: 23; 2006: 135), and Jeff Siegel (2008), substrate influence often operates by congruence with target language features rather than direct transfer from the substrate languages. The use of verb markers and the loss of verbal inflection constitute a major case of congruence. As John McWhorter, for whom the tendency toward periphrasis constitutes a universal in language contact situations – and a feature of pidginization, comments (2013: 410): 'Haitian Creole is analytic not because of an interruption of transmission, but because Fongbe is analytic ... and vernacular French varieties are often more analytic than even standard modern French.' Whereas the replacement of verbal inflection by pre-posed verb markers reflects convergence between the verb systems of vernacular French and Kwa languages like Fongbe and Ewe, a direct transfer in the verb system of HC is the combination of verb markers, for example, *Si m te pati yè, m **t av ap** kabicha nan kabann mwen kounye a* 'If I had left yesterday, I would be taking a nap in my bed now'. In the next sections, I provide examples of what I consider, on the one hand, congruences between the superstrate target and the substrate languages, and on the other, direct transfer from the latter.

13.3.3 Some cases of congruence

The definite determiner

The case of the post-posed definite article illustrates a complex case of congruence and direct transfer. As discussed in Section 13.2.3 above, in some North American varieties of French that, like FBCs, exhibit less divergence from early CF, the post-posed locative adverb *là* encodes nominal deixis without a pre-posed definite or demonstrative determiner: Old Mines (Missouri) French *liv-là* 'this book', *blé sec là* 'this dry wheat'. This adverb has also been re-analyzed in metropolitan and overseas vernacular varieties of French to express pre-supposition or emphasis, as in (8) above, reproduced as (9) below:

(9) ... il touchait éyou il était et pis   ... he touched where he was and
     là il l'enveloppait avec la seine   then he covered it with the draw net
     là ...   ... (as one usually does) (Stäbler
                                             1995: 66)

For the slave acquirers of CF – speakers of African Kwa languages like Fongbe or Ewe that have post-posed definite determiners – the frequently occurring invariable *là*, unlike the pre-posed definite article that occurred in at least five distinct oral forms (/l, lœ, la, le, lez/), provided a salient target-language form that coincided with the position of the definite article of the language or languages they had spoken before. Note, too, that the HC post-posed determiner is highly deictic, with a meaning intermediate between that of the French demonstrative and definite determiners.[25]

Manessy (1981, 1995) reports the use of post-posed *là* together with or without the pre-posed determiner corresponding to vernacular metropolitan colloquial French in African approximative French varieties, for example, *l'garçon là, il est fort* 'that boy is really strong' or *ballon là, c'est raté* 'that ball, it's been misplayed'. He labels this form '*article emphatique*'. Citing Lafage's (1985: 262) observation of this use in the colloquial French spoken in Togo, and her suggestion that it was a transfer from Ewe, he also draws attention to sentence-final use of *là* in Cameroun French. In this region, where Bantu languages are spoken, *là* is used in cases that correspond to those of sentential *LA* in HC (see Section 9.2.7, sentence (27c): *Pyè te pati a?* 'Has Peter left (as I thought he did)): *Il peut quand même comprendre quelques mots là* 'The fact is that he can still understand a few words'. This use also corresponds to those in Canadian and Louisiana French cited in (6) and (7) above.

However, as Claire Lefebvre (1988: 78–100) stresses, what the acquirers did transfer was not so much the definite determiner form of the substrate language(s) but primarily the semantic values it expresses, namely, definiteness. In French, the definite determiner expresses two semantic notions: definiteness (indicating previous mention or known identity) and generic. But in both Fongbe and HC the definite determiner only expresses definiteness:

(10a)   **Le** lait est sur **la** table.   'The milk (that we know about) is
                                                 on the table (that we know about or
                                                 previously mentioned).'

   Lèt   **la**   sou   tab   **la**.
   milk   DET   on   table   DET

As in Fongbe, the HC generic is expressed by the absence of the determiner:

(10b)   J'aime **le** lait.   'I like milk.'
        M renmen lèt.
        1SG like Ø milk

Also, unlike French, in which mass nouns are preceded by the partitive determiner (*du, de l', de la, des*), in both Fongbe and HC the determiner is absent in these cases:

(11)   **Le** lait est bon pour **les** enfants.   'Milk is good for children.'
        Lèt bon pou ti moun.
(12)   Je veux **du** lait.   'I want milk.'
        M vle lèt.

However, in discussing the Français Populaire d'Abidjan, an approximate variety of French used by speakers of several African languages in the

Ivory Coast area (not all of them belonging to the Kwa group, like Fongbe), Manessy (1995: 125) reports that the post-posed determiner *là* occurs only with specified nouns, as is the case with HC and Fongbe. Thus, in their generic sense, nouns occur without a determiner, for example, *je vais planté cafè* 'I'm going to plant coffee' versus the specific sense *cafè là ça donne pas* 'this coffee doesn't produce'. This raises the issue of whether this is a case of transfer from the local African languages or simply the application of the unmarked parameter, a second-language-acquisition strategy.

Interrogative (WH) words

The use of syntactic interrogatives composed of *ki* + noun constitutes a striking distinction between French and HC (see Section 9.3.2). To recapitulate, although HC does have monomorphemic WH words, *kouman* 'how', *konbe* 'how much', most WH forms are syntactic constructions consisting of the interrogative marker *ki* followed by a noun bearing a particular meaning, for example, *ki moun* (*ki* + person) 'who/whom'. Proponents of Relexification consider that the latter constructions result from substrate transfer. In Fongbe, the substrate language used by Claire Lefebvre (1988: 171–80), syntactic interrogatives are semantically identical to HC corresponding forms. However, in Fongbe the interrogative marker follows rather than precedes the noun; note that in the Fongbe examples the grave accent denotes a falling tone:

(13) ki moun 'which person'   person + which   mè tè
      ki lè 'which time'   time + which   hwènù tè

Claire Lefebvre (1988: 171–80) cites Brousseau's (1995) assumption that the French source of the interrogative marker *ki* is the French interrogative phrase *Lequel est-ce?* 'Which one is it?', from which is derived the HC *kilès ki/kiyès?* 'who/whom': *Kilès nan nou ki ta vle fè travay la?* 'Who among you wants to do the work?'[26] More persuasive sources are *qui* that functions as an interrogative animate subject: *Qui est venu?, Qui c'est qui est venu?* 'Who came?', *C'est qui ?* 'Who is it?' or better still, the interrogative adjective *quel* (*quels, quelle, quelles*) that enters into interrogative constructions matching those of HC: *quel homme* 'which man', *quelle heure* 'which time', *quelle chose* 'which thing', etc. As is the case in French, the list of nouns that follow the interrogative is open: *ki jou* 'which day', *ki chat* 'which cat', etc. Clearly, these appear to constitute the target form of the slave learners, particularly since Chaudenson (1996: 34), citing a historian of the French language (Marchello-Nizia, 1979: 167), points out that *quel* served as an interrogative pronoun up to the fifteenth century and that it was pronounced as /kø/ and then /ke/ in dialects of western France, alternating freely with /ki/. Finally, Chaudenson asks why these syntactic interrogatives must be associated exclusively with African substrate languages when they are attested in the Indian Ocean FBCs. For example, corresponding to *ki jan* (which alternates with *kouman*) 'how', Mauritian and Seychellois creoles also show bi- and monomorphemic WH words: *kouman/ki manier* (Carpooran 2009) and *koman/ki mangner*, respectively (D'Offay and Lionnet, 1982). In fact, Seychellois Creole also has *ki kote* 'where', *ki sa* 'what' and *ki sèl la* 'who'.

Clements and Mahboob (2000), following Muysken and Smith (1990), propose that bimorphemic WH words are more semantically transparent, and presumably less marked than monomorphemic ones. Thus, universal language principles would guide second-language acquirers to select them if some were present in the target input, and as indicated above, this was the case for CF in Saint-Domingue. To put it somewhat differently, in the competition-and-selection approach put forward by Mufwene (2001, 2006), learners typically select the more transparent option available in the feature pool.

Some cases of full transfers

Although there are certainly persuasive cases of some direct transfers, the Relexification Hypothesis' assumption of total transfer from African languages of the Guinea region supplemented by what is termed 'dialect leveling' from other languages is not tenable. Three clear cases of direct transfer are treated in this chapter. As McWhorter and Parkvall (2002: 199–202) suggest, persuasive cases for morphosyntactic direct transfers could be advanced for the use of the 3rd person singular pronoun *yo* as plural marker (*chat sa yo* 'these cats') and the use of body parts (*tèt* 'head', *kò* 'body') in reflexive constructions (*li touye kò li* 'he killed himself').[27]

Phrase-final emphatic markers

A signal difference between Standard French and HC is the use of sentence-final markers to indicate emphasis, or as Claire Lefebvre suggests (1998: 213), markers to express speakers' points of view. The examples given in Section 7.4 are repeated in (14) and (15) below):

(14)   M pa ka fè travay sa a *non!*   'I really can't do this job!'
        Ann ale *non*, nou deja an reta!   'Let's go, we're already late!'
        Ann manje *non*!   'Come on, let's eat!'
(15)   M byen *wi*!   'I'm FINE!'
        Chante *non*!   'Why don't you sing?'

Lefebvre points out that these two markers match corresponding monosyllabic forms in Fongbe, *ó* for *non* and *bó* for *wi*, with regard to their pragmatic function and their position in the sentence. She also notes that *non* does occur as an emphatic marker in colloquial French, but that its pragmatic function and syntactic characteristics differ markedly from those in HC. In *T'as fait ça, non!* 'The fact is that you did that!' or 'You did that, no?', *non* occurs with affirmative sentences, not negative ones as is the case in HC. Furthermore, unlike HC, there is a pause and an intonational break before *non*. However, congruence with LF cannot be ruled out completely, as is shown by the following example from Louisiana French (Valdman *et al.* 2010): *Ah foutre oui!* 'That's for sure!', literally, 'Ah, damn it, yes!'

Serial verbs

One of the features that differentiates HC most from French is verb serialization. As described in Section 7.6, most serial verb constructions consist of a focal verb that bears the central meaning and a deictic or modifying verb that narrows down the meaning of the focal verb. Deictic verbs are directional and are equivalent to English adverbs or French prepositions: *ale* indicates motion away from the speaker and *vini* toward the speaker.

(16a) Li **janbe** **ale** Fisi. 'He crossed over to Furcy.'
3SG cross go Furcy *Il a traversé pour aller à Furcy.*
(16b) Tidjo **kouri** **ale** lakay li. 'Tidjo ran over to his house.'
Tidjo run go house his *Tidjo a couru à sa maison.*
(16c) **Bwote** barik **vini** isit. 'Bring the barrel here.'
carry barrel come here *Apporte le tonneau ici.*
(16d) Li **rale** chèz la **vini**. 'He pulled the chair toward here.'
3SG pull chair the come *Il a tiré la chaise par ici.*

In combinations of focal and modifying verbs, the overall meaning is dependent on the situational context, and it is not clearly signaled by the modifying verb. In (17) the serial verb *mete kanpe* could mean 'to make something stand up' or, with regard to a school, 'to set it up'.

(17) Se Vilè ki **mete** lekòl la **kanpe**.
it's Vilaire who put school the standing
'It's Vilaire who established the school.'

McWhorter and Parkvall (2002: 198) analyze as benefactive serial verb constructions combinations with the verb *bay/ba* 'to give' (derived from French *bailler* 'to give'). However, as pointed out in Section 8.6.6, it appears that in serial constructions *bay/ba* has undergone grammaticalization from a verb with benefactive meaning to a preposition equivalent to English 'for' or 'to':

(18)　Jan **pote** liv yo **ba** Mari.　　'John brought the books to Mary.'
　　　John carry book PL give Mary　　*Jean a apporté les livres à Marie.*

Note that, in the French gloss, the prefix *a-* adjoined to the verb *porter* 'to carry', like *ba,* is equivalent to the preposition 'to' (motion toward the speaker). It contrasts with the prefix *en/em-* : *emporter* 'to carry, take away'.

Hugo Schuchardt (1914) was the first creolist to invoke substrate transfer in accounting for serial verbs in Atlantic creoles in his comparison of Sranan, the English-based creole of Surinam, to Ewe. For Derek Bickerton (1981: 120), West African languages and creoles 'invented serial verbs independently but for slightly different reasons'. Indeed, according to the Bioprogram Hypothesis serial verbs constitute one of the defining features of creoles. This hypothesis, however, encounters several problems. First, if serial verbs reflect the operation of the Bioprogram, they should be an unmarked linguistic feature present in most languages of the world. Serial verbs occur in geographically distant languages, for example, those of Papua New Guinea or East Asia (Mandarin Chinese). But they are absent in many more, including Bantu languages.

Second, Bickerton (1981: 119, cited by Nylander 1987: 82) claims it is unlikely that languages that have prepositions would develop serial verbs. Presumably, for him serial verbs reflect more innate linguistic features than prepositions. However, various Africanists identify African languages, like Baule[28], that have both prepositions and serial verbs.

The fact that serial verbs are generally absent in Indian Ocean FBCs, influenced in the case of Mauritian Creole by Bantu languages that lack this construction (Manessy 1995), but are widely attested in all Atlantic creoles, supports the claim that this structure may be a transfer from Niger-Congo languages like Fongbe or Ewe.

Clefting and predicate doubling

Section 10.3 presented a wide variety of clefting constructions, some of which involved verb doubling:

(19a)　Li **lavil**.　　　　　　'She's in town.'
(19b)　**Se lavil** li ye.　　　　'It's in town that she is.'

(20a)　Mwen **manje**.　　　　'I'm eating.'
(20b)　**Se manje** mwen **manje**.　'What I'm doing is eating.'

(21a) Jan **te travay**, li pa te dòmi. 'John had worked, he hadn't slept.'
(21b) **Se travay** Jan **te travay**, li pa te dòmi. 'What John had done is worked, he hadn't slept.'

Clefting is also a widespread feature of colloquial French. Traditionally referred to as **dislocation**, the topicalized or focalized element of a sentence may be clefted to the left or to the right. Example (22b) shows the topicalization of *le vélo de Jean*, whereas (22c) shows a double cleft: the topicalization of *Jean* and of *le vélo de Jean*. In (22b), the clefted direct object is replaced by the resumptive pronom *l'*. In (22c), note the replacement of both *de* and *le* by the possessive determiner referring to *le vélo de Jean*:

(22a) On a volé **le vélo de Jean**. 'Someone stole John's bike.'
(22b) **Le vélo de Jean**, on l'a volé. 'John's bike, someone stole it.'
(22c) **Jean, son vélo**, on l'a volé. 'John, his bike, someone stole it.'

In both right or left dislocation, the clefted element may be preceded by the introducer *c'est*:

(23a) Le lait de chèvre est **bon pour la santé**. 'Goat's milk is good for health.'
(23b) **C'est bon pour la santé**, le lait de chèvre. 'It's good for health, goat's milk.'
(23c) Le lait de chèvre, **c'est bon pour la santé**. 'Goat's milk, it's good for heatlh.'

Clefting is a key feature of Niger-Congo languages, and it also occurs in Bantu languages, notably Kintuba and Lingala (Mufwene 1987). Thus, speakers of these languages found in the target input a feature compatible with their own. However, what French does not have is doubling of a focalized verb or adjective. To topicalize the verb *voler* in (24a) it is necessary to resort to various syntactic modifications that do not involve doubling the verb, as is done in HC. Compare (24a) and (24b), and (25a) and (25b):

(24a) On a volé le vélo de Jean. 'Someone stole John's bike.'
(24b) **On l'a bien volé,** le vélo de Jean. 'The fact is that someone did indeed steal John's bike.'

(25a) Mari pa vle **travay**. 'Mary doesn't want to work.'
(25b) **Se travay** Mari pa vle **travay**. 'Mary really doesn't want to work.'

As Claire Lefebvre (1988: 363) clearly shows, Fongbe allows verb doubling:

(26) wá Jan wá (tróló) bɔ̀ Màrí yí
 rive Jan **rive** (epi) Mari pati
 arrive John **arrive** as soon and Mary leave
 'As soon as John arrived, Mary left.'

To be sure, there are differences between the matched Fongbe and HC sentences: the absence of the conjunction and the optionality of the coordinating conjunction *epi* in HC, as opposed to its obligatory use in Fongbe. Thus, although the extensive clefting that characterizes HC cannot be uniquely ascribed to substrate transfer, the doubling of predicates consisting of adjectives and verbs clearly can.

Summary

In accounting for the genesis of HC, I have adopted a non-exceptional view of the process of creolization put forward by Superstratists. For these creolists, FBCs result from the unguided acquisition of highly variable vernacular varieties of the French exported to France's seventeenth- and eighteenth-century plantation colonies, which were subsequently konéized locally into what can be broadly characterized as Colonial French. In addition to FBCs, phonological, grammatico-semantic, and lexical features of CF can be reconstructed by examining the structure of current North American varieties of French spoken in Louisiana, Acadia (the Canadian Maritime provinces), and Quebec, as well as in St. Barts and St. Thomas.

For Superstratists, FBCs did not evolve from a previous pidgin, as hypothesized by the Bioprogram and the Creole Prototype. They are not the result of children exposed to unlearnable pidgins resorting to their innate language faculty (the Bioprogram), nor do they involve the full transfer of the grammatico-semantic system of West African languages as claimed by the Relexification Hypothesis.

Historical evidence suggests that HC was not created originally in Saint-Domingue during the initial contact between a preponderant population of African slaves and a smaller number of European colonists. The plantation society phase, with which the emergence of HC is associated, was preceded by a homestead phase during which speakers of CF constituted the majority of the population, which was not yet segregated. Thus, early arriving slaves, depending on social conditions, had relatively full access to the emergent CF, variable though it was, and undoubtedly to French foreigner talk. The latter or some earlier developed varieties of

FBCs might have been introduced into Saint-Domingue from the French colonies that developed earlier in St. Kitts, Martinique, and Guadeloupe. As Saint-Domingue early creole texts attest, in the early stages of the development of the colony, the creole remained much closer to CF than do present-day varieties of the language. In the later stages of the Saint-Domingue colony, as the newly arriving slave population greatly outnumbered CF speakers, its acquisitional target shifted to approximations of CF spoken by creole slaves, that is, those born in Saint-Domingue, and seasoned African-born slaves.[29] The language then underwent the basilectalization that resulted in today's HC.

The superstratist view of the genesis of HC is not altogether incompatible with transfer from substrate African languages. Some of the apparent transfers, such as the post-position in noun phrases of the definite determiner and pronouns in the possessive construction reflect a congruence between morphosyntactic structures of African languages and CF. For example, what is most likely exclusively African in the HC determiner is not the fact that it is post-posed but rather the fact that it expresses deictic and specific reference. Unlike CF, generic reference in HC is marked by the absence of the determiner. What are likely total transfers from substrate languages are the sentence-final emphatic markers *wi* and *non*, verb serialization, and doubling in predicate-cleft constructions.

As incontrovertible evidence for substrate transfer, Robert Chaudenson (2003: 404–6) puts forward an exemplary case: the distinction in Réunion Creole between subject and object pronouns: *mi èm aou* 'I love you', *ou la tap amoin* 'you hit me'. He shows that Malagasy also distinguishes these two sets of pronouns:

	Réunion Creole		Malagasy	
	Subject	Object	Subject	Object
2SG	*ou*	*aou*	*ianao*	*anao*
3SG	*li*	*ali*	*izy*	*azy*
2PL	*zot*	*azot*	*ianareo*	*anareo*

Chaudenson's account of this particular feature of Réunion Creole is persuasive because: (1) there is clear matching between the putative substrate feature from Malagasy and that of the creole; (2) speakers of Malagasy constituted a large proportion of the slaves imported into Réunion during the initial period of settlement; (3) this grammatical distinction was present in the early stages of the colony; (4) it is absent in the other Indian Ocean creoles and in vernacular varieties of French which constituted the acquisitional target for the Malagasy slaves.

What is lacking in the case made by the Relexification hypothesis are, among other things: (1) evidence that the features of HC attributed to substratal transfer do not occur in other FBCs, especially in those of the Indian Ocean, where the proportion of slaves from West Africa was not preponderant during the formative period of these creoles; (2) sociohistorical data that indicate that the importation of slaves was massive during the initial establishment period of the Saint-Domingue colony, that is, the homestead (*habitation*) phase.

Notes

1. For a detailed refutation of the notion of 'creole exceptionalism' see DeGraff (2003).
2. Another approach in refuting the Creole Prototype hypothesis involves showing that languages that do not share the sociohistorical history of creoles do show these same three prototypical features (Gil 2001).
3. Holm (1989: 278) proposes a different definition of radicalness, namely, closeness of creoles to their African substrate languages and concomitant distance from their European superstrate.
4. Chaudenson (2003: 292–5) points out that the development of bimorphemic interrogative words, as well as the attestation of monomorphemic question words such as *outi* 'when', *comment* 'how', and *qu'o faire* 'why' in early Saint-Domingue texts, is an internal auto-regulatory process in French that favors analytic over synthetic features. The same development is found in the verb system, where verb markers replace inflection.
5. These authors also grant that recourse to substrate influence is not essential: '*Nous voulons souligner que nous ne nions nullement qu'une bonne partie des traits qui séparent les créoles du français standard moderne s'explique en effet fort bien sans que l'on ait recours à la pidginisation ou à l'influence du substrat* (We wish to emphasize that we do not deny at all that a good part of the features that distinguish creoles from modern standard French can very well be explained without recourse to pidginization or the influence of the substrate)'.
6. I am grateful to André Thibault (private communication) for this term .
7. Lefebvre and her colleagues' choice of Fongbe as the sole substrate language stems from methodological considerations. This does not entail that it was the one spoken by the majority of the early servile arrivals to Saint-Domingue. As that author emphasizes: '... the decision to conduct an in-depth study of one of the substratum languages rather than a general survey of the properties of all West African languages involved is the result of a *methodological* choice forced by time and resource limitations ... [and] does *not* imply that Fongbe was the only substratum language of Haitian Creole nor that Haitian is a relexified form of Fongbe' (C. Lefebvre 2008:

67). She adds that the choice of Fongbe rather than any other Kwa group language is not that significant given the fact that languages of that group and other Niger-Congo languages share many typological features. Where HC differs from Fongbe Lefebvre invokes reanalysis and dialect leveling. The choice of the term 'dialect' is curious inasmuch as she states (as above) that many different substratum African languages were involved, not different dialects of Fongbe. As Baudet (1981: 106) observes, Suzanne Sylvain's choice (1936) of Ewe as the West African substrate language was also determined by convenience. Presumably her primary data were based on that language. Lefebvre provides another argument for the choice of Fongbe, namely, the predominance of Fon cultural elements. It is indeed the case that the most widespread Vodou rite has its roots in Benin, where Fongbe is spoken (C. Lefebvre 2008: 66). However, it may well be that these religious practices were adopted by slaves who spoke other languages. Also, Geggus (2001) points out that owners of sugar plantations preferred slaves from Benin, many of whom probably spoke Kwa languages, rather than speakers of Bantu languages from the Central West African coast. Because sugar plantations held larger numbers of slaves than those that produced coffee, indigo, or cotton and were located in the plains of northern Saint-Domingue, close to Cap-Français (now Cap Haïtien), slaves from Benin who spoke Kwa languages might have exercised greater linguistic influence. A fundamental problem in identifying substrate languages spoken in the French Atlantic colonies is that, as pointed out by d'Ans (1987), Manessy (1995), and Chaudenson (2003), among others, incoming slaves were identified neither by language nor by ethnic group but by the term *nation*, which referred to the region where the port of embarkation was located. Slaves shipped, say, from the Guinea coast may have been captured far inland and would not be native speakers of the language predominant in the coastal region. After having consulted a variety of recent descriptions of Fongbe during a stay in Cotonou (Benin) – none cited by Lefebvre – Chaudenson (1996) points out divergences between these descriptions and Lefebvre's choice of Fongbe data.

8. This massive demographic input reflects the high level of mortality of slaves in what was no doubt the most brutal slavery system in the Americas.
9. In this regard, Hull echoes Jules Faine's hypothesis of the origin of FBCs in a *patois nautique* 'maritime dialect' (Faine 1939).
10. Note that Hull assumes that Acadian French is derived from the assumed Maritime French. It is generally accepted that this variety of overseas French has its roots in the dialects of western France. The direct link that this author posits between Acadian French and Louisiana French, on the one hand, and Missouri French, on the other, is reductionist. With regard to the latter variety, although there were contacts between French settlers in that region and the Louisiana colony, the influence from New France (present-day Quebec) was no doubt much stronger.

11. The term 'generation' that Chaudenson proposes is derived from computer technology not biology. A second-generation computer is one in which some components are adapted from a first-generation one, not one that has evolved entirely independently. Thus, for him Mauritian Creole is not a directly evolved variety of Bourbonnais. Simply put, it contains many elements, particularly at the lexical level, found in Bourbonnais (Chaudenson 2003: 82). To be cautious, Chaudenson in fact refers to *générations de parlers* 'generations of speech' rather than *générations de créoles*. This underscores the idea that at that time a local speech variety had not yet crystallized into Réunion (Bourbon Island) Creole. Presumably what was exported to Mauritius (Isle de France) was an approximative version of Colonial French.
12. My translation reflects the approximative pidginized nature of the French original.
13. Robert Chaudenson expresses some doubts about Boutin's authorship, as well as whether it reflects only early Saint-Domingue Creole (personal communication). The French priests who provided early descriptions of the speech varieties in use in the Caribbean colonies often travelled among them.
14. Recall that in the Capois dialect, as in Guadeloupean Creole, the possessive construction contains the preposition *a*. Corresponding to N + *mwen* that dialect shows N + *a* + *mwen*, for example, 'my husband': *mari a mwen*, realized in normal oral style as *maranm* /marãm/.
15. Highfield (1979) collected his data in Carénage, a neighborhood of Charlotte-Amalie, the main town of St. Thomas. In this neighborhood reside White descendants of speakers of SBP from the Sous le Vent (Leeward) part of St. Barts, who immigrated to St. Thomas in the late nineteenth century. The speech of the Carénage community, less exposed to St. Barts Creole and French than the original community in St. Barts, may be more conservative than that of the original homeland. For a detailed treatment of St. Barts French and St. Barts Creole and a historical and social description of the island, see Calvet and Chaudenson (1998), Maher (1990), and G. Lefebvre (1980). For the sake of convenience, the examples from Highfield have been re-transcribed using conventional orthographic considerations. In their phonologically based idiosyncratic transcription, *dans mon temps à mouin* is noted as *dâ mô tâ a mwê*. Calvet and Chaudenson use a similar type of notation adapted from Gilles Lefebvre's unpublished work (Lexique de Saint-Barthélemy), e.g., *le fanmiy du mòr.*
16. As pointed out in Section 9.2.4, in HC there exists a relic combination of *la* plus *yo* that preserves a structure combining the features of definiteness and plural. The same fusion of these two semantic features occurred in Guianese Creole where *yé la* was replaced by *ya*.
17. Some of these can still be found in vernacular varieties of metropolitan French. Robert Chaudenson indicates that he occasionally uses *être à* (personal communication). I also recently heard near Nice '*mon mari est après travailler* ... "my husband is working ..." ' (June 2013). *Etre à* is widely distributed geographically. It is attested in western France as well as in the

eastern Franco-Provençal region (Rhône-Alpes) (Rézeau 1991; Martin and Tuaillon 1999). In 1998, I heard in the Beaujolais region an older woman say: '*mon gendre est après cueillir de la lavande en Provence* "my son-in-law is picking lavender in Provence" ').

18. Most specialists of LF use capital letters for non-integrated English loanwords.

19. I adapt here the idiosyncratic transcriptions used by Highfield (1979) and Calvet and Chaudenson (1998). For example, Highfield (1979: 90) provides *chu ki va (je suis qui va), t é ki va (tu es qui va)* 'you're going'. *Chu* is an agglutination of *je suis*, reflected in current vernacular French *j'suis* /ʃwi/. In LF, the 1st person singular pronoun is often reduced to /z/: *Z'veux les enfants à d'êt' contents* (Rottet, 1995: 254), but the agglutination of *je suis* is also prevalent: *Ça c'est les enfants que j'sus si fier* 'These are the children I'm proud of' (Rottet 1995: 233).

20. The only extensive source for the lexicon of St. Barts is Gilles Lefebvre's unpublished 'Lexique de Saint-Barthélemy', which can only be consulted at the French Colonial Archives (Archives d'Outre-mer) in Aix-en-Provence. However, Highfield (1979) contains a valuable lexical list.

21. Examples of the various creoles represented here are taken from the following sources: **Lou** Valdman *et al.* (2007), **Haï(ti)** Valdman *et al.* (2007), **Gua(deloupe)** Ludwig *et al.* (1990), **Mart(inique)** Confiant (2007), **St-Luc(ia)** Mondésir and Carrington (1992), **Dom(inica)** Fontaine and Roberts (1991), **Guy(ane)** Barthélémi (2007), **Kar(iña)** A. W. Tobler (1987), **Réu(nion)**, **Rod(rigues)**, **Seych(elles)** Bollée (2000), **Maur(itius)** Baker and Hookoomsing (1987).

22. Three major journals serve as the principal venues for SLA research: *Language Learning*, *Studies in Second Language Acquisition* (SSLA), and *Second Language Research*.

23. Mervyn Alleyne (1971) distinguishes two varieties of Saint-Domingue Creole, a *créole de salon*, illustrated by the texts mentioned here, and the variety spoken by the field slaves. Although the term *créole de salon* erroneously suggests that it was used by the upper classes of Saint-Domingue, as many authors have warned, great care must be exercised in interpreting texts of the colonial period (Chaudenson 1977: 259; Carden and Stewart 1988: 26–7; C. Lefebvre 1988: 69). On the other hand, their relative uniformity does suggest that Saint-Domingue Creole had not progressed far toward the extensive basilectalization reflected by late-nineteenth- and early-twentieth-century texts such as Georges Sylvain (1901) provides.

24. However, Manessy (1983), the eminent French Africanist, casts doubt on this claim of Bantu substratum transfer. He points out that contemporary speakers of Bantu languages do not necessarily incorporate French articles in borrowings: *bureau* 'office, desk' > *bilô*, *craie* 'chalk' > *kèle*, although Salikoko Mufwene (personal communication) cites some French nouns borrowed into Lingala with their determiners: *maser* 'nun' (< ma sœur), *lopitalo* 'hospital' (< l'hôpital). Also, speakers of African languages other than Bantu ones

incorporate the French article: *du thé* 'tea' > [dyte], *du vin* 'wine' > [dyvẽ]. For Manessy the question is not why Mauritian Creole has more agglutinated forms than Atlantic FBCs but why the latter have so few. For him the default case is that unguided learners of French will incorporate the variable determiners into the noun. Furthermore, Chaudenson points out that many of the agglutinations claimed by Baker and Grant involve doublets, such as *barb/ labarb* 'beard' where one of the variants lacks the agglutinated article.

25. As Manessy (1995) suggests, in addition to their native language, West African slaves might have brought over area lingua francas used for interethnic contacts in their native homelands. Thus, substrate transfers might have multiple sources.

26. Corresponding to this form is the homonymous indefinite pronoun: *Se kèk moun ki di sa, men m pa konn kilès.* 'It was someone who said that, I don't know which one.'

27. With regard to this feature, these authors remark that it illustrates the superstratist tendency to posit transmission from vernacular or dialectal varieties of French of rare features whereas their presence in African languages is overwhelming.

28. Baule is a language spoken on the Ivory Coast that belongs to the Akan group of Niger-Congo languages and, thus, is distantly related to Fongbe.

29. In the context of American slavery the term 'seasoned slaves' refers to the purchase of slaves from British West Indian plantation colonies, notably Jamaica. There, slaves arriving from Africa underwent acculturation to the plantocratic system under often harsh conditions. Here, the term refers to a slave born in Africa who had acculturated to the servile condition in Saint-Domingue, and had acquired some competence in the earlier-developed creole.

References

Acosta, José de. 2002. *The Natural and Moral History of the Indies*. Edited by Jane Mangan; translated by Frances Lopez-Morillas. Durham, NC: Duke University Press.
Adam, Lucien. 1883. *Les Idiomes négro-aryen et maléo-aryen. Essai d'hybridologie linguistique*. Paris: Maisonneuve.
d'Alaux, Gustave. 1860. *L'Empereur Soulouque et son empire*. Paris: Michel Lévy Frères.
Alleyne, Mervyn C. 1971. Acculturation and the Cultural Matrix of Creolization. In Dell H. Hymes (ed.), *Pidginization and Creolization of Languages*. Cambridge: Cambridge University Press, pp. 169–87.
Alterpresse. Haïti: Le Plan National d'éducation en Regard des Problèmes Démographiques et Socioéconomiques du Pays. http://www.alterpresse.org/spip.php?article6882#.VBiBxMH5y0s
Andersen, Roger. 1983. Transfer to Somewhere. In Susan M. Gass and Larry Selinker (eds.), *Language Transfer in Language Learning*. Rowley, MA: Newbury House, pp. 177–201.
Andrade, Julieta de. 1984. *Cultura Crioula e Lanc-Patuá no Norte do Brasil*. São Paulo: Escola de Folclore.
Anglade, Pierre. 1998. *Inventaire étymologique des termes créoles des Caraïbes d'origine africaine*. Paris: L'Harmattan.
Anonby, Stan. 2007. A Report on the Creoles of Amapá. SIL Electronic Survey Report. SILESR 2007-020.
d'Ans, André-Michel. 1968. *Le Créole français d'Haïti. Etude des unités d'articulation, d'expansion et de communication*. The Hague/Paris: Mouton.
d'Ans, André-Michel. 1987. *Haïti: Paysage et société*. Paris: Karthala.
Baggioni, Daniel, and Didier de Robillard. 1990. *Ile Maurice: Une Francophonie paradoxale*. Paris: L'Harmattan.
Baissac, Charles. 1880. *Études sur le patois créole mauricien*. Nancy: Berger-Levrault.
Baker, Philip. 1972. *Kreol: A Description of Mauritian Creole*. London: Hurst.
Baker, Philip. 1982. On the Origin of the First Mauritians and of the Creole Language of Their Descendants: A Refutation of Chaudenson's 'Bourbonnais' Theory. In Philip Baker and Chris Corne (eds.), *Isle de France Creole: Affinities and Origins*. Ann Arbor: Karoma, pp. 131–260.
Baker, Philip. 1984. Agglutinated French Articles in Creole French: Their Evolutionary Significance. *Te Reo* 27: 89–129.
Baker, Philip, and Chris Corne. 1982. *Isle de France Creole: Affinities and Origins*. Ann Arbor: Karoma Press.

Baker, Philip, and Vinesh Y. Hookoomsing. 1987. *Diksyoner Kreol Morisyen.* Paris: L'Harmattan.
Baker, Philip, and Guillaume Fon Sing. 2007. *The Making of Mauritian Creole.* London: Battleridge Publications (Westminster Creolistic Series 9).
Barbotin, Maurice. 1994. *Dictionnaire du créole de Marie-Galante.* Hamburg: Buske.
Barthélémi, Georges. 2007. *Dictionnaire créole guyanais-français.* Matoury: Ibis Rouge Editions.
Bartoli, Matteo. 1945. *Saggi di Linguistica Spaziale.* Turin: Rosenberg & Sellier.
Baudet, Martha M. 1981. Identifying the African Grammatical Base in the Caribbean Creoles. In Arnold Highfield and Albert Valdman (eds.), *Historicity and Variation in Creole Studies.* Ann Arbor: Karoma Press, pp. 104–17.
Baudoux, Georges. 1979. *Sauvages et Civilisés – Impressions de Nouvelle-Calédonie: Les Blancs sont venus.* Vol 2. Nouméa: Publications de la Société d'Etudes historiques de la Nouvelle-Calédonie, pp. 255–304.
Belloncle, Guy. 1981. *Dix Années d'alphabétisation en Haïti.* Paris: Agence de coopération culturelle et technique.
Bentolila, Alain. 1987. Marques aspecto-temporelles en créole haïtien: De l'analyse synchronique à la formulation d'hypothèses diachroniques. *La Linguistique* 23.1: 103–22.
Bentolila, Alain, and Léon Ganni. 1981. Langues et problèmes d'éducation en Haïti. *Langages* 61: 117–27.
Bentolila, Alain *et al.* 1976. *Ti Diksyonnè Kreyòl-Franse* [Dictionnaire élémentaire créole haïtien-français]. Port-au-Prince: Editions Caraïbes.
Bernabé, Jean. 1976. Propositions pour un code orthographique intégré des créoles à base lexicale française. *Espace créole* 1: 25–57.
Bernabé, Jean. 1983. *Fondal-natal: Grammaire basilectale approchée des créoles guadeloupéens et martiniquais: approche sociolittéraire, sociolinguistique et syntaxique.* Paris: L'Harmattan.
Bernabé, Jean. 1987. *Grammaire créole, Fondas kréyol-la.* Paris: L'Harmattan.
Bernabé, Jean. 2001. *La Graphie créole.* Matoury: Ibis Rouge Editions.
Bernabé, Jean. 2003. *Guides de Capés du créole: Précis de syntaxe créole.* Matoury (French Guiana): Ibis Rouge Editions.
Bernabé, Jean, Patrick Chamoiseau, and Raphaël Confiant. 1993. *Éloge de la créolité.* Paris: Gallimard.
Bernadin de Saint-Pierre, Jacques-Henri. 1773. *Voyage à l'Isle de France, à l'Isle de Bourbon, au Cap de Bonne-Espérance, etc. Avec des observations nouvelles sur la nature et sur les hommes, par un officier du Roi.* Paris: Merlin.
Berrouët-Oriol, Robert. 2011. Le « Système » linguistique d'Yves Dejean conduit à une impasse. *Le Nouvelliste.* August 11, 2011.
Berrouët-Oriol, Robert, Darline Cothière, Robert Fournier, and Hugues St-Fort. 2011. *Aménagement linguistique en Haïti: enjeux, défis, propositions.* Montreal: Les Editions du CIDHICA et Editions de l'Université d'Etat d'Haïti.
Berry, Paul C. 1964. 'Writing Haitian Creole: Issues and Proposals for Orthography.' Mimeographed. New York: Hudson Institute.
Bickerton, Derek. 1981. *Roots of Language.* Ann Arbor: Karoma Press.

Bickerton, Derek. 1975. *Dynamics of a Creole System*. Cambridge: Cambridge University Press.
Bickerton, Derek. 1987. Beyond Roots: Knowing What's What. *Journal of Pidgin and Creole Languages* 2.2: 229–37.
Bollée, Annegret. 1977. *Le Créole français des Seychelles*.Tübingen: Niemeyer.
Bollée, Annegret. 1993. *Dictionnaire étymologique des créoles français de l'océan Indien*. Hamburg: Helmut Buske.
Bollée, Annegret. 2000. *Dictionnaire étymologique des créoles français de l'océan Indien. Deuxième Partie. Mots d'origine française*. A-D. Hamburg: Helmut Buske.
Bollée, Annegret. 2012. Etymologies créoles. Contribution du dictionnaire étymologique des créoles français d'Amérique (DECA) à l'histoire du vocabulaire régional antillais. In André Thibault (ed.), *Le Français dans les Antilles: études linguistiques*. Paris: L'Harmattan, pp. 31–50.
Bollée, Annegret, and Pamela Nembach. 2006. Diatopic Variation in Haitian Creole. In J. Clancy Clements, Thomas A. Klingler, Deborah Piston-Hatlen, and Kevin J. Rottet (eds.), *History, Society and Variation: In Honor of Albert Valdman*. Philadelphia and Amsterdam: John Benjamins, pp. 225–35.
Borde, Pierre-Gustave-Louis. 1876. *Histoire de l'Île de la Trinidad sous le gouvernement espagnol*. Paris: Maisonneuve.
Brasseur, Patrice. 1997. Créoles à base lexicale française et français marginaux d'Amérique du Nord: quelques points de comparaison. In Marie-Christine Hazaël-Massieux and Didier de Robillard (eds.), *Contacts de langues, contacts de culture, créolisation*. Paris: L'Harmattan, pp. 141–66.
Breen, Henry H. 1844. *St. Lucia: Historical, Statistical, and Descriptive*. London: Longman, Brown & Green.
Breton, Raymond (Père). 1664. *Grammaire caraïbe, suivie du catéchisme caraïbe*. Reprinted 1887. Paris: L. Adam & Ch. Leclerc.
Breton, Raymond (Père). 1666. *Dictionnaire François-Caraïbe*. Reprinted 1900. Leipzig: Jules Platzman.
Brousseau, Anne-Marie. 1995. Les Pronoms en créole haïtien, en français, et en fongbé. In Claire Lefebvre (ed.), *Research Report Prepared for FCAR on the Project L'Organisation des lexiques et des entrées lexicales* (Vol. 4). Quebec: Université du Québec à Montréal (UQUAM).
Buscher, Gertrud. 1969. Introduction. In John J. Thomas (ed.), *The Theory and Practice of Creole Grammar*. Reprint of 1869 edition. London (Port-of-Spain): New Beacon Books.
Byers, Bruce. 1988. 'Defining Norms in a Non-standard Language: A Study of Verb and Pronoun Variation in Cajun French.' Ph.D. dissertation (Indiana University).
Cadely, Jean-Robert. 1988. L'opposition /r/ et /w/ en Créole haïtien: Un Paradoxe résolu. *Canadian Journal of Linguistics* 3.2: 121–4.
Cadely, Jean-Robert. 1994. 'Aspects de la phonologie du créole haïtien.' Ph.D. dissertation (University of Quebec at Montreal (UQUAM)).

Cadette-Blasse, Antheia. 2008. Vers une didactique du français adaptée au context de Sainte-Lucie. In Robert Chaudenson (ed.), *Didactique du français en milieux francophones*. Paris: L'Harmattan, pp. 203–16.
Calvet, Louis-Jean, and Robert Chaudenson. 1998. *Saint-Barthélemy: Une Enigme linguistique*. Paris: Didier Edition (CIRELFA-Agence de la Francophonie).
Carayol, Michel, Robert Chaudenson, and Christian Barat. 1984, 1989, 1995. *Atlas linguistique et ethnographique de la Réunion*. 3 vols. Paris: CNRS.
Carden, Guy, and William A. Stewart. 1988. Binding Theory, Bioprogram, and Creolization: Evidence from Haitian Creole. *Journal of Pidgin and Creole Languages* 3: 1–68.
Carden, Guy, Morris Goodman, Rebecca Posner, and William Stewart. 1991. A 1671 French Creole Text from Martinique. Paper presented at the Meeting of the Society for Pidgin and Creole Linguistics, January 5, 1991, Chicago.
Carpooran, Arnaud. 2002. *Le Créole mauricien de poche*. Chennevières-sur-Marne: ASSIMIL.
Carpooran, Arnaud. 2009. *Diksyoner Morisien*. Saint-Croix (Mauritius): Keleksion Text Kreol Ltd.
Carrington, Lawrence D. 1984. *St. Lucian Creole: A Descriptive Analysis of Its Phonology and Morpho-Syntax*. Hamburg: Buske.
Célestin-Mégie, Emile. 1975. *Lanmou pa gin baryè*. Port-au-Prince: Editions Fardin.
Célestin-Mégie, Emile. 1977. *Lanmou pa gin baryè:2èm Epòk*. Port-au-Prince: Editions Fardin.
Cervinka-Taulier, Bernadette. 1992. 'Le Lexique du créole de la Guadeloupe: Héritage, créativité, prédictibilité' (3 vols.). Ph.D. dissertation (Université des Antilles et de la Guyane).
Césaire, Aimé. 1939. *Cahier d'un retour au pays natal*. Paris: Présence Africaine.
Chamoiseau, Patrick. 1992. *Texaco*. Paris: Gallimard.
Chanlatte, Juste (Comte de Rosiers). 1818. *L'Entrée du Roi en sa capitale en janvier 1818, an 15ème de l'indépendance d'Hayti*. Cap Haïtian (Haiti): Imprimerie royale de Sans-Souci.
Chatillon, M. 1984. Lettres du R. P. Jean Mongin: L'évangélisation des esclaves au XVIIe siècle. *Bulletin de la société d'histoire de la Guadeloupe*, 61–2.
Chaudenson, Robert. 1974. *Le Lexique du parler créole de la Réunion* (2 vols.). Paris: Champion.
Chaudenson, Robert. 1977. Toward the Reconstruction of the Social Matrix of Creole Language. In Albert Valdman (ed.), *Pidgins and Creole Linguistics*. Bloomington and London: Indiana University Press, pp. 259–77.
Chaudenson, Robert. 1979. A propos de la Genèse du créole mauricien: le peuplement de l'Ile de France de 1721–1735. *Études créoles* 1: 43–57.
Chaudenson, Robert. 1981. *Textes créoles anciens (La Réunion et Ile Maurice) comparaison et essai d'analyse*. Hamburg: Buske.
Chaudenson, Robert. 1992. *Des Iles, des hommes, des langues: essais sur la créolisation linguistique et culturelle*. Paris: L'Harmattan.
Chaudenson, Robert. 1994. A propos de Sabine Ehrhart, *Le Créole français de Saint-Louis (le tayo) en Nouvelle-Calédonie*. Etudes créoles 17.1: 128–42.

Chaudenson, Robert. 1996. Démystification de la relexification. *Études créoles* 19: 93–109.
Chaudenson, Robert. 2001. Le CAPES de créole(s): approche historique et linguistique. *Études créoles* 24.1: 37–79.
Chaudenson, Robert. 2003. *La Créolisation: théorie, applications, implications*. Paris: L'Harmattan.
Chaudenson, Robert (coordinator). 2008. *Didactique du français en milieux créolophones. Outils pédagogiques et formation des maîtres*. Paris: l'Harmattan.
Chaudenson, Robert. 2010. *La Genèse des créoles de l'Océan Indien*. Paris: L'Harmattan.
Chaudenson, Robert, and Pierre Vernet. 1983. *L'Ecole en créole: Étude comparée des réformes des systèmes éducatifs en Haïti et aux Seychelles*. Paris: ACCT.
Chaudenson, Robert, Michel Carayol, and Christian Barat. 1992. *Atlas linguistique ethnographique de Rodrigues* (3 vols.). Paris: ACCT.
Chauveau, Jean-Paul. 2012. Des Régionalismes de France dans le créole de Marie-Galante. In André Thibault (ed.), *Le Français dans les Antilles: études linguistiques*. Paris: L'Harmattan, pp. 51–100.
Chevillard, R. P. André. 1659. *Les Dessins de son Eminence de Richelieu pour l'Amérique*. Rennes: Jean Durand. (1973 Basse-Terre, Guadeloupe: Société d'Histoire de la Guadeloupe.)
CHISS (Centre Haitien d'investigation en sciences sociales). 1975. Le Projet expérimental sur le bilinguisme créole français au niveau de l'enseignement primaire en Haïti: bilan de la première année 1974–1975. *Bulletin d'Information du CHISS* 14: 1–35.
Churchill, Margaret A. 1957. 'Haitian Creole: Linguistic Analysis and Proposed Orthography.' MA thesis (Georgetown University).
Clark, Eve. 1985. Acquisition of Romance, with Special Reference to French. In Dan Isaac Slobin (ed.), *The Cross-Linguistic Study of Language Acquisition*. Hillsdale, NJ: Lawrence Erlbaum Associates.
Clements, Clancy J., and Ahmar Mahboob. 2000. *Wh*-Words and Question Formation in Pidgin/Creole Languages. In John McWhorter (ed.), *Language Change and Language Contact in Pidgins and Creoles*. Philadelphia and Amsterdam: John Benjamins, pp. 459–98.
Coelho, Adolfo. 1880. Os dialectos românicos ou neolatinos na Africa, Asia, e América. *Boletim da Sociedade de Geografia de Lisboa*. Republished in Jorge Morais-Barbosa (ed.), *Estudos linguisticos crioulos* (1967). Lisbon: Academia Internacional de Cultura Portuguesa.
Collins, Chris. 1997. Argument Sharing in Serial Verb Constructions. *Linguistic Inquiry* 28: 461–97.
Comrie, Bernard. 1976. *Aspect: An Introduction to the Study of Verbal Aspect and Related Problems*. Cambridge: Cambridge University Press.
Confiant, Raphaël. 1979. *Jik dèyè do Bondyé, nouvelles*. Martinique: Grif An Tè.
Confiant, Raphaël. 1988. *Le Nègre et l'amiral*. Paris: Grasset.
Confiant, Raphaël. 2007. *Dictionnaire créole martiniquais-français* (2 vols.). Matoury (Guiana): Ibis Rouge Editions.
Coriolan, Anne-Marie. 2010. Situation linguistique et éducative d'Haïti. *Études créoles* 1.2: 233–42.

Corne, Chris. 1977. *Seychelles Creole Grammar: Elements for Indian Ocean Proto-Creole Reconstruction*. Tübingen: Gunter Narr.
Corne, Chris. 1982. A Contrastive Analysis of Reunion and Isle de France Creole French: Two Typologically Contrastive Languages. In Philip Baker and Chris Corne. *Isle de France Creole: Affinities and Origins*. Ann Arbor: Karoma Press, pp. 8–129.
Corne, Chris. 1989. Un Créole à base lexicale française en Nouvelle Calédonie: le tayo ou le patois de Saint-Louis. *Etudes créoles* 12.2: 29–42.
Corne, Chris. 1995. A Contact-induced and Vernacularized Language: How Melanesian Is Tayo? In Philip Baker (ed.), *From Contact to Creole and Beyond*. London: Westminster University Press, pp. 121–48.
Corne, Chris. 1999. *From French to Creole: The Development of New Vernaculars in the French Colonial World*. London: University of Westminster Press.
Cornevin, Robert. 1982. *Haïti*. Paris: Presses Universitaires de France (Série: Que sais-je?).
Craig, Denis R. 1980. Models for Educational Policy in Creole Speaking Communities. In Albert Valdman and Arnold Highfield (eds.), *Theoretical Orientations in Creole Studies*. New York: Academic Press, pp. 245–65.
Damoiseau, Robert. 1987. Situation de communication et fonctionnement de la langue en créole haïtien. *Études créoles* 10.2: 90–106.
Damoiseau, Robert. 1988. Eléments pour une classification des verbaux en créole haïtien. *Études créoles* 11.1: 41–64.
Damoiseau, Robert. 1991. Exemples de procédures de réinterprétation d'un lexique français en créole haïtien. *Études créoles* 14: 1–43.
Damoiseau, Robert. 1996. Les Adjectifs en créole haïtien. In Daniel Véronique (ed.), *Matériaux pour l'étude des classes grammaticales dans les langues créoles*. Aix-en-Provence: Publications de l'Université de Provence, pp. 151–61.
Damoiseau, Robert. 2005a. *Eléments de grammaire comparée Français-Créole haïtien*. Matoury: Ibis Rouge Editions.
Damoiseau, Robert. 2005b. *Eléments de grammaire comparée Français-Créole guyanais*. Matoury: Ibis Rouge Editions.
Damoiseau, Robert. 2007. Le créole guyanais dans la famille des créoles à base lexicale francaise dans la zone américano-caraïbe. In Serge Mam-Lam-Fouk (ed.), *Comprendre la Guyane aujourd'hui*. Matoury: Ibis Rouge Editions, pp. 501–14.
Damoiseau, Robert, and Luc Guimbretière. 1994. Regards d'Haïtiens sur la langue française. *Espace créole* 8: 173–86.
Damoiseau, Robert, and Gérald Saint-Louis. 1986. Les Verbo-adjectivaux en créole haïtien. *Modèles linguistiques* 8: 103–35.
Darlow, Mark R. 1999. Fonctionnement des timbres dans *Les Amours de Bastien et Bastienne*. In Herbe Schneider (ed.), *Timbre und Vaudeville: Zur Geschichte und Problematik einer populären Gattung im 17 und 18 Jahrhundert*. Hilderheim/Zurich/New York: Georg Olms Verlag, pp. 126–223.
Daudier, Valéry. 2011. Un Téléthon pour reloger les déplacés de la Place St-Pierre, *Le Nouvelliste,* 11 March.
De Regt, Jacomina P. 1984. Basic Education in Haiti. In Charles R. Foster and Albert Valdman (eds.), *Haiti – Today and Tomorrow: An Interdisciplinary Study*. Lanham, MD: University Press of America, pp. 119–140.

DeGraff, Michel. 2001. Morphology in Creole Genesis: Linguistics and Ideology. In Michael Kenstowicz (ed.), *Ken Hale: A Life in Language*. Cambridge, MA: MIT Press, pp. 53–121.

DeGraff, Michel. 2003. Against Creole Exceptionalism. *Language* 79: 191–210.

DeGraff, Michel. 2005. Morphology and Word Order in Creolization and Beyond. In Guglielmo Cinque and Richard S. Kayne (eds.), *Comparative Syntax*. Oxford: Oxford University Press, pp. 293–372.

DeGraff, Michel. 2007. Haitian Creole. In John Holm and Peter Patrick (eds.), *Comparative Creole Syntax: Parallel Outlines of 18 Creole Grammars*. London: Battlebridge Publications (Westminster Creolistics Series).

DeGraff, Michel. 2009. Language Acquisition in Creolization and, thus, Language Change: Some Cartesian-Uniformitarian Boundary Conditions. *Language and Linguistics Compass* 3.4: 888–971.

Dejean, Yves. 1974. *Ti Liv òtograf kreyòl*. Montreal: Agence Libre du Québec.

Dejean, Yves. 1976. *Orthographe créole et passage au français*. Unpublished manuscript (from the author).

Dejean, Yves. 1980. *Comment écrire le créole d'Haïti*. Outremont (Québec): Collectif Paroles.

Dejean, Yves. n.d. Unpublished review of Lefebvre *et al.* (1982).

Dejean, Yves. 1993. An Overview of the Language Situation in Haiti. *International Journal of the Sociology of Language* 102: 73–83.

Dejean, Yves. 2006. *Yon Ekòl tèt anba nan yon peyi tèt anba*. Port-au-Prince: FOKAL.

Dejean, Yves. 2010. Creole and Education in Haïti. In Arthur Spears and Carole Berotte Joseph (eds.), *The Haitian Creole Language*. Lanham, MD: Lexington Books, pp. 199–216.

Dejean, Yves. 2011. *Haïti: Déménagement linguistique*. Alterpresse, http://www.alterpresse.org/spip.php?article11343#.VBiDasH5y0s

Desmarattes, Jean Lyonel. 1983. *Mouché Défas*. Port-au-Prince: Collection Créolade.

Dillard, Joey. 1970. Principles in the History of American English: Paradox, Virginity, and Cafeteria. *Florida FL Reporter* 8: 32–33.

D'Offay, Danielle, and Guy Lionnet. 1982. *Disyonner kreol-fransé*. Hamburg: Buske.

Doret, Frédéric. 1924. *Pour Amuser nos tout petits: initiation aux fables de la Fontaine, avec une introduction sur le créole*. Port-au-Prince: Sirius Books (Paris: Imprimerie des Orphelins-Apprentis d'Auteuil).

Du Tertre, Jean-Baptiste. 1667. *L'Histoire générale des Antilles habitées par les François*. Paris: Jolly.

Ducœurjoly, S. J. 1802. *Manuel des habitants de Saint-Domingue*. Paris: Lenoir.

Durizot Jno-Baptiste, Paulette. 1996. *La Question du créole à l'école en Guadeloupe*. Paris: L'Harmattan.

Ehrhart, Sabine. 1993. *Le Créole français de Saint-Louis (le tayo) en Nouvelle Calédonie*. Hamburg: Buske.

Etienne, Gérard. 1974. 'Le Créole du Nord d'Haïti: Etude des niveaux de structure.' Ph.D. dissertation (Université de Strasbourg).

Exmelin, Alexandre-Olivier. 1980 [1678]. *Histoire des Frères de la Côte. Filibustiers et Boucaniers des Antilles*. Paris: Editions Maritimes et d'Outre-Mer.

Faine, Jules. 1936. *Philologie créole: Études historiques et étymologiques sur la langue créole d'Haïti*. Port-au-Prince: Imprimerie de l'État.
Faine, Jules. 1939. *Le Créole dans l'univers: Études comparatives des parlers français*. Port-au-Prince: Imprimerie de l'Etat.
Faine, Jules. 1974. *Dictionnaire français-créole*. Montréal: Leméac.
Faraclas, Nicolas, Arthur K. Spears, Elizabeth Barrows, and Mayra C. Piñeiro. 2010. Orthography. In Arthur Spears and Carole Berotte-Joseph (eds.), *The Haitian Creole Language: History, Structure, Use, and Education*. Lanham, MD: Lexington Books, pp. 83–106.
Fattier, Dominique. 1994. Un Fragment colonial: Le Manuel des habitants de Saint-Dominique de S. J. Ducoeurjoly, 1802. Réflexions sur l'apprentissage et la créolisation. In Daniel Véronique (ed.), *Créolisation et acquisition des langues*. Aix-en-Provence: Publication de l'Université de Provence, pp. 53–77.
Fattier, Dominique. 1996. La Passion de Notre Seigneur en langage nègre: un scripta créole? *Études créoles* 19.2: 9–30.
Fattier, Dominique. 1998. 'Contribution à l'étude de la genèse d'un créole: l'Atlas Linguistique d'Haïti, cartes et commentaires (Vols. 1–6).' Ph.D. dissertation (doctorat d'État) (Université de Provence).
Fattier, Dominique. 2000. *Contribution à l'étude de la genèse d'un créole: L'atlas linguistique d'Haïti, cartes et commentaires. Thèse de doctoral d'Etat*. Villeneuve d'Ascq: Presses Universitaires du Septentrion.
Fattier, Dominique. 2003. Grammaticalisations en créole haïtien: morceaux choisis. *Creolica* 1: 1–17. Online: http://www.creolica.net/article.php3?id_article=19 (accessed May 5, 2010).
Fattier-Thomas, Dominique. 1984. De la variété rèk à la variété swa. Pratiques vivantes de la langue en Haïti. *Conjonction* 161.162: 39–51.
Férère, Gérard A. 1974. 'Haitian Creole Sound System, Form-classes, Texts.' Ph.D. dissertation (University of Pennsylvania).
Ferguson, Charles A. 1959. Diglossia. *Word* 15: 325–40.
Ferguson, James. 1987. *Papa Doc, Baby Doc: Haiti and the Duvaliers*. Oxford: Basil Blackwell.
Ferreira, Jo-Anne S., and Mervyn C. Alleyne. 2007. Comparative Perspectives on the Origins, Development and Structure of Amazonian (Karipúna) French Creole. In Magnus Huber and Viveka Velupillai (eds.), *Synchronic and Diachronic Perspectives on Contact Languages [CLL 33]*. Philadelphia and Amsterdam: John Benjamins, pp. 325–57.
Firmin, Anténor.1885. *De l'Egalité des races humaines*. Paris: Cotillon.
Firmin, Anténor. 1905. *M. Roosevelt, président des Etats-Unis et la République d'Haïti*. New York: Hamilton Bank Note Engraving and Printing Company.
Fishman, Joshua. 1971. *Sociolinguistics*. Rowley, MA: Newbury House.
Fleischman, Suzanne. 1982. *The Future in Thought and Language: Diachronic Evidence from Romance* (Cambridge Studies in Linguistics, 36). Cambridge: Cambridge University Press.
Fleischmann, Ulrich. 1984. Language, Literacy, and Underdevelopment. In Charles R. Foster and Albert Valdman (eds.), *Haiti – Today and Tomorrow: An Interdisciplinary Study*. Lanham, MD: University Press of America, pp. 101–17.

Fleischmann, Ulrich. 2010. L'Expérience témoin de Marbial, Haïti. *Études créoles* 1.2: 23–41.
Fong Sing, Guillaume. 2004. 'Les Phénomènes de grammaticalisation et de réanalyze dans le processus de créolisation: etude de la mise en place du système temps-mode-aspect et de l'évolution diachronique des particules préverbales en créole mauricien.' DEA thesis (University of Paris III).
Fontaine, M., and Peter A. Roberts. 1991. *Dominica's diksyonnè: Kwéyòl-Annglè*. Roseau, Dominica: The Folk Research Institute.
Fouchard, Jean. 1988. *Regards sur l'histoire*. Port-au-Prince: Deschamps.
Frank, David (ed.). 2001. *Kwéyòl Dictionary*. Castries: Ministry of Education.
Franketienne. 1975. *Dézafi, roman*. Port-au-Prince: Edition Fardin.
Freeman, Bryant C. 2010. *Haitian-English Dictionary*. Lawrence, KS: Institute of Haitian Studies.
Freeman, Bryant C. 2011. *English-Haitian Dictionary* (3 vols.). Lawrence, KS: Institute of Haitian Studies.
Freeman, Bryant C., and Jowel Laguerre. 2006. *Haitian-English Dictionary*. Port-au-Prince: La Presse Evangélique.
Frei, Henri. 1929. *La Grammaire des fautes*. Paris: Gueutner.
Frostin, Charles. 1975. *Les Révoltes blanches à Saint-Domingue aux XVII et XVIII siècles (Haïti avant 1789)*. Paris: Editions de l'École.
Froude, James Anthony. 1888. *The English in the West Indies: Or, the Bow of Ulysses*. London: Longmans.
Furetière, Antoine. 1690. *Dictionnaire universel, concernant les mots français tant vieux que modernes, et les termes de toutes les sciences et des arts...* (3 vols.). La Haye/Rotterdam: Arnout et Reinier Leers. Reprinted 1970: Geneva: Slatkine Reprints.
Garçon, Jacques. 2009. Anba bouch a Grann Mari; Labitid ak koutim. *Haïti en Marche*: 22–39.
Geggus, David. 2001. The French Slave Trade: An Overview. *William and Mary Quarterly* 58: 119–38.
Germain, Robert. 1976. *Grammaire créole*. Villejuif: Editions du Levain.
Gil, David. 2001. Creoles, Complexity, and Riau Indonesian. *Linguistic Typology* 5: 325–71.
Galliéron, Jules, and Édmond Édmont. 1902. *Atlas linguistique de la France 1902–1910*. Paris: Champion (9 vols.); supplement 1920.
Girod-Chantrans, Justin. 1785 (reprint 1980). *Voyage d'un Suisse dans différentes colonies d'Amérique*. Paris: Tallandier.
Givón, Talmy. 1991. Some Substantive Issues Concerning Verb Serialization: Grammatical vs. Cognitive Packaging. In Claire Lefebvre (ed.), *Serial Verbs: Grammatical, Comparative and Cognitive Approaches*. Philadelphia and Amsterdam: John Benjamins, pp. 137–84.
Goodman, Morris F. 1964. *A Comparative Study of Creole French Dialects*. The Hague: Mouton.
Gougenheim, Georges. 1929. *Etude sur les périphrases verbales de la langue française*. Paris: Nizet.

Grant, Anthony P. 1995. Article Agglutination in Creole French: A Wider Perspective. In Philip Baker (ed.), *From Contact to Creole and Beyond*. London: University of Westminster Press, pp. 149–75.

Grégoire, Henri-Baptiste Abbé. 1794. *Rapport sur la nécessité et les moyens d'anéantir les patois et d'universaliser la langue française*. http://books.google.com/books?id=8PB2RBNrLZYC&printsec=frontcover&source=gbs_ge_summary_r&cad=0#v=onepage&q&f=false (accessed June 23, 2014).

Grégoire, Antoine. 1947. *L'Apprentissage du langage: La troisième année et les années suivantes* (Vol. 2). Paris: Société d'Edition des Belles Lettres.

Grevisse, Maurice. 1969. *Le Bon Usage: Grammaire française avec des remarques sur la langue française d'aujourd'hui*. Gembloux: J. Duculot.

Grimes, Barbara F. 1996. *Ethnologue: Languages of the World*. 13th ed. Dallas: SIL International. Web version for 2005 (15th) edition, R. G. Gordon Jr. (ed.): <http://www.ethnologue.com/web.asp> (accessed April 27, 2005).

Guilbeau, John. 1950. 'The French Spoken in Lafourche Parish, Louisiana.' Ph.D. dissertation (University of North Carolina).

Hadjadj, Bernard. 2000. Education of All in Haiti Over the Last 20 Years. Assessment and Perspective. *Education of All in the Caribbean: Assessment 2000. Monograph Series 18*. Kingston, Jamaica: Office of the UNESCO Representative in the Caribbean.

Hall, Gwendolyn M. 2000. Introduction to the Louisiana Slave Database and the Louisiana Free Database: 1719–1820. In Gwendolyn M. Hall (ed.), *Databases for the Study of Afro-Louisiana History and Genealogy, 1699–1860*. Baton Rouge: Louisiana State University Press.

Hall, Robert A., Jr. 1953. *Haitian Creole: Grammar-Texts-Vocabulary*. Philadelphia: American Folklore Society (Memoirs 43).

Hall, Robert A., Jr. 1966. *Pidgin and Creole Languages*. Ithaca, NY: Cornell University Press.

Halliday, Michael A. K. 1973. *Explorations in the Functions of Language*. London: Edward Arnold.

Hancock, Ian. 1969. A Provisional Comparison of the English-based Atlantic Creoles. *African Language Review* 8: 7–72.

Hancock, Ian. 1979. *Readings in Creole Studies*. Ghent: Story-Scientia.

Hancock, Ian. 1985. A Preliminary Structural Sketch of Trinidad Creole French. With a Note on the Related Dialect of Güiria, Venezuela. *Amsterdam Creole Studies* 9: 27–39.

Harbour, Daniel. 2008. Klivaj predika, or predicate clefts in Haitian. *Lingua* 118.7: 853–71.

Hazaël-Massieux, Guy. 1983. Les Parties du discours en créole de la Guadeloupe. *Travaux du Cercle de Linguistique de l'Université de Provence* 1: 73–85.

Hazaël-Massieux, Guy. 1991. Genèse ou histoire de la modalité verbale en créole de la Guadeloupe. In Guy Hazaël-Massieux (ed.), *Modalisations en langues étrangères*. Aix-en-Provence: Publications de l'Université de Provence, pp. 17–30.

Hazaël-Massieux, Guy. 1992. Peut-on caractériser un créole par sa morphosyntaxe? Verbe et groupe verbal dans les créoles français. In *Lalies*, Actes des sessions de linguistique et de littérature. No 10. Paris: Presses de la Sorbonne Nouvelle.
Hazaël-Massieux, Guy. 1994. La Passion de Notre Seigneur selon Saint-Jean en langage nègre. *Études créoles* 17: 10–27.
Hazaël-Massieux, Marie-Christine. 1993. *Ecrire en créole: Oralité et écriture aux Antilles*. Paris: L'Harmattan.
Hazaël-Massieux, Marie-Christine. 2008. *Textes anciens en créole français de la Caraïbe: Histoire et analyse*. Paris: Editions Publibook.
Heinl, Robert D. and Nancy G. Heinl. 2005. *Written in Blood: The Story of the Haitian People, 1492–1995*. Rev.edn. Lanham, MD: University Press of America.
Hesseling, Dirk C. 1897. Het Hollandsch in Zuid-Afrika. *De Gids* 60.1: 138–62.
Highfield, Arnold R. 1979. *The French Dialect of St. Thomas. U.S. Virgin Islands*. Ann Arbor: Karoma Press.
Holm, John. 1988. *Pidgins and Creoles*. (Cambridge Language Surveys I). Cambridge: Cambridge University Press.
Holm, John. 1989. *Pidgins and Creoles*. (Cambridge Language Surveys II). Cambridge: Cambridge University Press.
Honorien, Louis. 2009. La Langue kréyòl. In Odile Reneau-Lescure and Laurence Goury (eds.), *Langues de Guyane*. La Roque D'Anthéron: Vents d'ailleurs, pp. 118–31.
Howe, Kate. 1990. *Haitian News Port-au-Prince Reader*. Wheaton, MD: Dunwoody Press.
Hugo, Victor. 1826 [1985]. *Bug-Jargal*. Reprinted in *Œuvres complètes*, Vol. 12. Paris: Robert Laffont.
Hull, Alexander. 1979. On the Origin and Chronology of the French-based Creoles. In Ian Hancock (ed.), *Readings in Creole Studies*. Ghent: Story-Scientia, pp. 201–16.
Hyppolite, Michelson P. 1949. *Les Origines des variations du créole haïtien*. Port-au-Prince: Imprimerie de l'Etat.
Hyppolite, Michelson P. 1951–56. *Contes dramatiques haïtiens* (vols. 1–2). Port-au-Prince: Imprimerie de l'Etat.
Idylles et chansons, ou, Essais de poësie créole par un habitant d'Hayti (1811). Philadelphia: J. Edwards.
James, C. L. R. 1938. *Black Jacobins: Toussaint L'Ouverture and the San Domingo Revolution*. New York: Random House.
Jansen, Silke. 2012. La Formation du français regional et des créoles antillais: l'apport du taïno. In André Thibault (ed.), *Le Français dans les Antilles: études linguistiques*, 101–140.
Jauze, Jean-Michel, and Jeannine Yeung Ching Yung. 1998. *La troisième île des Mascareignes*. Paris: L'Harmattan.
Jean-Baptiste, Rozevel. 1992. 'Etude syntactico-sémantique des zones de prédication et de détermination en créole haïtien: essai sur quelques micro-opérations.' Ph.D. dissertation (University of Paris V (René Descartes)).
Jean-Charles, Hervé L. 1987. 'Attitudes of Teachers and Parents toward French and Creole in Haiti.' Ph.D. dissertation (Stanford University Paolo Alto).

Jean-François, Lesly. 2006. 'Attitudes des éducateurs envers le français et le créole: le cas d'Haïti.' Ph.D. dissertation (Louisiana State University and Agricultural and Mechanical College).
Jennings, William. 1995. The First Generations of a Creole Society: Cayenne 1660–1700. In Philip Baker (ed.), *From Contact to Creole and Beyond*. London: University of Westminster Press, pp. 21–40.
Jespersen, Otto. 1922. *Language: Its Nature, Development, and Origin*. London: Allen and Unwin.
Joint, Louis-Auguste. 2006. *Système éducatif et inégalités sociales en Haïti*. Paris: L'Harmattan.
Joseph, Frantz. 1988. 'La Détermination nominale en créole haïtien.' Ph.D. dissertation (Université de Paris VII).
Joseph, Yves. 1980. Enquête pilote sur l'environnement linguistique de l'enfant haïtien. In Albert Valdman and Yves Joseph (eds.), *Créole et enseignement primaire en Haïti*. Bloomington: Indiana University Creole Institute, pp. 75–94.
Jourdain, Elodie. 1956. *Le Vocabulaire du parler créole de la Martinique*. Paris: Klincksieck.
Karam, Antoine. 1986. Les Esclaves de la sucrerie Noël. In Anne-Marie Bruleaux, Régine Calmont, and Serge Mam-Lam-Fouck (eds.), *2 Siècles d'esclavage en Guyane française*. Paris: L'Harmattan, pp. 63–74.
Kephart, Ronald. 1991. Creole French on Carriacou, Grenada: Texts and Commentary. *Florida Journal of Anthropology* (special publication) 7. 81–90.
Klingler, Thomas. 1992. 'A Descriptive Study of Creole Speech of Pointe Coupee Parish Louisiana with Focus on the Lexicon.' Ph.D. dissertation (Indiana University).
Klingler, Thomas. 2003. *If I Could Turn My Tongue Like That: The Creole Language of Pointe Coupée Parish, Louisiana*. Baton Rouge: Louisiana State Press.
Koopman, Hilda. 1982. Les Questions. In Claire Lefebvre, Hélène Magloire-Holly, and Nanie Piou (eds.), *Syntaxe de l'haïtien*. Ann Arbor: Karoma Press, pp. 204–33.
Koopman, Hilda, and Claire Lefebvre. 1981. 'Haitian Creole pou'. In Pieter C. Muysken (ed.), *Generative Studies on Creole Languages*. Dordrecht: Foris, pp. 201–21.
Koopman, Hilda, and Claire Lefebvre. 1982. PU: marqueur de mode, préposition et complémenteur. In Claire Lefebvre, Hélène Magloire-Holly, and Nanie Piou (eds.), *Syntaxe de l'haïtien*. Ann Arbor: Karoma Press, pp. 64–91.
Krashen, Stephen. 1988. *Second Language Acquisition and Second Language Learning*. New York: Prentice-Hall.
Kremnitz, Jorg. 1983. *Français et créole: ce qu'en pensent les enseignants. Le conflit linguistique à la Martinique*. Hamburg: Buske.
Kurath, Hans.1949. *A Word Geography of the Eastern United States*. Ann Arbor: University of Michigan Press.
Labov, William. 1992. *Sociolinguistic Patterns*. Philadelphia: University of Pennsylvania Press.
Labov, William. 2001. *Principles of Linguistic Change, I: Internal Factors, II: Social Factors*. Oxford: Blackwell.

Lafage, Suzanne. 1985. *Français écrit et parlé en pays Ewé (Sud-Congo)*. Paris: SELAF.
Laguerre, Pierre M. 2010. *Enseigner le créole et le français aux enfants haïtiens. Enjeux et perspectives*. Port-au-Prince: Deschamps.
Lainy, Rochambeau. 2010. 'Temps et aspect dans la structure de l'énonciation rapportée: comparaison entre le français et le créole haïtien.' Ph.D. dissertation (University of Rouen).
Lambert, Wallace E. et al. 1967. A Social Psychology of Bilingualism. *Journal of Social Issues* 23: 91–108.
Lambert, Wallace E., and Richard C. Tucker. 1972. *Bilingual Education of Children in the Saint Lambert Experiment*. Rowley, MA: Newbury House.
Le Dû, Jean, and Gyslaine Brun-Trigaud. 2011. *Atlas linguistique des Petites Antilles (ATLA)* (Vol. 1). Paris: Editions du Comité des Etudes Historiques et Scientifiques.
Le Page, Robert B., and Andrée Tabouret-Keller. 1985. *Acts of Identity: Creole-based Approaches to Language and Ethnicity*. Cambridge: Cambridge University Press.
Lefebvre, Claire. 1986. Relexification in Creole Genesis Revisited: The Case of Haitian Creole. In Pieter C. Muysken and Norval Smith (eds.), *Universals versus Substratum Influence in Creole Genesis*. Philadelphia and Amsterdam: John Benjamins, pp. 279–301.
Lefebvre, Claire. 1988. *Études syntaxiques, morphologiques et phonologiques*. Research report prepared for SSHRCC, FCAR, and PAFAC on the project Haiti-Fon. Université de Québec à Montréal (UQUAM).
Lefebvre, Claire. 1998. *Creole Genesis and the Acquisition of Grammar: The Case of Haitian Creole*. New York: Cambridge University Press.
Lefebvre, Claire. 2008. On the Principled Nature of the Respective Contributions of Substrate and Superstrate Languages to a Creole's Lexicon. In Susanne Michaelis (ed.), *Roots of Creole Structures: Weighing the Contribution of Substrates and Superstrates*. Philadelphia and Amsterdam: John Benjamins, pp. 197–223.
Lefebvre, Claire, Hélène Magloire-Holly, and Nanie Piou. 1982. *Syntaxe de l'haïtien*. Ann Arbor: Karoma Press.
Lefebvre, Gilles. 1976. Français régional et créole à Saint-Barthélemy. In Albert Valdman and Emile Snyder (eds), *Identité culturelle et francophonie dans les Amériques*. Quebec: Presses de l'Université Laval, pp. 122–46.
Lefebvre, Gilles. 1980. Créativités lexicales et créolité à Saint-Barthélemy. *Etudes créoles* 3: 27–44.
Lefebvre, Gilles. n.d. Lexique de Saint-Barthélemy. Unpublished manuscript.
Lionnet, Guy. 1972. *A Short History of the Seychelles*. Mahé: Imprimerie St. Fidèle.
Lipsky, John M. 1986. Bozal Spanish: Consistency and Parallel Structures. *Journal of Pidgin and Creole Languages* 1: 171–203.
Locher, Uli. 2010. Education in Haiti. In Arthur Spears and Carole Berotte-Joseph (eds.), *The Haitian Creole Language*. Lanham, MD: Lexington Books, pp. 177–98.
Locher, Uli, Thierry Milan, and Charles Pierre-Jacques. 1987. *Evaluation de la réforme éducative en Haïti*. Geneva: World Bank.

Lofficial, Frantz. 1979. *Créole-Français: une fausse querelle*. Quebec: Collectif Paroles.
Longuefosse, Mozart F. 1996. Pour un souffle nouveau de l'alphabétisation en Haïti. *Le Monde alphabétique* 8: 61–3.
Ludwig, Ralph. 1988. *Korpus: Texte des gesprochenen Französisch*. Tübingen: Narr.
Ludwig, Ralph. 1992. La Relative en créole guadeloupéen: l'évolution d'une technique grammaticale dans un context diglossique. *Études créoles* 15.2: 109–25.
Ludwig, Ralph, and Stefan Pfänder. 2003. La Particule là/la en français oral et en créole caribéen: grammaticalisation et contact de langue. In Sibylle Kriegel (ed.), *Grammaticalisation et réanalyze. Approche de la variation créole et français*. Paris: CNRS Editions, pp. 269–84.
Ludwig, Ralph, Danièle Montbrand, Hector Poullet, and Silvyàn Telchid. 1990. *Dictionnaire créole français*. Paris: Servedit/Editions Jasor.
Lumsden, John. 1999. Language Acquisition and Creolization. In Michel DeGraff (ed.), *Language Creation and Language Change: Creolization, Diachrony, and Development*. Cambridge, MA: MIT Press, pp. 129–57.
Lundahl, Mats. 1979. *Peasants and Poverty: A Study of Haiti*. London: Palgrave Macmillan.
Luxana, Vernet. 1997. *Haïti, Réforme du système éducatif et représentations attachées aux langues*. Paris: Institut Supérieur de Pédagogie.
McConnell, Ormonde H. n.d. *Mission Extraordinary: Haiti Diary*. Cincinnati: United Methodist Committee on Relief.
McConnell, Ormonde H., and Eugene Swan. 1945a. *You Can Learn Creole: A Simple Introduction to Haitian Creole for English Speaking People*. Port-au-Prince: Imprimerie de l'Etat.
McConnell, Ormonde H., and Eugene Swan. 1945b. *Let's Speak Creole*. Petit-Goave (Haïti): Imprimerie du Sauveur.
McWhorter, John. 1998. Identifying the Creole Prototype, Vindicating a Typological Class. *Language* 74: 788–818.
McWhorter, John. 2005. *Defining Creole*. New York: Oxford University Press.
McWhorter, John. 2013. It's Not Over: Why It Matters Whether There Is Such a Thing As a Creole. *Journal of Pidgin and Creole Languages* 28.2: 409–23.
McWhorter, John, and Mikaël Parkvall. 2002. Pas tout à fait du français: une étude créole. *Études créoles* 25.1: 179–231.
Maher, Julianne. 1990. Créole et patois à Saint-Barthélémy: diversité. *Études créoles* 13.1: 35–44.
Maher, Julianne. 1996. Fishermen, Farmers, and Traders: Language and Economic History in the French West Indies. *Language in Society* 25: 373–406.
Maher, Julianne. 1997. French and Creole on St. Barth and St. Thomas. In Albert Valdman (ed.), *French and Creole in Louisiana*. New York and London: Plenum Press, pp. 237–53.
Manessy, Gabriel. 1981. Expansion fonctionnelle et évolution. In Arnold Highfield and Albert Valdman (eds.), *Historicity and Variation in Creole Studies*. Ann Arbor: Karoma Press, pp. 79–90.
Manessy, Gabriel. 1983. Français, créoles français, français régionaux. Paper presented at IVe Colloque International des Etudes Créoles, Baton Rouge, Louisiana.

Manessy, Gabriel. 1995. *Créoles, pidgins, variétés véhiculaires: Procès et genèse.* Paris: CNRS Editions, pp. 77–90.
Manigat, Max. 2006. *Mots créoles du Nord d'Haïti.* Coconut Creek, FL: EducaVison.
March, Christian. 1996. *Le Discours des mères martiniquaises. Diglossie et créolité: un point de vue sociolinguistique.* Paris: L'Hartmann.
Marchand-Thébault, Marie-Thérèse. 1986. L'Esclavage en Guyane sous l'Ancien Régime. In Anne-Marie Bruleaux, Régine Calmont, and Serge Mam-Lam-Fouck (eds.), *2 Siècles d'esclavage en Guyane française.* Paris: L'Harmattan, pp. 11–62.
Marchello-Nizia, Christiane. 1979. *Histoire de la langue française des XIVe et XVe siècles.* Paris: Bordas.
Marshall, Margaret M. 1982. Bilingualism in Southern Louisiana: A Linguistic Analysis. *Anthropological Linguistics* 24.3: 308–24.
Marshall, Margaret M. 1990. The Origin of French Creole in Louisiana. *Regional Dimensions* 8: 23–40.
Martin, Jean-Baptiste, and Gaston Tuaillon. 1999. *Atlas linguistique et ethnographique du Jura et des Alpes du nord (Francoprovençal Central): La maison, l'homme, la morphologie* (Vol. 3). Paris: CNRS Éditions.
Martinez, Pierre. 1994. *Langues et sociétés aux Antilles: Saint-Martin.* Paris: Maisonneuve et Larose.
Mercier, Alfred. 1881. *L'Habitation Saint-Ybars ou maîtres et esclaves en Louisiane.* New Orleans: Imprimerie Franco-Américaine.
Michaelis, Susanne. 1993. *Temps et aspect en créole seychellois: valeurs et interférence.* Hamburg: Buske.
Ministère de l'Education Nationale et de la Formation Professionnelle (MENFP). 2010. *Vers la Refondation du Système Éducatif Haïtien Plan Opérationnel 2010–2015. Des Recommandations. De la Commission Présidentielle Éducation et Formation.* Port-au-Prince: MENFP.
Mondésir, Jones E., and Lawrence D. Carrington. 1992. *Dictionary of St. Lucian Creole.* Berlin/New York: Mouton de Gruyter.
Moreau de Saint-Méry, Louis Elie Médéric. 1797/1958. *Description topographique, physique, politique et historique de la partie françoise de l'Ile de Saint-Domingue* (3 vols.). Paris: Larose (reprinted 1958).
Morgan, Raleigh J. 1959. Structural Sketch of Saint Martin Creole. *Anthropological Linguistics* 1: 7–29.
Morisseau-Leroy, Félix. 1953. *Antigone en créole.* Pétionville: Morne Hercule.
Morrill, Warren T., and Bennet Dyke. 1965. A French Community in St. Thomas. *Caribbean Studies* 5.5: 39–47.
Mufwene, Salikoko S. 1987. An Issue on Predicate-Clefting: Evidence from Atlantic Creoles and African Languages. *Varia Creolica*: 71–89.
Mufwene, Salikoko S. 2001. *The Ecology of Language Evolution.* Cambridge: Cambridge University Press.
Mufwene, Salikoko S. 2006. Les Continua créoles, linguistiques et langagiers. In Raphaël Confiant and Robert Damoiseau (eds.), *A l'Arpanteur inspiré: Mélanges offerts à Jean Bernabé.* Matoury, French Guiana: Ibis Rouge Editions, pp. 185–97.

Mufwene, Salikoko S. 2008. *Language Evolution: Contact, Competition, and Change*. London: Continuum.
Mufwene, Salikoko S. 2010. SLA and the Emergence of Creoles. *Studies in Second Language Acquisition* 32.3: 359–400.
Mühlhäusler, Peter. 1986. *Pidgin and Creole Linguistics*. Oxford: Blackwell.
Muysken, Pieter C. 1981. Creole Tense/Mood/Aspect Systems: The Unmarked Case? In Pieter Muysken (ed.), *Generative Studies on Creole Languages*. Dordrecht: Foris, pp. 181–200.
Muysken, Pieter C., and Norval Smith. 1990. Question Words in Pidgin and Creole Languages. *Linguistics* 28: 883–903.
Neumann, Ingrid. 1985. *Le Créole de Breaux Bridge, Louisiane: Étude morphosyntaxique, textes, vocabulaire*. Hamburg: Buske.
Neumann-Holzschuh, Ingrid. 1987. *Textes anciens en créole louisianais*. Hamburg: Buske.
Neumann-Holzschuh, Ingrid. 2003. Les Formes verbales en créole: Un cas de réanalyse. In Sybille Kriegel (ed.), *Grammaticalisation et réanalyse. Approches de la variation créole et française*. Paris: CNRS-Editions (coll. CNRS Langage), pp. 69–86.
Neumann-Holzschuh, Ingrid. 2007. A propos du patois de Güiria (Venezuela). In Patrice Brasseur and Georges D. Véronique (eds.), *Mondes créoles et francophones*. Paris: L'Harmattan, pp. 100–16.
Neumann-Holzschuh, Ingrid. 2011. *Morceaux choisis du folklore louisianais: Matériaux pour l'étude diachronique du créole de la Louisiane*. Hamburg: Buske.
Nicholls, David. 1979. *From Dessalines to Duvalier: Race, Colour, and National Independence in Haiti*. New York: Vail-Ballou Press.
Nylander, Dudley K. 1987. Comment expliquer la présence des verbes sériels dans les langues créoles. *Études créoles* 10: 77–89.
Orjala, Paul. 1970. 'A Dialect Survey of Haitian Creole.' Ph.D dissertation (Hartford Seminary Foundation).
Pamphile, Leon D. 2008. *Clash of Cultures: America's Educational Strategies in Occupied Haiti, 1915–1934*. Lanham, MD: University Press of America.
Papen, Robert. 1978. 'The French-based Creoles of the Indian Ocean: An Analysis and Comparison.' Ph.D. dissertation (University of California San Diego).
Parépou, Alfred. 1882. *Atipa*. Paris: Auguste Ghio. (new editions: 1980. Paris: Editions Caribéennes; 1987. Paris: L'Harmattan.)
Parkvall, Mikael. 1995. The Role of St. Kitts in a New Scenario of French Creole Genesis. In Philip Baker (ed.), *From Contact to Creole and Beyond*. London: University of Westminster Press, pp. 149–76.
Peleman, Louis. 1976. *Diksyonnè Kréyòl-Fransé*. Port-au-Prince: Bon Nouvèl.
Pelleprat, Pierre R. P. 1655. *Relation des Pères de la Compagnie de Jésus dans les Iles et dans la terre ferme de l'Amérique méridionale*. Paris: Cramoisy.
Perdue, Clive. 1991. *Adult Language Acquisition: Cross Linguistic Perspectives* (2 vols.). Cambridge: Cambridge University Press.
Perrot, Marie-Eve. 1992. 'Aspects fondamentaux du métissage français/anglais dans le chiac de Moncton (Nouveau-Brunswick, Canada).' Ph.D. dissertation (Université de la Sorbonne nouvelle, Paris III).

Peyraud, Flore. 1983. 'Structure de l'énoncé en créole guyanais.' Ph.D dissertation (Université de Paris-III).
Phillips, John S. 1975. 'Vietnamese Contact French: Variation in a Contact Situation.' Ph.D dissertation (Indiana University).
Picoche, Jacqueline. 1977. *Précis de lexicographie française: l'étude et l'enseignement du vocabulaire*. Paris: Nathan.
Piou, Nanie. 1982a. Le Clivage du prédicat. In Claire Lefebvre, Hélène Magloire-Holly, and Nanie Piou (eds.), *Syntaxe de l'haïtien*. Ann Arbor: Karoma Press, pp. 122–51.
Piou, Nanie. 1982b. Le redoublement verbal. In Claire Lefebvre, Hélène Magloire-Holly, and Nanie Piou (eds.), *Syntaxe de l'haïtien*. Ann Arbor: Karoma Press, pp. 152–66.
Pompilus, Pradel. 1958. 'Lexique créole-français.' Complementary dissertation (University of Paris).
Pompilus, Pradel. 1973. *Contribution à l'étude comparée du créole et du français à partir du créole haïtien: Phonologie et lexique* (Vol. I). Port-au-Prince: Éditions Caraïbes.
Pompilus, Pradel. 1976. *Contribution à l'étude comparée du créole et du français à partir du créole haïtien: Morphologie et syntaxe* (Vol. II). Port-au-Prince: Éditions Caraïbes.
Pompilus, Pradel. 1980. Conclusion et recommandations. In Albert Valdman and Yves Joseph (eds.), *Créole et enseignement primaire en Haïti*. Bloomington: Indiana University Creole Institute, pp. 204–15.
Poullet, Robert, and Sylviane Telchid. 1990. *Le Créole sans peine (guadeloupéen)*. Paris: Assimil.
Pressoir, Charles-Fernand. 1947. *Débats sur le créole et le folklore*. Port-au-Prince: Imprimerie de l'Etat.
Pressoir, Charles-Fernand. 1954. *Méthode de français oral à l'usage de l'Haïtien débutant en 45 leçons (passage du créole au français). Conversation, grammaire, lecture, copie, dictées*. Port-au-Prince: Deschamps.
Price-Mars, Jean. 1928. *Ainsi parla l'oncle. Essais d'ethnographie*. New York: Parapsychological Foundation.
Prudent, Lambert-Felix. 1989. Ecrire le créole à la Martinique: Norme et conflit sociolinguistic. In Ralph Ludwig (ed.), *Les Créoles français entre l'oral et l'écrit*. Tübingen: Gunter Narr Verlag, pp. 65–80.
Racine, Marie Marcelle Buteau. 1970. 'Creole and French Lexico-semantic Conflicts. A Contribution to the Study of Languages in Contact in the Haitian Diglossic Situation.' *Dissertation Abstracts International* 32(02). 952A (University Microforms No. AAT-7119335). Ph.D. dissertation (Georgetown University, Washington, DC).
Renault-Lescure, Odile, and Laurence Goury. 2009. *Langues de Guyane*. La Roque D'Anthéron: Vents d'Ailleurs.
Rézeau, Pierre. 1991. *Dictionnaire du français régional de Poitou-Charentes et de Vendée*. Paris: Bonneton.
Rézeau, Pierre. 1997. Toward a Lexicography of French in Louisiana: Historical and Geographic Aspects. In Albert Valdman (ed.), *French and Creole in Louisiana*. New York/London: Plenum Press, pp. 315–32.

Roberts, Peter Arthur. 1971. "The Verb in Grenadian French Creole". MA dissertation (University of the West Indies).
Roberts, Sarah J. 1998. The Role of Diffusion in the Genesis of Hawaiian Creole. *Language* 74: 1–39.
Roberts, Sarah J. 2000. Nativization and the Genesis of Hawaiian Creole. In John McWhorter (ed.), *Language Change and Language Contact in Pidgins and Creoles*. Philadelphia and Amsterdam: John Benjamins, pp. 257–300.
Roberts, Sarah J. 2005. 'The Emergence of Hawai'i Creole English in the Early 20th Century. The Sociohistorical Context of Creole Genesis.' Ph.D. dissertation (Stanford University).
Ronceray, Hubert de, and Serge Petit-Frère. 1975. Projet expérimental sur le bilinguisme créole-français. *Bulletin d'Information du CHISS* 4.14: 1–35.
Rottet, Kevin J. 1995. 'Language Shift and Language Death in the Cajun French-speaking Communities of Terrebonne and Lafourche parishes, Louisiana.' Ph.D. dissertation (Indiana University).
Rottet, Kevin J. 2001. *Language Shift in the Coastal Marshes of Louisiana*. New York: Peter Lang.
Rousseau, Jean-Jacques. 1752. *Le Devin du village* (opéra).
Saint Jacques Fauquenoy, Marguerite. 1972. *Analyse structurelle du créole guyanais*. Paris: Klincksieck.
Saint-Jorre, Danielle, and Guy Lionnet. 1999. *Disksyonner kreol-franse, Dictionnaire créole Seychellois-français* (Annegret Bollée, ed.). Bamberg and Mahé: Difo Druck.
Saint-Quentin, Auguste de. 1872. *Introduction à l'histoire de Cayenne, suivie d'un recueil de contes, fables et chansons en créole avec traduction en regard*. Antibes: J. Marchand.
Sankoff, Gillian. 1977. Creolization and Syntactic Change in New Guinea Tok Pisin. In Ben G. Blount and Mary Sanchez (eds.), *Sociocultural Dimensions of Language Change*. New York: Academic Press, pp. 119–30.
Schieffelin, Bambi, and Rene Doucet. 1994. The 'Real' Haitian Creole: Metalinguistics and Orthographic Choice. *American Ethnologist* 21.1: 176–200.
Schuchardt, Hugo. 1882. Kreolische Studien. I. Ueber das Negerportugiesische von S. Thomé (Westafrika). *Sitzungsberichete der kaiserlichen Akademie der Wissenschaften zu Wien* 101.2: 889–917.
Schuchardt, Hugo. 1914. *Die Sprache der Saramakkaneger in Surinam*. Amsterdam: Johannes Müller.
Schwartz, Bonnie D., and Rex A. Sprouse. 1996. L2 Cognitive States and the Full Transfer/Full Access Mode. *Second Language Research* 12.1: 40–72.
Siegel, Jason F. 2011. *Clefting and Doubling in Haitian Creole: A Cyclic Linearization Account*. Unpublished manuscript. Indiana University-Bloomington.
Siegel, Jeff. 2006. Transmission of Transfer. In Umberto Ansaldo, Stephen Mathews, and Lisa Lim (eds.), *Deconstructing Creole*. Amsterdam and Philadelphia: John Benjamins, pp. 227–37.
Siegel, Jeff. 2008. *Emergence of Pidgin and Creole Languages*. Oxford: Oxford University Press.

Snow, Catherine E., and Charles A. Ferguson. 1977. *Talking to Children*. Cambridge: Cambridge University Press.
Spears, Arthur K. 1989. AP and VA Futures in Haitian Creole. *CUNY Forum: Papers in Linguistics* (City University of New York) 14: 204–10.
Spears, Arthur K. 1990. Tense, Mood, and Aspect in the Haitian Creole Preverbal Marker System. In John V. Singler (ed.), *Pidgin/Creole Tense, Modality, Aspect Systems*. Philadelphia and Amsterdam: John Benjamins, pp. 119–42.
Spears, Arthur K. 1991. Haitian Creole *Pou*. Unpublished manuscript.
Spears, Arthur K. 1993a. Foregrounding and Backgrounding in Haitian Creole Discourse. In Francis Byrne and Donald Windford (eds.), *Focus and Grammatical Relations in Creole Languages*. Philadelphia and Amsterdam: John Benjamins, pp. 249–65.
Spears, Arthur K. 1993b. Stem and So-called Anterior Forms in Haitian Creole: Atlantic Meets Pacific. In John Singler (ed.), *Pidgin and Creole Tense-Mood-Aspect*. Philadelphia and Amsterdam: John Benjamins, pp. 119–42.
Spears, Arthur K., and Carole Berotte Joseph. 2010. *The Haitian Creole Language*. Lanham, MD: Lexington Books.
Speedy, Karen. 1994. 'Mississippi and Tèche Creole: A Demographic and Linguistic Case for Separate Genesis in Louisiana.' MA thesis (University of Auckland).
Speedy, Karen. 1995. Mississippi and Tèche Creole: Two Separate Starting Points for Creole in Louisiana. In Philip Baker (ed.), *From Contact to Creole and Beyond*. London: Westminster University Press, pp. 97–111.
Speedy, Karin. 2007. Reunion Creole in New Caledonia: What Influence on Tayo? *Journal of Pidgin and Creole Languages* 22: 193–230.
Sprouse, Rex A. 2010. Full Transfer and Relexification and Creole Genesis. In Claire Lefebvre, Lydia White, and Christine Jourdan (eds.), *Acquisition and Creole Genesis*. Philadelphia and Amsterdam: John Benjamins, pp. 169–91.
Stäbler, Cynthia K. 1995. *Entwicklung mündlicher romanisher Syntax, Das Français cadien in Louisiana*. Tübingen: Gunter Narr.
Stein, Peter. 1982. *Connaissance et emploi des langues à l'Ile Maurice*. Hamburg: Burske.
Stein, Peter. 1984. *Kreolisch und Französisch*. Tübingen: Max Niemeyer.
Sterlin, M.-D. 1988. Les Différentes Caractéristiques de *pou* en créole haïtien. *Travaux de recherché sur le créole haïtien*. No. 3. Université du Québec à Montréal (UQUAM).
Syea, Anand. 1992. The Short and Long Form of Verbs in Mauritian Creole: Functionalism versus Formalism. *Theoretical Linguistics* 18.1: 61–97.
Syea, Anand. 1994. The Development of Genitives in Mauritian Creole. In Dany Adone and Ingo Plag (eds.), *Creolization and Language Change*. Tübingen: Niemeyer, pp. 85–107.
Syea, Anand. 1997. Copula, *WH*-trace, and the ECP in Mauritian Creole. *Linguistics* 35.1: 25–56.
Syea, Anand. 2013. *The Syntax of Mauritian Creole*. London and New York: Bloomsbury Academic.
Sylvain, Georges. 1901. *Cric? Crac! Fables de la Fontaine racontées par un montagnard haïtien et transcrites en vers créoles*. Paris: Ateliers Haïtiens.

Sylvain, Suzanne. 1936. *Le Créole haïtien: morphologie et syntaxe*. Wetteren (Belgique): de Meester; Port-au-Prince: chez l'auteur.
Tardieu, Charles. 1988. *L'Education en Haïti de la période coloniale jusqu'à nos jours*. Port-au-Prince: Imprimerie Henri Deschamps.
Targète, Jean, and Raphaël Urciolo. 1993. *Haitian Creole–English Dictionary*. Kensington, MD: Dunwoody Press.
Taylor, Douglas D. 1951. Structural Outline of Caribbean Creole. *Word* 7: 43–59.
Taylor, Douglas D. 1962. Le Créole de la Dominique. In *Encyclopédie de la Pléiade: Langages*. Paris: Gallimard, pp. 1022–49.
Taylor, Douglas D. 1977. *Languages of the West Indies*. Baltimore: Johns Hopkins University Press.
Thogmartin, Clyde. 1979. Old Mines, Missouri et la survivance du français dans la haute vallée du Mississippi. In Albert Valdman (ed.), *Le Français hors de France*. Paris: Champion, pp. 111–18.
Thomas, John J. 1869. *The Theory and Practice of Creole Grammar*. Port of Spain: The Chronicle Office Press. (1969 edition with an introduction by Gertrud Buscher, London: New Beacon.)
Thomas, John J. 1889. *Froudacity: West Indian Fables by James Anthony Froude*. Philadelphia: Gebbie and Company.
Thomas, Wayne P., and Virginia Collier. 1997. *School Effectiveness for Language Minority Students*. Resource Collection Series, No. 9. Washington, DC: National Clearinghouse for English Language Acquisition (NCELA).
Tinelli, Henry. 1970. 'Generative Phonology of Haitian Creole.' Ph.D. dissertation (University of Michigan, Ann Arbor).
Tobler, Alfred W. 1987. *Dicionário crioulo karipúna/português português/karipúna*. Brasilia: Summer Institute of Linguistics.
Tobler, Joy S. 1983. The Grammar of Karipúna Creole. *Série Lingüística* 10: 1–156. Brasilia: Summer Institute of Linguistics.
Tornquist, Lisa. 2000. 'Attitudes linguistiques vis-à-vis du vernaculaire francolouisianais dans le programme d'immersion en Louisiane.' Ph.D. dissertation (University of Louisiana-Lafayette).
Tourneux, Henry, and Maurice Barbotin.1990. *Dictionnaire pratique du créole de la Guadeloupe*. Paris: Karthala.
Trouillot, Jocelyne (Joslin Twouyo). n.d. *Diksyonè Kreyòl Karayib*. Port-au-Prince: Editions CUC (Université Caraïbe).
USAID. 1986. Haiti Project Paper: Incentives to Improve Basic Education. USAID: Washington, DC.
Valdman, Albert. 1968. Language Standardization in a Diglossia Situation: Haiti. In J. A. Fishman, Charles A. Ferguson, and J. Das Gupta (eds.), *Language Problems of Developing Nations*. New York: John Wiley and Sons, pp. 313–26.
Valdman, Albert. 1969. The Language Situation in Haiti. In Richard P. Schaedel (ed.), *Research and Resources of Haiti*. New York: Research Institute for the Study of Man, pp. 155–203.
Valdman, Albert. 1971. L'Evolution sociolinguistique des dialectes français créoles aux Antilles. *Français et Créole dans les Caraïbes*. Documents du Centre d'Etudes Régionales Antilles-Guyane (CERAG), 4: 5–20.

Valdman, Albert. 1976. *Introduction to French Phonology and Morphology.* Rowley, MA: Newbury House.
Valdman, Albert. 1978. *Le Créole: Structure, statut et origine.* Paris: Klincksieck.
Valdman, Albert. 1979. La Diglossie français-créole dans l'univers plantocratique. In Gabriel Mansessy and Paul Wald (eds.), *Plurilinguisme: Normes, situations, stratégies.* Paris: L'Harmattan, pp. 173–85.
Valdman, Albert. 1980. La Situation linguistique d'Haïti. In Albert Valdman and Yves Joseph (eds.), *Créole et enseignement primaire en Haïti.* Bloomington: Indiana University Creole Institute.
Valdman, Albert. 1989. Aspects sociolinguistiques de l'élaboration d'une norme écrite pour le créole haïtien. In Ralph Ludwig (ed.), *Les Créoles français entre l'oral et l'écrit.* Tübingen: Günter Narr Verlag, pp. 43–63.
Valdman, Albert. 1991. Decreolization or Dialect Contact in Haiti? In Frank Byrne and Theodore Huebner (eds.), *Development and Structures of Creole Languages: Essays in Honor of Derek Bickerton.* Philadelphia and Amsterdan: John Benjamins, pp. 75–88.
Valdman, Albert. 1992. On the socio-historical context in the development of Louisiana and Saint-Domingue Creoles. *Journal of French Language Studies* 2: 75–95.
Valdman, Albert. 1999. L'Orthographe du créole haïtien: au delà de l'alphabet. *Études créoles* 22.1: 81–96.
Valdman, Albert. 2004. L'Influence de la norme émergente du créole haïtien sur les variétés vernaculaires régionales. In A. Coveney, M.-A. Hintze, and C. Sanders (eds.), *Variation et francophonie.* Paris: L'Harmattan, pp. 37–51.
Valdman, Albert. 2005. Vers la standardisation du créole haïtien. *Revue française de linguistique appliquée* 10.1: 39–52.
Valdman, Albert. 2008. Sur la diffusion du créole haïtien standard. *Études créoles* 30: 165–92.
Valdman, Albert. 2010. French in the United States. In Kim Potowski (ed.), *Language Diversity in the United States.* Cambridge: Cambridge University Press, pp. 110–27.
Valdman, Albert, and Iskra Iskrova. 2003. A New Look at Nasalization in Haitian Creole. In Ingo Plag (ed.), *The Phonology and Morphology of Creole Languages.* Tübingen: Niemeyer, pp. 25–41.
Valdman, Albert, and Yves Joseph (eds.). 1980. *Créole et enseignement primaire en Haïti.* Bloomington: Indiana University Creole Institute, pp. 17–29.
Valdman, Albert, and Thomas A. Klingler. 1997. The Structure of Louisiana Creole. In Albert Valdman (ed.), *French and Creole in Louisiana.* New York: Plenum, pp. 109–44.
Valdman, Albert, Charles Pooser, and Jean-Baptiste Rozevel. 1996. *A Learners' Dictionary of Haitian Creole* (English–HC). Bloomington: Indiana University Creole Institute.
Valdman, Albert, Anne-José Villeneuve, and Jason F. Siegel. 2015. On the influence of the standard norm of Haitian Creole on the Cap Haïtien dialect: Evidence from sociolinguistic variation in the third person singular pronoun. *Journal of Pidgin and Creole Languages* 30(1): 1–43.

Valdman, Albert, Yves Joseph, Craige Roberts, and Sarah Yoder. 1981. *Haitian Creole–English–French Dictionary*. Bloomington: Indiana University Creole Institute.

Valdman, Albert, Iskra Iskrova, Nicolas André, and Jacques Pierre. 2007. *Haitian Creole–English Bilingual Dictionary*. Bloomington: Indiana University Creole Institute.

Valdman, Albert, Thomas A. Klingler, Margaret M. Marshall, and Kevin J. Rottet. 1998. *Dictionary of Louisiana Creole*. Bloomington: Indiana University Press.

Valdman, Albert, Kevin Rottet, Barry J. Ancelet, Thomas A. Klingler, Amanda LaFleur, Tamara Lindner, Michael D. Picone, and Dominique Ryon. 2010. *Dictionary of Louisiana French: As Spoken in Cajun, Creole, and American Indian Communities*. Oxford, MS: University Press of Mississippi.

Van Name, Addison. 1869–70. Contributions to Creole Grammar. *Transactions of the American Philological So*ciety 1: 123–67.

Vernet, Pierre. 1980. L'Ecriture du créole et ses réalités de fonctionnement. In Albert Valdman and Yves Joseph (eds.), *Créole et enseignement primaire en Haïti*. Bloomington: Indiana University Creole Institute, pp. 170–81.

Vidale, Akins. 2005. Biography: John Jacob Thomas. Triniview.com (accessed July 8, 2013).

Vilsaint, Féquière. 1991. *Diksyonè Anglè Kreyòl/English Kreyòl Dictionary*. Temple Terrace, FL: Educa Vision.

Vilsaint, Féquière, and Maude Heurtelou. 1994. *Diksyonè Kreyòl Vilsen*. Temple Terrace, FL: Educa Vision.

Volcy-Focard, Eugène. 1884. Le Patois de l'Ile Bourbon. *Bulletin de la Société des Sciences et des Arts* (Réunion) 179–29.

Wartburg, Walter von. 1922–28. *Französisches etymologisches Wörterbuch*. Bonn: F. Klopp.

Watbled, Jean-Philippe. 2003. Le Système verbal du créole réunionnais: flexion, auxiliaires, relation. *Etudes créoles* 27.1: 67–106.

Weinstein, Brian, and Aaron Segal. 1984. *Haiti: Political Failures, Cultural Successes*. New York: Praeger.

Whinnom, Keith. 1965. The Origin of the European-based Creoles and Pidgins. *Orbis* 14: 509–27.

Whinnom, Keith. 1971. Linguistic Hybridization and the 'Special Case' of Pidgins and Creoles. In Dell Hymes (ed.), *Pidginization and Creolization of Languages*. Cambridge: Cambridge University Press, pp. 91–115.

Wiesler, Hans. 1978. *La Scolarisation en Haïti*. Port-au-Prince: Institut Haïtien de Statistique.

Wiesler, Hans. 1987. *Evaluation de la réforme éducative en Haiti*. Geneva: World Bank.

Wood, Donald. 1968. *Trinidad in Transition: The Years after Slavery*. Oxford: Oxford University Press.

Zéphir, Flore. 1990. 'Language Choice, Language Use, Language Attitudes of the Haitian Bilingual Community.' Ph.D. dissertation (Indiana University, Bloomington).

Subject Index

abstract representation in HC 127, 132, 134
Acadian refugees 22
accents 59, 98, 122
adjectives
   comparison of 283
   post-nominal 194, 282
   superlative of 284
adult literacy programs 125, 373, 381
affrication 63, 76
African influence on HC 161, 183, 186
agents 189–90, 199–200
agglutination 44, 103, 105, 108, 132, 175, 279, 421–2, 429, 442–3
American occupation 9–12, 56, 119, 185–6, 358, 380
Amerindian influence on HC 182
analytic grammatical machinery 212
'Anglo-Saxon' letters 119, 122, 393
Aristide, Jean-Bertrand 12–13, 352, 375, 392
aspect 37, 44, 51, 102, 113, 189, 209–18, 224–5, 228, 230, 232, 240, 248–9, 261, 306–7, 347, 396, 411, 418–19
aspectual AUX
   attenuative: *manyen* 233
   completive: *fin, fek, sot* 230
   habitual: *konn* 231
   inchoative: *pete, pran, met(e), tonbe* 231
   intensifier: *peze* 232
assimilation 63, 69, 71, 76–7, 81, 87–8, 91, 93, 103, 127, 168, 173-4, 187, 268, 333
Atipa (Alfred Parépou) 40, 287

attitudes
   toward HC varieties 370
   toward French and HC 367
   purist, toward French 388

Baby Doc, *see* Duvalier, Jean-Claude
basic education 56, 74, 95, 357, 375, 378–9, 381, 383, 386, 389
basilectalization 426–8, 438, 442
beneficiary 203; *see also* patient
Bernard Reform (Réforme Bernard) 12, 369, 381, 383–6, 391–3
bi-unique representation /bi-uniqueness 60, 96–8, 116, 120, 122, 124, 136–7, 248
bilingual dictionaries 15–16, 29, 40, 108, 186
bilingual minority 15, 386, 391
Bioprogram 395–8, 401–3, 405–6, 425, 435, 437
Bois Caïman 8
Bon Nouvèl 125, 130–1, 365, 374, 391–3
Bonaparte, Napoleon 8, 46, 107
borrowing 144, 163, 167, 182, 245, 442
bougre 423
Boukan (magazine) 125, 374
Boukman (Vodou priest) 8, 136
Bourbon Island 43–4, 45–6, 48, 169, 403, 407, 412, 441
Bourbonnais 43–4, 48, 50, 398, 407–9, 441
Boyer, Jean-Pierre 9, 377
Bozals 7, 55, 112, 404, 414, 427–8
buccaneers 3, 7, 404

cafeteria principle 400
Cajun (Cadien) 20, 22
calquing 163
Capois, see Northern HC
cardinal numbers 128, 133, 143
Carenage 30, 32, 441
Caribs 25–6, 30, 33–4, 100, 169, 410
Carriacou 34
Cavelier, René-Robert, Sieur de La Salle 20–1
Cayenne 36–40, 135, 412
Centre Haïtien d'investigations en sciences sociales (CHISS), bilingual experiment 382–5, 394
Chagos Archipelago 52
changes of noun class 265–6
Chanlatte, Juste 112–13
Christophe, Henri 8, 184, 376
CF, see Colonial French
clauses
    completive 289–90
    conditional 250, 288, 290, 297
    conjunctive 289, 291, 310, 313
    relative 189, 282, 290, 293–5, 313, 351
    resultative 298
clefting 206, 268, 285, 288, 300–3, 305–14, 435–7
    and predicate doubling 435
co-official languages with French 364
Colonial French (CF) 14, 21–2, 30–1, 40, 42–3, 45–6, 48, 119, 166–7, 170–1, 174, 176, 177–9, 182, 251, 398, 407–8, 411–13, 416, 418–19, 421–4, 426–8, 430, 433
colonial Saint-Domingue texts 427
comment (rheme) 196, 301
complementizer
    direct object 296
    ke 296, 303, 351, 353
    ki 85, 93, 297
completives 24, 197, 210–11, 218, 225, 228, 230, 232, 249–50, 259, 261, 288–91, 306
complexification 4, 428

compounding 132, 144, 156, 159–60, 241
concrete representations in HC 127, 132
conditional mood 225, 227
conditional *ta* 299
congruence 429–30, 434, 438
conjunction *si* 297
consonant clusters 64–5, 87, 102, 108, 172, 318
consonant system of HC 61
constraints on reduplication and clefting 305
convergent approach 387
coordination 189, 241, 288, 313
copula
    zero copula 193–4, 196–7, 214, 290
    copula *se* 193–4
    copula *ye* 195
corpus planning 357–8, 360
correlative conjunctions 289
creative processes in the HC lexicon 143
Creole Academy 361
Creole Prototype 395, 398, 402, 415, 424, 437, 439
creoles
    Amapá French Creole 42
    Bayou Teche Creole 22
    Bhojpuri-influenced Creole 49
    Créole des Bas 46
    Créole des Hauts 4–7
    as exceptional languages 2, 395, 401–2
    Guadeloupean Creole (GC) 26–7, 30–1, 33, 36, 40, 134, 415, 441
    Guianese Creole (GuiC) 19, 22, 29, 36–8, 40–2, 287, 405, 409, 412, 415, 441
    Guïria Creole 36–7
    Hawaiian Creole English (HCE) 397–8, 402
    Louisiana Creole (LC) 13, 19–20, 22–5, 41–2, 56, 405, 409, 412, 415–16, 420

creoles – *continued*
  Mauritian Creole 42, 44, 47–9, 58, 407, 409
  Mississippi Valley Creole 22
  Réunion Creole (RC) 19, 29, 45, 54, 58, 167, 182, 405–6, 408, 421, 438, 441
  Rodrigues Creole (RodC) 43, 50, 52, 58, 408
  Saint-Domingue Creole 56, 76, 97, 100–1, 103, 108, 275, 329, 341, 392, 408–9, 412, 419, 428, 441–2
  second-generation creoles 408
  Seychellois Creole 51, 58, 188, 408, 416, 429, 433
  St. Barts Creole (SBC) 30–1, 408, 441
  third-generation creoles 407, 409
  Trinidadian Creole (TC) 35–7
  Uaça Creole 42
Cric? Crac! (Georges Sylvain) 113

definite futurity 212, 222
definition of the word 139
deictic function 417
deictico-temporal marker 418
delimitation of words 139
demarcation of word boundaries 132
deontic 199, 211, 226, 230, 234, 236, 240, 249–50, 307
derivation/derivational 144–7, 149, 152–5, 162, 164–5, 167, 185, 207, 311, 396
descriptive sentences 193, 201
Dessalines, Jean-Jacques 8–9, 358, 376
determiners
  definite 22–3, 36–7, 41–2, 67, 87–8, 92–3, 102, 127–8, 138, 191, 207, 208, 218, 257, 259, 264–5, 276, 278–9, 287, 295, 302, 329, 331–3, 354–5, 416–17, 430–1, 438
  demonstrative 42, 261, 264, 273, 279, 287, 313, 417, 430
  determiner system 257–68

indefinite 42, 85, 126–7, 131, 136, 258, 260, 278, 280, 286, 305, 356
  pre-determiners 254
deverbal adjectives 202
deverbals 148, 151
diacritics 98, 118, 121, 124
dialect geography studies 315
dialect surveys 318, 329
diglossia 14, 27
digraphs 98, 118, 136–7
direct transfer 429–30, 433
dislocation 301, 313, 436
distinctive features of phonemes 60, 63, 222
distribution of *r* and *w* 66
Dominica 13, 26–7, 32, 264, 409, 412
drop-out rate from schooling 380, 383, 388
durativity 214
Duvalier, François (Papa Doc) 12, 359, 373, 392
Duvalier, Jean-Claude (Baby Doc) 12, 77, 359, 375, 380
dynamic verbs 214, 249; *see also* non-stative verbs

educational reform 12, 121–2, 130, 134, 381, 384, 391, 394
elision 81–6, 91–4, 128, 130, 132, 134, 249, 276, 295
embedding 189, 196, 203, 284, 288, 289–90, 301, 305, 311–12
emphatic constructions 253, 271, 283
English influence on HC 34, 184, 418
L'Entrée du Roi en sa capitale 112
epilinguistic comments 336, 338
epistemic 199, 211, 230, 234, 236–7, 249
etymological spelling 40, 56, 97, 99, 113–16, 121, 136–7
etymology 16, 113, 116, 143, 167–9
Ewe 168, 183–4, 400, 430–1, 435, 440
exclamation *o* 302, 314

Subject Index   469

exclusive use of HC as instructional medium 386
expanded pidgin 4–5, 53
exposure to French 75, 364–5

focalization 54, 189, 195–6, 202, 204, 282–3, 288, 300–1, 303–7, 309, 311, 313
focus 195–6, 201–2, 207, 210, 253, 301, 303, 306, 310–12
Fongbe 3, 183–4, 400, 428–33, 435, 437, 439–40, 443
Fort Dauphin 44
Français Populaire d'Abidjan 431
French language
  schooling in 369
  as a second language 381, 384
  foreigner talk 100, 111, 411, 437
  liaison in 80–1, 92–3, 98, 108, 126, 175, 429
  periphrastic constructions in 248, 418
French Guiana 5, 13, 26, 28, 37–42, 44, 55, 57–8, 120, 135, 166, 369
French official proclamations 104, 106–7, 427–8
Frères de l'Instruction Chrétienne 130, 376, 379
front rounded vowels 46, 49, 59, 68, 72–6, 78, 88, 103, 105, 108, 137, 173, 296, 329, 330–1, 337, 347, 351–2, 354
fronting 54, 113, 196, 301, 387–8
futurity 102, 197, 211–16, 219, 222, 224, 248, 250, 252, 419

generations of creoles 407
glides, *see* semivowels
grammatical operator 196
graphic representation of Capois particularities 347
grègue 423
Grenada 26, 34–5, 409, 412
Guadeloupe 5, 13, 26–31, 35, 37, 44, 57, 99, 264, 369, 408–9, 412, 438

Haitian constitution (1983) 359
Haitian constitution (1987) 13, 360–2, 377, 388
HC /r/ 64
heads 199, 279
Hispaniola 5–7, 9, 25, 164, 182, 258, 403
homestead phase 7, 21, 45, 55, 399, 403, 407, 426–7, 437
homonymy of *yo* 273
hypercorrection 73–5, 329–30, 348, 356
hypothetical future 299

identification of lexemes 142–3
independence of Haiti 9
Institut pédagogique national, *see* orthographies, IPN
instrument 200, 202, 418
interlanguage 399, 402, 415, 425, 427
International Phonetic Alphabet (IPA), *see* orthographies
intermediate pidgin stage 398–9
interrogative (WH) words 432–3
introducers 192, 209, 212, 237–8, 249, 251
irrealis 24, 40, 214–15, 226, 249, 290, 398
isoglosses 317–18, 320

Jeannot et Thérèse 106, 356

Kanak languages 53–4
Karipúna 41
kreyòl pèp la 351–2
kreyòl rèk 351
kreyòl swa 15, 67, 76, 126, 187, 296, 316, 329–30, 351, 370, 392

Laborde bilingual experiment 383–5
Lanc-Patua (Patois Language) 42
language planning 13, 119, 121, 125–6, 133–4, 357–8, 360, 362
language preferences of urban teachers 366
latent consonant 98

leveling 335, 433, 440
lexemes, types of 140–1
lexifier language 395, 398
LF, see Louisiana French
linguistic ecology 357, 362–3
linguistic factors 19, 340, 342
linguistic issue in basic education 379
Lisette quitté la plaine (song) 104, 107
loanwords 65, 144, 149, 152, 163–4, 178, 185–6, 351, 442
loss of post-vocalic r 172
'lottery schools' (*écoles borlettes*) 389
Louisiana French (LF) 19–20, 65, 135, 152, 166–7, 173, 177–9, 182, 188, 214, 215, 270, 413–15, 417–19, 421–4, 428, 431, 434, 440, 442

McConnell-Laubach, see orthographies
Mahé 50
Manuel des habitants de Saint-Domingue (S. J. Ducœurjoly) 108, 420, 427
Maraval Valley 35
Marbial pilot project 372
marginal nasal vowels: *in* and *oun* 71
maritime French 406, 408, 440
marking of plural 22, 41, 262–5
Martelly, Michel 13, 222, 362, 365, 390
Martinique 5, 13, 26–9, 31, 33–5, 37, 44, 57, 99–100, 105, 111, 264, 369, 403, 408–10, 412, 438
Mauritius 13, 43–4, 47–52, 169, 171, 178, 405–7, 412, 441
migrant workers 425–6
minimal pair 60, 63, 68, 70–2, 77
Mission Alpha 375
modal AUX 209, 234, 238–40, 248–9, 306
modal introducers
 appearance: *sanble* 239
 exhortative: *annou/ann* 238
 necessity: *fòk/fò* 238

permission: *kite/te* 235, 238
preference: *pito* 238
prohibition: *piga/pinga* 239
modification of syllable structure 175
monogenesis 404–5, 407
monolingual dictionaries for HC 18, 49
mood 113, 189, 209–15, 225–7, 249–50
mood distinctions 225
morphemes
 bound 141, 145, 212
 identification of 142
 types of 141–2
multifunctionality of words in HC 190

nasal vowels 59, 63, 67–71, 76–7, 98, 114, 118–20, 123, 132, 137, 351
nasalization 61, 70–1, 77, 89, 105, 128, 131–2, 173, 331–4, 354–5
 of the definite determiner *LA* 331–2, 354
naturalistic SLA 427
negritude movement 12, 28, 55
neologisms 136, 146–7, 151–2, 155–6, 165, 171, 178, 187
New Caledonia 19, 52–4
NHC, see Northern HC
nominative-accusative 200
non-stative verbs 24, 42, 197, 214–16, 222, 225, 229, 248; *see also* dynamic verbs
norm, see standard variety
normalization 124–6, 130, 134–5
Northern HC (Capois/NHC) 15, 42, 65–7, 76–7, 87, 90–1, 94, 102–3, 113, 122–3, 187, 250, 270–1, 275–6, 287, 313, 318, 320–2, 324, 329, 334–47, 349–51, 353–6, 370, 388, 409, 415, 428, 441
nouns
 abstract 257
 common 257
 count 257, 266
 generic meaning of 257

mass 257, 260, 266
NP expansion, types of 255

objectives of orthographic systems 96
ONAAC (Office national d'alphabétisation et d'action communautaire) 120–1, 372–5, 393
ONEC (Office national d'education communautaire) 120–1, 371, 373–5, 393
onomasiological studies 316
onomatopoeia 144, 160–1, 183
oral vowels 68–9, 77, 118, 121–2, 173
orthographies
  autonomous 116, 120
  Faublas-Pressoir 29, 117, 119–22, 128, 133, 137, 360, 372, 393
  International Phonetic Alphabet (IPA) 56, 77, 117–18, 122
  IPN (Institut pédagogique national) 56, 117, 121–3, 125–7, 130, 133–4, 137, 172, 345, 354, 360, 374, 381, 383
  McConnell-Laubach 117–19, 120, 123, 137, 372
over-age students 379, 388
overseas French departments 26, 171
overt mark of past time 219

Papa Doc, see Duvalier, François
Partie de chasse du Roy, La (play) 112
Passion de Notre Seigneur selon Saint Jean en Langage Nègre, La 100, 404, 411
patient 199, 201; see also beneficiary
Patois de Saint-Louis 53
Pearl of the Antilles, Haiti called 7
Péralte, Charlemagne 11
Pétion, Alexandre 9, 376
phonemes 23, 36–7, 60–5, 68–9, 71–2, 76–7, 97–8, 118, 122–4, 142, 151, 167, 172, 186, 208, 278, 286, 329, 416
phonemic inventory 59
phonemic principle 59
phrase-final emphatic markers 206, 433

pidgins 2, 48, 53, 99, 101–2, 111, 145, 397–9, 401, 403, 405, 407
pidginization 399, 402, 439
pidginized foreigner talk 398, 403
pied-piping 295
Plan national d'éducation (PNEF) 388
polygenesis 404
polysemy/polysemous 139–40, 153–4, 188, 208, 224, 228, 232, 235, 248–9, 291, 314, 356, 429
Portuguese-based pidgin 401, 405
positive transfers 386
possessive constructions 36, 90–1, 94, 279, 388, 409
post-posed determiner *LA* 87, 264, 411, 432
pou 204, 209, 239–40, 248–9, 251, 272, 296, 342–3
predicate types in HC 192
prefixes 153–6
progressive 26, 83, 85, 88, 102, 128, 132, 135, 177, 197, 210–11, 213–15, 219, 225, 248, 259, 300, 320, 322–3, 343, 347, 398, 418–19, 422
progressivity 212–14, 216
pronouns
  demonstrative 273
  emphatic marker *li* 271
  interrogative pronouns and adverbs in HC 272–3
  personal pronoun modifiers 271–2
  personal pronouns in HC 269–74
proper plantation phase 403
PSUGO (Programme de scolarisation universelle gratuite et obligatoire) 390
punctuality 214

quantifiers (Quant) 143, 254, 262, 271

radicalness 397, 405–6, 439
realis 214–15
reduplication 135, 160–1, 167, 206, 283, 300, 303–5, 311–13
reflexives 200, 207–8, 274, 433
Réforme Bernard, see Bernard Reform

refugees from Saint-Domingue 22
relative pronoun 132, 138, 284, 293–5, 311, 313
relativized possessive 296
relativized prepositional complements 297
Relexification Hypothesis 395, 399, 401–2, 424–7, 432–3, 437, 439
retention of final consonants 175
Réunion 5, 13, 26, 43–8, 50–1, 54, 146, 167, 169, 171, 178, 320, 403, 406–7, 412, 416, 419–20, 438
rheme, *see* comment
Rodrigues Island 13, 43, 44, 50, 52, 171, 407, 412

safre 177, 424
Saint-Barthélemy (St. Barts) 30–2, 171, 173, 176, 188, 409, 413, 437, 441–2
Saint-Domingue Creole texts 101, 103–13, 341, 419
Saint-Quentin, Auguste de 36, 40–1, 58, 120, 399
Saint-Martin 29–30, 52
sandhi phenomena 428
schools in Haiti, types of 378
second-language acquisition 58, 395, 401, 403, 413, 424, 432
Secrétairerie à l'alphabétisation 375
semantic change 166, 178–9
semantic differences between HC and SF cognates 177–8
semasiological studies 317
semivowels (glides) 62, 66, 77, 86, 93, 119–20, 123, 278
sentential *LA* 267–8, 295, 418, 431
sex reference 285
Seychelles, The 13, 43, 50–2, 169, 171, 178, 407, 412
simple and complex symbols 98
single invariable verb form 415
slaver jargon 405
social factors 79, 91, 315, 334, 336, 339–40
sociolinguistic continuum 351
sociolinguistic indicators 336
source 203

Southern HC 15, 321, 323–4
Spanish influence 186
St. Barts Patois (SBP) 30, 173, 421
St. Barts Sous le Vent 30, 32, 441
St. Kitts (Saint-Christophe) 25, 26, 30–1, 408–13, 438
St. Lucia 26–7, 32–3
St. Thomas 30, 32, 437, 441
standard variety (norm) 56, 67, 94, 124, 171–2, 370, 403, 412, 418
standardization 13, 96, 124–5, 133
stative verbs 24, 102, 196, 214–18, 221–5, 248–9
status planning 357–8
stranding 54, 196, 295, 387
stress alternations in English 80
structural mechanisms 209–10, 248
subjunctive mood 226, 250
substrate 43, 53–4, 399–400, 413, 424–6, 428–33, 435–40, 443
suffixes
  agentive *-tè* 147, 151
  -al 145
  -ay/-aj (a) 149–150
  -è /-èz 149, 162
  -e/-en 142, 146, 148, 153
  -èt 151, 155
  -mann 142, 149
  verb-forming suffixes 151–2
  zero suffix 147–8
superstrate 398–400, 425–6, 428, 430, 439
Superstratist Hypothesis 402–3
survivals from older stages of French or from regional dialects 176
synthetic machinery 212
systematic phonological correspondences between HC and SF 171

Tayo 19, 52–4
te as an anti-perfect 220
temporal relations in complex sentences 299
tense 44, 51, 102, 113, 189, 191, 209–18, 221, 224, 241, 248, 250, 299–300, 347, 396, 410–11, 418, 421
tense-mood-aspect (TMA) markers

a(v)(a) 222
ap 214, 219
Ø 217–19
te 219
testing programs 386
texts from the Early Colonial Period 99
Theory and Practice of Creole Grammar, The (John Jacob Thomas) 35
Thomas, John Jacob 35
Tortuga Island 7, 25
total transfer 395, 426, 433, 438
Toussaint L'Ouverture 8–9, 57
transitional glides 76
transitional zones 320
Treaty of Ryswick (1697) 7, 404
Trinidad and Tobago 34–5
truncation 81–2, 84–5, 93, 228, 231, 251

US occupation, *see* American occupation

variants
   Northern HC (Capois) lexical 276, 323, 335–6, 338–41, 345–6, 349–50, 355
   peripheral and general lexical 326
   phonological 126, 208, 249, 286, 322, 328
   Southern HC lexical 323
variation
   diaphasic 95, 315–16, 354, 428
   diastratic 95, 315, 343, 354, 428
   geographical (topolectal) 73, 315–20, 322, 354
   lexical 321

   phonological 328
   sociolinguistic 14, 316, 331, 353–4
velar nasal 62–3
verb marker system 37, 214, 418
verbal semantic categories 211
verbs
   auxiliary 110, 191–2, 196–9, 207, 209, 212–13, 225, 227–9, 240, 248, 306, 311, 418
   compound 242
   deictic 243, 246, 249, 308–9
   ditransitive 204, 271–2, 341
   focal 243–7, 249, 434
   intransitive 150, 205–6, 310
   modifying 243–5, 247, 434
   multiple serial verb constructions 246
   passive and middle 201
   processive 216–19, 221, 223–4, 248
   resultative 216, 223–4, 248, 250
   serial 56, 158, 189, 209, 212, 240–6, 249, 308, 314, 434–5
   transitive 110, 147, 149, 199–204
Vocabulaire des isles 166, 169–70, 182, 186–7, 407–8, 412
vowel blending 86, 127
vowel loss 81–2, 84

weakened medial consonants 64
West African Pidgin English 401

yo as plural marker 433

Author Index

Acosta, J. 1
Adam, L. vii, 396, 399
d'Alaux, G. 136
Alleyne, M. 41–2, 103, 442
Alterpresse 334, 361
Andersen, R. 58
Andrade, J. 42
Anglade, P. 168–9
Anonby, S. 41
d'Ans, A.-M. 6, 15, 62, 65, 250, 409, 440

Baggioni, D. 47, 49
Baissac, C. 399
Baker, P. 44, 46, 48, 49, 50, 405, 429, 442–3
Barbotin, M. 27, 57
Barthélémi, G. 40, 442
Bartoli, M. 409
Baudet, M. 440
Baudoux, G. 58
Belloncle, G. 372, 374
Bentolila, A. 16, 121, 186, 218, 315, 367, 374
Bernabé, J. 26–9, 116
Berrouët-Oriol, R. 380, 391
Berry, P. 115–16, 121, 136
Bickerton, D. 214, 395, 397–8, 402, 405, 425, 435
Bollée, A. 44, 51, 168, 178, 182–3, 186, 188, 320, 442
Borde, P.-G.-L. 35
Brasseur, P. 414
Breen, H. 57
Breton, R. 33
Brousseau, A.-M. 165, 432
Buscher, G. 35
Byers, B. 420

Cadely, J.-R. 15, 64, 67
Cadette-Blasse, A. 34
Calvet, L.-J. 26, 30–1, 411, 416, 441–2
Carayol, M. 47, 320
Carden, G. 100, 200, 208, 442
Carpooran, A. 49, 433
Carrington, L. 34, 57, 442
Célestin-Mégie, E. 381
Cervinka-Taulier, B. 27
Césaire, A. 3, 28, 55
Chamoiseau, P. 28–9
Chanlatte, J. 112–13
Chatillon, M. 410
Chaudenson, R. xiv, 5, 15, 21, 25–8, 30–1, 33, 38–9, 43–51, 54, 146, 166, 169, 171, 182, 213, 252, 320, 370, 386–7, 395, 398, 403, 405, 407–8, 411, 416, 418–20, 426–7, 429, 432–3, 438–43
Chauveau, J.-P. 176
Chevillard, R.-P. 100, 410
CHISS (Centre Haitien d'investigation en sciences sociales) 382–4, 394
Churchill, M. 137
Clark, E. 413–14
Clements, C. 433
Coelho, A. vii, 395–6
Collins, C. 241
Comrie, B. 215
Confiant, R. 28, 29, 442
Coriolan, A.-M. 360
Corne, C. 41, 44, 46–51, 53–4, 405, 429
Cornevin, R. 7, 404
Craig, D. 381–2

Damoiseau, R. 15, 40, 153, 191, 197, 202, 216, 224, 249–50, 307, 369, 429

Darlow, M. 356
Daudier, V. 378
De Regt, J. 380
DeGraff, M. 2, 15, 153, 395–6, 400, 402, 426, 439
Dejean, Y. 15, 63, 65–6, 75, 77–8, 127, 134–6, 234–6, 240, 251, 360, 375, 386, 391–2
Desmarattes, J. 270, 287
Dillard, J. 400
D'Offay, D. 433
Doret, F. 115
Du Tertre, J.-B. 30
Ducœurjoly, S. 104, 108–10, 420, 427
Durizot Jno-Baptiste, P. 27

Ehrhart, S. 53
Etienne, F. 15, 153
Etienne, G. 15, 62–3, 341
Exmelin, A.-O. 404

Faine, J. vii, 2, 15, 16, 167, 187, 194–5, 233, 235, 240, 242, 250, 262, 264, 270, 427, 440
Faraclas, N. 95
Fattier, D. viii, xiv, 15, 73, 78, 135, 237, 251, 270–1, 273–4, 287, 315–16, 320, 322, 329–31, 341, 354, 419, 428
Fattier-Thomas, D. 351
Férère, G. 62, 77
Ferguson, C. 14, 427
Ferguson, J. 55–6
Ferreira, J.-A. 41–2
Firmin, A. 55–6
Fishman, J. 14
Fleischman, S. 250
Fleischmann, U. 119, 373
Fontaine, M. 33, 442
Fouchard, J. 375
Frank, D. 34
Freeman, B. 16, 56
Frei, H. 415
Frostin, C. 404
Froude, J. 36
Furetière, A. 2

Garçon, J. 347, 349–50

Geggus, D. 440
Germain, R. 27
Gil, D. 439
Gilliéron, J. 317–18
Girod-Chantrans, J. 2, 111
Givón, T. 241
Goodman, M. 36, 405
Gougenheim, G. 248, 418
Grant, A. 429, 443
Grégoire, H.-B. 417, 426
Grevisse, M. 237
Grimes, B. 42
Guilbeau, J. 414–15

Hadjadj, B. 374, 376
Hall, G. 21
Hall, R. vii, 4, 15, 65, 77, 146, 150, 243, 250–1, 393
Halliday, M. 55
Hancock, I. 37, 401, 405
Harbour, D. 304, 309, 311, 314
Hazaël-Massieux, G. 100, 135, 189, 409, 416, 419
Hazaël-Massieux, M.-C. xiv, 95, 100, 103, 106, 116, 134–5, 343, 356
Heinl, N. 6, 10, 11, 55
Heinl, R. 6, 10, 11, 55
Hesseling, D. vii, 396
Highfield, A. 30, 32, 415–17, 420, 441–2
Holm, J. 1, 26, 34, 35
Honorien, L. 40
Howe, K. 352
Hugo, V. 136
Hull, A. 405, 408, 440
Hyppolite, M. 73, 78, 318–20

James, C. 55
Jansen, S. 182
Jauze, J.-M. 50
Jean-Baptiste, R. xiii, 262, 266
Jean-Charles, H. 370, 393
Jean-François, L. 365, 369–70
Jennings, W. 39, 411
Jespersen, O. 397
Joint, L.-A. 376–7, 380, 391
Joseph, F. 15, 265, 287
Joseph, Y. 364–5, 383

Jourdain, E. 29

Karam, A. 39
Kephart, R. 34
Klingler, T. xiv, 19, 21–5, 31, 43, 56, 409, 421
Koopman, H. 239–40, 251, 296
Krashen, S. 426–7
Kremnitz, J. 28–9
Kurath, H. 316–17

Labov, W. 336
Lafage, S. 431
Laguerre, P. 16, 365, 378
Lainy, R. 15, 216, 219–20, 223, 299–300, 311, 313
Lambert, W. 380, 392–3
Le Dû, J. 26
Le Page, R. 33–4
Lefebvre, C. 3, 15, 206, 236, 239–40, 249, 251, 262, 395, 400, 425–6, 428–9, 431–4, 437, 439–42
Lefebvre, G. 30, 173
Lionnet, G. 51, 433
Lipsky, J. 55
Locher, U. 377, 379–80, 383, 385
Lofficial, F. 137
Longuefosse, M. 375
Ludwig, R. 27, 189, 417–18, 442
Lumsden, J. 426
Lundahl, M. 367
Luxana, V. 394

McConnell, O. 78, 117–20, 122–3, 125, 137, 372, 374, 393
McWhorter, J. 2, 153, 395–6, 398–9, 402, 415, 429, 433–4
Maher, J. 30–1, 441
Manessy, G. 39, 401, 428, 430, 432, 435, 442–3
Manigat, M. 183, 347, 365
March, C. 29
Marchand-Thébault, M.-T. 38
Marchello-Nizia, C. 432
Marshall, M. 19–20
Martin, J.-B. 442
Martinez, P. 30

Mercier, A. 23
Michaelis, S. 51
Mondésir, J. 34, 442
Moreau de Saint-Méry, L. 104–5, 108, 111
Morgan, R. 19
Morisseau-Leroy, F. 115
Morrill, W. 30, 32
Mufwene, S. xiv, 395, 402, 413, 424–7, 429, 433, 436, 442
Mühlhäusler, P. 4
Muysken, P. 401, 433

Neumann, I. 19, 22, 24, 25, 56, 409
Neumann-Holzschuh, I. 23, 24, 37, 56, 414
Nicholls, D. 55
Nylander, D. 435

Orjala, P. 77, 315–16, 319–20, 329, 355

Pamphile, L. 10
Papen, R. 42–4, 46–7, 52, 421
Parépou, A. 40, 287
Parkvall, M. 398–9, 402, 409, 415, 433–4
Peleman, L. 16
Pelleprat, P. 410–11, 413, 427
Perdue, C. 425
Perrot, M.-E. 418
Peyraud, F. 40
Phillips, J. 4, 420
Picoche, J. 179
Piou, N. 15, 306–8, 310–11
Pompilus, P. 15–16, 62–3, 65, 77, 121, 136, 384, 386–7
Poullet, R. 27
Pressoir, C.-F. 29, 78, 117, 119–22, 128, 133, 137, 360, 372, 386, 393
Price-Mars, J. 12
Prudent, L.-F. 135

Racine, M. 15
Renault-Lescure, O. 38
Rézeau, P. 179, 442
Roberts, P. 34
Roberts, S. 33, 398, 402
Ronceray, H. 382, 394

Rottet, K. 22, 414, 419, 442
Rousseau, J.-J. 106, 356

Saint Jacques Fauquenoy, M. 38, 40–1
Saint-Jorre, D. 51
Saint-Quentin, A. 36, 40–1, 58, 120, 399
Sankoff, G. 4
Schieffelin, B. 117
Schuchardt, H. vii, 396, 399, 435
Schwartz, B. 426
Siegel, Jason xiii, xiv, 305, 308, 310, 314
Siegel, Jeff 54, 399, 402, 429
Snow, C. 427
Spears, A. 214, 220, 225–7, 239–40, 250–1, 298, 300, 315
Speedy, K. 22, 54, 58
Sprouse, R. 425–6
Stäbler, C. 418, 430
Stein, P. 49, 188
Sterlin, M.-D. 239–40
Syea, A. 49, 251
Sylvain, G. 113–15, 442
Sylvain, S. vii, 15, 118, 146, 228–30, 233, 235, 239, 242, 250–1, 261, 263, 284–5, 287, 291, 299, 302–6, 311–12, 314, 400, 427–8, 440

Tardieu, C. 376
Targète, J. 16
Taylor, D. 33

Thogmartin, C. 417
Thomas, J. 35–6, 40, 399
Thomas, W. 380
Tinelli, H. 15, 62–3, 65
Tobler, A. 41, 442
Tornquist, L. 20
Tourneux, H. 27, 57
Trouillot, J. 18

Valdman, A. 15–17, 19–20, 22–5, 56, 62, 64–5, 69, 73–4, 84, 89, 93, 95, 100, 121, 124, 145–6, 152, 164–5, 174, 178, 182, 188, 233, 248, 250–1, 291, 316, 329, 331, 335–6, 353–6, 383, 395, 403, 412, 417, 421, 426, 428, 434, 442
Van Name, A. 395
Vernet, P. 15, 51, 124, 370
Vidale, A. 35–6
Vilsaint, F. 15–16, 18
Volcy-Focard, E. 46

Wartburg, W. 168
Watbled, J.-P. 47
Weinstein, B. 11, 55
Whinnom, K. 145, 401
Wiesler, H. 377, 385
Wood, D. 57

Zéphir, F. 15, 351